PHP Cookbook™

PHP Cookbook™

David Sklar and Adam Trachtenberg

O'REILLY®

Beijing · Cambridge · Farnham · Köln · Paris · Sebastopol · Taipei · Tokyo

Table of Contents

Preface

PHP is the engine behind millions of dynamic web applications. Its broad feature set, approachable syntax, and support for different operating systems and web servers have made it an ideal language for both rapid web development and the methodical construction of complex systems.

One of the major reasons for PHP's success as a web scripting language is its origins as a tool to process HTML forms and create web pages. This makes PHP very web-friendly. Additionally, it is a polyglot. PHP can speak to a multitude of databases, and it knows numerous Internet protocols. PHP also makes it simple to parse browser data and make HTTP requests. This web-specific focus carries over to the recipes and examples in the *PHP Cookbook*.

This book is a collection of solutions to common tasks in PHP. We've tried to include material that will appeal to everyone from newbies to wizards. If we've succeeded, you'll learn something (or perhaps many things) from the *PHP Cookbook*. There are tips in here for everyday PHP programmers as well as for people coming to PHP with experience in another language.

PHP, in source-code and binary forms, is available for download for free from *http://www.php.net/*. The PHP web site also contains installation instructions, comprehensive documentation, and pointers to online resources, user groups, mailing lists, and other PHP resources.

Who This Book Is For

This book is for programmers who need to solve problems with PHP. If you don't know any PHP, make this your second PHP book. The first should be *Programming PHP*, also from O'Reilly & Associates.

If you're already familiar with PHP, this book will help you overcome a specific problem and get on with your life (or at least your programming activities.) The *PHP Cookbook* can also show you how to accomplish a particular task in PHP, like sending email or writing a SOAP server, that you may already know how to do in another language. Programmers converting applications from other languages to PHP will find this book a trusty companion.

What Is in This Book

We don't expect that you'll sit down and read this book from cover to cover. (although we'll be happy if you do!). PHP programmers are constantly faced with a wide variety of challenges on a wide range of subjects. Turn to the *PHP Cookbook* when you encounter a problem you need to solve. Each recipe is a self-contained explanation that gives you a head start towards finishing your task. When a recipe refers to topics outside its scope, it contains pointers to related recipes and other online and offline resources.

If you choose to read an entire chapter at once, that's okay. The recipes generally flow from easy to hard, with example programs that "put it all together" at the end of many chapters. The chapter introduction provides an overview of the material covered in the chapter, including relevant background material, and points out a few highlighted recipes of special interest.

The book begins with four chapters about basic data types. Chapter 1 covers details like processing substrings, manipulating case, taking strings apart into smaller pieces, and parsing comma-separated data. Chapter 2 explains operations with floating-point numbers, random numbers, converting between bases, and number formatting. Chapter 3 shows you how to manipulate dates and times, format them, handle time zones and daylight saving time, and find time to microsecond precision. Chapter 4 covers array operations like iterating, merging, reversing, sorting, and extracting particular elements.

Next are three chapters that discuss program building blocks. Chapter 5 covers notable features of PHP's variable handling, like default values, static variables, and producing string representations of complex data types. The recipes in Chapter 6 deal with using functions in PHP: processing arguments, passing and returning variables by reference, creating functions at runtime, and scoping variables. Chapter 7 covers PHP's object-oriented capabilities, with recipes on using overloading and polymorphism, defining constructors, and cloning objects.

The heart of the book is five chapters devoted to topics that are central to web programming. Chapter 8 covers cookies, headers, authentication, configuration variables, and other fundamentals of web applications. Chapter 9 covers processing and validating form input, displaying multi-page forms, showing forms with error messages, and escaping special characters in user data. Chapter 10 explains the differences between text-file, DBM, and SQL databases and, using the PEAR DB database abstraction layer, shows how to assign unique ID values, retrieve rows, change data, escape quotes, and log debugging information. Chapter 11 focuses on retrieving

URLs and processing HTML but also touches on using templates and parsing server access logs. Chapter 12 covers XML and related formats, including the DOM, SAX, XSLT, XML-RPC, and SOAP.

The next section of the book is a series of chapters on other features and extensions of PHP that provide a lot of useful functionality. These are recipes that help you build applications that are more robust, secure, user-friendly, and efficient. Chapter 13 covers regular expressions, including matching a valid email address, capturing text inside of HTML tags, and using greedy or non-greedy matching. Chapter 14 discusses encryption, including generating and storing passwords, sharing encrypted data with others, storing encrypted data in a file or database, and using SSL. Chapter 15 shows you how to create graphics, with recipes on drawing text, lines, polygons, and curves. Chapter 16 helps you make your applications globally friendly and includes recipes on using locales and localizing text, dates and times, currency values, and images. Chapter 17 discusses network-related tasks, like reading and sending email messages and newsgroup posts, using FTP and LDAP, and doing DNS and Whois lookups.

Chapter 18 and Chapter 19 cover the filesystem. Chapter 18 focuses on files: opening and closing them, using temporary files, locking file, sending compressed files, and processing the contents of files. Chapter 19 deals with directories and file metadata, with recipes on changing file permissions and ownership, moving or deleting a file, and processing all files in a directory.

Last, there are two chapters on topics that extend the reach of what PHP can do. Chapter 20 covers using PHP outside of web programming. Its recipes cover command-line topics like parsing program arguments and reading passwords, as well as topics related to building client-side GUI applications with PHP-GTK like displaying widgets, responding to user actions, and displaying menus. Chapter 21 covers PEAR, the PHP Extension and Application Repository. PEAR is a collection of PHP code that provides various functions and extensions to PHP. We use PEAR modules throughout the book and Chapter 21 shows you how to install and upgrade them.

Other Resources

Web Sites

There is a tremendous amount of PHP reference material online. With everything from the annotated PHP manual to sites with periodic articles and tutorials, a fast Internet connection rivals a large bookshelf in PHP documentary usefulness. Here are some key sites:

The Annotated PHP Manual: http://www.php.net/manual/
    Available in seventeen languages, this includes both official documentation of functions and language features as well as user-contributed comments.

PHP mailing lists: http://www.php.net/mailing-lists.php
> There are many PHP mailing lists covering installation, programming, extending PHP, and various other topics. A read-only web interface to the mailing lists is at *http://news.php.net/*.

PHP Presentation archive: http://conf.php.net/
> A collection of presentations on PHP given at various conferences.

PEAR: http://pear.php.net/
> PEAR calls itself "a framework and distribution system for reuseable PHP components." You'll find lots of useful PHP classes and sample code there.

PHP.net: A Tourist's Guide: http://www.php.net/sites.php
> This is a guide to the various web sites under the *php.net* umbrella.

PHP Knowledge Base: http://php.faqts.com/
> Many questions and answers from the PHP community, as well as links to other resources.

PHP DevCenter: http://www.onlamp.com/php/
> A collection of PHP articles and tutorials with a good mix of introductory and advanced topics.

Books

This section lists books that are helpful references and tutorials for building applications with PHP. Most are specific to web-related programming; look for books on MySQL, HTML, XML, and HTTP.

At the end of the section, we've included a few books that are useful for every programmer regardless of language of choice. These works can make you a better programmer by teaching you how to think about programming as part of a larger pattern of problem solving.

- *Programming PHP* by Kevin Tatroe and Rasmus Lerdorf (O'Reilly).
- *HTML and XHTML: The Definitive Guide* by Chuck Musciano and Bill Kennedy (O'Reilly).
- *Dynamic HTML: The Definitive Guide* by Danny Goodman (O'Reilly).
- *Mastering Regular Expressions* by Jeffrey E. F. Friedl (O'Reilly).
- *XML in a Nutshell* by Elliotte Rusty Harold and W. Scott Means (O'Reilly).
- *MySQL Reference Manual*, by Michael "Monty" Widenius, David Axmark, and MySQL AB (O'Reilly); also available at *http://www.mysql.com/documentation/*.
- *MySQL*, by Paul DuBois (New Riders).
- *Web Security, Privacy, and Commerce* by Simson Garfinkel and Gene Spafford (O'Reilly).
- *Web Services Essentials*, by Ethan Cerami (O'Reilly).

- *HTTP Pocket Reference*, by Clinton Wong (O'Reilly).
- *The Practice of Programming*, by Brian W. Kernighan and Rob Pike (Addison-Wesley).
- *Programming Pearls* by Jon Louis Bentley (Addison-Wesley).
- *The Mythical Man-Month*, by Frederick P. Brooks (Addison-Wesley).

Conventions Used in This Book

Programming Conventions

We've generally omitted from examples in this book the `<?php` and `?>` opening and closing markers that begin and end a PHP program, except in examples where the body of the code includes an opening or closing marker. To minimize naming conflicts, function and class names in the *PHP Cookbook* begin with `pc_`.

The examples in this book were written to run under PHP Version 4.2.2. Sample code should work on both Unix and Windows, except where noted in the text. Some functions, notably the XML-related ones, were written to run under PHP Version 4.3.0. We've noted in the text when we depend on a feature not present in PHP Version 4.2.2.

Typesetting Conventions

The following typographic conventions are used in this book:

Italic
> Used for file and directory names, email addresses, and URLs, as well as for new terms where they are defined.

`Constant width`
> Used for code listings and for keywords, variables, functions, command options, parameters, class names, and HTML tags where they appear in the text.

`Constant width bold`
> Used to mark lines of output in code listings and command lines to be typed by the user.

`Constant width italic`
> Used as a general placeholder to indicate items that should be replaced by actual values in your own programs.

Comments and Questions

Please address comments and questions concerning this book to the publisher:

O'Reilly & Associates, Inc.
1005 Gravenstein Highway North
Sebastopol, CA 95472
(800) 998-9938 (in the United States or Canada)
(707) 829-0515 (international/local)
(707) 829-0104 (fax)

We have a web page for this book, where we list errata, examples, or any additional information. You can access this page at:

http://www.oreilly.com/catalog/phpckbk

To comment or ask technical questions about this book, send email to:

bookquestions@oreilly.com

For more information about books, conferences, Resource Centers, and the O'Reilly Network, see the O'Reilly web site at:

http://www.oreilly.com

Acknowledgments

Most importantly, thanks to everyone who has contributed their time, creativity, and skills to making PHP what it is today. This amazing volunteer effort has created not only hundreds of thousands of lines of source code, but also comprehensive documentation, a QA infrastructure, lots of add-on applications and libraries, and a thriving user community worldwide. It's a thrill and an honor to add the *PHP Cookbook* to the world of PHP.

Thanks also to our reviewers: Stig Bakken, Shane Caraveo, Ike DeLorenzo, Rasmus Lerdorf, Adam Morton, Ophir Prusak, Kevin Tatroe, and Nathan Torkington. They caught plenty of bugs and offered many helpful suggestions for making the book better. We would like to specially single out Nat Torkington for flooding us with a plethora of useful changes and suggested additions.

All the folks at Student.Net Publishing, Student.Com, and TVGrid.Com provided a fertile environment for exploring PHP. Our experiences there in large part made this book possible. Bret Martin and Miranda Productions provided hosting and infrastructure that let us collaborate remotely while writing. We're only four miles from each other, but in Manhattan, that's remote.

Last, but far from least, thanks to our editor Paula Ferguson. From her shockingly quick (to our friends) acceptance of our modest book proposal to her final handling of our requests for last-minute revisions, she's guided the *PHP Cookbook* with a steady hand through the O'Reilly publishing process. Without her, this book would never have made the transformation from idea into reality.

David Sklar

Thanks to Adam for writing this book with me (and catching all the places I used too many parentheses).

Thanks to my parents, who didn't really know what they were getting into when they bought me that 4K Radio Shack Color Computer 20 years ago.

Thanks to Susannah for unwavering love and support, and for reminding me at crucial moments that life's not a paragraph.

Adam Trachtenberg

It is hard to express the size of my debt to David for putting up with me over the course of working together on the *PHP Cookbook*. His comments drastically improved my writing and his unwavering punctuality helped keep me close to schedule.

Thanks to Coleco and its Adam computer, for making me the first kid on the block able to own a computer named after himself.

Thanks to all my friends and business-school classmates who grew tired of hearing me say "Sorry, I've got to go work on the book tonight" and who still talked to me after I took two weeks to return their phone calls.

A special thanks to Elizabeth Hondl. Her childlike fascination with web technologies proves that if you ask often enough, you just might make it in the book.

Thanks to my brother, parents, and entire family. So much of me comes from them. Their encouragement and love sustains me.

CHAPTER 1

Strings

1.0 Introduction

Strings in PHP are a sequence of characters, such as "We hold these truths to be self evident," or "Once upon a time," or even "111211211." When you read data from a file or output it to a web browser, your data is represented as strings.

Individual characters in strings can be referenced with array subscript style notation, as in C. The first character in the string is at index 0. For example:

```
$neighbor = 'Hilda';
print $neighbor[3];
d
```

However, PHP strings differ from C strings in that they are binary-safe (i.e., they can contain null bytes) and can grow and shrink on demand. Their size is limited only by the amount of memory that is available.

You can initialize strings three ways, similar in form and behavior to Perl and the Unix shell: with single quotes, with double quotes, and with the "here document" (heredoc) format. With single-quoted strings, the only special characters you need to escape inside a string are backslash and the single quote itself:

```
print 'I have gone to the store.';
print 'I\'ve gone to the store.';
print 'Would you pay $1.75 for 8 ounces of tap water?';
print 'In double-quoted strings, newline is represented by \n';
I have gone to the store.
I've gone to the store.
Would you pay $1.75 for 8 ounces of tap water?
In double-quoted strings, newline is represented by \n
```

Because PHP doesn't check for variable interpolation or almost any escape sequences in single-quoted strings, defining strings this way is straightforward and fast.

Double-quoted strings don't recognize escaped single quotes, but they do recognize interpolated variables and the escape sequences shown in Table 1-1.

Table 1-1. Double-quoted string escape sequences

Escape sequence	Character
\n	Newline (ASCII 10)
\r	Carriage return (ASCII 13)
\t	Tab (ASCII 9)
\\	Backslash
\$	Dollar sign
\"	Double quotes
\{	Left brace
\}	Right brace
\[	Left bracket
\]	Right bracket
\0 through \777	Octal value
\x0 through \xFF	Hex value

For example:

```
print "I've gone to the store.";
print "The sauce cost \$10.25.";
$cost = '$10.25';
print "The sauce cost $cost.";
print "The sauce cost \$\061\060.\x32\x35.";
I've gone to the store.
The sauce cost $10.25.
The sauce cost $10.25.
The sauce cost $10.25.
```

The last line of code prints the price of sauce correctly because the character 1 is ASCII code 49 decimal and 061 octal. Character 0 is ASCII 48 decimal and 060 octal; 2 is ASCII 50 decimal and 32 hex; and 5 is ASCII 53 decimal and 35 hex.

Heredoc-specified strings recognize all the interpolations and escapes of double-quoted strings, but they don't require double quotes to be escaped. Heredocs start with <<< and a token. That token (with no leading or trailing whitespace), followed by a semicolon to end the statement (if necessary), ends the heredoc. For example:

```
print <<< END
It's funny when signs say things like:
    Original "Root" Beer
    "Free" Gift
    Shoes cleaned while "you" wait
or have other misquoted words.
END;
It's funny when signs say things like:
    Original "Root" Beer
    "Free" Gift
    Shoes cleaned while "you" wait
or have other misquoted words.
```

With heredocs, newlines, spacing, and quotes are all preserved. The end-of-string identifier is usually all caps, by convention, and it is case sensitive. Thus, this is okay:

```
print <<< PARSLEY
It's easy to grow fresh:
Parsley
Chives
on your windowsill
PARSLEY;
```

So is this:

```
print <<< DOGS
If you like pets, yell out:
DOGS AND CATS ARE GREAT!
DOGS;
```

Heredocs are useful for printing out HTML with interpolated variables:

```
if ($remaining_cards > 0) {
    $url = '/deal.php';
    $text = 'Deal More Cards';
} else {
    $url = '/new-game.php';
    $text = 'Start a New Game';
}
print <<< HTML
There are <b>$remaining_cards</b> left.
<p>
<a href="$url">$text</a>
HTML;
```

In this case, the semicolon needs to go after the end-of-string delimiter, to tell PHP the statement is ended. In some cases, however, you shouldn't use the semicolon:

```
$a = <<< END
Once upon a time, there was a
END
. ' boy!';
print $a;
Once upon a time, there was a boy!
```

In this case, the expression needs to continue on the next line, so you don't use a semicolon. Note also that in order for PHP to recognize the end-of-string delimiter, the . string concatenation operator needs to go on a separate line from the end-of-string delimiter.

1.1 Accessing Substrings

You want to extract part of a string, starting at a particular place in the string. For example, you want the first eight characters of a username entered into a form.

Solution

Use substr( ) to select your substrings:

```
$substring = substr($string,$start,$length);
$username = substr($_REQUEST['username'],0,8);
```

Discussion

If $start and $length are positive, substr( ) returns $length characters in the string, starting at $start. The first character in the string is at position 0:

```
print substr('watch out for that tree',6,5);
out f
```

If you leave out $length, substr( ) returns the string from $start to the end of the original string:

```
print substr('watch out for that tree',17);
t tree
```

If $start plus $length goes past the end of the string, substr( ) returns all of the string from $start forward:

```
print substr('watch out for that tree',20,5);
ree
```

If $start is negative, substr( ) counts back from the end of the string to determine where your substring starts:

```
print substr('watch out for that tree',-6);
print substr('watch out for that tree',-17,5);
t tree
out f
```

If $length is negative, substr( ) counts back from the end of the string to determine where your substring ends:

```
print substr('watch out for that tree',15,-2);
print substr('watch out for that tree',-4,-1);
hat tr
tre
```

See Also

Documentation on substr( ) at *http://www.php.net/substr*.

1.2   Replacing Substrings

Problem

You want to replace a substring with a different string. For example, you want to obscure all but the last four digits of a credit card number before printing it.

Solution

Use substr_replace():

```
// Everything from position $start to the end of $old_string
// becomes $new_substring
$new_string = substr_replace($old_string,$new_substring,$start);

// $length characters, starting at position $start, become $new_substring
$new_string = substr_replace($old_string,$new_substring,$start,$length);
```

Discussion

Without the $length argument, substr_replace() replaces everything from $start to the end of the string. If $length is specified, only that many characters are replaced:

```
print substr_replace('My pet is a blue dog.','fish.',12);
print substr_replace('My pet is a blue dog.','green',12,4);
$credit_card = '4111 1111 1111 1111';
print substr_replace($credit_card,'xxxx ',0,strlen($credit_card)-4);
My pet is a fish.
My pet is a green dog.
xxxx 1111
```

If $start is negative, the new substring is placed at $start characters counting from the end of $old_string, not from the beginning:

```
print substr_replace('My pet is a blue dog.','fish.',-9);
print substr_replace('My pet is a blue dog.','green',-9,4);
My pet is a fish.
My pet is a green dog.
```

If $start and $length are 0, the new substring is inserted at the start of $old_string:

```
print substr_replace('My pet is a blue dog.','Title: ',0,0);
Title: My pet is a blue dog.
```

The function substr_replace() is useful when you've got text that's too big to display all at once, and you want to display some of the text with a link to the rest. For example, this displays the first 25 characters of a message with an ellipsis after it as a link to a page that displays more text:

```
$r = mysql_query("SELECT id,message FROM messages WHERE id = $id") or die();
$ob = mysql_fetch_object($r);
```

```
printf('<a href="more-text.php?id=%d">%s</a>',
       $ob->id, substr_replace($ob->message,' ...',25));
```

The *more-text.php* page can use the message ID passed in the query string to retrieve the full message and display it.

See Also

Documentation on substr_replace() at *http://www.php.net/substr-replace*.

1.3   Processing a String One Character at a Time

Problem

You need to process each character in a string individually.

Solution

Loop through each character in the string with for. This example counts the vowels in a string:

```
$string = "This weekend, I'm going shopping for a pet chicken.";
$vowels = 0;
for ($i = 0, $j = strlen($string); $i < $j; $i++) {
    if (strstr('aeiouAEIOU',$string[$i])) {
        $vowels++;
    }
}
```

Discussion

Processing a string a character at a time is an easy way to calculate the "Look and Say" sequence:

```
function lookandsay($s) {
    // initialize the return value to the empty string
    $r = '';
    /* $m holds the character we're counting, initialize to the first
    // character in the string */
    $m = $s[0];
    // $n is the number of $m's we've seen, initialize to 1
    $n = 1;
    for ($i = 1, $j = strlen($s); $i < $j; $i++) {
        // if this character is the same as the last one
        if ($s[$i] == $m) {
            // increment the count of this character
            $n++;
        } else {
```

```
            // otherwise, add the count and character to the return value
            $r .= $n.$m;
            // set the character we're looking for to the current one
            $m = $s[$i];
            // and reset the count to 1
            $n = 1;
        }
    }
    // return the built up string as well as the last count and character //
    return $r.$n.$m;
}

for ($i = 0, $s = 1; $i < 10; $i++) {
    $s = lookandsay($s);
    print "$s\n";
}
1
11
21
1211
111221
312211
13112221
1113213211
31131211131221
13211311123113112211
```

It's called the "Look and Say" sequence because each element is what you get by looking at the previous element and saying what's in it. For example, looking at the first element, 1, you say "one one." So the second element is "11." That's two ones, so the third element is "21." Similarly, that's one two and one one, so the fourth element is "1211," and so on.

See Also

Documentation on for at *http://www.php.net/for*; more about the "Look and Say" sequence at *http://mathworld.wolfram.com/LookandSaySequence.html*.

1.4   Reversing a String by Word or Character

Problem

You want to reverse the words or the characters in a string.

Solution

Use strrev( ) to reverse by character:

```
print strrev('This is not a palindrome.');
.emordnilap a ton si sihT
```

To reverse by words, explode the string by word boundary, reverse the words, then rejoin:

```
$s = "Once upon a time there was a turtle.";
// break the string up into words
$words = explode(' ',$s);
// reverse the array of words
$words = array_reverse($words);
// rebuild the string
$s = join(' ',$words);
print $s;
turtle. a was there time a upon Once
```

Discussion

Reversing a string by words can also be done all in one line:

```
$reversed_s = join(' ',array_reverse(explode(' ',$s)));
```

See Also

Recipe 18.7 discusses the implications of using something other than a space character as your word boundary; documentation on strrev( ) at *http://www.php.net/strrev* and array_reverse( ) at *http://www.php.net/array-reverse*.

1.5   Expanding and Compressing Tabs

Problem

You want to change spaces to tabs (or tabs to spaces) in a string while keeping text aligned with tab stops. For example, you want to display formatted text to users in a standardized way.

Solution

Use str_replace( ) to switch spaces to tabs or tabs to spaces:

```
$r = mysql_query("SELECT message FROM messages WHERE id = 1") or die();
$ob = mysql_fetch_object($r);
$tabbed = str_replace(' ',"\t",$ob->message);
$spaced = str_replace("\t",' ',$ob->message);

print "With Tabs: <pre>$tabbed</pre>";
print "With Spaces: <pre>$spaced</pre>";
```

Using str_replace() for conversion, however, doesn't respect tab stops. If you want tab stops every eight characters, a line beginning with a five-letter word and a tab should have that tab replaced with three spaces, not one. Use the pc_tab_expand() function shown in Example 1-1 to turn tabs to spaces in a way that respects tab stops.

Example 1-1. pc_tab_expand()

```
function pc_tab_expand($a) {
  $tab_stop = 8;
  while (strstr($a,"\t")) {
    $a = preg_replace('/^([^\t]*)(\t+)/e',
                      "'\\1'.str_repeat(' ',strlen('\\2') *
                      $tab_stop - strlen('\\1') % $tab_stop)",$a);
  }
  return $a;
}

$spaced = pc_tab_expand($ob->message);
```

You can use the pc_tab_unexpand() function shown in Example 1-2 to turn spaces back to tabs.

Example 1-2. pc_tab_unexpand()

```
function pc_tab_unexpand($x) {
  $tab_stop = 8;

  $lines = explode("\n",$x);
  for ($i = 0, $j = count($lines); $i < $j; $i++) {
    $lines[$i] = pc_tab_expand($lines[$i]);
    $e = preg_split("/(.\{$tab_stop})/",$lines[$i],-1,PREG_SPLIT_DELIM_CAPTURE);
    $lastbit = array_pop($e);
    if (!isset($lastbit)) { $lastbit = ''; }
    if ($lastbit == str_repeat(' ',$tab_stop)) { $lastbit = "\t"; }
    for ($m = 0, $n = count($e); $m < $n; $m++) {
      $e[$m] = preg_replace('/ +$',"\t",$e[$m]);
    }
    $lines[$i] = join('',$e).$lastbit;
  }
  $x = join("\n", $lines);
  return $x;
}

$tabbed = pc_tab_unexpand($ob->message);
```

Both functions take a string as an argument and return the string appropriately modified.

Discussion

Each function assumes tab stops are every eight spaces, but that can be modified by changing the setting of the $tab_stop variable.

The regular expression in pc_tab_expand( ) matches both a group of tabs and all the text in a line before that group of tabs. It needs to match the text before the tabs because the length of that text affects how many spaces the tabs should be replaced so that subsequent text is aligned with the next tab stop. The function doesn't just replace each tab with eight spaces; it adjusts text after tabs to line up with tab stops.

Similarly, pc_tab_unexpand( ) doesn't just look for eight consecutive spaces and then replace them with one tab character. It divides up each line into eight-character chunks and then substitutes ending whitespace in those chunks (at least two spaces) with tabs. This not only preserves text alignment with tab stops; it also saves space in the string.

See Also

Documentation on str_replace( ) at *http://www.php.net/str-replace*.

1.6 Controlling Case

Problem

You need to capitalize, lowercase, or otherwise modify the case of letters in a string. For example, you want to capitalize the initial letters of names but lowercase the rest.

Solution

Use ucfirst( ) or ucwords( ) to capitalize the first letter of one or more words:

```
print ucfirst("how do you do today?");
print ucwords("the prince of wales");
How do you do today?
The Prince Of Wales
```

Use strtolower( ) or strtoupper( ) to modify the case of entire strings:

```
print strtoupper("i'm not yelling!");
// Tags must be lowercase to be XHTML compliant
print strtolower('<A HREF="one.php">one</A>');
I'M NOT YELLING!
<a href="one.php">one</a>
```

Discussion

Use ucfirst( ) to capitalize the first character in a string:

```
print ucfirst('monkey face');
print ucfirst('1 monkey face');
Monkey face
1 monkey face
```

Note that the second line of output is not "1 Monkey face".

Use ucwords( ) to capitalize the first character of each word in a string:

```
print ucwords('1 monkey face');
print ucwords("don't play zone defense against the philadelphia 76-ers");
1 Monkey Face
Don't Play Zone Defense Against The Philadelphia 76-ers
```

As expected, ucwords( ) doesn't capitalize the "t" in "don't." But it also doesn't capitalize the "e" in "76-ers." For ucwords( ), a word is any sequence of nonwhitespace characters that follows one or more whitespace characters. Since both ' and - aren't whitespace characters, ucwords( ) doesn't consider the "t" in "don't" or the "e" in "76-ers" to be word-starting characters.

Both ucfirst( ) and ucwords( ) don't change the case of nonfirst letters:

```
print ucfirst('macWorld says I should get a iBook');
print ucwords('eTunaFish.com might buy itunaFish.Com!');
MacWorld says I should get a iBook
ETunaFish.com Might Buy ItunaFish.Com!
```

The functions strtolower( ) and strtoupper( ) work on entire strings, not just individual characters. All alphabetic characters are changed to lowercase by strtolower( ) and strtoupper( ) changes all alphabetic characters to uppercase:

```
print strtolower("I programmed the WOPR and the TRS-80.");
print strtoupper('"since feeling is first" is a poem by e. e. cummings.');
i programmed the wopr and the trs-80.
"SINCE FEELING IS FIRST" IS A POEM BY E. E. CUMMINGS.
```

When determining upper- and lowercase, these functions respect your locale settings.

See Also

For more information about locale settings, see Chapter 16; documentation on ucfirst( ) at *http://www.php.net/ucfirst*, ucwords( ) at *http://www.php.net/ucwords*, strtolower( ) at *http://www.php.net/strtolower*, and strtoupper( ) at *http://www.php.net/strtoupper*.

1.7 Interpolating Functions and Expressions Within Strings

Problem

You want to include the results of executing a function or expression within a string.

Solution

Use the string concatenation operator (.) when the value you want to include can't be inside the string:

```
print 'You have '.($_REQUEST['boys'] + $_REQUEST['girls']).' children.';
print "The word '$word' is ".strlen($word).' characters long.';
print 'You owe '.$amounts['payment'].' immediately';
print "My circle's diameter is ".$circle->getDiameter().' inches.';
```

Discussion

You can put variables, object properties, and array elements (if the subscript is unquoted) directly in double-quoted strings:

```
print "I have $children children.";
print "You owe $amounts[payment] immediately.";
print "My circle's diameter is $circle->diameter inches.";
```

Direct interpolation or using string concatenation also works with heredocs. Interpolating with string concatenation in heredocs can look a little strange because the heredoc delimiter and the string concatenation operator have to be on separate lines:

```
print <<< END
Right now, the time is
END
. strftime('%c') . <<< END
 but tomorrow it will be
END
. strftime('%c',time() + 86400);
```

Also, if you're interpolating with heredocs, make sure to include appropriate spacing for the whole string to appear properly. In the previous example, "Right now the time" has to include a trailing space, and "but tomorrow it will be" has to include leading and trailing spaces.

See Also

For the syntax to interpolate variable variables (like ${"amount_$i"}), see Recipe 5.4; documentation on the string concatenation operator at *http://www.php.net/ language.operators.string*.

1.8   Trimming Blanks from a String

Problem

You want to remove whitespace from the beginning or end of a string. For example, you want to clean up user input before validating it.

Solution

Use `ltrim()`, `rtrim()`, or `trim()`. `ltrim()` removes whitespace from the beginning of a string, `rtrim()` from the end of a string, and `trim()` from both the beginning and end of a string:

```
$zipcode = trim($_REQUEST['zipcode']);
$no_linefeed = rtrim($_REQUEST['text']);
$name = ltrim($_REQUEST['name']);
```

Discussion

For these functions, whitespace is defined as the following characters: newline, carriage return, space, horizontal and vertical tab, and null.

Trimming whitespace off of strings saves storage space and can make for more precise display of formatted data or text within <pre> tags, for example. If you are doing comparisons with user input, you should trim the data first, so that someone who mistakenly enters "98052   " as their Zip Code isn't forced to fix an error that really isn't. Trimming before exact text comparisons also ensures that, for example, "salami\n" equals "salami." It's also a good idea to normalize string data by trimming it before storing it in a database.

The `trim()` functions can also remove user-specified characters from strings. Pass the characters you want to remove as a second argument. You can indicate a range of characters with two dots between the first and last characters in the range.

```
// Remove numerals and space from the beginning of the line
print ltrim('10 PRINT A$',' 0..9');
// Remove semicolon from the end of the line
print rtrim('SELECT * FROM turtles;',';');
PRINT A$
SELECT * FROM turtles
```

PHP also provides `chop()` as an alias for `rtrim()`. However, you're best off using `rtrim()` instead, because PHP's `chop()` behaves differently than Perl's `chop()` (which is deprecated in favor of `chomp()`, anyway) and using it can confuse others when they read your code.

See Also

Documentation on trim( ) at *http://www.php.net/trim*, ltrim( ) at *http://www.php.net/ltrim*, and rtrim( ) at *http://www.php.net/rtrim*.

1.9   Parsing Comma-Separated Data

Problem

You have data in comma-separated values (CSV) format, for example a file exported from Excel or a database, and you want to extract the records and fields into a format you can manipulate in PHP.

Solution

If the CSV data is in a file (or available via a URL), open the file with fopen( ) and read in the data with fgetcsv( ). This prints out the data in an HTML table:

```
$fp = fopen('sample2.csv','r') or die("can't open file");
print "<table>\n";
while($csv_line = fgetcsv($fp,1024)) {
    print '<tr>';
    for ($i = 0, $j = count($csv_line); $i < $j; $i++) {
        print '<td>'.$csv_line[$i].'</td>';
    }
    print "</tr>\n";
}
print '</table>\n';
fclose($fp) or die("can't close file");
```

Discussion

The second argument to fgetcsv( ) must be longer than the maximum length of a line in your CSV file. (Don't forget to count the end-of-line whitespace.) If you read in CSV lines longer than 1K, change the 1024 used in this recipe to something that accommodates your line length.

You can pass fgetcsv( ) an optional third argument, a delimiter to use instead of a comma (,). Using a different delimiter however, somewhat defeats the purpose of CSV as an easy way to exchange tabular data.

Don't be tempted to bypass fgetcsv( ) and just read a line in and explode( ) on the commas. CSV is more complicated than that, in order to deal with embedded commas and double quotes. Using fgetcsv( ) protects you and your code from subtle errors.

See Also

Documentation on fgetcsv() at *http://www.php.net/fgetcsv.*

1.10 Parsing Fixed-Width Delimited Data

Problem

You need to break apart fixed-width records in strings.

Solution

Use substr():

```
$fp = fopen('fixed-width-records.txt','r') or die ("can't open file");
while ($s = fgets($fp,1024)) {
    $fields[1] = substr($s,0,10);  // first field:  first 10 characters of the line
    $fields[2] = substr($s,10,5);  // second field: next 5 characters of the line
    $fields[3] = substr($s,15,12); // third field:  next 12 characters of the line
    // a function to do something with the fields
    process_fields($fields);
}
fclose($fp) or die("can't close file");
```

Or unpack():

```
$fp = fopen('fixed-width-records.txt','r') or die ("can't open file");
while ($s = fgets($fp,1024)) {
    // an associative array with keys "title", "author", and "publication_year"
    $fields = unpack('A25title/A14author/A4publication_year',$s);
    // a function to do something with the fields
    process_fields($fields);
}
fclose($fp) or die("can't close file");
```

Discussion

Data in which each field is allotted a fixed number of characters per line may look like this list of books, titles, and publication dates:

```
$booklist=<<<END
Elmer Gantry          Sinclair Lewis1927
The Scarlatti InheritanceRobert Ludlum 1971
The Parsifal Mosaic   Robert Ludlum 1982
Sophie's Choice       William Styron1979
END;
```

In each line, the title occupies the first 25 characters, the author's name the next 14 characters, and the publication year the next 4 characters. Knowing those field widths, it's straightforward to use substr() to parse the fields into an array:

```
$books = explode("\n",$booklist);

for($i = 0, $j = count($books); $i < $j; $i++) {
    $book_array[$i]['title'] = substr($books[$i],0,25);
    $book_array[$i]['author'] = substr($books[$i],25,14);
    $book_array[$i]['publication_year'] = substr($books[$i],39,4);
}
```

Exploding $booklist into an array of lines makes the looping code the same whether it's operating over a string or a series of lines read in from a file.

The loop can be made more flexible by specifying the field names and widths in a separate array that can be passed to a parsing function, as shown in the pc_fixed_width_substr() function in Example 1-3.

Example 1-3. pc_fixed_width_substr()

```
function pc_fixed_width_substr($fields,$data) {
    $r = array();
    for ($i = 0, $j = count($data); $i < $j; $i++) {
        $line_pos = 0;
        foreach($fields as $field_name => $field_length) {
            $r[$i][$field_name] = rtrim(substr($data[$i],$line_pos,$field_length));
            $line_pos += $field_length;
        }
    }
    return $r;
}

$book_fields = array('title' => 25,
                     'author' => 14,
                     'publication_year' => 4);

$book_array = pc_fixed_width_substr($book_fields,$books);
```

The variable $line_pos keeps track of the start of each field, and is advanced by the previous field's width as the code moves through each line. Use rtrim() to remove trailing whitespace from each field.

You can use unpack() as a substitute for substr() to extract fields. Instead of specifying the field names and widths as an associative array, create a format string for unpack(). A fixed-width field extractor using unpack() looks like the pc_fixed_width_unpack() function shown in Example 1-4.

Example 1-4. pc_fixed_width_unpack()

```
function pc_fixed_width_unpack($format_string,$data) {
    $r = array();
    for ($i = 0, $j = count($data); $i < $j; $i++) {
        $r[$i] = unpack($format_string,$data[$i]);
    }
    return $r;
}
```

Example 1-4. pc_fixed_width_unpack() (continued)

```
$book_array = pc_fixed_width_unpack('A25title/A14author/A4publication_year',
                                    $books);
```

Because the A format to unpack( ) means "space padded string," there's no need to rtrim( ) off the trailing spaces.

Once the fields have been parsed into $book_array by either function, the data can be printed as an HTML table, for example:

```
$book_array = pc_fixed_width_unpack('A25title/A14author/A4publication_year',
                                    $books);
print "<table>\n";
// print a header row
print '<tr><td>';
print join('</td><td>',array_keys($book_array[0]));
print "</td></tr>\n";
// print each data row
foreach ($book_array as $row) {
    print '<tr><td>';
    print join('</td><td>',array_values($row));
    print "</td></tr>\n";
}
print '</table>\n';
```

Joining data on </td><td> produces a table row that is missing its first <td> and last </td>. We produce a complete table row by printing out <tr><td> before the joined data and </td></tr> after the joined data.

Both substr( ) and unpack( ) have equivalent capabilities when the fixed-width fields are strings, but unpack( ) is the better solution when the elements of the fields aren't just strings.

See Also

For more information about unpack( ), see Recipe 1.13 and *http://www.php.net/ unpack*; Recipe 4.8 discusses join( ).

1.11   Taking Strings Apart

Problem

You need to break a string into pieces. For example, you want to access each line that a user enters in a <textarea> form field.

Solution

Use explode( ) if what separates the pieces is a constant string:

```
$words = explode(' ','My sentence is not very complicated');
```

Use split( ) or preg_split( ) if you need a POSIX or Perl regular expression to describe the separator:

```
$words = split(' +','This sentence  has  some extra whitespace  in it.');
$words = preg_split('/\d\. /','my day: 1. get up 2. get dressed 3. eat toast');
$lines = preg_split('/[\n\r]+/',$_REQUEST['textarea']);
```

Use spliti( ) or the /i flag to preg_split( ) for case-insensitive separator matching:

```
$words = spliti(' x ','31 inches x 22 inches X 9 inches');
$words = preg_split('/ x /i','31 inches x 22 inches X 9 inches');
```

Discussion

The simplest solution of the bunch is explode( ). Pass it your separator string, the string to be separated, and an optional limit on how many elements should be returned:

```
$dwarves = 'dopey,sleepy,happy,grumpy,sneezy,bashful,doc';
$dwarf_array = explode(',',$dwarves);
```

Now $dwarf_array is a seven element array:

```
print_r($dwarf_array);
Array
(
    [0] => dopey
    [1] => sleepy
    [2] => happy
    [3] => grumpy
    [4] => sneezy
    [5] => bashful
    [6] => doc
)
```

If the specified limit is less than the number of possible chunks, the last chunk contains the remainder:

```
$dwarf_array = explode(',',$dwarves,5);
print_r($dwarf_array);
Array
(
    [0] => dopey
    [1] => sleepy
    [2] => happy
    [3] => grumpy
    [4] => sneezy,bashful,doc
)
```

The separator is treated literally by explode( ). If you specify a comma and a space as a separator, it breaks the string only on a comma followed by a space—not on a comma or a space.

With split( ), you have more flexibility. Instead of a string literal as a separator, it uses a POSIX regular expression:

```
$more_dwarves = 'cheeky,fatso, wonder boy, chunky,growly, groggy, winky';
$more_dwarf_array = split(', ?',$more_dwarves);
```

This regular expression splits on a comma followed by an optional space, which treats all the new dwarves properly. Those with a space in their name aren't broken up, but everyone is broken apart whether they are separated by "," or ", ":

```
print_r($more_dwarf_array);
Array
(
    [0] => cheeky
    [1] => fatso
    [2] => wonder boy
    [3] => chunky
    [4] => growly
    [5] => groggy
    [6] => winky
)
```

Similar to split( ) is preg_split( ), which uses a Perl-compatible regular-expression engine instead of a POSIX regular-expression engine. With preg_split( ), you can take advantage of various Perlish regular-expression extensions, as well as tricks such as including the separator text in the returned array of strings:

```
$math = "3 + 2 / 7 - 9";
$stack = preg_split('/ *([+\-\/*]) */',$math,-1,PREG_SPLIT_DELIM_CAPTURE);
print_r($stack);
Array
(
    [0] => 3
    [1] => +
    [2] => 2
    [3] => /
    [4] => 7
    [5] => -
    [6] => 9
)
```

The separator regular expression looks for the four mathematical operators (+, -, /, *), surrounded by optional leading or trailing spaces. The PREG_SPLIT_DELIM_CAPTURE flag tells preg_split( ) to include the matches as part of the separator regular expression in parentheses in the returned array of strings. Only the mathematical operator character class is in parentheses, so the returned array doesn't have any spaces in it.

See Also

Regular expressions are discussed in more detail in Chapter 13; documentation on explode() at *http://www.php.net/explode*, split() at *http://www.php.net/split*, and preg_split() at *http://www.php.net/preg-split*.

1.12   Wrapping Text at a Certain Line Length

Problem

You need to wrap lines in a string. For example, you want to display text in <pre>/ </pre> tags but have it stay within a regularly sized browser window.

Solution

Use wordwrap():

```
$s = "Four score and seven years ago our fathers brought forth on this continen
t a new nation, conceived in liberty and dedicated to the proposition that all
men are created equal.";

print "<pre>\n".wordwrap($s)."\n</pre>";
<pre>
Four score and seven years ago our fathers brought forth on this continent
a new nation, conceived in liberty and dedicated to the proposition that
all men are created equal.
</pre>
```

Discussion

By default, wordwrap() wraps text at 75 characters per line. An optional second argument specifies different line length:

```
print wordwrap($s,50);
Four score and seven years ago our fathers brought
forth on this continent a new nation, conceived in
liberty and dedicated to the proposition that all
men are created equal.
```

Other characters besides "\n" can be used for linebreaks. For double spacing, use "\n\n":

```
print wordwrap($s,50,"\n\n");
Four score and seven years ago our fathers brought

forth on this continent a new nation, conceived in

liberty and dedicated to the proposition that all

men are created equal.
```

There is an optional fourth argument to wordwrap( ) that controls the treatment of words that are longer than the specified line length. If this argument is 1, these words are wrapped. Otherwise, they span past the specified line length:

```
print wordwrap('jabberwocky',5);
print wordwrap('jabberwocky',5,"\n",1);
jabberwocky

jabbe
rwock
y
```

See Also

Documentation on wordwrap( ) at *http://www.php.net/wordwrap*.

1.13   Storing Binary Data in Strings

Problem

You want to parse a string that contains values encoded as a binary structure or encode values into a string. For example, you want to store numbers in their binary representation instead of as sequences of ASCII characters.

Solution

Use pack( ) to store binary data in a string:

```
$packed = pack('S4',1974,106,28225,32725);
```

Use unpack( ) to extract binary data from a string:

```
$nums = unpack('S4',$packed);
```

Discussion

The first argument to pack( ) is a format string that describes how to encode the data that's passed in the rest of the arguments. The format string S4 tells pack( ) to produce four unsigned short 16-bit numbers in machine byte order from its input data. Given 1974, 106, 28225, and 32725 as input, this returns eight bytes: 182, 7, 106, 0, 65, 110, 213, and 127. Each two-byte pair corresponds to one of the input numbers: 7 * 256 + 182 is 1974; 0 * 256 + 106 is 106; 110 * 256 + 65 = 28225; 127 * 256 + 213 = 32725.

The first argument to unpack( ) is also a format string, and the second argument is the data to decode. Passing a format string of S4, the eight-byte sequence that pack( ) produced returns a four-element array of the original numbers:

```
print_r($nums);
Array
(
    [1] => 1974
    [2] => 106
    [3] => 28225
    [4] => 32725
)
```

In unpack( ), format characters and their count can be followed by a string to be used as an array key. For example:

```
$nums = unpack('S4num',$packed);
print_r($nums);
Array
(
    [num1] => 1974
    [num2] => 106
    [num3] => 28225
    [num4] => 32725
)
```

Multiple format characters must be separated with / in unpack( ):

```
$nums = unpack('S1a/S1b/S1c/S1d',$packed);
print_r($nums);
Array
(
    [a] => 1974
    [b] => 106
    [c] => 28225
    [d] => 32725
)
```

The format characters that can be used with pack( ) and unpack( ) are listed in Table 1-2.

Table 1-2. Format characters for pack() and unpack()

Format character	Data type
a	NUL-padded string
A	Space-padded string
h	Hex string, low nibble first
H	Hex string, high nibble first
c	signed char
C	unsigned char
s	signed short (16 bit, machine byte order)
S	unsigned short (16 bit, machine byte order)
n	unsigned short (16 bit, big endian byte order)
v	unsigned short (16 bit, little endian byte order)

Table 1-2. Format characters for pack() and unpack() (continued)

Format character	Data type
i	signed int (machine-dependent size and byte order)
I	unsigned int (machine-dependent size and byte order)
l	signed long (32 bit, machine byte order)
L	unsigned long (32 bit, machine byte order)
N	unsigned long (32 bit, big endian byte order)
V	unsigned long (32 bit, little endian byte order)
f	float (machine dependent size and representation)
d	double (machine dependent size and representation)
x	NUL byte
X	Back up one byte
@	NUL-fill to absolute position

For a, A, h, and H, a number after the format character indicates how long the string is. For example, A25 means a 25-character space-padded string. For other format characters, a following number means how many of that type appear consecutively in a string. Use * to take the rest of the available data.

You can convert between data types with unpack(). This example fills the array $ascii with the ASCII values of each character in $s:

```
$s = 'platypus';
$ascii = unpack('c*',$s);
print_r($ascii);
Array
(
    [1] => 112
    [2] => 108
    [3] => 97
    [4] => 116
    [5] => 121
    [6] => 112
    [7] => 117
    [8] => 115
)
```

See Also

Documentation on pack() at *http://www.php.net/pack* and unpack() at *http://www.php.net/unpack*.

CHAPTER 2

Numbers

2.0   Introduction

In everyday life, numbers are easy to identify. They're 3:00 P.M., as in the current time, or $1.29, as in the cost of a pint of milk. Maybe they're like π, the ratio of the circumference to the diameter of a circle. They can be pretty large, like Avogadro's number, which is about 6×10^{23}. In PHP, numbers can be all these things.

However, PHP doesn't treat all these numbers as "numbers." Instead, it breaks them down into two groups: integers and floating-point numbers. Integers are whole numbers, such as -4, 0, 5, and 1,975. Floating-point numbers are decimal numbers, such as -1.23, 0.0, 3.14159, and 9.9999999999.

Conveniently, most of the time PHP doesn't make you worry about the differences between the two because it automatically converts integers to floating-point numbers and floating-point numbers to integers. This conveniently allows you to ignore the underlying details. It also means 3/2 is 1.5, not 1, as it would be in some programming languages. PHP also automatically converts from strings to numbers and back. For instance, 1+"1" is 2.

However, sometimes this blissful ignorance can cause trouble. First, numbers can't be infinitely large or small; there's a minimum size of 2.2e-308 and a maximum size of about 1.8e308.* If you need larger (or smaller) numbers, you must use the BCMath or GMP libraries, which are discussed in Recipe 2.13.

Next, floating-point numbers aren't guaranteed to be exactly correct but only correct plus or a minus a small amount. Now, this amount is small enough for most occasions, but you can end up with problems in certain instances. For instance, humans automatically convert 6 followed by an endless string of 9s after the decimal point to 7, but PHP thinks it's 6 with a bunch of 9s. Therefore, if you ask PHP for the

---

* These numbers are actually platform-specific, but the values are common because they are from the 64-bit IEEE standard 754.

integer value of that number, it returns 6, not 7. For similar reasons, if the digit located in the 200th decimal place is significant, floating-point numbers aren't useful. Again, the BCMath and GMP libraries ride to the rescue. But, for most occasions, PHP behaves very nicely when playing with numbers and lets you treat them just as you do in real life.

2.1 Checking Whether a String Contains a Valid Number

Problem

You want to ensure that a string contains a number. For example, you want to validate an age that the user has typed into a form input field.

Solution

Use is_numeric():

```
if (is_numeric('five')) { /* false */ }

if (is_numeric(5))      { /* true  */ }
if (is_numeric('5'))    { /* true  */ }

if (is_numeric(-5))     { /* true  */ }
if (is_numeric('-5'))   { /* true  */ }
```

Discussion

Besides working on numbers, is_numeric() can also be applied to numeric strings. The distinction here is that the integer 5 and the string 5 technically aren't the same in PHP.*

Helpfully, is_numeric() properly parses decimal numbers, such as 5.1; however, numbers with thousands separators, such as 5,100, cause is_numeric() to return false.

To strip the thousands separators from your number before calling is_numeric() use str_replace():

```
is_numeric(str_replace($number, ',', ''));
```

---

* The most glaring example of this difference came during the transition from PHP 3 to PHP 4. In PHP 3, empty('0') returned false, but as of PHP 4, it returns true. On the other hand, empty(0) has always returned true and still does. (Actually, you need to call empty() on *variables* containing '0' and 0.) See the Introduction to Chapter 5 for details.

To check if your number is a specific type, there are a variety of self-explanatorily named related functions: is_bool(), is_float() (or is_double() or is_real(); they're all the same), and is_int() (or is_integer() or is_long()).

See Also

Documentation on is_numeric() at *http://www.php.net/is-numeric* and str_replace() at *http://www.php.net/str-replace*.

2.2   Comparing Floating-Point Numbers

Problem

You want to check whether two floating-point numbers are equal.

Solution

Use a small delta value, and check if the numbers are equal within that delta:

```
$delta = 0.00001;

$a = 1.00000001;
$b = 1.00000000;

if (abs($a - $b) < $delta) { /* $a and $b are equal */ }
```

Discussion

Floating-point numbers are represented in binary form with only a finite number of bits for the mantissa and the exponent. You get overflows when you exceed those bits. As a result, sometimes PHP (and other languages, too) don't believe two equal numbers are actually equal because they may differ toward the very end.

To avoid this problem, instead of checking if $a == $b, make sure the first number is within a very small amount ($delta) of the second one. The size of your delta should be the smallest amount of difference you care about between two numbers. Then use abs() to get the absolute value of the difference.

See Also

Recipe 2.3 for information on rounding floating-point numbers; documentation on floating-point numbers in PHP at *http://www.php.net/language.types.float*.

2.3   Rounding Floating-Point Numbers

Problem

You want to round a floating-point number, either to an integer value or to a set number of decimal places.

Solution

To round a number to the closest integer, use round():

```
$number = round(2.4);    // $number = 2
```

To round up, use ceil():

```
$number = ceil(2.4);    // $number = 3
```

To round down, use floor():

```
$number = floor(2.4);    // $number = 2
```

Discussion

If a number falls exactly between two integers, its behavior is undefined:

```
$number = round(2.5);    // $number is 2 or 3!
```

Be careful! As we mention in Recipe 2.2, floating-point numbers don't always work out to exact values because of how they're stored internally by the computer. This can create situations in which the obvious answer isn't. A value you expect to have a decimal part of "0.5" might instead be ".499999...9" (with a whole bunch of 9s) or ".500000...1" (with many 0s and a trailing 1). If you want to ensure that a number is rounded up as you might expect, add a small delta value to it before rounding:

```
$delta = 0.0000001;
$number = round(2.5 + $delta);    // $number = 3
```

To keep a set number of digits after the decimal point, round() accepts an optional precision argument. For example, if you are calculating the total price for the items in a user's shopping cart:

```
$cart = 54.23;
$tax = $cart * .05;
$total = $cart + $tax;        // $total = 56.9415

$final = round($total, 2);    // $final = 56.94
```

See Also

Recipe 2.2 for information on comparing floating-point numbers; documentation on round() at *http://www.php.net/round*.

2.4   Operating on a Series of Integers

Problem

You want to apply a piece of code over a range of integers.

Solution

Use the range() function, which returns an array populated with integers:

```
foreach(range($start,$end) as $i) {
    plot_point($i);
}
```

Instead of using range(), it can be more efficient to use a for loop. Also, you can increment using values other than 1. For example:

```
for ($i = $start; $i <= $end; $i += $increment) {
    plot_point($i);
}
```

Discussion

Loops like this are common. For instance, you could be plotting a function and need to calculate the results for multiple points on the graph. Or, you could be NASA counting down until the launch of the Space Shuttle Columbia.

In the first example, range() returns an array with values from $start to $end. Then foreach pulls out each element and assigns it to $i inside of the loop. The advantage of using range() is its brevity, but this technique has a few disadvantages. For one, a large array can take up unnecessary memory. Also, you're forced to increment the series one number at a time, so you can't loop through a series of even integers, for example.

As of PHP 4.1, it is valid for $start to be larger than $end. In this case, the numbers returned by range() are in descending order. Also, you can use iterate over character sequences:

```
print_r(range('l', 'p'));
Array
(
    [0] => l
    [1] => m
    [2] => n
    [3] => o
    [4] => p
)
```

The for loop method just uses a single integer and avoids the array entirely. While it's longer, you have greater control over the loop, because you can increment and

---

decrement $i more freely. Also, you can modify $i from inside the loop, something you can't do with range( ), because PHP reads in the entire array when it enters the loop, and changes to the array don't effect the sequence of elements.

See Also

Recipe 4.3 for details on initializing an array to a range of integers; documentation on range( ) at *http://www.php.net/range*.

2.5   Generating Random Numbers Within a Range

Problem

You want to generate a random number within a range of numbers.

Solution

Use mt_rand( ):

```
// random number between $upper and $lower, inclusive
$random_number = mt_rand($lower, $upper);
```

Discussion

Generating random numbers is useful when you want to display a random image on a page, randomize the starting position of a game, select a random record from a database, or generate a unique session identifier.

To generate a random number between two end points, pass mt_rand( ) two arguments:

```
$random_number = mt_rand(1, 100);
```

Calling mt_rand( ) without any arguments returns a number between 0 and the maximum random number, which is returned by mt_getrandmax( ).

Generating truly random numbers is hard for computers to do. Computers excel at following instructions methodically; they're not so good at spontaneity. If you want to instruct a computer to return random numbers, you need to give it a specific set of repeatable commands; the very fact that they're repeatable undermines the desired randomness.

PHP has two different random number generators, a classic function called rand( ) and a better function called mt_rand( ). MT stands for Mersenne Twister, which is named for the French monk and mathematician Marin Mersenne and the type of

prime numbers he's associated with. The algorithm is based on these prime numbers. Since mt_rand( ) is more random and faster than rand( ), we prefer it to rand( ).

If you're running a version of PHP earlier than 4.2, before using mt_rand( ) (or rand( ))
for the first time in a script, you need to seed the generator, by calling mt_srand( ) (or
srand( )). The *seed* is a number the random function uses as the basis for generating
the random numbers it returns; it's how to solve the repeatable versus random
dilemma mentioned earlier. Use the value returned by microtime( ), a high-precision
time function, to get a seed that changes very quickly and is unlikely to repeat—quali-
ties desirable in a good seed. After the initial seed, you don't need to reseed the ran-
domizer. PHP 4.2 and later automatically handles seeding for you, but if you
manually provide a seed before calling mt_rand( ) for the first time, PHP doesn't alter
it by substituting a new seed of its own.

If you want to select a random record from a database—an easy way is to find the
total number of fields inside the table—select a random number in that range, and
then request that row from the database:

```
$sth = $dbh->query('SELECT COUNT(*) AS count FROM quotes');
if ($row = $sth->fetchRow()) {
    $count = $row[0];
} else {
    die ($row->getMessage());
}

$random = mt_rand(0, $count - 1);

$sth = $dbh->query("SELECT quote FROM quotes LIMIT $random,1");
while ($row = $sth->fetchRow()) {
    print $row[0] . "\n";
}
```

This snippet finds the total number of rows in the table, computes a random number inside that range, and then uses LIMIT $random,1 to SELECT one line from the
table starting at position $random.

Alternatively, if you're using MySQL 3.23 or above, you can do this:

```
$sth = $dbh->query('SELECT quote FROM quotes ORDER BY RAND() LIMIT 1');
while ($row = $sth->fetchRow()) {
    print $row[0] . "\n";
}
```

In this case, MySQL randomizes the lines, and then the first row is returned.

See Also

Recipe 2.6 for how to generate biased random numbers; documentation on mt_rand( )
at *http://www.php.net/mt-rand* and rand( ) at *http://www.php.net/rand*; the MySQL
Manual on RAND( ) at *http://www.mysql.com/doc/M/a/Mathematical_functions.html*.

2.6   Generating Biased Random Numbers

Problem

You want to generate random numbers, but you want these numbers to be somewhat biased, so that numbers in certain ranges appear more frequently than others. For example, you want to spread out a series of banner ad impressions in proportion to the number of impressions remaining for each ad campaign.

Solution

Use the pc_rand_weighted() function shown in Example 2-1.

Example 2-1. pc_rand_weighted()

```
// returns the weighted randomly selected key
function pc_rand_weighted($numbers) {
    $total = 0;
    foreach ($numbers as $number => $weight) {
        $total += $weight;
        $distribution[$number] = $total;
    }
    $rand = mt_rand(0, $total - 1);
    foreach ($distribution as $number => $weights) {
        if ($rand < $weights) { return $number; }
    }
}
```

Discussion

Imagine if instead of an array in which the values are the number of remaining impressions, you have an array of ads in which each ad occurs exactly as many times as its remaining number of impressions. You can simply pick an unweighted random place within the array, and that'd be the ad that shows.

This technique can consume a lot of memory if you have millions of impressions remaining. Instead, you can calculate how large that array would be (by totalling the remaining impressions), pick a random number within the size of the make-believe array, and then go through the array figuring out which ad corresponds to the number you picked. For instance:

```
$ads = array('ford' => 12234, // advertiser, remaining impressions
             'att'  => 33424,
             'ibm'  => 16823);

$ad = pc_rand_weighted($ads);
```

See Also

Recipe 2.5 for how to generate random numbers within a range.

2.7   Taking Logarithms

Problem

You want to take the logarithm of a number.

Solution

For logs using base *e* (natural log), use log( ):

```
$log = log(10);          // 2.30258092994
```

For logs using base 10, use log10( ):

```
$log10 = log10(10);      // 1
```

For logs using other bases, use pc_logn( ):

```
function pc_logn($number, $base) {
    return log($number) / log($base);
}

$log2 = pc_logn(10, 2); // 3.3219280948874
```

Discussion

Both log( ) and log10( ) are defined only for numbers that are greater than zero. The pc_logn( ) function uses the change of base formula, which says that the log of a number in base n is equal to the log of that number, divided by the log of n.

See Also

Documentation on log( ) at *http://www.php.net/log* and log10( ) at *http://www.php.net/log10*.

2.8   Calculating Exponents

Problem

You want to raise a number to a power.

Solution

To raise *e* to a power, use exp( ):

```
$exp = exp(2);        // 7.3890560989307
```

To raise it to any power, use pow( ):

```
$exp = pow( 2, M_E); // 6.5808859910179

$pow = pow( 2, 10);   // 1024
$pow = pow( 2, -2);   // 0.25
$pow = pow( 2, 2.5);  // 5.6568542494924

$pow = pow(-2, 10);   // 1024
$pow = pow( 2, -2);   // 0.25
$pow = pow(-2, -2.5); // NAN (Error: Not a Number)
```

Discussion

The built-in constant M_E is an approximation of the value of *e*. It equals 2.718281828459045 2354. So exp($n) and pow(M_E, $n) are identical.

It's easy to create very large numbers using exp( ) and pow( ); if you outgrow PHP's maximum size (almost 1.8e308), see Recipe 2.13 for how to use the arbitrary precision functions. With these functions, PHP returns INF, infinity, if the result is too large and NAN, not-a-number, on an error.

See Also

Documentation on pow( ) at *http://www.php.net/pow*, exp( ) at *http://www.php.net/exp*, and information on predefined mathematical constants at *http://www.php.net/math*.

2.9   Formatting Numbers

Problem

You have a number and you want to print it with thousands and decimals separators. For instance, you want to display prices for items in a shopping cart.

Solution

Use the number_format( ) function to format as an integer:

```
$number = 1234.56;
print number_format($number);    // 1,235 because number is rounded up
```

Specify a number of decimal places to format as a decimal:

```
print number_format($number, 2); // 1,234.56
```

Discussion

The `number_format()` function formats a number by inserting the correct decimal and thousands separators for your locale. If you want to manually specify these values, pass them as the third and fourth parameters:

```
$number = 1234.56;
print number_format($number, 2, '@', '#'); // 1#234@56
```

The third argument is used as the decimal point and the last separates thousands. If you use these options, you must specify both arguments.

By default, `number_format()` rounds the number to the nearest integer. If you want to preserve the entire number, but you don't know ahead of time how many digits follow the decimal point in your number, use this:

```
$number = 1234.56; // your number
list($int, $dec) = explode('.', $number);
print number_format($number, strlen($dec));
```

See Also

Documentation on `number_format()` at *http://www.php.net/number-format*.

2.10   Printing Correct Plurals

Problem

You want to correctly pluralize words based on the value of a variable. For instance, you are returning text that depends on the number of matches found by a search.

Solution

Use a conditional expression:

```
$number = 4;
print "Your search returned $number " . ($number == 1 ? 'hit' : 'hits') . '.';
Your search returned 4 hits.
```

Discussion

It's slightly shorter to write the line as:

```
print "Your search returned $number hit" . ($number == 1 ? '' : 's') . '.';
```

However, for odd pluralizations, such as "person" versus "people," we find it clearer to break out the entire word rather than just the letter.

Another option is to use one function for all pluralization, as shown in the pc_may_pluralize() function in Example 2-2.

Example 2-2. pc_may_pluralize()

```
function pc_may_pluralize($singular_word, $amount_of) {

    // array of special plurals
    $plurals = array(
        'fish' => 'fish',
        'person' => 'people',
    );

    // only one
    if (1 == $amount_of) {
        return $singular_word;
    }

    // more than one, special plural
    if (isset($plurals[$singular_word])) {
        return $plurals[$singular_word];
    }

    // more than one, standard plural: add 's' to end of word
    return $singular_word . 's';
}
```

Here are some examples:

```
$number_of_fish = 1;
print "I ate $number_of_fish " . pc_may_pluralize('fish', $number_of_fish) . '.';

$number_of_people = 4;
print 'Soylent Green is ' . pc_may_pluralize('person', $number_of_people) . '!';
I ate 1 fish.
Soylent Green is people!
```

If you plan to have multiple plurals inside your code, using a function such as pc_may_pluralize() increases readability. To use the function, pass pc_may_pluralize() the singular form of the word as the first argument and the amount as the second. Inside the function, there's a large array, $plurals, that holds all the special cases. If the $amount is 1, you return the original word. If it's greater, you return the special pluralized word, if it exists. As a default, just add an "s" to the end of the word.

2.11 Calculating Trigonometric Functions

Problem

You want to use trigonometric functions, such as sine, cosine, and tangent.

Solution

PHP supports many trigonometric functions natively: sin( ), cos( ), and tan( ):

```
$cos = cos(2.1232);
```

You can also use their inverses: asin( ), acos( ), and atan( ):

```
$atan = atan(1.2);
```

Discussion

These functions assume their arguments are in radians, not degrees. (See Recipe 2.12 if this is a problem.)

The function atan2( ) takes two variables $x and $y, and computes atan($x/$y). However, it always returns the correct sign because it uses both parameters when finding the quadrant of the result.

For secant, cosecant, and cotangent, you should manually calculate the reciprocal values of sin( ), cos( ), and tan( ):

```
$n = .707;

$secant    = 1 / sin($n);
$cosecant  = 1 / cos($n);
$cotangent = 1 / tan($n);
```

Starting in PHP 4.1, you can also use hyperbolic functions: sinh( ), cosh( ), and tanh( ), plus, of course, asin( ), cosh( ), and atanh( ). The inverse functions, however, aren't supported on Windows.

See Also

Recipe 2.12 for how to perform trig operations in degrees, not radians; documentation on sin( ) at *http://www.php.net/sin*, cos( ) at *http://www.php.net/cos*, tan( ) at *http://www.php.net/tan*, asin( ) at *http://www.php.net/asin*, acos( ) at *http://www.php.net/acos*, atan( ) at *http://www.php.net/atan*, and atan2( ) at *http://www.php.net/atan2*.

2.12 Doing Trigonometry in Degrees, not Radians

Problem

You have numbers in degrees but want to use the trigonometric functions.

Solution

Use deg2rad( ) and rad2deg( ) on your input and output:

```
$cosine = rad2deg(cos(deg2rad($degree)));
```

Discussion

By definition, 360 degrees is equal to 2π radians, so it's easy to manually convert between the two formats. However, these functions use PHP's internal value of π, so you're assured a high-precision answer. To access this number for other calculations, use the constant M_PI, which is 3.14159265358979323846.

There is no built-in support for gradians. This is considered a feature, not a bug.

See Also

Recipe 2.12 for trig basics; documentation on deg2rad( ) at *http://www.php.net/ deg2rad* and rad2deg( ) at *http://www.php.net/rad2deg*.

2.13 Handling Very Large or Very Small Numbers

Problem

You need to use numbers that are too large (or small) for PHP's built-in floating-point numbers.

Solution

Use either the BCMath or GMP libraries.

Using BCMath:

```
$sum = bcadd('1234567812345678', '8765432187654321');

// $sum is now the string '9999999999999999'
print $sum;
```

Using GMP:

```
$sum = gmp_add('1234567812345678', '8765432187654321');

// $sum is now a GMP resource, not a string; use gmp_strval() to convert
print gmp_strval($sum);
```

Discussion

The BCMath library is easy to use. You pass in your numbers as strings, and the function return the sum (or difference, product, etc.) as a string. However, the range of actions you can apply to numbers using BCMath is limited to basic arithmetic.

The GMP library is available as of PHP 4.0.4. While most members of the GMP family of functions accept integers and strings as arguments, they prefer to pass numbers around as resources, which are essentially pointers to the numbers. So, unlike BCMath functions, which return strings, GMP functions return only resources. You then pass the resource to any GMP function, and it acts as your number.

The only downside is when you want to view or use the resource with a non-GMP function, you need to explicitly convert it using gmp_strval() or gmp_intval().

GMP functions are liberal in what they accept. For instance:

```
$four = gmp_add(2, 2);           // You can pass integers
$eight = gmp_add('4', '4');      // Or strings
$twelve = gmp_add($four, $eight); // Or GMP resources
print gmp_strval($twelve);       // Prints 12
```

However, you can do many more things with GMP numbers than addition, such as raising a number to a power, computing large factorials very quickly, finding a greatest common divisor (GCD), and other fancy mathematical stuff:

```
// Raising a number to a power
$pow = gmp_pow(2, 10);           // 1024

// Computing large factorials very quickly
$factorial = gmp_fact(20);       // 2432902008176640000

// Finding a GCD
$gcd = gmp_gcd (123, 456);       // 3

// Other fancy mathematical stuff
$legdendre = gmp_legendre(1, 7); // 1
```

The BCMath and GMP libraries aren't necessarily enabled with all PHP configurations. As of PHP 4.0.4, BCMath is bundled with PHP, so it's likely to be available. However, GMP isn't bundled with PHP, so you'll need to download, install it, and instruct PHP to use it during the configuration process. Check the values of function_defined('bcadd') and function_defined('gmp_init') to see if you can use BCMath and GMP.

See Also

Documentation on BCMath at *http://www.php.net/bc* and GMP at *http://www.php.net/gmp*.

2.14 Converting Between Bases

Problem

You need to convert a number from one base to another.

Solution

Use the base_convert() function:

```
$hex = 'a1';                        // hexadecimal number (base 16)

// convert from base 16 to base 10
$decimal = base_convert($hex, 16, 10); // $decimal is now 161
```

Discussion

The base_convert() function changes a string in one base to the correct string in another. It works for all bases from 2 to 36 inclusive, using the letters a through z as additional symbols for bases above 10. The first argument is the number to be converted, followed by the base it is in and the base you want it to become.

There are also a few specialized functions for conversions to and from base 10 and the most commonly used other bases of 2, 8, and 16. They're bindec() and decbin(), octdec() and decoct(), and hexdec() and dechex():

```
// convert to base 10
print bindec(11011); // 27
print octdec(33);    // 27
print hexdec('1b');  // 27

// convert from base 10
print decbin(27);    // 11011
print decoct(27);    // 33
print dechex(27);    // 1b
```

Another alternative is to use sprintf(), which allows you to convert decimal numbers to binary, octal, and hexadecimal numbers with a wide range of formatting, such as leading 0s and a choice between upper- and lowercase letters for hexadecimal numbers.

For instance, say you want to print out HTML color values:

```
printf('#%02X%02X%02X', 0, 102, 204); // #0066CC
```

See Also

Documentation on base_convert( ) at *http://www.php.net/base-convert* and sprintf( ) formatting options at *http://www.php.net/sprintf.*

2.15   Calculating Using Numbers in Bases Other Than Decimal

Problem

You want to perform mathematical operations with numbers formatted not in decimal, but in octal or hexadecimal. For example, you want to calculate web-safe colors in hexadecimal.

Solution

Prefix the number with a leading symbol, so PHP knows it isn't in base 10. The following values are all equal:

```
0144  // base 8
 100  // base 10
0x64  // base 16
```

Here's how to count from decimal 1 to 15 using hexadecimal notation:

```
for ($i = 0x1; $i < 0x10; $i++) { print "$i\n"; }
```

Discussion

Even if you use hexadecimally formatted numbers in a for loop, by default, all numbers are printed in decimal. In other words, the code in the Solution doesn't print out "..., 8, 9, a, b, ...". To print in hexadecimal, use one of the methods listed in Recipe 2.14. Here's an example:

```
for ($i = 0x1; $i < 0x10; $i++) { print dechex($i) . "\n"; }
```

For most calculations, it's easier to use decimal. Sometimes, however, it's more logical to switch to another base, for example, when using the 216 web-safe colors. Every web color code is of the form *RRGGBB*, where *RR* is the red color, *GG* is the green color, and *BB* is the blue color. Each color is actually a two-digit hexadecimal number between 0 and FF.

What makes web-safe colors special is that *RR*, *GG*, and *BB* each must be one of the following six numbers: 00, 33, 66, 99, CC, and FF (in decimal: 0, 51, 102, 153, 204, 255). So, 003366 is web-safe, but 112233 is not. Web-safe colors render without dithering on a 256-color display.

When creating a list of these numbers, use hexadecimal notation in this triple-loop to reinforce the list's hexadecimal basis:

```
for ($rr = 0; $rr <= 0xFF; $rr += 0x33)
    for ($gg = 0; $gg <= 0xFF; $gg += 0x33)
        for ($bb = 0; $bb <= 0xFF; $bb += 0x33)
            printf("%02X%02X%02X\n", $rr, $gg, $bb);
```

Here the loops compute all possible web-safe colors. However, instead of stepping through them in decimal, you use hexadecimal notation, because it reinforces the hexadecimal link between the numbers. Print them out using `printf()` to format them as uppercase hexadecimal numbers at least two digits long. One-digit numbers are passed with a leading zero.

See Also

Recipe 2.14 for details on converting between bases; Chapter 3, "Web Design Principles for Print Designers," in *Web Design in a Nutshell* (O'Reilly).

CHAPTER 3
Dates and Times

3.0   Introduction

Displaying and manipulating dates and times seems simple at first but gets more difficult depending on how diverse and complicated your users are. Do your users span more than one time zone? Probably so, unless you are building an intranet or a site with a very specific geographical audience. Is your audience frightened away by timestamps that look like "2002-07-20 14:56:34 EDT" or do they need to be calmed with familiar representations like "Saturday July 20, 2000 (2:56 P.M.)." Calculating the number of hours between today at 10 A.M. and today at 7 P.M. is pretty easy. How about between today at 3 A.M. and noon on the first day of next month? Finding the difference between dates is discussed in Recipes 3.5 and 3.6.

These calculations and manipulations are made even more hectic by daylight saving (or summer) time (DST). Thanks to DST, there are times that don't exist (in most of the United States, 2 A.M. to 3 A.M. on the first Sunday in April) and times that exist twice (in most of the United States, 1 A.M. to 2 A.M. on the last Sunday in October). Some of your users may live in places that observe DST, some may not. Recipes 3.11 and 3.12 provide ways to work with time zones and DST.

Programmatic time handling is made much easier by two conventions. First, treat time internally as Coordinated Universal Time (abbreviated UTC and also known as GMT, Greenwich Mean Time), the patriarch of the time-zone family with no DST or summer time observance. This is the time zone at 0 degrees longitude, and all other time zones are expressed as offsets (either positive or negative) from it. Second, treat time not as an array of different values for month, day, year, minute, second, etc., but as seconds elapsed since the Unix epoch: midnight on January 1, 1970 (UTC, of course). This makes calculating intervals much easier, and PHP has plenty of functions to help you move easily between epoch timestamps and human-readable time representations.

The function `mktime()` produces epoch timestamps from a given set of time parts, while `date()`, given an epoch timestamp, returns a formatted time string. You can use these functions, for example, to find on what day of the week New Year's Day 1986 occurred:

```
$stamp = mktime(0,0,0,1,1,1986);
print date('l',$stamp);
Wednesday
```

This use of mktime( ) returns the epoch timestamp at midnight on January 1, 1986. The l format character to date( ) tells it to return the full name of the day of the week that corresponds to the given epoch timestamp. Recipe 3.4 details the many format characters available to date( ).

In this book, the phrase *epoch timestamp* refers to a count of seconds since the Unix epoch. *Time parts* (or *date parts* or *time and date parts*) means an array or group of time and date components such as day, month, year, hour, minute, and second. *Formatted time string* (or *formatted date string*, etc.) means a string that contains some particular grouping of time and date parts, for example "2002-03-12," "Wednesday, 11:23 A.M.," or "February 25."

If you used epoch timestamps as your internal time representation, you avoided any Y2K issues, because the difference between 946702799 (1999-12-31 23:59:59 UTC) and 946702800 (2000-01-01 00:00:00 UTC) is treated just like the difference between any other two timestamps. You may, however, run into a Y2038 problem. January 19, 2038 at 3:14:07 A.M. (UTC) is 2147483647 seconds after midnight January 1, 1970. What's special about 2147483647? It's $2^{31} - 1$, which is the largest integer expressible when 32 bits represent a signed integer. (The 32nd bit is used for the sign.)

The solution? At some point before January 19, 2038, make sure you trade up to hardware that uses, say, a 64-bit quantity for time storage. This buys you about another 292 billion years. (Just 39 bits would be enough to last you until about 10680, well after the impact of the Y10K bug has leveled the Earth's cold fusion factories and faster-than-light travel stations.) 2038 might seem far off right now, but so did 2000 to COBOL programmers in the 1950s and 1960s. Don't repeat their mistake!

3.1   Finding the Current Date and Time

Problem

You want to know what the time or date is.

Solution

Use strftime( ) or date( ) for a formatted time string:

```
print strftime('%c');
print date('r');
```

```
Mon Aug 12 18:23:45 2002
Mon, 12 Aug 2002 18:23:45 -0400
```

Use getdate() or localtime() if you want time parts:

```
$now_1 = getdate();
$now_2 = localtime();
print "$now_1[hours]:$now_1[minutes]:$now_1[seconds]";
print "$now_2[2]:$now_2[1]:$now_2[0]";
18:23:45
18:23:45
```

Discussion

The functions strftime() and date() can produce a variety of formatted time and date strings. They are discussed in more detail in Recipe 3.4. Both localtime() and getdate(), on the other hand, return arrays whose elements are the different pieces of the specified date and time.

The associative array getdate() returns has the key/value pairs listed in Table 3-1.

Table 3-1. Return array from getdate()

Key	Value
seconds	Seconds
minutes	Minutes
hours	Hours
mday	Day of the month
wday	Day of the week, numeric (Sunday is 0, Saturday is 6)
mon	Month, numeric
year	Year, numeric
yday	Day of the year, numeric (e.g., 299)
weekday	Day of the week, textual, full (e.g., "Friday")
month	Month, textual, full (e.g., "January")

For example, here's how to use getdate() to print out the month, day, and year:

```
$a = getdate();
printf('%s %d, %d',$a['month'],$a['mday'],$a['year']);
August 7, 2002
```

Pass getdate() an epoch timestamp as an argument to make the returned array the appropriate values for local time at that timestamp. For example, the month, day, and year at epoch timestamp 163727100 is:

```
$a = getdate(163727100);
printf('%s %d, %d',$a['month'],$a['mday'],$a['year']);
March 10, 1975
```

The function localtime() returns an array of time and date parts. It also takes an epoch timestamp as an optional first argument, as well as a boolean as an optional second argument. If that second argument is true, localtime() returns an associative array instead of a numerically indexed array. The keys of that array are the same as the members of the tm_struct structure that the C function localtime() returns, as shown in Table 3-2.

Table 3-2. Return array from localtime()

Numeric position	Key	Value
0	tm_sec	Second
1	tm_min	Minutes
2	tm_hour	Hour
3	tm_mday	Day of the month
4	tm_mon	Month of the year (January is 0)
5	tm_year	Years since 1900
6	tm_wday	Day of the week
7	tm_yday	Day of the year
8	tm_isdst	Is daylight saving time in effect?

For example, here's how to use localtime() to print out today's date in month/day/year format:

```
$a = localtime();
$a[4] += 1;
$a[5] += 1900;
print "$a[4]/$a[3]/$a[5]";
8/7/2002
```

The month is incremented by 1 before printing since localtime() starts counting months with 0 for January, but we want to display 1 if the current month is January. Similarly, the year is incremented by 1900 because localtime() starts counting years with 0 for 1900.

Like getdate(), localtime() accepts an epoch timestamp as an optional first argument to produce time parts for that timestamp:

```
$a = localtime(163727100);
$a[4] += 1;
$a[5] += 1900;
print "$a[4]/$a[3]/$a[5]";
3/10/1975
```

See Also

Documentation on strftime() at *http://www.php.net/strftime*, date() at *http://www.php.net/date*, getdate() at *http://www.php.net/getdate*, and localtime() at *http://www.php.net/localtime*.

3.2   Converting Time and Date Parts to an Epoch Timestamp

Problem

You want to know what epoch timestamp corresponds to a set of time and date parts.

Solution

Use mktime() if your time and date parts are in the local time zone:

```
// 7:45:03 PM on March 10, 1975, local time
$then = mktime(19,45,3,3,10,1975);
```

Use gmmktime() if your time and date parts are in GMT:

```
// 7:45:03 PM on March 10, 1975, in GMT
$then = gmmktime(19,45,3,3,10,1975);
```

Pass no arguments to get the current date and time in the local or UTC time zone:

```
$now = mktime();
$now_utc = gmmktime();
```

Discussion

The functions mktime() and gmmktime() each take a date and time's parts (hour, minute, second, month, day, year, DST flag) and return the appropriate Unix epoch timestamp. The components are treated as local time by mktime(), while gmmktime() treats them as a date and time in UTC. For both functions, a seventh argument, the DST flag (1 if DST is being observed, 0 if not), is optional. These functions return sensible results only for times within the epoch. Most systems store epoch time-stamps in a 32-bit signed integer, so "within the epoch" means between 8:45:51 P.M. December 13, 1901 UTC and 3:14:07 A.M. January 19, 2038 UTC.

In the following example, $stamp_now is the epoch timestamp when mktime() is called and $stamp_future is the epoch timestamp for 3:25 P.M. on June 4, 2012:

```
$stamp_now = mktime();
$stamp_future = mktime(15,25,0,6,4,2012);
```

```
print $stamp_now;
print $stamp_future;
1028782421
1338837900
```

Both epoch timestamps can be fed back to strftime() to produce formatted time strings:

```
print strftime('%c',$stamp_now);
print strftime('%c',$stamp_future);
Thu Aug  8 00:53:41 2002
Mon Jun 4 15:25:00 2012
```

Because the previous calls to mktime() were made on a computer set to EDT (which is four hours behind GMT), using gmmktime() instead produces epoch timestamps that are 14400 seconds (four hours) smaller:

```
$stamp_now = gmmktime();
$stamp_future = gmmktime(15,25,0,6,4,2012);

print $stamp_now;
print $stamp_future;
1028768021
1338823500
```

Feeding these gmmktime()-generated epoch timestamps back to strftime() produces formatting time strings that are also four hours earlier:

```
print strftime('%c',$stamp_now);
print strftime('%c',$stamp_future);
Wed Aug  7 20:53:41 2002
Mon Jun 4 11:25:00 2012
```

See Also

Recipe 3.3 for how to convert an epoch timestamp back to time and date parts; documentation on mktime() at *http://www.php.net/mktime* and gmmktime() at *http://www.php.net/gmmktime*.

3.3   Converting an Epoch Timestamp to Time and Date Parts

Problem

You want the set of time and date parts that corresponds to an epoch timestamp.

Solution

Pass an epoch timestamp to getdate( ):

```
$time_parts = getdate(163727100);
```

Discussion

The time parts returned by getdate( ) are detailed in Table 3-1. These time parts are in local time. If you want time parts in another time zone corresponding to a particular epoch timestamp, see Recipe 3.11.

See Also

Recipe 3.2 for how to convert time and date parts back to epoch timestamps; Recipe 3.11 for how to deal with time zones; documentation on getdate( ) at *http://www.php.net/getdate*.

3.4 Printing a Date or Time in a Specified Format

Problem

You need to print out a date or time formatted in a particular way.

Solution

Use date( ) or strftime( ):

```
print strftime('%c');
print date('m/d/Y');
Tue Jul 30 11:31:08 2002
07/30/2002
```

Discussion

Both date( ) and strftime( ) are flexible functions that can produce a formatted time string with a variety of components. The formatting characters for these functions are listed in Table 3-3. The Windows column indicates whether the formatting character is supported by strftime( ) on Windows systems.

Table 3-3. strftime() and date() format characters

Type	strftime()	date()	Description	Range	Windows
Hour	%H	H	Hour, numeric, 24-hour clock	00–23	Yes
Hour	%I	h	Hour, numeric, 12-hour clock	01–12	Yes
Hour	%k		Hour, numeric, 24-hour clock, leading zero as space	0–23	No
Hour	%l		Hour, numeric, 12-hour clock, leading zero as space	1–12	No
Hour	%p	A	AM or PM designation for current locale		Yes
Hour	%P	a	am/pm designation for current locale		No
Hour		G	Hour, numeric, 24-hour clock, leading zero trimmed	0–23	No
Hour		g	Hour, numeric, 12-hour clock, leading zero trimmed	0–1	No
Minute	%M	I	Minute, numeric	00–59	Yes
Second	%S	s	Second, numeric	00–61[a]	Yes
Day	%d	d	Day of the month, numeric	01–31	Yes
Day	%e		Day of the month, numeric, leading zero as space	1–31	No
Day	%j	z	Day of the year, numeric	001–366 for strftime(); 0–365 for date()	Yes
Day	%u		Day of the week, numeric (Monday is 1)	1–7	No
Day	%w	w	Day of the week, numeric (Sunday is 0)	0–6	Yes
Day		j	Day of the month, numeric, leading zero trimmed	1–31	No
Day		S	English ordinal suffix for day of the month, textual	"st," "th," "nd," "rd"	No
Week	%a	D	Abbreviated weekday name, text for current locale		Yes
Week	%A	l	Full weekday name, text for current locale		Yes
Week	%U		Week number in the year; numeric; first Sunday is the first day of the first week	00–53	Yes
Week	%V	W	ISO 8601:1988 week number in the year; numeric; week 1 is the first week that has at least 4 days in the current year; Monday is the first day of the week	01–53	No
Week	%W		Week number in the year; numeric; first Monday is the first day of the first week	00–53	Yes
Month	%B	F	Full month name, text for current locale		Yes
Month	%b	M	Abbreviated month name, text for current locale		Yes

Table 3-3. strftime() and date() format characters (continued)

Type	strftime()	date()	Description	Range	Windows
Month	%h		Same as %b		No
Month	%m	m	Month, numeric	01–12	Yes
Month		n	Month, numeric, leading zero trimmed	1–12	No
Month		t	Month length in days, numeric	28, 29, 30, 31	No
Year	%C		Century, numeric	00–99	No
Year	%g		Like %G, but without the century	00–99	No
Year	%G		ISO 8601 year with century; numeric; the four-digit year corresponding to the ISO week number; same as %y except if the ISO week number belongs to the previous or next year, that year is used instead		No
Year	%y	y	Year without century, numeric	00–99	Yes
Year	%Y	Y	Year, numeric, including century		Yes
Year		L	Leap year flag (yes is 1)	0, 1	No
Timezone	%z	O	Hour offset from GMT, +/-HHMM (e.g., −0400, +0230)	−1200–+1200	Yes, but acts like %Z
Timezone	%Z	T	Time zone, name, or abbreviation; textual		Yes
Timezone		I	Daylight saving time flag (yes is 1)	0, 1	No
Timezone		Z	Seconds offset from GMT; west of GMT is negative, east of GMT is positive	−43200–43200	No
Compound	%c		Standard date and time format for current locale		Yes
Compound	%D		Same as %m/%d/%y		No
Compound	%F		Same as %Y-%m-%d		No
Compound	%r		Time in AM or PM notation for current locale		No
Compound	%R		Time in 24-hour notation for current locale		No
Compound	%T		Time in 24-hour notation (same as %H:%M:%S)		No
Compound	%x		Standard date format for current locale (without time)		Yes
Compound	%X		Standard time format for current locale (without date)		Yes
Compound		r	RFC 822 formatted date (e.g., "Thu, 22 Aug 2002 16:01:07 +0200")		No
Other	%s	U	Seconds since the epoch		No
Other		B	Swatch Internet time		No
Formatting	%%		Literal % character		Yes
Formatting	%n		Newline character		No
Formatting	%t		Tab character		No

[a] The range for seconds extends to 61 to account for leap seconds.

The first argument to each function is a format string, and the second argument is an epoch timestamp. If you leave out the second argument, both functions default to the current date and time. While date() and strftime() operate over local time, they each have UTC-centric counterparts (gmdate() and gmstrftime()).

The formatting characters for date() are PHP-specific, but strftime() uses the C-library strftime() function. This may make strftime() more understandable to someone coming to PHP from another language, but it also makes its behavior slightly different on various platforms. Windows doesn't support as many strftime() formatting commands as most Unix-based systems. Also, strftime() expects its formatting characters to each be preceded by a % (think printf()), so it's easier to produce strings with lots of interpolated time and date values in them.

For example, at 12:49 P.M. on July 15, 2002, the code to print out:

```
It's after 12 pm on July 15, 2002
```

with strftime() looks like:

```
print strftime("It's after %I %P on %B %d, %Y");
```

With date() it looks like:

```
print "It's after ".date('h a').' on '.date('F d, Y');
```

Non-date-related characters in a format string are fine for strftime(), because it looks for the % character to decide where to interpolate the appropriate time information. However, date() doesn't have such a delimiter, so about the only extras you can tuck into the formatting string are spaces and punctuation. If you pass strftime()'s formatting string to date():

```
print date("It's after %I %P on %B%d, %Y");
```

you'd almost certainly not want what you'd get:

```
131'44 pmf31eMon, 15 Jul 2002 12:49:44 -0400 %1 %P o7 %742%15, %2002
```

To generate time parts with date() that are easy to interpolate, group all time and date parts from date() into one string, separating the different components with a delimiter that date() won't translate into anything and that isn't itself part of one of your substrings. Then, using explode() with that delimiter character, put each piece of the return value from date() in an array, which is easily interpolated in your output string:

```
$ar = explode(':',date("h a:F d, Y"));
print "It's after $ar[0] on $ar[1]";
```

See Also

Documentation on date() at *http://www.php.net/date* and strftime() at *http://www.php.net/strftime*; on Unix-based systems, *man strftime* for your system-specific

strftime() options; on Windows, see *http://msdn.microsoft.com/library/*
default.asp?url=/library/en-us/vclib/html/_crt_strftime.2c_.wcsftime.asp for strftime()
details.

3.5   Finding the Difference of Two Dates

Problem

You want to find the elapsed time between two dates. For example, you want to tell
a user how long it's been since she last logged onto your site.

Solution

Convert both dates to epoch timestamps and subtract one from the other. Use this
code to separate the difference into weeks, days, hours, minutes, and seconds:

```
// 7:32:56 pm on May 10, 1965
$epoch_1 = mktime(19,32,56,5,10,1965);
// 4:29:11 am on November 20, 1962
$epoch_2 = mktime(4,29,11,11,20,1962);

$diff_seconds  = $epoch_1 - $epoch_2;
$diff_weeks    = floor($diff_seconds/604800);
$diff_seconds -= $diff_weeks   * 604800;
$diff_days     = floor($diff_seconds/86400);
$diff_seconds -= $diff_days    * 86400;
$diff_hours    = floor($diff_seconds/3600);
$diff_seconds -= $diff_hours   * 3600;
$diff_minutes  = floor($diff_seconds/60);
$diff_seconds -= $diff_minutes * 60;

print "The two dates have $diff_weeks weeks, $diff_days days, ";
print "$diff_hours hours, $diff_minutes minutes, and $diff_seconds ";
print "seconds elapsed between them.";
The two dates have 128 weeks, 6 days, 14 hours, 3 minutes,
and 45 seconds elapsed between them.
```

Note that the difference isn't divided into larger chunks than weeks (i.e., months or
years) because those chunks have variable length and wouldn't give an accurate
count of the time difference calculated.

Discussion

There are a few strange things going on here that you should be aware of. First of all,
1962 and 1965 precede the beginning of the epoch. Fortunately, mktime() fails gracefully here and produces negative epoch timestamps for each. This is okay because the
absolute time value of either of these questionable timestamps isn't necessary, just

the difference between the two. As long as epoch timestamps for the dates fall within the range of a signed integer, their difference is calculated correctly.

Next, a wall clock (or calendar) reflects a slightly different amount of time change between these two dates, because they are on different sides of a DST switch. The result subtracting epoch timestamps gives is the correct amount of *elapsed* time, but the perceived human time change is an hour off. For example, on the Sunday morning in April when DST is activated, what's the difference between 1:30 A.M. and 4:30 A.M.? It seems like three hours, but the epoch timestamps for these two times are only 7,200 seconds apart—two hours. When a local clock springs forward an hour (or falls back an hour in October), the steady march of epoch timestamps takes no notice. Truly, only two hours have passed, although our clock manipulations make it seem like three.

If you want to measure actual elapsed time (and you usually do), this method is fine. If you're more concerned with the difference in what a clock says at two points in time, use Julian days to compute the interval, as discussed in Recipe 3.6.

To tell a user the elapsed time since her last login, you need to find the difference between the login time and her last login time:

```
$epoch_1 = time();
$r = mysql_query("SELECT UNIX_TIMESTAMP(last_login) AS login
                  FROM user WHERE id = $id") or die();
$ob = mysql_fetch_object($r);
$epoch_2 = $ob->login;

$diff_seconds  = $epoch_1 - $epoch_2;
$diff_weeks    = floor($diff_seconds/604800);
$diff_seconds -= $diff_weeks    * 604800;
$diff_days     = floor($diff_seconds/86400);
$diff_seconds -= $diff_days      * 86400;
$diff_hours    = floor($diff_seconds/3600);
$diff_seconds -= $diff_hours     * 3600;
$diff_minutes  = floor($diff_seconds/60);
$diff_seconds -= $diff_minutes * 60;

print "You last logged in $diff_weeks weeks, $diff_days days, ";
print "$diff_hours hours, $diff_minutes minutes, and $diff_seconds ago.";
```

See Also

Recipe 3.6 to find the difference between two dates with Julian days; Recipe 3.10 for adding and subtracting from a date; documentation on MySQL's UNIX_TIMESTAMP() function at *http://www.mysql.com/doc/D/a/Date_and_time_functions.html*.

3.6   Finding the Difference of Two Dates with Julian Days

Problem

You want to find the difference of two dates measured by what a clock would say, not the actual elapsed time.

Solution

Use gregoriantojd() to get the Julian day for a set of date parts, then subtract one Julian day from the other to find the date difference. Then convert the time parts to seconds and subtract one from the other to find the time difference. If the time difference is less than 0, decrease the date difference by one and adjust the time difference to apply to the previous day. Here's the code:

```
$diff_date = gregoriantojd($date_1_mo, $date_1_dy, $date_1_yr) -
             gregoriantojd($date_2_mo, $date_2_dy, $date_2_yr);
$diff_time = $date_1_hr * 3600 + $date_1_mn * 60 + $date_1_sc -
             $date_2_hr * 3600 - $date_2_mn * 60 - $date_2_sc;
if ($diff_time < 0) {
   $diff_date--;
   $diff_time = 86400 - $diff_time;
}
```

Discussion

Finding differences with Julian days lets you operate outside the range of epoch seconds and also accounts for DST differences.

If you have the components of your two days in arrays:

```
// 7:32:56 pm on May 10, 1965
list($date_1_yr, $date_1_mo, $date_1_dy, $date_1_hr, $date_1_mn, $date_1_sc)=
   array(1965, 5, 10, 19, 32, 56);
// 4:29:11 am on November 20, 1962
list($date_2_yr, $date_2_mo, $date_2_dy, $date_2_hr, $date_2_mn, $date_2_sc)=
   array(1962, 11, 20, 4, 29, 11);

$diff_date = gregoriantojd($date_1_mo, $date_1_dy, $date_1_yr) -
             gregoriantojd($date_2_mo, $date_2_dy, $date_2_yr);
$diff_time = $date_1_hr * 3600 + $date_1_mn * 60 + $date_1_sc -
             $date_2_hr * 3600 - $date_2_mn * 60 - $date_2_sc;
if ($diff_time < 0) {
   $diff_date--;
   $diff_time = 86400 - $diff_time;
}
```

```
$diff_weeks = floor($diff_date/7); $diff_date -= $diff_weeks * 7;
$diff_hours = floor($diff_time/3600); $diff_time -= $diff_hours * 3600;
$diff_minutes = floor($diff_time/60); $diff_time -= $diff_minutes * 60;

print "The two dates have $diff_weeks weeks, $diff_date days, ";
print "$diff_hours hours, $diff_minutes minutes, and $diff_time ";
print "seconds between them.";
The two dates have 128 weeks, 6 days, 15 hours, 3 minutes,
and 45 seconds between them.
```

This method produces a time difference based on clock time, which is why the result shows an hour more of difference than in Recipe 3.5. May 10 is during DST, and November 11 is during standard time.

The function gregoriantojd() is part of PHP's calendar extension, and so is available only if that extension is loaded.

See Also

Recipe 3.5 to find the difference between two dates in elapsed time; Recipe 3.10 for adding and subtracting from a date; documentation on gregoriantojd() at *http://www.php.net/gregoriantojd*; an overview of the Julian Day system is at *http://tycho.usno.navy.mil/mjd.html*.

3.7   Finding the Day in a Week, Month, Year, or the Week Number in a Year

Problem

You want to know the day or week of the year, the day of the week, or the day of the month. For example, you want to print a special message every Monday, or on the first of every month.

Solution

Use the appropriate arguments to date() or strftime():

```
print strftime("Today is day %d of the month and %j of the year.");
print 'Today is day '.date('d').' of the month and '.date('z').' of the year.';
```

Discussion

The two functions date() and strftime() don't behave identically. Days of the year start with 0 for date(), but with 1 for strftime(). Table 3-4 contains all the day and week number format characters date() and strftime() understand.

Table 3-4. Day and week number format characters

Type	strftime()	date()	Description	Range
Day	%d	d	Day of the month, numeric	01–31
Day	%j	z	Day of the year, numeric	001–366 for strftime( );0–365 for date( )
Day	%u		Day of the week, numeric (Monday is 1)	1–7
Day	%w	w	Day of the week, numeric (Sunday is 0)	0–6
Day	%W		ISO 8601 day of the week, numeric (Monday is the first day of the week)	0–6
Week	%U		Week number in the year; numeric; first Sunday is the first day of the first week	00–53
Week	%V	W	ISO 8601:1988 week number in the year; numeric; week 1 is the first week that has at least four days in the current year; Monday is the first day of the week	01–53

To print out something only on Mondays, use the w formatting character to date( ) or the %w string with strftime( ):

```
if (1 == date('w')) {
    print "Welcome to the beginning of your work week.";
}

if (1 == strftime('%w')) {
    print "Only 4 more days until the weekend!";
}
```

There are different ways to calculate week numbers and days in a week, so be careful to choose the appropriate one. The ISO standard (ISO 8601), says that weeks begin on Mondays and that the days in the week are numbered 1 (Monday) through 7 (Sunday). Week 1 in a year is the first week in a year with a Thursday in that year. This means the first week in a year is the first week with a majority of its days in that year. These week numbers range from 01 to 53.

Other week number standards range from 00 to 53, with days in a year's week 53 potentially overlapping with days in the following year's week 00.

As long as you're consistent within your programs, you shouldn't run into any trouble, but be careful when interfacing with other PHP programs or your database. For example, MySQL's DAYOFWEEK( ) function treats Sunday as the first day of the week, but numbers the days 1 to 7, which is the ODBC standard. Its WEEKDAY( ) function, however, treats Monday as the first day of the week and numbers the days from 0 to 6. Its WEEK( ) function lets you choose whether weeks should start on Sunday or Monday, but it's incompatible with the ISO standard.

See Also

Documentation on date() at *http://www.php.net/date* and strftime() at *http://www.php.net/strftime*; MySQL's DAYOFWEEK(), WEEKDAY(), and WEEK() functions are documented at *http://www.mysql.com/doc/D/a/Date_and_time_functions.html*.

3.8 Validating a Date

Problem

You want to check if a date is valid. For example, you want to make sure a user hasn't provided a birthdate such as February 30, 1962.

Solution

Use checkdate():

```
$valid = checkdate($month,$day,$year);
```

Discussion

The function checkdate() returns true if $month is between 1 and 12, $year is between 1 and 32767, and $day is between 1 and the correct maximum number of days for $month and $year. Leap years are correctly handled by checkdate(), and dates are rendered using the Gregorian calendar.

Because checkdate() has such a broad range of valid years, you should do additional validation on user input if, for example, you're expecting a valid birthdate. *The Guinness Book of World Records* says the oldest person ever reached 122. To check that a birthdate indicates a user between 18 and 122 years old, use the pc_checkbirthdate() function shown in Example 3-1.

Example 3-1. pc_checkbirthdate()

```
function pc_checkbirthdate($month,$day,$year) {
    $min_age = 18;
    $max_age = 122;

    if (! checkdate($month,$day,$year)) {
        return false;
    }

    list($this_year,$this_month,$this_day) = explode(',',date('Y,m,d'));

    $min_year = $this_year - $max_age;
    $max_year = $this_year - $min_age;
```

Example 3-1. pc_checkbirthdate() (continued)

```
    print "$min_year,$max_year,$month,$day,$year\n";

    if (($year > $min_year) && ($year < $max_year)) {
        return true;
    } elseif (($year == $max_year) &&
            (($month < $this_month) ||
             (($month == $this_month) && ($day <= $this_day)))) {
        return true;
    } elseif (($year == $min_year) &&
            (($month > $this_month) ||
             (($month == $this_month && ($day > $this_day))))) {
        return true;
    } else {
        return false;
    }
}
```

Here is some sample usage:

```
// check December 3, 1974
if (pc_checkbirthdate(12,3,1974)) {
    print "You may use this web site.";
} else {
    print "You are too young to proceed.";
    exit();
}
```

This function first uses checkdate() to make sure that $month, $day, and $year represent a valid date. Various comparisons then make sure that the supplied date is in the range set by $min_age and $max_age.

If $year is noninclusively between $min_year and $max_year, the date is definitely within the range, and the function returns true. If not, some additional checks are required. If $year equals $max_year (e.g., in 2002, $year is 1984), $month must be before the current month. If $month equals the current month, $day must be before or equal to the current day. If $year equals $min_year (e.g., in 2002, $year is 1880), $month must be after the current month. If $month equals the current month, $day must be after the current day. If none of these conditions are met, the supplied date is outside the appropriate range, and the function returns false.

The function returns true if the supplied date is exactly $min_age years before the current date, but false if the supplied date is exactly $max_age years after the current date. That is, it would let you through on your 18th birthday, but not on your 123rd.

See Also

Documentation on checkdate() at *http://www.php.net/checkdate*; information about *The Guinness Book*'s oldest person is at *http://www.guinnessworldrecords.com* (navigate to "The Human Body," "Age and Youth," and then "Oldest Woman Ever").

3.9   Parsing Dates and Times from Strings

Problem

You need to get a date or time in a string into a format you can use in calculations. For example, you want to convert date expressions such as "last Thursday" into an epoch timestamp.

Solution

The simplest way to parse a date or time string is with strtotime(), which turns a variety of human-readable date and time strings into epoch timestamps:

```
$a = strtotime('march 10'); // defaults to the current year
```

Discussion

The grammar strtotime() uses is both complicated and comprehensive so the best way to get comfortable with it is to try out lots of different time expressions. If you're curious about its nuts and bolts, check out *ext/standard/parsedate.y* in the PHP source distribution.

The function strtotime() understands words about the current time:

```
$a = strtotime('now');
print strftime('%c',$a);
$a = strtotime('today');
print strftime('%c',$a);
Mon Aug 12 20:35:10 2002
Mon Aug 12 20:35:10 2002
```

It understands different ways to identify a time and date:

```
$a = strtotime('5/12/1994');
print strftime('%c',$a);
$a = strtotime('12 may 1994');
print strftime('%c',$a);
Thu May 12 00:00:00 1994
Thu May 12 00:00:00 1994
```

It understands relative times and dates:

```
$a = strtotime('last thursday');   // On August 12, 2002
print strftime('%c',$a);
$a = strtotime('2001-07-12 2pm + 1 month');
print strftime('%c',$a);
Thu Aug  8 00:00:00 2002
Mon Aug 12 14:00:00 2002
```

It understands time zones. When the following is run from a computer in EDT, it prints out the same time:

```
$a = strtotime('2002-07-12 2pm edt + 1 month');
print strftime('%c',$a);
Mon Aug 12 14:00:00 2002
```

However, when the following is run from a computer in EDT, it prints out the time in EDT when it is 2 P.M. in MDT (two hours before EDT):

```
$a = strtotime('2002-07-12 2pm mdt + 1 month');
print strftime('%c',$a);
Mon Aug 12 16:00:00 2002
```

If the date and time you want to parse out of a string are in a format you know in advance, instead of calling strtotime(), you can build a regular expression that grabs the different date and time parts you need. For example, here's how to parse "YYYY-MM-DD HH:MM:SS" dates, such as a MySQL DATETIME field:

```
$date = '1974-12-03 05:12:56';
preg_match('/(\d{4})-(\d{2})-(\d{2}) (\d{2}):(\d{2}):(\d{2})/',$date,$date_parts);
```

This puts the year, month, day, hour, minute, and second into $date_parts[1] through $date_parts[6]. (preg_match() puts the entire matched expression into $date_parts[0].)

You can use regular expressions to pull the date and time out of a larger string that might also contain other information (from user input, or a file you're reading), but if you're sure about the position of the date in the string you're parsing, you can use substr() to make it even faster:

```
$date_parts[0] = substr($date,0,4);
$date_parts[1] = substr($date,5,2);
$date_parts[2] = substr($date,8,2);
$date_parts[3] = substr($date,11,2);
$date_parts[4] = substr($date,14,2);
$date_parts[5] = substr($date,17,2);
```

You can also use split();

```
$ar = split('[- :]',$date);
print_r($ar);
Array
(
    [0] => 1974
    [1] => 12
    [2] => 03
    [3] => 05
    [4] => 12
    [5] => 56
)
```

Be careful: PHP converts between numbers and strings without any prompting, but numbers beginning with a 0 are considered to be in octal (base 8). So, 03 and 05 are 3 and 5; but, 08 and 09 are *not* 8 and 9.

preg_match( ) and strtotime( ) are equally efficient in parsing a date format such as "YYYY-MM-DD HH:MM:SS", but ereg( ) is about four times slower than either. If you need the individual parts of the date string, preg_match( ) is more convenient, but strtotime( ) is obviously much more flexible.

See Also

Documentation on strtotime( ) at *http://www.php.net/strtotime*; the grammar for strtotime( ) is available at *http://cvs.php.net/cvs.php/php4/ext/standard/parsedate.y*.

3.10   Adding to or Subtracting from a Date

Problem

You need to add or subtract an interval from a date.

Solution

Depending on how your date and interval are represented, use strtotime( ) or some simple arithmetic.

If you have your date and interval in appropriate formats, the easiest thing to do is use strtotime( ):

```
$birthday = 'March 10, 1975';
$whoopee_made = strtotime("$birthday - 9 months ago");
```

If your date in an epoch timestamp and you can express your interval in seconds, subtract the interval from the timestamp:

```
$birthday = 163727100;
$gestation = 36 * 7 * 86400; // 36 weeks
$whoopee_made = $birthday - $gestation;
```

Discussion

Using strtotime( ) is good for intervals that are of varying lengths, like months. If you can't use strtotime( ), you can convert your date to an epoch timestamp and add or subtract the appropriate interval in seconds. This is mostly useful for intervals of a fixed time, such as days or weeks:

```
$now = time();
$next_week = $now + 7 * 86400;
```

Using this method, however, you can run into problems if the endpoints of your interval are on different sides of a DST switch. In this case, one of your fixed length days isn't 86,400 seconds long; it's either 82,800 or 90,000 seconds long, depending on the season. If you use UTC exclusively in your application, you don't have to worry about this. But if you have to use local time, you can count days without worrying about this hiccup with Julian days. You can convert between epoch timestamps and Julian days with unixtojd() and jdtounix():

```
$now = time();
$today = unixtojd($now);
$next_week = jdtounix($today + 7);
// don't forget to add back hours, minutes, and seconds
$next_week += 3600 * date('H',$now) + 60 * date('i',$now) + date('s',$now);
```

The functions unixtojd() and jdtounix() are part of PHP's calendar extension, so they are only available if that extension is loaded.

See Also

Recipe 3.5 for finding the difference between two dates in elapsed time; Recipe 3.6 for finding the difference between two dates in Julian days; documentation on strtotime() at *http://www.php.net/strtotime*, unixtojd() at *http://www.php.net/unixtojd*, and jdtounix() at *http://www.php.net/jdtounix*.

3.11   Calculating Time with Time Zones

Problem

You need to calculate times in different time zones. For example, you want to give users information adjusted to their local time, not the local time of your server.

Solution

For simple calculations, you can explicitly add or subtract the offsets between two time zones:

```
// If local time is EST
$time_parts = localtime();
// California (PST) is three hours earlier
$california_time_parts = localtime(time() - 3 * 3600);
```

On Unix-based systems, if you don't know the offsets between time zones, just set the TZ environment variable to your target time zone:

```
putenv('TZ=PST8PDT');
$california_time_parts = localtime();
```

Discussion

Before we sink too deeply into the ins and outs of time zones, we want to pass along the disclaimer that the U.S. Naval Observatory offers at *http://tycho.usno.navy.mil/tzones.html*. Namely, official worldwide time-zone information is somewhat fragile "because nations are sovereign powers that can and do change their timekeeping systems as they see fit." So, remembering that we are at the mercy of the vagaries of international relations, here are some ways to cope with Earth's many time zones.

For a relatively simple treatment of offsets between time zones, use an array in your program that has the various time zones' offsets from UTC. Once you determine what time zone your user is in, just add that offset to the appropriate UTC time and the functions that print out UTC time (e.g., gmdate(), gmstrftime()) can print out the correct adjusted time.

```
// Find the current time
$now = time();

// California is 8 hours behind UTC
$now += $pc_timezones['PST'];

// Use gmdate() or gmstrftime() to print California-appropriate time
print gmstrftime('%c',$now);
```

The previous code uses this $pc_timezones array, which contains offsets from UTC:

```
// From Perl's Time::Timezone
$pc_timezones = array(
  'GMT'  =>  0,             // Greenwich Mean
  'UTC'  =>  0,             // Universal (Coordinated)
  'WET'  =>  0,             // Western European
  'WAT'  =>  -1*3600,       // West Africa
  'AT'   =>  -2*3600,       // Azores
  'NFT'  =>  -3*3600-1800,  // Newfoundland
  'AST'  =>  -4*3600,       // Atlantic Standard
  'EST'  =>  -5*3600,       // Eastern Standard
  'CST'  =>  -6*3600,       // Central Standard
  'MST'  =>  -7*3600,       // Mountain Standard
  'PST'  =>  -8*3600,       // Pacific Standard
  'YST'  =>  -9*3600,       // Yukon Standard
  'HST'  =>  -10*3600,      // Hawaii Standard
  'CAT'  =>  -10*3600,      // Central Alaska
  'AHST' =>  -10*3600,      // Alaska-Hawaii Standard
  'NT'   =>  -11*3600,      // Nome
  'IDLW' =>  -12*3600,      // International Date Line West
  'CET'  =>  +1*3600,       // Central European
  'MET'  =>  +1*3600,       // Middle European
  'MEWT' =>  +1*3600,       // Middle European Winter
  'SWT'  =>  +1*3600,       // Swedish Winter
  'FWT'  =>  +1*3600,       // French Winter
  'EET'  =>  +2*3600,       // Eastern Europe, USSR Zone 1
  'BT'   =>  +3*3600,       // Baghdad, USSR Zone 2
  'IT'   =>  +3*3600+1800,  // Iran
```

```
    'ZP4'  =>  +4*3600,       // USSR Zone 3
    'ZP5'  =>  +5*3600,       // USSR Zone 4
    'IST'  =>  +5*3600+1800,  // Indian Standard
    'ZP6'  =>  +6*3600,       // USSR Zone 5
    'SST'  =>  +7*3600,       // South Sumatra, USSR Zone 6
    'WAST' =>  +7*3600,       // West Australian Standard
    'JT'   =>  +7*3600+1800,  // Java
    'CCT'  =>  +8*3600,       // China Coast, USSR Zone 7
    'JST'  =>  +9*3600,       // Japan Standard, USSR Zone 8
    'CAST' =>  +9*3600+1800,  // Central Australian Standard
    'EAST' =>  +10*3600,      // Eastern Australian Standard
    'GST'  =>  +10*3600,      // Guam Standard, USSR Zone 9
    'NZT'  =>  +12*3600,      // New Zealand
    'NZST' =>  +12*3600,      // New Zealand Standard
    'IDLE' =>  +12*3600       // International Date Line East
);
```

On Unix systems, you can use the *zoneinfo* library to do the conversions. This makes your code more compact and also transparently handles DST, as discussed in Recipe 3.12.

To take advantage of *zoneinfo* in PHP, do all your internal date math with epoch timestamps. Generate them from time parts with the pc_mktime() function shown in Example 3-2.

Example 3-2. pc_mktime()

```
function pc_mktime($tz,$hr,$min,$sec,$mon,$day,$yr) {
    putenv("TZ=$tz");
    $a = mktime($hr,$min,$sec,$mon,$day,$yr);
    putenv('TZ=EST5EDT');   // change EST5EDT to your server's time zone!
    return $a;
}
```

Calling putenv() before mktime() fools the system functions mktime() uses into thinking they're in a different time zone. After the call to mktime(), the correct time zone has to be restored. On the East Coast of the United States, that's EST5EDT. Change this to the appropriate value for your computer's location (see Table 3-5).

Time parts are turned into epoch timestamps by pc_mktime(). Its counterpart, to turn epoch timestamps into formatted time strings and time parts, is pc_strftime(), shown in Example 3-3.

Example 3-3. pc_strftime()

```
function pc_strftime($tz,$format,$timestamp) {
    putenv("TZ=$tz");
    $a = strftime($format,$timestamp);
    putenv('TZ=EST5EDT');   // change EST5EDT to your server's time zone!
    return $a;
}
```

This example uses the same system-function-fooling pc_mktime() does to get the right results from strftime().

The great thing about these functions is that you don't have to worry about the offsets from UTC of different time zones, whether DST is in effect, or any other irregularities of time-zone differences. You just set the appropriate zone and let your system's libraries do the rest.

Note that the value of the $tz variable in both these functions should not be a time-zone name but a *zoneinfo* zone. *zoneinfo* zones are more specific than time zones, because they correspond to particular places. Table 3-5 contains mappings for appropriate *zoneinfo* zones for some UTC offsets. The last column indicates whether the zone observes DST.

Table 3-5. zoneinfo zones

UTC offset (hours)	UTC offset (seconds)	zoneinfo zone	DST?
−12	−43200	Etc/GMT+12	No
−11	−39600	Pacific/Midway	No
−10	−36000	US/Aleutian	Yes
−10	−36000	Pacific/Honolulu	No
−9	−32400	America/Anchorage	Yes
−9	−32400	Etc/GMT+9	No
−8	−28800	PST8PDT	Yes
−8	−28800	America/Dawson_Creek	No
−7	−25200	MST7MDT	Yes
−7	−25200	MST	No
−6	−21600	CST6CDT	Yes
−6	−21600	Canada/Saskatchewan	No
−5	−18000	EST5EDT	Yes
−5	−18000	EST	No
−4	−14400	America/Halifax	Yes
−4	−14400	America/Puerto_Rico	No
−3.5	−12600	America/St_Johns	Yes
−3	−10800	America/Buenos_Aires	No
0	0	Europe/London	Yes
0	0	GMT	No
1	3600	CET	Yes
1	3600	GMT-1	No
2	7200	EET	No
2	7200	GMT-2	No
3	10800	Asia/Baghdad	Yes

Table 3-5. zoneinfo zones (continued)

UTC offset (hours)	UTC offset (seconds)	zoneinfo zone	DST?
3	10800	GMT-3	No
3.5	12600	Asia/Tehran	Yes
4	14400	Asia/Dubai	No
4	14400	Asia/Baku	Yes
4.5	16200	Asia/Kabul	No
5	18000	Asia/Tashkent	No
5.5	19800	Asia/Calcutta	No
5.75	20700	Asia/Katmandu	No
6	21600	Asia/Novosibirsk	Yes
6	21600	Etc/GMT-6	No
6.5	23400	Asia/Rangoon	No
7	25200	Asia/Jakarta	No
8	28800	Hongkong	No
9	32400	Japan	No
9.5	34200	Australia/Darwin	No
10	36000	Australia/Sydney	Yes
10	36000	Pacific/Guam	No
12	43200	Etc/GMT-13	No
12	43200	Pacific/Auckland	Yes

Countries around the world don't begin and end DST observance on the same days or at the same times. To calculate time appropriately for an international DST-observing location, pick a *zoneinfo* zone that matches your desired location as specifically as possible.

See Also

Recipe 3.12 for dealing with DST; documentation on putenv( ) at *http://www.php.net/putenv*, localtime( ) at *http://www.php.net/localtime*, gmdate( ) at *http://www.php.net/gmdate*, and gmstrftime( ) at *http://www.php.net/gmstrftime*; *zoneinfo* zone names and longitude and latitude coordinates for hundreds of places around the world are available at *ftp://elsie.nci.nih.gov/pub/tzdata2002c.tar.gz*; many links to historical and technical information about time zones can be found at *http://www.twinsun.com/tz/tz-link.htm*.

3.12 Accounting for Daylight Saving Time

Problem

You need to make sure your time calculations properly consider DST.

Solution

The *zoneinfo* library calculates the effects of DST properly. If you are using a Unix-based system, take advantage of *zoneinfo* with putenv():

```
putenv('TZ=MST7MDT');
print strftime('%c');
```

If you can't use *zoneinfo*, you can modify hardcoded time-zone offsets based on whether the local time zone is currently observing DST. Use localtime() to determine the current DST observance status:

```
// Find the current UTC time
$now = time();

// California is 8 hours behind UTC
$now -= 8 * 3600;

// Is it DST?
$ar = localtime($now,true);
if ($ar['tm_isdst']) { $now += 3600; }

// Use gmdate() or gmstrftime() to print California-appropriate time
print gmstrftime('%c',$now);
```

Discussion

Altering an epoch timestamp by the amount of a time zone's offset from UTC and then using gmdate() or gmstrftime() to print out time zone-appropriate functions is flexible—it works from any time zone—but the DST calculations are slightly inaccurate. For the brief intervals when the server's DST status is different from the target time zone's, the results are incorrect. For example, at 3:30 A.M. EDT on the first Sunday in April (after the switch to DST), it's still before the switch (11:30 P.M.) in the Pacific time zone. A server in Eastern time using this method calculates California time to be seven hours behind UTC, whereas it's actually eight hours. At 6:00 A.M. EDT (3:00 A.M. PDT), both Pacific and Eastern time are observing DST, and the calculation is correct again (putting California at seven hours behind UTC).

See Also

Recipe 3.11 for dealing with time zones; documentation on putenv() at *http://www.php.net/putenv*, localtime() at *http://www.php.net/localtime*, gmdate() at *http://www.php.net/gmdate*, and gmstrftime() at *http://www.php.net/gmstrftime*; a detailed presentation on DST is at *http://webexhibits.org/daylightsaving/*.

3.13   Generating a High-Precision Time

Problem

You need to measure time with finer than one-second resolution, for example to generate a unique ID.

Solution

Use microtime():

```
list($microseconds,$seconds) = explode(' ',microtime());
```

Discussion

The function microtime() returns a string that contains the microseconds part of elapsed time since the epoch, a space, and seconds since the epoch. For example, a return value of 0.41644100 1026683258 means that 1026683258.41644100 seconds have elapsed since the epoch. A string is returned instead of a double because the double doesn't have enough capacity to hold the entire value with microsecond precision.

Time including microseconds is useful for generating unique IDs. When combined with the current process ID, it guarantees a unique ID, as long as a process doesn't generate more than one ID per microsecond:

```
list($microseconds,$seconds) = explode(' ',microtime());
$id = $seconds.$microseconds.getmypid();
```

However, this method is not as foolproof on multithreaded systems, where there is a nonzero (but very tiny) chance that two threads of the same process could call microtime() simultaneously.

See Also

Documentation on microtime() at *http://www.php.net/microtime*.

3.14 Generating Time Ranges

Problem

You need to know all the days in a week or a month. For example, you want to print out a list of appointments for a week.

Solution

Identify your start date using time() and strftime(). If your interval has a fixed length, you can loop through that many days. If not, you need to test each subsequent day for membership in your desired range.

For example, a week has seven days, so you can use a fixed loop to generate all the days in the current week:

```
// generate a time range for this week
$now = time();

// If it's before 3 AM, increment $now, so we don't get caught by DST
// when moving back to the beginning of the week
if (3 < strftime('%H', $now)) { $now += 7200; }

// What day of the week is today?
$today = strftime('%w', $now);

// How many days ago was the start of the week?
$start_day = $now - (86400 * $today);

// Print out each day of the week
for ($i = 0; $i < 7; $i++) {
  print strftime('%c',$start_day + 86400 * $i);
}
```

Discussion

A particular month or year could have a variable number of days, so you need to compute the end of the time range based on the specifics of that month or year. To loop through every day in a month, find the epoch timestamps for the first day of the month and the first day of the next month. The loop variable, $day is incremented a day at a time (86400 seconds) until it's no longer less than the epoch timestamp at the beginning of the next month:

```
// Generate a time range for this month
$now = time();
```

```
// If it's before 3 AM, increment $now, so we don't get caught by DST
// when moving back to the beginning of the month
if (3 < strftime('%H', $now)) { $now += 7200; }

// What month is this?
$this_month = strftime('%m',$now);

// Epoch timestamp for midnight on the first day of this month
$day = mktime(0,0,0,$this_month,1);
// Epoch timestamp for midnight on the first day of next month
$month_end = mktime(0,0,0,$this_month+1,1);

while ($day < $month_end) {
  print strftime('%c',$day);
  $day += 86400;
}
```

See Also

Documentation on `time()` at *http://www.php.net/time* and `strftime()` at *http://www.php.net/strftime*.

3.15 Using Non-Gregorian Calendars

Problem

You want to use a non-Gregorian calendar, such as a Julian, Jewish, or French Republican calendar.

Solution

PHP's calendar extension provides conversion functions for working with the Julian calendar, as well as the French Republican and Jewish calendars. To use these functions, the calendar extension must be loaded.

These functions use the Julian day count (which is different than the Julian calendar) as their intermediate format to move information between them.

The two functions `jdtogregorian()` and `gregoriantojd()` convert between Julian days and the familiar Gregorian calendar:

```
$jd = gregoriantojd(3,9,1876);      // March 9, 1876; $jd = 2406323

$gregorian = jdtogregorian($jd);    // $gregorian = 3/9/1876
```

The valid range for the Gregorian calendar is 4714 BCE to 9999 CE.

Discussion

To convert between Julian days and the Julian calendar, use jdtojulian() and juliantojd():

```
// February 29, 1900 (not a Gregorian leap year)
$jd = juliantojd(2,29,1900);      // $jd = 2415092
$julian = jdtojulian($jd);        // $julian = 2/29/1900
$gregorian = jdtogregorian($jd);  // $gregorian = 3/13/1900
```

The valid range for the Julian calendar is 4713 BCE to 9999 CE, but since it was created in 46 BCE, you run the risk of annoying Julian calendar purists if you use it for dates before that.

To convert between Julian days and the French Republican calendar, use jdtofrench() and frenchtojd():

```
$jd = frenchtojd(8,13,11);        // 13 floréal XI; $jd = 2379714
$french = jdtofrench($jd);        // $french = 8/13/11
$gregorian = jdtofregorian($jd);  // $gregorian = 5/3/1803; sale of Louisiana to U.S.
```

The valid range for the French Republican calendar is September 1792 to September 1806, which is small, but since the calendar was only in use from October 1793 to January 1806, it's comprehensive enough.

To convert between Julian days and the Jewish calendar, use jdtojewish() and jewishtojd():

```
$jd = JewishToJD(6,14,5761);      // Adar 14, 5761; $jd = 2451978
$jewish = JDToJewish($jd);        // $jewish = 6/14/5761
$gregorian = JDToGregorian($jd);  // $gregorian = 3/9/2001
```

The valid range for the Jewish calendar starts with 3761 BCE (year 1 on the Jewish calendar).

See Also

Documentation for the calendar functions at *http://www.php.net/calendar*; the history of the Gregorian calendar is explained at *http://scienceworld.wolfram.com/astronomy/GregorianCalendar.html*.

3.16   Program: Calendar

The pc_calendar() function shown in Example 3-4 prints out a month's calendar, similar to the Unix *cal* program. Here's how you can use the function:

```
// print the calendar for the current month
list($month,$year) = explode(',',date('m,Y'));
pc_calendar($month,$year);
```

The pc_calendar() function prints out a table with a month's calendar in it. It provides links to the previous and next month and highlights the current day.

Example 3-4. pc_calendar()

```php
<?php
function pc_calendar($month,$year,$opts = '') {
    // set default options //
    if (! is_array($opts)) { $opts = array(); }
    if (! isset($opts['today_color'])) { $opts['today_color'] = '#FFFF00'; }
    if (! isset($opts['month_link'])) {
        $opts['month_link'] =
            '<a href="'.$_SERVER['PHP_SELF'].'?month=%d&year=%d">%s</a>';
    }

    list($this_month,$this_year,$this_day) = split(',',strftime('%m,%Y,%d'));
    $day_highlight = (($this_month == $month) && ($this_year == $year));

    list($prev_month,$prev_year) =
        split(',',strftime('%m,%Y',mktime(0,0,0,$month-1,1,$year)));
    $prev_month_link = sprintf($opts['month_link'],$prev_month,$prev_year,'&lt;');

    list($next_month,$next_year) =
        split(',',strftime('%m,%Y',mktime(0,0,0,$month+1,1,$year)));
    $next_month_link = sprintf($opts['month_link'],$next_month,$next_year,'&gt;');

?>
<table border="0" cellspacing="0" cellpadding="2" align="center">
    <tr>
            <td align="left">
                    <?php print $prev_month_link ?>
            </td>
            <td colspan="5" align="center">
            <?php print strftime('%B %Y',mktime(0,0,0,$month,1,$year)); ?>
            </td>
            <td align="right">
                    <?php print $next_month_link ?>
            </td>
    </tr>
<?php
    $totaldays = date('t',mktime(0,0,0,$month,1,$year));

    // print out days of the week
    print '<tr>';
    $weekdays = array('Su','Mo','Tu','We','Th','Fr','Sa');
    while (list($k,$v) = each($weekdays)) {
        print '<td align="center">'.$v.'</td>';
    }
    print '</tr><tr>';
    // align the first day of the month with the right week day
    $day_offset = date("w",mktime(0, 0, 0, $month, 1, $year));
    if ($day_offset > 0) {
        for ($i = 0; $i < $day_offset; $i++) { print '<td> </td>'; }
    }
    $yesterday = time() - 86400;
```

Example 3-4. pc_calendar() (continued)

```
    // print out the days
    for ($day = 1; $day <= $totaldays; $day++) {
        $day_secs = mktime(0,0,0,$month,$day,$year);
        if ($day_secs >= $yesterday) {
            if ($day_highlight && ($day == $this_day)) {
                print sprintf('<td align="center" bgcolor="%s">%d</td>',
                              $opts['today_color'],$day);
            } else {
                print sprintf('<td align="center">%d</td>',$day);
            }
        } else {
            print sprintf('<td align="center">%d</td>',$day);
        }
        $day_offset++;

        // start a new row each week //
        if ($day_offset == 7) {
            $day_offset = 0;
            print "</tr>\n";
            if ($day < $totaldays) { print '<tr>'; }
        }
    }
    // fill in the last week with blanks //
    if ($day_offset > 0) { $day_offset = 7 - $day_offset; }
    if ($day_offset > 0) {
        for ($i = 0; $i < $day_offset; $i++) { print '<td> </td>'; }
    }
    print '</tr></table>';
}
?>
```

The pc_calendar() function begins by checking options passed to it in $opts. The color that the current day is highlighted with can be passed as an RGB value in $opts['today_color']. This defaults to #FFFF00, bright yellow. Also, you can pass a printf()-style format string in $opts['month_link'] to change how the links to the previous and next months are printed.

Next, the function sets $day_highlight to true if the month and year for the calendar match the current month and year. The links to the previous month and next month are put into $prev_month_link and $next_month_link using the format string in $opts['month_link'].

pc_calendar() then prints out the top of the HTML table that contains the calendar and a table row of weekday abbreviations. Using the day of the week returned from strftime('%w'), blank table cells are printed so the first day of the month is aligned with the appropriate day of the week. For example, if the first day of the month is a Tuesday, two blank cells have to be printed to occupy the slots under Sunday and Monday in the first row of the table.

After this preliminary information has been printed, pc_calendar( ) loops through all the days in the month. It prints a plain table cell for most days, but a table cell with a different background color for the current day. When $day_offset reaches 7, a week has completed, and a new table row needs to start.

Once a table cell has been printed for each day in the month, blank cells are added to fill out the last row of the table. For example, if the last day of the month is a Thursday, two cells are added to occupy the slots under Friday and Saturday. Last, the table is closed, and the calendar is complete.

CHAPTER 4

Arrays

4.0 Introduction

Arrays are lists: lists of people, lists of sizes, lists of books. To store a group of related items in a variable, use an array. Like a list on a piece of paper, the elements in array have an order. Usually, each new item comes after the last entry in the array, but just as you can wedge a new entry between a pair of lines already in a paper list, you can do the same with arrays in PHP.

In many languages, there is only one type of array: what is called a *numerical array* (or just an array). In a numerical array, if you want to find an entry, you need to know its position within the array, known as an *index*. Positions are identified by numbers: they start at 0 and work upwards one by one.

In some languages, there is also another type of array: an *associative array*, also known as a *hash*. In an associative array, indexes aren't integers, but strings. So, in a numerical array of U.S. presidents, "Abraham Lincoln" might have index 16; in the associative-array version, the index might be "Honest." However, while numerical arrays have a strict ordering imposed by their keys, associative arrays frequently make no guarantees about the key ordering. Elements are added in a certain order, but there's no way to determine the order later.

In a few languages, there are both numerical and associative arrays. But, usually the numerical array $presidents and the associative array $presidents are distinct arrays. Each array type has a specific behavior, and you need to operate on them accordingly. PHP has both numerical and associative arrays, but they don't behave independently.

In PHP, numerical arrays *are* associative arrays, and associative arrays *are* numerical arrays. So, which kind are they really? Both and neither. The line between them constantly blurs back and forth from one to another. At first, this can be disorienting, especially if you're used to rigid behavior, but soon you'll find this flexibility an asset.

To assign multiple values to an array in one step, use `array( )`:

```
$fruits = array('Apples', 'Bananas', 'Cantaloupes', 'Dates');
```

Now, the value of `$fruits[2]` is `'Cantaloupes'`.

`array( )` is very handy when you have a short list of known values. The same array is also produced by:

```
$fruits[0] = 'Apples';
$fruits[1] = 'Bananas';
$fruits[2] = 'Cantaloupes';
$fruits[3] = 'Dates';
```

and:

```
$fruits[] = 'Apples';
$fruits[] = 'Bananas';
$fruits[] = 'Cantaloupes';
$fruits[] = 'Dates';
```

Assigning a value to an array with an empty subscript is shorthand for adding a new element to the end of the array. So, PHP looks up the length of `$fruits` and uses that as the position for the value you're assigning. This assumes, of course, that `$fruits` isn't set to a scalar value, such as 3, and isn't an object. PHP complains if you try to treat a nonarray as an array; however, if this is the first time you're using this variable, PHP automatically converts it to an array and begins indexing at 0.

An identical feature is the function `array_push( )`, which pushes a new value on top of the array stack. However, the `$foo[ ]` notation is the more traditional PHP style; it's also faster. But, sometimes, using `array_push( )` more accurately conveys the stack nature of what you're trying to do, especially when combined with `array_pop( )`, which removes the last element from an array and returns it.

So far, we've placed integers and strings only inside arrays. However, PHP allows you to assign any data type you want to an array element: booleans, integers, floating-point numbers, strings, objects, resources, `NULL`, and even other arrays. So, you can pull arrays or objects directly from a database and place them into an array:

```
while ($row = mysql_fetch_row($r)) {
    $fruits[] = $row;
}

while ($obj = mysql_fetch_object($s)) {
    $vegetables[] = $obj;
}
```

The first while statement creates an array of arrays; the second creates an array of objects. See Recipe 4.2 for more on storing multiple elements per key.

To define an array not using integer keys but string keys, you can also use array(), but specify the key/value pairs with =>:

```
$fruits = array('red' => 'Apples', 'yellow' => 'Bananas',
                'beige' => 'Cantaloupes', 'brown' => 'Dates');
```

Now, the value of $fruits['beige'] is 'Cantaloupes'. This is shorthand for:

```
$fruits['red'] = 'Apples';
$fruits['yellow'] = 'Bananas';
$fruits['beige'] = 'Cantaloupes';
$fruits['brown'] = 'Dates';
```

Each array can only hold one unique value for each key. Adding:

```
$fruits['red'] = 'Strawberry';
```

overwrites the value of 'Apples'. However, you can always add another key at a later time:

```
$fruits['orange'] = 'Orange';
```

The more you program in PHP, the more you find yourself using associative arrays instead of numerical ones. Instead of creating a numeric array with string values, you can create an associative array and place your values as its keys. If you want, you can then store additional information in the element's value. There's no speed penalty for doing this, and PHP preserves the ordering. Plus, looking up or changing a value is easy because you already know the key.

The easiest way to cycle though an array and operate on all or some of the elements inside is to use foreach:

```
$fruits = array('red' => 'Apples', 'yellow' => 'Bananas',
                'beige' => 'Cantaloupes', 'brown' => 'Dates');

foreach ($fruits as $color => $fruit) {
    print "$fruit are $color.\n";
}
Apples are red.
Bananas are yellow.
Cantaloupes are beige.
Dates are brown.
```

Each time through the loop, PHP assigns the next key to $color and the key's value to $fruit. When there are no elements left in the array, the loop finishes.

To break an array apart into individual variables, use list():

```
$fruits = array('Apples', 'Bananas', 'Cantaloupes', 'Dates');

list($red, $yellow, $beige, $brown) = $fruits;
```

4.1 Specifying an Array Not Beginning at Element 0

Problem

You want to assign multiple elements to an array in one step, but you don't want the first index to be 0.

Solution

Instruct array( ) to use a different index using the => syntax:

```
$presidents = array(1 => 'Washington', 'Adams', 'Jefferson', 'Madison');
```

Discussion

Arrays in PHP, like most, but not all, computer languages begin with the first entry located at index 0. Sometimes, however, the data you're storing makes more sense if the list begins at 1. (And we're not just talking to recovering Pascal programmers here.)

In the Solution, George Washington is the first president, not the zeroth, so if you wish to print a list of the presidents, it's simpler to do this:

```
foreach ($presidents as $number => $president) {
    print "$number: $president\n";
}
```

than this:

```
foreach ($presidents as $number => $president) {
    $number++;
    print "$number: $president\n";
}
```

The feature isn't restricted to the number 1; any integer works:

```
$reconstruction_presidents = array(16 => 'Lincoln', 'Johnson', 'Grant');
```

Also, you can use => multiple times in one call:*

```
$whig_presidents = array(9 => 'Harrison', 'Tyler', 12 => 'Taylor', 'Fillmore');
```

PHP even allows you to use negative numbers in the array( ) call. (In fact, this method works for noninteger keys, too.) What you'll get is technically an associative

---

* John Tyler was elected as Harrison's Vice President under the Whig Party platform but was expelled from the party shortly after assuming the presidency following the death of Harrison.

array, although as we said, the line between numeric arrays and associative arrays is often blurred in PHP; this is just another one of these cases.

```
$us_leaders = array(-1 => 'George II', 'George III', 'Washington');
```

If Washington is the first U.S. leader, George III is the zeroth, and his grandfather George II is the negative-first.

Of course, you can mix and match numeric and string keys in one array() definition, but it's confusing and very rarely needed:

```
$presidents = array(1 => 'Washington', 'Adams', 'Honest' => 'Lincoln', 'Jefferson');
```

This is equivalent to:

```
$presidents[1]        = 'Washington';  // Key is 1
$presidents[]         = 'Adams';       // Key is 1 + 1 => 2
$presidents['Honest'] = 'Lincoln';     // Key is 'Honest'
$presidents[]         = 'Jefferson';   // Key is 2 + 1 => 3
```

See Also

Documentation on array() at *http://www.php.net/array*.

4.2   Storing Multiple Elements per Key in an Array

Problem

You want to associate multiple elements with a single key.

Solution

Store the multiple elements in an array:

```
$fruits = array('red' => array('strawberry','apple'),
                'yellow' => array('banana'));
```

Or, use an object:

```
while ($obj = mysql_fetch_object($r)) {
    $fruits[] = $obj;
}
```

Discussion

In PHP, keys are unique per array, so you can't associate more than one entry in a key without overwriting the old value. Instead, store your values in an anonymous array:

```
$fruits['red'][] = 'strawberry';
$fruits['red'][] = 'apple';
$fruits['yellow'][] = 'banana';
```

Or, if you're processing items in a loop:

```
while (list($color,$fruit) = mysql_fetch_array($r)) {
    $fruits[$color][] = $fruit;
}
```

To print the entries, loop through the array:

```
foreach ($fruits as $color=>$color_fruit) {
    // $color_fruit is an array
    foreach ($color_fruit as $fruit) {
        print "$fruit is colored $color.<br>";
    }
}
```

Or use the pc_array_to_comma_string() function from Recipe 4.9.

```
foreach ($fruits as $color=>$color_fruit) {
    print "$color colored fruits include " .
        pc_array_to_comma_string($color_fruit) . "<br>";
}
```

See Also

Recipe 4.9 for how to print arrays with commas.

4.3 Initializing an Array to a Range of Integers

Problem

You want to assign a series of consecutive integers to an array.

Solution

Use range($start, $stop):

```
$cards = range(1, 52);
```

Discussion

For increments other than 1, you can use:

```
function pc_array_range($start, $stop, $step) {
    $array = array();
    for ($i = $start; $i <= $stop; $i += $step) {
        $array[] = $i;
    }
    return $array;
}
```

So, for odd numbers:

```
$odd = pc_array_range(1, 52, 2);
```

And, for even numbers:

```
$even = pc_array_range(2, 52, 2);
```

See Also

Recipe 2.4 for how to operate on a series of integers; documentation on range( ) at *http://www.php.net/range*.

4.4   Iterating Through an Array

Problem

You want to cycle though an array and operate on all or some of the elements inside.

Solution

Use foreach:

```
foreach ($array as $value) {
    // Act on $value
}
```

Or, to get an array's keys and values:

```
foreach ($array as $key => $value) {
    // Act II
}
```

Another technique is to use for:

```
for ($key = 0, $size = count($array); $key < $size; $key++) {
    // Act III
}
```

Finally, you can use each( ) in combination with list( ) and while:

```
reset($array) // reset internal pointer to beginning of array
while (list($key, $value) = each ($array)) {
    // Final Act
}
```

Discussion

A foreach loop is the shortest way to iterate through an array:

```
// foreach with values
foreach ($items as $cost) {
    ...
```

```
    }

// foreach with keys and values
foreach($items as $item => $cost) {
    ...
}
```

With foreach, PHP iterates over a copy of the array instead of the actual array. In contrast, when using each( ) and for, PHP iterates over the original array. So, if you modify the array inside the loop, you may (or may not) get the behavior you expect.

If you want to modify the array, reference it directly:

```
reset($items);
while (list($item, $cost) = each($items)) {
    if (! in_stock($item)) {
        unset($items[$item]);          // address the array directly
    }
}
```

The variables returned by each( ) aren't aliases for the original values in the array: they're copies, so, if you modify them, it's not reflected in the array. That's why you need to modify $items[$item] instead of $item.

When using each( ), PHP keeps track of where you are inside the loop. After completing a first pass through, to begin again at the start, call reset( ) to move the pointer back to the front of the array. Otherwise, each( ) returns false.

The for loop works only for arrays with consecutive integer keys. Unless you're modifying the size of your array, it's inefficient to recompute the count( ) of $items each time through the loop, so we always use a $size variable to hold the array's size:

```
for ($item = 0, $size = count($items); $item < $size; $item++) {
    ...
}
```

If you prefer to count efficiently with one variable, count backwards:

```
for ($item = count($items) - 1; $item >= 0; $item--) {
    ...
}
```

The associative version of the for loop is:

```
for (reset($array); $key = key($array); next($array) ) {
    ...
}
```

This fails if any element holds a string that evaluates to false, so a perfectly normal value such as 0 causes the loop to end early.

Finally, use array_map( ) to hand off each element to a function for processing:

```
// lowercase all words
$lc = array_map('strtolower', $words);
```

The first argument to array_map( ) is a function to modify an individual element, and the second is the array to be iterated through.

Generally, we find these functions less flexible than the previous methods, but they are well-suited for the processing and merging of multiple arrays.

If you're unsure if the data you'll be processing is a scalar or an array, you need to protect against calling foreach with a non-array. One method is to use is_array( ):

```
if (is_array($items)) {
    // foreach loop code for array
} else {
    // code for scalar
}
```

Another method is to coerce all variables into array form using settype( ):

```
settype($items, 'array');
// loop code for arrays
```

This turns a scalar value into a one element array and cleans up your code at the expense of a little overhead.

See Also

Documentation on for at *http://www.php.net/for*, foreach at *http://www.php.net/ foreach*, while at *http://www.php.net/while*, each( ) at *http://www.php.net/each*, reset( ) at *http://www.php.net/reset*, and array_map( ) at *http://www.php.net/array-map*.

4.5   Deleting Elements from an Array

Problem

You want to remove one or more elements from an array.

Solution

To delete one element, use unset( ):

```
unset($array[3]);
unset($array['foo']);
```

To delete multiple noncontiguous elements, also use unset( ):

```
unset($array[3], $array[5]);
unset($array['foo'], $array['bar']);
```

To delete multiple contiguous elements, use array_splice( ):

```
array_splice($array, $offset, $length);
```

Discussion

Using these functions removes all references to these elements from PHP. If you want to keep a key in the array, but with an empty value, assign the empty string to the element:

```
$array[3] = $array['foo'] = '';
```

Besides syntax, there's a logical difference between using unset() and assigning '' to the element. The first says "This doesn't exist anymore," while the second says "This still exists, but its value is the empty string."

If you're dealing with numbers, assigning 0 may be a better alternative. So, if a company stopped production of the model XL1000 sprocket, it would update its inventory with:

```
unset($products['XL1000']);
```

However, if it temporarily ran out of XL1000 sprockets, but was planning to receive a new shipment from the plant later this week, this is better:

```
$products['XL1000'] = 0;
```

If you unset() an element, PHP adjusts the array so that looping still works correctly. It doesn't compact the array to fill in the missing holes. This is what we mean when we say that all arrays are associative, even when they appear to be numeric. Here's an example:

```
// create a "numeric" array
$animals = array('ant', 'bee', 'cat', 'dog', 'elk', 'fox');
print $animals[1];  // prints 'bee'
print $animals[2];  // prints 'cat'
count($animals);    // returns 6

// unset()
unset($animals[1]); // removes element $animals[1] = 'bee'
print $animals[1];  // prints '' and throws an E_NOTICE error
print $animals[2];  // still prints 'cat'
count($animals);    // returns 5, even though $array[5] is 'fox'

// add new element
$animals[] = 'gnu'; // add new element (not Unix)
print $animals[1];  // prints '', still empty
print $animals[6];  // prints 'gnu', this is where 'gnu' ended up
count($animals);    // returns 6

// assign ''
$animals[2] = '';   // zero out value
print $animals[2];  // prints ''
count($animals);    // returns 6, count does not decrease
```

To compact the array into a densely filled numeric array, use array_values():

```
$animals = array_values($animals);
```

Alternatively, array_splice( ) automatically reindexes arrays to avoid leaving holes:

```
// create a "numeric" array
$animals = array('ant', 'bee', 'cat', 'dog', 'elk', 'fox');
array_splice($animals, 2, 2);
print_r($animals);
Array
(
    [0] => ant
    [1] => bee
    [2] => elk
    [3] => fox
)
```

This is useful if you're using the array as a queue and want to remove items from the queue while still allowing random access. To safely remove the first or last element from an array, use array_shift( ) and array_pop( ), respectively.

However, if you find yourself often running into problems because of holes in arrays, you may not be "thinking PHP." Look at the ways to iterate through the array in Recipe 4.4 that don't involve using a for loop.

See Also

Recipe 4.4 for iteration techniques; documentation on unset( ) at *http://www.php.net/unset*, array_splice( ) at *http://www.php.net/array-splice*, and array_values( ) at *http://www.php.net/array-values*.

4.6   Changing Array Size

Problem

You want to modify the size of an array, either by making it larger or smaller than its current size.

Solution

Use array_pad( ) to make an array grow:

```
// start at three
$array = array('apple', 'banana', 'coconut');

// grow to five
$array = array_pad($array, 5, '');
```

Now, count($array) is 5, and the last two elements contain the empty string.

To reduce an array, you can use `array_splice()`:

```
// no assignment to $array
array_splice($array, 2);
```

This removes all but the first two elements from $array.

Discussion

Arrays aren't a predeclared size in PHP, so you can resize them on the fly.

To pad an array, use `array_pad()`. The first argument is the array to be padded. The next argument is the size and direction you want to pad. To pad to the right, use a positive integer; to pad to the left, use a negative one. The third argument is the value to be assigned to the newly created entries. The function returns a modified array and doesn't alter the original.

Here are some examples:

```
// make a four-element array with 'dates' to the right
$array = array('apple', 'banana', 'coconut');
$array = array_pad($array, 4, 'dates');
print_r($array);
Array
(
    [0] => apple
    [1] => banana
    [2] => coconut
    [3] => dates
)

// make a six-element array with 'zucchinis' to the left
$array = array_pad($array, -6, 'zucchini');
print_r($array);
Array
(
    [0] => zucchini
    [1] => zucchini
    [2] => apple
    [3] => banana
    [4] => coconut
    [5] => dates
)
```

Be careful. `array_pad($array, 4, 'dates')` makes sure an $array is *at least* four elements long, it doesn't add four *new* elements. In this case, if $array was already four elements or larger, `array_pad()` would return an unaltered $array.

Also, if you declare a value for a fourth element, $array[4]:

```
$array = array('apple', 'banana', 'coconut');
$array[4] = 'dates';
```

you end up with a four-element array with indexes 0, 1, 2, and 4:

```
Array
(
    [0] => apple
    [1] => banana
    [2] => coconut
    [4] => dates
)
```

PHP essentially turns this into an associative array that happens to have integer keys.

The array_splice( ) function, unlike array_pad( ), has the side-effect of modifying the original array. It returns the spliced out array. That's why you don't assign the return value to $array. However, like array_pad( ), you can splice from either the right or left. So, calling array_splice( ) with a value of –2 chops off the last two elements from the end:

```
// make a four-element array
$array = array('apple', 'banana', 'coconut', 'dates');

// shrink to three elements
array_splice($array, 3);

// remove last element, equivalent to array_pop()
array_splice($array, -1);

// only remaining fruits are apple and banana
print_r($array);
Array
(
    [0] => apple
    [1] => banana
)
```

See Also

Documentation on array_pad( ) at *http://www.php.net/array-pad* and array_splice( ) at *http://www.php.net/array-splice*.

4.7   Appending One Array to Another

Problem

You want to combine two arrays into one.

Solution

Use array_merge( ):

```
$garden = array_merge($fruits, $vegetables);
```

Discussion

The array_merge( ) function works with both predefined arrays and arrays defined in place using array( ):

```
$p_languages = array('Perl', 'PHP');
$p_languages = array_merge($p_languages, array('Python'));
print_r($p_languages);
Array
(
    [0] => PHP
    [1] => Perl
    [2] => Python
)
```

Accordingly, merged arrays can be either preexisting arrays, as with $p_languages, or anonymous arrays, as with array('Python').

You can't use array_push( ), because PHP won't automatically flatten out the array into series of independent variables, and you'll end up with a nested array. Thus:

```
array_push($p_languages, array('Python'));
print_r($p_languages);
Array
(
    [0] => PHP
    [1] => Perl
    [2] => Array
        (
            [0] => Python
        )

)
```

Merging arrays with only numerical keys causes the arrays to get renumbered, so values aren't lost. Merging arrays with string keys causes the second array to overwrite the value of any duplicated keys. Arrays with both types of keys exhibit both types of behavior. For example:

```
$lc = array('a', 'b' => 'b'); // lower-case letters as values
$uc = array('A', 'b' => 'B'); // upper-case letters as values
$ac = array_merge($lc, $uc); // all-cases?
print_r($ac);
Array
(
    [0] => a
    [b] => B
    [1] => A
)
```

The uppercase A has been renumbered from index 0 to index 1, to avoid a collision, and merged onto the end. The uppercase B has overwritten the lowercase b and replaced it in the original place within the array.

The + operator can also merge arrays. The array on the right overwrites any identically named keys found on the left. It doesn't do any reordering to prevent collisions. Using the previous example:

```
print_r($a + $b);
print_r($b + $a);
Array
(
    [0] => a
    [b] => b
)
Array
(
    [0] => A
    [b] => B
)
```

Since a and A both have a key of 0, and b and B both have a key of b, you end up with a total of only two elements in the merged arrays.

In the first case, $a + $b becomes just $b, and in the other, $b + $a becomes $a.

However, if you had two distinctly keyed arrays, this wouldn't be a problem, and the new array would be the union of the two arrays.

See Also

Documentation on array_merge( ) at *http://www.php.net/array-merge*.

4.8   Turning an Array into a String

Problem

You have an array, and you want to convert it into a nicely formatted string.

Solution

Use join( ):

```
// make a comma delimited list
$string = join(',', $array);
```

Or loop yourself:

```
$string = '';

foreach ($array as $key => $value) {
    $string .= ",$value";
}

$string = substr($string, 1); // remove leading ","
```

Discussion

If you can use join( ), do; it's faster than any PHP-based loop. However, join( ) isn't very flexible. First, it places a delimiter only between elements, not around them. To wrap elements inside HTML bold tags and separate them with commas, do this:

```
$left  = '<b>';
$right = '</b>';

$html = $left . join("$right,$left", $html) . $right;
```

Second, join( ) doesn't allow you to discriminate against values. If you want to include a subset of entries, you need to loop yourself:

```
$string = '';

foreach ($fields as $key => $value) {
    // don't include password
    if ('password' != $key) {
        $string .= ",<b>$value</b>";
    }
}

$string = substr($string, 1); // remove leading ","
```

Notice that a separator is always added to each value, then stripped off outside the loop. While it's somewhat wasteful to add something that will be later subtracted, it's far cleaner and efficient (in most cases) then attempting to embed logic inside of the loop. To wit:

```
$string = '';
foreach ($fields as $key => $value) {
    // don't include password
    if ('password' != $value) {
        if (!empty($string)) { $string .= ','; }
        $string .= "<b>$value</b>";
    }
}
```

Now you have to check $string every time you append a value. That's worse than the simple substr( ) call. Also, prepend the delimiter (in this case a comma) instead of appending it because it's faster to shorten a string from the front than the rear.

See Also

Recipe 4.9 for printing an array with commas; documentation on join( ) at *http://www.php.net/join* and substr( ) at *http://www.php.net/substr*.

4.9   Printing an Array with Commas

Problem

You want to print out an array with commas separating the elements and with an "and" before the last element if there are more than two elements in the array.

Solution

Use the pc_array_to_comma_string() function shown in Example 4-1, which returns the correct string.

Example 4-1. pc_array_to_comma_string()

```
function pc_array_to_comma_string($array) {

    switch (count($array)) {
    case 0:
        return '';

    case 1:
        return reset($array);

    case 2:
        return join(' and ', $array);

    default:
        $last = array_pop($array);
        return join(', ', $array) . ", and $last";
    }
}
```

Discussion

If you have a list of items to print, it's useful to print them in a grammatically correct fashion. It looks awkward to display text like this:

```
$thundercats = array('Lion-O', 'Panthro', 'Tygra', 'Cheetara', 'Snarf');
print 'ThunderCat good guys include ' . join(', ', $thundercats) . '.';
ThunderCat good guys include Lion-O, Panthro, Tygra, Cheetara, Snarf.
```

This implementation of this function isn't completely straightforward, since we want pc_array_to_comma_string() to work with all arrays, not just numeric ones beginning at 0. If restricted only to that subset, for an array of size one, you return $array[0]. But, if the array doesn't begin at 0, $array[0] is empty. So, you can use the fact that reset(), which resets an array's internal pointer, also returns the value of the first array element.

For similar reasons, you call array_pop( ) to grab the end element, instead of assuming it's located at $array[count($array)-1]. This allows you to use join( ) on $array.

Also note that the code for case 2 actually also works correctly for case 1. And, the default code works (though inefficiently) for case 2; however, the transitive property doesn't apply, so you can't use the default code on elements of size 1.

See Also

Recipe 4.8 for turning an array into a string; documentation on join( ) at *http://www.php.net/join*, array_pop( ) at *http://www.php.net/array-pop*, and reset( ) at *http://www.php.net/reset*.

4.10   Checking if a Key Is in an Array

Problem

You want to know if an array contains a certain key.

Solution

Use isset( ):

```
if (isset($array['key'])) { /* there is a value for 'key' in $array */ }
```

Discussion

You can check the definedness of an array element just as you'd for any other variable. See the Introduction to Chapter 5 for more information about the truth value of variables.

See Also

Documentation on isset( ) at *http://www.php.net/isset*.

4.11   Checking if an Element Is in an Array

Problem

You want to know if an array contains a certain value.

Solution

Use in_array():

```
if (in_array($value, $array)) {
    // an element has $value as its value in array $array
}
```

Discussion

Use in_array() to check if an element of an array holds a value:

```
$book_collection = array('Emma', 'Pride and Prejudice', 'Northhanger Abbey');
$book = 'Sense and Sensibility';

if (in_array($book, $book_collection)) {
    echo 'Own it.';
} else {
    echo 'Need it.';
}
```

The default behavior of in_array() is to compare items using the == operator. To use the strict equality check, ===, pass true as the third parameter to in_array():

```
$array = array(1, '2', 'three');

in_array(0, $array);          // true!
in_array(0, $array, true);    // false
in_array(1, $array);          // true
in_array(1, $array, true);    // true
in_array(2, $array);          // true
in_array(2, $array, true);    // false
```

The first check, in_array(0, $array), evaluates to true because to compare the number 0 against the string three, PHP casts three to an integer. Since three isn't a numeric string, as is 2, it becomes 0. Therefore, in_array() thinks there's a match.

Consequently, when comparing numbers against data that may contain strings, it's safest to use a strict comparison.

If you find yourself calling in_array() multiple times on the same array, it may be better to use an associative array, with the original array elements as the keys in the new associative array. Looking up entries using in_array() takes linear time; with an associative array, it takes constant time.

If you can't create the associative array directly but need to convert from a traditional one with integer keys, use array_flip() to swap the keys and values of an array:

```
$book_collection = array('Emma',
                         'Pride and Prejudice',
                         'Northhanger Abbey');
```

```
// convert from numeric array to associative array
$book_collection = array_flip($book_collection);
$book = 'Sense and Sensibility';

if (isset($book_collection[$book])) {
    echo 'Own it.';
} else {
    echo 'Need it.';
}
```

Note that doing this condenses multiple keys with the same value into one element in the flipped array.

See Also

Recipe 4.12 for determining the position of an element in an array; documentation on in_array() at *http://www.php.net/in-array* and array_flip() at *http://www.php.net/array-flip*.

4.12 Finding the Position of an Element in an Array

Problem

You want know if an element is in an array, and, if it is, you want to know where it is located.

Solution

Use array_search(). It returns the key of the found element or false:

```
$position = array_search($value, $array);
if ($position !== false) {
    // the element in position $position has $value as its value in array $array
}
```

Discussion

Use in_array() to find if an array contains a value; use array_search() to discover where that value is located. However, because array_search() gracefully handles searches in which the value isn't found, it's better to use array_search() instead of in_array(). The speed difference is minute, and the extra information is potentially useful:

```
$favorite_foods = array(1 => 'artichokes', 'bread', 'cauliflower', 'deviled eggs');
$food = 'cauliflower';
$position = array_search($food, $favorite_foods);
```

```
    if ($position !== false) {
        echo "My #$position favorite food is $food";
    } else {
        echo "Blech! I hate $food!";
    }
```

Use the !== check against false because if your string is found in the array at position 0, the if evaluates to a logical false, which isn't what is meant or wanted.

If a value is in the array multiple times, array_search() is only guaranteed to return one of the instances, not the first instance.

See Also

Recipe 4.11 for checking whether an element is in an array; documentation on array_search() at *http://www.php.net/array-search*; for more sophisticated searching of arrays using regular expression, see preg_replace() at *http://www.php.net/preg-replace* and Chapter 13.

4.13   Finding Elements That Pass a Certain Test

Problem

You want to locate entries in an array that meet certain requirements.

Solution

Use a foreach loop:

```
    $movies = array(...);

    foreach ($movies as $movie) {
        if ($movie['box_office_gross'] < 5000000) { $flops[] = $movie; }
    }
```

Or array_filter():

```
    $movies = array(...);

    function flops($movie) {
        return ($movie['box_office_gross'] < 5000000) ? 1 : 0;
    }

    $flops = array_filter($movies, 'flops');
```

Discussion

The foreach loops are simple; you scroll through the data and append elements to the return array that match your criteria.

If you want only the first such element, exit the loop using break:

```
foreach ($movies as $movie) {
    if ($movie['box_office_gross'] > 200000000) { $blockbuster = $movie; break; }
}
```

You can also return directly from a function:

```
function blockbuster($movies) {
    foreach ($movies as $movie) {
        if ($movie['box_office_gross'] > 200000000) { return $movie; }
    }
}
```

With array_filter(), however, you first create a callback function that returns true for values you want to keep and false for values you don't. Using array_filter(), you then instruct PHP to process the array as you do in the foreach.

It's impossible to bail out early from array_filter(), so foreach provides more flexibility and is simpler to understand. Also, it's one of the few cases in which the built-in PHP function doesn't clearly outperform user-level code.

See Also

Documentation on array_filter() at *http://www.php.net/array-filter*.

4.14 Finding the Largest or Smallest Valued Element in an Array

Problem

You have an array of elements, and you want to find the largest or smallest valued element. For example, you want to find the appropriate scale when creating a histogram.

Solution

To find the largest element, use max():

```
$largest = max($array);
```

To find the smallest element, use min():

```
$smallest = min($array);
```

Discussion

Normally, max() returns the larger of two elements, but if you pass it an array, it searches the entire array instead. Unfortunately, there's no way to find the index of the largest element using max( ). To do that, you must sort the array in reverse order to put the largest element in position 0:

```
arsort($array);
```

Now the value of the largest element is $array[0].

If you don't want to disturb the order of the original array, make a copy and sort the copy:

```
$copy = $array;
arsort($copy);
```

The same concept applies to min( ) but use asort( ) instead of arsort( ).

See Also

Recipe 4.16 for sorting an array; documentation on max( ) at *http://www.php.net/max*, min( ) at *http://www.php.net/min*, arsort( ) at *http://www.php.net/arsort*, and asort( ) at *http://www.php.net/min*.

4.15   Reversing an Array

Problem

You want to reverse the order of the elements in an array.

Solution

Use array_reverse( ):

```
$array = array('Zero', 'One', 'Two');
$reversed = array_reverse($array);
```

Discussion

The array_reverse( ) function reverses the elements in an array. However, it's often possible to avoid this operation. If you wish to reverse an array you've just sorted, modify the sort to do the inverse. If you want to reverse a list you're about to loop through and process, just invert the loop. Instead of:

```
for ($i = 0, $size = count($array); $i < $size; $i++) {
    ...
}
```

do the following:

```
for ($i = count($array) - 1; $i >=0 ; $i--) {
    ...
}
```

However, as always, use a for loop only on a tightly packed array.

Another alternative would be, if possible, to invert the order elements are placed into the array. For instance, if you're populating an array from a series of rows returned from a database, you should be able to modify the query to ORDER DESC. See your database manual for the exact syntax for your database.

See Also

Documentation on array_reverse( ) at *http://www.php.net/array-reverse.*

4.16   Sorting an Array

Problem

You want to sort an array in a specific way.

Solution

To sort an array using the traditional definition of sort, use sort( ):

```
$states = array('Delaware', 'Pennsylvania', 'New Jersey');
sort($states);
```

To sort numerically, pass SORT_NUMERIC as the second argument to sort( ).

```
$scores = array(1, 10, 2, 20);
sort($scores, SORT_NUMERIC);
```

This resorts the numbers in ascending order (1, 2, 10, 20) instead of lexicographical order (1, 10, 2, 20).

Discussion

The sort( ) function doesn't preserve the key/value association between elements; instead, entries are reindexed starting at 0 and going upward. (The one exception to this rule is a one-element array; its lone element doesn't have its index reset to 0. This is fixed as of PHP 4.2.3.)

To preserve the key/value links, use asort( ). The asort( ) function is normally used for associative arrays, but it can also be useful when the indexes of the entries are meaningful:

```
$states = array(1 => 'Delaware', 'Pennsylvania', 'New Jersey');
asort($states);

while (list($rank, $state) = each($states)) {
    print "$state was the #$rank state to join the United States\n";

}
```

Use `natsort()` to sort the array using a natural sorting algorithm. Under natural sorting, you can mix strings and numbers inside your elements and still get the right answer.

```
$tests = array('test1.php', 'test10.php', 'test11.php', 'test2.php');
natsort($tests);
```

The elements are now ordered: `'test1.php'`, `'test2.php'`, `'test10.php'`, and `'test11.php'`. With natural sorting, the number 10 comes after the number 2; the opposite occurs under traditional sorting. For case-insensitive natural sorting, use `natcasesort()`.

To sort the array in reverse order, use `rsort()` or `arsort()`, which is like `rsort()` but also preserves keys. There is no `natrsort()` or `natcasersort()`. You can also pass `SORT_NUMERIC` into these functions.

See Also

Recipe 4.17 for sorting with a custom comparison function and Recipe 4.18 for sorting multiple arrays; documentation on `sort()` at *http://www.php.net/sort*, `asort()` at *http://www.php.net/asort*, `natsort()` at *http://www.php.net/natsort*, `natcasesort()` at *http://www.php.net/natcasesort*, `rsort()` at *http://www.php.net/rsort*, and `arsort()` at *http://www.php.net/arsort*.

4.17   Sorting an Array by a Computable Field

Problem

You want to define your own sorting routine.

Solution

Use `usort()` in combination with a custom comparison function:

```
// sort in reverse natural order
function natrsort($a, $b) {
    return strnatcmp($b, $a);
}

$tests = array('test1.php', 'test10.php', 'test11.php', 'test2.php');
usort($tests, 'natrsort');
```

Discussion

The comparison function must return a value greater that 0 if $a > $b, 0 if $a == $b, and a value less than 0 if $a < $b. To sort in reverse, do the opposite. The function in the Solution, `strnatcmp()`, obeys those rules.

To reverse the sort, instead of multiplying the return value of strnatcmp($a, $b) by -1, switch the order of the arguments to strnatcmp($b, $a).

The sort function doesn't need to be a wrapper for an existing sort. For instance, the pc_date_sort( ) function, shown in Example 4-2, shows how to sort dates.

Example 4-2. pc_date_sort()

```
// expects dates in the form of "MM/DD/YYYY"
function pc_date_sort($a, $b) {
    list($a_month, $a_day, $a_year) = explode('/', $a);
    list($b_month, $b_day, $b_year) = explode('/', $b);

    if ($a_year  > $b_year ) return  1;
    if ($a_year  < $b_year ) return -1;

    if ($a_month > $b_month) return  1;
    if ($a_month < $b_month) return -1;

    if ($a_day   > $b_day  ) return  1;
    if ($a_day   < $b_day  ) return -1;

    return 0;
}

$dates = array('12/14/2000', '08/10/2001', '08/07/1999');
usort($dates, 'pc_date_sort');
```

While sorting, usort( ) frequently recomputes the sort function's return values each time it's needed to compare two elements, which slows the sort. To avoid unnecessary work, you can cache the comparison values, as shown in pc_array_sort( ) in Example 4-3.

Example 4-3. pc_array_sort()

```
function pc_array_sort($array, $map_func, $sort_func = '') {
    $mapped = array_map($map_func, $array);    // cache $map_func() values

    if ('' == $sort_func) {
        asort($mapped);                        // asort() is faster then usort()
    } else {
        uasort($mapped, $sort_func);           // need to preserve keys
    }

    while (list($key) = each($mapped)) {
        $sorted[] = $array[$key];              // use sorted keys
    }

    return $sorted;
}
```

To avoid unnecessary work, pc_array_sort() uses a temporary array, $mapped, to cache the return values. It then sorts $mapped, using either the default sort order or a user-specified sorting routine. Importantly, it uses a sort that preserves the key/value relationship. By default, it uses asort() because asort() is faster than uasort(). (Slowness in uasort() is the whole reason for pc_array_sort() after all.) Finally, it creates a sorted array, $sorted, using the sorted keys in $mapped to index the values in the original array.

For small arrays or simple sort functions, usort() is faster, but as the number of computations grows, pc_array_sort() surpasses usort(). The following example sorts elements by their string lengths—a relatively quick custom sort:

```
function pc_u_length($a, $b) {
    $a = strlen($a);
    $b = strlen($b);

    if ($a == $b) return  0;
    if ($a  > $b) return  1;
                  return -1;
}

function pc_map_length($a) {
    return strlen($a);
}

$tests = array('one', 'two', 'three', 'four', 'five',
               'six', 'seven', 'eight', 'nine', 'ten');

// faster for < 5 elements using pc_u_length()
usort($tests, 'pc_u_length');

// faster for >= 5 elements using pc_map_length()
$tests = pc_array_sort($tests, 'pc_map_length');
```

Here, pc_array_sort() is faster than usort() once the array reaches five elements.

See Also

Recipe 4.16 for basic sorting and Recipe 4.18 for sorting multiple arrays; documentation on usort() at *http://www.php.net/usort*, asort() at *http://www.php.net/asort*, and array_map() at *http://www.php.net/array-map*.

4.18 Sorting Multiple Arrays

Problem

You want to sort multiple arrays or an array with multiple dimensions.

Solution

Use array_multisort():

To sort multiple arrays simultaneously, pass multiple arrays to array_multisort():

```
$colors = array('Red', 'White', 'Blue');
$cities = array('Boston', 'New York', 'Chicago');

array_multisort($colors, $cities);
print_r($colors);
print_r($cities);
Array
(
    [0] => Blue
    [1] => Red
    [2] => White
)
Array
(
    [0] => Chicago
    [1] => Boston
    [2] => New York
)
```

To sort multiple dimensions within a single array, pass the specific array elements:

```
$stuff = array('colors' => array('Red', 'White', 'Blue'),
               'cities' => array('Boston', 'New York', 'Chicago'));

array_multisort($stuff['colors'], $stuff['cities']);
print_r($stuff);
Array
(
    [colors] => Array
        (
            [0] => Blue
            [1] => Red
            [2] => White
        )

    [cities] => Array
        (
            [0] => Chicago
            [1] => Boston
            [2] => New York
        )

)
```

To modify the sort type, as in sort(), pass in SORT_REGULAR, SORT_NUMERIC, or SORT_STRING after the array. To modify the sort order, unlike in sort(), pass in SORT_ASC or SORT_DESC after the array. You can also pass in both a sort type and a sort order after the array.

Discussion

The `array_multisort()` function can sort several arrays at once or a multidimensional array by one or more dimensions. The arrays are treated as columns of a table to be sorted by rows. The first array is the main one to sort by; all the items in the other arrays are reordered based on the sorted order of the first array. If items in the first array compare as equal, the sort order is determined by the second array, and so on.

The default sorting values are SORT_REGULAR and SORT_ASC, and they're reset after each array, so there's no reason to pass either of these two values, except for clarity.

```
$numbers = array(0, 1, 2, 3);
$letters = array('a', 'b', 'c', 'd');
array_multisort($numbers, SORT_NUMERIC, SORT_DESC,
                $letters, SORT_STRING , SORT_DESC);
```

This example reverses the arrays.

See Also

Recipe 4.16 for simple sorting and Recipe 4.17 for sorting with a custom function; documentation on `array_multisort()` at *http://www.php.net/array-multisort*.

4.19   Sorting an Array Using a Method Instead of a Function

Problem

You want to define a custom sorting routine to order an array. However, instead of using a function, you want to use an object method.

Solution

Pass in an array holding a class name and method in place of the function name:

```
usort($access_times, array('dates', 'compare'));
```

Discussion

As with a custom sort function, the object method needs to take two input arguments and return 1, 0, or −1, depending if the first parameter is larger than, equal to, or less than the second:

```
class pc_sort {
    // reverse-order string comparison
    function strrcmp($a, $b) {
```

```
        return strcmp($b, $a);
    }
}

usort($words, array('pc_sort', 'strrcmp'));
```

See Also

Chapter 7 for more on classes and objects; Recipe 4.17 for more on custom sorting of arrays.

4.20   Randomizing an Array

Problem

You want to scramble the elements of an array in a random order.

Solution

If you're running PHP 4.3 or above, use shuffle( ):

```
shuffle($array);
```

If you're running an earlier version, use the pc_array_shuffle( ) function shown in Example 4-4.

Example 4-4. pc_array_shuffle()

```
function pc_array_shuffle($array) {
    $i = count($array);

    while(--$i) {
        $j = mt_rand(0, $i);

        if ($i != $j) {
            // swap elements
            $tmp = $array[$j];
            $array[$j] = $array[$i];
            $array[$i] = $tmp;
        }
    }

    return $array;
}
```

Here's an example:

```
$cards = range(1,52); // deal out 52 "cards"
$cards = pc_array_shuffle($cards);
```

Discussion

There's already a shuffle() function in PHP to shuffle arrays, but as of PHP 4.2.2, it doesn't do its job correctly. The built-in shuffling algorithm tends to favor certain permutations more than others. Elements end up looking randomized, but since each element doesn't have the same chance of ending up in each position, it's not a true shuffle. This is fixed in PHP 4.3.

pc_array_shuffle(), known as the Fisher-Yates shuffle, equally distributes the elements throughout the array. Use it if you run a version of PHP earlier than 4.3. Unlike shuffle(), this function returns the scrambled array instead of modifying it in-place. It also requires a tightly packed array with integer keys.

See Also

Recipe 4.21 for a function that simulates shuffling a deck of cards; documentation on shuffle() at *http://www.php.net/shuffle*.

4.21 Shuffling a Deck of Cards

Problem

You want to shuffle a deck of cards and deal them out.

Solution

Create a array of 52 integers, shuffle them, and map them to cards:

```
$suits = array('Clubs', 'Diamonds', 'Hearts', 'Spades');
$cards = array('Ace', 2, 3, 4, 5, 6, 7, 8, 9, 10, 'Jack', 'Queen', 'King');

$deck = pc_array_shuffle(range(0, 51));

while (($draw = array_pop($deck)) != NULL) {
    print $cards[$draw / 4] . ' of ' . $suits[$draw % 4] . "\n";
}
```

This code uses the pc_array_shuffle() function from Recipe 4.20.

Discussion

Here, a pair of arrays, $suits and $cards, is created to hold the English representation of a card. The numbers 0 through 51 are randomly arranged and assigned to $deck. To deal a card, just pop them off the top of the array, treating the array like a literal deck of cards.

It's necessary to add the check against NULL inside the while, otherwise the loop terminates when you draw the zeroth card. If you modify the deck to contain the numbers 1 through 52, the mathematics of deciding which number belongs to which card becomes more complex.

To deal multiple cards at once, call array_slice():

```
array_slice($deck, $cards * -1);
```

See Also

Recipe 4.20 for a function that randomizes an array; documentation on array_slice() at *http://www.php.net/array-slice*.

4.22   Removing Duplicate Elements from an Array

Problem

You want to eliminate duplicates from an array.

Solution

If the array is already complete, use array_unique(), which returns a new array that contains no duplicate values:

```
$unique = array_unique($array);
```

If you create the array while processing results, here is a technique for numerical arrays:

```
foreach ($_REQUEST['fruits'] as $fruit) {
    if (!in_array($array, $fruit)) { $array[] = $fruit; }
}
```

Here's one for associative arrays:

```
foreach ($_REQUEST['fruits'] as $fruit) {
    $array[$fruit] = $fruit;
}
```

Discussion

Once processing is completed, array_unique() is the best way to eliminate duplicates. But, if you're inside a loop, you can eliminate the duplicate entries from appearing by checking if they're already in the array.

An even faster method than using in_array() is to create a hybrid array in which the key and the value for each element are the same. This eliminates the linear check of in_array() but still allows you to take advantage of the array family of functions that operate over the values of an array instead of the keys.

In fact, it's faster to use the associative array method and then call array_values() on the result (or, for that matter, array_keys(), but array_values() is slightly faster) than to create a numeric array directly with the overhead of in_array().

See Also

Documentation on array_unique() at *http://www.php.net/array-unique*.

4.23   Finding the Union, Intersection, or Difference of Two Arrays

Problem

You have a pair of arrays, and you want to find their union (all the elements), intersection (elements in both, not just one), or difference (in one but not both).

Solution

To compute the union:

```
$union = array_unique(array_merge($a, $b));
```

To compute the intersection:

```
$intersection = array_intersect($a, $b);
```

To find the simple difference:

```
$difference = array_diff($a, $b);
```

And for the symmetric difference:

```
$difference = array_merge(array_diff($a, $b), array_diff($b, $a));
```

Discussion

Many necessary components for these calculations are built into PHP, it's just a matter of combining them in the proper sequence.

To find the union, you merge the two arrays to create one giant array with all values. But, array_merge() allows duplicate values when merging two numeric arrays, so you call array_unique() to filter them out. This can leave gaps between entries because array_unique() doesn't compact the array. It isn't a problem, however, as foreach and each() handle sparsely filled arrays without a hitch.

The function to calculate the intersection is simply named array_intersection() and requires no additional work on your part.

The array_diff() function returns an array containing all the unique elements in $old that aren't in $new. This is known as the *simple difference*:

```
$old = array('To', 'be', 'or', 'not', 'to', 'be');
$new = array('To', 'be', 'or', 'whatever');
$difference = array_diff($old, $new);
Array
(
    [3] => not
    [4] => to
)
```

The resulting array, $difference contains 'not' and 'to', because array_diff() is case-sensitive. It doesn't contain 'whatever' because it doesn't appear in $old.

To get a reverse difference, or in other words, to find the unique elements in $new that are lacking in $old, flip the arguments:

```
$old = array('To', 'be', 'or', 'not', 'to', 'be');
$new = array('To', 'be', 'or', 'whatever');
$reverse_diff = array_diff($new, $old);
Array
(
    [3] => whatever
)
```

The $reverse_diff array contains only 'whatever'.

If you want to apply a function or other filter to array_diff(), roll your own diffing algorithm:

```
// implement case-insensitive diffing; diff -i

$seen = array();
foreach ($new as $n) {
    $seen[strtolower($n)]++;
}

foreach ($old as $o) {
    $o = strtolower($o);
    if (!$seen[$o]) { $diff[$o] = $o; }
}
```

The first foreach builds an associative array lookup table. You then loop through $old and, if you can't find an entry in our lookup, add the element to $diff.

It can be a little faster to combine array_diff() with array_map():

```
$diff = array_diff(array_map('strtolower', $old), array_map('strtolower', $new));
```

The symmetric difference is what's in $a, but not $b, and what's in $b, but not $a:

```
$difference = array_merge(array_diff($a, $b), array_diff($b, $a));
```

Once stated, the algorithm is straightforward. You call array_diff() twice and find the two differences. Then you merge them together into one array. There's no need to call array_unique(), since you've intentionally constructed these arrays to have nothing in common.

See Also

Documentation on array_unique() at *http://www.php.net/array-unique*, array_intersect() at *http://www.php.net/array-intersect*, array_diff() at *http://www.php.net/array-diff*, array_merge() at *http://www.php.net/array-merge*, and array_map() at *http://www.php.net/array-map*.

4.24 Finding All Element Combinations of an Array

Problem

You want to find all combinations of sets containing some or all of the elements in an array, also called the *power set*.

Solution

Use the pc_array_power_set() function shown in Example 4-5.

Example 4-5. pc_array_power_set()

```
function pc_array_power_set($array) {
    // initialize by adding the empty set
    $results = array(array());

    foreach ($array as $element)
        foreach ($results as $combination)
            array_push($results, array_merge(array($element), $combination));

    return $results;
}
```

This returns an array of arrays holding every combination of elements, including the empty set. For example:

```
$set = array('A', 'B', 'C');
$power_set = pc_array_power_set($set);
```

$power_set contains eight arrays:

```
array();
array('A');
array('B');
array('C');
array('A', 'B');
array('A', 'C');
array('B', 'C');
array('A', 'B', 'C');
```

Discussion

First, you include the empty set, {}, in the results. After all, one potential combination of a set is to take no elements from it.

The rest of this function relies on the nature of combinations and PHP's implementation of foreach. Each new element added to the array increases the number of combinations. The new combinations are all the old combinations alongside the new element; a two-element array containing A and B generates four possible combinations: {}, {A}, {B}, and {A, B}. Adding C to this set keeps the four previous combinations but also adds four new combinations: {C}, {A, C}, {B, C}, and {A, B, C}.

Therefore, the outer foreach loop moves through every element of the list; the inner foreach loops through every previous combination created by earlier elements. This is the tricky bit; you need to know exactly how PHP behaves during a foreach.

The array_merge() function combines the element with the earlier combinations. Note, however, the $results array added to the new array with array_push() is the one that's cycled through in the foreach. Normally, adding entries to $results causes an infinite loop, but not in PHP, because PHP operates over a copy of the original list. But, when you pop back up a level to the outer loop, and reexecute the foreach with the next $element, it's reset. So, you can operate directly on $results in place and use it as a stack to hold your combinations. By keeping everything as arrays, you're given far more flexibility when it comes to printing out or further subdividing the combinations at a later time.

To remove the empty set, replace the opening line of:

```
// initialize by adding the empty set
$results = array(array());
```

with:

```
// initialize by adding the first element
$results = array(array(array_pop($array)));
```

Since a one-element array has only one combination—itself—popping off an element is identical to making the first pass through the loop. The double foreach statements don't know they're really starting their processing with the second element in the array.

To print the results with tabs between elements inside the combination and returns between each combination, use the following:

```
$array = array('Adam', 'Bret', 'Ceff', 'Dave');

foreach (pc_array_power_set($array) as $combination) {
    print join("\t", $combination) . "\n";
}
```

Here's how to print only three-element sized combinations:

```
foreach (pc_array_power_set($set) as $combination) {
    if (3 == count($combination)) {
        print join("\t", $combination) . "\n";
    }
}
```

Iterating over a large set of elements takes a long time. A set of n elements generates 2^{n+1} sets. In other words, as n grows by 1, the number of elements doubles.

See Also

Recipe 4.25 for a function that finds all permutation of an array.

4.25   Finding All Permutations of an Array

Problem

You have an array of elements and want to compute all the different ways they can be ordered.

Solution

Use one of the two permutation algorithms discussed next.

Discussion

The pc_permute() function shown in Example 4-6 is a PHP modification of a basic recursive function.

Example 4-6. pc_permute()

```
function pc_permute($items, $perms = array()) {
    if (empty($items)) {
        print join(' ', $perms) . "\n";
    } else {
        for ($i = count($items) - 1; $i >= 0; --$i) {
            $newitems = $items;
            $newperms = $perms;
```

Example 4-6. pc_permute() (continued)

```
            list($foo) = array_splice($newitems, $i, 1);
            array_unshift($newperms, $foo);
            pc_permute($newitems, $newperms);
        }
    }
}
```

For example:

```
    pc_permute(split(' ', 'she sells seashells'));
    she sells seashells
    she seashells sells
    sells she seashells
    sells seashells she
    seashells she sells
    seashells sells she
```

However, while this recursion is elegant, it's inefficient, because it's making copies all over the place. Also, it's not easy to modify the function to return the values instead of printing them out without resorting to a global variable.

The pc_next_permutation() function shown in Example 4-7, however, is a little slicker. It combines an idea of Mark-Jason Dominus from *Perl Cookbook* by Tom Christianson and Nathan Torkington (O'Reilly) with an algorithm from Edsger Dijkstra's classic text *A Discipline of Programming* (Prentice-Hall).

Example 4-7. pc_next_permutation()

```
function pc_next_permutation($p, $size) {
    // slide down the array looking for where we're smaller than the next guy
    for ($i = $size - 1; $p[$i] >= $p[$i+1]; --$i) { }

    // if this doesn't occur, we've finished our permutations
    // the array is reversed: (1, 2, 3, 4) => (4, 3, 2, 1)
    if ($i == -1) { return false; }

    // slide down the array looking for a bigger number than what we found before
    for ($j = $size; $p[$j] <= $p[$i]; --$j) { }

    // swap them
    $tmp = $p[$i]; $p[$i] = $p[$j]; $p[$j] = $tmp;

    // now reverse the elements in between by swapping the ends
    for (++$i, $j = $size; $i < $j; ++$i, --$j) {
        $tmp = $p[$i]; $p[$i] = $p[$j]; $p[$j] = $tmp;
    }

    return $p;
}

$set = split(' ', 'she sells seashells'); // like array('she', 'sells', 'seashells')
$size = count($set) - 1;
```

Example 4-7. pc_next_permutation() (continued)

```
$perm = range(0, $size);
$j = 0;

do {
    foreach ($perm as $i) { $perms[$j][] = $set[$i]; }
} while ($perm = pc_next_permutation($perm, $size) and ++$j);

foreach ($perms as $p) {
    print join(' ', $p) . "\n";
}
```

Dominus's idea is that instead of manipulating the array itself, you can create permutations of integers. You then map the repositioned integers back onto the elements of the array to calculate the true permutation—a nifty idea.

However, this technique still has some shortcomings. Most importantly, to us as PHP programmers, it frequently pops, pushes, and splices arrays, something that's very Perl-centric. Next, when calculating the permutation of integers, it goes through a series of steps to come up with each permutation; because it doesn't remember previous permutations, it therefore begins each time from the original permutation. Why redo work if you can help it?

Dijkstra's algorithm solves this by taking a permutation of a series of integers and returning the next largest permutation. The code is optimized based upon that assumption. By starting with the smallest pattern (which is just the integers in ascending order) and working your way upwards, you can scroll through all permutations one at a time, by plugging the previous permutation back into the function to get the next one. There are hardly any swaps, even in the final swap loop in which you flip the tail.

There's a side benefit. Dominus's recipe needs the total number of permutations for a given pattern. Since this is the factorial of the number of elements in the set, that's a potentially expensive calculation, even with memoization. Instead of computing that number, it's faster to return false from pc_next_permutation() when you notice that $i == -1. When that occurs, you're forced outside the array, and you've exhausted the permutations for the phrase.

Two final notes of implementation. Since the size of the set is invariant, you capture it once using count() and pass it into pc_next_permutation(); this is faster than repeatedly calling count() inside the function. Also, since the set is guaranteed by its construction to have unique elements, i.e., there is one and only one instance of each integer, we don't need to need to check for equality inside the first two for loops. However, you should include them in case you want to use this recipe on other numeric sets, in which duplicates might occur.

See Also

Recipe 4.24 for a function that finds the power set of an array; Recipe 4.19 in the *Perl Cookbook* (O'Reilly); Chapter 3, *A Discipline of Programming* (Prentice-Hall).

4.26 Program: Printing an Array in a Horizontally Columned HTML Table

Converting an array into a horizontally columned table places a fixed number of elements in a row. The first set goes in the opening table row, the second set goes in the next row, and so forth. Finally, you reach the final row, where you might need to optionally pad the row with empty table data cells.

The function pc_grid_horizontal( ), shown in Example 4-8, lets you specify an array and number of columns. It assumes your table width is 100%, but you can alter the $table_width variable to change this.

Example 4-8. pc_grid_horizontal()

```
function pc_grid_horizontal($array, $size) {

    // compute <td> width %ages
    $table_width = 100;
    $width = intval($table_width / $size);

    // define how our <tr> and <td> tags appear
    // sprintf() requires us to use %% to get literal %
    $tr = '<tr align="center">';
    $td = "<td width=\"$width%%\">%s</td>";

    // open table
    $grid = "<table width=\"$table_width%\">$tr";

    // loop through entries and display in rows of size $sized
    // $i keeps track of when we need a new table tow
    $i = 0;
    foreach ($array as $e) {
        $grid .= sprintf($td, $e);
        $i++;

        // end of a row
        // close it up and open a new one
        if (!($i % $size)) {
            $grid .= "</tr>$tr";
        }
    }

    // pad out remaining cells with blanks
    while ($i % $size) {
        $grid .= sprintf($td, ' ');
```

Example 4-8. pc_grid_horizontal() (continued)

```
        $i++;
    }

    // add </tr>, if necessary
    $end_tr_len = strlen($tr) * -1;
    if (substr($grid, $end_tr_len) != $tr) {
        $grid .= '</tr>';
    } else {
        $grid = substr($grid, 0, $end_tr_len);
    }

    // close table
    $grid .= '</table>';

    return $grid;
}
```

The function begins by calculating the width of each <td> as a percentage of the total table size. Depending on the number of columns and the overall size, the sum of the <td> widths might not equal the <table> width, but this shouldn't effect the displayed HTML in a noticeable fashion. Next, define the <td> and <tr> tags, using printf-style formatting notation. To get the literal % needed for the <td> width percentage, use a double %%.

The meat of the function is the foreach loop through the array in which we append each <td> to the $grid. If you reach the end of a row, which happens when the total number of elements processed is a multiple of number of elements in a row, you close and then reopen the <tr>.

Once you finish adding all the elements, you need to pad the final row with blank or empty <td> elements. Put a nonbreaking space inside the data cell instead of leaving it empty to make the table renders properly in the browser. Now, make sure there isn't an extra <tr> at the end of grid, which occurs when the number of elements is an exact multiple of the width (in other words, if you didn't need to add padding cells). Finally, you can close the table.

For example, let's print the names of the 50 U.S. states in a six-column table:

```
// establish connection to database
$dsn = 'mysql://user:password@localhost/table';
$dbh = DB::connect($dsn);
if (DB::isError($dbh)) { die ($dbh->getMessage()); }

// query the database for the 50 states
$sql = "SELECT state FROM states";
$sth = $dbh->query($sql);

// load data into array from database
while ($row = $sth->fetchRow(DB_FETCHMODE_ASSOC)) {
```

```
    $states[] = $row['state'];
}

// generate the HTML table
$grid = pc_grid_horizontal($states, 6);

// and print it out
print $grid;
```

When rendered in a browser, it looks like Figure 4-1.

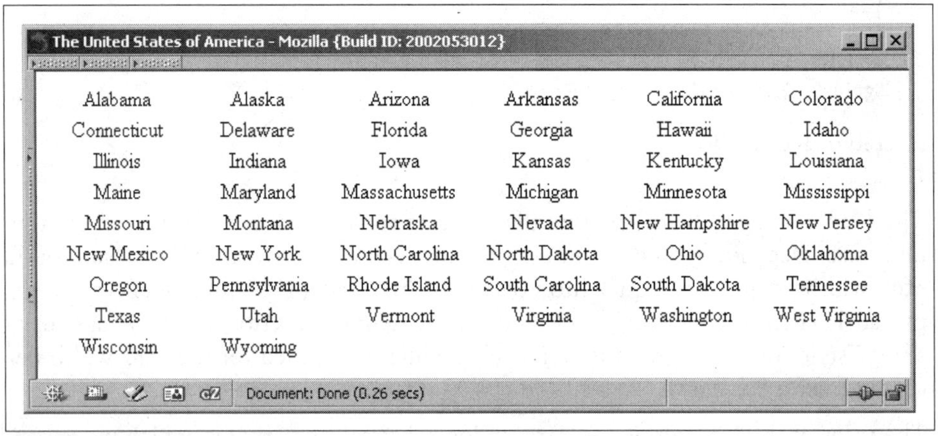

Figure 4-1. The United States of America

Because 50 doesn't divide evenly by six, there are four extra padding cells in the last row.

Variables

5.0 Introduction

Along with conditional logic, variables are the core of what makes computer programs powerful and flexible. If you think of a variable as a bucket with a name that holds a value, PHP lets you have plain old buckets, buckets that contain the name of other buckets, buckets with numbers or strings in them, buckets holding arrays of other buckets, buckets full of objects, and just about any other variation on that analogy you can think of.

A variable is either set or unset. A variable with any value assigned to it, true or false, empty or nonempty, is set. The function isset( ) returns true when passed a variable that's set. The only way to turn a variable that's set into one that's unset is to call unset( ) on the variable. Scalars, arrays, and objects can all be passed to unset( ). You can also pass unset( ) multiple variables to unset them all:

```
unset($vegetables);
unset($vegetables[12]);
unset($earth, $moon, $stars);
```

If a variable is present in the query string of a URL, even if it has no value assigned to it, it is set. Thus:

```
http://www.example.com/set.php?chimps=&monkeys=12
```

sets $_GET['monkeys'] to 12 and $_GET['chimps'] to the empty string.

All unset variables are also empty. Set variables may be empty or nonempty. Empty variables have values that evaluate to false as a boolean: the integer 0, the double 0.0, the empty string, the string "0", the boolean false, an array with no elements, an object with no variables or methods, and NULL. Everything else is nonempty. This includes the string "00", and the string " ", containing just a space character.

Variables evaluate to either true or false. The values listed earlier that evaluate to false as a boolean are the complete set of what's false in PHP. Every other value is true. The distinction between empty and false is that emptiness is only possible for variables. Constants and return values from functions can be `false`, but they can't be empty. For example, the following is valid because $first_name is a variable:

```
if (empty($first_name)) { .. }
```

On the other hand, these two examples return parse errors because 0 (a constant) and the return value from get_first_name() can't be empty:

```
if (empty(0)) { .. }
if (empty(get_first_name())) { .. }
```

5.1   Avoiding == Versus = Confusion

Problem

You don't want to accidentally assign values when comparing a variable and a constant.

Solution

Use:

```
if (12 == $dwarves) { ... }
```

instead of:

```
if ($dwarves == 12) { ... }
```

Putting the constant on the left triggers a parse error with the assignment operator. In other words, PHP complains when you write:

```
if (12 = $dwarves) { ... }
```

but:

```
if ($dwarves = 12) { ... }
```

silently executes, assigning 12 to the variable $dwarves, and then executing the code inside the block. ($dwarves = 12 evaluates to 12, which is true.)

Discussion

Putting a constant on the left side of a comparison coerces the comparison to the type of the constant. This causes problems when you are comparing an integer with a variable that could be an integer or a string. 0 == $dwarves is true when $dwarves is 0, but it's also true when $dwarves is sleepy. Since an integer (0) is on the left side of the comparison, PHP converts what's on the right (the string sleepy) to an integer (0) before comparing. To avoid this, use the identity operator, 0 === $dwarves, instead.

See Also

Documentation for = at *http://www.php.net/language.operators.assignment.php* and for == and === at *http://www.php.net/manual/language.operators.comparison.php*.

5.2   Establishing a Default Value

Problem

You want to assign a default value to a variable that doesn't already have a value. It often happens that you want a hardcoded default value for a variable that can be overridden from form input or through an environment variable.

Solution

Use isset() to assign a default to a variable that may already have a value:

```
if (! isset($cars)) { $cars = $default_cars; }
```

Use the ternary (a ? b : c) operator to give a new variable a (possibly default) value:

```
$cars = isset($_REQUEST['cars']) ? $_REQUEST['cars'] : $default_cars;
```

Discussion

Using isset() is essential when assigning default values. Without it, the nondefault value can't be 0 or anything else that evaluates to false. Consider this assignment:

```
$cars = $_REQUEST['cars'] ? $_REQUEST['cars'] : $default_cars;
```

If $_REQUEST['cars'] is 0, $cars is set to $default_cars even though 0 may be a valid value for $cars.

You can use an array of defaults to set multiple default values easily. The keys in the defaults array are variable names, and the values in the array are the defaults for each variable:

```
$defaults = array('emperors'  => array('Rudolf II','Caligula'),
                  'vegetable' => 'celery',
                  'acres'     => 15);

foreach ($defaults as $k => $v) {
    if (! isset($GLOBALS[$k])) { $GLOBALS[$k] = $v; }
}
```

Because the variables are set in the global namespace, the previous code doesn't work for setting function-private defaults. To do that, use variable variables:

```
foreach ($defaults as $k => $v) {
    if (! isset($$k)) { $$k = $v; }
}
```

See Also

Documentation on `isset()` at *http://www.php.net/isset*; variable variables are discussed in Recipe 5.4 and at *http://www.php.net/language.variables.variable*.

5.3   Exchanging Values Without Using Temporary Variables

Problem

You want to exchange the values in two variables without using additional variables for storage.

Solution

To swap $a and $b:

```
list($a,$b) = array($b,$a);
```

Discussion

PHP's `list()` language construct lets you assign values from an array to individual variables. Its counterpart on the right side of the expression, `array()`, lets you construct arrays from individual values. Assigning the array that `array()` returns to the variables in the `list()` lets you juggle the order of those values. This works with more than two values, as well:

```
list($yesterday,$today,$tomorrow) = array($today,$tomorrow,$yesterday);
```

This method isn't faster than using temporary variables, so you should use it for clarity, but not speed.

See Also

Documentation on `list()` at *http://www.php.net/list* and `array()` at *http://www.php.net/array*.

5.4   Creating a Dynamic Variable Name

Problem

You want to construct a variable's name dynamically. For example, you want to use variable names that match the field names from a database query.

Solution

Use PHP's variable variable syntax by prepending a $ to a variable whose value is the variable name you want:

```
$animal = 'turtles';
$turtles = 103;
print $$animal;
103
```

Discussion

The previous example prints 103. Because $animal = 'turtles', $$animal is $turtles, which equals 103.

Using curly braces, you can construct more complicated expressions that indicate variable names:

```
$stooges = array('Moe','Larry','Curly');
$stooge_moe = 'Moses Horwitz';
$stooge_larry = 'Louis Feinberg';
$stooge_curly = 'Jerome Horwitz';

foreach ($stooges as $s) {
  print "$s's real name was ${'stooge_'.strtolower($s)}.\n";
}
Moe's real name was Moses Horwitz.
Larry's real name was Louis Feinberg.
Curly's real name was Jerome Horwitz.
```

PHP evaluates the expression between the curly braces and uses it as a variable name. That expression can even have function calls in it, such as strtolower().

Variable variables are also useful when iterating through similarly named variables. Say you are querying a database table that has fields named title_1, title_2, etc. If you want to check if a title matches any of those values, the easiest way is to loop through them like this:

```
for ($i = 1; $i <= $n; $i++) {
    $t = "title_$i";
    if ($title == $$t) { /* match */ }
}
```

Of course, it would be more straightforward to store these values in an array, but if you are maintaining old code that uses this technique (and you can't change it), variable variables are helpful.

The curly brace syntax is also necessary in resolving ambiguity about array elements. The variable variable $$donkeys[12] could have two meanings. The first is "take what's in the 12th element of the $donkeys array and use that as a variable name." Write this as: ${$donkeys[12]}. The second is, "use what's in the scalar $donkeys as an array name and look in the 12th element of that array." Write this as: `${$donkeys}[12]`.

See Also

http://www.php.net/language.variables.variable for documentation on variable variables.

5.5   Using Static Variables

Problem

You want a local variable to retain its value between invocations of a function.

Solution

Declare the variable as static:

```
function track_times_called() {
    static $i = 0;
    $i++;
    return $i;
}
```

Discussion

Declaring a variable static causes its value to be remembered by a function. So, if there are subsequent calls to the function, you can access the value of the saved variable. The pc_check_the_count() function shown in Example 5-1 uses static variables to keep track of the strikes and balls for a baseball batter.

Example 5-1. pc_check_the_count()

```
function pc_check_the_count($pitch) {
    static $strikes = 0;
    static $balls   = 0;

    switch ($pitch) {
    case 'foul':
        if (2 == $strikes) break; // nothing happens if 2 strikes
        // otherwise, act like a strike
    case 'strike':
        $strikes++;
        break;
    case 'ball':
        $balls++;
        break;
    }
```

Example 5-1. pc_check_the_count() (continued)

```
    if (3 == $strikes) {
        $strikes = $balls = 0;
        return 'strike out';
    }
    if (4 == $balls) {
        $strikes = $balls = 0;
        return 'walk';
    }
    return 'at bat';
}

$what_happened = check_the_count($pitch);
```

In pc_check_the_count( ), the logic of what happens to the batter depending on the pitch count is in the switch statement inside the function. You can instead return the number of strikes and balls, but this requires you to place the checks for striking out, walking, and staying at the plate in multiple places in the code.

While static variables retain their values between function calls, they do so only during one invocation of a script. A static variable accessed in one request doesn't keep its value for the next request to the same page.

See Also

Documentation on static variables at *http://www.php.net/language.variables.scope.*

5.6   Sharing Variables Between Processes

Problem

You want a way to share information between processes that provides fast access to the shared data.

Solution

Store the data in a shared memory segment, and guarantee exclusive access to the shared memory with a semaphore:

```
$semaphore_id = 100;
$segment_id   = 200;
// get a handle to the semaphore associated with the shared memory
// segment we want
$sem = sem_get($semaphore_id,1,0600);
// ensure exclusive access to the semaphore
sem_acquire($sem) or die("Can't acquire semaphore");
// get a handle to our shared memory segment
$shm = shm_attach($segment_id,16384,0600);
```

```
// retrieve a value from the shared memory segment
$population = shm_get_var($shm,'population');
// manipulate the value
$population += ($births + $immigrants - $deaths - $emigrants);
// store the value back in the shared memory segment
shm_put_var($shm,'population',$population);
// release the handle to the shared memory segment
shm_detach($shm);
// release the semaphore so other processes can acquire it
sem_release($sem);
```

Discussion

A shared memory segment is a slice of your machine's RAM that different processes (such as the multiple web server processes that handle requests) can access. A semaphore makes sure that the different processes don't step on each other's toes when they access the shared memory segment. Before a process can use the segment, it needs to get control of the semaphore. When it's done with the segment, it releases the semaphore for another process to grab.

To get control of a semaphore, use sem_get( ) to find the semaphore's ID. The first argument to sem_get( ) is an integer semaphore key. You can make the key any integer you want, as long as all programs that need to access this particular semaphore use the same key. If a semaphore with the specified key doesn't already exist, it's created, the maximum number of processes that can access the semaphore is set to the second argument of sem_get( ) (in this case, 1), and the semaphore's permissions are set to sem_get( )'s third argument (0600). These permissions work just like file permissions, so 0600 means that the user that created the semaphore can read it and write to it. In this context, user doesn't just mean the process that created the semaphore but any process with the same user ID. Permissions of 0600 should be appropriate for most uses, in which web server processes run as the same user.

sem_get( ) returns an identifier that points to the underlying system semaphore. Use this ID to gain control of the semaphore with sem_acquire( ). This function waits until the semaphore can be acquired (perhaps waiting until other processes release the semaphore) and then returns true. It returns false on error. Errors include invalid permissions or not enough memory to create the semaphore. Once the semaphore is acquired, you can read from the shared memory segment.

First, establish a link to the particular shared memory segment with shm_attach( ). As with sem_get( ), the first argument to shm_attach( ) is an integer key. This time, however it identifies the desired segment, not the semaphore. If the segment with the specified key doesn't exist, the other arguments create it. The second argument (16384) is the size in bytes of the segment, and the last argument (0600) are the permissions on the segment. shm_attach(200,16384,0600) creates a 16K shared memory segment that can be read from and written to only by the user who created it. The function returns the identifier you need to read from and write to the shared memory segment.

After attaching to the segment, pull variables out of it with shm_get_var($shm, 'population'). This looks in the shared memory segment identified by $shm and retrieves the value of the variable called population. You can store any type of variable in shared memory. Once the variable is retrieved, it can be operated on like other variables. shm_put_var($shm,'population',$population) puts the value of $population back into the shared memory segment as a variable called population.

You're now done with the shared memory statement. Detach from it with shm_detach() and release the semaphore with sem_release() so another process can use it.

Shared memory's chief advantage is that it's fast. But since it's stored in RAM, it can't hold too much data, and it doesn't persist when a machine is rebooted (unless you take special steps to write the information in shared memory to disk before shutdown and then load it into memory again at startup). Also, shared memory is not available on Windows.

See Also

Recipe 8.27 includes a program that uses shared memory; documentation on shared memory and semaphore functions at *http://www.php.net/sem*.

5.7 Encapsulating Complex Data Types as a String

Problem

You want a string representation of an array or object for storage in a file or database. This string should be easily reconstitutable into the original array or object.

Solution

Use serialize() to encode variables and their values into a textual form:

```
$pantry = array('sugar' => '2 lbs.','butter' => '3 sticks');
$fp = fopen('/tmp/pantry','w') or die ("Can't open pantry");
fputs($fp,serialize($pantry));
fclose($fp);
```

To recreate the variables, use unserialize():

```
$new_pantry = unserialize(join('',file('/tmp/pantry')));
```

Discussion

The serialized string that is reconstituted into $pantry looks like:

```
a:2:{s:5:"sugar";s:6:"2 lbs.";s:6:"butter";s:8:"3 sticks";}
```

This stores enough information to bring back all the values in the array, but the variable name itself isn't stored in the serialized representation.

When passing serialized data from page to page in a URL, call urlencode( ) on the data to make sure URL metacharacters are escaped in it:

```
$shopping_cart = array('Poppy Seed Bagel' => 2,
                       'Plain Bagel' => 1,
                       'Lox' => 4);
print '<a href="next.php?cart='.urlencode(serialize($shopping_cart)).'">Next</a>';
```

The magic_quotes_gpc and magic_quotes_runtime configuration settings affect data being passed to unserialize( ). If magic_quotes_gpc is on, data passed in URLs, POST variables, or cookies must be processed with stripslashes( ) before it's unserialized:

```
$new_cart = unserialize(stripslashes($cart)); // if magic_quotes_gpc is on
$new_cart = unserialize($cart);                // if magic_quotes_gpc is off
```

If magic_quotes_runtime is on, serialized data stored in a file must be processed with addslashes( ) when writing and stripslashes( ) when reading:

```
$fp = fopen('/tmp/cart','w');
fputs($fp,addslashes(serialize($a)));
fclose($fp);

// if magic_quotes_runtime is on
$new_cart = unserialize(stripslashes(join('',file('/tmp/cart'))));
// if magic_quotes_runtime is off
$new_cart = unserialize(join('',file('/tmp/cart')));
```

Serialized data read from a database must also be processed with stripslashes( ) when magic_quotes_runtime is on:

```
mysql_query(
    "INSERT INTO cart (id,data) VALUES (1,'".addslashes(serialize($cart))."')");

$r = mysql_query('SELECT data FROM cart WHERE id = 1');
$ob = mysql_fetch_object($r);
// if magic_quotes_runtime is on
$new_cart = unserialize(stripslashes($ob->data));
// if magic_quotes_runtime is off
$new_cart = unserialize($ob->data);
```

Serialized data going into a database always needs to have addslashes( ) called on it (or another database-appropriate escaping method) to ensure it's saved properly.

See Also

Recipe 10.7 for information on escaping data for a database.

5.8 Dumping Variable Contents as Strings

Problem

You want to inspect the values stored in a variable. It may be a complicated nested array or object, so you can't just print it out or loop through it.

Solution

Use print_r() or var_dump():

```
$array = array("name" => "frank", 12, array(3, 4));

print_r($array);
Array
(
    [name] => frank
    [0] => 12
    [1] => Array
        (
            [0] => 3
            [1] => 4
        )
)
var_dump($array);
array(3) {
  ["name"]=>
  string(5) "frank"
  [0]=>
  int(12)
  [1]=>
  array(2) {
    [0]=>
    int(3)
    [1]=>
    int(4)
  }
}
```

Discussion

The output of print_r() is more concise and easier to read. The output of var_dump(), however, gives data types and lengths for each variable.

Since these functions recursively work their way through variables, if you have references within a variable pointing back to the variable itself, you can end up with an infinite loop. Both functions stop themselves from printing variable information forever, though. Once print_r() has seen a variable once, it prints *RECURSION* instead of printing information about the variable again and continues iterating through the rest of the information it has to print. When var_dump( ) sees a variable more than three times, it throws a fatal error and ends script execution. Consider the arrays $user_1 and $user_2, which reference each other through their friend elements:

```
$user_1 = array('name' => 'Max Bialystock',
                'username' => 'max');

$user_2 = array('name' => 'Leo Bloom',
                'username' => 'leo');

// Max and Leo are friends
$user_2['friend'] = &$user_1;
$user_1['friend'] = &$user_2;

// Max and Leo have jobs
$user_1['job'] = 'Swindler';
$user_2['job'] = 'Accountant';
```

The output of print_r($user_2) is:

```
Array
(
    [name] => Leo Bloom
    [username] => leo
    [friend] => Array
        (
            [name] => Max Bialystock
            [username] => max
            [friend] => Array
                (
                    [name] => Leo Bloom
                    [username] => leo
                    [friend] => Array
 *RECURSION*
                    [job] => Accountant
                )

            [job] => Swindler
        )

    [job] => Accountant
)
```

When print_r( ) sees the reference to $user_1 the second time, it prints *RECURSION* instead of descending into the array. It then continues on its way, printing the remaining elements of $user_1 and $user_2.

Confronted with recursion, var_dump( ) behaves differently:

```
array(4) {
  ["name"]=>
  string(9) "Leo Bloom"
  ["username"]=>
  string(3) "leo"
  ["friend"]=>
```

```
&array(4) {
  ["name"]=>
  string(14) "Max Bialystock"
  ["username"]=>
  string(3) "max"
  ["friend"]=>
  &array(4) {
    ["name"]=>
    string(9) "Leo Bloom"
    ["username"]=>
    string(3) "leo"
    ["friend"]=>
    &array(4) {
      ["name"]=>
      string(14) "Max Bialystock"
      ["username"]=>
      string(3) "max"
      ["friend"]=>
      &array(4) {
        ["name"]=>
        string(9) "Leo Bloom"
        ["username"]=>
        string(3) "leo"
        ["friend"]=>
        &array(4) {
          ["name"]=>
          string(14) "Max Bialystock"
          ["username"]=>
          string(3) "max"
          ["friend"]=>
          &array(4) {
            ["name"]=>
            string(9) "Leo Bloom"
            ["username"]=>
            string(3) "leo"
            ["friend"]=>
            &array(4) {
<br />
<b>Fatal error</b>:  Nesting level too deep - recursive dependency? in
<b>var-dump.php</b> on line <b>15</b><br />
```

It's not until the fourth appearance of the reference to $user_1 that var_dump() stops recursing. When it does, it throws a fatal error, and no more variable dumping (or script execution) occurs.

Even though print_r() and var_dump() print their results instead of returning them, you can capture the data without printing it using output buffering:

```
ob_start();
var_dump($user);
$dump = ob_get_contents();
ob_end_clean();
```

This puts the results of var_dump($user) in $dump.

See Also

Output buffering is discussed in Recipe 8.12; error handling with PEAR's DB module, shown in Recipe 10.8, uses output buffering with print_r( ) to save error messages; documentation on print_r( ) at *http://www.php.net/print-r* and var_dump( ) at *http://www.php.net/var-dump*.

Functions

6.0 Introduction

Functions help you create organized and reusable code. They allow you to abstract out details so your code becomes more flexible and more readable. Without functions, it is impossible to write easily maintainable programs because you're constantly updating identical blocks of code in multiple places and in multiple files.

With a function you pass a number of arguments in and get a value back:

```
// add two numbers together
function add($a, $b) {
    return $a + $b;
}

$total = add(2, 2);    // 4
```

To declare a function, use the `function` keyword, followed by the name of the function and any parameters in parentheses. To invoke a function, simply use the function name, specifying argument values for any parameters to the function. If the function returns a value, you can assign the result of the function to a variable, as shown in the previous example.

You don't need to predeclare a function before you call it. PHP parses the entire file before it begins executing, so you can intermix function declarations and invocations. You can't, however, redefine a function in PHP. If PHP encounters a function with an identical name to one it's already found, it throws a fatal error and dies.

Sometimes, the standard procedure of passing in a fixed number of arguments and getting one value back doesn't quite fit a particular situation in your code. Maybe you don't know ahead of time exactly how many parameters your function needs to accept. Or, you do know your parameters, but they're almost always the same values, so it's tedious to continue to repass them. Or, you want to return more than one value from your function.

This chapter helps you use PHP to solve these types of problems. We begin by detailing different ways to pass arguments to a function. Recipes 6.1 through 6.5 cover passing arguments by value, reference, and as named parameters; assigning default parameter values; and functions with a variable number of parameters.

The next four recipes are all about returning values from a function. Recipe 6.6 describes returning by reference, Recipe 6.7 covers returning more than one variable, Recipe 6.8 describes how to skip selected return values, and Recipe 6.9 talks about the best way to return and check for failure from a function. The final three recipes show how to call variable functions, deal with variable scoping problems, and dynamically create a function. There's one recipe on function variables located in Chapter 5; if you want a variable to maintain its value between function invocations, see Recipe 5.5.

6.1 Accessing Function Parameters

Problem

You want to access the values passed to a function.

Solution

Use the names from the function prototype:

```
function commercial_sponsorship($letter, $number) {
    print "This episode of Sesame Street is brought to you by ";
    print "the letter $letter and number $number.\n";
}

commercial_sponsorship('G', 3);
commercial_sponsorship($another_letter, $another_number);
```

Discussion

Inside the function, it doesn't matter whether the values are passed in as strings, numbers, arrays, or another kind of variable. You can treat them all the same and refer to them using the names from the prototype.

Unlike in C, you don't need to (and, in fact, can't) describe the type of variable being passed in. PHP keeps track of this for you.

Also, unless specified, all values being passed into and out of a function are passed by value, not by reference. This means PHP makes a copy of the value and provides you with that copy to access and manipulate. Therefore, any changes you make to your copy don't alter the original value. Here's an example:

```
function add_one($number) {
    $number++;
}

$number = 1;
add_one($number);
print "$number\n";
1
```

If the variable was passed by reference, the value of $number would be 2.

In many languages, passing variables by reference also has the additional benefit of being significantly faster than by value. While this is also true in PHP, the speed difference is marginal. For that reason, we suggest passing variables by reference only when actually necessary and never as a performance-enhancing trick.

See Also

Recipe 6.3 to pass values by reference and Recipe 6.6 to return values by reference.

6.2   Setting Default Values for Function Parameters

Problem

You want a parameter to have a default value if the function's caller doesn't pass it. For example, a function to draw a table might have a parameter for border width, which defaults to 1 if no width is given.

Solution

Assign the default value to the parameters inside the function prototype:

```
function wrap_html_tag($string, $tag = 'b') {
    return "<$tag>$string</$tag>";
}
```

Discussion

The example in the Solution sets the default tag value to b, for bold. For example:

```
$string = 'I am some HTML';
wrap_html_tag($string);
```

returns:

```
<b>I am some HTML</b>
```

This example:

```
wrap_html_tag($string, 'i');
```

returns:

```
<i>I am some HTML</i>
```

There are two important things to remember when assigning default values. First, all parameters with default values must appear after parameters without defaults. Otherwise, PHP can't tell which parameters are omitted and should take the default value, and which arguments are overriding the default. So, wrap_html_tag() can't be defined as:

```
function wrap_html_tag($tag = 'i', $string)
```

If you do this and pass wrap_html_tag() only a single argument, PHP assigns the value to $tag and issues a warning complaining of a missing second argument.

Second, the assigned value must be a constant—a string or a number. It can't be a variable. Again, using wrap_html_tag() as our example, you can't do this:

```
$my_favorite_html_tag = 'i';

function wrap_html_tag($string, $tag = $my_favorite_html_tag) {
    ...
}
```

If you want to assign a default of nothing, one solution is to assign the empty string to your parameter:

```
function wrap_html_tag($string, $tag = '') {
    if (empty($tag)) return $string;
    return "<$tag>$string</$tag>";
}
```

This function returns the original string, if no value is passed in for the $tag. Or, if a (nonempty) tag is passed in, it returns the string wrapped inside of tags.

Depending on circumstances, another option for the $tag default value is either 0 or NULL. In wrap_html_tag(), you don't want to allow an empty valued-tag. However, in some cases, the empty string can be an acceptable option. For instance, join() is often called on the empty string, after calling file(), to place a file into a string. Also, as the following code shows, you can use a default message if no argument is provided but an empty message if the empty string is passed:

```
function pc_log_db_error($message = NULL) {
    if (is_null($message)) {
        $message = 'Couldn't connect to DB';
    }

    error_log("[DB] [$message]");
}
```

See Also

Recipe 6.5 on creating functions that take a variable number of arguments.

6.3   Passing Values by Reference

Problem

You want to pass a variable to a function and have it retain any changes made to its value inside the function.

Solution

To instruct a function to accept an argument passed by reference instead of value, prepend an & to the parameter name in the function prototype:

```
function wrap_html_tag(&$string, $tag = 'b') {
    $string = "<$tag>$string</$tag>";
}
```

Now there's no need to return the string because the original is modified in-place.

Discussion

Passing a variable to a function by reference allows you to avoid the work of returning the variable and assigning the return value to the original variable. It is also useful when you want a function to return a boolean success value of true or false, but you still want to modify argument values with the function.

You can't switch between passing a parameter by value or reference; it's either one or the other. In other words, there's no way to tell PHP to optionally treat the variable as a reference or as a value.

Actually, that statement isn't 100% true. If the configuration directive allow_call_ time_pass_reference is enabled, PHP lets you optionally pass a value by reference by prepending an ampersand to the variable's name. However, this feature has been deprecated since PHP 4.0 Beta 4, and PHP issues explicit warnings that this feature may go away in the future when you employ call-time pass-by-reference. Caveat coder.

Also, if a parameter is declared to accept a value by reference, you can't pass a constant string (or number, etc.), or PHP will die with a fatal error.

See Also

Recipe 6.6 on returning values by reference.

6.4   Using Named Parameters

Problem

You want to specify your arguments to a function by name, instead of simply their position in the function invocation.

Solution

Have the function use one parameter but make it an associative array:

```
function image($img) {
    $tag  = '<img src="' . $img['src'] . '" ';
    $tag .= 'alt="' . ($img['alt'] ? $img['alt'] : '') .'">';
    return $tag;
}

$image = image(array('src' => 'cow.png', 'alt' => 'cows say moo'));
$image = image(array('src' => 'pig.jpeg'));
```

Discussion

While using named parameters makes the code inside your functions more complex, it ensures the calling code is easier to read. Since a function lives in one place but is called in many, this makes for more understandable code.

When you use this technique, PHP doesn't complain if you accidentally misspell a parameter's name, so you need to be careful because the parser won't catch these types of mistakes. Also, you can't take advantage of PHP's ability to assign a default value for a parameter. Luckily, you can work around this deficit with some simple code at the top of the function:

```
function image($img) {
    if (! isset($img['src']))    { $img['src']    = 'cow.png';      }
    if (! isset($img['alt']))    { $img['alt']    = 'milk factory'; }
    if (! isset($img['height'])) { $img['height'] = 100;            }
    if (! isset($img['width']))  { $img['width']  = 50;             }
    ...
}
```

Using the isset() function, check to see if a value for each parameter is set; if not, assign a default value.

Alternatively, you can write a short function to handle this:

```
function pc_assign_defaults($array, $defaults) {
    $a = array();
    foreach ($defaults as $d => $v) {
        $a[$d] = isset($array[$d]) ? $array[$d] : $v;
    }
```

```
        return $a;
    }
```

This function loops through a series of keys from an array of defaults and checks if a given array, $array, has a value set. If it doesn't, the function assigns a default value from $defaults. To use it in the previous snippet, replace the top lines with:

```
function image($img) {
    $defaults = array('src'    => 'cow.png',
                      'alt'    => 'milk factory',
                      'height' => 100,
                      'width'  => 50
                     );
    $img = pc_assign_defaults($img, $defaults);
    ...
}
```

This is nicer because it introduces more flexibility into the code. If you want to modify how defaults are assigned, you only need to change it inside pc_assign_defaults() and not in hundreds of lines of code inside various functions. Also, it's clearer to have an array of name/value pairs and one line that assigns the defaults instead of intermixing the two concepts in a series of almost identical repeated lines.

See Also

Recipe 6.5 on creating functions that accept a variable number of arguments.

6.5   Creating Functions That Take a Variable Number of Arguments

Problem

You want to define a function that takes a variable number of arguments.

Solution

Pass an array and place the variable arguments inside the array:

```
// find the "average" of a group of numbers
function mean($numbers) {
    // initialize to avoid warnings
    $sum = 0;

    // the number of elements in the array
    $size = count($numbers);

    // iterate through the array and add up the numbers
    for ($i = 0; $i < $size; $i++) {
```

```
        $sum += $numbers[$i];
    }

    // divide by the amount of numbers
    $average = $sum / $size;

    // return average
    return $average;
}

$mean = mean(array(96, 93, 97));
```

Discussion

There are two good solutions, depending on your coding style and preferences. The more traditional PHP method is the one described in the Solution. We prefer this method because using arrays in PHP is a frequent activity; therefore, all programmers are familiar with arrays and their behavior.

So, while this method creates some additional overhead, bundling variables is commonplace. It's done in Recipe 6.4 to create named parameters and in Recipe 6.7 to return more than one value from a function. Also, inside the function, the syntax to access and manipulate the array involves basic commands such as $array[$i] and count($array).

However, this can seem clunky, so PHP provides an alternative and allows you direct access to the argument list:

```
// find the "average" of a group of numbers
function mean() {
    // initialize to avoid warnings
    $sum = 0;

    // the number of arguments passed to the function
    $size = func_num_args();

    // iterate through the arguments and add up the numbers
    for ($i = 0; $i < $size; $i++) {
        $sum += func_get_arg($i);
    }

    // divide by the amount of numbers
    $average = $sum / $size;

    // return average
    return $average;
}

$mean = mean(96, 93, 97);
```

This example uses a set of functions that return data based on the arguments passed to the function they are called from. First, func_num_args() returns an integer with the number of arguments passed into its invoking function—in this case, mean(). From there, you can then call func_get_arg() to find the specific argument value for each position.

When you call mean(96, 93, 97), func_num_args() returns 3. The first argument is in position 0, so you iterate from 0 to 2, not 1 to 3. That's what happens inside the for loop where $i goes from 0 to less than $size. As you can see, this is the same logic used in the first example in which an array was passed. If you're worried about the potential overhead from using func_get_arg() inside a loop, don't be. This version is actually faster than the array passing method.

There is a third version of this function that uses func_num_args() to return an array containing all the values passed to the function. It ends up looking like hybrid between the previous two functions:

```php
// find the "average" of a group of numbers
function mean() {
    // initialize to avoid warnings
    $sum = 0;

    // load the arguments into $numbers
    $numbers = func_get_args();

    // the number of elements in the array
    $size = count($numbers);

    // iterate through the array and add up the numbers
    for ($i = 0; $i < $size; $i++) {
        $sum += $numbers[$i];
    }

    // divide by the amount of numbers
    $average = $sum / $size;

    // return average
    return $average;
}

$mean = mean(96, 93, 97);
```

Here you have the dual advantages of not needing to place the numbers inside a temporary array when passing them into mean(), but inside the function you can continue to treat them as if you did. Unfortunately, this method is slightly slower than the first two.

See Also

Recipe 6.7 on returning multiple values from a function; documentation on func_num_arg() at *http://www.php.net/func-num-arg*, func_get_arg() at *http://www.php.net/func-get-arg*, and func_get_args() at *http://www.php.net/func-get-args*.

6.6   Returning Values by Reference

Problem

You want to return a value by reference, not by value. This allows you to avoid making a duplicate copy of a variable.

Solution

The syntax for returning a variable by reference is similar to passing it by reference. However, instead of placing an & before the parameter, place it before the name of the function:

```
function &wrap_html_tag($string, $tag = 'b') {
    return "<$tag>$string</$tag>";
}
```

Also, you must use the =& assignment operator instead of plain = when invoking the function:

```
$html =& wrap_html_tag($string);
```

Discussion

Unlike passing values into functions, in which an argument is either passed by value or by reference, you can optionally choose not to assign a reference and just take the returned value. Just use = instead of =&, and PHP assigns the value instead of the reference.

See Also

Recipe 6.3 on passing values by reference.

6.7   Returning More Than One Value

Problem

You want to return more than one value from a function.

Solution

Return an array and use list( ) to separate elements:

```
function averages($stats) {
    ...
    return array($median, $mean, $mode);
```

```
    }

    list($median, $mean, $mode) = averages($stats);
```

Discussion

From a performance perspective, this isn't a great idea. There is a bit of overhead because PHP is forced to first create an array and then dispose of it. That's what is happening in this example:

```
function time_parts($time) {
    return explode(':', $time);
}

list($hour, $minute, $second) = time_parts('12:34:56');
```

You pass in a time string as you might see on a digital clock and call explode() to break it apart as array elements. When time_parts() returns, use list() to take each element and store it in a scalar variable. Although this is a little inefficient, the other possible solutions are worse because they can lead to confusing code.

One alternative is to pass the values in by reference. However, this is somewhat clumsy and can be nonintuitive since it doesn't always make logical sense to pass the necessary variables into the function. For instance:

```
function time_parts($time, &$hour, &$minute, &$second) {
    list($hour, $minute, $second) = explode(':', $time);
}

time_parts('12:34:56', $hour, $minute, $second);
```

Without knowledge of the function prototype, there's no way to look at this and know $hour, $minute, and $second are, in essence, the return values of time_parts().

You can also use global variables, but this clutters the global namespace and also makes it difficult to easily see which variables are being silently modified in the function. For example:

```
function time_parts($time) {
    global $hour, $minute, $second;
    list($hour, $minute, $second) = explode(':', $time);
}

time_parts('12:34:56');
```

Again, here it's clear because the function is directly above the call, but if the function is in a different file or written by another person, it'd be more mysterious and thus open to creating a subtle bug.

Our advice is that if you modify a value inside a function, return that value and assign it to a variable unless you have a very good reason, such as significant performance issues. It's cleaner and easier to understand and maintain.

See Also

Recipe 6.3 on passing values by reference and Recipe 6.11 for information on variable scoping.

6.8   Skipping Selected Return Values

Problem

A function returns multiple values, but you only care about some of them.

Solution

Omit variables inside of list():

```
// Only care about minutes
function time_parts($time) {
    return explode(':', $time);
}

list(, $minute,) = time_parts('12:34:56');
```

Discussion

Even though it looks like there's a mistake in the code, the code in the Solution is valid PHP. This is most frequently seen when a programmer is iterating through an array using each( ), but cares only about the array values:

```
while (list(,$value) = each($array)) {
    process($value);
}
```

However, this is more clearly written using a foreach:

```
foreach ($array as $value) {
    process($value);
}
```

To reduce confusion, we don't often use this feature, but if a function returns many values, and you only want one or two of them, this technique can come in handy. One example of this case is if you read in fields using fgetcsv( ), which returns an array holding the fields from the line. In that case, you can use the following:

```
while ($fields = fgetcsv($fh, 4096)) {
    print $fields[2] . "\n";  // the third field
}
```

If it's an internally written function and not built-in, you could also make the returning array have string keys, because it's hard to remember, for example, that array element 2 is associated with 'rank':

```
while ($fields = read_fields($filename)) {
    $rank = $fields['rank']; // the third field is now called rank
    print "$rank\n";
}
```

However, here's the most efficient method:

```
while (list(,,$rank,,) = fgetcsv($fh, 4096)) {
    print "$rank\n";          // directly assign $rank
}
```

Be careful you don't miscount the amount of commas; you'll end up with a bug.

See Also

Recipe 1.9 for more on reading files using `fgetcsv()`.

6.9   Returning Failure

Problem

You want to indicate failure from a function.

Solution

Return false:

```
function lookup($name) {
    if (empty($name)) { return false; }
    ...
}

if (false !== lookup($name)) { /* act upon lookup */ }
```

Discussion

In PHP, non-true values aren't standardized and can easily cause errors. As a result, it's best if all your functions return the defined `false` keyword because this works best when checking a logical value.

Other possibilities are `''` or 0. However, while all three evaluate to non-true inside an `if`, there's actually a difference among them. Also, sometimes a return value of 0 is a meaningful result, but you still want to be able to also return failure.

For example, `strpos()` returns the location of the first substring within a string. If the substring isn't found, `strpos()` returns `false`. If it is found, it returns an integer with the position. Therefore, to find a substring position, you might write:

```
if (strpos($string, $substring)) { /* found it! */ }
```

However, if $substring is found at the exact start of $string, the value returned is 0. Unfortunately, inside the if, this evaluates to false, so the conditional is not executed. Here's the correct way to handle the return value of strpos():

```
if (false !== strpos($string, $substring)) { /* found it! */ }
```

Also, false is always guaranteed to be false—in the current version of PHP and forever more. Other values may not guarantee this. For example, in PHP 3, empty('0') was true, but it changed to false in PHP 4.

See Also

The introduction to Chapter 5 for more on the truth values of variables; documentation on strpos() at *http://www.php.net/strpos* and empty() at *http://www.php.net/ empty*; information on migrating from PHP 3 to PHP 4 at *http://www.php.net/ migration4*.

6.10   Calling Variable Functions

Problem

You want to call different functions depending on a variable's value.

Solution

Use variable variables:

```
function eat_fruit($fruit) { print "chewing $fruit."; }

$function = 'eat_fruit';
$fruit = 'kiwi';

$function($fruit); // calls eat_fruit()
```

Discussion

If you have multiple possibilities to call, use an associative array of function names:

```
$dispatch = array(
    'add'      => 'do_add',
    'commit'   => 'do_commit',
    'checkout' => 'do_checkout',
    'update'   => 'do_update'
);

$cmd = (isset($_REQUEST['command']) ? $_REQUEST['command'] : '');

if (array_key_exists($cmd, $dispatch)) {
    $function = $dispatch[$cmd];
```

```
        $function(); // call function
    } else {
        error_log("Unknown command $cmd");
    }
```

This code takes the command name from a request and executes that function. Note the check to see that the command is in a list of acceptable command. This prevents your code from calling whatever function was passed in from a request, such as phpinfo(). This makes your code more secure and allows you to easily log errors.

Another advantage is that you can map multiple commands to the same function, so you can have a long and a short name:

```
$dispatch = array(
    'add'      => 'do_add',
    'commit'   => 'do_commit',   'ci' => 'do_commit',
    'checkout' => 'do_checkout', 'co' => 'do_checkout',
    'update'   => 'do_update',   'up' => 'do_update'
);
```

See Also

Recipe 5.4 for more on variable variables.

6.11 Accessing a Global Variable Inside a Function

Problem

You need to access a global variable inside a function.

Solution

Bring the global variable into local scope with the global keyword:

```
function eat_fruit($fruit) {
    global $chew_count;

    for ($i = $chew_count; $i > 0; $i--) {
        ...
    }
}
```

Or reference it directly in $GLOBALS:

```
function eat_fruit($fruit) {
    for ($i = $GLOBALS['chew_count']; $i > 0; $i--) {
        ...
    }
}
```

Discussion

If you use a number of global variables inside a function, the global keyword may make the syntax of the function easier to understand, especially if the global variables are interpolated in strings.

You can use the global keyword to bring multiple global variables into local scope by specifying the variables as a comma-separated list:

```
global $age,$gender,shoe_size;
```

You can also specify the names of global variables using variable variables:

```
$which_var = 'age';
global $$which_var; // refers to the global variable $age
```

However, if you call unset() on a variable brought into local scope using the global keyword, the variable is unset only within the function. To unset the variable in the global scope, you must call unset() on the element of the $GLOBALS array:

```
$food = 'pizza';
$drink = 'beer';

function party() {
    global $food, $drink;

    unset($food);              // eat pizza
    unset($GLOBALS['drink']); // drink beer
}

print "$food: $drink\n";
party();
print "$food: $drink\n";
pizza: beer
pizza:
```

You can see that $food stayed the same, while $drink was unset. Declaring a variable global inside a function is similar to assigning a reference of the global variable to the local one:

```
$food = &GLOBALS['food'];
```

See Also

Documentation on variable scope at *http://www.php.net/variables.scope* and variable references at *http://www.php.net/language.references*.

6.12   Creating Dynamic Functions

Problem

You want to create and define a function as your program is running.

Solution

Use create_function():

```
$add = create_function('$i,$j', 'return $i+$j;');

$add(1, 1); // returns 2
```

Discussion

The first parameter to create_function() is a string that contains the arguments for the function, and the second is the function body. Using create_function() is exceptionally slow, so if you can predefine the function, it's best to do so.

The most frequently used case of create_function() in action is to create custom sorting functions for usort() or array_walk():

```
// sort files in reverse natural order
usort($files, create_function('$a, $b', 'return strnatcmp($b, $a);'));
```

See Also

Recipe 4.17 for information on usort(); documentation on create_function() at *http://www.php.net/create-function* and on usort() at *http://www.php.net/usort*.

Classes and Objects

7.0 Introduction

At first, PHP wasn't an object-oriented (OO) language. As it evolved, more and more object-oriented features appeared. First, you could define classes, but there were no constructors. Then, constructors appeared, but there were no destructors. Slowly but surely, as more people began to push the limits of PHP's syntax, additional features were added to satisfy the demand.

However, if you're the type of person who wishes PHP to be a true OO language, you'll probably be disappointed. At its heart, PHP is a procedural language. It isn't Java. But, if you're the type of person who wants to use some OO features in your code, PHP is probably right for you.

A *class* is a package containing two things: data and methods to access and modify that data. The data portion consists of variables; they're known as *properties*. The other part of a class is a set of functions that can alter a class' properties; they're called *methods*.

When we define a class, we don't define an object that can be accessed and manipulated. Instead, we define a template for an object. From this blueprint, we create malleable objects through a process known as *instantiation*. A program can have multiple objects of the same class, just as a person can have more than one book or many pieces of fruit.

Classes also live in a defined hierarchy. At the top of the chain, there is a generic class. In PHP, this class is named stdClass, for "standard class." Each class down the line is more specialized than its parent. For example, a parent class could be a building. Buildings can be further divided into residential and commercial. Residential buildings can be further subdivided into houses and apartment buildings, and so forth.

Both houses and apartment buildings have the same set of properties as all residential buildings, just as residential and commercial buildings share some things in common. When classes are used to express these parent-child relationships, the child class inherits the properties and methods defined in the parent class. This allows you to reuse the code from the parent class and requires you to write code only to adapt the new child to its specialized circumstances. This is called *inheritance* and is one of the major advantages of classes over functions. The process of defining a child class from a parent is known as *subclassing* or *extending*.

Objects play another role in PHP outside their traditional OO position. Since PHP can't use more than one namespace, the ability for a class to package multiple properties into a single object is extremely helpful. It allows clearly demarcated separate areas for variables.

Classes in PHP are easy to define and create:

```
class guest_book {
    var $comments;
    var $last_visitor;

    function update($comment, $visitor) {
        ...
    }

}
```

The `class` keyword defines an class, just as `function` defines a function. Properties are declared using the `var` keyword. Method declaration is identical to how functions are defined.

The `new` keyword instantiates an object:

```
$gb = new guest_book;
```

Object instantiation is covered in more detail in Recipe 7.1.

Inside a class, you can optionally declare properties using `var`. There's no requirement to do so, but it is a useful way to reveal all the class' variables. Since PHP doesn't force you to predeclare all your variables, it's possible to create one inside a class without PHP throwing an error or otherwise letting you know. This can cause the list of variables at the top of a class definition to be misleading, because it's not the same as the list of variables actually in the class.

Besides declaring a property, you can also assign it a value:

```
var $last_visitor = 'Donnan';
```

You can assign constant values only using this construct:

```
var $last_visitor = 'Donnan';       // okay
var $last_visitor = 9;              // okay
var $last_visitor = array('Jesse'); // okay
var $last_visitor = pick_visitor(); // bad
var $last_visitor = 'Chris' . '9';  // bad
```

If you try to assign something else, PHP dies with a parse error.

To assign a non-constant value to a variable, do it from a method inside the class.

```
var $last_visitor;

function update($comment, $visitor) {
    if (!empty($comment)) {
        array_unshift($this->comments, $comment);
        $this->last_visitor = $visitor;
    }
}
```

If the visitor left a comment, you add it to the top of the array of comments and set that person as the latest visitor to the guest book. The variable $this is a special variable that refers to the current object. So, to access the $size property of an object from inside that object, refer to $this->size.

To assign nonconstant values to variables upon instantiation, assign them in the class constructor. The *class constructor* is a method automatically called when a new object is created, and it has the same name as your class:

```
class guest_book {
    var $comments;
    var $last_visitor;

    function guest_book($user) {
        $dbh  =  mysql_connect('localhost', 'username', 'password');
        $db   =  mysql_select_db('sites');
        $user =  mysql_real_escape_string($user);
        $sql  = "SELECT comments, last_visitor FROM guest_books WHERE user='$user'";
        $r    =  mysql_query($sql);

        if ($obj = mysql_fetch_object($r)) {
            $this->comments = $obj->comments;
            $this->last_visitor = $obj->last_visitor;
        }
    }
}

$gb = new guest_book('stewart');
```

Constructors are covered in Recipe 7.2. Note that mysql_real_escape_string() is new as of PHP 4.3; for earlier versions, use mysql_escape_string().

Be careful not to mistakenly type $this->$size. This is legal, but it's not the same as $this->size. Instead, it accesses the property of the object whose name is the value stored in the $size variable. More often then not, $size is undefined, so $this->$size appears empty. For more on variable property names, see Recipe 6.5.

Besides using -> to access a method or member variable, you can also use ::. This syntax can access static methods in a class. These methods are identical for every instance of an class, because they can't rely on instance-specific data. For example:

```
class convert {
    // convert from Celsius to Fahrenheit
    function c2f($degrees) {
        return (1.8 * $degrees) + 32;
    }
}

$f = convert::c2f(100); // 212
```

To implement inheritance by extending an existing class, use the extends keyword:

```
class xhtml extends xml {

}
```

Child classes inherit parent methods and can optionally choose to implement their own specific versions:

```
class DB {
    var $result;

    function getResult() {
        return $this->result;
    }

    function query($sql) {
        error_log("query() must be overridden by a database-specific child");
        return false;
    }
}

class MySQL extends DB {
    function query($sql) {
        $this->result = mysql_query($sql);
    }
}
```

The MySQL class above inherits the getResult() method unchanged from the parent DB class, but has its own MySQL-specific query() method.

Preface the method name with parent:: to explicitly call a parent method:

```
function escape($sql) {
    $safe_sql = mysql_real_escape_string($sql); // escape special characters
    $safe_sql = parent::escape($safe_sql); // parent method adds '' around $sql
    return $safe_sql;
}
```

Recipe 7.7 covers accessing overridden methods.

The underlying engine powering PHP is named Zend. PHP 4 uses Zend Engine 1; PHP 5 will use an updated version—Zend Engine 2 (ZE2). ZE2 has an entirely new object model that allows PHP to support many new object-oriented features: constructors and destructors, private methods, exception handling, cloning, and nested classes. In this chapter, we mention when there's a difference in syntax or features between PHP 4 and what's supported by ZE2, so you can plan for the future.

7.1   Instantiating Objects

Problem

You want to create a new instance of an object.

Solution

Define the class, then use new to create an instance of the class:

```
class user {
    function load_info($username) {
        // load profile from database
    }
}

$user = new user;
$user->load_info($_REQUEST['username']);
```

Discussion

You can instantiate multiple instances of the same object:

```
$adam = new user;
$adam->load_info('adam');

$dave = new user;
$dave->load_info('adam');
```

These are two independent objects that happen to have identical information. They're like identical twins; they may start off the same, but they go on to live separate lives.

See Also

Recipe 7.4 for more on copying objects; Recipe 7.5 for more on copying objects by reference; documentation on classes and objects at *http://www.php.net/oop*.

7.2   Defining Object Constructors

Problem

You want to define a method that is called when an object is instantiated. For example, you want to automatically load information from a database into an object when it's created.

Solution

Define a method with the same name as the class:

```
class user {
    function user($username, $password) {
        ...
    }
}
```

Discussion

If a function has the same name as its class, it acts as a constructor:

```
class user {
    var $username;

    function user($username, $password) {
        if ($this->validate_user($username, $password)) {
            $this->username = $username;
        }
    }
}
```

```
$user = new user('Grif', 'Mistoffelees'); // using built-in constructor
```

PHP hasn't always had support for constructors. So people made pseudo-constructors by adopting a naming convention and calling that function after creation:

```
class user {
    ...

    init($username, $password) { ... }
}
```

```
$user = new user();
$user->init($username, $password);
```

If you see this, it's usually a result of legacy code.

However, having a standard name for all constructors makes it easier to call your parent's constructor (because you don't need to know the name of the parent class) and also doesn't require you to modify the constructor if you rename your class name. With Zend Engine 2, the naming conventions of constructors have been modified, and the new constructor name is __construct( ). However, for backwards compatibility, if this method isn't found, PHP tries to call a constructor with the same name as the class.

See Also

Recipe 7.7 for more on calling parent constructors; documentation on object constructors at *http://www.php.net/oop.constructor*.

7.3 Destroying an Object

Problem

You want to eliminate an object.

Solution

Objects are automatically destroyed when a script terminates. To force the destruction of an object, use unset( ):

```
$car = new car; // buy new car
...
unset($car);    // car wreck
```

Discussion

It's not normally necessary to manually clean up objects, but if you have a large loop, unset( ) can help keep memory usage from spiraling out of control.

PHP 4 doesn't have destructors, however Zend Engine 2 supports them with the __destruct( ) method.

See Also

Documentation on unset( ) at *http://www.php.net/unset*.

7.4 Cloning Objects

Problem

You want to make a copy of an existing object. For instance, you have an object containing a message posting and you want to copy it as the basis for a reply message.

Solution

Use = to assign the object to a new variable:

```
$rabbit = new rabbit;
$rabbit->eat();
$rabbit->hop();
$baby = $rabbit;
```

Discussion

In PHP, all that's needed to make a copy of an object is to assign it to a new variable. From then on, each instance of the object has an independent life and modifying one has no effect upon the other:

```
class person {
    var $name;

    function person ($name) {
        $this->name = $name;
    }
}

$adam = new person('adam');
print $adam->name;    // adam
$dave = $adam;
$dave->name = 'dave';
print $dave->name;    // dave
print $adam->name;    // still adam
```

Zend Engine 2 allows explicit object cloning via a __clone() method that is called whenever an object is copied. This provides more finely-grained control over exactly which properties are duplicated.

See Also

Recipe 7.5 for more on assigning objects by reference.

7.5   Assigning Object References

Problem

You want to link two objects, so when you update one, you also update the other.

Solution

Use =& to assign one object to another by reference:

```
$adam = new user;
$dave =& $adam;
```

Discussion

When you do an object assignment using =, you create a new copy of an object. So, modifying one doesn't alter the other. But when you use =&, the two objects point at each other, so any changes made in the first are also made in the second:

```
$adam = new user;
$adam->load_info('adam');

$dave =& $adam;
$dave->load_info('dave');
```

The values in $adam are equal to those of $dave.

See Also

Recipe 7.4 for more on copying object; documentation on references at *http://www.php.net/references*.

7.6 Calling Methods on an Object Returned by Another Method

Problem

You need to call a method on an object returned by another method.

Solution

Assign the object to a temporary variable, and then call the method of that temporary variable:

```
$orange = $fruit->get('citrus');
$orange->peel();
```

Discussion

This is necessary because a parse error results from:

```
$fruit->get('citrus')->peel();
```

Zend Engine 2 supports direct dereferencing of objects returned from a method so this workaround is no longer necessary.

7.7   Accessing Overridden Methods

Problem

You want to access a method in the parent class that's been overridden in the child.

Solution

Prefix parent:: to the method name:

```
class shape {
    function draw() {
        // write to screen
    }
}

class circle extends shape {
    function draw($origin, $radius) {
        // validate data
        if ($radius > 0) {
            parent::draw();
            return true;
        }

        return false;
    }
}
```

Discussion

When you override a parent method by defining one in the child, the parent method isn't called unless you explicitly reference it.

In the Solution, we override the draw() method in the child class, circle, because you want to accept circle specific parameters and validate the data. However, in this case, we still want to perform the generic shape::draw() action, which does the actual drawing, so we call parent::draw() inside your method if $radius is greater than 0.

Only code inside the class can use parent::. Calling parent::draw() from outside the class gets you a parse error. For example, if circle::draw() checked only the radius, but you also wanted to call shape::draw(), this wouldn't work:[*]

```
$circle = new circle;
if ($circle->draw($origin, $radius)) {
    $circle->parent::draw();
}
```

---

[*] In fact, it fails with the error unexpected T_PAAMAYIM_NEKUDOTAYIM, which is Hebrew for "double-colon."

If you want to call the constructor belonging to an object's parent but don't know the parent's class name, use get_parent_class() to dynamically identify the parent, then combine that with parent:: to call the parent's constructor:

```
class circle extends shape {

    function circle() {
        $parent = get_parent_class($this);
        parent::$parent();
    }
}
```

The function get_parent_class() takes a class name or an object and returns the name of the object's parent. In order to maintain generality, pass $this, which is the reference to the current object. In this case, the function returns shape. Then, use parent:: to ensure PHP explicitly calls the constructor in the parent class. Calling $parent() without parent:: runs the risk of calling a method in circle that overrides the parent definition.

The call to parent::$parent() may look a little odd. However, PHP just substitutes in the parent class name for the $parent variable. Then, because there are ( )s after the variable, PHP knows it should make a method call.

It's possible to hardcode the call to parent::shape() directly into the circle constructor:

```
function circle() {
    parent::shape();
}
```

However, this isn't as flexible as using get_parent_class(). It is faster, so if you know your object hierarchy isn't going to change, that may be a trade-off you can benefit from.

Last, you can't chain the parent:: keyword to work back to a "grandparent" class, so, parent::parent::foo() doesn't work.

See Also

Recipe 7.2 for more on object constructors; documentation on class parents at *http://www.php.net/keyword.parent* and on get_parent_class() at *http://www.php.net/get-parent-class*.

7.8 Using Property Overloading

Problem

You want handler functions to execute whenever you read and write object properties. This lets you write generalized code to handle property access in your class.

Solution

Use the experimental overload extension and write __get() and __set() methods to intercept property requests.

Discussion

Property overloading allows you to seamlessly obscure from the user the actual location of your object's properties and the data structure you use to store them.

For example, the pc_user class shown in Example 7-1 stores variables in an array, $data.

Example 7-1. pc_user class

```
require_once 'DB.php';

class pc_user {

    var $data = array();

    function pc_user($user) {
        /* connect to database and load information on
         * the user named $user into $this->data
         */

        $dsn = 'mysql://user:password@localhost/test';
        $dbh = DB::connect($dsn);
        if (DB::isError($dbh)) { die ($dbh->getMessage()); }

        $user = $dbh->quote($user);
        $sql = "SELECT name,email,age,gender FROM users WHERE user LIKE '$user'";
        if ($data = $dbh->getAssoc($sql)) {
            foreach($data as $key => $value) {
                $this->data[$key] = $value;
            }
        }
    }

    function __get($property_name, &$property_value) {
        if (isset($this->data[$property_name])) {
            $property_value = $this->data[$property_name];
```

Example 7-1. pc_user class (continued)

```
        return true;
    }

    return false;
}

function __set($property_name, $property_value) {
    $this->data[$property_name] = $property_value;
    return true;
}
}
```

Here's how to use the pc_user class:

```
overload('pc_user');

$user = new pc_user('johnwood');
$name = $user->name;                    // reads $user->data['name']
$user->email = 'jonathan@wopr.mil'; // sets  $user->data['email']
```

The class constructor connects to the users table in the database and retrieves information about the user named $user. When you set data, __set() rewrites the element inside of $data. Likewise, use __get() to trap the call and return the correct array element.

Using an array as the alternate variable storage source doesn't provide many benefits over a nonoverloaded object, but this feature isn't restricted to simple arrays. For instance, you can make $this->email return the get_name() method of an email object. You can also avoid pulling all the user information from the database at once and request it on demand. Another alternative is to use a more persistent storage mechanism, such as files, shared memory, or a database to hold data.

See Also

Recipe 6.7 for information on storing objects in external sources; documentation on the overload extension at *http://www.php.net/overload*.

7.9   Using Method Polymorphism

Problem

You want to execute different code depending on the number and type of arguments passed to a method.

Solution

PHP doesn't support method polymorphism as a built-in feature. However, you can emulate it using various type-checking functions. The following `combine()` function uses `is_numeric()`, `is_string()`, `is_array()`, and `is_bool()`:

```
// combine() adds numbers, concatenates strings, merges arrays,
// and ANDs bitwise and boolean arguments
function combine($a, $b) {
    if (is_numeric($a) && is_numeric($b)) {
        return $a + $b;
    }

    if (is_string($a)  && is_string($b))  {
        return "$a$b";
    }

    if (is_array($a)   && is_array($b))   {
        return array_merge($a, $b);
    }

    if (is_bool($a)    && is_bool($b))    {
        return $a & $b;
    }

    return false;
}
```

Discussion

Because PHP doesn't allow you to declare a variable's type in a method prototype, it can't conditionally execute a different method based on the method's signature, as can Java and C++. You can, instead, make one function and use a `switch` statement to manually recreate this feature.

For example, PHP lets you edit images using GD. It can be handy in an image class to be able to pass in either the location of the image (remote or local) or the handle PHP has assigned to an existing image stream. Example 7-2 shows a `pc_Image` class that does just that.

Example 7-2. pc_Image class

```
class pc_Image {

    var $handle;

    function ImageCreate($image) {
        if (is_string($image)) {
            // simple file type guessing

            // grab file suffix
            $info = pathinfo($image);
```

Example 7-2. pc_Image class (continued)

```
        $extension = strtolower($info['extension']);
        switch ($extension) {
        case 'jpg':
        case 'jpeg':
            $this->handle = ImageCreateFromJPEG($image);
            break;
        case 'png':
            $this->handle = ImageCreateFromPNG($image);
            break;
        default:
            die('Images must be JPEGs or PNGs.');
        }
    } elseif (is_resource($image)) {
        $this->handle = $image;
    } else {
        die('Variables must be strings or resources.');
    }
  }
}
```

In this case, any string passed in is treated as the location of a file, so we use
pathinfo() to grab the file extension. Once we know the extension, we try to guess
which ImageCreateFrom() function accurately opens the image and create a handle.

If it's not a string, we're dealing directly with a GD stream, which is of type resource.
Since there's no conversion necessary, we assign the stream directly to $handle. Of
course, if you're using this class in a production environment, you'd be more robust
in your error handling.

Method polymorphism also encompasses methods with differing numbers of arguments. The code to find the number of arguments inside a method is identical to
how you process variable argument functions using func_num_args(). This is discussed in Recipe 6.5.

See Also

Recipe 6.5 for variable argument functions; documentation on is_string() at *http://
www.php.net/is-string*, is_resource() at *http://www.php.net/is-resource*, and
pathinfo() at *http://www.php.net/pathinfo*.

7.10 Finding the Methods and Properties of an Object

Problem

You want to inspect an object to see what methods and properties it has, which lets you write code that works on any generic object, regardless of type.

Solution

Use get_class_methods() and get_class_vars() to probe an object for information:

```
// learn about cars
$car_methods = get_class_methods('car');
$car_vars    = get_class_vars('car');

// act on our knowledge
if (in_array('speed_away', $car_methods)) {
    $getaway_van = new car;
    $getaway_van->speed_away();
}
```

Discussion

It's rare to have an object and be unable to examine the actual code to see how it's described. Still, these functions can be useful for projects you want to apply to a whole range of different classes, such as creating automated class documentation, generic object debuggers, and state savers, like serialize().

Both get_class_methods() and get_class_vars() return an array of values. In get_class_methods(), the keys are numbers, and the values are the method names. For get_class_vars(), both variable names and default values (assigned using var) are returned, with the variable name as the key and the default value, if any, as the value.

Another useful function is get_object_vars(). Unlike its sister function get_class_vars(), get_object_vars() returns variable information about a specific instance of an object, instead of a generic newly created object.

As a result, you can use it to check the status of an object as it currently exists in a program:

```
$clunker = new car;
$clunker_vars = get_object_vars($clunker); // we pass the object, not the class
```

Since you want information about a specific object, you pass the object and not its class name. But, get_object_vars() returns information in the same format as get_class_vars().

This makes it easy to write quick scripts to see if you're adding new class variables:

```
$new_vars = array_diff(array_keys(get_object_vars($clunker)),
                       array_keys(get_class_vars('car')));
```

You extract the variable names using array_keys(). Then, with the help of array_diff(), you find which variables are in the $clunker object that aren't defined in the car class.

If you just need a quick view at an object instance, and don't want to fiddle with get_class_vars(), use either var_dump(), var_export(), or print_r() to print the object's values. Each of these three functions prints out information in a slightly different way; var_export() can optionally return the information, instead of displaying it.

See Also

Recipe 5.8 for more on printing variables; documentation on get_class_vars() at *http://www.php.net/get-class-vars*, get_class_methods() at *http://www.php.net/get-class-methods*, get_object_vars() at *http://www.php.net/get-object-vars*, var_dump() at *http://www.php.net/var-dump*, var_export() at *http://www.php.net/var-export*, and print_r() at *http://www.php.net/print-r*.

7.11 Adding Properties to a Base Object

Problem

You want to create an object and add properties to it, but you don't want to formally define it as a specific class. This is useful when you have a function that requires an object with certain properties, such as what's returned from mysql_fetch_object() or imap_header().

Solution

Use the built-in base class, stdClass:

```
$pickle = new stdClass;
$pickle->type = 'fullsour';
```

Discussion

Just as array() returns an empty array, creating an object of the type stdClass provides you with an object without properties or methods.

Like objects belonging to other classes, you can create new object properties, assign them values, and check those properties:

```
$guss = new stdClass;

$guss->location = 'Essex';
print "$guss->location\n";
$guss->location = 'Orchard';
print "$guss->location\n";
Essex
Orchard
```

Methods, however, can't be defined after an object is instantiated.

It is useful to create objects of stdClass when you have a function that takes a generic object, such as one returned from a database fetching function, but you don't want to actually make a database request. For example:

```
function pc_format_address($obj) {
    return "$obj->name <$obj->email>";
}

$sql = "SELECT name, email FROM users WHERE id=$id";
$dbh = mysql_query($sql);
$obj = mysql_fetch_object($dbh);
print pc_format_address($obj);
David Sklar <david@example.com>
```

The pc_print_address() function takes a name and email address and converts it to a format as you might see in the To and From fields in an email program. Here's how to call this function without calling mysql_fetch_object():

```
$obj = new stdClass;
$obj->name = 'Adam Trachtenberg';
$obj->email = 'adam@example.com';
print pc_format_address($obj);
Adam Trachtenberg <adam@example.com>
```

7.12 Creating a Class Dynamically

Problem

You want to create a class, but you don't know everything about it until your code is executed.

Solution

Use eval() with interpolated variables:

```
eval("class van extends $parent_class {
    function van() {
        \$this->$parent_class();
    }
```

```
};");

$mystery_machine = new van;
```

Discussion

While it's okay in PHP to use variable names to call functions or create objects, it's not okay to define functions and classes in a similar manner:

```
$van();                    // okay
$van = new $parent_class   // okay
function $van() {};        // bad
class $parent_class {};    // bad
```

Trying to do either of the last two examples results in a parser error because PHP expects a string, and you supplied a variable.

So, if you want to make a class named $van and you don't know beforehand what's going to be stored in $van, you need to employ eval() to do your dirty work:

```
eval("class $van {};");
```

There is a performance hit whenever you call eval(), so high traffic sites should try to restructure their code to avoid this technique when possible. Also, if you're defining your class based on input from users, be sure to escape any potentially dangerous characters.

See Also

Recipe 7.13 to instantiate an object dynamically; documentation on eval() at *http:// www.php.net/eval.*

7.13   Instantiating an Object Dynamically

Problem

You want to instantiate an object, but you don't know the name of the class until your code is executed. For example, you want to localize your site by creating an object belonging to a specific language. However, until the page is requested, you don't know which language to select.

Solution

Use a variable for your class name:

```
$language = $_REQUEST['language'];
$valid_langs = array('en_US' => 'US English',
                     'en_GB' => 'British English',
```

```
                        'es_US' => 'US Spanish',
                        'fr_CA' => 'Canadian French');

    if (isset($valid_langs[$language]) && class_exists($language)) {
        $lang = new $language;
    }
```

Discussion

Sometimes you may not know the class name you want to instantiate at runtime, but you know part of it. For instance, to provide your class hierarchy a pseudo-namespace, you may prefix a leading series of characters in front of all class names; this is why we often use pc_ to represent *PHP Cookbook* or PEAR uses Net_ before all Networking classes.

However, while this is legal PHP:

```
    $class_name = 'Net_Ping';
    $class = new $class_name;              // new Net_Ping
```

This is not:

```
    $partial_class_name = 'Ping';
    $class = new "Net_$partial_class_name"; // new Net_Ping
```

This, however, is okay:

```
    $partial_class_name = 'Ping';
    $class_prefix = 'Net_';

    $class_name = "$class_prefix$partial_class_name";
    $class = new $class_name;              // new Net_Ping
```

So, you can't instantiate an object when its class name is defined using variable concatenation in the same step. However, because you can use simple variable names, the solution is to preconcatenate the class name.

See Also

Recipe 6.4 for more on variable variables; Recipe 7.12 for more on defining a class dynamically; documentation on class_exists( ) at *http://www.php.net/class-exists*.

CHAPTER 8
Web Basics

8.0 Introduction

Web programming is probably why you're reading this book. It's why the first version of PHP was written and what continues to make it so popular today. With PHP, it's easy to write dynamic web programs that do almost anything. Other chapters cover various PHP capabilities, like graphics, regular expressions, database access, and file I/O. These capabilities are all part of web programming, but this chapter focuses on some web-specific concepts and organizational topics that will make your web programming stronger.

Recipes 8.1, 8.2, and 8.3 show how to set, read, and delete cookies. A cookie is a small text string that the server instructs the browser to send along with requests the browser makes. Normally, HTTP requests aren't "stateful"; each request can't be connected to a previous one. A cookie, however, can link different requests by the same user. This makes it easier to build features such as shopping carts or to keep track of a user's search history.

Recipe 8.4 shows how to redirect users to a different web page than the one they requested. Recipe 8.5 explains the session module, which lets you easily associate persistent data with a user as he moves through your site. Recipe 8.6 demonstrates how to store session information in a database, which increases the scalability and flexibility of your web site. Discovering the features of a user's browser is shown in Recipe 8.7. Recipe 8.8 shows the details of constructing a URL that includes a GET query string, including proper encoding of special characters and handling of HTML entities.

The next two recipes demonstrate how to use authentication, which lets you protect your web pages with passwords. PHP's special features for dealing with HTTP Basic authentication are explained in Recipe 8.9. Sometimes it's a better idea to roll your own authentication method using cookies, as shown in Recipe 8.10.

The three following recipes deal with output control. Recipe 8.11 shows how to force output to be sent to the browser. Recipe 8.12 explains the output buffering functions. Output buffers enable you to capture output that would otherwise be printed or delay output until an entire page is processed. Automatic compression of output is shown in Recipe 8.13.

Recipes 8.14 to 8.19 cover error handling topics, including controlling where errors are printed, writing custom functions to handle error processing, and adding debugging assistance information to your programs. Recipe 8.18 includes strategies for avoiding the common "headers already sent" error message, such as using the output buffering discussed in Recipe 8.12.

The next four recipes show how to interact with external variables: environment variables and PHP configuration settings. Recipes 8.20 and 8.21 discuss environment variables, while Recipes 8.22 and 8.23 discuss reading and changing PHP configuration settings. If Apache is your web server, you can use the techniques in Recipe 8.24 to communicate with other Apache modules from within your PHP programs.

Recipe 8.25 demonstrates a few methods for profiling and benchmarking your code. By finding where your programs spend most of their time, you can focus your development efforts on improving the code that has the most noticeable speed-up effect to your users.

This chapter also includes two programs that assist in web site maintenance. Program 8.26 validates user accounts by sending an email message with a customized link to each new user. If the user doesn't visit the link within a week of receiving the message, the account is deleted. Program 8.27 monitors requests in real time on a per-user basis and blocks requests from users that flood your site with traffic.

8.1   Setting Cookies

Problem

You want to set a cookie.

Solution

Use setcookie():

```
setcookie('flavor','chocolate chip');
```

Discussion

Cookies are sent with the HTTP headers, so setcookie() must be called before any output is generated.

You can pass additional arguments to setcookie( ) to control cookie behavior. The third argument to setcookie( ) is an expiration time, expressed as an epoch time-stamp. For example, this cookie expires at noon GMT on December 3, 2004:

```
setcookie('flavor','chocolate chip',1102075200);
```

If the third argument to setcookie( ) is missing (or empty), the cookie expires when the browser is closed. Also, many systems can't handle a cookie expiration time greater than 2147483647, because that's the largest epoch timestamp that fits in a 32-bit integer, as discussed in the introduction to Chapter 3.

The fourth argument to setcookie( ) is a path. The cookie is sent back to the server only when pages whose path begin with the specified string are requested. For example, the following cookie is sent back only to pages whose path begins with */products/*:

```
setcookie('flavor','chocolate chip','','/products/');
```

The page that's setting this cookie doesn't have to have a URL that begins with */products/*, but the following cookie is sent back only to pages that do.

The fifth argument to setcookie( ) is a domain. The cookie is sent back to the server only when pages whose hostname ends with the specified domain are requested. For example, the first cookie in the following code is sent back to all hosts in the *example.com* domain, but the second cookie is sent only with requests to the host *jeannie.example.com*:

```
setcookie('flavor','chocolate chip','','','.example.com');
setcookie('flavor','chocolate chip','','','jeannie.example.com');
```

If the first cookie's domain was just *example.com* instead of *.example.com*, it would be sent only to the single host *example.com* (and not *www.example.com* or *jeannie.example.com*).

The last optional argument to setcookie( ) is a flag that if set to 1, instructs the browser only to send the cookie over an SSL connection. This can be useful if the cookie contains sensitive information, but remember that the data in the cookie is stored in the clear on the user's computer.

Different browsers handle cookies in slightly different ways, especially with regard to how strictly they match path and domain strings and how they determine priority between different cookies of the same name. The setcookie( ) page of the online manual has helpful clarifications of these differences.

See Also

Recipe 8.2 shows how to read cookie values; Recipe 8.3 shows how to delete cookies; Recipe 8.12 explains output buffering; Recipe 8.18 shows how to avoid the "headers already sent" error message that sometimes occurs when calling setcookie( ); documentation on setcookie( ) at *http://www.php.net/setcookie*; an expanded cookie specification is detailed in RFC 2965 at *http://www.faqs.org/rfcs/rfc2965.html*.

8.2   Reading Cookie Values

Problem

You want to read the value of a cookie that's been previously set.

Solution

Look in the $_COOKIE superglobal array:

```
if (isset($_COOKIE['flavor'])) {
    print "You ate a $_COOKIE[flavor] cookie.";
}
```

Discussion

A cookie's value isn't available in $_COOKIE during the request in which the cookie is set. In other words, the setcookie() function doesn't alter the value of $_COOKIE. On subsequent requests, however, each cookie is stored in $_COOKIE. If register_globals is on, cookie values are also assigned to global variables.

When a browser sends a cookie back to the server, it sends only the value. You can't access the cookie's domain, path, expiration time, or secure status through $_COOKIE because the browser doesn't send that to the server.

To print the names and values of all cookies sent in a particular request, loop through the $_COOKIE array:

```
foreach ($_COOKIE as $cookie_name => $cookie_value) {
    print "$cookie_name = $cookie_value<br>";
}
```

See Also

Recipe 8.1 shows how to set cookies; Recipe 8.3 shows how to delete cookies; Recipe 8.12 explains output buffering; Recipe 8.18 shows how to avoid the "headers already sent" error message that sometimes occurs when calling setcookie(); Recipe 9.7 for information on register_globals.

8.3   Deleting Cookies

Problem

You want to delete a cookie so a browser doesn't send it back to the server.

Solution

Call setcookie( ) with no value for the cookie and an expiration time in the past:

```
setcookie('flavor','',time()-86400);
```

Discussion

It's a good idea to make the expiration time a few hours or an entire day in the past, in case your server and the user's computer have unsynchronized clocks. For example, if your server thinks it's 3:06 P.M. and a user's computer thinks it's 3:02 P.M., a cookie with an expiration time of 3:05 P.M. isn't deleted by that user's computer even though the time is in the past for the server.

The call to setcookie( ) that deletes a cookie has to have the same arguments (except for value and time) that the call to setcookie( ) that set the cookie did, so include the path, domain, and secure flag if necessary.

See Also

Recipe 8.1 shows how to set cookies; Recipe 8.2 shows how to read cookie values; Recipe 8.12 explains output buffering; Recipe 8.18 shows how to avoid the "headers already sent" error message that sometimes occurs when calling setcookie( ); documentation on setcookie( ) at *http://www.php.net/setcookie.*

8.4   Redirecting to a Different Location

Problem

You want to automatically send a user to a new URL. For example, after successfully saving form data, you want to redirect a user to a page that confirms the data.

Solution

Before any output is printed, use header( ) to send a Location header with the new URL:

```
header('Location: http://www.example.com/');
```

Discussion

If you want to pass variables to the new page, you can include them in the query string of the URL:

```
header('Location: http://www.example.com/?monkey=turtle');
```

The URL that you are redirecting a user to is retrieved with GET. You can't redirect someone to retrieve a URL via POST. You can, however, send other headers along with the Location header. This is especially useful with the Window-target header, which indicates a particular named frame or window in which to load the new URL:

```
header('Window-target: main');
header('Location: http://www.example.com/');
```

The redirect URL must include the protocol and hostname; it can't just be a pathname:

```
// Good Redirect
header('Location: http://www.example.com/catalog/food/pemmican.php');

// Bad Redirect
header('Location: /catalog/food/pemmican.php');
```

See Also

Documentation on header( ) at *http://www.php.net/header*.

8.5   Using Session Tracking

Problem

You want to maintain information about a user as she moves through your site.

Solution

Use the session module. The session_start() function initializes a session, and accessing an element in the global $_SESSION array tells PHP to keep track of the corresponding variable.

```
session_start();
$_SESSION['visits']++;
print 'You have visited here '.$_SESSION['visits'].' times.';
```

Discussion

To start a session automatically on each request, set session.auto_start to 1 in *php.ini*. With session.auto_start, there's no need to call session_start().

The session functions keep track of users by issuing them cookies with a randomly generated session IDs. If PHP detects that a user doesn't accept the session ID cookie, it automatically adds the session ID to URLs and forms.* For example, consider this code that prints a URL:

```
print '<a href="train.php">Take the A Train</a>';
```

If sessions are enabled, but a user doesn't accept cookies, what's sent to the browser is something like:

```
<a href="train.php?PHPSESSID=2eb89f3344520d11969a79aea6bd2fdd">Take the A Train</a>
```

In this example, the session name is PHPSESSID and the session ID is 2eb89f3344520d11969a79aea6bd2fdd. PHP adds those to the URL so they are passed along to the next page. Forms are modified to include a hidden element that passes the session ID. Redirects with the Location header aren't automatically modified, so you have to add a session ID to them yourself using the SID constant:

```
$redirect_url = 'http://www.example.com/airplane.php';
if (defined('SID') && (! isset($_COOKIE[session_name()]))) {
    $redirect_url .= '?' . SID;
}

header("Location: $redirect_url");
```

The session_name() function returns the name of the cookie that the session ID is stored in, so this code appends the SID constant only to $redirect_url if the constant is defined, and the session cookie isn't set.

By default, PHP stores session data in files in the */tmp* directory on your server. Each session is stored in its own file. To change the directory in which the files are saved, set the session.save_path configuration directive in *php.ini* to the new directory. You can also call session_save_path() with the new directory to change directories, but you need to do this before accessing any session variables.

See Also

Documentation on session_start() at *http://www.php.net/session-start*, session_save_path() at *http://www.php.net/session-save-path*; the session module has a number of configuration directives that help you do things like manage how long sessions can last and how they are cached; these are detailed in the "Sessions" section of the online manual at *http://www.php.net/session*.

---

* Before PHP 4.2.0, this behavior had to be explicitly enabled by building PHP with the --enable-trans-sid configuration setting.

8.6 Storing Sessions in a Database

Problem

You want to store session data in a database instead of in files. If multiple web servers all have access to the same database, the session data is then mirrored across all the web servers.

Solution

Set session.save_handler to user in *php.ini* and use the pc_DB_Session class shown in Example 8-1. For example:

```
$s = new pc_DB_Session('mysql://user:password@localhost/db');
ini_get('session.auto_start') or session_start();
```

Discussion

One of the most powerful aspects of the session module is its abstraction of how sessions get saved. The session_set_save_handler() function tells PHP to use different functions for the various session operations such as saving a session and reading session data. The pc_DB_Session class stores the session data in a database. If this database is shared between multiple web servers, users' session information is portable across all those web servers. So, if you have a bunch of web servers behind a load balancer, you don't need any fancy tricks to ensure that a user's session data is accurate no matter which web server they get sent to.

To use pc_DB_Session, pass a data source name (DSN) to the class when you instantiate it. The session data is stored in a table called php_session whose structure is:

```
CREATE TABLE php_session (
    id CHAR(32) NOT NULL,
    data MEDIUMBLOB,
    last_access INT UNSIGNED NOT NULL,
    PRIMARY KEY(id)
)
```

If you want the table name to be different than php_session, set session.save_path in *php.ini* to your new table name. Example 8-1 shows the pc_DB_Session class.

Example 8-1. pc_DB_Session class

```
require 'PEAR.php';
require 'DB.php';

class pc_DB_Session extends PEAR {

    var $_dbh;
    var $_table;
```

Example 8-1. pc_DB_Session class (continued)

```
var $_connected = false;
var $_gc_maxlifetime;
var $_prh_read;
var $error = null;

/**
 * Constructor
 */
function pc_DB_Session($dsn = null) {
    if (is_null($dsn)) {
        $this->error = PEAR::raiseError('No DSN specified');
        return;
    }

    $this->_gc_maxlifetime = ini_get('session.gc_maxlifetime');
    // Sessions last for a day unless otherwise specified.
    if (! $this->_gc_maxlifetime) {
        $this->_gc_maxlifetime = 86400;
    }

    $this->_table = ini_get('session.save_path');
    if ((! $this->_table) || ('/tmp' == $this->_table)) {
        $this->_table = 'php_session';
    }

    $this->_dbh = DB::connect($dsn);
    if (DB::isError($this->_dbh)) {
        $this->error = $this->_dbh;
        return;
    }

    $this->_prh_read = $this->_dbh->prepare(
        "SELECT data FROM $this->_table WHERE id LIKE ? AND last_access >= ?");
    if (DB::isError($this->_prh_read)) {
        $this->error = $this->_prh_read;
        return;
    }

    if (! session_set_save_handler(array(&$this,'_open'),
                                   array(&$this,'_close'),
                                   array(&$this,'_read'),
                                   array(&$this,'_write'),
                                   array(&$this,'_destroy'),
                                   array(&$this,'_gc'))) {
        $this->error = PEAR::raiseError('session_set_save_handler() failed');
        return;
    }

    return $this->_connected = true;
}
```

Example 8-1. pc_DB_Session class (continued)

```
function _open() {
    return $this->_connected;
}

function _close() {
    return $this->_connected;
}

function _read($id) {
    if (! $this->_connected) { return false; }
    $sth =
        $this->_dbh->execute($this->_prh_read,
                            array($id,time() - $this->_gc_maxlifetime));
    if (DB::isError($sth)) {
        $this->error = $sth;
        return '';
    } else {
        if (($sth->numRows() == 1) &&
            ($ar = $sth->fetchRow(DB_FETCHMODE_ORDERED))) {
            return $ar[0];
        } else {
            return '';
        }
    }
}

function _write($id,$data) {
    $sth = $this->_dbh->query(
        "REPLACE INTO $this->_table (id,data,last_access) VALUES (?,?,?)",
        array($id,$data,time()));
    if (DB::isError($sth)) {
        $this->error = $sth;
        return false;
    } else {
        return true;
    }
}

function _destroy($id) {
    $sth = $this->_dbh->query("DELETE FROM $this->_table WHERE id LIKE ?",
                            array($id));
    if (DB::isError($sth)) {
        $this->error = $sth;
        return false;
    } else {
        return true;
    }
}

function _gc($maxlifetime) {
    $sth = $this->_dbh->query("DELETE FROM $this->_table WHERE last_access < ?",
                            array(time() - $maxlifetime));
```

Example 8-1. pc_DB_Session class (continued)

```
    if (DB::isError($sth)) {
        $this->error = $sth;
        return false;
    } else {
        return true;
    }
}
}
```

The `pc_DB_Session::_write()` method uses a MySQL-specific SQL command, `REPLACE INTO`, which updates an existing record or inserts a new one, depending on whether there is already a record in the database with the given id field. If you use a different database, modify the `_write()` function to accomplish the same task. For instance, delete the existing row (if any), and insert a new one, all inside a transaction:

```
function _write($id,$data) {
    $sth = $this->_dbh->query('BEGIN WORK');
    if (DB::isError($sth)) {
        $this->error = $sth;
        return false;
    }
    $sth = $this->_dbh->query("DELETE FROM $this->_table WHERE id LIKE ?",
                              array($id));
    if (DB::isError($sth)) {
        $this->error = $sth;
        $this->_dbh->query('ROLLBACK');
        return false;
    }
    $sth = $this->_dbh->query(
        "INSERT INTO $this->_table (id,data,last_access) VALUES (?,?,?)",
        array($id,$data,time()));
    if (DB::isError($sth)) {
        $this->error = $sth;
        $this->_dbh->query('ROLLBACK');
        return false;
    }
    $sth = $this->_dbh->query('COMMIT');
    if (DB::isError($sth)) {
        $this->error = $sth;
        $this->_dbh->query('ROLLBACK');
        return false;
    }
        return true;
}
```

See Also

Documentation on `session_set_save_handler()` at *http://www.php.net/session-set-save-handler*; a handler using PostgreSQL is available at *http://www.zend.com/codex.php?id=456&single=1*; the format for data source names is discussed in Recipe 10.3.

8.7   Detecting Different Browsers

Problem

You want to generate content based on the capabilities of a user's browser.

Solution

Use the object returned by get_browser() to determine a browser's capabilities:

```
$browser = get_browser();

if ($browser->frames) {
    // print out a frame-based layout
} elseif ($browser->tables) {
    // print out a table-based layout
} else {
    // print out a boring layout
}
```

Discussion

The get_browser() function examines the environment variable $_ENV['HTTP_USER_AGENT'] (set by the web server) and compares it to browsers listed in an external browser capability file. Due to licensing issues, PHP isn't distributed with a browser capability file. The "Obtaining PHP" section of the PHP FAQ (*http://www.php.net/faq.obtaining*) lists *http://www.cyscape.com/asp/browscap/* and *http://www.amrein.com/apps/page.asp?Q=InowDownload* as sources for a browser capabilities file, and there is also one at *http://asp.net.do/browscap.zip*.

Once you download a browser capability file, you need to tell PHP where to find it by setting the browscap configuration directive to the pathname of the file. If you use PHP as a CGI, set the directive in the *php.ini* file:

```
browscap=/usr/local/lib/browscap.txt
```

If you use Apache, you need to set the directive in your Apache configuration file:

```
php_value browscap "/usr/local/lib/browscap.txt"
```

Many of the capabilities get_browser() finds are shown in Table 8-1. For user-configurable capabilities such as javascript or cookies though, get_browser() just tells you if the browser can support those functions. It doesn't tell you if the user has disabled the functions. If JavaScript is turned off in a JavaScript-capable browser or a user refuses to accept cookies when the browser prompts him, get_browser() still indicates that the browser supports those functions.

Table 8-1. Browser capability object properties

Property	Description
platform	Operating system the browser is running on (e.g., Windows, Macintosh, UNIX, Win32, Linux, MacPPC)
version	Full browser version (e.g., 5.0, 3.5, 6.0b2)
majorver	Major browser version (e.g., 5, 3, 6)
minorver	Minor browser version (e.g., 0, 5, 02)
frames	1 if the browser supports frames
tables	1 if the browser supports tables
cookies	1 if the browser supports cookies
backgroundsounds	1 if the browser supports background sounds with \<embed> or \<bgsound>
vbscript	1 if the browser supports VBScript
javascript	1 if the browser supports JavaScript
javaapplets	1 if the browser can run Java applets
activexcontrols	1 if the browser can run ActiveX controls

See Also

Documentation on get_browser( ) at *http://www.php.net/get-browser*.

8.8   Building a GET Query String

Problem

You need to construct a link that includes name/value pairs in a query string.

Solution

Encode the names and values with urlencode( ) and use join( ) to create the query string:

```
$vars = array('name' => 'Oscar the Grouch',
              'color' => 'green',
              'favorite_punctuation' => '#');
$safe_vars = array();
foreach ($vars as $name => $value) {
    $safe_vars[] = urlencode($name).'='.urlencode($value);
}

$url = '/muppet/select.php?' . join('&',$safe_vars);
```

Discussion

The URL built in the solution is:

```
/muppet/select.php?name=Oscar+the+Grouch&color=green&favorite_punctuation=%23
```

The query string has spaces encoded as +. Special characters such as # are hex-encoded as %23 because the ASCII value of # is 35, which is 23 in hexadecimal.

Although urlencode() prevents any special characters in the variable names or values from disrupting the constructed URL, you may have problems if your variable names begin with the names of HTML entities. Consider this partial URL for retrieving information about a stereo system:

```
/stereo.php?speakers=12&cdplayer=52&amp=10
```

The HTML entity for ampersand (&) is & so a browser may interpret that URL as:

```
/stereo.php?speakers=12&cdplayer=52&=10
```

To prevent embedded entities from corrupting your URLs, you have three choices. The first is to choose variable names that can't be confused with entities, such as _amp instead of amp. The second is to convert characters with HTML entity equivalents to those entities before printing out the URL. Use htmlentities():

```
$url = '/muppet/select.php?' . htmlentities(join('&',$safe_vars));
```

The resulting URL is:

```
/muppet/select.php?name=Oscar+the+Grouch&color=green&favorite_punctuation=%23
```

Your third choice is to change the argument separator from & to ; by setting the configuration directive arg_separator.input to ;. You then join name-value pairs with ; to produce a query string:

```
/muppet/select.php?name=Oscar+the+Grouch;color=green;favorite_punctuation=%23
```

You may run into trouble with any GET method URLs that you can't explicitly construct with semicolons, such as a form with its method set to GET, because your users' browsers use & as the argument separator.

Because many browsers don't support using ; as an argument separator, the easiest way to avoid problems with entities in URLs is to choose variable names that don't overlap with entity names. If you don't have complete control over variable names, however, use htmlentities() to protect your URLs from entity decoding.

See Also

Documentation on urlencode() at *http://www.php.net/urlencode* and htmlentities() at *http://www.php.net/htmlentities*.

8.9   Using HTTP Basic Authentication

Problem

You want to use PHP to protect parts of your web site with passwords. Instead of storing the passwords in an external file and letting the web server handle the authentication, you want the password verification logic to be in a PHP program.

Solution

The $_SERVER['PHP_AUTH_USER'] and $_SERVER['PHP_AUTH_PW'] global variables contain the username and password supplied by the user, if any. To deny access to a page, send a WWW-Authenticate header identifying the authentication realm as part of a response with status code 401:

```
header('WWW-Authenticate: Basic realm="My Website"');
header('HTTP/1.0 401 Unauthorized');
echo "You need to enter a valid username and password.";
exit;
```

Discussion

When a browser sees a 401 header, it pops up a dialog box for a username and password. Those authentication credentials (the username and password), if accepted by the server, are associated with the realm in the WWW-Authenticate header. Code that checks authentication credentials needs to be executed before any output is sent to the browser, since it might send headers. For example, you can use a function such as pc_validate(), shown in Example 8-2.

Example 8-2. pc_validate()

```
function pc_validate($user,$pass) {
    /* replace with appropriate username and password checking,
       such as checking a database */
    $users = array('david' => 'fadj&32',
                   'adam'  => '8HEj838');

    if (isset($users[$user]) && ($users[$user] == $pass)) {
        return true;
    } else {
        return false;
    }
}
```

Here's an example of how to use pc_validate():

```
if (! pc_validate($_SERVER['PHP_AUTH_USER'], $_SERVER['PHP_AUTH_PW'])) {
    header('WWW-Authenticate: Basic realm="My Website"');
    header('HTTP/1.0 401 Unauthorized');
```

```
        echo "You need to enter a valid username and password.";
        exit;
    }
```

Replace the contents of the pc_validate() function with appropriate logic to determine if a user entered the correct password. You can also change the realm string from "My Website" and the message that gets printed if a user hits "cancel" in their browser's authentication box from "You need to enter a valid username and password."

HTTP Basic authentication can't be used if you're running PHP as a CGI. If you can't run PHP as a server module, you can use cookie authentication, discussed in Recipe 8.10.

Another issue with HTTP Basic authentication is that it provides no simple way for a user to log out, other then to exit his browser. The PHP online manual has a few suggestions for log out methods that work with varying degrees of success with different server and browser combinations at *http://www.php.net/features.http-auth*.

There is a straightforward way, however, to force a user to log out after a fixed time interval: include a time calculation in the realm string. Browsers use the same username and password combination every time they're asked for credentials in the same realm. By changing the realm name, the browser is forced to ask the user for new credentials. For example, this forces a log out every night at midnight:

```
if (! pc_validate($_SERVER['PHP_AUTH_USER'],$_SERVER['PHP_AUTH_PW'])) {
    $realm = 'My Website for '.date('Y-m-d');
    header('WWW-Authenticate: Basic realm="'.$realm.'"');
    header('HTTP/1.0 401 Unauthorized');
    echo "You need to enter a valid username and password.";
    exit;
}
```

You can also have a user-specific timeout without changing the realm name by storing the time that a user logs in or accesses a protected page. The pc_validate() function in Example 8-3 stores login time in a database and forces a log out if it's been more than 15 minutes since the user last requested a protected page.

Example 8-3. pc_validate2()

```
function pc_validate2($user,$pass) {
    $safe_user = strtr(addslashes($user),array('_' => '\_', '%' => '\%'));
    $r = mysql_query("SELECT password,last_access
                    FROM users WHERE user LIKE '$safe_user'");

    if (mysql_numrows($r) == 1) {
        $ob = mysql_fetch_object($r);
        if ($ob->password == $pass) {
            $now = time();
            if (($now - $ob->last_access) > (15 * 60)) {
                return false;
            } else {
```

Example 8-3. pc_validate2() (continued)

```
            // update the last access time
            mysql_query("UPDATE users SET last_access = NOW()
                        WHERE user LIKE '$safe_user'");
            return true;
        }
    }
} else {
    return false;
}
}
```

For example:

```
if (! pc_validate($_SERVER['PHP_AUTH_USER'],$_SERVER['PHP_AUTH_PW'])) {
    header('WWW-Authenticate: Basic realm="My Website"');
    header('HTTP/1.0 401 Unauthorized');
    echo "You need to enter a valid username and password.";
    exit;
}
```

See Also

Recipe 8.10; the HTTP Authentication section of the PHP online manual at *http://www.php.net/features.http-auth*.

8.10   Using Cookie Authentication

Problem

You want more control over the user login procedure, such as presenting your own login form.

Solution

Store authentication status in a cookie or as part of a session. When a user logs in successfully, put their username in a cookie. Also include a hash of the username and a secret word so a user can't just make up an authentication cookie with a username in it:

```
$secret_word = 'if i ate spinach';
if (pc_validate($_REQUEST['username'],$_REQUEST['password'])) {
    setcookie('login',
            $_REQUEST['username'].'.'.md5($_REQUEST['username'].$secret_word));
}
```

Discussion

When using cookie authentication, you have to display your own login form:

```
<form method="post" action="login.php">
Username: <input type="text" name="username"> <br>
Password: <input type="password" name="password"> <br>
<input type="submit" value="Log In">
</form>
```

You can use the same pc_validate( ) function from the Recipe 8.9 to verify the username and password. The only difference is that you pass it $_REQUEST['username'] and $_REQUEST['password'] as the credentials instead of $_SERVER['PHP_AUTH_USER'] and $_SERVER['PHP_AUTH_PW']. If the password checks out, send back a cookie that contains a username and a hash of the username, and a secret word. The hash prevents a user from faking a login just by sending a cookie with a username in it.

Once the user has logged in, a page just needs to verify that a valid login cookie was sent in order to do special things for that logged-in user:

```
unset($username);
if ($_COOKIE['login']) {
    list($c_username,$cookie_hash) = split(',',$_COOKIE['login']);
    if (md5($c_username.$secret_word) == $cookie_hash) {
        $username = $c_username;
    } else {
        print "You have sent a bad cookie.";
    }
}

if ($username) {
    print "Welcome, $username.";
} else {
    print "Welcome, anonymous user.";
}
```

If you use the built-in session support, you can add the username and hash to the session and avoid sending a separate cookie. When someone logs in, set an additional variable in the session instead of sending a cookie:

```
if (pc_validate($_REQUEST['username'],$_REQUEST['password'])) {
    $_SESSION['login'] =
        $_REQUEST['username'].','.md5($_REQUEST['username'].$secret_word));
}
```

The verification code is almost the same; it just uses $_SESSION instead of $_COOKIE:

```
unset($username);
if ($_SESSION['login']) {
    list($c_username,$cookie_hash) = explode(',',$_SESSION['login']);
    if (md5($c_username.$secret_word) == $cookie_hash) {
        $username = $c_username;
```

```
    } else {
        print "You have tampered with your session.";
    }
}
```

Using cookie or session authentication instead of HTTP Basic authentication makes it much easier for users to log out: you just delete their login cookie or remove the login variable from their session. Another advantage of storing authentication information in a session is that you can link users' browsing activities while logged in to their browsing activities before they log in or after they log out. With HTTP Basic authentication, you have no way of tying the requests with a username to the requests that the same user made before they supplied a username. Looking for requests from the same IP address is error-prone, especially if the user is behind a firewall or proxy server. If you are using sessions, you can modify the login procedure to log the connection between session ID and username:

```
if (pc_validate($_REQUEST['username'],$_REQUEST['password'])) {
    $_SESSION['login'] =
        $_REQUEST['username'].',.'.md5($_REQUEST['username'].$secret_word));
    error_log('Session id '.session_id().' log in as '.$_REQUEST['username']);
}
```

This example writes a message to the error log, but it could just as easily record the information in a database that you could use in your analysis of site usage and traffic.

One danger of using session IDs is that sessions are hijackable. If Alice guesses Bob's session ID, she can masquerade as Bob to the web server. The session module has two optional configuration directives that help you make session IDs harder to guess. The session.entropy_file directive contains a path to a device or file that generates randomness, such as *(dev/random* or *(dev/urandom*. The session.entropy_length directive holds the number of bytes to be read from the entropy file when creating session IDs.

No matter how hard session IDs are to guess, they can also be stolen if they are sent in clear text between your server and a user's browser. HTTP Basic authentication also has this problem. Use SSL to guard against network sniffing, as described in Recipe 14.10.

See Also

Recipe 8.9; Recipe 8.17 discusses logging errors; Recipe 14.3 discusses verifying data with hashes; documentation on setcookie() at *http://www.php.net/setcookie* and on md5() at *http://www.php.net/md5*.

8.11 Flushing Output to the Browser

Problem

You want to force output to be sent to the browser. For example, before doing a slow database query, you want to give the user a status update.

Solution

Use flush():

```
print 'Finding identical snowflakes...';
flush();
$sth = $dbh->query(
    'SELECT shape,COUNT(*) AS c FROM snowflakes GROUP BY shape HAVING c > 1');
```

Discussion

The flush() function sends all output that PHP has internally buffered to the web server, but the web server may have internal buffering of its own that delays when the data reaches the browser. Additionally, some browsers don't display data immediately upon receiving it, and some versions of Internet Explorer don't display a page until they've received at least 256 bytes. To force IE to display content, print blank spaces at the beginning of the page:

```
print str_repeat(' ',300);
print 'Finding identical snowflakes...';
flush();
$sth = $dbh->query(
    'SELECT shape,COUNT(*) AS c FROM snowflakes GROUP BY shape HAVING c > 1');
```

See Also

Recipe 18.17; documentation on flush() at *http://www.php.net/flush*.

8.12 Buffering Output to the Browser

Problem

You want to start generating output before you're finished sending headers or cookies.

Solution

Call ob_start() at the top of your page and ob_end_flush() at the bottom. You can then intermix commands that generate output and commands that send headers. The output won't be sent until ob_end_flush() is called:

```
<?php ob_start(); ?>

I haven't decided if I want to send a cookie yet.

<?php setcookie('heron','great blue'); ?>

Yes, sending that cookie was the right decision.

<?php ob_end_flush(); ?>
```

Discussion

You can pass ob_start() the name of a callback function to process the output buffer with that function. This is useful for postprocessing all the content in a page, such as hiding email addresses from address-harvesting robots:

```
<?php
function mangle_email($s) {
    return preg_replace('/([^@\s]+)@([-a-z0-9]+\.)+[a-z]{2,}/is',
                        '<$1@...>',
                        $s);
}

ob_start('mangle_email');
?>

I would not like spam sent to ronald@example.com!

<?php ob_end_flush(); ?>
```

The mangle_email() function transforms the output to:

```
I would not like spam sent to <ronald@...>!
```

The output_buffering configuration directive turns output buffering on for all pages:

```
output_buffering = On
```

Similarly, output_handler sets an output buffer processing callback to be used on all pages:

```
output_handler=mangle_email
```

Setting an output_handler automatically sets output_buffering to on.

See Also

Recipe 10.10 uses output buffering in a database error logging function; documentation on ob_start() at *http://www.php.net/ob-start*, ob_end_flush() at *http://www.php.net/ob-end-flush*, and output buffering at *http://www.php.net/outcontrol*.

8.13 Compressing Web Output with gzip

Problem

You want to send compressed content to browsers that support automatic decompression.

Solution

Add this setting to your *php.ini* file:

```
zlib.output_compression=1
```

Discussion

Browsers tell the server that they can accept compressed responses with the Accept-Encoding header. If a browser sends Accept-Encoding: gzip or Accept-Encoding: deflate, and PHP is built with the *zlib* extension, the zlib.output_compression configuration directive tells PHP to compress the output with the appropriate algorithm before sending it back to the browser. The browser uncompresses the data before displaying it.

You can adjust the compression level with the zlib.output_compression_level configuration directive:

```
; minimal compression
zlib.output_compression_level=1

; maximal compression
zlib.output_compression_level=9
```

At higher compression levels, less data needs to be sent from the server to the browser, but more server CPU time must be used to compress the data.

See Also

Documentation on the *zlib* extension at *http://www.php.net/zlib*.

8.14   Hiding Error Messages from Users

Problem

You don't want PHP error messages visible to users.

Solution

Set the following values in your *php.ini* or web server configuration file:

```
display_errors =off
log_errors     =on
```

These settings tell PHP not to display errors as HTML to the browser but to put them in the server's error log.

Discussion

When `log_errors` is set to `on`, error messages are written to the server's error log. If you want PHP errors to be written to a separate file, set the `error_log` configuration directive with the name of that file:

```
error_log   = /var/log/php.error.log
```

If `error_log` is set to `syslog`, PHP error messages are sent to the system logger using *syslog(3)* on Unix and to the Event Log on Windows NT.

There are lots of error messages you want to show your users, such as telling them they've filled in a form incorrectly, but you should shield your users from internal errors that may reflect a problem with your code. There are two reasons for this. First, these errors appear unprofessional (to expert users) and confusing (to novice users). If something goes wrong when saving form input to a database, check the return code from the database query and display a message to your users apologizing and asking them to come back later. Showing them a cryptic error message straight from PHP doesn't inspire confidence in your web site.

Second, displaying these errors to users is a security risk. Depending on your database and the type of error, the error message may contain information about how to log in to your database or server and how it is structured. Malicious users can use this information to mount an attack on your web site.

For example, if your database server is down, and you attempt to connect to it with `mysql_connect()`, PHP generates the following warning:

```
<br>
<b>Warning</b>:  Can't connect to MySQL server on 'db.example.com' (111) in
<b>/www/docroot/example.php</b> on line <b>3</b><br>
```

If this warning message is sent to a user's browser, he learns that your database server is called *db.example.com* and can mount an attack on it.

See Also

Recipe 8.17 for how to log errors; documentation on PHP configuration directives at *http://www.php.net/configuration*.

8.15 Tuning Error Handling

Problem

You want to alter the error-logging sensitivity on a particular page. This lets you control what types of errors are reported.

Solution

To adjust the types of errors PHP complains about, use error_reporting():

```
error_reporting(E_ALL);                // everything
error_reporting(E_ERROR | E_PARSE);    // only major problems
error_reporting(E_ALL & ~E_NOTICE);    // everything but notices
```

Discussion

Every error generated has an error type associated with it. For example, if you try to array_pop() a string, PHP complains that "This argument needs to be an array," since you can only pop arrays. The error type associated with this message is E_NOTICE, a nonfatal runtime problem.

By default, the error reporting level is E_ALL & ~E_NOTICE, which means all error types except notices. The & is a logical AND, and the ~ is a logical NOT. However, the *php.ini-recommended* configuration file sets the error reporting level to E_ALL, which is all error types.

Error messages flagged as notices are runtime problems that are less serious than warnings. They're not necessarily wrong, but they indicate a potential problem. One example of an E_NOTICE is "Undefined variable," which occurs if you try to use a variable without previously assigning it a value:

```
// Generates an E_NOTICE
foreach ($array as $value) {
    $html .= $value;
}

// Doesn't generate any error message
$html = '';
```

```
foreach ($array as $value) {
    $html .= $value;
}
```

In the first case, the first time though the foreach, $html is undefined. So, when you append to it, PHP lets you know you're appending to an undefined variable. In the second case, the empty string is assigned to $html above the loop to avoid the E_NOTICE. The previous two code snippets generate identical code because the default value of a variable is the empty string. The E_NOTICE can be helpful because, for example, you may have misspelled a variable name:

```
foreach ($array as $value) {
    $hmtl .= $value; // oops! that should be $html
}

$html = ''
foreach ($array as $value) {
    $hmtl .= $value; // oops! that should be $html
}
```

A custom error-handling function can parse errors based on their type and take an appropriate action. A complete list of error types is shown in Table 8-2.

Table 8-2. Error types

Value	Constant	Description	Catchable
1	E_ERROR	Nonrecoverable error	No
2	E_WARNING	Recoverable error	Yes
4	E_PARSE	Parser error	No
8	E_NOTICE	Possible error	Yes
16	E_CORE_ERROR	Like E_ERROR but generated by the PHP core	No
32	E_CORE_WARNING	Like E_WARNING but generated by the PHP core	No
64	E_COMPILE_ERROR	Like E_ERROR but generated by the Zend Engine	No
128	E_COMPILE_WARNING	Like E_WARNING but generated by the Zend Engine	No
256	E_USER_ERROR	Like E_ERROR but triggered by calling trigger_error()	Yes
512	E_USER_WARNING	Like E_WARNING but triggered by calling trigger_error()	Yes
1024	E_USER_NOTICE	Like E_NOTICE but triggered by calling trigger_error()	Yes
2047	E_ALL	Everything	n/a

Errors labeled catchable can be processed by the function registered using set_error_handler(). The others indicate such a serious problem that they're not safe to be handled by users, and PHP must take care of them.

See Also

Recipe 8.16 shows how to set up a custom error handler; documentation on error_reporting() at *http://www.php.net/error-reporting* and set_error_handler() at *http://www.php.net/set-error-handler*; for more information about errors, see *http://www.php.net/ref.errorfunc.php*.

8.16 Using a Custom Error Handler

Problem

You want to create a custom error handler that lets you control how PHP reports errors.

Solution

To set up your own error function, use set_error_handler():

```
set_error_handler('pc_error_handler');

function pc_error_handler($errno, $error, $file, $line) {
    $message = "[ERROR][$errno][$error][$file:$line]";
    error_log($message);
}
```

Discussion

A custom error handling function can parse errors based on their type and take the appropriate action. See Table 8-2 in Recipe 8.15 for a list of error types.

Pass set_error_handler() the name of a function, and PHP forwards all errors to that function. The error handling function can take up to five parameters. The first parameter is the error type, such as 8 for E_NOTICE. The second is the message thrown by the error, such as "Undefined variable: html". The third and fourth arguments are the name of the file and the line number in which PHP detected the error. The final parameter is an array holding all the variables defined in the current scope and their values.

For example, in this code $html is appended to without first being assigned an initial value:

```
error_reporting(E_ALL);
set_error_handler('pc_error_handler');

function pc_error_handler($errno, $error, $file, $line, $context) {
    $message = "[ERROR][$errno][$error][$file:$line]";
    print "$message";
```

```
        print_r($context);
}

$form = array('one','two');

foreach ($form as $line) {
    $html .= "<b>$line</b>";
}
```

When the "Undefined variable" error is generated, pc_error_handler() prints:

```
[ERROR][8][Undefined variable:  html][err-all.php:16]
```

After the initial error message, pc_error_handler() also prints a large array containing all the globals, environment, request, and session variables.

Errors labeled catchable in Table 8-2 can be processed by the function registered using set_error_handler(). The others indicate such a serious problem that they're not safe to be handled by users and PHP must take care of them.

See Also

Recipe 8.15 lists the different error types; documentation on set_error_handler() at *http://www.php.net/set-error-handler*.

8.17   Logging Errors

Problem

You want to write program errors to a log. These errors can include everything from parser errors and files not being found to bad database queries and dropped connections.

Solution

Use error_log() to write to the error log:

```
// LDAP error
if (ldap_errno($ldap)) {
    error_log("LDAP Error #" . ldap_errno($ldap) . ": " . ldap_error($ldap));
}
```

Discussion

Logging errors facilitates debugging. Smart error logging makes it easier to fix bugs. Always log information about what caused the error:

```
$r = mysql_query($sql);
if (! $r) {
```

```
    $error = mysql_error();
    error_log('[DB: query @'.$_SERVER['REQUEST_URI'].']'."[$sql]: $error");
} else {
    // process results
}
```

You're not getting all the debugging help you could be if you simply log that an error occurred without any supporting information:

```
$r = mysql_query($sql);
if (! $r) {
    error_log("bad query");
} else {
    // process result
}
```

Another useful technique is to include the __FILE__ and __LINE__ constants in your error messages:

```
error_log('['.__FILE__.']'.'['.__LINE__."]: $error");
```

The __FILE__ constant is the current filename, and __LINE__ is the current line number.

See Also

Recipe 8.14 for hiding error messages from users; documentation on error_log( ) at *http://www.php.net/error-log*.

8.18 Eliminating "headers already sent" Errors

Problem

You are trying to send a HTTP header or cookie using header( ) or setcookie( ), but PHP reports a "headers already sent" error message.

Solution

This error happens when you send nonheader output before calling header( ) or setcookie( ).

Rewrite your code so any output happens after sending headers:

```
// good
setcookie("name", $name);
print "Hello $name!";

// bad
print "Hello $name!";
setcookie("name", $name);
```

```
// good
<?php setcookie("name",$name); ?>
<html><title>Hello</title>
```

Discussion

An HTTP message has a header and a body, which are sent to the client in that order. Once you begin sending the body, you can't send any more headers. So, if you call setcookie() after printing some HTML, PHP can't send the appropriate Cookie header.

Also, remove trailing whitespace in any include files. When you include a file with blank lines outside <?php ?> tags, the blank lines are sent to the browser. Use trim() to remove leading and trailing blank lines from files:

```
$file = '/path/to/file.php';

// backup
copy($file, "$file.bak") or die("Can't copy $file: $php_errormsg);

// read and trim
$contents = trim(join('',file($file)));

// write
$fh = fopen($file, 'w')  or die("Can't open $file for writing: $php_errormsg);
if (-1 == fwrite($fh, $contents)) { die("Can't write to $file: $php_errormsg); }
fclose($fh)               or die("Can't close $file: $php_errormsg);
```

Instead of processing files on a one-by-one basis, it may be more convenient to do so on a directory-by-directory basis. Recipe 19.7 describes how to process all the files in a directory.

If you don't want to worry about blank lines disrupting the sending of headers, turn on output buffering. Output buffering prevents PHP from immediately sending all output to the client. If you buffer your output, you can intermix headers and body text with abandon. However, it may seem to users that your server takes longer to fulfill their requests since they have to wait slightly longer before the browser displays any output.

See Also

Recipe 8.12 discusses output buffering; Recipe 19.7 for processing all files in a directory; documentation on header() at *http://www.php.net/header*.

8.19 Logging Debugging Information

Problem

You want to make debugging easier by adding statements to print out variables. But, you want to easily be able to switch back and forth from production and debug modes.

Solution

Put a function that conditionally prints out messages based on a defined constant in a page included using the `auto_prepend_file` configuration setting. Save the following code to *debug.php*:

```
// turn debugging on
define('DEBUG',true);

// generic debugging function
function pc_debug($message) {
    if (defined('DEBUG') && DEBUG) {
        error_log($message);
    }
}
```

Set the `auto_prepend_file` directive in *php.ini*:

```
auto_prepend_file=debug.php
```

Now call `pc_debug()` from your code to print out debugging information:

```
$sql = 'SELECT color, shape, smell FROM vegetables';
pc_debug("[sql: $sql]"); // only printed if DEBUG is true
$r = mysql_query($sql);
```

Discussion

Debugging code is a necessary side-effect of writing code. There are a variety of techniques to help you quickly locate and squash your bugs. Many of these involve including scaffolding that helps ensure the correctness of your code. The more complicated the program, the more scaffolding needed. Fred Brooks, in *The Mythical Man-Month*, guesses that there's "half as much code in scaffolding as there is in product." Proper planning ahead of time allows you to integrate the scaffolding into your programming logic in a clean and efficient fashion. This requires you to think out beforehand what you want to measure and record and how you plan on sorting through the data gathered by your scaffolding.

One technique for sifting through the information is to assign different priority levels to different types of debugging comments. Then the debug function prints information only if it's higher than the current priority level.

```
define('DEBUG',2);

function pc_debug($message, $level = 0) {
    if (defined('DEBUG') && ($level > DEBUG) {
        error_log($message);
    }
}

$sql = 'SELECT color, shape, smell FROM vegetables';
pc_debug("[sql: $sql]", 1); // not printed, since 1 < 2
pc_debug("[sql: $sql]", 3); // printed, since 3 > 2
```

Another technique is to write wrapper functions to include additional information to help with performance tuning, such as the time it takes to execute a database query.

```
function getmicrotime(){
    $mtime = microtime();
    $mtime = explode(' ',$mtime);
    return ($mtime[1] + $mtime[0]);
}

function db_query($sql) {
    if (defined('DEBUG') && DEBUG) {
        // start timing the query if DEBUG is on
        $DEBUG_STRING = "[sql: $sql]<br>\n";
        $starttime = getmicrotime();
    }

    $r = mysql_query($sql);

    if (! $r) {
        $error = mysql_error();
        error_log('[DB: query @'.$_SERVER['REQUEST_URI']."][$sql]: $error");
    } elseif (defined(DEBUG) && DEBUG) {
        // the query didn't fail and DEBUG is turned on, so finish timing it
        $endtime = getmicrotime();
        $elapsedtime = $endtime - $starttime;
        $DEBUG_STRING .= "[time: $elapsedtime]<br>\n";
        error_log($DEBUG_STRING);
    }

    return $r;
}
```

Here, instead of just printing out the SQL to the error log, you also record the number of seconds it takes MySQL to perform the request. This lets you see if certain queries are taking too long.

The getmicrotime() function converts the output of microtime() into a format that allows you to easily perform addition and subtraction upon the numbers.

See Also

Documentation on define() at *http://www.php.net/define*, defined() at *http://www.php.net/defined*, and error_log() at *http://www.php.net/error-log*; *The Mythical Man-Month*, by Frederick P. Brooks (Addison-Wesley).

8.20 Reading Environment Variables

Problem

You want to get the value of an environment variable.

Solution

Read the value from the $_ENV superglobal array:

```
$name = $_ENV['USER'];
```

Discussion

Environment variables are named values associated with a process. For instance, in Unix, you can check the value of $_ENV['HOME'] to find the home directory of a user:

```
print $_ENV['HOME']; // user's home directory
/home/adam
```

Early versions of PHP automatically created PHP variables for all environment variables by default. As of 4.1.0, *php.ini-recommended* disables this because of speed considerations; however *php.ini-dist* continues to enable environment variable loading for backward compatibility.

The $_ENV array is created only if the value of the variables_order configuration directive contains E. If $_ENV isn't available, use getenv() to retrieve an environment variable:

```
$path = getenv('PATH');
```

The getenv() function isn't available if you're running PHP as an ISAPI module.

See Also

Recipe 8.21 on setting environment variables; documentation on getenv() at *http://www.php.net/getenv*; information on environment variables in PHP at *http://www.php.net/reserved.variables.php#reserved.variables.environment*.

8.21   Setting Environment Variables

Problem

You want to set an environment variable in a script or in your server configuration. Setting environment variables in your server configuration on a host-by-host basis allows you to configure virtual hosts differently.

Solution

To set an environment variable in a script, use putenv( ):

```
putenv('ORACLE_SID=ORACLE'); // configure oci extension
```

To set an environment variable in your Apache *httpd.conf* file, use SetEnv:

```
SetEnv DATABASE_PASSWORD password
```

Discussion

An advantage of setting variables in *httpd.conf* is that you can set more restrictive read permissions on it than on your PHP scripts. Since PHP files need to be readable by the web-server process, this generally allows other users on the system to view them. By storing passwords in *httpd.conf*, you can avoid placing a password in a publicly available file. Also, if you have multiple hostnames that map to the same document root, you can configure your scripts to behave differently based on the hostnames.

For example, you could have *members.example.com* and *guests.example.com*. The members version requires authentication and allows users additional access. The guests version provides a restricted set of options, but without authentication:

```
$version = $_ENV['SITE_VERSION'];

// redirect to http://guest.example.com, if user fails to sign in correctly
if ('members' == $version) {
    if (!authenticate_user($_REQUEST['username'], $_REQUEST['password'])) {
        header('Location: http://guest.example.com/');
        exit;
    }
}

include_once "${version}_header"; // load custom header
```

See Also

Recipe 8.20 on getting the values of environment variables; documentation on putenv() at *http://www.php.net/putenv*; information on setting environment variables in Apache at *http://httpd.apache.org/docs/mod/mod_env.html*.

8.22 Reading Configuration Variables

Problem

You want to get the value of a PHP configuration setting.

Solution

Use ini_get():

```
// find out the include path:
$include_path = ini_get('include_path');
```

Discussion

To get all configuration variable values in one step, call ini_get_all(). It returns the variables in an associative array, and each array element is itself an associative array. The second array has three elements: a global value for the setting, a local value, and an access code:

```
// put all configuration variables in an associative array
$vars = ini_get_all();
print_r($vars['include_path']);
Array
(
    [global_value] => .:/usr/local/lib/php/
    [local_value] => .:/usr/local/lib/php/
    [access] => 7
)
```

The global_value is the value set from the *php.ini* file; the local_value is adjusted to account for any changes made in the web server's configuration file, any relevant *.htaccess* files, and the current script. The value of access is a numeric constant representing the places where this value can be altered. Table 8-3 explains the values for access. Note that the name access is a little misleading in this respect, as the setting's value can always be checked, but not adjusted.

Table 8-3. Access values

Value	PHP constant	Meaning
1	PHP_INI_USER	Any script, using ini_set()
2	PHP_INI_PERDIR	Directory level, using .htaccess
4	PHP_INI_SYSTEM	System level, using php.ini or httpd.conf
7	PHP_INI_ALL	Everywhere: scripts, directories, and the system

A value of 6 means the setting can be changed in both the directory and system level, as 2 + 4 = 6. In practice, there are no variables modifiable only in PHP_INI_USER or PHP_INI_PERDIR, and all variables are modifiable in PHP_INI_SYSTEM, so everything has a value of 4, 6, or 7.

You can also get variables belonging to a specific extension by passing the extension name to ini_get_all():

```
// return just the session module specific variables
$session = ini_get_all('session');
```

By convention, the variables for an extension are prefixed with the extension name and a period. So, all the session variables begin with session. and all the Java variables begin with java., for example.

Since ini_get() returns the current value for a configuration directive, if you want to check the original value from the *php.ini* file, use get_cfg_var():

```
$original = get_cfg_var('sendmail_from'); // have we changed our address?
```

The value returned by get_cfg_var() is the same as what appears in the global_value element of the array returned by ini_get_all().

See Also

Recipe 8.23 on setting configuration variables; documentation on ini_get() at *http://www.php.net/ini-get*, ini_get_all() at *http://www.php.net/ini-get-all*, and get_cfg_var() at *http://www.php.net/get-cfg-var*; a complete list of configuration variables and when they can be modified at *http://www.php.net/function.ini-set.php*.

8.23   Setting Configuration Variables

Problem

You want to change the value of a PHP configuration setting.

Solution

Use ini_set():

```
// add a directory to the include path
ini_set('include_path', ini_get('include_path') . ':/home/fezzik/php');
```

Discussion

Configuration variables are not permanently changed by ini_set(). The new value lasts only for the duration of the request in which ini_set() is called. To make a persistent modification, alter the values stored in the *php.ini* file.

It isn't meaningful to alter certain variables, such as asp_tags or register_globals because by the time you call ini_set() to modify the setting, it's too late to change the behavior the setting affects. If a variable can't be changed, ini_set() returns false.

However, it is useful to alter configuration variables in certain pages. For example, if you're running a script from the command line, set html_errors to off.

To reset a variable back to its original setting, use ini_restore():

```
ini_restore('sendmail_from'); // go back to the default value
```

See Also

Recipe 8.22 on getting values of configuration variables; documentation on ini_set() at *http://www.php.net/ini-set* and ini_restore() at *http://www.php.net/ini-restore*.

8.24 Communicating Within Apache

Problem

You want to communicate from PHP to other parts of the Apache request process. This includes setting variables in the *access_log*.

Solution

Use apache_note():

```
// get value
$session = apache_note('session');

// set value
apache_note('session', $session);
```

Discussion

When Apache processes a request from a client, it goes through a series of steps; PHP plays only one part in the entire chain. Apache also remaps URLs, authenticates users, logs requests, and more. While processing a request, each handler has access to a set of key/value pairs called the *notes table*. The apache_note() function provides access to the notes table to retrieve information set by handlers earlier on in the process and leave information for handlers later on.

For example, if you use the session module to track users and preserve variables across requests, you can integrate this with your log file analysis so you can determine the average number of page views per user. Use apache_note() in combination with the logging module to write the session ID directly to the *access_log* for each request:

```
// retrieve the session ID and add it to Apache's notes table
apache_note('session_id', session_id());
```

Then, modify your *httpd.conf* file to add this string to your LogFormat:

```
%{session_id}n
```

The trailing n tells Apache to use a variable stored in its notes table by another module.

If PHP is built with the --enable-memory-limit configuration option, it stores the peak memory usage of each request in a note called mod_php_memory_usage. Add the memory usage information to a LogFormat with:

```
%{mod_php_memory_usage}n
```

See Also

Documentation on apache_note() at *http://www.php.net/apache-note*; information on logging in Apache at *http://httpd.apache.org/docs/mod/mod_log_config.html*.

8.25   Profiling Code

Problem

You have a block of code and you want to profile it to see how long each statement takes to execute.

Solution

Use the PEAR Benchmark module:

```
require 'Benchmark/Timer.php';

$timer =& new Benchmark_Timer(true);
```

```
$timer->start();
// some setup code here
$timer->setMarker('setup');
// some more code executed here
$timer->setMarker('middle');
// even yet still more code here
$timer->setmarker('done');
// and a last bit of code here
$timer->stop();

$timer->display();
```

Discussion

Calling setMarker() records the time. The display() method prints out a list of markers, the time they were set, and the elapsed time from the previous marker:

```
---------------------------------------------------------------------
marker    time index           ex time                    perct
---------------------------------------------------------------------
Start     1029433375.42507400  -                          0.00%
---------------------------------------------------------------------
setup     1029433375.42554800  0.00047397613525391       29.77%
---------------------------------------------------------------------
middle    1029433375.42568700  0.00013899803161621        8.73%
---------------------------------------------------------------------
done      1029433375.42582000  0.00013303756713867        8.36%
---------------------------------------------------------------------
Stop      1029433375.42666600  0.00084602832794189       53.14%
---------------------------------------------------------------------
total     -                    0.0015920400619507       100.00%
---------------------------------------------------------------------
```

The Benchmark module also includes the Benchmark_Iterate class, which can be used to time many executions of a single function:

```
require 'Benchmark/Iterate.php';

$timer =& new Benchmark_Iterate;

// a sample function to time
function use_preg($ar) {
    for ($i = 0, $j = count($ar); $i < $j; $i++) {
        if (preg_match('/gouda/',$ar[$i])) {
            // it's gouda
        }
    }
}

// another sample function to time
function use_equals($ar) {
    for ($i = 0, $j = count($ar); $i < $j; $i++) {
        if ('gouda' == $ar[$i]) {
            // it's gouda
```

```
            }
        }
    }

    // run use_preg() 1000 times
    $timer->run(1000,'use_preg',
                    array('gouda','swiss','gruyere','muenster','whiz'));
    $results = $timer->get();
    print "Mean execution time for use_preg(): $results[mean]\n";

    // run use_equals() 1000 times
    $timer->run(1000,'use_equals',
                    array('gouda','swiss','gruyere','muenster','whiz'));
    $results = $timer->get();
    print "Mean execution time for use_equals(): $results[mean]\n";
```

The Benchmark_Iterate::get() method returns an associative array. The mean element of this array holds the mean execution time for each iteration of the function. The iterations element holds the number of iterations. The execution time of each iteration of the function is stored in an array element with an integer key. For example, the time of the first iteration is in $results[1], and the time of the 37th iteration is in $results[37].

To automatically record the elapsed execution time after every line of PHP code, use the declare construct and the ticks directive:

```
function profile($display = false) {
    static $times;

    switch ($display) {
    case false:
        // add the current time to the list of recorded times
        $times[] = microtime();
        break;
    case true:
        // return elapsed times in microseconds
        $start = array_shift($times);

        $start_mt = explode(' ', $start);
        $start_total = doubleval($start_mt[0]) + $start_mt[1];

        foreach ($times as $stop) {
            $stop_mt = explode(' ', $stop);
            $stop_total = doubleval($stop_mt[0]) + $stop_mt[1];
            $elapsed[] = $stop_total - $start_total;
        }

        unset($times);
        return $elapsed;
        break;
    }
}
```

```
// register tick handler
register_tick_function('profile');

// clock the start time
profile();

// execute code, recording time for every statement execution
declare (ticks = 1) {
    foreach ($_SERVER['argv'] as $arg) {
        print strlen($arg);
    }
}

// print out elapsed times
$i = 0;
foreach (profile(true) as $time) {
    $i++;
    print "Line $i: $time\n";
}
```

The ticks directive allows you to execute a function on a repeatable basis for a block of code. The number assigned to ticks is how many statements go by before the functions that are registered using register_tick_function() are executed.

In the previous example, we register a single function and have the profile() function execute for every statement inside the declare block. If there are two elements in $_SERVER['argv'], profile() is executed four times: once for each time through the foreach loop, and once each time the print strlen($arg) line is executed.

You can also set things up to call two functions every three statements:

```
register_tick_function('profile');
register_tick_function('backup');

declare (ticks = 3) {
    // code...
}
```

You can also pass additional parameters into the registered functions, which can be object methods instead of regular functions:

```
// pass "parameter" into profile()
register_tick_function('profile', 'parameter');

// call $car->drive();
$car = new Vehicle;
register_tick_function(array($car, 'drive'));
```

If you want to execute an object method, pass the object and the name of the method in encapsulated within an array. This lets the register_tick_function() know you're referring to an object instead of a function.

Call unregister_tick_function() to remove a function from the list of tick functions:

```
unregister_tick_function('profile');
```

See Also

http://pear.php.net/package-info.php?package=Benchmark for information on the PEAR Benchmark class; documentation on register_tick_function() at *http://www.php.net/register-tick-function*, unregister_tick_function() at *http://www.php.net/unregister-tick-function*, and declare at http://www.php.net/declare.

8.26 Program: Website Account (De)activator

When users sign up for your web site, it's helpful to know that they've provided you with a correct email address. To validate the email address they provide, send an email to the address they supply when they sign up. If they don't visit a special URL included in the email after a few days, deactivate their account.

This system has three parts. The first is the *notify-user.php* program that sends an email to a new user and asks them to visit a verification URL, shown in Example 8-4. The second, shown in Example 8-5, is the *verify-user.php* page that handles the verification URL and marks users as valid. The third is the *delete-user.php* program that deactivates accounts of users who don't visit the verification URL after a certain amount of time. This program is shown in Example 8-6.

Here's the SQL to create the table that user information is stored in:

```
CREATE TABLE users (
  email VARCHAR(255) NOT NULL,
  created_on DATETIME NOT NULL,
  verify_string VARCHAR(16) NOT NULL,
  verified TINYINT UNSIGNED
);
```

You probably want to store more information than this about your users, but this is all that's needed to verify them. When creating a user's account, save information to the users table, and send the user an email telling them how to verify their account. The code in Example 8-4 assumes that user's email address is stored in the variable $email.

Example 8-4. notify-user.php

```
// generate verify_string
$verify_string = '';
for ($i = 0; $i < 16; $i++) {
    $verify_string .= chr(mt_rand(32,126));
}

// insert user into database
if (! mysql_query("INSERT INTO users (email,created_on,verify_string,verified)
    VALUES ('".addslashes($email)."',NOW(),'".addslashes($verify_string)."',0)")) {
    error_log("Can't insert user: ".mysql_error());
    exit;
}
```

Example 8-4. notify-user.php (continued)

```php
$verify_string = urlencode($verify_string);
$safe_email = urlencode($email);

$verify_url = "http://www.example.com/verify.php";

$mail_body=<<<_MAIL_
To $email:

Please click on the following link to verify your account creation:

$verify_url?email=$safe_email&verify_string=$verify_string

If you do not verify your account in the next seven days, it will be
deleted.
_MAIL_;

mail($email,"User Verification",$mail_body);
```

The verification page users go to when they follow the link in the email message updates the users table if the proper information has been provided, as shown in Example 8-5.

Example 8-5. verify-user.php

```php
$safe_email = addslashes($_REQUEST['email']);
$safe_verify_string = addslashes($_REQUEST['verify_string']);

if ($r = mysql_query("UPDATE users SET verified = 1 WHERE email
    LIKE '$safe_email' AND
    verify_string = '$safe_verify_string' AND verified = 0")) {
    if (mysql_affected_rows() == 1) {
        print "Thank you, your account is verified.";
    } else {
        print "Sorry, you could not be verified.";
    }
} else {
    print "Please try again later due to a database error.";
}
```

The user's verification status is updated only if the email address and verify string provided match a row in the database that has not already been verified. The last step is the short program that deletes unverified users after the appropriate interval, as shown in Example 8-6.

Example 8-6. delete-user.php

```php
$window = 7; // in days

if ($r = mysql_query("DELETE FROM users WHERE verified = 0 AND
    created_on < DATE_SUB(NOW(),INTERVAL $window DAY)")) {
    if ($deleted_users = mysql_affected_rows()) {
```

Example 8-6. delete-user.php (continued)

```
        print "Deactivated $deleted_users users.\n";
    }
} else {
    print "Can't delete users: ".mysql_error();
}
```

Run this program once a day to scrub the users table of users that haven't been verified. If you want to change how long users have to verify themselves, adjust the value of $window, and update the text of the email message sent to users to reflect the new value.

8.27   Program: Abusive User Checker

Shared memory's speed makes it an ideal way to store data different web server processes need to access frequently when a file or database would be too slow. Example 8-7 shows the pc_Web_Abuse_Check class, which uses shared memory to track accesses to web pages in order to cut off users that abuse a site by bombarding it with requests.

Example 8-7. pc_Web_Abuse_Check class

```
class pc_Web_Abuse_Check {
  var $sem_key;
  var $shm_key;
  var $shm_size;
  var $recalc_seconds;
  var $pageview_threshold;
  var $sem;
  var $shm;
  var $data;
  var $exclude;
  var $block_message;

  function pc_Web_Abuse_Check() {
    $this->sem_key = 5000;
    $this->shm_key = 5001;
    $this->shm_size = 16000;
    $this->recalc_seconds = 60;
    $this->pageview_threshold = 30;

    $this->exclude['/ok-to-bombard.html'] = 1;
    $this->block_message =<<<END
<html>
<head><title>403 Forbidden</title></head>
<body>
<h1>Forbidden</h1>
You have been blocked from retrieving pages from this site due to
abusive repetitive activity from your account. If you believe this
is an error, please contact
```

Example 8-7. pc_Web_Abuse_Check class (continued)

```
<a href="mailto:webmaster@example.com?subject=Site+Abuse">webmaster@example.com</a>.
</body>
</html>
END;
  }

  function get_lock() {
    $this->sem = sem_get($this->sem_key,1,0600);
    if (sem_acquire($this->sem)) {
      $this->shm = shm_attach($this->shm_key,$this->shm_size,0600);
      $this->data = shm_get_var($this->shm,'data');
    } else {
      error_log("Can't acquire semaphore $this->sem_key");
    }
  }

  function release_lock() {
    if (isset($this->data)) {
      shm_put_var($this->shm,'data',$this->data);
    }
    shm_detach($this->shm);
    sem_release($this->sem);
  }

  function check_abuse($user) {
    $this->get_lock();
    if ($this->data['abusive_users'][$user]) {
      // if user is on the list release the semaphore & memory
      $this->release_lock();
      //  serve the "you are blocked" page
      header('HTTP/1.0 403 Forbidden');
      print $this->block_message;
      return true;
    } else {
     // mark this user looking at a page at this time
     $now = time();
     if (! $this->exclude[$_SERVER['PHP_SELF']]) {
       $this->data['user_traffic'][$user]++;
     }
     // (sometimes) tote up the list and add bad people
     if (! $this->data['traffic_start']) {
       $this->data['traffic_start'] = $now;
     } else {
       if (($now - $this->data['traffic_start']) > $this->recalc_seconds) {
         while (list($k,$v) = each($this->data['user_traffic'])) {
           if ($v > $this->pageview_threshold) {
             $this->data['abusive_users'][$k] = $v;
             // log the user's addition to the abusive user list
             error_log("Abuse: [$k] (from ".$_SERVER['REMOTE_ADDR'].')');
           }
         }
         $this->data['traffic_start'] = $now;
```

Example 8-7. pc_Web_Abuse_Check class (continued)

```
        $this->data['user_traffic'] = array();
      }
    }
    $this->release_lock();
    }
    return false;
  }
}
```

To use this class, call its check_abuse() method at the top of a page, passing it the username of a logged in user:

```
// get_logged_in_user_name() is a function that finds out if a user is logged in
if ($user = get_logged_in_user_name()) {
    $abuse = new pc_Web_Abuse_Check();
    if ($abuse->check_abuse($user)) {
        exit;
    }
}
```

The check_abuse() method secures exclusive access to the shared memory segment in which information about users and traffic is stored with the get_lock() method. If the current user is already on the list of abusive users, it releases its lock on the shared memory, prints out an error page to the user, and returns true. The error page is defined in the class's constructor.

If the user isn't on the abusive user list, and the current page (stored in $_SERVER['PHP_SELF']) isn't on a list of pages to exclude from abuse checking, the count of pages that the user has looked at is incremented. The list of pages to exclude is also defined in the constructor. By calling check_abuse() at the top of every page and putting pages that don't count as potentially abusive in the $exclude array, you ensure that an abusive user will see the error page even when retrieving a page that doesn't count towards the abuse threshold. This makes your site behave more consistently.

The next section of check_abuse() is responsible for adding users to the abusive users list. If more than $this->recalc_seconds have passed since the last time it added users to the abusive users list, it looks at each user's pageview count and if any are over $this->pageview_threshold, they are added to the abusive users list, and a message is put in the error log. The code that sets $this->data['traffic_start'] if it's not already set is executed only the very first time check_abuse() is called. After adding any new abusive users, check_abuse() resets the count of users and pageviews and starts a new interval until the next time the abusive users list is updated. After releasing its lock on the shared memory segment, it returns false.

All the information check_abuse() needs for its calculations, such as the abusive user list, recent pageview counts for users, and the last time abusive users were calculated, is stored inside a single associative array, $data. This makes reading the values from and writing the values to shared memory easier than if the information was stored in separate variables, because only one call to shm_get_var( ) and shm_put_var( ) are necessary.

The pc_Web_Abuse_Check class blocks abusive users, but it doesn't provide any reporting capabilities or a way to add or remove specific users from the list. Example 8-8 shows the *abuse-manage.php* program, which lets you manage the abusive user data.

Example 8-8. abuse-manage.php

```
// the pc_Web_Abuse_Check class is defined in abuse-check.php
require 'abuse-check.php';

$abuse = new pc_Web_Abuse_Check();
$now = time();

// process commands, if any
$abuse->get_lock();
switch ($_REQUEST['cmd']) {
    case 'clear':
      $abuse->data['traffic_start'] = 0;
      $abuse->data['abusive_users'] = array();
      $abuse->data['user_traffic'] = array();
      break;
    case 'add':
      $abuse->data['abusive_users'][$_REQUEST['user']] = 'web @ '.strftime('%c',$now);
      break;
    case 'remove':
      $abuse->data['abusive_users'][$_REQUEST['user']] = 0;
      break;
}
$abuse->release_lock();

// now the relevant info is in $abuse->data

print 'It is now <b>'.strftime('%c',$now).'</b><br>';
print 'Current interval started at <b>'.strftime('%c',$abuse->data['traffic_start']);
print '</b> ('.($now - $abuse->data['traffic_start']).' seconds ago).<p>';

print 'Traffic in the current interval:<br>';
if (count($abuse->data['user_traffic'])) {
  print '<table border="1"><tr><th>User</th><th>Pages</th></tr>';
  while (list($user,$pages) = each($abuse->data['user_traffic'])) {
    print "<tr><td>$user</td><td>$pages</td></tr>";
  }
  print "</table>";
} else {
  print "<i>No traffic.</i>";
}
print '<p>Abusive Users:';

if ($abuse->data['abusive_users']) {
  print '<table border="1"><tr><th>User</th><th>Pages</th></tr>';
  while (list($user,$pages) = each($abuse->data['abusive_users'])) {
```

Example 8-8. abuse-manage.php (continued)

```
    if (0 === $pages) {
      $pages = 'Removed';
      $remove_command = '';
    } else {
      $remove_command =
        "<a href=\"$_SERVER[PHP_SELF]?cmd=remove&user=".urlencode($user)."\">remove</a>";
    }
    print "<tr><td>$user</td><td>$pages</td><td>$remove_command</td></tr>";
  }
  print '</table>';
} else {
  print "<i>No abusive users.</i>";
}

print<<<END
<form method="post" action="$_SERVER[PHP_SELF]">
<input type="hidden" name="cmd" value="add">
Add this user to the abusive users list:
<input type="text" name="user" value="">
<br>
<input type="submit" value="Add User">
</form>
<hr>
<form method="post" action="$_SERVER[PHP_SELF]">
<input type="hidden" name="cmd" value="clear">
<input type="submit" value="Clear the abusive users list">
END;
```

Example 8-8 prints out information about current user page view counts and the current abusive user list, as shown in Figure 8-1. It also lets you add or remove specific users from the list and clear the whole list.

When it removes users from the abusive users list, instead of:

```
unset($abuse->data['abusive_users'][$_REQUEST['user']])
```

it sets the following to 0:

```
$abuse->data['abusive_users'][$_REQUEST['user']]
```

This still causes check_abuse() to return false, but it allows the page to explicitly note that the user was on the abusive users list but was removed. This is helpful to know in case a user that was removed starts causing trouble again.

When a user is added to the abusive users list, instead of recording a pageview count, the script records the time the user was added. This is helpful in tracking down who or why the user was manually added to the list.

If you deploy pc_Web_Abuse_Check and this maintenance page on your server, make sure that the maintenance page is protected by a password or otherwise inaccessible to the general public. Obviously, this code isn't very helpful if abusive users can remove themselves from the list of abusive users.

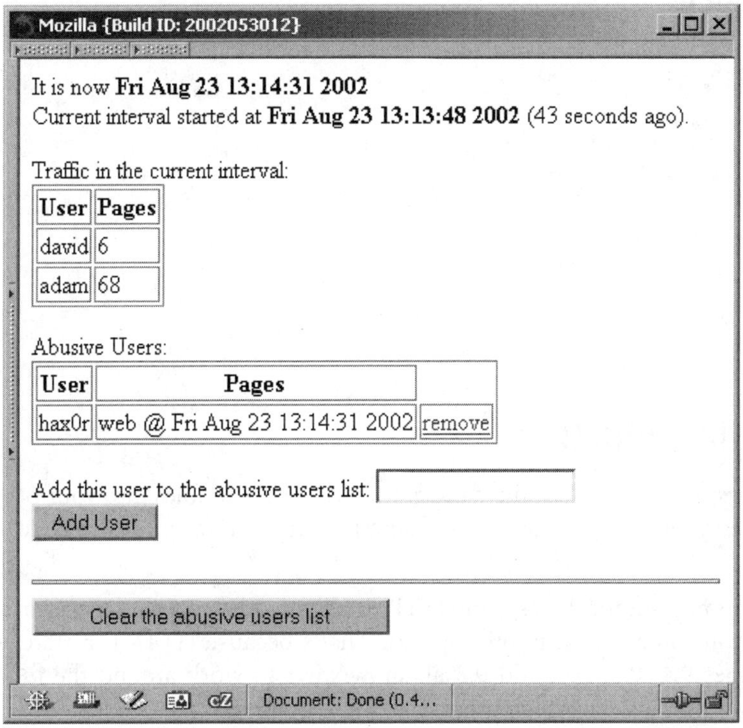

Figure 8-1. Abusive users

CHAPTER 9

Forms

9.0 Introduction

The genius of PHP is its seamless integration of form variables into your programs. It makes web programming smooth and simple, from web form to PHP code to HTML output.

There's no built-in mechanism in HTTP to allow you to save information from one page so you can access it in other pages. That's because HTTP is a stateless protocol. Recipes 9.1, 9.3, 9.4, and 9.5 all show ways to work around the fundamental problem of figuring out which user is making which requests to your web server.

Processing data from the user is the other main topic of this chapter. You should never trust the data coming from the browser, so it's imperative to always validate all fields, even hidden form elements. Validation takes many forms, from ensuring the data match certain criteria, as discussed in Recipe 9.2, to escaping HTML entities to allow the safe display of user entered data, as covered in Recipe 9.8. Furthermore, Recipe 9.7 tells how to protect the security of your web server, and Recipe 9.6 covers how to process files uploaded by a user.

Whenever PHP processes a page, it checks for GET and POST form variables, uploaded files, applicable cookies, and web server and environment variables. These are then directly accessible in the following arrays: `$_GET`, `$_POST`, `$_FILES`, `$_COOKIE`, `$_SERVER`, and `$_ENV`. They hold, respectively, all variables set by GET requests, POST requests, uploaded files, cookies, the web server, and the environment. There's also `$_REQUEST`, which is one giant array that contains the values from the other six arrays.

When placing elements inside of `$_REQUEST`, if two arrays both have a key with the same name, PHP falls back upon the `variables_order` configuration directive. By default, `variables_order` is EGPCS (or GPCS, if you're using the *php.ini-recommended* configuration file). So, PHP first adds environment variables to `$_REQUEST` and then adds GET, POST, cookie, and web server variables to the array, in this order. For instance, since C comes after P in the default order, a cookie named username over-writes a POST variable named username.

If you don't have access to PHP's configuration files, you can use ini_get() to check a setting:

```
print ini_get('variables_order');
EGPCS
```

You may need to do this because your ISP doesn't let you view configuration set-tings or because your script may run on someone else's server. You can also use phpinfo() to view settings. However, if you can't rely on the value of variables_order, you should directly access $_GET and $_POST instead of using $_REQUEST.

The arrays containing external variables, such as $_REQUEST, are superglobals. As such, they don't need to be declared as global inside of a function or class. It also means you probably shouldn't assign anything to these variables, or you'll overwrite the data stored in them.

Prior to PHP 4.1, these superglobal variables didn't exist. Instead there were regular arrays named $HTTP_COOKIE_VARS, $HTTP_ENV_VARS, $HTTP_GET_VARS, $HTTP_POST_VARS, $HTTP_POST_FILES, and $HTTP_SERVER_VARS. These arrays are still available for legacy reasons, but the newer arrays are easier to work with. These older arrays are popu-lated only if the track_vars configuration directive is on, but, as of PHP 4.0.3, this feature is always enabled.

Finally, if the register_globals configuration directive is on, all these variables are also available as variables in the global namespace. So, $_GET['password'] is also just $password. While convenient, this introduces major security problems because mali-cious users can easily set variables from the outside and overwrite trusted internal variables. Starting with PHP 4.2, register_globals defaults to off.

With this knowledge, here is a basic script to put things together. The form asks the user to enter his first name, then replies with a welcome message. The HTML for the form looks like this:

```
<form action="/hello.php" method="post">
What is your first name?
<input type="text" name="first_name">
<input type="submit" value="Say Hello">
</form>
```

The name of the text input element inside the form is first_name. Also, the method of the form is post. This means that when the form is submitted, $_POST['first_name'] will hold whatever string the user typed in. (It could also be empty, of course, if he didn't type anything.)

For simplicity, however, let's assume the value in the variable is valid. (The term "valid" is open for definition, depending on certain criteria, such as not being empty, not being an attempt to break into the system, etc.) This allows us to omit the error checking stage, which is important but gets in the way of this simple example. So, here is a simple *hello.php* script to process the form:

```
echo 'Hello ' . $_POST['first_name'] . '!';
```

If the user's first name is Joe, PHP prints out:

```
Hello Joe!
```

9.1   Processing Form Input

Problem

You want to use the same HTML page to emit a form and then process the data entered into it. In other words, you're trying to avoid a proliferation of pages that each handle different steps in a transaction.

Solution

Use a hidden field in the form to tell your program that it's supposed to be processing the form. In this case, the hidden field is named stage and has a value of process:

```
if (isset($_POST['stage']) && ('process' == $_POST['stage'])) {
    process_form();
} else {
    print_form();
}
```

Discussion

During the early days of the Web, when people created forms, they made two pages: a static HTML page with the form and a script that processed the form and returned a dynamically generated response to the user. This was a little unwieldy, because *form.html* led to *form.cgi* and if you changed one page, you needed to also remember to edit the other, or your script might break.

Forms are easier to maintain when all parts live in the same file and context dictates which sections to display. Use a hidden form field named stage to track your position in the flow of the form process; it acts as a trigger for the steps that return the proper HTML to the user. Sometimes, however, it's not possible to design your code to do this; for example, when your form is processed by a script on someone else's server.

When writing the HTML for your form, however, don't hardcode the path to your page directly into the action. This makes it impossible to rename or relocate your page without also editing it. Instead, PHP supplies a helpful variable:

```
$_SERVER['PHP_SELF']
```

This variable is an alias to the URL of the current page. So, set the value of the action attribute to that value, and your form always resubmits, even if you've moved the file to a new place on the server.

So, the example in the introduction of this chapter is now:

```
if (isset($_POST['stage']) && ('process' == $_POST['stage'])) {
    process_form();
} else {
    print_form();
}

function print_form() {
    echo <<<END
        <form action="$_SERVER[PHP_SELF]" method="post">
        What is your first name?
        <input type="text" name="first_name">
        <input type="hidden" name="stage" value="process">
        <input type="submit" value="Say Hello">
        </form>
END;
}

function process_form() {
    echo 'Hello ' . $_POST['first_name'] . '!';
}
```

If your form has more than one step, just set stage to a new value for each step.

See Also

Recipe 9.3 for handling multipage forms.

9.2   Validating Form Input

Problem

You want to ensure data entered from a form passes certain criteria.

Solution

Create a function that takes a string to validate and returns true if the string passes a check and false if it doesn't. Inside the function, use regular expressions and comparisons to check the data. For example, Example 9-1 shows the pc_validate_zipcode() function, which validates a U.S. Zip Code.

Example 9-1. pc_validate_zipcode()

```
function pc_validate_zipcode($zipcode) {
    return preg_match('/^[0-9]{5}([- ]?[0-9]{4})?$/', $zipcode);
}
```

Here's how to use it:

```
if (pc_validate_zipcode($_REQUEST['zipcode'])) {
    // U.S. Zip Code is okay, can proceed
    process_data();
} else {
    // this is not an okay Zip Code, print an error message
    print "Your ZIP Code is should be 5 digits (or 9 digits, if you're ";
    print "using ZIP+4).";
    print_form();
}
```

Discussion

Deciding what constitutes valid and invalid data is almost more of a philosophical task than a straightforward matter of following a series of fixed steps. In many cases, what may be perfectly fine in one situation won't be correct in another.

The easiest check is making sure the field isn't blank. The empty() function best handles this problem.

Next come relatively easy checks, such as the case of a U.S. Zip Code. Usually, a regular expression or two can solve these problems. For example:

```
/^[0-9]{5}([- ]?[0-9]{4})?$/
```

finds all valid U.S. Zip Codes.

Sometimes, however, coming up with the correct regular expression is difficult. If you want to verify that someone has entered only two names, such as "Alfred Aho," you can check against:

```
/^[A-Za-z]+ +[A-Za-z]+$/
```

However, Tim O'Reilly can't pass this test. An alternative is /^\S+\s+\S+$/; but then Donald E. Knuth is rejected. So think carefully about the entire range of valid input before writing your regular expression.

In some instances, even with regular expressions, it becomes difficult to check if the field is legal. One particularly popular and tricky task is validating an email address, as discussed in Recipe 13.6. Another is how to make sure a user has correctly entered the name of her U.S. state. You can check against a listing of names, but what if she enters her postal service abbreviation? Will MA instead of Massachusetts work? What about Mass.?

One way to avoid this issue is to present the user with a dropdown list of pregenerated choices. Using a select element, users are forced by the form's design to select a state in the format that always works, which can reduce errors. This, however, presents another series of difficulties. What if the user lives some place that isn't one of the choices? What if the range of choices is so large this isn't a feasible solution?

There are a number of ways to solve these types of problems. First, you can provide an "other" option in the list, so that a non-U.S. user can successfully complete the form. (Otherwise, she'll probably just pick a place at random, so she can continue using your site.) Next, you can divide the registration process into a two-part sequence. For a long list of options, a user begins by picking the letter of the alphabet his choice begins with; then, a new page provides him with a list containing only the choices beginning with that letter.

Finally, there are even trickier problems. What do you do when you want to make sure the user has correctly entered information, but you don't want to tell her you did so? A situation where this is important is a sweepstakes; in a sweepstakes, there's often a special code box on the entry form in which a user enters a string—AD78DQ—from an email or flier she's received. You want to make sure there are no typos, or your program won't count her as a valid entrant. You also don't want to allow her to just guess codes, because then she could try out those codes and crack the system.

The solution is to have two input boxes. A user enters her code twice; if the two fields match, you accept the data as legal and then (silently) validate the data. If the fields don't match, you reject the entry and have the user fix it. This procedure eliminates typos and doesn't reveal how the code validation algorithm works; it can also prevent misspelled email addresses.

Finally, PHP performs server-side validation. Server-side validation requires that a request be made to the server, and a page returned in response; as a result, it can be slow. It's also possible to do client-side validation using JavaScript. While client-side validation is faster, it exposes your code to the user and may not work if the client doesn't support JavaScript or has disabled it. Therefore, you should always duplicate all client-side validation code on the server.

See Also

Recipe 13.6 for a regular expression for validating email addresses; Chapter 7, "Validation on the Server and Client," of *Web Database Applications with PHP and MySQL* (Hugh Williams and David Lane, O'Reilly).

9.3   Working with Multipage Forms

Problem

You want to use a form that displays more than one page and preserve data from one page to the next.

Solution

Use session tracking:

```
session_start();
$_SESSION['username'] = $_GET['username'];
```

You can also include variables from a form's earlier pages as hidden input fields in its later pages:

```
<input type="hidden" name="username"
     value="<?php echo htmlentities($_GET['username']); ?>">
```

Discussion

Whenever possible, use session tracking. It's more secure because users can't modify session variables. To begin a session, call `session_start()`; this creates a new session or resumes an existing one. Note that this step is unnecessary if you've enabled `session.auto_start` in your *php.ini* file. Variables assigned to `$_SESSION` are automatically propagated. In the Solution example, the form's username variable is preserved by assigning `$_GET['username']` to `$_SESSION['username']`.

To access this value on a subsequent request, call `session_start()` and then check `$_SESSION['username']`:

```
session_start();
$username = htmlentities($_SESSION['username']);
print "Hello $username.";
```

In this case, if you don't call `session_start()`, `$_SESSION` isn't set.

Be sure to secure the server and location where your session files are located (the filesystem, database, etc.); otherwise your system will be vulnerable to identity spoofing.

If session tracking isn't enabled for your PHP installation, you can use hidden form variables as a replacement. However, passing data using hidden form elements isn't secure because anyone can edit these fields and fake a request; with a little work, you can increase the security to a reliable level.

The most basic way to use hidden fields is to include them inside your form.

```
<form action="<?php echo $_SERVER['PHP_SELF']; ?>"
     method="get">

<input type="hidden" name="username"
     value="<?php echo htmlentities($_GET['username']); ?>">
```

When this form is resubmitted, `$_GET['username']` holds its previous value unless someone has modified it.

A more complex but secure solution is to convert your variables to a string using `serialize()`, compute a secret hash of the data, and place both pieces of information in the form. Then, on the next request, validate the data and unserialize it. If it fails the validation test, you'll know someone has tried to modify the information.

The pc_encode() encoding function shown in Example 9-2 takes the data to encode in the form of an array.

Example 9-2. pc_encode()

```
$secret = 'Foo25bAr52baZ';

function pc_encode($data) {
  $data = serialize($data);
  $hash = md5($GLOBALS['secret'] . $data);
  return array($data, $hash);
}
```

In function pc_encode(), the data is serialized into a string, a validation hash is computed, and those variables are returned.

The pc_decode() function shown in Example 9-3 undoes the work of its counterpart.

Example 9-3. pc_decode()

```
function pc_decode($data, $hash) {
  if (!empty($data) && !empty($hash)) {
    if (md5($GLOBALS['secret'] . $data) == $hash) {
      return unserialize($data);
    } else {
      error_log("Validation Error: Data has been modified");
      return false;
    }
  }
  return false;
}
```

The pc_decode() function recreates the hash of the secret word and compares it to the hash value from the form. If they're equal, $data is valid, so it's unserialized. If it flunks the test, the function writes a message to the error log and returns false.

These functions go together like this:

```
<?php
$secret = 'Foo25bAr52baZ';

// Load in and validate old data
if (! $data = pc_decode($_GET['data'], $_GET['hash'])) {
  // crack attempt
}

// Process form (new form data is in $_GET)

// Update $data
$data['username'] = $_GET['username'];
```

```
$data['stage']++;
unset($data['password']);

// Encode results
list ($data, $hash) = pc_encode($data);

// Store data and hash inside the form
?>
<form action="<?php echo $_SERVER['PHP_SELF']; ?>" method="get">
...

<input type="hidden" name="data"
       value="<?php echo htmlentities($data); ?>">
<input type="hidden" name="hash"
       value="<?php echo htmlentities($hash); ?>">
</form>
```

At the top of the script, we pass pc_decode() the variables from the form for decoding. Once the information is loaded into $data, form processing can proceed by checking in $_GET for new variables and in $data for old ones. Once that's complete, update $data to hold the new values and then encode it, calculating a new hash in the process. Finally, print out the new form and include $data and $hash as hidden variables.

See Also

Recipes 8.5 and 8.6 for information on using the session module; Recipe 9.8 for details on using htmlentities() to escape control characters in HTML output; Recipe 14.3 for information on verifying data with hashes; documentation on session tracking at *http://www.php.net/session* and in Recipe 8.4; documentation on serialize() at *http://www.php.net/serialize* and unserialize() at *http://www.php.net/unserialize*.

9.4   Redisplaying Forms with Preserved Information and Error Messages

Problem

When there's a problem with data entered in a form, you want to print out error messages alongside the problem fields, instead of a generic error message at the top of the form. You also want to preserve the values the user typed into the form the first time.

Solution

Use an array, $errors, and store your messages in the array indexed by the name of the field.

```
if (! pc_validate_zipcode($_REQUEST['zipcode'])) {
    $errors['zipcode'] = "This is is a bad ZIP Code. ZIP Codes must "
                        . "have 5 numbers and no letters.";
}
```

When you redisplay the form, you can display each error by its field and include the original value in the field:

```
echo $errors['zipcode'];
$value = isset($_REQUEST['zipcode']) ?
                htmlentities($_REQUEST['zipcode']) : '';
echo "<input type=\"text\" name=\"zipcode\" value=\"$value\">";
```

Discussion

If your users encounter errors when filling out a long form, you can increase the overall usability of your form if you highlight exactly where the errors need to be fixed.

Consolidating all errors in a single array has many advantages. First, you can easily check if your validation process has located any items that need correction; just use count($errors). This method is easier than trying to keep track of this fact in a separate variable, especially if the flow is complex or spread out over multiple functions. Example 9-4 shows the pc_validate_form() validation function, which uses an $errors array.

Example 9-4. pc_validate_form()

```
function pc_validate_form() {
  if (! pc_validate_zipcode($_POST['zipcode'])) {
    $errors['zipcode'] = "ZIP Codes are 5 numbers";
  }

  if (! pc_validate_email($_POST['email'])) {
    $errors['email'] = "Email addresses look like user@example.com";
  }

  return $errors;
}
```

This is clean code because all errors are stored in one variable. You can easily pass around the variable if you don't want it to live in the global scope.

Using the variable name as the key preserves the links between the field that caused the error and the actual error message itself. These links also make it easy to loop through items when displaying errors.

You can automate the repetitive task of printing the form; the pc_print_form() function in Example 9-5 shows how.

Example 9-5. pc_print_form()

```
function pc_print_form($errors) {
    $fields = array('name'   => 'Name',
                    'rank'   => 'Rank',
                    'serial' => 'Serial');

    if (count($errors)) {
        echo 'Please correct the errors in the form below.';
    }

    echo '<table>';

    // print out the errors and form variables
    foreach ($fields as $field => $field_name) {
        // open row
        echo '<tr><td>';

        // print error
        if (!empty($errors[$field])) {
            echo $errors[$field];
        } else {
            echo ' '; // to prevent odd looking tables
        }

        echo "</td><td>";

        // print name and input
        $value = isset($_REQUEST[$field]) ?
                        htmlentities($_REQUEST[$field]) : '';

        echo "$field_name: ";
        echo "<input type=\"text\" name=\"$field\" value=\"$value\">";
        echo '</td></tr>';
    }

    echo '</table>';
}
```

The complex part of pc_print_form() comes from the $fields array. The key is the variable name; the value is the pretty display name. By defining them at the top of the function, you can create a loop and use foreach to iterate through the values; otherwise, you need three separate lines of identical code. This integrates with the variable name as a key in $errors, because you can find the error message inside the loop just by checking $errors[$field].

If you want to extend this example beyond input fields of type text, modify $fields to include more meta-information about your form fields:

```
$fields = array('name' => array('name' => 'Name', 'type' => 'text'),
                'rank' => array('name' => 'Rank', 'type' => 'password'),
                'serial' => array('name' => 'Serial', 'type' => 'hidden')
                );
```

See Also

Recipe 9.2 for simple form validation.

9.5   Guarding Against Multiple Submission of the Same Form

Problem

You want to prevent people from submitting the same form multiple times.

Solution

Generate a unique identifier and store the token as a hidden field in the form. Before processing the form, check to see if that token has already been submitted. If it hasn't, you can proceed; if it has, you should generate an error.

When creating the form, use uniqid( ) to get a unique identifier:

```
<?php
$unique_id = uniqid(microtime(),1);
...
?>
<input type="hidden" name="unique_id" value="<?php echo $unique_id; ?>">
</form>
```

Then, when processing, look for this ID:

```
$unique_id  = $dbh->quote($_GET['unique_id']);
$sth = $dbh->query("SELECT * FROM database WHERE unique_id = $unique_id");

if ($sth->numRows()) {
    // already submitted, throw an error
} else {
    // act upon the data
}
```

Discussion

For a variety of reasons, users often resubmit a form. Usually it's a slip-of-the-mouse: double-clicking the Submit button. They may hit their web browser's Back button to edit or recheck information, but then they re-hit Submit instead of Forward. It can be intentional: they're trying to stuff the ballot box for an online survey or sweepstakes.

Our Solution prevents the nonmalicious attack and can slow down the malicious user. It won't, however, eliminate all fraudulent use: more complicated work is required for that.

The Solution does prevent your database from being cluttered with too many copies of the same record. By generating a token that's placed in the form, you can uniquely identify that specific instance of the form, even when cookies is disabled. When you then save the form's data, you store the token alongside it. That allows you to easily check if you've already seen this form and record the database it belongs to.

Start by adding an extra column to your database table—unique_id—to hold the identifier. When you insert data for a record, add the ID also. For example:

```
$username  = $dbh->quote($_GET['username']);
$unique_id = $dbh->quote($_GET['unique_id']);

$sth = $dbh->query("INSERT INTO members ( username,  unique_id)
                         VALUES ($username, $unique_id)");
```

By associating the exact row in the database with the form, you can more easily handle a resubmission. There's no correct answer here; it depends on your situation. In some cases, you'll want to ignore the second posting all together. In others, you'll want to check if the record has changed, and, if so, present the user with a dialog box asking if they want to update the record with the new information or keep the old data. Finally, to reflect the second form submission, you could update the record silently, and the user never learns of a problem.

All these possibilities should be considered given the specifics of the interaction. Our opinion is there's no reason to allow the deficits of HTTP to dictate the user experience. So, while the third choice, silently updating the record, isn't what normally happens, in many ways this is the most natural option. Applications we've developed with this method are more user friendly; the other two methods confuse or frustrate most users.

It's tempting to avoid generating a random token and instead use a number one greater then the number of records already in the database. The token and the primary key will thus be the same, and you don't need to use an extra column. There are (at least) two problems with this method. First, it creates a race condition. What happens when a second person starts the form before the first person has completed it? The second form will then have the same token as the first, and conflicts will occur. This can be worked around by creating a new blank record in the database when the form is requested, so the second person will get a number one higher than the first. However, this can lead to empty rows in the database if users opt not to complete the form.

The other reason not do this is because it makes it trivial to edit another record in the database by manually adjusting the ID to a different number. Depending on your security settings, a fake GET or POST submission allows the data to be altered without difficulty. A long random token, however, can't be guessed merely by moving to a different integer.

See Also

Recipe 14.3 for more details on verifying data with hashes; documentation on uniqid( ) at *http://www.php.net/uniqid*.

9.6   Processing Uploaded Files

Problem

You want to process a file uploaded by a user.

Solution

Use the $_FILES array:

```
// from <input name="event" type="file">
if (is_uploaded_file($_FILES['event']['tmp_name'])) {
    readfile($_FILES['event']['tmp_name']); // print file on screen
}
```

Discussion

Starting in PHP 4.1, all uploaded files appear in the $_FILES superglobal array. For each file, there are four pieces of information:

name
: The name assigned to the form input element

type
: The MIME type of the file

size
: The size of the file in bytes

tmp_name
: The location in which the file is temporarily stored on the server.

If you're using an earlier version of PHP, you need to use $HTTP_POST_FILES instead.

After you've selected a file from that array, use is_uploaded_file( ) to confirm that the file you're about to process is a legitimate file resulting from a user upload, then process it as you would other files on the system. Always do this. If you blindly trust the filename supplied by the user, someone can alter the request and add names such as */etc/passwd* to the list for processing.

You can also move the file to a permanent location; use move_uploaded_file() to safely transfer the file:

```
// move the file: move_uploaded_file() also does a check of the file's
// legitimacy, so there's no need to also call is_uploaded_file()
move_uploaded_file($_FILES['event']['tmp_name'], '/path/to/file.txt');
```

Note that the value stored in tmp_name is the complete path to the file, not just the base name. Use basename() to chop off the leading directories if needed.

Be sure to check that PHP has permission to read and write to both the directory in which temporary files are saved (see the upload_tmp_dir configuration directive to check where this is) and the location in which you're trying to copy the file. This can often be user nobody or apache, instead of your personal username. Because of this, if you're running under safe_mode, copying a file to a new location will probably not allow you to access it again.

Processing files can often be a subtle task because not all browsers submit the same information. It's important to do it correctly, however, or you open yourself up to a possible security hole. You are, after all, allowing strangers to upload any file they choose to your machine; malicious people may see this as an opportunity to crack into or crash the computer.

As a result, PHP has a number of features that allow you to place restrictions on uploaded files, including the ability to completely turn off file uploads all together. So, if you're experiencing difficulty processing uploaded files, check that your file isn't being rejected because it seems to pose a security risk.

To do such a check first, make sure file_uploads is set to On inside your configuration file. Next, make sure your file size isn't larger than upload_max_filesize; this defaults to 2 MB, which stops someone trying to crash the machine by filling up the hard drive with a giant file. Additionally, there's a post_max_size directive, which controls the maximum size of all the POST data allowed in a single request; its initial setting is 8 MB.

From the perspective of browser differences and user error, if you can't get $_FILES to populate with information, make sure you add enctype="multipart/form-data" to the form's opening tag; PHP needs this to trigger processing. If you can't do so, you need to manually parse $HTTP_RAW_POST_DATA. (See RFCs 1521 and 1522 for the MIME specification at *http://www.faqs.org/rfcs/rfc1521.html* and *http://www.faqs.org/rfcs/rfc1522.html*.)

Also, if no file is selected for uploading, versions of PHP prior to 4.1 set tmp_name to none; newer versions set it to the empty string. PHP 4.2.1 allows files of length 0. To be sure a file was uploaded and isn't empty (although blank files may be what you want, depending on the circumstances), you need to make sure tmp_name is set and size is greater than 0. Last, not all browsers necessarily send the same MIME type for a file; what they send depends on their knowledge of different file types.

See Also

Documentation on handling file uploads at *http://www.php.net/features.file-upload* and on basename() at *http://www.php.net/basename.*

9.7 Securing PHP's Form Processing

Problem

You want to securely process form input variables and not allow someone to maliciously alter variables in your code.

Solution

Disable the register_globals configuration directive and access variables only from the $_REQUEST array. To be even more secure, use $_GET, $_POST, and $_COOKIE to make sure you know exactly where your variables are coming from.

To do this, make sure this line appears in your *php.ini* file:

```
register_globals = Off
```

As of PHP 4.2, this is the default configuration.

Discussion

When register_globals is set on, external variables, including those from forms and cookies, are imported directly into the global namespace. This is a great convenience, but it can also open up some security holes if you're not very diligent about checking your variables and where they're defined. Why? Because there may be a variable you use internally that isn't supposed to be accessible from the outside but has its value rewritten without your knowledge.

Here is a simple example. You have a page in which a user enters a username and password. If they are validated, you return her user identification number and use that numerical identifier to look up and print out her personal information:

```
// assume magic_quotes_gpc is set to Off
$username = $dbh->quote($_GET['username']);
$password = $dbh->quote($_GET['password']);

$sth = $dbh->query("SELECT id FROM users WHERE username = $username AND
                    password = $password");

if (1 == $sth->numRows()) {
    $row = $sth->fetchRow(DB_FETCHMODE_OBJECT);
    $id = $row->id;
```

```
    } else {
        "Print bad username and password";
    }

    if (!empty($id)) {
        $sth = $dbh->query("SELECT * FROM profile WHERE id = $id");
    }
```

Normally, $id is set only by your program and is a result of a verified database lookup. However, if someone alters the GET string, and passes in a value for $id, with register_globals enabled, even after a bad username and password lookup, your script still executes the second database query and returns results. Without register_globals, $id remains unset because only $_REQUEST['id'] (and $_GET['id']) are set.

Of course, there are other ways to solve this problem, even when using register_globals. You can restructure your code not to allow such a loophole.

```
    $sth = $dbh->query("SELECT id FROM users WHERE username = $username AND
                        password = $password");

    if (1 == $sth->numRows()) {
        $row = $sth->fetchRow(DB_FETCHMODE_OBJECT);
        $id = $row->id;
        if (!empty($id)) {
            $sth = $dbh->query("SELECT * FROM profile WHERE id = $id");
        }
    } else {
        "Print bad username and password";
    }
```

Now you use $id only when it's been explicitly set from a database call. Sometimes, however, it is difficult to do this because of how your program is laid out. Another solution is to manually unset( ) or initialize all variables at the top of your script:

```
    unset($id);
```

This removes the bad $id value before it gets a chance to affect your code. However, because PHP doesn't require variable initialization, it's possible to forget to do this in one place; a bug can then slip in without a warning from PHP.

See Also

Documentation on register_globals at *http://www.php.net/security.registerglobals.php.*

9.8 Escaping Control Characters from User Data

Problem

You want to securely display user-entered data on an HTML page.

Solution

For HTML you wish to display as plain text, with embedded links and other tags, use `htmlentities()`:

```
echo htmlentities('<p>O'Reilly & Associates</p>');
&lt;p&gt;O'Reilly & Associates&lt;/p&gt;
```

Discussion

PHP has a pair of functions to escape characters in HTML. The most basic is `htmlspecialchars()`, which escapes four characters: < > " and &. Depending on optional parameters, it can also translate ' instead of or in addition to ". For more complex encoding, use `htmlentities()`; it expands on `htmlspecialchars()` to encode any character that has an HTML entity.

```
$html = "<a href='fletch.html'>Stew's favorite movie.</a>\n";
print htmlspecialchars($html);                // double-quotes
print htmlspecialchars($html, ENT_QUOTES);    // single- and double-quotes
print htmlspecialchars($html, ENT_NOQUOTES);  // neither
&lt;a href=&quot;fletch.html&quot;&gt;Stew's favorite movie.&lt;/a&gt;
&lt;a href=&quot;fletch.html&quot;&gt;Stew&#039;s favorite movie.&lt;/a&gt;
&lt;a href="fletch.html"&gt;Stew's favorite movie.&lt;/a&gt;
```

Both functions allow you to pass in a character encoding table that defines what characters map to what entities. To retrieve either table used by the previous functions, use `get_html_translation_table()` and pass in `HTML_ENTITIES` or `HTML_SPECIALCHARS`. This returns an array that maps characters to entities; you can use it as the basis for your own table.

```
$copyright = "Copyright © 2003 O'Reilly & Associates\n";
$table = get_html_translation_table(); // get <, >, ", and &
$table[©] = '&copy;'            // add ©
print strtr($copyright, $table);
Copyright &copy; 2003 O'Reilly &amp; Associates
```

See Also

Recipes 13.8, 18.20, and 10.7; documentation on `htmlentities()` at *http://www.php.net/htmlentities* and `htmlspecialchars()` at *http://www.php.net/htmlspecialchars*.

9.9 Handling Remote Variables with Periods in Their Names

Problem

You want to process a variable with a period in its name, but when a form is submitted, you can't find the variable.

Solution

Replace the period in the variable's name with an underscore. For example, if you have a form input element named foo.bar, you access it inside PHP as the variable $_REQUEST['foo_bar'].

Discussion

Because PHP uses the period as a string concatenation operator, a form variable called animal.height is automatically converted to animal_height, which avoids creating an ambiguity for the parser. While $_REQUEST['animal.height'] lacks these ambiguities, for legacy and consistency reasons, this happens regardless of your register_globals settings.

You usually deal with automatic variable name conversion when you process an image used to submit a form. For instance: you have a street map showing the location of your stores, and you want people to click on one for additional information. Here's an example:

```
<input type="image" name="locations" src="locations.gif">
```

When a user clicks on the image, the x and y coordinates are submitted as locations.x and locations.y. So, in PHP, to find where a user clicked, you need to check $_REQUEST['locations_x'] and $_REQUEST['locations_y'].

It's possible, through a series of manipulations, to create a variable inside PHP with a period:

```
${"a.b"} = 123; // forced coercion using {}

$var = "c.d";   // indirect variable naming
$$var = 456;

print ${"a.b"} . "\n";
print $$var . "\n";
123
456
```

This is generally frowned on because of the awkward syntax.

See Also

Documentation on variables from outside PHP at *http://www.php.net/language. variables.external.php*.

9.10 Using Form Elements with Multiple Options

Problem

You have a form element with multiple values, such as a checkbox or select element, but PHP sees only one value.

Solution

Place brackets ([ ]) after the variable name:

```
<input type="checkbox" name="boroughs[]" value="bronx"> The Bronx
<input type="checkbox" name="boroughs[]" value="brooklyn"> Brooklyn
<input type="checkbox" name="boroughs[]" value="manhattan"> Manhattan
<input type="checkbox" name="boroughs[]" value="queens"> Queens
<input type="checkbox" name="boroughs[]" value="statenisland"> Staten Island
```

Inside your program, treat the variable as an array:

```
print 'I love ' . join(' and ', $boroughs) . '!';
```

Discussion

By placing [ ] after the variable name, you tell PHP to treat it as an array instead of a scalar. When it sees another value assigned to that variable, PHP auto-expands the size of the array and places the new value at the end. If the first three boxes in the Solution were checked, it's as if you'd written this code at the top of the script:

```
$boroughs[] = "bronx";
$boroughs[] = "brooklyn";
$boroughs[] = "manhattan";
```

You can use this to return information from a database that matches multiple records:

```
foreach ($_GET['boroughs'] as $b) {
  $boroughs[] = strtr($dbh->quote($b),array('_' => '\_', '%' => '\%'));
}
$locations = join(',', $boroughs);

$dbh->query("SELECT address FROM locations WHERE borough IN ($locations)");
```

This syntax also works with multidimensional arrays:

```
<input type="checkbox" name="population[NY][NYC]" value="8008278">New York...
```

If checked, this form element sets $population['NY']['NYC']$ to 8008278.

Placing a [ ] after a variable's name can cause problems in JavaScript when you try to address your elements. Instead of addressing the element by its name, use the numerical ID. You can also place the element name inside single quotes. Another way is to assign the element an ID, perhaps the name without the [ ], and use that ID instead. Given:

```
<form>
<input type="checkbox" name="myName[]" value="myValue" id="myName">
</form>
```

the following three refer to the same form element:

```
document.forms[0].elements[0];            // using numerical IDs
document.forms[0].elements['myName[]'];   // using the name with quotes
document.forms[0].elements['myName'];     // using ID you assigned
```

See Also

The introduction to Chapter 4 for more on arrays.

9.11 Creating Dropdown Menus Based on the Current Date

Problem

You want to create a series of dropdown menus that are based automatically on the current date.

Solution

Use date() to find the current time in the web server's time zone and loop through the days with mktime().

The following code generates option values for today and the six days that follow. In this case, "today" is January 1, 2002.

```
list($hour, $minute, $second, $month, $day, $year) =
                            split(':', date('h:i:s:m:d:Y'));

// print out one week's worth of days
for ($i = 0; $i < 7; ++$i) {
    $timestamp = mktime($hour, $minute, $second, $month, $day + $i, $year);
    $date = date("D, F j, Y", $timestamp);

    print "<option value=\"$timestamp\">$date</option>\n";
}
```

```
<option value="946746000">Tue, January 1, 2002</option>
<option value="946832400">Wed, January 2, 2002</option>
<option value="946918800">Thu, January 3, 2002</option>
<option value="947005200">Fri, January 4, 2002</option>
<option value="947091600">Sat, January 5, 2002</option>
<option value="947178000">Sun, January 6, 2002</option>
<option value="947264400">Mon, January 7, 2002</option>
```

Discussion

In the Solution, we set the value for each date as its Unix timestamp representation because we find this easier to handle inside our programs. Of course, you can use any format you find most useful and appropriate.

Don't be tempted to eliminate the calls to mktime(); dates and times aren't as consistent as you'd hope. Depending on what you're doing, you might not get the results you want. For example:

```
$timestamp = mktime(0, 0, 0, 10, 24, 2002); // October 24, 2002
$one_day = 60 * 60 * 24; // number of seconds in a day

// print out one week's worth of days
for ($i = 0; $i < 7; ++$i) {
    $date = date("D, F j, Y", $timestamp);

    print "<option value=\"$timestamp\">$date</option>";

    $timestamp += $one_day;
}
```
```
<option value="972619200">Fri, October 25, 2002</option>
<option value="972705600">Sat, October 26, 2002</option>
<option value="972792000">Sun, October 27, 2002</option>
<option value="972878400">Sun, October 27, 2002</option>
<option value="972964800">Mon, October 28, 2002</option>
<option value="973051200">Tue, October 29, 2002</option>
<option value="973137600">Wed, October 30, 2002</option>
```

This script should print out the month, day, and year for a seven-day period starting October 24, 2002. However, it doesn't work as expected.

Why are there two "Sun, October 27, 2002"s? The answer: daylight saving time. It's not true that the number of seconds in a day stays constant; in fact, it's almost guaranteed to change. Worst of all, if you're not near either of the change-over dates, you're liable to miss this bug during testing.

See Also

Chapter 3, particularly Recipe 3.12, but also Recipes 3.1, 3.2, 3.4, 3.10, and 3.13; documentation on date() at *http://www.php.net/date* and mktime() at *http://www.php.net/mktime*.

CHAPTER 10

Database Access

10.0 Introduction

Databases are central to many web applications. A database can hold almost any collection of information you may want to search and update, such as a user list, a product catalog, or recent headlines. One reason why PHP is such a great web programming language is its extensive database support. PHP can interact with (at last count) 17 different databases, some relational and some not. The relational databases it can talk to are DB++, FrontBase, Informix, Interbase, Ingres II, Microsoft SQL Server, mSQL, MySQL, Oracle, Ovrimos SQL Server, PostgreSQL, SESAM, and Sybase. The nonrelational databases it can talk to are dBase, filePro, HyperWave, and the DBM family of flat-file databases. It also has ODBC support, so even if your favorite database isn't in the list, as long as it supports ODBC, you can use it with PHP.

If your data storage needs are simple and you don't need to serve many users, you may be able to use a plaintext file as a makeshift database. This is discussed in Recipe 10.1. Text files require no special database software but are appropriate only for lightly used, basic applications. A text file can't handle structured data well; if your data changes a lot, it's inefficient to store it in a plain file instead of a database.

DBM flat-file databases, discussed in Recipe 10.2, offer more robustness and efficiency than flat files but still limit the structure of your data to key/value pairs. They scale better than plaintext files, especially for read-only (or read-almost-always) data.

PHP really shines, though, when paired with a SQL database. This combination is used for most of the recipes in this chapter. SQL databases can be complicated, but they are extremely powerful. To use PHP with a particular SQL database, PHP must be explicitly told to include support for that database when it is compiled. If PHP is built to support dynamic module loading, the database support can also be built as a dynamic module.

Many SQL examples in this chapter use a table of information about Zodiac signs. The table's structure is:

```
CREATE TABLE zodiac (
  id INT UNSIGNED NOT NULL,
  sign CHAR(11),
  symbol CHAR(13),
  planet CHAR(7),
  element CHAR(5),
  start_month TINYINT,
  start_day TINYINT,
  end_month TINYINT,
  end_day TINYINT,
  PRIMARY KEY(id)
);
```

And the data in the table is:

```
INSERT INTO zodiac VALUES (1,'Aries','Ram','Mars','fire',3,21,4,19);
INSERT INTO zodiac VALUES (2,'Taurus','Bull','Venus','earth',4,20,5,20);
INSERT INTO zodiac VALUES (3,'Gemini','Twins','Mercury','air',5,21,6,21);
INSERT INTO zodiac VALUES (4,'Cancer','Crab','Moon','water',6,22,7,22);
INSERT INTO zodiac VALUES (5,'Leo','Lion','Sun','fire',7,23,8,22);
INSERT INTO zodiac VALUES (6,'Virgo','Virgin','Mercury','earth',8,23,9,22);
INSERT INTO zodiac VALUES (7,'Libra','Scales','Venus','air',9,23,10,23);
INSERT INTO zodiac VALUES (8,'Scorpio','Scorpion','Mars','water',10,24,11,21);
INSERT INTO zodiac VALUES (9,'Sagittarius','Archer','Jupiter','fire',11,22,12,21);
INSERT INTO zodiac VALUES (10,'Capricorn','Goat','Saturn','earth',12,22,1,19);
INSERT INTO zodiac VALUES (11,'Aquarius','Water Carrier','Uranus','air',1,20,2,18);
INSERT INTO zodiac VALUES (12,'Pisces','Fishes','Neptune','water',2,19,3,20);
```

The specific functions required to talk to the database differ with each database, but each follows a similar pattern. Connecting to the database returns a database connection handle. You use the connection handle to create statement handles, which are associated with particular queries. A query statement handle then gets the results of that query.

This example retrieves all the rows from the zodiac table with Oracle, using the OCI8 interface:

```
if (! $dbh = OCILogon('david', 'foo!bar','ORAINST')) {
    die("Can't connect: ".OCIError());
}

if (! $sth = OCIParse($dbh,'SELECT * FROM zodiac')) {
    die("Can't parse query: ".OCIError());
}

if (! OCIExecute($sth)) {
    die("Can't execute query: ".OCIError());
}

$cols = OCINumCols($sth);
while (OCIFetch($sth)) {
```

```
    for ($i = 1; $i <= $cols; $i++) {
        print OCIResult($sth,$i);
        print " ";
    }
    print "\n";
}
```

The `OCILogin()` function connects to a given Oracle instance with a username and password. You can leave out the third argument (the instance) if the environment variable `ORACLE_SID` is set to the desired Oracle instance. A statement handle is returned from `OCIParse()`, and `OCIExecute()` runs the query. Each time `OCIFetch()` is called, the next row in the result is retrieved into a result buffer. The value of a particular column of the current row in the result buffer is retrieved by `OCIResult()`.

Here's the same example using PostgreSQL:

```
if (! $dbh = pg_connect('dbname=test user=david password=foo!bar')) {
    die("Can't connect: ".pg_errormessage());
}

if (! $sth = pg_exec($dbh,'SELECT * FROM zodiac')) {
    die("Can't execute query: ".pg_errormessage());
}

for ($i = 0, $j = pg_numrows($sth); $i < $j; $i++) {
    $ar = pg_fetch_row($sth,$i);
    foreach ($ar as $col) {
        print "$col ";
    }
    print "\n";
}
```

In this case, `pg_connect()` connects to PostgreSQL using the provided database name, user, and password. The query is run by `pg_exec()`. There's no need for a separate parse and execute step as with Oracle. Because `pg_fetch_row()` retrieves a specific row from the result set into an array, you loop over all the rows (using `pg_numrows()` to get the total number of rows) and print out each element in the array.

Here's the same exercise with MySQL:

```
if (! $dbh = mysql_connect('localhost','david','foo!bar')) {
    die("Can't connect: ".mysql_error());
}

mysql_select_db('test');

if (! $sth = mysql_query('SELECT * FROM zodiac')) {
    die("Can't execute query: ".mysql_error());
}

while ($ar = mysql_fetch_row($sth)) {
    foreach ($ar as $col) {
```

```
        print "$col ";
    }
    print "\n";
}
```

First, `mysql_connect( )` returns a database handle using the provided hostname, username, and password. You then use `mysql_select_db( )` to indicate which database to use. The query is executed by `mysql_query( )`. The `mysql_fetch_row( )` function retrieves the next row in the result set and NULL when there are no more rows; use a while loop to retrieve all the rows.

Each example prints out all the data in the zodiac table, one row per line, with spaces between each field, as shown here:

```
Aries Ram Mars fire 3 21 4 19
Taurus Bull Venus earth 4 20 5 20
Gemini Twins Mercury air 5 21 6 21
Cancer Crab Moon water 6 22 7 22
Leo Lion Sun fire 7 23 8 22
Virgo Virgin Mercury earth 8 23 9 22
Libra Scales Venus air 9 23 10 23
Scorpio Scorpion Mars water 20 24 11 21
Sagittarius Archer Jupiter fire 11 22 12 21
Capricorn Goat Saturn earth 12 22 1 19
Aquarius Water Carrier Uranus air 1 20 2 18
Pisces Fishes Neptune water 2 19 3 20
```

Recipes 10.4 through 10.8 cover the basics of sending queries to the database and getting the results back, as well as using queries that change the data in the database.

There are a number of options and optimizations for each database PHP supports. Most database interfaces support persistent connections with separate connection functions. In the previous three examples, you would use `OCIPLogon( )`, `pg_pconnect( )`, and `mysql_pconnect( )` for persistent instead of single-request connections.

If you require a database-specific set of functions, the PHP online manual section for each database has many useful tips for proper configuration and use. If you can, use a database abstraction layer instead. Starting with Recipe 10.3, all the SQL examples use the PEAR DB database abstraction layer, which minimizes the amount of code that has to change to make the examples work on different databases. Here's code that can display all the rows in the zodiac table using DB and MySQL:

```
require 'DB.php';
$dbh = DB::connect('mysql://david:foo!bar@localhost/test');
$sth = $dbh->query('SELECT * FROM zodiac');
while ($row = $sth->fetchRow()) {
    print join(' ',$row)."\n";
}
```

The only thing that needs to change to make this code work on another database is the argument passed to `DB::connect( )`, which specifies what database to connect to. However, a database abstraction layer doesn't make SQL completely portable. Each database vendor generally has custom SQL extensions that enable handy features on one database and don't work at all on another database.

While it's possible to write SQL that works on different databases with a minimum of changes, tuning a database for speed and efficiency is not portable. Having portable database interactions can be a useful goal, but it needs to be balanced with the likelihood of your code being used with multiple databases. If you're writing code for wide distribution, working with many databases is a plus. If your code is an internal project, however, you probably don't need to be as concerned with database independence.

Whatever database you're using, you're probably going to be capturing information from HTML form fields and storing that information in the database. Some characters, such as the apostrophe and backslash, have special meaning in SQL, so you have to be careful if your form data contains those characters. PHP has a feature called "magic quotes" to make this easier. When the configuration setting magic_quotes_gpc is on, variables coming from GET requests, POST requests, and cookies have single quotes, double quotes, backslashes, and nulls escaped with a backslash. You can also turn on magic_quotes_runtime to automatically escape quotes, backslashes, and nulls from external sources such as database queries or text files. For example, if magic_quotes_runtime is on, and you read a file into an array with file( ), the special characters in that array are backslash-escaped.

For example, if $_REQUESTS['excuse'] is "Ferris wasn't sick," and magic_quotes_gpc is on, this query executes successfully:

```
$dbh->query("INSERT INTO excuses (truth) VALUES ('" . $_REQUESTS['excuse'] . ')');
```

Without the magic quotes, the apostrophe in "wasn't" signals the end of the string to the database, and the query produces a syntax error. To instruct magic_quotes_gpc and magic_quotes_runtime to escape single quotes with another single quote instead of a backslash, set magic_quotes_sybase to on. Recipe 10.9 discusses escaping special characters in queries. General debugging techniques you can use to handle errors resulting from database queries are covered in Recipe 10.10.

The remaining recipes cover database tasks that are more involved than just simple queries. Recipe 10.11 shows how to automatically generate unique ID values you can use as record identifiers. Recipe 10.12 covers building queries at runtime from a list of fields. This makes it easier to manage INSERT and UPDATE queries that involve a lot of columns. Recipe 10.13 demonstrates how to display links that let you page through a result set, displaying a few records on each page. To speed up your database access, you can cache queries and their results, as explained in Recipe 10.14.

10.1 Using Text-File Databases

Problem

You want a lightweight way to store information between requests.

Solution

Use a text file with advisory locking to prevent conflicts. You can store data in the text file in any useful format (CSV, pipe-delimited, etc.) One convenient way is to put all the data you want to store in one variable (a big associative array) and then store the output of calling serialize( ) on the variable:

```
$data_file = '/tmp/data';

// open the file for reading and writing
$fh = fopen($data_file,'a+') or die($php_errormsg);
rewind($fh)                  or die($php_errormsg);

// get an exclusive lock on the file
flock($fh,LOCK_EX)           or die($php_errormsg);

// read in and unserialize the data
$serialized_data = fread($fh,filesize($data_file)) or die($php_errormsg);
$data = unserialize($serialized_data);

/*
 * do whatever you need to with $data ...
 */

// reserialize the data
$serialized_data = serialize($data);

// clear out the file
rewind($fh)                  or die($php_errormsg);
ftruncate($fp,0)             or die($php_errormsg);

// write the data back to the file and release the lock
if (-1 == (fwrite($fh,$serialized_data))) { die($php_errormsg); }
fflush($fh)                  or die($php_errormsg);
flock($fh,LOCK_UN)           or die($php_errormsg);
fclose($fh)                  or die($php_errormsg);
```

Discussion

Storing your data in a text file doesn't require any additional database software to be installed, but that's pretty much its only advantage. Its main disadvantages are clumsiness and inefficiency. At the beginning of a request, you've got to lock your text file and haul out all your data from it, even if you're only using a little bit of the data.

Until you unlock the file at the end of the request, all other processes have to wait around, doing nothing, which means all your users are waiting too. One of the great assets of databases is that they give you structured access to your data, so you only lock (and load into memory) the data you actually care about. The text file solution doesn't do that.

What's worse, the locking you can do with a text file isn't nearly as robust as what you can do with a database. Because flock( ) provides a kind of file locking called advisory locking, the only thing that prevents multiple processes from stepping on each other and trashing your data is politeness and diligent programming. There's no guarantee your data is safe from an innocently incompetent or intentionally malicious program.

See Also

Recipe 5.7 discusses serializing data; Recipe 18.24 goes into the details of file locking; documentation on flock( ) at *http://www.php.net/flock*, serialize( ) at *http://www.php.net/serialize*, and unserialize( ) at *http://www.php.net/unserialize*.

10.2   Using DBM Databases

Problem

You want a more stable and scalable way to store simple data than what text files offer.

Solution

Use the DBA abstraction layer to access a DBM-style database:

```
$dbh = dba_open('fish.db','c','gdbm') or die($php_errormsg);

// retrieve and change values
if (dba_exists('flounder',$dbh)) {
  $flounder_count = dba_fetch('flounder',$dbh);
  $flounder_count++;
  dba_replace('flounder',$flounder_count,$dbh);
  print "Updated the flounder count.";
} else {
  dba_insert('flounder',1,$dbh);
  print "Started the flounder count.";
}

// no more tilapia
dba_delete('tilapia',$dbh);
```

```
// what fish do we have?
for ($key = dba_firstkey($dbh);  $key !== false; $key = dba_nextkey($dbh)) {
    $value = dba_fetch($key,$dbh);
    print "$key: $value\n";
}

dba_close($dbh);
```

Discussion

PHP can support a few different kinds of DBM backends: GDBM, NDBM, DB2, DB3, DBM, and CDB. The DBA abstraction layer lets you use the same functions on any DBM backend. All these backends store key/value pairs. You can iterate through all the keys in a database, retrieve the value associated with a particular key, and find if a particular key exists. Both the keys and the values are strings.

The following program maintains a list of usernames and passwords in a DBM database. The username is the first command-line argument, and the password is the second argument. If the given username already exists in the database, the password is changed to the given password; otherwise the user and password combination are added to the database:

```
$user = $_SERVER['argv'][1];
$password = $_SERVER['argv'][2];

$data_file = '/tmp/users.db';

$dbh = dba_open($data_file,'c','gdbm') or die("Can't open db $data_file");

if (dba_exists($user,$dbh)) {
    print "User $user exists. Changing password.";
} else {
    print "Adding user $user.";
}

dba_replace($user,$password,$dbh) or die("Can't write to database $data_file");

dba_close($dbh);
```

The dba_open( ) function returns a handle to a DBM file (or false on error). It takes three arguments. The first is the filename of the DBM file. The second argument is the mode for opening the file. A mode of 'r' opens an existing database for read-only access, and 'w' opens an existing database for read-write access. The 'c' mode opens a database for read-write access and creates the database if it doesn't already exist. Last, 'n' does the same thing as 'c', but if the database already exists, 'n' empties it. The third argument to dba_open( ) is which DBM handler to use; this example uses 'gdbm'. To find what DBM handlers are compiled into your PHP installation, look at the "DBA" section of the output from phpinfo( ). The "Supported handlers" line gives you your choices.

To find if a key has been set in a DBM database, use dba_exists( ). It takes two arguments: a string key and a DBM file handle. It looks for the key in the DBM file and returns true if it finds the key (or false if it doesn't). The dba_replace( ) function takes three arguments: a string key, a string value, and a DBM file handle. It puts the key/value pair into the DBM file. If an entry already exists with the given key, it overwrites that entry with the new value.

To close a database, call dba_close( ). A DBM file opened with dba_open( ) is automatically closed at the end of a request, but you need to call dba_close( ) explicitly to close persistent connections created with dba_popen( ).

You can use dba_firstkey( ) and dba_nextkey( ) to iterate through all the keys in a DBM file and dba_fetch( ) to retrieve the values associated with each key. This program calculates the total length of all passwords in a DBM file:

```
$data_file = '/tmp/users.db';
$total_length = 0;
if (! ($dbh = dba_open($data_file,'r','gdbm'))) {
    die("Can't open database $data_file");
}

$k = dba_firstkey($dbh);
while ($k) {
    $total_length += strlen(dba_fetch($k,$dbh));
    $k = dba_nextkey($dbh);
}

print "Total length of all passwords is $total_length characters.";

dba_close($dbh);
```

The dba_firstkey( ) function initializes $k to the first key in the DBM file. Each time through the while loop, dba_fetch( ) retrieves the value associated with key $k and $total_length is incremented by the length of the value (calculated with strlen( )). With dba_nextkey( ), $k is set to the next key in the file.

You can use serialize( ) to store complex data in a DBM file, just like in a text file. However, the data in the DBM file can be indexed by a key:

```
$dbh = dba_open('users.db','c','gdbm') or die($php_errormsg);

// read in and unserialize the data
if ($exists = dba_exists($_REQUEST['username'],$dbh)) {
    $serialized_data = dba_fetch($_REQUEST['username'],$dbh) or die($php_errormsg);
    $data = unserialize($serialized_data);
} else {
    $data = array();
}

// update values
if ($_REQUEST['new_password']) {
```

```
    $data['password'] = $_REQUEST['new_password'];
}
$data['last_access'] = time();

// write data back to file
if ($exists) {
    dba_replace($_REQUEST['username'],serialize($data),$dbh);
} else {
    dba_insert($_REQUEST['username'],serialize($data),$dbh);
}

dba_close($dbh);
```

While this example can store multiple users' data in the same file, you can't search, for example, a user's last access time, without looping through each key in the file. Structured data like this belongs in a SQL database.

Each DBM handler has different behavior in some areas. For example, GDBM provides internal locking. If one process has opened a GDBM file in read-write mode, other calls to dba_open( ) to open the same file in read-write mode will fail. The DB3 handler, however, provides no such internal locking; you need to do that with additional code, as discussed for text files in Recipe 18.24. Two DBA functions are also database-specific: dba_optimize( ) and dba_sync( ). The dba_optimize( ) function calls a handler-specific DBM file-optimization function. Currently, this is implemented only for GDBM, for which its gdbm_reorganize( ) function is called. The dba_sync( ) function calls a handler-specific DBM file synchronizing function. For DB2 and DB3, their sync( ) function is called. For GDBM, its gdbm_sync( ) function is called. Nothing happens for other DBM handlers.

Using a DBM database is a step up from a text file but it lacks most features of a SQL database. Your data structure is limited to key/value pairs, and locking robustness varies greatly depending on the DBM handler. Still, DBM handlers can be a good choice for heavily accessed read-only data; for example, the Internet Movie Database uses DBM databases.

See Also

Recipe 5.7 discusses serializing data; Recipe 18.24 studies the details of file locking; documentation on the DBA functions at *http://www.php.net/dba*; for more information on the DB2 and DB3 DBM handlers, see *http://www.sleepycat.com/ faq.html#program*; for GDBM, check out *http://www.gnu.org/directory/gdbm.html* or *http://www.mit.edu:8001/afs/athena.mit.edu/project/gnu/doc/html/gdbm_toc.html*; CDB info is at *http://cr.yp.to/cdb.html*; the Internet Movie Database's technical specifications are at *http://us.imdb.com/Help/Classes/Master/tech-info*.

10.3   Connecting to a SQL Database

Problem

You want access to a SQL database.

Solution

Use the connect( ) method of PEAR DB:

```
require 'DB.php';

$dsn = 'mysql://david:foo!bar@localhost/test';

$dbh = DB::connect($dsn);
if (DB::isError($dbh)) { die ($dbh->getMessage()); }
```

Discussion

To use PEAR DB, you must download it from PEAR at:

http://pear.php.net/package-info.php?package=DB

After loading the DB functions from *DB.php*, connect to the database with DB::
connect( ), execute the query with $dbh->query( ), and retrieve each row with $sth->
fetchRow( ). The Solution example connects to MySQL. To connect to Oracle
instead, you just need to change $dsn. This variable holds the data source name
(DSN), a string that specifies which database to connect to and how to connect to it.
Here's the value for Oracle:

```
$dsn = 'oci8://david:foo!bar@ORAINST';
```

For PostgreSQL, $dsn is:

```
$dsn = 'pgsql://david:foo!bar@unix(/tmp/.s.PGSQL.5432)/test';
```

The PostgreSQL DSN is a little more complicated because it specifies that the connection should be made using a local Unix socket (whose pathname is */tmp/
.s.PGSQL.5432*) instead of a TCP/IP connection. In general, the form of a data
source name is:

database_interface://user:password@hostname/database

The *database_interface* part of the DSN is the kind of database you're using, such as
Oracle, MySQL, etc. Currently, PEAR supports 10 database backends, as listed in
Table 10-1.

Table 10-1. PEAR DB backends

Name	Database
fbsql	FrontBase
ibase	Interbase
ifx	Informix
msql	Mini-SQL
mssql	Microsoft SQL Server
mysql	MySQL
oci8	Oracle (using the OCI8 interface)
odbc	ODBC
pgsql	PostgreSQL
sybase	Sybase

To use a particular PEAR DB backend, PHP must be built with support for the database that corresponds to the backend. Note that to use the Oracle OCI8 backend, PHP must have the OCI8 extension (--with-oci8 when building). The older PHP oracle extension (--with-oracle) isn't compatible with PEAR DB.

user and *password* are the username and password to use to connect to the database. *hostname* is usually the hostname that the database is running on, but it can also be the name of an instance (for Oracle) or the special syntax used previously to indicate a local socket. *database* is the name of the logical database to use, such as what you'd specify with the *dbname* parameter in pg_connect( ) or the argument to mysql_select_db( ).

PEAR DB is by no means the only database abstraction layer available for PHP. We've chosen to focus on it because it's easy to use and widely available. Other database abstraction layers include ADOdb (*http://php.weblogs.com/ADODB*), Metabase (*http://en.static.phpclasses.org/browse.html/package/20.html*), the DB_Sql class in PHPLib (*http://phplib.sourceforge.net/*), and MDB (*http://pear.php.net/package-info.php?package=MDB*).

See Also

Recipe 10.4 for querying a SQL database; Recipe 10.6 for modifying a SQL database; Pear DB at *http://pear.php.net/package-info.php?package=DB*; documentation on DB::connect( ) at *http://pear.php.net/manual/en/core.db.tut_connect.php* and *http://pear.php.net/manual/en/core.db.connect.php*; information on DSNs at *http://pear.php.net/manual/en/core.db.tut_dsn.php*.

10.4   Querying a SQL Database

Problem

You want to retrieve some data from your database.

Solution

Use DB::query( ) from PEAR DB to send the SQL query to the database, and then
DB_Result::fetchRow( ) or DB_Result::fetchInto( ) to retrieve each row of the
result:

```
// using fetchRow()
$sth = $dbh->query("SELECT sign FROM zodiac WHERE element LIKE 'fire'");
if (DB::isError($sth)) { die($sth->getMessage()); }

while($row = $sth->fetchRow()) {
    print $row[0]."\n";
}

// using fetchInto()
$sth = $dbh->query("SELECT sign FROM zodiac WHERE element LIKE 'fire'");
if (DB::isError($sth)) { die($sth->getMessage()); }

while($sth->fetchInto($row)) {
    print $row[0]."\n";
}
```

Discussion

The fetchRow( ) method returns data, while fetchInto( ) puts the data into a variable you pass it. Both fetchRow( ) and fetchInto( ) return NULL when no more rows
are available. If either encounter an error when retrieving a row, they return a DB_
Error object, just as the DB::connect( ) and DB::query( ) methods do. You can insert
a check for this inside your loop:

```
while($row = $sth->fetchRow()) {
    if (DB::isError($row)) { die($row->getMessage()); }
    print $row[0]."\n";
}
```

If magic_quotes_gpc is on, you can use form variables directly in your queries:

```
$sth = $dbh->query(
    "SELECT sign FROM zodiac WHERE element LIKE '" . $_REQUEST['element'] . "'");
```

If not, escape the value with DB::quote( ), or use a placeholder in the query:

```
$sth = $dbh->query("SELECT sign FROM zodiac WHERE element LIKE " .
                    $dbh->quote($_REQUEST['element']));
```

```
$sth = $dbh->query('SELECT sign FROM zodiac WHERE element LIKE ?',
                   array($_REQUEST['element']));
```

Recipe 10.9 goes into detail about when you need to quote values and how to do it.

By default, fetchRow( ) and fetchInto( ) put data in numeric arrays. You can tell them to use associative arrays or objects by passing an additional parameter to either method. For associative arrays, use DB_FETCHMODE_ASSOC:

```
while($row = $sth->fetchRow(DB_FETCHMODE_ASSOC)) {
    print $row['sign']."\n";
}

while($sth->fetchInto($row,DB_FETCHMODE_ASSOC)) {
    print $row['sign']."\n";
}
```

For objects, use DB_FETCHMODE_OBJECT:

```
while($row = $sth->fetchRow(DB_FETCHMODE_OBJECT)) {
    print $row->sign."\n";
}

while($sth->fetchInto($row,DB_FETCHMODE_OBJECT)) {
    print $row->sign."\n";
}
```

Whatever the fetch mode, the methods still return NULL when there is no more data to retrieve and a DB_Error object on error. The default numeric array behavior can be specified with DB_FETCHMODE_ORDERED. You can set a fetch mode to be used in all subsequent calls to fetchRow( ) or fetchInto( ) with DB::setFetchMode( ):

```
$dbh->setFetchMode(DB_FETCHMODE_OBJECT);

while($row = $sth->fetchRow()) {
    print $row->sign."\n";
}

// subsequent queries and calls to fetchRow() also return objects
```

See Also

Recipe 10.3 for connecting to a SQL database; Recipe 10.6 for modifying a SQL database; Recipe 10.9 details how to quote data for safe inclusion in queries; documentation on DB::query( ) at *http://pear.php.net/manual/en/core.db.tut_query.php* and *http://pear.php.net/manual/en/core.db.query.php*, fetching at *http://pear.php.net/manual/en/core.db.tut_fetch.php*, DB_Result::fetchRow( ) at *http://pear.php.net/manual/en/core.db.fetchrow.php*, DB_Result::fetchInto( ) at *http://pear.php.net/manual/en/core.db.fetchinto.php*, and DB::setFetchMode( ) at *http://pear.php.net/manual/en/core.db.setfetchmode.php*.

10.5   Retrieving Rows Without a Loop

Problem

You want a concise way to execute a query and retrieve the data it returns.

Solution

With PEAR DB, use DB::getRow( ) to retrieve the first (or only) row from a query:

```
$row = $dbh->getRow("SELECT planet,symbol FROM zodiac WHERE sign LIKE 'Pisces'");
```

Use DB::getAll( ) to retrieve all rows from a query:

```
$rows = $dbh->getAll("SELECT planet,symbol FROM zodiac WHERE element LIKE 'fire'");
```

Use DB::getOne( ) to retrieve just one column from one row:

```
$col = $dbh->getOne("SELECT symbol FROM zodiac WHERE sign = 'Libra'");
```

Use DB::getCol( ) to retrieve a column from all rows:

```
$cols = $dbh->getCol('SELECT symbol FROM zodiac');
```

Use DB::getAssoc( ) to retrieve all rows from a query into an associative array indexed by the first column of the query:

```
$assoc = $dbh->getAssoc(
    "SELECT sign,symbol,planet FROM zodiac WHERE element LIKE 'water'");
```

Discussion

All these functions return a DB_Error object if an error occurs in executing a query or retrieving the results. If the query returns no results, getRow( ) and getOne( ) return NULL; getAll( ), getCol( ), and getAssoc( ) return an empty array.

When returning results, getRow( ) returns an array or object, depending on the current fetch mode. The getAll( ) method returns an array of arrays or array of objects, also depending on the fetch mode. The single result getOne( ) returns is usually a string, because PHP database drivers generally cast retrieved results into strings. Similarly, getCol( ) returns an array of results whose values are usually strings. The results from getAssoc( ) are returned as an array. The type of elements of that array are controlled by the fetch mode.

Like DB::query( ), you can pass these functions a query with placeholders in it and an array of parameters to fill the placeholders. The parameters are properly quoted when they replace the placeholders in the query:

```
$row = $dbh->getRow('SELECT planet,symbol FROM zodiac WHERE sign LIKE ?',
                    array('Pisces'));
```

The parameter array is the second argument to each of these functions, except getCol( ) and getAssoc( ). For these two functions, the parameter array is the third argument. The second argument to getCol( ) is a column number to return if you don't want the first column (column number 0). For example, this returns the values of the planet column:

```
$cols = $dbh->getCol('SELECT symbol,planet FROM zodiac',1);
```

The second argument to getAssoc( ) is a boolean that tells the function whether to force the values in the associative array it returns to be arrays themselves even if they could be scalars. Take this query for example:

```
$assoc = $dbh->getAssoc(
    "SELECT sign,symbol FROM zodiac WHERE element LIKE 'water'");
print_r($assoc);
Array
(
    [Cancer] => Crab
    [Scorpio] => Scorpion
    [Pisces] => Fishes
)
```

Because the query passed to getAssoc( ) asks only for two columns, the first column is the array key, and the second column is the scalar array value. Here's how to force the array values to be one-element arrays:

```
$assoc = $dbh->getAssoc(
    "SELECT sign,symbol FROM zodiac WHERE element LIKE 'water'",true);
print_r($assoc);
Array
(
    [Cancer] => Array
        (
            [0] => Crab
        )
    [Scorpio] => Array
        (
            [0] => Scorpion
        )
    [Pisces] => Array
        (
            [0] => Fishes
        )
)
```

Just as fetchRow( ) and fetchInto( ) do, getRow( ), getAssoc( ), and getAll( ) put data in numeric arrays by default. You can pass them a fetch mode (the third argument to getRow( ) or getAll( ), the fourth argument to getAssoc( )). They also respect the fetch mode set by DB::setFetchMode( ).

See Also

Recipe 10.4 for more on the fetch mode; documentation on fetching at *http://pear.php.net/manual/en/core.db.tut_fetch.php*, DB::getRow( ) at *http://pear.php.net/manual/en/core.db.getrow.php*, DB::getAll( ) at *http://pear.php.net/manual/en/core.db.getall.php*, DB::getOne( ) at *http://pear.php.net/manual/en/core.db.getone.php*, DB::getCol( ) at *http://pear.php.net/manual/en/core.db.getcol.php*, and DB::getAssoc( ) at *http://pear.php.net/manual/en/core.db.getassoc.php*.

10.6   Modifying Data in a SQL Database

Problem

You want to add, remove, or change data in a SQL database.

Solution

With PEAR DB, use DB::query( ) to send an INSERT, DELETE, or UPDATE command:

```
$dbh->query("INSERT INTO family (id,name) VALUES (1,'Vito')");

$dbh->query("DELETE FROM family WHERE name LIKE 'Fredo'");

$dbh->query("UPDATE family SET is_naive = 1 WHERE name LIKE 'Kay'");
```

You can also prepare a query with DB::prepare( ) and execute it with DB::execute( ):

```
$prh = $dbh->prepare('INSERT INTO family (id,name) VALUES (?,?)');
$dbh->execute($prh,array(1,'Vito'));

$prh = $dbh->prepare('DELETE FROM family WHERE name LIKE ?');
$dbh->execute($prh,array('Fredo'));

$prh = $dbh->prepare('UPDATE family SET is_naive = ? WHERE name LIKE ?');
$dbh->execute($prh,array(1,'Kay'));
```

Discussion

The query( ) method sends to the database whatever it's passed, so it can be used for queries that retrieve data or queries that modify data.

The prepare( ) and execute( ) methods are especially useful for queries that you want to execute multiple times. Once you've prepared a query, you can execute it with new values without re-preparing it:

```
$prh = $dbh->prepare('DELETE FROM family WHERE name LIKE ?');
$dbh->execute($prh,array('Fredo'));
$dbh->execute($prh,array('Sonny'));
$dbh->execute($prh,array('Luca Brasi'));
```

See Also

Recipe 10.3 for connecting to a SQL database; Recipe 10.4 for querying a SQL database; Recipe 10.7 discusses prepare( ) and execute( ) in detail; documentation on DB::query( ) at *http://pear.php.net/manual/en/core.db.query.php*, DB::prepare( ) at *http://pear.php.net/manual/en/core.db.prepare.php*, and DB::execute( ) at *http://pear.php.net/manual/en/core.db.execute.php*.

10.7 Repeating Queries Efficiently

Problem

You want to run the same query multiple times, substituting in different values each time.

Solution

With PEAR DB, set up the query with DB::prepare( ) and then run the query with DB::execute( ). The placeholders in the query passed to prepare( ) are replaced with data by execute( ):

```
$prh = $dbh->prepare("SELECT sign FROM zodiac WHERE element LIKE ?");

$sth = $dbh->execute($prh,array('fire'));
while($sth->fetchInto($row)) {
    print $row[0]."\n";
}

$sth = $dbh->execute($prh,array('water'));
while($sth->fetchInto($row)) {
    print $row[0]."\n";
}
```

Discussion

In the Solution, the first execute( ) runs the query:

```
SELECT sign FROM zodiac WHERE element LIKE 'fire'
```

The second runs:

```
SELECT sign FROM zodiac WHERE element LIKE 'water'
```

Each time, execute( ) substitutes the value in its second argument for the ? placeholder. If there is more than one placeholder, put the arguments in the array in the order they should appear in the query:

```
$prh = $dbh->prepare(
    "SELECT sign FROM zodiac WHERE element LIKE ? OR planet LIKE ?");
```

```
// SELECT sign FROM zodiac WHERE element LIKE 'earth' OR planet LIKE 'Mars'
$sth = $dbh->execute($prh,array('earth','Mars'));
```

Values that replace a ? placeholder are appropriately quoted. To insert the contents of a file instead, use the & placeholder and pass execute( ) the filename:

```
/* The structure of the pictures table is:
    CREATE TABLE pictures (
        mime_type CHAR(20),
        data      LONGBLOB
    )
*/

$prh = $dbh->prepare('INSERT INTO pictures (mime_type,data) VALUES (?,&)');
$sth = $dbh->execute($prh,array('image/jpeg','test.jpeg'));
```

To tell execute( ) not to quote a value, use the ! parameter. This is dangerous when applied to user input; it's useful, however, when one of the values is not a scalar, but a database function. For example, this query uses the NOW( ) function to insert the current date and time in a DATETIME column:

```
$prh = $dbh->prepare("INSERT INTO warnings (message,message_time) VALUES (?,!)");
$dbh->execute($prh,array("Don't cross the streams!",NOW()));
```

To execute a prepared statement many times with different arguments each time, use executeMultiple( ). Instead of just passing it one array of arguments as with execute( ), you pass it an array of argument arrays:

```
$prh = $dbh->prepare('INSERT INTO pictures (mime_type,data) VALUES (?,&)');

$ar = array(array('image/jpeg','earth.jpeg'),
            array('image/gif','wind.gif'),
            array('image/jpeg','fire.jpeg'));

$sth = $dbh->executeMultiple($prh,$ar);
```

You must declare the array first and then pass it to executeMultiple( ), or PHP gives an error that says you are passing executeMultiple( ) a parameter by reference. Although executeMultiple( ) loops through each argument in the array, if it encounters an error part-way through, it doesn't continue on with the rest of the arguments. If all queries succeed, executeMultiple( ) returns the constant DB_OK. Because executeMultiple( ) never returns a result object, you can't use it for queries that return data.

The Interbase and OCI8 DB backends take advantage of native database features so that prepare( )/execute( ) is more efficient than query( ) for INSERT/UPDATE/DELETE queries. The Interbase backend uses the ibase_prepare( ) and ibase_execute( ) functions, and the OCI8 backend uses the OCIParse( ), OCIBindByName( ), and OCIExecute( ) functions. Other database backends construct queries to execute by interpolating the supplied values for the placeholders.

See Also

Documentation on `DB::prepare()` at *http://pear.php.net/manual/en/core.db.prepare.php*, `DB::execute()` at *http://pear.php.net/manual/en/core.db.execute.php*, and `DB::executeMultiple()` at *http://pear.php.net/manual/en/core.db.executemultiple.php*; an overview of executing queries is at *http://pear.php.net/manual/en/core.db.tut_execute.php*.

10.8   Finding the Number of Rows Returned by a Query

Problem

You want to know how many rows a `SELECT` query returned, or you want to know how many rows were changed by an `INSERT`, `UPDATE`, or `DELETE` query.

Solution

To find the number of rows returned by a `SELECT` query, use PEAR DB's `DB_Result::numRows()`:

```
// query
$sth = $dbh->query('SELECT * FROM zodiac WHERE element LIKE ?', array('water'));
$water_rows = $sth->numRows();

// prepare and execute
$prh = $dbh->prepare('SELECT * FROM zodiac WHERE element LIKE ?');
$sth = $dbh->execute($prh,array('fire'));
$fire_rows = $sth->numRows();
```

To find the number of rows changed by an `INSERT`, `UPDATE`, or `DELETE` query, use `DB::affectedRows()`:

```
$sth = $dbh->query('DELETE FROM zodiac WHERE element LIKE ?',array('fire'));
$deleted_rows = $dbh->affectedRows();

$prh = $dbh->prepare('INSERT INTO zodiac (sign,symbol) VALUES (?,?)',
                     array('Leap Day','Kangaroo'));
$dbh->execute($prh,$sth);
$inserted_rows = $dbh->affectedRows();

$dbh->query('UPDATE zodiac SET planet = ? WHERE sign LIKE ?',
            array('Trantor','Leap Day'));
$updated_rows = $dbh->affectedRows();
```

Discussion

The number of rows in a result set is a property of that result set, so that numRows( ) is called on the statement handle and not the database handle. The number of rows affected by a data manipulation query, however, can't be a property of a result set, because those queries don't return result sets. As a result, affectedRows( ) is a method of the database handle.

See Also

Documentation on DB_Result::numRows( ) at *http://pear.php.net/manual/en/core.db.numrows.php* and DB::affectedRows( ) at *http://pear.php.net/manual/en/core.db.affectedrows.php*.

10.9 Escaping Quotes

Problem

You need to make text or binary data safe for queries.

Solution

Write all your queries with placeholders and pass values to fill the placeholders in an array:

```
$sth = $dbh->query('UPDATE zodiac SET planet = ? WHERE id = 2',
                   array('Melmac'));

$rows = $dbh->getAll('SELECT * FROM zodiac WHERE planet LIKE ?',
                     array('M%'));
```

You can also use PEAR DB's DB::quote( ) to escape special characters and make sure strings are appropriately marked (usually with single quotes around them):

```
$planet = $dbh->quote($planet);
$dbh->query("UPDATE zodiac SET planet = $planet WHERE id = 2");
```

If $planet is Melmac, $dbh->quote($planet) if you are using MySQL returns 'Melmac'. If $planet is Ork's Moon, $dbh->quote($planet) returns 'Ork\'s Moon'.

Discussion

The DB::quote( ) method makes sure that text or binary data is appropriately quoted, but you also need to quote the SQL wildcard characters % and _ to ensure that SELECT statements return the right results. If $planet is set to Melm%, this query returns rows with planet set to Melmac, Melmacko, Melmacedonia, or anything else beginning with Melm:

```
$planet = $dbh->quote($planet);
$dbh->query("SELECT * FROM zodiac WHERE planet LIKE $planet");
```

Because % is the SQL wildcard meaning "match any number of characters" (like * in shell globbing) and _ is the SQL wildcard meaning "match one character" (like ? in shell globbing), those need to be backslash-escaped as well. Use strtr( ) to escape them:

```
$planet = $dbh->quote($planet);
$planet = strtr($planet,array('_' => '\_', '%' => '\%'));
$dbh->query("SELECT * FROM zodiac WHERE planet LIKE $planet");
```

strtr( ) must be called after DB::quote( ). Otherwise, DB::quote( ) would backslash-escape the backslashes strtr( ) adds. With DB::quote( ) first, Melm_ is turned into Melm_, which is interpreted by the database to mean "the string M e l m followed by a literal underscore character." With DB::quote( ) after strtr( ), Melm_ is turned into Melm_, which is interpreted by the database to mean "the string Melm followed by a literal backslash character, followed by the underscore wildcard."

A quote method is defined in the DB base class, but some of the database-specific subclasses override that method to provide appropriate quoting behavior for the particular database in use. By using DB::quote( ) instead of replacing specific characters, your program is more portable.

Quoting of placeholder values happens even if magic_quotes_gpc or magic_quotes_runtime is turned on. Similarly, if you call DB::quote( ) on a value when magic quotes are active, the value gets quoted anyway. For maximum portability, remove the magic quotes-supplied backslashes before you use a query with placeholders or call DB::quote( ):

```
$fruit = ini_get('magic_quotes_gpc') ? stripslashes($_REQUEST['fruit']) :
    $_REQUEST['fruit'];

$dbh->query('UPDATE orchard SET trees = trees - 1 WHERE fruit LIKE ?',
            array($fruit));
```

See Also

Documentation on DB::quote( ) at *http://pear.php.net/manual/en/core.db.quote.php* and magic quotes at *http://www.php.net/manual/en/ref.info.php#ini.magic-quotes-gpc*.

10.10 Logging Debugging Information and Errors

Problem

You want access to information to help you debug database problems. For example, when a query fails, you want to see what error message the database returns.

Solution

Use DB::isError( ) to investigate the results of a single query:

```
$sth = $dbh->query("SELECT aroma FROM zodiac WHERE element LIKE 'fire'");
DB::isError($sth) and print 'Database Error: '.$sth->getMessage();
```

Use DB::setErrorHandling( ) to automatically take action on any database error:

```
$dbh->setErrorHandling(PEAR_ERROR_PRINT);
$sth = $dbh->query("SELECT aroma FROM zodiac WHERE element LIKE 'fire'");
```

Discussion

When they encounter an error, most PEAR DB methods return an DB_Error object.
The DB::isError( ) method returns true if it's passed a DB_Error object, so you can
use that to test the results of individual queries. The DB_Error class is a subclass of
PEAR::Error, so you can use methods such as getMessage( ) to display information
about the error. If you want to display everything in the error object, use print_r( ):

```
$sth = $dbh->query('SELECT aroma FROM zodiac WHERE element LIKE 'fire'");
if (DB::isError($sth)) {
    print_r($sth);
}
```

Since there is no aroma column in the zodiac table, this prints:

```
db_error Object
(
    [error_message_prefix] =>
    [mode] => 1
    [level] => 1024
    [code] => -19
    [message] => DB Error: no such field
    [userinfo] => SELECT aroma FROM zodiac WHERE element LIKE 'fire' \
[nativecode=1054 ** Unknown column 'aroma' in 'field list']
    [callback] =>
)
```

Using setErrorHandling( ) lets you define a behavior that's invoked automatically
whenever there's a database error. Tell setErrorHandling( ) what to do by passing it
a PEAR_ERROR constant. The PEAR_ERROR_PRINT constant prints the error message, but
program execution continues:

```
$dbh->setErrorHandling(PEAR_ERROR_PRINT);
$sth = $dbh->query("SELECT aroma FROM zodiac WHERE element LIKE 'fire'");
```

This prints:

```
DB Error: no such field
```

To print out an error message and then quit, use PEAR_ERROR_DIE. You can also use
the PEAR_ERROR_CALLBACK constant to run a custom function when an error is raised.
This custom function can print out even more detailed information:

```
function pc_log_error($error_obj) {
    error_log(sprintf("%s (%s)",$error_obj->message,$error_obj->userinfo));
}

$dbh->setErrorHandling(PEAR_ERROR_CALLBACK,'pc_log_error');
$sth = $dbh->query("SELECT aroma FROM zodiac WHERE element LIKE 'fire'");
```

When the incorrect SQL in the $dbh->query( ) method raises an error, pc_log_error( )
is called with the DB_Error object passed to it. The pc_log_error( ) callback uses the
properties of the DB_Error object to print a more complete message to the error log:

```
DB Error: no such field (SELECT aroma FROM zodiac WHERE element
LIKE 'fire' [nativecode=Unknown column 'aroma' in 'field list'])
```

To capture all the data in the error object and write it to the error log, use print_r( )
with output buffering in the error callback:

```
function pc_log_error($error_obj) {
    ob_start();
    print_r($error_obj);
    $dump = ob_get_contents();
    ob_end_clean();
    error_log('Database Error: '.$dump);
}

$dbh->setErrorHandling(PEAR_ERROR_CALLBACK,'pc_log_error');
$sth = $dbh->query("SELECT aroma FROM zodiac WHERE element LIKE 'fire'");
```

This includes all of the error object's fields in the error log message:

```
Database Error: db_error Object
(
    [error_message_prefix] =>
    [mode] => 16
    [level] => 1024
    [code] => -19
    [message] => DB Error: no such field
    [userinfo] => SELECT aroma FROM zodiac WHERE element LIKE 'fire' \
[nativecode=1054 ** Unknown column 'aroma' in 'field list']
    [callback] => pc_log_error
)
```

You can also have a DB_Error generate an internal PHP error with PEAR_ERROR_
TRIGGER:

```
$dbh->setErrorHandling(PEAR_ERROR_TRIGGER);
$sth = $dbh->query("SELECT aroma FROM zodiac WHERE element LIKE 'fire'");
```

With the PEAR_ERROR_TRIGGER constant, setErrorHandling( ) uses PHP's trigger_
error( ) function to generate an internal error. This error is handled by PHP's default
error handler or a user-defined error handler set by set_error_handler( ). By default,
the internal error is an E_USER_NOTICE:

```
<br />
<b>Notice</b>:  DB Error: no such field in <b>/usr/local/lib/php/PEAR.php</b> \
on line <b>593</b><br />
```

Make the error an E_USER_WARNING or E_USER_ERROR by passing a second argument to setErrorHandling( ):

```
$dbh->setErrorHandling(PEAR_ERROR_TRIGGER,E_USER_ERROR);
$sth = $dbh->query("SELECT aroma FROM zodiac WHERE element LIKE 'fire'");
```

If the error is an E_USER_ERROR, program execution terminates after displaying the error message:

```
<br />
<b>Fatal error</b>:  DB Error: no such field in <b>/usr/local/lib/php/PEAR.php</b>
on line <b>593</b><br />
```

See Also

Recipe 8.12 for a discussion of output buffering; Recipes 8.15 through 8.17 for discussions on error handling and writing a custom error handler; documentation on DB::isError( ) at *http://pear.php.net/manual/en/core.db.iserror.php*, the PEAR_Error class at *http://pear.php.net/manual/en/class.pear-error.php*, trigger_error( ) at *http://www.php.net/trigger-error*, and set_error_handler( ) at *http://www.php.net/set-error-handler*.

10.11 Assigning Unique ID Values Automatically

Problem

You want to use an incrementing sequence of integers for unique IDs. For example, you want to assign unique IDs to users, articles, or other objects as you add them to your database.

Solution

With PEAR DB, use DB::nextId( ) with a sequence name to get the next integer in a sequence:

```
$id = $dbh->nextId('user_ids');
```

Discussion

By default, the sequence is created if it doesn't already exist, and the first ID in the sequence is 1. You can use the integer returned from nextId( ) in subsequent INSERT statements:

```
$id = $dbh->nextId('user_ids');
$dbh->query("INSERT INTO users (id,name) VALUES ($id,'david')");
```

This inserts a record into the users table with an id of 1 and a name of david. To prevent a sequence from being created if it doesn't already exist, pass false as a second argument to nextId( ):

```
$id = $dbh->nextId('user_ids',false);
$dbh->query("INSERT INTO users (id,name) VALUES ($id,'david')");
```

To create a sequence, use createSequence( ); to drop a sequence, use dropSequence( ):

```
$dbh->createSequence('flowers');
$id = $dbh->nextId('flowers');
$dbh->dropSequence('flowers');
```

A DB_Error object is returned if you try to create a sequence that already exists or drop a sequence that doesn't.

See Also

Documentation on DB::nextId( ) at *http://pear.php.net/manual/en/core.db.nextid.php*, DB::createSequence( ) at *http://pear.php.net/manual/en/core.db.createsequence.php*, and DB::dropSequence( ) at *http://pear.php.net/manual/en/core.db.dropsequence.php*.

10.12 Building Queries Programmatically

Problem

You want to construct an INSERT or UPDATE query from an array of field names. For example, you want to insert a new user into your database. Instead of hardcoding each field of user information (such as username, email address, postal address, birthdate, etc.), you put the field names in an array and use the array to build the query. This is easier to maintain, especially if you need to conditionally INSERT or UPDATE with the same set of fields.

Solution

To construct an UPDATE query, build an array of field/value pairs and then join( ) together each element of that array:

```
$fields = array('symbol','planet','element');

$update_fields = array();
foreach ($fields as $field) {
    $update_fields[] = "$field = " . $dbh->quote($GLOBALS[$field]);
}
$sql = 'UPDATE zodiac SET ' . join(',',$update_fields)
    . ' WHERE sign = ' . $dbh->quote($sign);
```

For an INSERT query, construct an array of values in the same order as the fields, and build the query by applying join( ) to each array:

```
$fields = array('symbol','planet','element');

$insert_values = array();
foreach ($fields as $field) {
    $insert_values[] = $dbh->quote($GLOBALS[$field]);
}
$sql = 'INSERT INTO zodiac (' . join(',',$fields) . ') VALUES ('
        . join(',',$insert_values) . ')';
```

If you have PEAR DB Version 1.3 or later, use the DB::autoPrepare( ) method:

```
$fields = array('symbol','planet','element');

// UPDATE: specify the WHERE clause
$update_prh = $dbh->autoPrepare('zodiac',$fields,DB_AUTOQUERY_UPDATE,
                                'sign = ?');
$update_values = array();
foreach ($fields as $field) { $update_values[] = $GLOBALS[$field]; }
$update_values[] = $GLOBALS['sign'];
$dbh->execute($update_prh,$update_values);

// INSERT: no WHERE clause
$insert_prh = $dbh->autoPrepare('zodiac',$fields,DB_AUTOQUERY_INSERT);
$insert_values = array();
foreach ($fields as $field) { $insert_values[] = $GLOBALS[$field]; }
$dbh->execute($insert_prh,$insert_values);
```

Discussion

The DB::autoPrepare( ) method is concise and easy to use if you have a recent version of DB. PHP 4.2.2 comes with DB 1.2. Newer versions of DB can be downloaded from PEAR. Use method_exists( ) to check whether your version of DB supports autoPrepare( ):

```
if (method_exists($dbh,'autoPrepare')) {
    $prh = $dbh->autoPrepare('zodiac',$fields,DB_AUTOQUERY_UPDATE','sign = ?');
    // ...
} else {
    error_log("Can't use autoPrepare");
    exit;
}
```

If you can't use DB::autoPrepare( ), the array-manipulation techniques shown in the Solution accomplish the same thing. If you use sequence-generated integers as primary keys, you can combine the two query-construction techniques into one function. That function determines whether a record exists and then generates the correct query, including a new ID, as shown in the pc_build_query( ) function in Example 10-1.

Example 10-1. pc_build_query()

```
function pc_build_query($dbh,$key_field,$fields,$table) {

    if (! empty($_REQUEST[$key_field])) {
```

Example 10-1. pc_build_query() (continued)

```
        $update_fields = array();
        foreach ($fields as $field) {
            $update_fields[] = "$field = ".$dbh->quote($_REQUEST[$field]);
        }
        return "UPDATE $table SET " . join(',',$update_fields) .
            " WHERE $key_field = ".$_REQUEST[$key_field];
    } else {
        $insert_values = array();
        foreach ($fields as $field) {
            $insert_values[] = $dbh->quote($_REQUEST[$field]);
        }
        $next_id = $dbh->nextId($table);
        return "INSERT INTO $table ($key_field," . join(',',$fields) .
            ") VALUES ($next_id," . join(',',$insert_values) . ')';
    }
}
```

Using this function, you can make a simple page to edit all the information in the zodiac table:

```
require 'DB.php';

$dbh = DB::connect('mysql://test:@localhost/test');
$dbh->setFetchMode(DB_FETCHMODE_OBJECT);

$fields = array('sign','symbol','planet','element',
                'start_month','start_day','end_month','end_day');

switch ($_REQUEST['cmd']) {
 case 'edit':
    $row = $dbh->getRow('SELECT ' . join(',',$fields) .
                        " FROM zodiac WHERE id = ?",array($_REQUEST['id']));
 case 'add':
    print '<form method="post" action="'.$_SERVER['PHP_SELF'].'">';
    print '<input type="hidden" name="cmd" value="save">';
    print '<table>';
    if ('edit' == $_REQUEST['cmd']) {
        printf('<input type="hidden" name="id" value="%d">',
            $_REQUEST['id']);
    }
    foreach ($fields as $field) {
        if ('edit' == $_REQUEST['cmd']) {
            $value = htmlspecialchars($row->$field);
        } else {
            $value = '';
        }
        printf('<tr><td>%s: </td><td><input type="text" name="%s" value="%s">',
            $field,$field,$value);
        printf('</td></tr>');
    }
    print '<tr><td></td><td><input type="submit" value="Save"></td></tr>';
    print '</table></form>';
    break;
```

```
case 'save':
    $sql = pc_build_query($dbh,'id',$fields,'zodiac');
    if (DB::isError($sth = $dbh->query($sql))) {
        print "Couldn't add info: ".$sth->getMessage();
    } else {
        print "Added info.";
    }
    print '<hr>';
default:
    $sth = $dbh->query('SELECT id,sign FROM zodiac');
    print '<ul>';
    while ($row = $sth->fetchRow()) {
        printf('<li> <a href="%s?cmd=edit&id=%s">%s</a>',
               $_SERVER['PHP_SELF'],$row->id,$row->sign);
    }
    print '<hr><li> <a href="'.$_SERVER['PHP_SELF'].'?cmd=add">Add New</a>';
    print '</ul>';
    break;
}
```

The switch statement controls what action the program takes based on the value of $_REQUEST['cmd']. If $_REQUEST['cmd'] is add or edit, the program displays a form with textboxes for each field in the $fields array, as shown in Figure 10-1. If $_REQUEST['cmd'] is edit, values for the row with the supplied $id are loaded from the database and displayed as defaults. If $_REQUEST['cmd'] is save, the program uses pc_build_query( ) to generate an appropriate query to either INSERT or UPDATE the data in the database. After saving (or if no $_REQUEST['cmd'] is specified), the program displays a list of all zodiac signs, as shown in Figure 10-2.

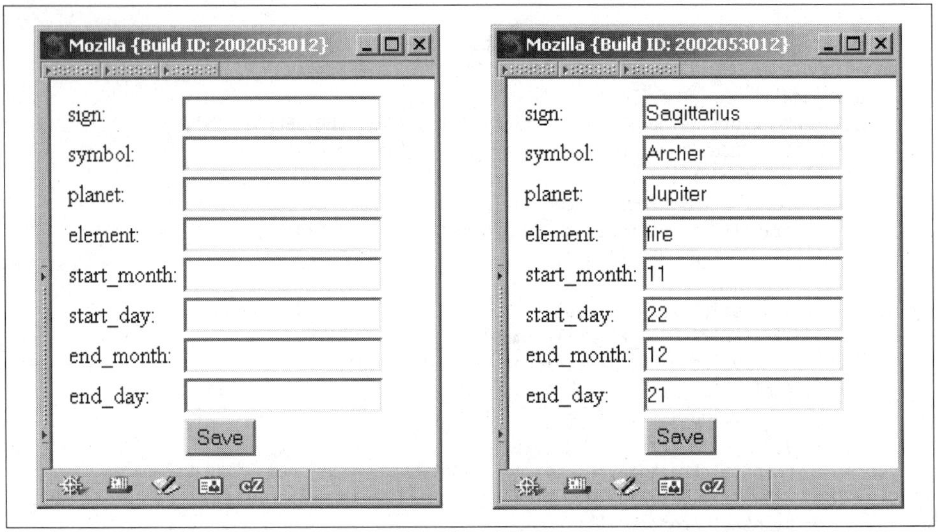

Figure 10-1. Adding and editing a record

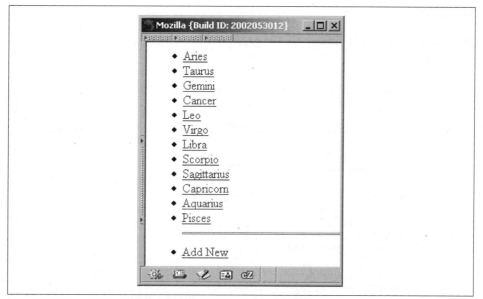

Figure 10-2. Listing records

Whether pc_build_query( ) builds an INSERT or UPDATE statement is based on the presence of the request variable $_REQUEST['id'] (because id is passed in $key_field). If $_REQUEST['id'] is not empty, the function builds an UPDATE query to change the row with that ID. If $_REQUEST['id'] is empty (or it hasn't been set at all), the function generates a new ID with nextId( ) and uses that new ID in an INSERT query that adds a row to the table.

See Also

Documentation on DB::autoPrepare( ) at *http://pear.php.net/manual/en/core.db.autoprepare.php*; new versions of PEAR DB are available at *http://pear.php.net/package-info.php?package=DB*.

10.13 Making Paginated Links for a Series of Records

Problem

You want to display a large dataset a page at a time and provide links that move through the dataset.

Solution

Use the PEAR DB_Pager class:

```
require 'DB/Pager.php';

$offset = intval($_REQUEST['offset']);
$per_page = 3;

$sth = $dbh->limitQuery('SELECT * FROM zodiac ORDER BY id', $offset, $per_page);
// display each row on this page
while ($v = $sth->fetchRow()) {
    print "$v->sign, $v->symbol ($v->id)<br>";
}
$data = DB_Pager::getData($offset, $per_page, $sth->numRows());

// a link to the previous page
printf('<a href="%s?offset=%d">&lt;&lt;Prev</a> |',
        $_SERVER['PHP_SELF'],$data['prev']);

// direct links to each page
foreach ($data['pages'] as $page => $start) {
    printf(' <a href="%s?offset=%d">%d</a> |',$_SERVER['PHP_SELF'],$start,$page);
}

// a link to the next page
printf(' <a href="%s?offset=%d">Next&gt;&gt;</a>',
        $_SERVER['PHP_SELF'],$data['next']);

// display which records are on this page
printf("<br>(Displaying %d - %d of %d)",
        $data['from'],$data['to'],$data['numrows']);
```

If you don't have DB_Pager or you do but don't want to use it, you can roll your own indexed link display using the pc_indexed_links( ) and pc_print_link( ) functions shown in the Discussion in Examples 10-2 and 10-3.

```
$offset = intval($_REQUEST['offset']);
if (! $offset) { $offset = 1; }
$per_page = 5;
$total = $dbh->getOne('SELECT COUNT(*) FROM zodiac');

$sql = $dbh->modifyLimitQuery('SELECT * FROM zodiac ORDER BY id',
                                $offset - 1,$per_page);
$ar = $dbh->getAll($sql);
foreach ($ar as $k => $v) {
    print "$v->sign, $v->symbol ($v->id)<br>";
}

pc_indexed_links($total,$offset,$per_page);
printf("<br>(Displaying %d - %d of %d)",$offset,$offset+$k,$total);
```

Discussion

DB_Pager is designed specifically to paginate results that come from a PEAR DB query. To use it, create a DB_Pager object and tell it what query to use, what offset into the result set to start at, and how many items belong on each page. It calculates the correct pagination.

The $pager->build( ) method calculates the appropriate rows to return and other page-specific variables. DB_Pager provides a fetchRow( ) method to retrieve the results in the same way the DB class operates. (You can also use fetchInto( ) with DB_ Pager). However, while it provides all the data you need to build appropriate links, it also leaves it up to you to build those links. The offset the previous page starts at is in $data['prev'], and $data['next'] is the offset of the next page. The $data['pages'] array contains page numbers and their starting offsets. The output when $offset is 0 is shown in Figure 10-3.

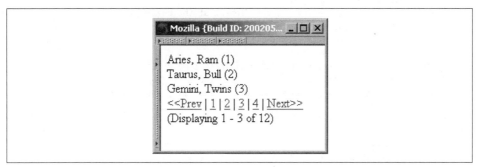

Figure 10-3. Paginated results with DB_Pager

All the page numbers, "<<Prev" and "Next>>," are links. "<<Prev" and "1" point to the current page; the others point to their corresponding pages. On page 4, the "Next>>" link points back to page 1. (But on page 1, the "<<Prev" link doesn't point to page 4.) The numbers in the links refer to page numbers, not element numbers.

If DB_Pager isn't available, you can use the pc_print_link( ) and pc_indexed_links( ) functions shown in Examples 10-2 and 10-3 to produce properly formatted links.

Example 10-2. pc_print_link()

```
function pc_print_link($inactive,$text,$offset='') {

    if ($inactive) {
        printf('<font color="#666666">%s</font>',$text);
    } else {
        printf('<a href="%s?offset=%d">%s</a>',$_SERVER['PHP_SELF'],$offset,$text);
    }
}
```

Example 10-3. pc_indexed_links()

```
function pc_indexed_links($total,$offset,$per_page) {
    $separator = ' | ';

    // print "<<Prev" link
    pc_print_link($offset == 1, '&lt;&lt;Prev', $offset - $per_page);


    // print all groupings except last one
    for ($start = 1, $end = $per_page;
        $end < $total;
        $start += $per_page, $end += $per_page) {

        print $separator;
        pc_print_link($offset == $start, "$start-$end", $start);
    }

    /* print the last grouping -
     * at this point, $start points to the element at the beginning
     * of the last grouping
     */

    /* the text should only contain a range if there's more than
     * one element on the last page. For example, the last grouping
     * of 11 elements with 5 per page should just say "11", not "11-11"
     */
    $end = ($total > $start) ? "-$total" : '';

    print $separator;
    pc_print_link($offset == $start, "$start$end", $start);

    // print "Next>>" link
    print $separator;
    pc_print_link($offset == $start, 'Next&gt;&gt;',$offset + $per_page);
}
```

To use these functions, retrieve the correct subset of the data using DB::
modifyLimitQuery( ) and then print it out. Call pc_indexed_links( ) to display the
indexed links:

```
$offset = intval($_REQUEST['offset']);
if (! $offset) { $offset = 1; }
$per_page = 5;
$total = $dbh->getOne('SELECT COUNT(*) FROM zodiac');

$sql = $dbh->modifyLimitQuery('SELECT * FROM zodiac ORDER BY id',
                              $offset - 1,$per_page);
$ar = $dbh->getAll($sql);
foreach ($ar as $k => $v) {
    print "$v->sign, $v->symbol ($v->id)<br>";
}
```

```
pc_indexed_links($total,$offset,$per_page);
printf("<br>(Displaying %d - %d of %d)",$offset,$offset+$k,$total);
```

After connecting to the database, you need to make sure $offset has an appropriate value. $offset is the beginning record in the result set that should be displayed. To start at the beginning of the result set, $offset should be 1. The variable $per_page is set to how many records to display on each page, and $total is the total number of records in the entire result set. For this example, all the Zodiac records are displayed, so $total is set to the count of all the rows in the entire table.

The SQL query that retrieves information in the proper order is:

```
SELECT * FROM zodiac ORDER BY id
```

Use modifyLimitQuery( ) to restrict the rows being retrieved. You'll want to retrieve $per_page rows, starting at $offset - 1, because the first row is 0, not 1, to the database. The modifyLimitQuery( ) method applies the correct database-specific logic to restrict what rows are returned by the query.

The relevant rows are retrieved by $dbh->getAll($sql), and then information is displayed from each row. After the rows, pc_indexed_links( ) provides navigation links. The output when $offset is not set (or is 1) is shown in Figure 10-4.

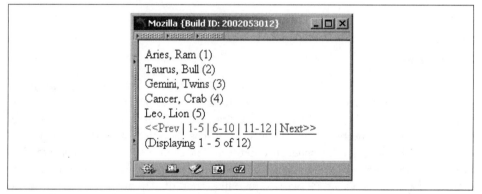

Figure 10-4. Paginated results with pc_indexed_links()

In Figure 10-4, "6-10", "11-12", and "Next>>" are links to the same page with adjusted $offset arguments, while "<<Prev" and "1-5" are greyed out, because what they would link to is what's currently displayed.

See Also

Information on DB_Pager at *http://pear.php.net/package-info.php?package=DB_Pager*.

10.14 Caching Queries and Results

Problem

You don't want to rerun potentially expensive database queries when the results haven't changed.

Solution

Use PEAR's Cache_DB package. It wraps the DB database abstraction layer with an object that has similar methods and that automatically caches the results of SELECT queries:

```
require 'Cache/DB.php';

$cache = new Cache_DB;
$cache->connect('mysql://test:@localhost/test');

$sth = $cache->query("SELECT sign FROM zodiac WHERE element LIKE 'fire'");

while($row = $sth->fetchRow()) {
    print $row['sign']."\n";
}
```

Discussion

Using Cache_DB is almost the same as using DB, but there are some crucial differences. First, *Cache/DB.php* is required instead of *DB.php*. The *Cache/DB.php* file then loads the appropriate DB classes. Instead of creating a database handle with the DB::connect( ) method, you instantiate a Cache_DB object with the new operator and then call the object's connect( ) method. The syntax of $cache->connect( ) is the same, however, so you just pass it the DSN that identifies the database. The query( ) method of Cache_DB works just like that of DB, however there are no prepare( ) and execute( ) methods in Cache_DB. query( ) returns a statement handle that supports fetchRow( ) and fetchInto( ), but the default fetch mode is DB_FETCH_ ASSOC, not DB_FETCH_ORDERED.

The first time a particular SELECT statement is passed to $cache->query( ), Cache_DB executes the statement and returns the results, just like DB, but it also saves the results in a file whose name is a hash of the query. If the same SELECT statement is passed to $cache->query( ) again, Cache_DB retrieves the results from the file instead of running the query in the database.

By default, Cache_DB creates its cache files in a subdirectory of the current directory called *db_query*. You can change this by passing a directory name as part of an options array as a second argument to the `Cache_DB` constructor. This sets the cache directory to */tmp/db_query*:

```
$cache = new Cache_DB('file',array('cache_dir' => '/tmp/'));
```

The first argument, `file`, tells `Cache_DB` what container to use to store the cached data. `file` is the default, but you need to include it here to specify the container options in the second argument. The relevant container option is `cache_dir`, which tells `Cache_DB` where to create the *db_query* subdirectory. Including a trailing slash is required.

By default, entries stay in the cache for one hour. You can adjust this by passing a different value (in seconds) when creating a new `Cache_DB` object. Here's how to keep entries in the cache for one day, 86,400 seconds:

```
$cache = new Cache_DB('file',array('cache_dir' => '.',
                                   'filename_prefix' => 'query_'),86400);
```

Because the expiration time is the third argument, you have to pass the defaults for the first two arguments as well.

The cache isn't altered if you change the database with an `INSERT`, `UPDATE`, or `DELETE` query. If there are cached `SELECT` statements that refer to data no longer in the database, you need to explicitly remove everything from the cache with the `$cache->flush( )` method:

```
$cache->flush('db_cache');
```

It's very important to include the `db_cache` argument to `flush( )`. The PEAR `Cache` system supports dividing up the cached items into different groups, and the `Cache_DB` object puts everything it's keeping track of in the `db_cache` group. Leaving out the group argument results in deleting the files in the base cache directory (which is probably the directory you're running your script from).

The file container stores each result in a file whose name is based on an MD5 hash of the query that generated the particular result. Because MD5 is case-sensitive, the file container is case-sensitive, too. This means that if the results of `SELECT * FROM zodiac` are in the cache, and you run the query `SELECT * from zodiac`, the results aren't found in the cache, and the query is run again. Maintaining consistent capitalization, spacing, and field ordering when constructing your SQL queries results in more efficient cache usage.

Although this recipe focuses on the file container, the PEAR `Cache` system supports a number of other containers that hold cached data, such as shared memory, PHPLib sessions, databases via the dbx library, and msession sessions. To use a different container, pass the appropriate container name as the first argument when creating a new `Cache_DB` object:

```
$cache = new Cache_DB('shm');
```

See Also

Information about the PEAR Cache system and the different containers at *http:// pear.php.net/package-info.php?package=Cache*.

10.15 Program: Storing a Threaded Message Board

Storing and retrieving threaded messages requires extra care to display the threads in the correct order. Finding the children of each message and building the tree of message relationships can easily lead to a recursive web of queries. Users generally look at a list of messages and read individual messages far more often then they post messages. With a little extra processing when saving a new message to the database, the query that retrieves a list of messages to display is simpler and much more efficient.

Store messages in a table structured like this:

```
CREATE TABLE pc_message (
    id INT UNSIGNED NOT NULL,
    posted_on DATETIME NOT NULL,
    author CHAR(255),
    subject CHAR(255),
    body MEDIUMTEXT,
    thread_id INT UNSIGNED NOT NULL,
    parent_id INT UNSIGNED NOT NULL,
    level INT UNSIGNED NOT NULL,
    thread_pos INT UNSIGNED NOT NULL,
    PRIMARY KEY(id)
);
```

The primary key, id, is a unique integer that identifies a particular message. The time and date that a message is posted is stored in posted_on, and author, subject, and body are (surprise!) a message's author, subject, and body. The remaining four fields keep track of the threading relationships between messages. The integer thread_id identifies each thread. All messages in a particular thread have the same thread_id. If a message is a reply to another message, parent_id is the id of the replied-to message. level is how many replies into a thread a message is. The first message in a thread has level 0. A reply to that level 0 message has level 1, and a reply to that level 1 message has level 2. Multiple messages in a thread can have the same level and the same parent_id. For example, if someone starts off a thread with a message about the merits of BeOS over CP/M, the angry replies to that message from CP/M's legions of fans all have level 1 and a parent_id equal to the id of the original message.

The last field, thread_pos, is what makes the easy display of messages possible. When displayed, all messages in a thread are ordered by their thread_pos value.

Here are the rules for calculating thread_pos:

- The first message in a thread has thread_pos = 0.
- For a new message N, if there are no messages in the thread with the same parent as N, N's thread_pos is one greater than its parent's thread_pos.
- For a new message N, if there are messages in the thread with the same parent as N, N's thread_pos is one greater than the biggest thread_pos of all the messages with the same parent as N.
- After new message N's thread_pos is determined, all messages in the same thread with a thread_pos value greater than or equal to N's have their thread_pos value incremented by 1 (to make room for N).

The message board program, *message.php*, shown in Example 10-4 saves messages and properly calculates thread_pos. Sample output is shown in Figure 10-5.

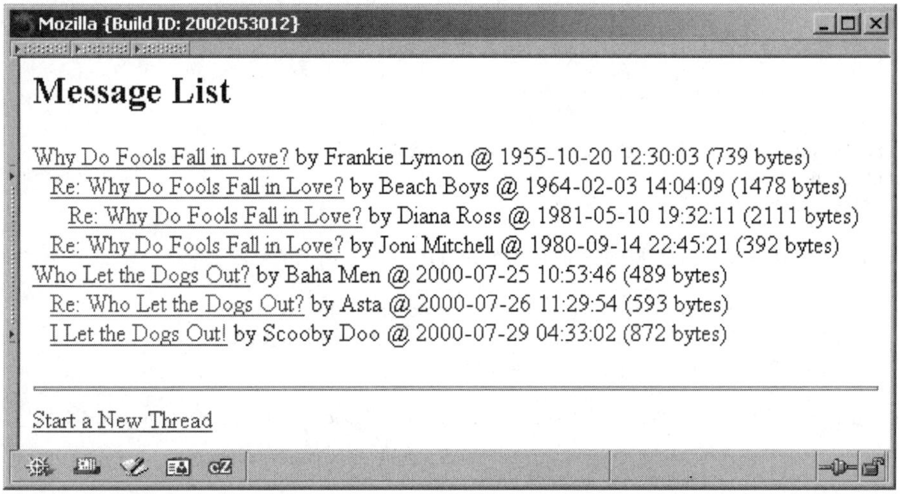

Figure 10-5. A threaded message board

Example 10-4. message.php

```
require 'DB.php';

// a helpful database debugging function
function log_die($ob) { print '<pre>'; print_r($ob); print '</pre>'; }

// connect to the database
$dbh = DB::connect('mysql://test:@localhost/test') or die("Can't connect");
if (DB::isError($dbh)) { log_die($dbh); }
$dbh->setFetchMode(DB_FETCHMODE_OBJECT);
PEAR::setErrorHandling(PEAR_ERROR_CALLBACK,'log_die');
```

Example 10-4. message.php (continued)

```
// The value of $_REQUEST['cmd'] tells us what to do
switch ($_REQUEST['cmd']) {
case 'read':                        // read an individual message
    pc_message_read();
    break;
case 'post':                        // display the form to post a message
    pc_message_post();
    break;
case 'save':                        // save a posted message
    if (pc_message_validate()) {    // if the message is valid,
        pc_message_save();          // then save it
        pc_message_list();          // and display the message list
    } else {
        pc_message_post();          // otherwise, redisplay the posting form
    }
    break;
case 'list':                        // display a message list by default
default:
    pc_message_list();
    break;
}

// pc_message_save() saves the message to the database
function pc_message_save() {
    global $dbh;

    $parent_id = intval($_REQUEST['parent_id']);

    /* MySQL syntax for making sure pc_message doesn't change while
     * we're working with it. We also have to lock the tables that
     * hold the thread and pc_message sequences
     */
    $dbh->query('LOCK TABLES pc_message WRITE, thread_seq WRITE, pc_message_seq WRITE');

    // is this message a reply?
    if ($parent_id) {

        // get the thread, level, and thread_pos of the parent message
        $parent = $dbh->getRow("SELECT thread_id,level,thread_pos
                                FROM pc_message
                                WHERE id = $parent_id");

        // a reply's level is one greater than its parents
        $level = $parent->level + 1;

        /* what's the biggest thread_pos in this thread among messages
           with the same parent? */
        $thread_pos = $dbh->getOne("SELECT MAX(thread_pos) FROM pc_message
            WHERE thread_id = $parent->thread_id AND parent_id = $parent_id");

        // are there existing replies to this parent?
        if ($thread_pos) {
            // this thread_pos goes after the biggest existing one
```

Example 10-4. message.php (continued)

```
            $thread_pos++;
        } else {
            // this is the first reply, so put it right after the parent
            $thread_pos = $parent->thread_pos + 1;
        }

        /* increment the thread_pos of all messages in the thread that
           come after this one */
        $dbh->query("UPDATE pc_message SET thread_pos = thread_pos + 1
            WHERE thread_id = $parent->thread_id AND thread_pos >= $thread_pos");

        // the new message should be saved with the parent's thread_id
        $thread_id = $parent->thread_id;
    } else {
        // the message is not a reply, so it's the start of a new thread
        $thread_id = $dbh->nextId('thread');
        $level = 0;
        $thread_pos = 0;
    }

    // get a new id for this message
    $id = $dbh->nextId('pc_message');

    /* insert the message into the database. Using prepare() and execute()
       makes sure that all fields are properly quoted */
    $prh =
        $dbh->prepare("INSERT INTO pc_message (id,thread_id,parent_id,
                        thread_pos,posted_on,level,author,subject,body)
                        VALUES (?,?,?,?,NOW(),?,?,?,?)");

    $dbh->execute($prh,array($id,$thread_id,$parent_id,$thread_pos,$level,
                            $_REQUEST['author'],$_REQUEST['subject'],
                            $_REQUEST['body']));


    // Tell MySQL that others can use the pc_message table now
    $dbh->query('UNLOCK TABLES');
}

// pc_message_list() displays a list of all messages
function pc_message_list() {
    global $dbh;

    print '<h2>Message List</h2><p>';

    /* order the messages by their thread (thread_id) and their position
       within the thread (thread_pos) */
    $sth = $dbh->query("SELECT id,author,subject,LENGTH(body) AS body_length,
                        posted_on,level FROM pc_message
                        ORDER BY thread_id,thread_pos");
```

Example 10-4. message.php (continued)

```
    while ($row = $sth->fetchRow()) {
        // indent messages with level > 0
        print str_repeat(' ',4 * $row->level);
        // print out information about the message with a link to read it
        print<<<_HTML_
<a href="$_SERVER[PHP_SELF]?cmd=read&id=$row->id">$row->subject</a> by
$row->author @ $row->posted_on ($row->body_length bytes)
<br>
_HTML_;
    }

    // provide a way to post a non-reply message
    printf('<hr><a href="%s?cmd=post">Start a New Thread</a>',
        $_SERVER['PHP_SELF']);
}

// pc_message_read() displays an individual message
function pc_message_read() {
    global $dbh;

    /* make sure the message id we're passed is an integer and really
       represents a message */
    $id = intval($_REQUEST['id']) or die("Bad message id");
    if (! ($msg = $dbh->getRow(
        "SELECT author,subject,body,posted_on FROM pc_message WHERE id = $id"))) {
        die("Bad message id");
    }

    /* don't display user-entered HTML, but display newlines as
       HTML line breaks */
    $body = nl2br(strip_tags($msg->body));

    // display the message with links to reply and return to the message list
    print<<<_HTML_
<h2>$msg->subject</h2>
<h3>by $msg->author</h3>
<p>
$body
<hr>
<a href="$_SERVER[PHP_SELF]?cmd=post&parent_id=$id">Reply</a>
<br>
<a href="$_SERVER[PHP_SELF]?cmd=list">List Messages</a>
_HTML_;
}

// pc_message_post() displays the form for posting a message
function pc_message_post() {
    global $dbh,$form_errors;

    foreach (array('author','subject','body') as $field) {
        // escape characters in default field values
        $$field = htmlspecialchars($_REQUEST[$field]);
```

Example 10-4. message.php (continued)

```
        // make the error messages display in red
        if ($form_errors[$field]) {
            $form_errors[$field] = '<font color="red">' .
                $form_errors[$field] . '</font><br>';
        }
    }

    // is this message a reply
    if ($parent_id = intval($_REQUEST['parent_id'])) {

        // send the parent_id along when the form is submitted
        $parent_field =
            sprintf('<input type="hidden" name="parent_id" value="%d">',
                    $parent_id);

        // if no subject's been passed in, use the subject of the parent
        if (! $subject) {
            $parent_subject = $dbh->getOne('SELECT subject FROM pc_message
                                    WHERE id = ?',array($parent_id));
            /* prefix 'Re: ' to the parent subject if it exists and
                doesn't already have a 'Re:' */
            $subject = htmlspecialchars($parent_subject);
            if ($parent_subject && (! preg_match('/^re:/i',$parent_subject))) {
                $subject = "Re: $subject";
            }
        }
    }

    // display the posting form, with errors and default values
    print<<<_HTML_
<form method="post" action="$_SERVER[PHP_SELF]">
<table>
<tr>
 <td>Your Name:</td>
 <td>$form_errors[author]<input type="text" name="author" value="$author">
</td>
<tr>
 <td>Subject:</td>
 <td>$form_errors[subject]<input type="text" name="subject" value="$subject">
</td>
<tr>
 <td>Message:</td>
 <td>$form_errors[body]<textarea rows="4" cols="30" wrap="physical"
name="body">$body</textarea>
</td>
<tr><td colspan="2"><input type="submit" value="Post Message"></td></tr>
</table>
$parent_field
<input type="hidden" name="cmd" value="save">
</form>
```

Example 10-4. message.php (continued)

```
_HTML_;
}

// pc_message_validate() makes sure something is entered in each field
function pc_message_validate() {
    global $form_errors;

    $form_errors = array();

    if (! $_REQUEST['author']) {
        $form_errors['author'] = 'Please enter your name.';
    }
    if (! $_REQUEST['subject']) {
        $form_errors['subject'] = 'Please enter a message subject.';
    }
    if (! $_REQUEST['body']) {
        $form_errors['body'] = 'Please enter a message body.';
    }

    if (count($form_errors)) {
        return false;
    } else {
        return true;
    }
}
```

To properly handle concurrent usage, pc_message_save( ) needs exclusive access to the msg table between the time it starts calculating the thread_pos of the new message and when it actually inserts the new message into the database. We've used MySQL's LOCK TABLE and UNLOCK TABLES commands to accomplish this. With other databases, the syntax may vary, or you may need to start a transaction at the beginning of the function and commit the transaction at the end.

The level field can be used when displaying messages to limit what you retrieve from the database. If discussion threads become very deep, this can help prevent your pages from growing too large. For example, here's how to display just the first message in each thread and any replies to that first message:

```
$sth = $dbh->query(
    "SELECT * FROM msg WHERE level <= 1 ORDER BY thread_id,thread_pos");
while ($row = $sth->fetchRow()) {
    // display each message
}
```

If you're interested in having a discussion group on your web site, you may want to use one of the existing PHP message board packages. The most popular is Phorum (*http://www.phorum.org/*), and there are a number of others listed at *http://www.zend.com/apps.php?CID=261*.

CHAPTER 11

Web Automation

11.0 Introduction

Most of the time, PHP is part of a web server, sending content to browsers. Even when you run it from the command line, it usually performs a task and then prints some output. PHP can also be useful, however, playing the role of a web browser— retrieving URLs and then operating on the content. Most recipes in this chapter cover retrieving URLs and processing the results, although there are a few other tasks in here as well, such as using templates and processing server logs.

There are four ways to retrieve a remote URL in PHP. Choosing one method over another depends on your needs for simplicity, control, and portability. The four methods are to use fopen( ), fsockopen( ), the cURL extension, or the HTTP_Request class from PEAR.

Using fopen( ) is simple and convenient. We discuss it in Recipe 11.1. The fopen( ) function automatically follows redirects, so if you use this function to retrieve the directory *http://www.example.com/people* and the server redirects you to *http://www.example.com/people/*, you'll get the contents of the directory index page, not a message telling you that the URL has moved. The fopen( ) function also works with both HTTP and FTP. The downsides to fopen( ) include: it can handle only HTTP GET requests (not HEAD or POST), you can't send additional headers or any cookies with the request, and you can retrieve only the response body with it, not response headers.

Using fsockopen( ) requires more work but gives you more flexibility. We use fsockopen( ) in Recipe 11.2. After opening a socket with fsockopen( ), you need to print the appropriate HTTP request to that socket and then read and parse the response. This lets you add headers to the request and gives you access to all the response headers. However, you need to have additional code to properly parse the response and take any appropriate action, such as following a redirect.

If you have access to the cURL extension or PEAR's HTTP_Request class, you should use those rather than fsockopen( ). cURL supports a number of different protocols (including HTTPS, discussed in Recipe 11.5) and gives you access to response headers. We use cURL in most of the recipes in this chapter. To use cURL, you must have the cURL library installed, available at *http://curl.haxx.se*. Also, PHP must be built with the --with-curl configuration option.

PEAR's HTTP_Request class, which we use in Recipes 11.2, 11.3, and 11.4, doesn't support HTTPS, but does give you access to headers and can use any HTTP method. If this PEAR module isn't installed on your system, you can download it from *http://pear.php.net/get/HTTP_Request*. As long as the module's files are in your include_path, you can use it, making it a very portable solution.

Recipe 11.6 helps you go behind the scenes of an HTTP request to examine the headers in a request and response. If a request you're making from a program isn't giving you the results you're looking for, examining the headers often provides clues as to what's wrong.

Once you've retrieved the contents of a web page into a program, use Recipes 11.7 through 11.11 to help you manipulate those page contents. Recipe 11.7 demonstrates how to mark up certain words in a page with blocks of color. This technique is useful for highlighting search terms, for example. Recipe 11.8 provides a function to find all the links in a page. This is an essential building block for a web spider or a link checker. Converting between plain ASCII and HTML is covered in Recipes 11.9 and 11.10. Recipe 11.11 shows how to remove all HTML and PHP tags from a web page.

Another kind of page manipulation is using a templating system. Discussed in Recipe 11.12, templates give you freedom to change the look and feel of your web pages without changing the PHP plumbing that populates the pages with dynamic data. Similarly, you can make changes to the code that drives the pages without affecting the look and feel. Recipe 11.13 discusses a common server administration task—parsing your web server's access log files.

Two sample programs use the link extractor from Recipe 11.8. The program in Recipe 11.14 scans the links in a page and reports which are still valid, which have been moved, and which no longer work. The program in Recipe 11.15 reports on the freshness of links. It tells you when a linked-to page was last modified and if it's been moved.

11.1 Fetching a URL with the GET Method

Problem

You want to retrieve the contents of a URL. For example, you want to include part of one web page in another page's content.

Solution

Pass the URL to fopen( ) and get the contents of the page with fread( ):

```
$page = '';
$fh = fopen('http://www.example.com/robots.txt','r') or die($php_errormsg);
while (! feof($fh)) {
    $page .= fread($fh,1048576);
}
fclose($fh);
```

You can use the cURL extension:

```
$c = curl_init('http://www.example.com/robots.txt');
curl_setopt($c, CURLOPT_RETURNTRANSFER, 1);
$page = curl_exec($c);
curl_close($c);
```

You can also use the HTTP_Request class from PEAR:

```
require 'HTTP/Request.php';

$r = new HTTP_Request('http://www.example.com/robots.txt');
$r->sendRequest();
$page = $r->getResponseBody();
```

Discussion

You can put a username and password in the URL if you need to retrieve a protected page. In this example, the username is david, and the password is hax0r. Here's how to do it with fopen( ):

```
$fh = fopen('http://david:hax0r@www.example.com/secrets.html','r')
    or die($php_errormsg);
while (! feof($fh)) {
    $page .= fread($fh,1048576);
}
fclose($fh);
```

Here's how to do it with cURL:

```
$c = curl_init('http://www.example.com/secrets.html');
curl_setopt($c, CURLOPT_RETURNTRANSFER, 1);
curl_setopt($c, CURLOPT_USERPWD, 'david:hax0r');
$page = curl_exec($c);
curl_close($c);
```

Here's how to do it with HTTP_Request:

```
$r = new HTTP_Request('http://www.example.com/secrets.html');
$r->setBasicAuth('david','hax0r');
$r->sendRequest();
$page = $r->getResponseBody();
```

While fopen( ) follows redirects in Location response headers, HTTP_Request does not. cURL follows them only when the CURLOPT_FOLLOWLOCATION option is set:

```
$c = curl_init('http://www.example.com/directory');
curl_setopt($c, CURLOPT_RETURNTRANSFER, 1);
curl_setopt($c, CURLOPT_FOLLOWLOCATION, 1);
$page = curl_exec($c);
curl_close($c);
```

cURL can do a few different things with the page it retrieves. If the CURLOPT_RETURNTRANSFER option is set, curl_exec( ) returns a string containing the page:

```
$c = curl_init('http://www.example.com/files.html');
curl_setopt($c, CURLOPT_RETURNTRANSFER, 1);
$page = curl_exec($c);
curl_close($c);
```

To write the retrieved page to a file, open a file handle for writing with fopen( ) and set the CURLOPT_FILE option to the file handle:

```
$fh = fopen('local-copy-of-files.html','w') or die($php_errormsg);
$c = curl_init('http://www.example.com/files.html');
curl_setopt($c, CURLOPT_FILE, $fh);
curl_exec($c);
curl_close($c);
```

To pass the cURL resource and the contents of the retrieved page to a function, set the CURLOPT_WRITEFUNCTION option to the name of the function:

```
// save the URL and the page contents in a database
function save_page($c,$page) {
    $info = curl_getinfo($c);
    mysql_query("INSERT INTO pages (url,page) VALUES ('" .
                mysql_escape_string($info['url']) . "', '" .
                mysql_escape_string($page) . "')");
}

$c = curl_init('http://www.example.com/files.html');
curl_setopt($c, CURLOPT_WRITEFUNCTION, 'save_page');
curl_exec($c);
curl_close($c);
```

If none of CURLOPT_RETURNTRANSFER, CURLOPT_FILE, or CURLOPT_WRITEFUNCTION is set, cURL prints out the contents of the returned page.

The fopen() function and the include and require directives can retrieve remote files only if URL fopen wrappers are enabled. URL fopen wrappers are enabled by default and are controlled by the allow_url_fopen configuration directive. On Windows, however, include and require can't retrieve remote files in versions of PHP earlier than 4.3, even if allow_url_fopen is on.

See Also

Recipe 11.2 for fetching a URL with the POST method; Recipe 18.3 discusses opening remote files with fopen(); documentation on fopen() at *http://www.php.net/ fopen*, include at *http://www.php.net/include*, curl_init( ) at *http://www.php.net/curl-init*, curl_setopt( ) at *http://www.php.net/curl-setopt*, curl_exec( ) at *http:// www.php.net/curl-exec*, and curl_close( ) at *http://www.php.net/curl-close*; the PEAR HTTP_Request class at *http://pear.php.net/package-info.php?package=HTTP_Request*.

11.2   Fetching a URL with the POST Method

Problem

You want to retrieve a URL with the POST method, not the default GET method. For example, you want to submit an HTML form.

Solution

Use the cURL extension with the CURLOPT_POST option set:

```
$c = curl_init('http://www.example.com/submit.php');
curl_setopt($c, CURLOPT_POST, 1);
curl_setopt($c, CURLOPT_POSTFIELDS, 'monkey=uncle&rhino=aunt');
curl_setopt($c, CURLOPT_RETURNTRANSFER, 1);
$page = curl_exec($c);
curl_close($c);
```

If the cURL extension isn't available, use the PEAR HTTP_Request class:

```
require 'HTTP/Request.php';

$r = new HTTP_Request('http://www.example.com/submit.php');
$r->setMethod(HTTP_REQUEST_METHOD_POST);
$r->addPostData('monkey','uncle');
$r->addPostData('rhino','aunt');
$r->sendRequest();
$page = $r->getResponseBody();
```

Discussion

Sending a POST method request requires special handling of any arguments. In a GET request, these arguments are in the query string, but in a POST request, they go in the request body. Additionally, the request needs a Content-Length header that tells the server the size of the content to expect in the request body.

Because of the argument handling and additional headers, you can't use fopen( ) to make a POST request. If neither cURL nor HTTP_Request are available, use the pc_post_request( ) function, shown in Example 11-1, which makes the connection to the remote web server with fsockopen( ).

Example 11-1. pc_post_request()

```
function pc_post_request($host,$url,$content='') {
    $timeout = 2;
    $a = array();
    if (is_array($content)) {
        foreach ($content as $k => $v) {
            array_push($a,urlencode($k).'='.urlencode($v));
        }
    }
    $content_string = join('&',$a);
    $content_length = strlen($content_string);
    $request_body = "POST $url HTTP/1.0
Host: $host
Content-type: application/x-www-form-urlencoded
Content-length: $content_length

$content_string";

    $sh = fsockopen($host,80,&$errno,&$errstr,$timeout)
        or die("can't open socket to $host: $errno $errstr");

    fputs($sh,$request_body);
    $response = '';
    while (! feof($sh)) {
        $response .= fread($sh,16384);
    }
    fclose($sh) or die("Can't close socket handle: $php_errormsg");

    list($response_headers,$response_body) = explode("\r\n\r\n",$response,2);
    $response_header_lines = explode("\r\n",$response_headers);

    // first line of headers is the HTTP response code
    $http_response_line = array_shift($response_header_lines);
    if (preg_match('@^HTTP/[0-9]\.[0-9] ([0-9]{3})@',$http_response_line,
                   $matches)) {
        $response_code = $matches[1];
    }

    // put the rest of the headers in an array
    $response_header_array = array();
    foreach ($response_header_lines as $header_line) {
        list($header,$value) = explode(': ',$header_line,2);
        $response_header_array[$header] = $value;
    }

    return array($response_code,$response_header_array,$response_body);
}
```

Call pc_post_request( ) like this:

```
list($code,$headers,$body) = pc_post_request('www.example.com','/submit.php',
                                    array('monkey' => 'uncle',
                                          'rhino' => 'aunt'));
```

Retrieving a URL with POST instead of GET is especially useful if the URL is very long, more than 200 characters or so. The HTTP 1.1 specification in RFC 2616 doesn't place a maximum length on URLs, so behavior varies among different web and proxy servers. If you retrieve URLs with GET and receive unexpected results or results with status code 414 ("Request-URI Too Long"), convert the request to a POST request.

See Also

Recipe 11.1 for fetching a URL with the GET method; documentation on curl_setopt( ) at *http://www.php.net/curl-setopt* and fsockopen( ) at *http://www.php.net/fsockopen*; the PEAR HTTP_Request class at *http://pear.php.net/package-info.php?package=HTTP_Request*; RFC 2616 is available at *http://www.faqs.org/rfcs/rfc2616.html*.

11.3   Fetching a URL with Cookies

Problem

You want to retrieve a page that requires a cookie to be sent with the request for the page.

Solution

Use the cURL extension and the CURLOPT_COOKIE option:

```
$c = curl_init('http://www.example.com/needs-cookies.php');
curl_setopt($c, CURLOPT_VERBOSE, 1);
curl_setopt($c, CURLOPT_COOKIE, 'user=ellen; activity=swimming');
curl_setopt($c, CURLOPT_RETURNTRANSFER, 1);
$page = curl_exec($c);
curl_close($c);
```

If cURL isn't available, use the addHeader( ) method in the PEAR HTTP_Request class:

```
require 'HTTP/Request.php';

$r = new HTTP_Request('http://www.example.com/needs-cookies.php');
$r->addHeader('Cookie','user=ellen; activity=swimming');
$r->sendRequest();
$page = $r->getResponseBody();
```

Discussion

Cookies are sent to the server in the Cookie request header. The cURL extension has a cookie-specific option, but with HTTP_Request, you have to add the Cookie header just as with other request headers. Multiple cookie values are sent in a semicolon-delimited list. The examples in the Solution send two cookies: one named user with value ellen and one named activity with value swimming.

To request a page that sets cookies and then make subsequent requests that include those newly set cookies, use cURL's "cookie jar" feature. On the first request, set CURLOPT_COOKIEJAR to the name of a file to store the cookies in. On subsequent requests, set CURLOPT_COOKIEFILE to the same filename, and cURL reads the cookies from the file and sends them along with the request. This is especially useful for a sequence of requests in which the first request logs into a site that sets session or authentication cookies, and then the rest of the requests need to include those cookies to be valid:

```
$cookie_jar = tempnam('/tmp','cookie');

// log in
$c = curl_init('https://bank.example.com/login.php?user=donald&password=b1gmoney$');
curl_setopt($c, CURLOPT_RETURNTRANSFER, 1);
curl_setopt($c, CURLOPT_COOKIEJAR, $cookie_jar);
$page = curl_exec($c);
curl_close($c);

// retrieve account balance
$c = curl_init('http://bank.example.com/balance.php?account=checking');
curl_setopt($c, CURLOPT_RETURNTRANSFER, 1);
curl_setopt($c, CURLOPT_COOKIEFILE, $cookie_jar);
$page = curl_exec($c);
curl_close($c);

// make a deposit
$c = curl_init('http://bank.example.com/deposit.php');
curl_setopt($c, CURLOPT_POST, 1);
curl_setopt($c, CURLOPT_POSTFIELDS, 'account=checking&amount=122.44');
curl_setopt($c, CURLOPT_RETURNTRANSFER, 1);
curl_setopt($c, CURLOPT_COOKIEFILE, $cookie_jar);
$page = curl_exec($c);
curl_close($c);

// remove the cookie jar
unlink($cookie_jar) or die("Can't unlink $cookie_jar");
```

Be careful where you store the cookie jar. It needs to be in a place your web server has write access to, but if other users can read the file, they may be able to poach the authentication credentials stored in the cookies.

See Also

Documentation on curl_setopt( ) at *http://www.php.net/curl-setopt*; the PEAR HTTP_
Request class at *http://pear.php.net/package-info.php?package=HTTP_Request*

11.4   Fetching a URL with Headers

Problem

You want to retrieve a URL that requires specific headers to be sent with the request
for the page.

Solution

Use the cURL extension and the CURLOPT_HTTPHEADER option:

```
$c = curl_init('http://www.example.com/special-header.php');
curl_setopt($c, CURLOPT_RETURNTRANSFER, 1);
curl_setopt($c, CURLOPT_HTTPHEADER, array('X-Factor: 12', 'My-Header: Bob'));
$page = curl_exec($c);
curl_close($c);
```

If cURL isn't available, use the addHeader( ) method in HTTP_Request:

```
require 'HTTP/Request.php';

$r = new HTTP_Request('http://www.example.com/special-header.php');
$r->addHeader('X-Factor',12);
$r->addHeader('My-Header','Bob');
$r->sendRequest();
$page = $r->getResponseBody();
```

Discussion

cURL has special options for setting the Referer and User-Agent request headers—
CURLOPT_REFERER and CURLOPT_USERAGENT:

```
$c = curl_init('http://www.example.com/submit.php');
curl_setopt($c, CURLOPT_VERBOSE, 1);
curl_setopt($c, CURLOPT_RETURNTRANSFER, 1);
curl_setopt($c, CURLOPT_REFERER, 'http://www.example.com/form.php');
curl_setopt($c, CURLOPT_USERAGENT, 'CURL via PHP');
$page = curl_exec($c);
curl_close($c);
```

See Also

Recipe 11.13 explains why "referrer" is often misspelled "referer" in web programming contexts; documentation on curl_setopt( ) at *http://www.php.net/curl-setopt*; the PEAR HTTP_Request class at *http://pear.php.net/package-info.php?package=HTTP_Request*.

11.5   Fetching an HTTPS URL

Problem

You want to retrieve a secure URL.

Solution

Use the cURL extension with an HTTPS URL:

```
$c = curl_init('https://secure.example.com/accountbalance.php');
curl_setopt($c, CURLOPT_RETURNTRANSFER, 1);
$page = curl_exec($c);
curl_close($c);
```

Discussion

To retrieve secure URLs, the cURL extension needs access to an SSL library, such as OpenSSL. This library must be available when PHP and the cURL extension are built. Aside from this additional library requirement, cURL treats secure URLs just like regular ones. You can provide the same cURL options to secure requests, such as changing the request method or adding POST data.

See Also

The OpenSSL Project at *http://www.openssl.org/*.

11.6   Debugging the Raw HTTP Exchange

Problem

You want to analyze the HTTP request a browser makes to your server and the corresponding HTTP response. For example, your server doesn't supply the expected response to a particular request so you want to see exactly what the components of the request are.

Solution

For simple requests, connect to the web server with *telnet* and type in the request
headers:

```
% telnet www.example.com 80
Trying 10.1.1.1...
Connected to www.example.com.
Escape character is '^]'.
GET / HTTP/1.0
Host: www.example.com

HTTP/1.1 200 OK
Date: Sat, 17 Aug 2002 06:10:19 GMT
Server: Apache/1.3.26 (Unix) PHP/4.2.2 mod_ssl/2.8.9 OpenSSL/0.9.6d
X-Powered-By: PHP/4.2.2
Connection: close
Content-Type: text/html

// ... the page body ...
```

Discussion

When you type in request headers, the web server doesn't know that it's just you
typing and not a web browser submitting a request. However, some web servers have
timeouts on how long they'll wait for a request, so it can be useful to pretype the
request and then just paste it into *telnet*. The first line of the request contains the
request method (GET), a space and the path of the file you want (/), and then a space
and the protocol you're using (HTTP/1.0). The next line, the Host header, tells the
server which virtual host to use if many are sharing the same IP address. A blank line
tells the server that the request is over; it then spits back its response: first headers,
then a blank line, and then the body of the response.

Pasting text into *telnet* can get tedious, and it's even harder to make requests with the
POST method that way. If you make a request with HTTP_Request, you can retrieve
the response headers and the response body with the getResponseHeader( ) and
getResponseBody( ) methods:

```
require 'HTTP/Request.php';

$r = new HTTP_Request('http://www.example.com/submit.php');
$r->setMethod(HTTP_REQUEST_METHOD_POST);
$r->addPostData('monkey','uncle');
$r->sendRequest();

$response_headers = $r->getResponseHeader();
$response_body    = $r->getResponseBody();
```

To retrieve a specific response header, pass the header name to getResponseHeader( ).
Without an argument, getResponseHeader( ) returns an array containing all the

response headers. HTTP_Request doesn't save the outgoing request in a variable, but you can reconstruct it by calling the private _buildRequest( ) method:

```
require 'HTTP/Request.php';

$r = new HTTP_Request('http://www.example.com/submit.php');
$r->setMethod(HTTP_REQUEST_METHOD_POST);
$r->addPostData('monkey','uncle');

print $r->_buildRequest();
```

The request that's printed is:

```
POST /submit.php HTTP/1.1
User-Agent: PEAR HTTP_Request class ( http://pear.php.net/ )
Content-Type: application/x-www-form-urlencoded
Connection: close
Host: www.example.com
Content-Length: 12

monkey=uncle
```

With cURL, to include response headers in the output from curl_exec( ), set the CURLOPT_HEADER option:

```
$c = curl_init('http://www.example.com/submit.php');
curl_setopt($c, CURLOPT_HEADER, 1);
curl_setopt($c, CURLOPT_POST, 1);
curl_setopt($c, CURLOPT_POSTFIELDS, 'monkey=uncle&rhino=aunt');
curl_setopt($c, CURLOPT_RETURNTRANSFER, 1);
$response_headers_and_page = curl_exec($c);
curl_close($c);
```

To write the response headers directly to a file, open a file handle with fopen( ) and set CURLOPT_WRITEHEADER to that file handle:

```
$fh = fopen('/tmp/curl-response-headers.txt','w') or die($php_errormsg);
$c = curl_init('http://www.example.com/submit.php');
curl_setopt($c, CURLOPT_POST, 1);
curl_setopt($c, CURLOPT_POSTFIELDS, 'monkey=uncle&rhino=aunt');
curl_setopt($c, CURLOPT_RETURNTRANSFER, 1);
curl_setopt($c, CURLOPT_WRITEHEADER, $fh);
$page = curl_exec($c);
curl_close($c);
fclose($fh) or die($php_errormsg);
```

The cURL module's CURLOPT_VERBOSE option causes curl_exec( ) and curl_close( ) to print out debugging information to standard error, including the contents of the request:

```
$c = curl_init('http://www.example.com/submit.php');
curl_setopt($c, CURLOPT_VERBOSE, 1);
curl_setopt($c, CURLOPT_POST, 1);
curl_setopt($c, CURLOPT_POSTFIELDS, 'monkey=uncle&rhino=aunt');
curl_setopt($c, CURLOPT_RETURNTRANSFER, 1);
```

```
$page = curl_exec($c);
curl_close($c);
```

This prints:

```
* Connected to www.example.com (10.1.1.1)
> POST /submit.php HTTP/1.1
Host: www.example.com
Pragma: no-cache
Accept: image/gif, image/x-xbitmap, image/jpeg, image/pjpeg, */*
Content-Length: 23
Content-Type: application/x-www-form-urlencoded

monkey=uncle&rhino=aunt* Connection #0 left intact
* Closing connection #0
```

Because cURL prints the debugging information to standard error and not standard output, it can't be captured with output buffering, as Recipe 10.10 does with print_r( ). You can, however, open a file handle for writing and set CURLOUT_STDERR to that file handle to divert the debugging information to a file:

```
$fh = fopen('/tmp/curl.out','w') or die($php_errormsg);
$c = curl_init('http://www.example.com/submit.php');
curl_setopt($c, CURLOPT_VERBOSE, 1);
curl_setopt($c, CURLOPT_POST, 1);
curl_setopt($c, CURLOPT_POSTFIELDS, 'monkey=uncle&rhino=aunt');
curl_setopt($c, CURLOPT_RETURNTRANSFER, 1);
curl_setopt($c, CURLOPT_STDERR, $fh);
$page = curl_exec($c);
curl_close($c);
fclose($fh) or die($php_errormsg);
```

See Also

Recipe 10.10 for output buffering; documentation on curl_setopt( ) at *http://www.php.net/curl-setopt*; the PEAR HTTP_Request class at *http://pear.php.net/package-info.php?package=HTTP_Request*; the syntax of an HTTP request is defined in RFC 2616 and available at *http://www.faqs.org/rfcs/rfc2616.html*.

11.7   Marking Up a Web Page

Problem

You want to display a web page, for example a search result, with certain words highlighted.

Solution

Use preg_replace( ) with an array of patterns and replacements:

```
$patterns = array('\bdog\b/', '\bcat\b');
$replacements = array('<b style="color:black;background-color=#FFFF00">dog</b>',
                      '<b style='color:black;background-color=#FF9900">cat</b>');
while ($page) {
    if (preg_match('{^([^<]*)?(</?[^>]+?>)?(.*)$}',$page,$matches)) {
        print preg_replace($patterns,$replacements,$matches[1]);
        print $matches[2];
        $page = $matches[3];
    }
}
```

Discussion

The regular expression used with preg_match( ) matches as much text as possible before an HTML tag, then an HTML tag, and then the rest of the content. The text before the HTML tag has the highlighting applied to it, the HTML tag is printed out without any highlighting, and the rest of the content has the same match applied to it. This prevents any highlighting of words that occur inside HTML tags (in URLs or alt text, for example) which would prevent the page from displaying properly.

The following program retrieves the URL in $url and highlights the words in the $words array. Words are not highlighted when they are part of larger words because they are matched with the \b Perl-compatible regular expression operator for finding word boundaries.

```
$colors = array('FFFF00','FF9900','FF0000','FF00FF',
                '99FF33','33FFCC','FF99FF','00CC33');

// build search and replace patterns for regex
$patterns = array();
$replacements = array();
for ($i = 0, $j = count($words); $i < $j; $i++) {
    $patterns[$i] = '/\b'.preg_quote($words[$i], '/').'\b/';
    $replacements[$i] = '<b style="color:black;background-color:#' .
                        $colors[$i % 8] .'">' . $words[$i] . '</b>';
}

// retrieve page
$fh = fopen($url,'r') or die($php_errormsg);
while (! feof($fh)) {
    $s .= fread($fh,4096);
}
fclose($fh);

if ($j) {
    while ($s) {
        if (preg_match('{^([^<]*)?(</?[^>]+?>)?(.*)$}s',$s,$matches)) {
            print preg_replace($patterns,$replacements,$matches[1]);
```

```
            print $matches[2];
            $s = $matches[3];
        }
    }
} else {
    print $s;
}
```

See Also

Recipe 13.7 for information on capturing text inside HTML tags; documentation on preg_match() at *http://www.php.net/preg-match* and preg_replace() at *http://www.php.net/preg-replace*.

11.8   Extracting Links from an HTML File

Problem

You need to extract the URLs that are specified inside an HTML document.

Solution

Use the pc_link_extractor() function shown in Example 11-2.

Example 11-2. pc_link_extractor()
```
function pc_link_extractor($s) {
  $a = array();
  if (preg_match_all('/<a\s+.*?href=[\"\']?([^\"\' >]*)[\"\']?[^>]*>(.*?)<\/a>/i',
                $s,$matches,PREG_SET_ORDER)) {
    foreach($matches as $match) {
      array_push($a,array($match[1],$match[2]));
    }
  }
  return $a;
}
```

For example:
```
    $links = pc_link_extractor($page);
```

Discussion

The pc_link_extractor() function returns an array. Each element of that array is itself a two-element array. The first element is the target of the link, and the second element is the text that is linked. For example:
```
    $links=<<<END
    Click <a href="http://www.oreilly.com">here</a> to visit a computer book
```

```
publisher. Click <a href="http://www.sklar.com">over here</a> to visit
a computer book author.
END;

$a = pc_link_extractor($links);
print_r($a);
Array
(
    [0] => Array
        (
            [0] => http://www.oreilly.com
            [1] => here
        )
    [1] => Array
        (
            [0] => http://www.sklar.com
            [1] => over here
        )
)
```

The regular expression in pc_link_extractor( ) won't work on all links, such as
those that are constructed with JavaScript or some hexadecimal escapes, but it
should function on the majority of reasonably well-formed HTML.

See Also

Recipe 13.7 for information on capturing text inside HTML tags; documentation on
preg_match_all( ) at *http://www.php.net/preg-match-all*.

11.9   Converting ASCII to HTML

Problem

You want to turn plaintext into reasonably formatted HTML.

Solution

First, encode entities with htmlentities( ); then, transform the text into various
HTML structures. The pc_ascii2html( ) function shown in Example 11-3 has basic
transformations for links and paragraph breaks.

Example 11-3. pc_ascii2html()

```
function pc_ascii2html($s) {
  $s = htmlentities($s);
  $grafs = split("\n\n",$s);
  for ($i = 0, $j = count($grafs); $i < $j; $i++) {
    // Link to what seem to be http or ftp URLs
    $grafs[$i] = preg_replace('/((ht|f)tp:\/\/[^\s&]+)/',
```

Example 11-3. pc_ascii2html() (continued)

```
                          '<a href="$1">$1</a>',$grafs[$i]);

    // Link to email addresses
    $grafs[$i] = preg_replace('/[^@\s]+@([-a-z0-9]+\.)+[a-z]{2,}/i',
        '<a href="mailto:$1">$1</a>',$grafs[$i]);

    // Begin with a new paragraph
    $grafs[$i] = '<p>'.$grafs[$i].'</p>';
  }
  return join("\n\n",$grafs);
}
```

Discussion

The more you know about what the ASCII text looks like, the better your HTML conversion can be. For example, if emphasis is indicated with *asterisks* or /slashes/ around words, you can add rules that take care of that, as follows:

```
$grafs[$i] = preg_replace('/(\A|\s)\*([^*]+)\*(\s|\z)/',
                          '$1<b>$2</b>$3',$grafs[$i]);
$grafs[$i] = preg_replace('{(\A|\s)/([^/]+)/(\s|\z)}',
                          '$1<i>$2</i>$3',$grafs[$i]);
```

See Also

Documentation on preg_replace( ) at *http://www.php.net/preg-replace*.

11.10 Converting HTML to ASCII

Problem

You need to convert HTML to readable, formatted ASCII text.

Solution

If you have access to an external program that formats HTML as ASCII, such as *lynx*, call it like so:

```
$file = escapeshellarg($file);
$ascii = `lynx -dump $file`;
```

Discussion

If you can't use an external formatter, the pc_html2ascii( ) function shown in Example 11-4 handles a reasonable subset of HTML (no tables or frames, though).

Example 11-4. pc_html2ascii()

```
function pc_html2ascii($s) {
  // convert links
  $s = preg_replace('/<a\s+.*?href="?([^\" >]*)"?[^>]*>(.*?)<\/a>/i',
                    '$2 ($1)', $s);

  // convert <br>, <hr>, <p>, <div> to line breaks
  $s = preg_replace('@<(b|h)r[^>]*>@i',"\n",$s);
  $s = preg_replace('@<p[^>]*>@i',"\n\n",$s);
  $s = preg_replace('@<div[^>]*>(.*)</div>@i',"\n".'$1'."\n",$s);

  // convert bold and italic
  $s = preg_replace('@<b[^>]*>(.*?)</b>@i','*$1*',$s);
  $s = preg_replace('@<i[^>]*>(.*?)</i>@i','/$1/',$s);

  // decode named entities
  $s = strtr($s,array_flip(get_html_translation_table(HTML_ENTITIES)));

  // decode numbered entities
  $s = preg_replace('//e','chr(\\1)',$s);

  // remove any remaining tags
  $s = strip_tags($s);

  return $s;
}
```

See Also

Recipe 9.8 for more on get_html_translation_table(); documentation on preg_replace( ) at *http://www.php.net/preg-replace*, get_html_translation_table( ) at *http://www.php.net/get-html-translation-table*, and strip_tags( ) at *http://www.php.net/strip-tags*.

11.11 Removing HTML and PHP Tags

Problem

You want to remove HTML and PHP tags from a string or file.

Solution

Use strip_tags( ) to remove HTML and PHP tags from a string:

```
$html = '<a href="http://www.oreilly.com">I <b>love computer books.</b></a>';
print strip_tags($html);
I love computer books.
```

Use fgetss( ) to remove them from a file as you read in lines:

```
$fh = fopen('test.html','r') or die($php_errormsg);
while ($s = fgetss($fh,1024)) {
    print $s;
}
fclose($fh)                    or die($php_errormsg);
```

Discussion

While fgetss( ) is convenient if you need to strip tags from a file as you read it in, it may get confused if tags span lines or if they span the buffer that fgetss( ) reads from the file. At the price of increased memory usage, reading the entire file into a string provides better results:

```
$no_tags = strip_tags(join('',file('test.html')));
```

Both strip_tags( ) and fgetss( ) can be told not to remove certain tags by specifying those tags as a last argument. The tag specification is case-insensitive, and for pairs of tags, you only have to specify the opening tag. For example, this removes all but <b></b> tags from $html:

```
$html = '<a href="http://www.oreilly.com">I <b>love</b> computer books.</a>';
print strip_tags($html,'<b>');
I <b>love</b> computer books.
```

See Also

Documentation on strip_tags( ) at *http://www.php.net/strip-tags* and fgetss( ) at *http://www.php.net/fgetss*.

11.12 Using Smarty Templates

Problem

You want to separate code and design in your pages. Designers can work on the HTML files without dealing with the PHP code, and programmers can work on the PHP files without worrying about design.

Solution

Use a templating system. One easy-to-use template system is called Smarty. In a Smarty template, strings between curly braces are replaced with new values:

```
Hello, {$name}
```

The PHP code that creates a page sets up the variables and then displays the template like this:

```
require 'Smarty.class.php';

$smarty = new Smarty;
$smarty->assign('name','Ruby');
$smarty->display('hello.tpl');
```

Discussion

Here's a Smarty template for displaying rows retrieved from a database:

```
<html>
<head><title>cheeses</title></head>
<body>
<table border="1">
<tr>
  <th>cheese</th>
  <th>country</th>
  <th>price</th>
</tr>
{section name=id loop=$results}
<tr>
  <td>{$results[id]->cheese}</td>
  <td>{$results[id]->country}</td>
  <td>{$results[id]->price}</td>
</tr>
{/section}
</table>
</body>
</html>
```

Here's the corresponding PHP file that loads the data from the database and then displays the template, stored in *food.tpl*:

```
require 'Smarty.class.php';

mysql_connect('localhost','test','test');
mysql_select_db('test');

$r = mysql_query('SELECT * FROM cheese');
while ($ob = mysql_fetch_object($r)) {
    $ob->price = sprintf('$%.02f',$ob->price);
    $results[] = $ob;

}
$smarty = new Smarty;
$smarty->assign('results',$results);
$smarty->display('food.tpl');
```

After including the base class for the templating engine (*Smarty.class.php*), you retrieve and format the results from the database and store them in an array. To generate the templated page, just instantiate a new $smarty object, tell $smarty to pay attention to the $results variable, and then tell $smarty to display the template.

Smarty is easy to install: just copy a few files to your include_path and make a few directories. You can find full instructions at *http://smarty.php.net/manual/en/ installing.smarty.basic.html*. Use Smarty with discipline to preserve the value of having templates in the first place—separating your logic and your presentation. A template engine has its own scripting language you use to interpolate variables, execute loops, and do other simple logic. Try to keep that to a minimum in your templates and load up your PHP files with the programming.

See Also

The Smarty home page at *http://smarty.php.net/*.

11.13 Parsing a Web Server Log File

Problem

You want to do calculations based on the information in your web server's access log file.

Solution

Open the file and parse each line with a regular expression that matches the log file format. This regular expression matches the NCSA Combined Log Format:

```
$pattern = '/^([^ ]+) ([^ ]+) ([^ ]+) (\[[^\]]+\]) "(.*)" (.*) (.*)" ([0-9\-]+)
    ([0-9\-]+) "(.*)" "(.*)"$/';
```

Discussion

This program parses the NCSA Combined Log Format lines and displays a list of pages sorted by the number of requests for each page:

```
$log_file = '/usr/local/apache/logs/access.log';
$pattern = '/^([^ ]+) ([^ ]+) ([^ ]+) (\[[^\]]+\]) "(.*)" (.*) (.*)" ([0-9\-]+)
    ([0-9\-]+) "(.*)" "(.*)"$/';

$fh = fopen($log_file,'r') or die($php_errormsg);
$i = 1;
$requests = array();
while (! feof($fh)) {
    // read each line and trim off leading/trailing whitespace
    if ($s = trim(fgets($fh,16384))) {
        // match the line to the pattern
        if (preg_match($pattern,$s,$matches)) {
```

```
        /* put each part of the match in an appropriately-named
         * variable */
        list($whole_match,$remote_host,$logname,$user,$time,
            $method,$request,$protocol,$status,$bytes,$referer,
            $user_agent) = $matches;
        // keep track of the count of each request
        $requests[$request]++;
    } else {
        // complain if the line didn't match the pattern
        error_log("Can't parse line $i: $s");
    }
  }
  $i++;
}
fclose($fh) or die($php_errormsg);

// sort the array (in reverse) by number of requests
arsort($requests);

// print formatted results
foreach ($requests as $request => $accesses) {
    printf("%6d    %s\n",$accesses,$request);
}
```

The pattern used in preg_match( ) matches Combined Log Format lines such as:

```
10.1.1.162 - david [20/Jul/2001:13:05:02 -0400] "GET /sklar.css HTTP/1.0" 200
278 "-" "Mozilla/4.77 [en] (WinNT; U)"
10.1.1.248 - - [14/Mar/2002:13:31:37 -0500] "GET /php-cookbook/colors.html
HTTP/1.1" 200 460 "-" "Mozilla/4.0 (compatible; MSIE 5.5; Windows NT 5.0)"
```

In the first line, 10.1.1.162 is the IP address that the request came from. Depending on the server configuration, this could be a hostname instead. When the $matches array is assigned to the list of separate variables, the hostname is stored in $remote_host. The next hyphen (-) means that the remote host didn't supply a username via *identd*,* so $logname is set to -.

The string david is a username provided by the browser using HTTP Basic Authentication and is put in $user. The date and time of the request, stored in $time, is in brackets. This date and time format isn't understood by strtotime( ), so if you wanted to do calculations based on request date and time, you have to do some further processing to extract each piece of the formatted time string. Next, in quotes, is the first line of the request. This is composed of the method (GET, POST, HEAD, etc.) which is stored in $method; the requested URI, which is stored in $request, and the protocol, which is stored in $protocol. For GET requests, the query string is part of the URI. For POST requests, the request body that contains the variables isn't logged.

---

* *identd*, defined in RFC 1413, is supposed to be a good way to identify users remotely. However, it's not very secure or reliable. A good explanation of why is at *http://www.clock.org/~fair/opinion/identd.html*.

After the request comes the request status, stored in $status. Status 200 means the request was successful. After the status is the size in bytes of the response, stored in $bytes. The last two elements of the line, each in quotes, are the referring page if any, stored in $referer* and the user agent string identifying the browser that made the request, stored in $user_agent.

Once the log file line has been parsed into distinct variables, you can do the needed calculations. In this case, just keep a counter in the $requests array of how many times each URI is requested. After looping through all lines in the file, print out a sorted, formatted list of requests and counts.

Calculating statistics this way from web server access logs is easy, but it's not very flexible. The program needs to be modified for different kinds of reports, restricted date ranges, report formatting, and many other features. A better solution for comprehensive web site statistics is to use a program such as *analog*, available for free at *http://www.analog.cx*. It has many types of reports and configuration options that should satisfy just about every need you may have.

See Also

Documentation on preg_match() at *http://www.php.net/preg-match*; information about common log file formats is available at *http://httpd.apache.org/docs/logs.html*.

11.14 Program: Finding Stale Links

The *stale-links.php* program in Example 11-5 produces a list of links in a page and their status. It tells you if the links are okay, if they've been moved somewhere else, or if they're bad. Run the program by passing it a URL to scan for links:

```
% stale-links.php http://www.oreilly.com/
http://www.oreilly.com/index.html: OK
http://www.oreillynet.com: OK
http://conferences.oreilly.com: OK
http://international.oreilly.com: OK
http://safari.oreilly.com: MOVED: mainhom.asp?home
...
```

The *stale-links.php* program uses the cURL extension to retrieve web pages. First, it retrieves the URL specified on the command line. Once a page has been retrieved, the program uses the pc_link_extractor() function from Recipe 11.8 to get a list of links in the page. Then, after prepending a base URL to each link if necessary, the link is retrieved. Because we need just the headers of these responses, we use the

---

* The correct way to spell this word is "referrer." However, since the original HTTP specification (RFC 1945) misspelled it as "referer," the three-R spelling is frequently used in context.

HEAD method instead of GET by setting the CURLOPT_NOBODY option. Setting CURLOPT_HEADER tells curl_exec( ) to include the response headers in the string it returns. Based on the response code, the status of the link is printed, along with its new location if it's been moved.

Example 11-5. stale-links.php

```php
function_exists('curl_exec') or die('CURL extension required');

function pc_link_extractor($s) {
    $a = array();
    if (preg_match_all('/<A\s+.*?HREF=[\"\']?([^\"\' >]*)[\"\']?[^>]*>(.*?)<\/A>/i',
                        $s,$matches,PREG_SET_ORDER)) {
        foreach($matches as $match) {
            array_push($a,array($match[1],$match[2]));
        }
    }
    return $a;
}

$url = $_SERVER['argv'][1];

// retrieve URL
$c = curl_init($url);
curl_setopt($c, CURLOPT_RETURNTRANSFER, 1);
curl_setopt($c, CURLOPT_FOLLOWLOCATION,1);
$page = curl_exec($c);
$info = curl_getinfo($c);
curl_close($c);

// compute base url from url
// this doesn't pay attention to a <base> tag in the page
$url_parts = parse_url($info['url']);
if ('' == $url_parts['path']) { $url_parts['path'] = '/'; }
$base_path = preg_replace('<^(.*/)([^/]*)$>','\\1',$url_parts['path']);
$base_url = sprintf('%s://%s%s%s',
                    $url_parts['scheme'],
                    ($url_parts['username'] || $url_parts['password']) ?
                    "$url_parts[username]:$url_parts[password]@" : '',
                    $url_parts['host'],
                    $url_parts['path']);

// keep track of the links we visit so we don't visit each more than once
$seen_links = array();

if ($page) {
    $links = pc_link_extractor($page);
    foreach ($links as $link) {
        // resolve relative links
        if (! (preg_match('{^(http|https|mailto):}',$link[0]))) {
            $link[0] = $base_url.$link[0];
        }
```

Example 11-5. stale-links.php (continued)

```
    // skip this link if we've seen it already
    if ($seen_links[$link[0]]) {
        continue;
    }

    // mark this link as seen
    $seen_links[$link[0]] = true;

    // print the link we're visiting
    print $link[0].': ';
    flush();

    // visit the link
    $c = curl_init($link[0]);
    curl_setopt($c, CURLOPT_RETURNTRANSFER, 1);
    curl_setopt($c, CURLOPT_NOBODY, 1);
    curl_setopt($c, CURLOPT_HEADER, 1);
    $link_headers = curl_exec($c);
    $curl_info = curl_getinfo($c);
    curl_close($c);

    switch (intval($curl_info['http_code']/100)) {
    case 2:
        // 2xx response codes mean the page is OK
        $status = 'OK';
        break;
    case 3:
        // 3xx response codes mean redirection
        $status = 'MOVED';
        if (preg_match('/^Location: (.*)$/m',$link_headers,$matches)) {
            $location = trim($matches[1]);
            $status .= ": $location";
        }
        break;
    default:
        // other response codes mean errors
        $status = "ERROR: $curl_info[http_code]";
        break;
    }

    print "$status\n";
    }
}
```

11.15 Program: Finding Fresh Links

Example 11-6, *fresh-links.php*, is a modification of the program in Recipe 11.14 that
produces a list of links and their last modified time. If the server on which a URL
lives doesn't provide a last modified time, the program reports the URL's last modified time as the time the URL was requested. If the program can't retrieve the URL

---

successfully, it prints out the status code it got when it tried to retrieve the URL. Run the program by passing it a URL to scan for links:

```
% fresh-links.php http://www.oreilly.com
http://www.oreilly.com/index.html: Fri Aug 16 16:48:34 2002
http://www.oreillynet.com: Mon Aug 19 10:18:54 2002
http://conferences.oreilly.com: Fri Aug 16 19:41:46 2002
http://international.oreilly.com: Fri Mar 29 18:06:32 2002
http://safari.oreilly.com: 302
http://www.oreilly.com/catalog/search.html: Tue Apr  2 19:05:57 2002
http://www.oreilly.com/oreilly/press/: 302
...
```

This output is from a run of the program at about 10:20 A.M. EDT on August 19, 2002. The link to *http://www.oreillynet.com* is very fresh, but the others are of varying ages. The link to *http://www.oreilly.com/oreilly/press/* doesn't have a last modified time next to it; it has instead, an HTTP status code (302). This means it's been moved elsewhere, as reported by the output of *stale-links.php* in Recipe 11.14.

The program to find fresh links is conceptually almost identical to the program to find stale links. It uses the same pc_link_extractor( ) function from Recipe 11.9; however, it uses the HTTP_Request class instead of cURL to retrieve URLs. The code to get the base URL specified on the command line is inside a loop so that it can follow any redirects that are returned.

Once a page has been retrieved, the program uses the pc_link_extractor( ) function to get a list of links in the page. Then, after prepending a base URL to each link if necessary, sendRequest( ) is called on each link found in the original page. Since we need just the headers of these responses, we use the HEAD method instead of GET. Instead of printing out a new location for moved links, however, it prints out a formatted version of the Last-Modified header if it's available.

Example 11-6. fresh-links.php

```
require 'HTTP/Request.php';

function pc_link_extractor($s) {
    $a = array();
    if (preg_match_all('/<A\s+.*?HREF=[\"\']?([^\"\' >]*)[\"\']?[^>]*>(.*?)<\/A>/i',
                    $s,$matches,PREG_SET_ORDER)) {
        foreach($matches as $match) {
            array_push($a,array($match[1],$match[2]));
        }
    }
    return $a;
}

$url = $_SERVER['argv'][1];

// retrieve URLs in a loop to follow redirects
$done = 0;
```

Example 11-6. fresh-links.php (continued)

```php
while (! $done) {
    $req = new HTTP_Request($url);
    $req->sendRequest();
    if ($response_code = $req->getResponseCode()) {
        if ((intval($response_code/100) == 3) &&
            ($location = $req->getResponseHeader('Location'))) {
            $url = $location;
        } else {
            $done = 1;
        }
    } else {
        return false;
    }
}

// compute base url from url
// this doesn't pay attention to a <base> tag in the page
$base_url = preg_replace('{^(.*/)([^/]*)$}','\\1',$req->_url->getURL());

// keep track of the links we visit so we don't visit each more than once
$seen_links = array();

if ($body = $req->getResponseBody()) {
    $links = pc_link_extractor($body);
    foreach ($links as $link) {
        // skip https URLs
        if (preg_match('{^https://}',$link[0])) {
            continue;
        }
        // resolve relative links
        if (! (preg_match('{^(http|mailto):}',$link[0]))) {
            $link[0] = $base_url.$link[0];
        }
        // skip this link if we've seen it already
        if ($seen_links[$link[0]]) {
            continue;
        }

        // mark this link as seen
        $seen_links[$link[0]] = true;

        // print the link we're visiting
        print $link[0].': ';
        flush();

        // visit the link
        $req2 = new HTTP_Request($link[0],
                              array('method' => HTTP_REQUEST_METHOD_HEAD));
        $now = time();
        $req2->sendRequest();
        $response_code = $req2->getResponseCode();
```

Example 11-6. fresh-links.php (continued)

```php
        // if the retrieval is successful
        if ($response_code == 200) {
            // get the Last-Modified header
            if ($lm = $req2->getResponseHeader('Last-Modified')) {
                $lm_utc = strtotime($lm);
            } else {
                // or set Last-Modified to now
                $lm_utc = $now;
            }
            print strftime('%c',$lm_utc);
        } else {
            // otherwise, print the response code
            print $response_code;
        }
        print "\n";
    }
}
```

CHAPTER 12

XML

12.0 Introduction

Recently, XML has gained popularity as a data-exchange and message-passing format. As web services become more widespread, XML plays an even more important role in a developer's life. With the help of a few extensions, PHP lets you read and write XML for every occasion.

XML provides developers with a structured way to mark up data with tags arranged in a tree-like hierarchy. One perspective on XML is to treat it as CSV on steroids. You can use XML to store records broken into a series of fields. But, instead of merely separating each field with a comma, you can include a field name, type, and attributes alongside the data.

Another view of XML is as a document representation language. For instance, the *PHP Cookbook* was written using XML. The book is divided into chapters; each chapter into recipes; and each recipe into Problem, Solution, and Discussion sections. Within any individual section, we further subdivide the text into paragraphs, tables, figures, and examples. An article on a web page can similarly be divided into the page title and headline, the authors of the piece, the story itself, and any sidebars, related links, and additional content.

XML text looks similar to HTML. Both use tags bracketed by < and > for marking up text. But XML is both stricter and looser than HTML. It's stricter because all container tags must be properly closed. No opening elements are allowed without a corresponding closing tag. It's looser because you're not forced to use a set list of tags, such as <a>, <img>, and <h1>. Instead, you have the freedom to choose a series of tag names that best describe your data.

Other key differences between XML and HTML are case-sensitivity, attribute quoting, and whitespace. In HTML, <B> and <b> are the same bold tag; in XML, they're two different tags. In HTML, you can often omit quotation marks around attributes; XML, however, requires them. So, you must always write:

```
<element attribute="value">
```

Additionally, HTML parsers generally ignore whitespace, so a run of 20 consecutive spaces is treated the same as one space. XML parsers preserve whitespace, unless explicitly instructed otherwise. Because all elements must be closed, empty elements must end with />. For instance in HTML, the line break is <br>, while in XML, it's written as <br />.*

There is another restriction on XML documents. Since XML documents can be parsed into a tree of elements, the outermost element is known as the *root element*. Just as a tree has only one trunk, an XML document must have exactly one root element. In the previous book example, this means chapters must be bundled inside a book tag. If you want to place multiple books inside a document, you need to package them inside a bookcase or another container. This limitation applies only to the document root. Again, just like trees can have multiple branches off of the trunk, it's legal to store multiple books inside a bookcase.

This chapter doesn't aim to teach you XML; for an introduction to XML, see *Learning XML*, by Erik T. Ray. A solid nuts-and-bolts guide to all aspects of XML is *XML in a Nutshell*, by Elliotte Rusty Harold and W. Scott Means. Both books are published by O'Reilly & Associates.

Now that we've covered the rules, here's an example: if you are a librarian and want to convert your card catalog to XML, start with this basic set of XML tags:

```
<book>
    <title>PHP Cookbook</title>
    <author>Sklar, David and Trachtenberg, Adam</author>
    <subject>PHP</subject>
</book>
```

From there, you can add new elements or modify existing ones. For example, <author> can be divided into first and last name, or you can allow for multiple records so two authors aren't placed in one field.

The first three recipes in this chapter cover writing and reading XML. Recipe 12.1 shows how to write XML without additional tools. To use the DOM XML extension to write XML in a standardized fashion, see Recipe 12.2. Reading XML using DOM is the topic of Recipe 12.3.

But XML isn't an end by itself. Once you've gathered all your XML, the real question is "What do you do with it?" With an event-based parser, as described in Recipe 12.4, you can make element tags trigger actions, such as storing data into easily manipulated structures or reformatting the text.

---

* This is why nl2br( ) outputs <br />; its output is XML-compatible.

With XSLT, you can take a XSL stylesheet and turn XML into viewable output. By separating content from presentation, you can make one stylesheet for web browsers, another for PDAs, and a third for cell phones, all without changing the content itself. This is the subject of Recipe 12.5.

You can use a protocol such as XML-RPC or SOAP to exchange XML messages between yourself and a server, or to act as a server yourself. You can thus put your card catalog on the Internet and allow other programmers to query the catalog and retrieve book records in a format that's easy for them to parse and display in their applications. Another use would be to set up an RSS feed that gets updated whenever the library gets a new book in stock. XML-RPC clients and servers are the subjects of Recipes 12.6 and 12.7, respectively. Recipes 12.8 and 12.9 cover SOAP clients and servers. WDDX, a data exchange format that originated with the ColdFusion language, is the topic of Recipe 12.10. Reading RSS feeds, a popular XML-based headline syndication format, is covered in Recipe 12.11.

As with many bleeding-edge technologies, some of PHP's XML tools are not feature-complete and bug-free. However, XML is an area of active development in the PHP community; new features are added and bugs are fixed on a regular basis. As a result, many XML functions documented here are still experimental. Sometimes, all that means is that the function is 99% complete, but there may be a few small bugs lying around. Other times, it means that the name or the behavior of the function could be completely changed. If a function is in a highly unstable state, we mention it in the recipe.

We've documented the functions as they're currently planned to work in PHP 4.3. Because XML is such an important area, it made no sense to omit these recipes from the book. Also, we wanted to make sure that the latest functions are used in our examples. This can, however, lead to small problems if the function names and prototypes change. If you find that a recipe isn't working as you'd expect it to, please check the online PHP manual or the errata section of the catalog page for the *PHP Cookbook, http://www.oreilly.com/catalog/phpckbk.*

12.1 Generating XML Manually

Problem

You want to generate XML. For instance, you want to provide an XML version of your data for another program to parse.

Solution

Loop through your data and print it out surrounded by the correct XML tags:

```
header('Content-Type: text/xml');
print '<?xml version="1.0"?>' . "\n";
print "<shows>\n";

$shows = array(array('name'     => 'Simpsons',
                     'channel'  => 'FOX',
                     'start'    => '8:00 PM',
                     'duration' => '30'),

              array('name'     => 'Law & Order',
                    'channel'  => 'NBC',
                    'start'    => '8:00 PM',
                    'duration' => '60'));

foreach ($shows as $show) {
    print "    <show>\n";
    foreach($show as $tag => $data) {
        print "        <$tag>" . htmlspecialchars($data) . "</$tag>\n";
    }
    print "    </show>\n";
}

print "</shows>\n";
```

Discussion

Printing out XML manually mostly involves lots of foreach loops as you iterate through arrays. However, there are a few tricky details. First, you need to call header( ) to set the correct Content-Type header for the document. Since you're sending XML instead of HTML, it should be text/xml.

Next, depending on your settings for the short_open_tag configuration directive, trying to print the XML declaration may accidentally turn on PHP processing. Since the <? of <?xml version="1.0"?> is the short PHP open tag, to print the declaration to the browser you need to either disable the directive or print the line from within PHP. We do the latter in the Solution.

Last, entities must be escaped. For example, the & in the show Law & Order needs to be &. Call htmlspecialchars( ) to escape your data.

The output from the example in the Solution is:

```
<?xml version="1.0"?>
<shows>
    <show>
        <name>Simpsons</name>
        <channel>FOX</channel>
        <start>8:00 PM</start>
```

```
        <duration>30</duration>
    </show>
    <show>
        <name>Law &amp; Order</name>
        <channel>NBC</channel>
        <start>8:00 PM</start>
        <duration>60</duration>
    </show>
</shows>
```

See Also

Recipe 12.2 for generating XML using DOM; Recipe 12.3 for reading XML with DOM; documentation on htmlspecialchars( ) at *http://www.php.net/htmlspecialchars*.

12.2   Generating XML with the DOM

Problem

You want to generate XML but want to do it in an organized way instead of using print and loops.

Solution

Use PHP's DOM XML extension to create a DOM object; then, call dump_mem( ) or dump_file( ) to generate a well-formed XML document:

```
// create a new document
$dom = domxml_new_doc('1.0');

// create the root element, <book>, and append it to the document
$book = $dom->append_child($dom->create_element('book'));

// create the title element and append it to $book
$title = $book->append_child($dom->create_element('title'));

// set the text and the cover attribute for $title
$title->append_child($dom->create_text_node('PHP Cookbook'));
$title->set_attribute('cover', 'soft');

// create and append author elements to $book
$sklar = $book->append_child($dom->create_element('author'));
// create and append the text for each element
$sklar->append_child($dom->create_text_node('Sklar'));

$trachtenberg = $book->append_child($dom->create_element('author'));
$trachtenberg->append_child($dom->create_text_node('Trachtenberg'));
```

```
// print a nicely formatted version of the DOM document as XML
echo $dom->dump_mem(true);
<?xml version="1.0"?>
<book>
  <title cover="soft">PHP Cookbook</title>
  <author>Sklar</author>
  <author>Trachtenberg</author>
</book>
```

Discussion

A single element is known as a *node*. Nodes can be of a dozen different types, but the three most popular are elements, attributes, and text. Given this:

```
<book cover="soft">PHP Cookbook</book>
```

PHP's DOM XML functions refer to book as type XML_ELEMENT_NODE, cover="soft" maps to an XML_ATTRIBUTE_NODE, and PHP Cookbook is a XML_TEXT_NODE.

For DOM parsing, PHP uses libxml, developed for the Gnome project. You can download it from *http://www.xmlsoft.org*. To activate it, configure PHP with --with-dom.

The revamped PHP 4.3 DOM XML functions follow a pattern. You create an object as either an element or a text node, add and set any attributes you want, and then append it to the tree in the spot it belongs.

Before creating elements, create a new document, passing the XML version as the sole argument:

```
$dom = domxml_new_doc('1.0');
```

Now create new elements belonging to the document. Despite being associated with a specific document, nodes don't join the document tree until appended:

```
$book_element = $dom->create_element('book');
$book = $dom->append_child($book_element);
```

Here a new book element is created and assigned to the object $book_element. To create the document root, append $book_element as a child of the $dom document. The result, $book, refers to the specific element and its location within the DOM object.

All nodes are created by calling a method on $dom. Once a node is created, it can be appended to any element in the tree. The element from which we call the append_child( ) method determines the location in the tree where the node is placed. In the previous case, $book_element is appended to $dom. The element appended to $dom is the top-level node, or the *root node*.

You can also append a new child element to $book. Since $book is a child of $dom, the new element is, by extension, a grandchild of $dom:

```
$title_element = $dom->create_element('title');
$title = $book->append_child($title_element);
```

By calling $book->append_child( ), this code places the $title_element element under the $book element.

To add the text inside the <title></title> tags, create a text node using create_text_node( ) and append it to $title:

```
$text_node = $dom->create_text_node('PHP Cookbook');
$title->append_child($text_node);
```

Since $title is already added to the document, there's no need to reappend it to $book.

The order in which you append children to nodes isn't important. The following four lines, which first append the text node to $title_element and then to $book, are equivalent to the previous code:

```
$title_element = $dom->create_element('title');
$text_node = $dom->create_text_node('PHP Cookbook');

$title_element->append_child($text_node);
$book->append_child($title_element);
```

To add an attribute, call set_attribute( ) upon a node, passing the attribute name and value as arguments:

```
$title->set_attribute('cover', 'soft');
```

If you print the title element now, it looks like this:

```
<title cover="soft">PHP Cookbook</title>
```

Once you're finished, you can output the document as a string or to a file:

```
// put the string representation of the XML document in $books
$books = $dom->dump_mem( );

// write the XML document to books.xml
$dom->dump_file('books.xml', false, true);
```

The only parameter dump_mem( ) takes is an optional boolean value. An empty value or false means "return the string as one long line." A true value causes the XML to be nicely formatted with child nodes indented, like this:

```
<?xml version="1.0"?>
<book>
  <title cover="soft">PHP Cookbook</title>
</book>
```

You can pass up to three values to dump_file( ). The first one, which is mandatory, is the filename. The second is whether the file should be compressed with *gzip*. The final value is the same pretty formatting option as dump_mem( ).

See Also

Recipe 12.1 for writing XML without DOM; Recipe 12.3 for parsing XML with DOM; documentation on domxml_new_dom( ) at *http://www.php.net/domxml-new-dom* and the DOM functions in general at *http://www.php.net/domxml*; more information about the underlying DOM C library at *http://xmlsoft.org/*.

12.3 Parsing XML with the DOM

Problem

You want to parse an XML file using the DOM API. This puts the file into a tree, which you can process using DOM functions. With the DOM, it's easy to search for and retrieve elements that fit a certain set of criteria.

Solution

Use PHP's DOM XML extension. Here's how to read XML from a file:

```
$dom = domxml_open_file('books.xml');
```

Here's how to read XML from a variable:

```
$dom = domxml_open_mem($books);
```

You can also get just a single node. Here's how to get the root node:

```
$root = $dom->document_element( );
```

Here's how to do a depth-first recursion to process all the nodes in a document:

```
function process_node($node) {
    if ($node->has_child_nodes( )) {
        foreach($node->child_nodes( ) as $n) {
            process_node($n);
        }
    }

    // process leaves
    if ($node->node_type( ) == XML_TEXT_NODE) {
        $content = rtrim($node->node_value( ));
        if (!empty($content)) {
            print "$content\n";
        }
    }

}
process_node($root);
```

Discussion

The W3C's DOM provides a platform- and language-neutral method that specifies the structure and content of a document. Using the DOM, you can read an XML document into a tree of nodes and then maneuver through the tree to locate information about a particular element or elements that match your criteria. This is called *tree-based parsing*. In contrast, the non-DOM XML functions allow you to do event-based parsing.

Additionally, you can modify the structure by creating, editing, and deleting nodes. In fact, you can use the DOM XML functions to author a new XML document from scratch; see Recipe 12.2

One of the major advantages of the DOM is that by following the W3C's specification, many languages implement DOM functions in a similar manner. Therefore, the work of translating logic and instructions from one application to another is considerably simplified. PHP 4.3 comes with an updated series of DOM functions that are in stricter compliance with the DOM standard than previous versions of PHP. However, the functions are not yet 100% compliant. Future PHP versions should bring a closer alignment, but this may break some applications that need minor updates. Check the DOM XML material in the online PHP Manual at *http://www.php.net/domxml* for changes. Functions available in earlier versions of PHP are available, but deprecated.

The DOM is large and complex. For more information, read the specification at *http://www.w3.org/DOM/* or pick up a copy of *XML in a Nutshell*; Chapter 18 discusses the DOM.

For DOM parsing, PHP uses *libxml*, developed for the Gnome project. You can download it from *http://www.xmlsoft.org*. To activate it, configure PHP with `--with-dom`.

DOM functions in PHP are object-oriented. To move from one node to another, call methods such as `$node->child_nodes( )`, which returns an array of node objects, and `$node->parent_node( )`, which returns the parent node object. Therefore, to process a node, check its type and call a corresponding method:

```
// $node is the DOM parsed node <book cover="soft">PHP Cookbook</book>
$type = $node->node_type();

switch($type) {
case XML_ELEMENT_NODE:
    // I'm a tag. I have a tagname property.
    print $node->node_name(); // prints the tagname property: "book"
    print $node->node_value(); // null
    break;
case XML_ATTRIBUTE_NODE:
    // I'm an attribute. I have a name and a value property.
    print $node->node_name(); // prints the name property: "cover"
    print $node->node_value(); // prints the value property: "soft"
    break;
```

```
    case XML_TEXT_NODE:
        // I'm a piece of text inside an element.
        // I have a name and a content property.
        print $node->node_name();  // prints the name property: "#text"
        print $node->node_value(); // prints the content property: "PHP Cookbook"
        break;
    default:
        // another type
        break;
}
```

To automatically search through a DOM tree for specific elements, use get_
elements_by_tagname( ). Here's how to do so with multiple book records:

```
<books>
    <book>
        <title>PHP Cookbook</title>
        <author>Sklar</author>
        <author>Trachtenberg</author>
        <subject>PHP</subject>
    </book>
    <book>
        <title>Perl Cookbook</title>
        <author>Christiansen</author>
        <author>Torkington</author>
        <subject>Perl</subject>
    </book>
</books>
```

Here's how to find all authors:

```
// find and print all authors
$authors = $dom->get_elements_by_tagname('author');

// loop through author elements
foreach ($authors as $author) {
    // child_nodes( ) hold the author values
    $text_nodes = $author->child_nodes( );

    foreach ($text_nodes as $text) {
        print $text->node_value( );
    }
    print "\n";
}
```

The get_elements_by_tagname( ) function returns an array of element node objects.
By looping through each element's children, you can get to the text node associated
with that element. From there, you can pull out the node values, which in this case
are the names of the book authors, such as Sklar and Trachtenberg.

See Also

Recipe 12.1 for writing XML without DOM; Recipe 12.2 for writing XML with DOM; Recipe 12.4 for event-based XML parsing; documentation on domxml_open_file( ) at *http://www.php.net/domxml-open-file*, domxml_open_mem( ) at *http://www.php.net/domxml-open-mem*, and the DOM functions in general at *http://www.php.net/domxml*; more information about the underlying DOM C library at *http://xmlsoft.org/*.

12.4   Parsing XML with SAX

Problem

You want to parse an XML document and format it on an event basis, such as when the parser encounters a new opening or closing element tag. For instance, you want to turn an RSS feed into HTML.

Solution

Use the parsing functions in PHP's XML extension:

```
$xml = xml_parser_create();
$obj = new Parser_Object;  // a class to assist with parsing

xml_set_object($xml,$obj);
xml_set_element_handler($xml, 'start_element', 'end_element');
xml_set_character_data_handler($xml, 'character_data');
xml_parser_set_option($xml, XML_OPTION_CASE_FOLDING, false);

$fp = fopen('data.xml', 'r') or die("Can't read XML data.");
while ($data = fread($fp, 4096)) {
  xml_parse($xml, $data, feof($fp)) or die("Can't parse XML data");
}
fclose($fp);

xml_parser_free($xml);
```

Discussion

These XML parsing functions require the *expat* library. However, because Apache 1.3.7 and later is bundled with *expat*, this library is already installed on most machines. Therefore, PHP enables these functions by default, and you don't need to explicitly configure PHP to support XML.

expat parses XML documents and allows you to configure the parser to call functions when it encounters different parts of the file, such as an opening or closing element tag or character data (the text between tags). Based on the tag name, you can then choose whether to format or ignore the data. This is known as *event-based parsing* and contrasts with DOM XML, which use a tree-based parser.

A popular API for event-based XML parsing is SAX: Simple API for XML. Originally developed only for Java, SAX has spread to other languages. PHP's XML functions follow SAX conventions. For more on the latest version of SAX—SAX2—see *SAX2* by David Brownell (O'Reilly).

PHP supports two interfaces to *expat*: a procedural one and an object-oriented one. Since the procedural interface practically forces you to use global variables to accomplish any meaningful task, we prefer the object-oriented version. With the object-oriented interface, you can bind an object to the parser and interact with the object while processing XML. This allows you to use object properties instead of global variables.

Here's an example application of *expat* that shows how to process an RSS feed and transform it into HTML. For more on RSS, see Recipe 12.11. The script starts with the standard XML processing code, followed by the objects created to parse RSS specifically:

```php
$xml = xml_parser_create();
$rss = new pc_RSS_parser;

xml_set_object($xml, $rss);
xml_set_element_handler($xml, 'start_element', 'end_element');
xml_set_character_data_handler($xml, 'character_data');
xml_parser_set_option($xml, XML_OPTION_CASE_FOLDING, false);

$feed = 'http://pear.php.net/rss.php';
$fp = fopen($feed, 'r') or die("Can't read RSS data.");
while ($data = fread($fp, 4096)) {
    xml_parse($xml, $data, feof($fp)) or die("Can't parse RSS data");
}
fclose($fp);

xml_parser_free($xml);
```

After creating a new XML parser and an instance of the pc_RSS_parser class, configure the parser. First, bind the object to the parser; this tells the parser to call the object's methods instead of global functions. Then call xml_set_element_handler() and xml_set_character_data_handler() to specify the method names the parser should call when it encounters elements and character data. The first argument to both functions is the parser instance; the other arguments are the function names. With xml_set_element_handler(), the middle and last arguments are the functions to call when a tag opens and closes, respectively. The xml_set_character_data_handler() function takes only one additional argument—the function to call when it processes character data.

Because an object has been associated with our parser, when that parser finds the string <tag>data</tag>, it calls $rss->start_element() when it reaches <tag>; $rss->

character_data( ) when it reaches data; and $rss->end_element( ) when it reaches </tag>. The parser can't be configured to automatically call individual methods for each specific tag; instead, you must handle this yourself. However, the PEAR package XML_Transform provides an easy way to assign handlers on a tag-by-by basis.

The last XML parser configuration option tells the parser not to automatically convert all tags to uppercase. By default, the parser folds tags into capital letters, so <tag> and <TAG> both become the same element. Since XML is case-sensitive, and most feeds use lowercase element names, this feature should be disabled.

With the parser configured, feed the data to the parser:

```php
$feed = 'http://pear.php.net/rss.php';
$fp = fopen($feed, 'r') or die("Can't read RSS data.");
while ($data = fread($fp, 4096)) {
  xml_parse($xml, $data, feof($fp)) or die("Can't parse RSS data");
}
fclose($fp);
```

In order to curb memory usage, load the file in 4096-byte chunks, and feed each piece to the parser one at a time. This requires you to write the handler functions that will accommodate text arriving in multiple calls and not assume the entire string comes in all at once.

Last, while PHP cleans up any open parsers when the request ends, you can also manually close the parser by calling xml_parser_free( ).

Now that the generic parsing is properly set up, add the pc_RSS_item and pc_RSS_parser classes, as shown in Examples 12-1 and 12-2, to handle a RSS document.

Example 12-1. pc_RSS_item

```php
class pc_RSS_item {

  var $title = '';
  var $description = '';
  var $link = '';

  function display() {
    printf('<p><a href="%s">%s</a><br />%s</p>',
           $this->link,htmlspecialchars($this->title),
           htmlspecialchars($this->description));
  }
}
```

Example 12-2. pc_RSS_parser

```php
class pc_RSS_parser {

  var $tag;
  var $item;
```

Example 12-2. pc_RSS_parser (continued)

```
function start_element($parser, $tag, $attributes) {
  if ('item' == $tag) {
    $this->item = new pc_RSS_item;
  } elseif (!empty($this->item)) {
    $this->tag = $tag;
  }
}

function end_element($parser, $tag) {
  if ('item' == $tag) {
    $this->item->display();
    unset($this->item);
  }
}

function character_data($parser, $data) {
  if (!empty($this->item)) {
    if (isset($this->item->{$this->tag})) {
      $this->item->{$this->tag} .= trim($data);
    }
  }
}
}
```

The pc_RSS_item class provides an interface to an individual feed item. This removes the details of displaying each item from the general parsing code and makes it easy to reset the data for a new item by calling unset( ).

The pc_RSS_item::display( ) method prints out an HTML-formatted RSS item. It calls htmlspecialchars( ) to reencode any necessary entities, because *expat* decodes them into regular characters while parsing the document. This reencoding, however, breaks on feeds that place HTML in the title and description instead of plaintext.

Within pc_RSS_parser( ), the start_element( ) method takes three parameters: the XML parser, the name of the tag, and an array of attribute/value pairs (if any) from the element. PHP automatically supplies these values to the handler as part of the parsing process.

The start_element( ) method checks the value of $tag. If it's item, the parser's found a new RSS item, and a new pc_RSS_item object is instantiated. Otherwise, it checks to see if $this->item is empty( ); if it isn't, the parser is inside an item element. It's then necessary to record the tag's name, so that the character_data( ) method knows which property to assign its value to. If it is empty, this part of the RSS feed isn't necessary for our application, and it's ignored.

When the parser finds a closing item tag, the corresponding end_element( ) method first prints the RSS item, then cleans up by deleting the object.

Finally, the character_data( ) method is responsible for assigning the values of title, description, and link to the RSS item. After making sure it's inside an item element, it checks that the current tag is one of the properties of pc_RSS_item. Without this check, if the parser encountered an element other than those three, its value would also be assigned to the object. The { }s are needed to set the object property dereferencing order. Notice how trim($data) is appended to the property instead of a direct assignment. This is done to handle cases in which the character data is split across the 4096-byte chunks retrieved by fread( ); it also removes the surrounding whitespace found in the RSS feed.

If you run the code on this sample RSS feed:

```
<?xml version="1.0"?>
<rss version="0.93">
<channel>
  <title>PHP Announcements</title>
  <link>http://www.php.net/</link>
  <description>All the latest information on PHP.</description>

  <item>
    <title>PHP 5.0 Released!</title>
    <link>http://www.php.net/downloads.php</link>
    <description>The newest version of PHP is now available.</description>
  </item>
</channel>
</rss>
```

It produces this HTML:

```
<p><a href="http://www.php.net/downloads.php">PHP 5.0 Released!</a><br />
The newest version of PHP is now available.</p>
```

See Also

Recipe 12.3 for tree-based XML parsing with DOM; Recipe 12.11 for more on parsing RSS; documentation on xml_parser_create( ) at *http://www.php.net/xml-parser-create*, xml_element_handler( ) at *http://www.php.net/xml-element-handler*, xml_character_handler( ) at *http://www.php.net/xml-character-handler*, xml_parse( ) at *http://www.php.net/xml-parse*, and the XML functions in general at *http://www.php.net/xml*; the official SAX site at *http://www.saxproject.org/*.

12.5   Transforming XML with XSLT

Problem

You have a XML document and a XSL stylesheet. You want to transform the document using XSLT and capture the results. This lets you apply stylesheets to your data and create different versions of your content for different media.

Solution

Use PHP's XSLT extension:

```
$xml = 'data.xml';
$xsl = 'stylesheet.xsl';

$xslt = xslt_create();
$results = xslt_process($xslt, $xml, $xsl);

if (!$results) {
    error_log("XSLT Error: #".xslt_errno($xslt).": ".xslt_error($xslt));
}

xslt_free($xslt);
```

The transformed text is stored in `$results`.

Discussion

XML documents describe the content of data, but they don't contain any information about how those data should be displayed. However, when XML content is coupled with a stylesheet described using XSL (eXtensible Stylesheet Language), the content is displayed according to specific visual rules.

The glue between XML and XSL is XSLT, which stands for eXtensible Stylesheet Language Transformations. These transformations apply the series of rules enumerated in the stylesheet to your XML data. So, just as PHP parses your code and combines it with user input to create a dynamic page, an XSLT program uses XSL and XML to output a new page that contains more XML, HTML, or any other format you can describe.

There are a few XSLT programs available, each with different features and limitations. PHP currently supports only the Sablotron XSLT processor, but in the future you'll be able to use other programs, such as Xalan and Libxslt. You can download Sablotron from *http://www.gingerall.com*. To enable Sablotron for XSLT processing, configure PHP with both --enable-xslt and --with-xslt-sablot.

Processing documents takes a few steps. First, you need to grab a handle to a new instance of an XSLT processor with xslt_create(). Then, to transform the files, use xslt_process() to make the transformation and check the results:

```
$xml = 'data.xml';
$xsl = 'stylesheet.xsl';

$xslt = xslt_create();
$results = xslt_process($xslt, $xml, $xsl);
```

You start by defining variables to store the filenames for the XML data and the XSL stylesheet. They're the first two parameters to the transforming function, xslt_ process( ). If the fourth argument is missing, as it is here, or set to NULL, the function returns the results. Otherwise, it writes the resulting data to the filename passed:

```
xslt_process($xslt, $xml, $xsl, 'data.html');
```

If you want to provide your XML and XSL data from variables instead of files, call xslt_process( ) with a fifth parameter, which allows you to substitute string place-holders for your files:

```
// grab data from database
$r = mysql_query("SELECT pages.page AS xml, templates.template AS xsl
                  FROM pages, templates
                  WHERE pages.id=$id AND templates.id=pages.template")
    or die("$php_errormsg");

$obj = mysql_fetch_object($r);
$xml = $obj->xml;
$xsl = $obj->xsl;

// map the strings to args
$args = array('/_xml' => $xml,
              '/_xsl' => $xsl);

$results = xslt_process($xslt, 'arg:/_xml', 'arg:/_xsl', NULL, $args);
```

When reading and writing files, Sablotron supports two types of URIs. The PHP default is file:, so Sablotron looks for the data on the filesystem. Sablotron also uses a custom URI of arg:, which allows users to alternatively pass in data using arguments. That's the feature used here.

In the previous example, the data for the XML and XSL comes from a database, but, it can arrive from anywhere, such as a remote URL or POSTed data. Once you've obtained the data, create the $args array. This sets up mappings between the argument names and the variable names. The keys of the associative array are the argument names passed to xslt_process( ); the values are the variables holding the data. By convention, /_xml and /_xsl are the argument names; however, you can use others.

Then call xslt_process( ) and in place of data.xml, use arg:/_xml, with arg: being the string that lets the extension know to look in the $args array. Because you're passing in $args as the fifth parameter, you need to pass NULL as the fourth argument; this makes sure the function returns the results.

Error checking is done using xslt_error( ) and xslt_errno( ) functions:

```
if (!$results) {
    error_log('XSLT Error: #' . xslt_errno($xslt) . ': ' . xslt_error($xslt));
}
```

The xslt_error( ) function returns a formatted message describing the error, while xslt_errno( ) provides a numeric error code.

To set up your own custom error handling code, register a function using xslt_set_error_handler( ). If there are errors, that function is automatically called instead of any built-in error handler.

```
function xslt_error_handler($processor, $level, $number, $messages) {
    error_log("XSLT Error: #$level");
}

xslt_set_error_handler($xslt, 'xslt_error_handler');
```

Finally, PHP cleans up any open XSLT processors when the request ends, but here's how to manually close the processor and free its memory:

```
xslt_free($xslt);
```

See Also

Documentation on xslt_create( ) at *http://www.php.net/xslt-create*, xslt_process( ) at *http://www.php.net/xslt-process*, xslt_errno( ) at *http://www.php.net/xslt-errno*, xslt_error( ) at *http://www.php.net/xslt-error*, xslt_error_handler( ) at *http://www.php.net/xslt-error-handler*, and xslt_free( ) at *http://www.php.net/xslt-free*; *XSLT*, by Doug Tidwell (O'Reilly).

12.6   Sending XML-RPC Requests

Problem

You want to be an XML-RPC client and make requests of a server. XML-RPC lets PHP make function calls to web servers, even if they don't use PHP. The retrieved data is then automatically converted to PHP variables for use in your application.

Solution

Use PHP's built-in XML-RPC extension with some helper functions. As of PHP 4.1, PHP bundles the *xmlrpc-epi* extension. Unfortunately, xmlrpc-epi does not have any native C functions for taking a XML-RPC formatted string and making a request. However, the folks behind xmlrpc-epi have a series of helper functions written in PHP available for download at *http://xmlrpc-epi.sourceforge.net/*. The only file used here is the one named *utils.php*, which is located in *xmlrpc_php/index.php*. To install it, just copy that file to a location where PHP can find it in its include_path.

Here's some client code that calls a function on an XML-RPC server that returns state names:

```
// this is the default file name from the package
// kept here to avoid confusion over the file name
require 'utils.php';
```

```
// server settings
$host = 'betty.userland.com';
$port = 80;
$uri = '/RPC2';

// request settings
// pass in a number from 1-50; get the nth state in alphabetical order
// 1 is Alabama, 50 is Wyoming
$method = 'examples.getStateName';
$args = array(32); // data to be passed

// make associative array out of these variables
$request = compact('host', 'port', 'uri', 'method', 'args');

// this function makes the XML-RPC request
$result = xu_rpc_http_concise($request);

print "I love $result!\n";
```

Discussion

XML-RPC, a format created by Userland Software, allows you to make a request to a web server using HTTP. The request itself is a specially formatted XML document. As a client, you build up an XML request to send that fits with the XML-RPC specification. You then send it to the server, and the server replies with an XML document. You then parse the XML to find the results. In the Solution, the XML-RPC server returns a state name, so the code prints:

```
I love New York!
```

Unlike earlier implementations of XML-RPC, which were coded in PHP, the current bundled extension is written in C, so there is a significant speed increase in processing time. To enable this extension while configuring PHP, add `--with-xmlrpc`.

The server settings tell PHP which web site to contact to make the request. The `$host` is the hostname of the machine; `$port` is the port the web server is running on, which is usually port 80; and `$uri` is the pathname to the XML-RPC server you wish to contact. This request is equivalent to *http://betty.userland.com:80/RPC2*. If no port is given, the function defaults to port 80, and the default URI is the web server root, /.

The request settings are the function to call and the data to pass to the function. The method `examples.getStateName` takes an integer from 1 to 50 and returns a string with the name of the U.S. state, in alphabetical order. In XML-RPC, method names can have periods, while in PHP, they cannot. If they could, the PHP equivalent to passing 32 as the argument to the XML-RPC call to `examples.getStateName` is calling a function named `examples.getStateName( )`:

```
examples.getStateName(32);
```

In XML-RPC, it looks like this:

```
<?xml version='1.0' encoding="iso-8859-1" ?>
<methodCall>
<methodName>examples.getStateName</methodName>
<params><param><value>
   <int>32</int>
  </value>
 </param>
</params>
</methodCall>
```

The server settings and request information go into a single associative array that is passed to xu_rpc_http_concise( ). As a shortcut, call compact( ), which is identical to:

```
$request = array('host'   => $host,
                 'port'   => $port,
                 'uri'    => $uri,
                 'method' => $method,
                 'args'   => $args);
```

The xu_rpc_http_concise( ) function makes the XML-RPC call and returns the results. Since the return value is a string, you can print $results directly. If the XML-RPC call returns multiple values, xu_rpc_http_concise( ) returns an array.

There are 10 different parameters that can be passed in the array to xu_rpc_http_concise( ), but the only one that's required is host. The parameters are shown in Table 12-1.

Table 12-1. Parameters for xu_rpc_http_concise()

Name	Description
host	Server hostname
uri	Server URI (default /)
port	Server port (default 80)
method	Name of method to call
args	Arguments to pass to method
debug	Debug level (0 to 2: 0 is none, 2 is lots)
timeout	Number of seconds before timing out the request; a value of 0 means never timeout
user	Username for Basic HTTP Authentication, if necessary
pass	Password for Basic HTTP Authentication, if necessary
secure	Use SSL for encrypted transmissions; requires PHP to be built with SSL support (pass any true value)

See Also

Recipe 12.7 for more on XML-RPC servers; PHP helper functions for use with the xmlrpc-epi extension at *http://xmlrpc-epi.sourceforge.net/*; *Programming Web Services with XML-RPC*, by Simon St. Laurent, Joe Johnston, and Edd Dumbill (O'Reilly); more on XML-RPC at *http://www.xml-rpc.com*

12.7 Receiving XML-RPC Requests

Problem

You want to create an XML-RPC server and respond to XML-RPC requests. This allows any XML-RPC-enabled client to ask your server questions and you to reply with data.

Solution

Use PHP's XML-RPC extension. Here is a PHP version of the Userland XML-RPC demonstration application that returns an ISO 8601 string with the current date and time:

```
// this is the function exposed as "get_time()"
function return_time($method, $args) {
    return date('Ymd\THis');
}

$server = xmlrpc_server_create() or die("Can't create server");
xmlrpc_server_register_method($server, 'return_time', 'get_time')
    or die("Can't register method.");

$request = $GLOBALS['HTTP_RAW_POST_DATA'];
$options = array('output_type' => 'xml', 'version' => 'xmlrpc');

print xmlrpc_server_call_method($server, $request, NULL, $options)
    or die("Can't call method");

xmlrpc_server_destroy($server);
```

Discussion

Since the bundled XML-RPC extension, xmlrpc-epi, is written in C, it processes XML-RPC requests in a speedy and efficient fashion. Add `--with-xmlrpc` to your configure string to enable this extension during compile time. For more on XML-RPC, see Recipe 12.6.

The Solution begins with a definition of the PHP function to associate with the XML-RPC method. The name of the function is `return_time()`. This is later linked with the `get_time()` XML-RPC method:

```
function return_time($method, $args) {
    return date('Ymd\THis');
}
```

The function returns an ISO 8601-formatted string with the current date and time. We escape the T inside the call to date( ) because the specification requires a literal T to divide the date part and the time part. For August 21, 2002 at 3:03:51 P.M., the return value is 20020821T150351.

The function is automatically called with two parameters: the name of the XML-RPC method the server is responding to and an array of method arguments passed by the XML-RPC client to the server. In this example, the server ignores both variables.

Next, create the XML-RPC server and register the get_time( ) method:

```
$server = xmlrpc_server_create() or die("Can't create server");
xmlrpc_server_register_method($server, 'return_time', 'get_time');
```

We create a new server and assign it to $server, then call xmlrpc_server_register_method( ) with three parameters. The first is the newly created server, the second is the name of the method to register, and the third is the name of the PHP function to handle the request.

Now that everything is configured, tell the XML-RPC server to dispatch the method for processing and print the results to the client:

```
$request = $GLOBALS['HTTP_RAW_POST_DATA'];
$options = array('output_type' => 'xml', 'version' => 'xmlrpc');

print xmlrpc_server_call_method($server, $request, NULL, $options);
```

The client request comes in as POST data. PHP converts HTTP POST data to variables, but this is XML-RPC data, so the server needs to access the unparsed data, which is stored in $GLOBALS['HTTP_RAW_POST_DATA']. In this example, the request XML looks like this:

```
<?xml version="1.0" encoding="iso-8859-1"?>
<methodCall>
<methodName>get_time</methodName>
<params/></methodCall>
```

Thus, the server is responding to the get_time( ) method, and it expects no parameters.

We also configure the response options to output the results in XML and interpret the request as XML-RPC. These two variables are then passed to xmlrpc_server_call_method( ) along with the XML-RPC server, $server. The third parameter to this function is for any user data you wish to provide; in this case, there is none, so we pass NULL.

The xmlrpc_server_call_method( ) function decodes the variables, calls the correct function to handle the method, and encodes the response into XML-RPC. To reply to the client, all you need to do is print out what xmlrpc_server_call_method( ) returns.

Finally, clean up with a call to xmlrpc_server_destroy( ):

```
xmlrpc_server_destroy($server);
```

Using the XML-RPC client code from Recipe 12.6, you can make a request and find the time, as follows:

```
require 'utils.php';

$output = array('output_type' => 'xml', 'version' => 'xmlrpc');
$result = xu_rpc_http_concise(array(
                        'method'  => 'get_time',
                        'host'    => 'clock.example.com',
                        'port'    => 80,
                        'uri'     => '/time-xmlrpc.php',
                        'output'  => $output));

print "The local time is $result.\n";
The local time is 20020821T162615.
```

It is legal to associate multiple methods with a single XML-RPC server. You can also associate multiple methods with the same PHP function. For example, we can create a server that replies to two methods: get_gmtime( ) and get_time( ). The first method, get_gmtime( ), is similar to get_time( ), but it replies with the current time in GMT. To handle this, you can extend get_time( ) to take an optional parameter, which is the name of a time zone to use when computing the current time.

Here's how to change the return_time( ) function to handle both methods:

```
function return_time($method, $args) {
    if ('get_gmtime' == $method) {
        $tz = 'GMT';
    } elseif (!empty($args[0])) {
        $tz = $args[0];
    } else {
        // use local time zone
        $tz = '';
    }

    if ($tz) { putenv("TZ=$tz"); }
    $date = date('Ymd\THis');
    if ($tz) { putenv('TZ=EST5EDT'); } // change EST5EDT to your server's zone

    return $date;
}
```

This function uses both the $method and $args parameters. At the top of the function, we check if the request is for get_gmtime. If so, the time zone is set to GMT. If it isn't, see if an alternate time zone is specified as an argument by checking $args[0]. If neither check is true, we keep the current time zone.

To configure the server to handle the new method, add only one new line:

```
xmlrpc_server_register_method($server, 'return_time', 'get_gmtime');
```

This maps get_gmtime( ) to return_time( ).

Here's an example of a client in action. The first request is for get_time( ) with no parameters; the second calls get_time( ) with a time zone of PST8PDT, which is three hours behind the server; the last request is for the new get_gmtime( ) method, which is four hours ahead of the server's time zone.

```
require 'utils.php';

$output = array('output_type' => 'xml', 'version' => 'xmlrpc');

// get_time( )
$result = xu_rpc_http_concise(array(
                          'method'  => 'get_time',
                          'host'    => 'clock.example.com',
                          'port'    => 80,
                          'uri'     => '/time.php',
                          'output'  => $output));

print "The local time is $result.\n";

// get_time('PST8PDT')
$result = xu_rpc_http_concise(array(
                          'method'  => 'get_time',
                          'args'    => array('PST8PDT'),
                          'host'    => 'clock.example.com',
                          'port'    => 80,
                          'uri'     => '/time.php',
                          'output'  => $output));

print "The time in PST8PDT is $result.\n";

// get_gmtime( )
$result = xu_rpc_http_concise(array(
                          'method'  => 'get_gmtime',
                          'host'    => 'clock.example.com',
                          'port'    => 80,
                          'uri'     => '/time.php',
                          'output'  => $output));

print "The time in GMT is $result.\n";
The local time is 20020821T162615.
The time in PST8PDT is 20020821T132615.
The time in GMT is 20020821T202615.
```

See Also

Recipe 12.6 for more information about XML-RPC clients; documentation on xmlrpc_server_create( ) at *http://www.php.net/xmlrpc-server-create*, xmlrpc_server_register_method( ) at *http://www.php.net/xmlrpc-server-register-method*, xmlrpc_server_call_method( ) at *http://www.php.net/xmlrpc-server-call-method*, and xmlrpc_server_destroy( ) at *http://www.php.net/xmlrpc-server-destroy*; *Programming Web Services with XML-RPC* by Simon St. Laurent, Joe Johnston, and Edd Dumbill

(O'Reilly); more on XML-RPC at *http://www.xml-rpc.com*; the original current time XML-RPC server at *http://www.xmlrpc.com/currentTime*.

12.8   Sending SOAP Requests

Problem

You want to send a SOAP request. Creating a SOAP client allows you to gather information from SOAP servers, regardless of their operating system and middleware software.

Solution

Use PEAR's SOAP classes. Here's some client code that uses the GoogleSearch SOAP service:

```
require 'SOAP/Client.php';

$query = 'php'; // your Google search terms

$soap = new SOAP_Client('http://api.google.com/search/beta2');

$params = array(
        new SOAP_Value('key',        'string',  'your google key'),
        new SOAP_Value('q',          'string',  $query),
        new SOAP_Value('start',      'int',      0),
        new SOAP_Value('maxResults', 'int',     10),
        new SOAP_Value('filter',     'boolean', false),
        new SOAP_Value('restrict',   'string',  ''),
        new SOAP_Value('safeSearch', 'boolean', false),
        new SOAP_Value('lr',         'string',  'lang_en'),
        new SOAP_Value('ie',         'string',  ''),
        new SOAP_Value('oe',         'string',  ''));

$hits = $soap->call('doGoogleSearch', $params, 'urn:GoogleSearch');

foreach ($hits->resultElements as $hit) {
    printf('<a href="%s">%s</a><br />', $hit->URL, $hit->title);
}
```

Discussion

The Simple Object Access Protocol (SOAP), is, like XML-RPC, a method for exchanging information over HTTP. It uses XML as its message format, which makes it easy to create and parse. As a result, because it's platform- and language-independent, SOAP is available on many platforms and in many languages, including

PHP. To make a SOAP request, you instantiate a new SOAP_Client object and pass the constructor the location of the page to make the request:

```
$soap = new SOAP_Client('http://api.google.com/search/beta2');
```

Currently, two different types of communications methods are supported: HTTP and SMTP. Secure HTTP is also allowed, if SSL is built into your version of PHP. To choose one of these methods, begin your URL with http, https, or mailto.

After creating a SOAP_Client object, you use its call( ) method to call a remote function:

```
$query = 'php';

$params = array(
            new SOAP_Value('key',        'string',  'your google key'),
            new SOAP_Value('q',          'string',  $query),
            new SOAP_Value('start',      'int',     0),
            new SOAP_Value('maxResults', 'int',     10),
            new SOAP_Value('filter',     'boolean', false),
            new SOAP_Value('restrict',   'string',  ''),
            new SOAP_Value('safeSearch', 'boolean', false),
            new SOAP_Value('lr',         'string',  'lang_en'),
            new SOAP_Value('ie',         'string',  ''),
            new SOAP_Value('oe',         'string',  ''));

$hits = $soap->call('doGoogleSearch', $params, 'urn:GoogleSearch');
```

The $params array holds a collection of SOAP_Value objects. A SOAP_Value object is instantiated with three arguments: the name, type, and value of the parameter you're passing to the SOAP server. These vary from message to message, depending upon the SOAP functions available on the server.

The real action happens with the SOAP_Client::call( ) method, which takes a few arguments. The first is the method you want the server to execute; here, it's doGoogleSearch. The second argument is an array of parameters that gets passed to the function on the SOAP server. The third argument, urn:GoogleSearch, is the SOAP namespace; it allows the server to know that doGoogleSearch belongs in the GoogleSearch namespace. With namespaces, a more generally named search method doesn't cause a conflict with another more specific search method.

There's a fourth parameter that's unused here: soapAction. If you want to provide the SOAP server with a URI indicating the intent of the request, you can add one here. Unfortunately, the definition of the word "intent" varies from implementation to implementation. The current consensus is that soapAction shouldn't be used until its meaning is further clarified. The PEAR SOAP server doesn't use this field, but other vendors may assign their own meanings.

Upon successful execution, the function returns an object containing the server's response. If an error occurs, the function returns a PEAR_Error object. Google returns all sorts of information, but here we just iterate through the $resultElements array and pull out the URL and title of each hit for display:

```
foreach ($hits->resultElements as $hit) {
    printf('<a href="%s">%s</a><br />', $hit->URL, $hit->title);
}
```

This results in:

```
<a href="http://www.php.net/"><b>PHP</b>: Hypertext Preprocessor</a>
<a href="http://www.php.net/downloads.php"><b>PHP</b>: Downloads</a>
<a href="http://phpnuke.org/"><b>PHP</b>-Nuke</a>
<a href="http://www.phpbuilder.com/">PHPBuilder.com</a>
<a href="http://php.resourceindex.com/">The <b>PHP</b> Resource Index</a>
<a href="http://www.php.com/"><b>PHP</b>.com: Home</a>
<a href="http://www.php.org/"><b>PHP</b>.org</a>
<a href="http://php.weblogs.com/"><b>PHP</b> Everywhere:</a>
<a href="http://www.php3.org/"></a>
<a href="http://gtk.php.net/"><b>PHP</b>-GTK</a>
```

You can also use Web Services Definition Language (WSDL), to implement the request. With WSDL, you don't need to explicitly enumerate the parameter keys or the SOAP namespace:

```
require 'SOAP/Client.php';

$wsdl_url = 'http://api.google.com/GoogleSearch.wsdl';
$WSDL = new SOAP_WSDL($wsdl_url);
$soap = $WSDL->getProxy();

$hits = $soap->doGoogleSearch('your google key',$query,0,10,
                         true,'',false,'lang_en','','');
```

This code is equivalent to the longer previous example. The SOAP_WSDL object takes a URL for the GoogleSearch WSDL file and automatically loads the specification from that URL. Instead of making $soap a SOAP_Client, call SOAP_WSDL::getProxy() to create a GoogleSearch object.

This new object has methods with the same name as the GoogleSearch SOAP methods. So, instead of passing doGoogleSearch as the first parameter to SOAP_Client::call(), you call $soap->doGoogleSearch(). The $params array becomes the arguments for the method, without any array encapsulation or SOAP_Value instantiations necessary. Also, because it's set in the WSDL file, the namespace doesn't need to be specified.

See Also

Recipe 12.9 for more on SOAP servers; Recipe 20.10 for an example of a SOAP client in a PHP-GTK application; PEAR's SOAP classes at *http://pear.php.net/package-info.php?package=SOAP*; *Programming Web Services with SOAP*, by Doug Tidwell,

James Snell, and Pavel Kulchenko (O'Reilly); information on the Google SOAP service at *http://www.google.com/apis/*.

12.9   Receiving SOAP Requests

Problem

You want to create an SOAP server and respond to SOAP requests. If your server responds to SOAP requests, anyone on the Internet that has a SOAP client can make requests of your server.

Solution

Use PEAR's `SOAP_Server` class. Here's a server that returns the current date and time:

```
require 'SOAP/Server.php';

class pc_SOAP_return_time {
    var $method_namespace = 'urn:pc_SOAP_return_time';

    function return_time() {
        return date('Ymd\THis');
    }
}

$rt = new pc_SOAP_return_time( );

$server = new SOAP_Server;
$server->addObjectMap($rt);
$server->service($HTTP_RAW_POST_DATA);
```

Discussion

There are three steps to creating a SOAP server with PEAR's `SOAP_Server` class:

1. Create a class to process SOAP methods and instantiate it
2. Create an instance of a SOAP server and associate the processing object with the server
3. Instruct the SOAP server to process the request and reply to the SOAP client

The PEAR `SOAP_Server` class uses objects to handle SOAP requests. A request-handling class needs a `$method_namespace` property that specifies the SOAP namespace for the class. In this case, it's `urn:pc_SOAP_return_time`. Object methods then map to SOAP procedure names within the namespace. The actual PHP class name isn't exposed via SOAP, so the fact that both the name of the class and its `$method_namespace` are identical is a matter of convenience, not of necessity:

```
class pc_SOAP_return_time {
    var $method_namespace = 'urn:pc_SOAP_return_time';

    function return_time( ) {
        return date('Ymd\THis');
    }
}

$rt = new pc_SOAP_return_time( );
```

Once the class is defined, you create an instance of the class to link methods with the
SOAP server object. Before mapping the procedures to the class methods, however,
you first must instantiate a SOAP_Server object:

```
$server = new SOAP_Server;
$server->addObjectMap($rt);
$server->service($GLOBALS['HTTP_RAW_POST_DATA']);
```

Once that's done, call SOAP_Server::addObjectMap( ) with the object to tell the SOAP
server about the methods the object provides. Now the server is ready to reply to all
SOAP requests within the namespace for which you've defined methods.

To tell the server to respond to the request, call SOAP_Server::service( ) and pass the
SOAP envelope. Because the envelope arrives via POST, you pass $GLOBALS['HTTP_
RAW_POST_DATA']. This provides the server with the complete request, because the
class takes care of the necessary parsing.

To call this procedure using a PEAR SOAP client, use this code:

```
require 'SOAP/Client.php';
$soapclient = new SOAP_Client('http://clock.example.com/time-soap.php');
$result = $soapclient->call('return_time', array( ),
                           array('namespace' => 'urn:pc_SOAP_return_time'));
print "The local time is $result.\n";
```

This prints:

```
The local time is 20020821T132615.
```

To extend the method to read in parameters, you need to alter the method prototype to include parameter names and then modify the client request to include data
for the additional arguments. This example modifies the SOAP procedure to accept
an optional time zone argument:

```
class pc_SOAP_return_time {
    var $method_namespace = 'urn:pc_SOAP_return_time';

    function return_time($tz='') {
        if ($tz) { putenv("TZ=$tz"); }
        $date = date('Ymd\THis');
        if ($tz) { putenv('TZ=EST5EDT'); } // change EST5EDT to your server's zone
        return $date
    }
}
```

The second parameter in the client's call now takes a tz option:

```
$result = $soapclient->call('return_time', array('tz' => 'PST8PDT'),
                           array('namespace' => 'urn:pc_SOAP_return_time'));
```

With the new settings, the server returns a time three hours behind the previous one:

```
20020821T202615
```

See Also

Recipe 12.8 for more on SOAP clients; PEAR's SOAP classes at *http://pear.php.net/package-info.php?package=SOAP*; *Programming Web Services with SOAP* (O'Reilly); the original SOAP current time application at *http://www.soapware.org/currentTime*.

12.10 Exchanging Data with WDDX

Problem

You want to serialize data in WDDX format for transmission or unserialize WDDX data you've received. This allows you to communicate with anyone who speaks WDDX.

Solution

Use PHP's WDDX extension. Serialize multiple variables using wddx_serialize_vars():

```
$a = 'string data';
$b = 123;
$c = 'rye';
$d = 'pastrami';
$array = array('c', 'd');

$wddx = wddx_serialize_vars('a', 'b', $array);
```

You can also start the WDDX packet with wddx_packet_start() and add data as it arrives with wddx_add_vars():

```
$wddx = wddx_packet_start('Some of my favorite things');

// loop through data
while ($array = mysql_fetch_array($r)) {
    $thing = $array['thing'];
    wddx_add_vars($wddx, 'thing');
}

$wddx = wddx_packet_end($wddx);
```

Use wddx_deserialize() to deserialize data:

```
// $wddx holds a WDDX packet
$vars = wddx_deserialize($wddx);
```

Discussion

WDDX stands for Web Distributed Data eXchange and was one of the first XML formats to share information in a language-neutral fashion. Invented by the company behind ColdFusion, WDDX gained a lot of popularity in 1999, but doesn't have much momentum at the present.

Instead, many people have begun to use SOAP as a replacement for WDDX. But WDDX does have the advantage of simplicity, so if the information you're exchanging is basic, WDDX may be a good choice. Also, due to its origins, it's very easy to read and write WDDX packets in ColdFusion, so if you need to communicate with a ColdFusion application, WDDX is helpful.

WDDX requires the *expat* library, available with Apache 1.3.7 and higher or from *http://www.jclark.com/xml/expat.html*. Configure PHP with --with-xml and --enable-wddx.

The example in the Solution produces the following XML (formatted to be easier to read):

```
<wddxPacket version='1.0'>
<header/>
<data>
    <struct>
        <var name='a'><string>string data</string></var>
        <var name='b'><number>123</number></var>
        <var name='c'><string>rye</string></var>
        <var name='d'><string>pastrami</string></var>
    </struct>
</data>
</wddxPacket>
```

Variables are wrapped inside <var> tags with the variable name assigned as the value for the name attribute. Inside there is another set of tags that indicate the variable type: string, number, dateTime, boolean, array, binary, or recordSet. Finally, you have the data itself.

You can also serialize one variable at a time using wddx_serialize_value:

```
// one variable
$s = wddx_serialize_value('Serialized', 'An optional comment');
```

This results in the following XML:

```
<wddxPacket version='1.0'>
<header>
    <comment>An optional comment</comment>
</header>
<data>
    <string>Serialized</string>
</data>
</wddxPacket>
```

See Also

Documentation on WDDX at *http://www.php.net/wddx*; more information at *http://www.openwddx.org*; Chapter 20, "Sharing Data with WDDX," from *Programming ColdFusion*, by Rob Brooks-Bilson (O'Reilly).

12.11 Reading RSS Feeds

Problem

You want to retrieve an RSS feed and look at the items. This allows you to incorporate newsfeeds from multiple web sites into your application.

Solution

Use the PEAR XML_RSS class. Here's an example that reads the RSS feed for the *php.announce* mailing list:

```
require 'XML/RSS.php';

$feed = 'http://news.php.net/group.php?group=php.announce&format=rss';

$rss =& new XML_RSS($feed);
$rss->parse();

print "<ul>\n";
foreach ($rss->getItems() as $item) {
    print '<li><a href="' . $item['link'] . '">' . $item['title'] . "</a></li>\n";
}
print "</ul>\n";
```

Discussion

RSS, which stands for RDF Site Summary, is an easy-to-use headline or article syndication format written in XML.* Many news web sites, such as Slashdot and O'Reilly's Meerkat, provide RSS feeds that update whenever new stories are published. Weblogs have also embraced RSS and having an RSS feed for your blog is a standard feature. The PHP web site also publishes RSS feeds for most PHP mailing lists.

Retrieving and parsing a RSS feed is simple:

```
$feed = 'http://news.php.net/group.php?group=php.announce&format=rss';

$rss =& new XML_RSS($feed);
$rss->parse();
```

---

* RDF stands for Resource Definition Framework. RSS also stands for Rich Site Summary.

This example makes $rss a new XML_RSS object and sets the feed to the RSS feed for the *php.announce* mailing list. The feed is then parsed by XML_RSS::parse( ) and stored internally within $rss.

RSS items are then retrieved as an associative array using XML_RSS:getItems( ):

```
print "<ul>\n";

foreach ($rss->getItems() as $item) {
    print '<li><a href="' . $item['link'] . '">' . $item['title'] . "</a></li>\n";
}

print "</ul>\n";
```

This foreach loop creates an unordered list of items with the item title linking back to the URL associated with the complete article, as shown in Figure 12-1. Besides the required title and link fields, an item can have an optional description field that contains a brief write-up about the item.

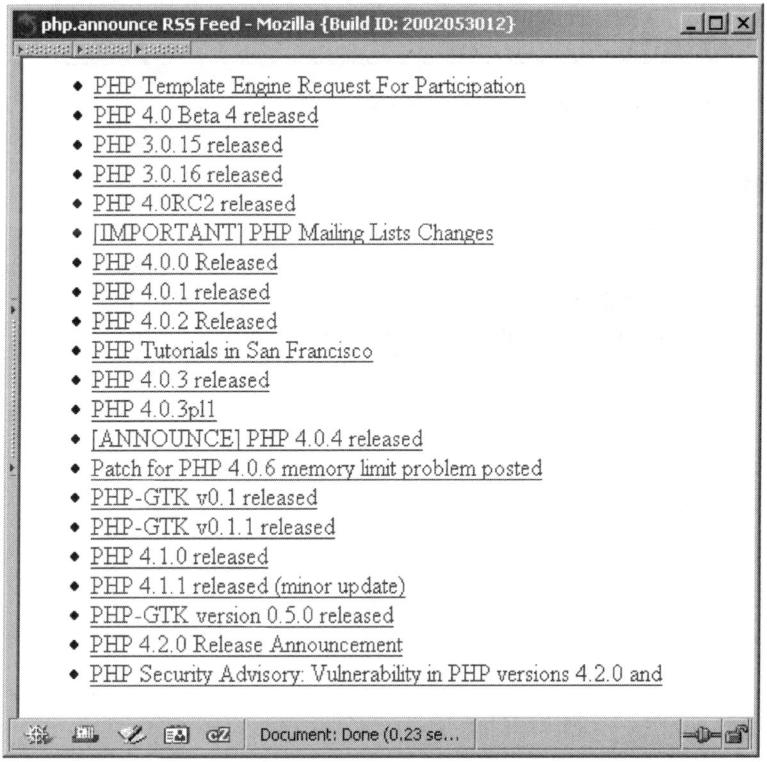

Figure 12-1. php.announce RSS feed

Each channel also has an entry with information about the feed, as shown in Figure 12-2. To retrieve that data, call XML_RSS::getChannelInfo( ):

```
$feed = 'http://news.php.net/group.php?group=php.announce&format=rss';
$rss =& new XML_RSS($feed);

$rss->parse();

print "<ul>\n";

foreach ($rss->getChannelInfo() as $key => $value) {
    print "<li>$key: $value</li>\n";
}

print "</ul>\n";
```

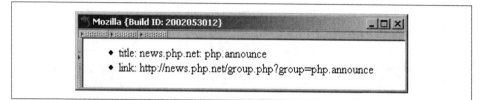

Figure 12-2. php.announce RSS channel information

See Also

Recipe 12.4 for how to process an RSS feed and transform it to HTML; PEAR's XML_RSS class at *http://pear.php.net/package-info.php?package=XML_RSS*; more information on RSS at *http://groups.yahoo.com/group/rss-dev/files/specification.html*; O'Reilly Network's Meerkat at *http://www.oreillynet.com/meerkat/*.

CHAPTER 13

Regular Expressions

13.0 Introduction

Regular expressions are a powerful tool for matching and manipulating text. While not as fast as plain-vanilla string matching, regular expressions are extremely flexible; they allow you to construct patterns to match almost any conceivable combination of characters with a simple, albeit terse and somewhat opaque syntax.

In PHP, you can use regular expression functions to find text that matches certain criteria. Once located, you can choose to modify or replace all or part of the matching substrings. For example, this regular expression turns text email addresses into `mailto:` hyperlinks:

```
$html = preg_replace('/[^@\s]+@([-a-z0-9]+\.)+[a-z]{2,}/i',
                     '<a href="mailto:$0">$0</a>', $text);
```

As you can see, regular expressions are handy when transforming plain text into HTML and vice versa. Luckily, since these are such popular subjects, PHP has many built-in functions to handle these tasks. Recipe 9.8 tells how to escape HTML entities, Recipe 11.11 covers stripping HTML tags, and Recipes 11.9 and 11.10 show how to convert ASCII to HTML and HTML to ASCII, respectively. For more on matching and validating email addresses, see Recipe 13.6.

Over the years, the functionality of regular expressions has grown from its basic roots to incorporate increasingly useful features. As a result, PHP offers two different sets of regular-expression functions. The first set includes the traditional (or POSIX) functions, all beginning with ereg (for extended regular expressions; the ereg functions themselves are already an extension of the original feature set). The other set includes the Perl family of functions, prefaced with preg (for Perl-compatible regular expressions).

The preg functions use a library that mimics the regular expression functionality of the Perl programming language. This is a good thing because Perl allows you to do a variety of handy things with regular expressions, including nongreedy matching, forward and backward assertions, and even recursive patterns.

In general, there's no longer any reason to use the ereg functions. They offer fewer features, and they're slower than preg functions. However, the ereg functions existed in PHP for many years prior to the introduction of the preg functions, so many programmers still use them because of legacy code or out of habit. Thankfully, the prototypes for the two sets of functions are identical, so it's easy to switch back and forth from one to another in your mind without too much confusion. (We list how to do this while avoiding the major gotchas in Recipe 13.1.)

The basics of regular expressions are simple to understand. You combine a sequence of characters to form a pattern. You then compare strings of text to this pattern and look for matches. In the pattern, most characters represent themselves. So, to find if a string of HTML contains an image tag, do this:

```
if (preg_match('/<img /', $html)) {
    // found an opening image tag
}
```

The `preg_match()` function compares the pattern of `"<img "` against the contents of `$html`. If it finds a match, it returns 1; if it doesn't, it returns 0. The `/` characters are called *pattern delimiters*; they set off the start and end of the pattern.

A few characters, however, are special. The special nature of these characters are what transforms regular expressions beyond the feature set of `strstr()` and `strpos()`. These characters are called *metacharacters*. The most frequently used *metacharacters* include the period (.), asterisk (*), plus (+), and question mark (?). To match an actual metacharacter, precede the character with a backslash(\).

- The period matches any character, so the pattern `/.at/` matches `bat`, `cat`, and even `rat`.
- The asterisk means match 0 or more of the preceding object. (Right now, the only objects we know about are characters.)
- The plus is similar to asterisk, but it matches 1 or more instead of 0 or more. So, `/.+at/` matches `brat`, `sprat`, and even `catastrophe`, but not `at`. To match `at`, replace the + with a *.
- The question mark matches 0 or 1 objects.

To apply * and + to objects greater than one character, place the sequence of characters inside parentheses. Parentheses allow you to group characters for more complicated matching and also capture the part of the pattern that falls inside them. A captured sequence can be referenced in `preg_replace()` to alter a string, and all captured matches can be stored in an array that's passed as a third parameter to `preg_match()` and `preg_match_all()`. The `preg_match_all()` function is similar to `preg_match()`, but it finds all possible matches inside a string, instead of stopping at the first match. Here are some examples:

```
if (preg_match('/<title>.+<\/title>/', $html)) {
    // page has a title
}

if (preg_match_all('/<li>/', $html, $matches)) {
    print 'Page has ' . count($matches[0]) . " list items\n";
}

// turn bold into italic
$italics = preg_replace('/(<\/?)b(>)/', '$1i$2', $bold);
```

If you want to match strings with a specific set of letters, create a character class with the letters you want. A *character class* is a sequence of characters placed inside square brackets. The caret (^) and the dollar sign ($) anchor the pattern at the beginning and the end of the string, respectively. Without them, a match can occur anywhere in the string. So, to match only vowels, make a character class containing a, e, i, o, and u; start your pattern with ^; and end it with $:

```
preg_match('/^[aeiou]+$/', $string); // only vowels
```

If it's easier to define what you're looking for by its complement, use that. To make a character class match the complement of what's inside it, begin the class with a caret. A caret outside a character class anchors a pattern at the beginning of a string; a caret inside a character class means "match everything except what's listed in the square brackets":

```
preg_match('/^[^aeiou]+$/', $string) // only non-vowels
```

Note that the opposite of [aeiou] isn't [bcdfghjklmnpqrstvwxyz]. The character class [^aeiou] also matches uppercase vowels such as AEIOU, numbers such as 123, URLs such as http://www.cnpq.br/, and even emoticons such as :).

The vertical bar (|), also known as the pipe, specifies alternatives. For example:

```
// find a gif or a jpeg
preg_match('/(gif|jpeg)/', $images);
```

Beside metacharacters, there are also metasymbols. *Metasymbols* are like metacharacters, but are longer than one character in length. Some useful metasymbols are \w (match any word character, [a-zA-Z0-9_]); \d (match any digit, [0-9]); \s (match any whitespace character), and \b (match a word boundary). Here's how to find all numbers that aren't part of another word:

```
// find digits not touching other words
preg_match_all('/\b\d+\b/', $html, $matches);
```

This matches 123, 76!, and 38-years-old, but not 2nd.

Here's a pattern that is the regular expression equivalent of trim():

```
// delete leading whitespace or trailing whitespace
$trimmed = preg_replace('/(^\s+)|(\s+$)/', '', $string);
```

Finally, there are pattern modifiers. Modifiers effect the entire pattern, not just a character or group of characters. Pattern modifiers are placed after the trailing pattern delimiter. For example, the letter i makes a regular expression pattern case-insensitive:

```
// strict match lower-case image tags only (XHTML compliant)
if (preg_match('/<img[^>]+>/', $html)) {
    ...
}

// match both upper and lower-case image tags
if (preg_match('/<img[^>]+>/i', $html)) {
    ...
}
```

We've covered just a small subset of the world of regular expressions. We provide some additional details in later recipes, but the PHP web site also has some very useful information on POSIX regular expressions at *http://www.php.net/regex* and on Perl-compatible regular expressions at *http://www.php.net/pcre*. The links from this last page to "Pattern Modifiers" and "Pattern Syntax" are especially detailed and informative.

The best books on this topic are *Mastering Regular Expressions* by Jeffrey Friedl, and *Programming Perl* by Larry Wall, Tom Christiansen, and Jon Orwant, both published by O'Reilly. (Since the Perl-compatible regular expressions are based on Perl's regular expressions, we don't feel too bad suggesting a book on Perl.)

13.1 Switching From ereg to preg

Problem

You want to convert from using ereg functions to preg functions.

Solution

First, you have to add delimiters to your patterns:

```
preg_match('/pattern/', 'string')
```

For eregi() case-insensitive matching, use the /i modifier instead:

```
preg_match('/pattern/i', 'string');
```

When using integers instead of strings as patterns or replacement values, convert the number to hexadecimal and specify it using an escape sequence:

```
$hex = dechex($number);
preg_match("/\x$hex/", 'string');
```

Discussion

There are a few major differences between ereg and preg. First, when you use preg functions, the pattern isn't just the string pattern; it also needs delimiters, as in Perl, so it's /pattern/ instead.* So:

```
ereg('pattern', 'string');
```

becomes:

```
preg_match('/pattern/', 'string');
```

When choosing your pattern delimiters, don't put your delimiter character inside the regular-expression pattern, or you'll close the pattern early. If you can't find a way to avoid this problem, you need to escape any instances of your delimiters using the backslash. Instead of doing this by hand, call addcslashes().

For example, if you use / as your delimiter:

```
$ereg_pattern = '<b>.+</b>';
$preg_pattern = addcslashes($ereg_pattern, '/');
```

The value of $preg_pattern is now <b>.+<\/b>.

The preg functions don't have a parallel series of case-insensitive functions. They have a case-insensitive modifier instead. To convert, change:

```
eregi('pattern', 'string');
```

to:

```
preg_match('/pattern/i', 'string');
```

Adding the i after the closing delimiter makes the change.

Finally, there is one last obscure difference. If you use a number (not a string) as a pattern or replacement value in ereg_replace(), it's assumed you are referring to the ASCII value of a character. Therefore, since 9 is the ASCII representation of tab (i.e., \t), this code inserts tabs at the beginning of each line:

```
$tab = 9;
$replaced = ereg_replace('^', $tab, $string);
```

Here's how to convert linefeed endings:

```
$converted = ereg_replace(10, 12, $text);
```

To avoid this feature in ereg functions, use this instead:

```
$tab = '9';
```

On the other hand, preg_replace() treats the number 9 as the number 9, not as a tab substitute. To convert these character codes for use in preg_replace(), convert them to hexadecimal and prefix them with \x. For example, 9 becomes \x9 or \x09, and 12

---

* Or {}, <>, ||, ##, or whatever your favorite delimiters are. PHP supports them all.

becomes \x0c. Alternatively, you can use \t, \r, and \n for tabs, carriage returns, and linefeeds, respectively.

See Also

Documentation on ereg() at *http://www.php.net/ereg*, preg_match() at *http://www.php.net/preg-match*, and addcslashes() at *http://www.php.net/addcslashes*.

13.2   Matching Words

Problem

You want to pull out all words from a string.

Solution

The key to this is carefully defining what you mean by a word. Once you've created your definition, use the special character types to create your regular expression:

```
/\S+/        // everything that isn't whitespace
/[A-Z'-]+/i  // all upper and lowercase letters, apostrophes, and hyphens
```

Discussion

The simple question "what is a word?" is surprisingly complicated. While the Perl compatible regular expressions have a built-in word character type, specified by \w, it's important to understand exactly how PHP defines a word. Otherwise, your results may not be what you expect.

Normally, because it comes directly from Perl's definition of a word, \w encompasses all letters, digits, and underscores; this means a_z is a word, but the email address php@example.com is not.

In this recipe, we only consider English words, but other languages use different alphabets. Because Perl-compatible regular expressions use the current locale to define its settings, altering the locale can switch the definition of a letter, which then redefines the meaning of a word.

To combat this, you may want to explicitly enumerate the characters belonging to your words inside a character class. To add a nonstandard character, use \ddd, where ddd is a character's octal code.

See Also

Recipe 16.2 for information about setting locales.

13.3   Finding the nth Occurrence of a Match

Problem

You want to find the *n*th word match instead of the first one.

Solution

Use `preg_match_all()` to pull all the matches into an array; then pick out the specific matches you're interested in:

```
preg_match_all ("/$pattern/$modifiers", $string, $matches)

foreach($matches[1] as $match) {
    print "$match\n";
}
```

Discussion

Unlike in Perl, PHP's Perl-compatible regular expressions don't support the /g modifier that allows you to loop through the string one match at a time. You need to use `preg_match_all()` instead of `preg_match()`.

The `preg_match_all()` function returns a two-dimensional array. The first element holds an array of matches of the complete pattern. The second element also holds an array of matches, but of the parenthesized submatches within each complete match. So, to get the third potato, you access the third element of the second element of the `$matches` array:

```
$potatoes = 'one potato two potato three potato four';
preg_match_all("/(\w+)\s+potato\b/", $potatoes, $matches);
print $matches[1][2];
three
```

Instead of returning an array divided into full matches and then submatches, `preg_match_all()` returns an array divided by matches, with each submatch inside. To trigger this, pass `PREG_SET_ORDER` in as the fourth argument. Now, three isn't in `$matches[1][2]`, as previously, but in `$matches[2][1]`.

Check the return value of `preg_match_all()` to find the number of matches:

```
print preg_match_all("/(\w+)\s+potato\b/", $potatoes, $matches);
3
```

Note that there are only three matches, not four, because there's no trailing potato after the word four in the string.

See Also

Documentation on `preg_match_all( )` at *http://www.php.net/preg-match-all*.

13.4 Choosing Greedy or Nongreedy Matches

Problem

You want your pattern to match the smallest possible string instead of the largest.

Solution

Place a ? after a quantifier to alter that portion of the pattern:

```
// find all bolded sections
preg_match_all('#<b>.+?</b>#', $html, $matches);
```

Or, use the U pattern modifier ending to invert all quantifiers from greedy to non-greedy:

```
// find all bolded sections
preg_match_all('#<b>.+</b>#U', $html, $matches);
```

Discussion

By default, all regular expressions in PHP are what's known as *greedy*. This means a quantifier always tries to match as many characters as possible.

For example, take the pattern p.*, which matches a p and then 0 or more characters, and match it against the string php. A greedy regular expression finds one match, because after it grabs the opening p, it continues on and also matches the hp. A non-greedy regular expression, on the other hand, finds a pair of matches. As before, it matches the p and also the h, but then instead of continuing on, it backs off and leaves the final p uncaptured. A second match then goes ahead and takes the closing letter.

The following code shows that the greedy match finds only one hit; the nongreedy ones find two:

```
print preg_match_all('/p.*/', "php");  // greedy
print preg_match_all('/p.*?/', "php"); // nongreedy
print preg_match_all('/p.*/U', "php"); // nongreedy
1
2
2
```

Greedy matching is also known as *maximal matching* and nongreedy matching can be called *minimal matching*, because these options match either the maximum or minimum number of characters possible.

Initially, all regular expressions were strictly greedy. Therefore, you can't use this syntax with ereg() or ereg_replace(). Greedy matching isn't supported by the older engine that powers these functions; instead, you must use Perl-compatible functions.

Nongreedy matching is frequently useful when trying to perform simplistic HTML parsing. Let's say you want to find all text between bold tags. With greedy matching, you get this:

```
$html = '<b>I am bold.</b> <i>I am italic.</i> <b>I am also bold.</b>';
preg_match_all('#<b>(.+)</b>#', $html, $bolds);
print_r($bolds[1]);
Array
(
    [0] => I am bold.</b> <i>I am italic.</i> <b>I am also bold.

)
```

Because there's a second set of bold tags, the pattern extends past the first </b>, which makes it impossible to correctly break up the HTML. If you use minimal matching, each set of tags is self-contained:

```
$html = '<b>I am bold.</b> <i>I am italic.</i> <b>I am also bold.</b>';
preg_match_all('#<b>(.+?)</b>#', $html, $bolds);
print_r($bolds[1]);
Array
(
    [0] => I am bold.
    [1] => I am also bold.
)
```

Of course, this can break down if your markup isn't 100% valid, and there are stray bold tags lying around.* If your goal is just to remove all (or some) HTML tags from a block of text, you're better off not using a regular expression. Instead, use the built-in function strip_tags(); it's faster and it works correctly. See Recipe 11.11 for more details.

Finally, even though the idea of nongreedy matching comes from Perl, the -U modifier is incompatible with Perl and is unique to PHP's Perl-compatible regular expressions. It inverts all quantifiers, turning them from greedy to nongreedy and also the reverse. So, to get a greedy quantifier inside of a pattern operating under a trailing /U, just add a ? to the end, the same way you would normally turn a greedy quantifier into a nongreedy one.

---

* It's possible to have valid HTML and still get into trouble. For instance, if you have bold tags inside a comment. A true HTML parser ignores this section, but our pattern won't.

See Also

Recipe 13.8 for more on capturing text inside HTML tags; Recipe 11.11 for more on stripping HTML tags; documentation on preg_match_all() at *http://www.php.net/ preg-match-all*.

13.5   Matching a Valid Email Address

Problem

You want to check if an email address is valid.

Solution

This is a popular question and everyone has a different answer, depending on their definition of valid. If valid means a mailbox belonging to a legitimate user at an existing hostname, the real answer is that you can't do it correctly, so don't even bother. However, sometimes a regular expression can help weed out some simple typos and obvious bogus attempts. That said, our favorite pattern that doesn't require maintenance is:

```
/^[^@\s]+@([-a-z0-9]+\.)+[a-z]{2,}$/i
```

If the IMAP extension is enabled, you can also use imap_rfc822_parse_adrlist():

```
$parsed = imap_rfc822_parse_adrlist($email_address, $default_host)
if ('INVALID_ADDRESS' == $parsed['mailbox']) {
    // bad address
}
```

Ironically, because this function is so RFC-compliant, it may not give the results you expect.

Discussion

The pattern in the Solution accepts any email address that has a name of any sequence of characters that isn't a @ or whitespace. After the @, you need at least one domain name consisting of the letters a-z, the numbers 0-9, and the hyphen, separated by periods, and proceed it with as many subdomains you want. Finally, you end with either a two-digit country code or another top-level domain, such as .com or .edu.

The solution pattern is handy because it still works if ICANN adds new top-level domains. However, it does allow through a few false positives. This more strict pattern explicitly enumerates the current noncountry top-level domains:

```
/
    ^                     # anchor at the beginning
```

```
  [^@\s]+        # name is all characters except @ and whitespace
  @              # the @ divides name and domain
  (
     [-a-z0-9]+  # (sub)domains are letters, numbers, and hyphens
     \.          # separated by a period
  )+             # and we can have one or more of them
  (
     [a-z]{2}    # TLDs can be a two-letter alphabetical country code
     |com|net    # or one of
     |edu|org    # many
     |gov|mil    # possible
     |int|biz    # three-letter
     |pro        # combinations
     |info|arpa  # or even
     |aero|coop  # a few
     |name       # four-letter ones
     |museum     # plus one that's six-letters long!
  )
  $              # anchor at the end
/ix              # and everything is case-insensitive
```

Both patterns are intentionally liberal in what they accept, because we assume you're only trying to make sure someone doesn't accidentally leave off their top-level domain or type in something fake such as "not telling." For instance, there's no domain "-.com", but "foo@-.com" flies through without a blip. (It wouldn't be hard to modify the pattern to correct this, but that's left as an exercise for you.) On the other hand, it is legal to have an address of "Tim O'Reilly@oreilly.com", and our pattern won't accept this. However, spaces in email addresses are rare; because a space almost always represents a mistake, we flag that address as bad.

The canonical definition of what's a valid address is documented in RFC 822; however, writing code to handle all cases isn't a pretty task. Here's one example of what you need to consider: people are allowed to embed comments inside addresses! Comments are set inside parentheses, so it's valid to write:

```
Tim (is the man @ computer books) @ oreilly.com
```

That's equivalent to "tim@oreilly.com". (So, again, the pattern fails on that address.)

Alternatively, the IMAP extension has an RFC 822-compliant address parser. This parser correctly navigates through whitespace comments and other oddities, but it allows obvious mistakes because it assumes that addresses without hostnames are local:

```
$email = 'stephen(his account)@ example(his host)';
$parsed = imap_rfc822_parse_adrlist($email,'');
print_r($parsed);
Array
(
    [0] => stdClass Object
        (
            [mailbox] => stephen
```

```
            [host] => example
            [personal] => his host
    )

)
```

Reassembling the mailbox and host, you get "stephen@example", which probably isn't what you want. The empty string you must pass in as the second argument defeats your ability to check for valid hostnames.

Some people like behind-the-scenes processing such as DNS lookups, to check if the address is valid. This doesn't make much sense because that technique won't always work, and you may end up rejecting perfectly valid people from your site, due to no fault of their own. (Also, its unlikely a mail administrator would fix his mail handling just to work around one web site's email validation scheme.)

Another consideration when validating email addresses is that it doesn't take too much work for a user to enter a completely legal and working address that isn't his. For instance, one of the authors used to have a bad habit of entering "billg@microsoft.com" when signing up for Microsoft's web sites because "Hey! Maybe Bill doesn't know about that new version of Internet Explorer?"

If the primary concern is to avoid typos, make people enter their address twice, and compare the two. If they match, it's probably correct. Also, filter out popular bogus addresses, such as "president@whitehouse.gov" and the previously mentioned "billg@microsoft.com". (This does have the downside of not letting The President of the United States of America or Bill Gates sign up for your site.)

However, if you need to ensure people actually have access to the email address they provide, one technique is to send a message to their address and require them to either reply to the message or go to a page on your site and type in a special code printed in the body of the message to confirm their sign-up. If you do choose the special code route, we suggest that you don't generate a random string of letters, such as HSD5nbAD18. Since it looks like garbage, it's hard to retype it correctly. Instead, use a word list and create code words such as television4coatrack. While, on occasion, it's possible to divine hidden meanings in these combos, you can cut the error rate and your support costs.

See Also

Recipe 8.5 for information about generating good passwords; Recipe 8.26 for a web site account deactivation program; documentation on imap_rfc822_parse_adrlist() at *http://www.php.net/imap-rfc822-parse-adrlist*.

13.6   Finding All Lines in a File That Match a Pattern

Problem

You want to find all the lines in a file that match a pattern.

Solution

Read the file into an array and use `preg_grep()`.

Discussion

There are two ways to do this. Here's the faster method:

```
$pattern = "/\bo'reilly\b/i"; // only O'Reilly books
$ora_books = preg_grep($pattern, file('/path/to/your/file.txt'));
```

Use the `file()` command to automatically load each line of the file into an array element and `preg_grep()` to filter the bad lines out.

Here's the more efficient method:

```
$fh = fopen('/path/to/your/file.txt', 'r') or die($php_errormsg);
while (!feof($fh)) {
    $line = fgets($fh, 4096);
    if (preg_match($pattern, $line)) { $ora_books[] = $line; }
}
fclose($fh);
```

Since the first method reads in everything all at once, it's about three times faster then the second way, which parses the file line by line but uses less memory. One downside, however, is that because the regular expression works only on one line at a time, the second method doesn't find strings that span multiple lines.

See Also

Recipe 18.5 on reading files into strings; documentation on `preg_grep()` at *http://www.php.net/preg-grep*.

13.7   Capturing Text Inside HTML Tags

Problem

You want to capture text inside HTML tags. For example, you want to find all the headings in a HTML document.

Solution

Read the HTML file into a string and use nongreedy matching in your pattern:

```
$html = join('',file($file));
preg_match('#<h([1-6])>(.+?)</h\1>#is', $html, $matches);
```

In this example, $matches[2] contains an array of captured headings.

Discussion

True parsing of HTML is difficult using a simple regular expression. This is one advantage of using XHTML; it's significantly easier to validate and parse.

For instance, the pattern in the Solution is smart enough to find only matching headings, so <h1>Dr. Strangelove<h1> is okay, because it's wrapped inside <h1> tags, but not <h2>How I Learned to Stop Worrying and Love the Bomb</h3>, because the opening tag is an <h2> while the closing tag is not.

This technique also works for finding all text inside bold and italic tags:

```
$html = join('',file($file));
preg_match('#<([bi])>(.+?)</\1>#is', $html, $matches);
```

However, it breaks on nested headings. Using that regular expression on:

```
<b>Dr. Strangelove or: <i>How I Learned to Stop Worrying and Love the Bomb</i></b>
```

doesn't capture the text inside the <i> tags as a separate item.

This wasn't a problem earlier; because headings are block level elements, it's illegal to nest them. However, as inline elements, nested bold and italic tags are valid.

Captured text can be processed by looping through the array of matches. For example, this code parses a document for its headings and pretty-prints them with indentation according to the heading level:

```
$html = join('',file($file));
preg_match('#<h([1-6])>(.+?)</h\1>#is', $html, $matches);

for ($i = 0, $j = count($matches[0]); $i < $j; $i++) {
  print str_repeat(' ', 2 * ($matches[1][$i] - 1)) . $matches[2][$i] . "\n";
}
```

So, with one representation of this recipe in HTML:

```
$html =<<<_END_
<h1>PHP Cookbook</h1>

Other Chapters
<h2>Regular Expressions</h2>

Other Recipes
<h3>Capturing Text Inside of HTML Tags</h3>
```

```
<h4>Problem</h4>
<h4>Solution</h4>
<h4>Discussion</h4>
<h4>See Also</h4>

_END_;

preg_match_all('#<h([1-6])>(.+?)</h\1>#is', $html, $matches);

for ($i = 0, $j = count($matches[0]); $i < $j; $i++) {
  print str_repeat(' ', 2 * ($matches[1][$i] - 1)) . $matches[2][$i] . "\n";
}
```

You get:

```
PHP Cookbook
    Regular Expressions
        Capturing Text Inside of HTML Tags
            Problem
            Solution
            Discussion
            See Also
```

By capturing the heading level and heading text separately, you can directly access the level and treat it as an integer when calculating the indentation size. To avoid a two-space indent for all lines, subtract 1 from the level.

See Also

Recipe 11.7 for information on marking up a web page and Recipe 11.8 for extracting links from an HTML file; documentation on preg_match() at *http://www.php.net/ preg-match* and str_repeat() at *http://www.php.net/str-repeat*.

13.8 Escaping Special Characters in a Regular Expression

Problem

You want to have characters such as * or + treated as literals, not as metacharacters, inside a regular expression. This is useful when allowing users to type in search strings you want to use inside a regular expression.

Solution

Use preg_quote() to escape Perl-compatible regular-expression metacharacters:

```
$pattern = preg_quote('The Education of H*Y*M*A*N K*A*P*L*A*N').':(\d+)';
if (preg_match("/$pattern/",$book_rank,$matches)) {
```

```
        print "Leo Rosten's book ranked: ".$matches[1];
    }
```

Use quotemeta() to escape POSIX metacharacters:

```
$pattern = quotemeta('M*A*S*H').':[0-9]+';
if (ereg($pattern,$tv_show_rank,$matches)) {
    print 'Radar, Hot Lips, and the gang ranked: '.$matches[1];
}
```

Discussion

Here are the characters that preg_quote() escapes:

. \ + * ? ^ $ [ ] ( ) { } < > = ! | :

Here are the characters that quotemeta() escapes:

. \ + * ? ^ $ [ ] ( )

These functions escape the metacharacters with backslash.

The quotemeta() function doesn't match all POSIX metacharacters. The characters {, }, and | are also valid metacharacters but aren't converted. This is another good reason to use preg_match() instead of ereg().

You can also pass preg_quote() an additional character to escape as a second argument. It's useful to pass your pattern delimiter (usually /) as this argument so it also gets escaped. This is important if you incorporate user input into a regular-expression pattern. The following code expects $_REQUEST['search_term'] from a web form and searches for words beginning with $_REQUEST['search_term'] in a string $s:

```
$search_term = preg_quote($_REQUEST['search_term'],'/');
if (preg_match("/\b$search_term/i",$s)) {
    print 'match!';
}
```

Using preg_quote() ensures the regular expression is interpreted properly if, for example, a Magnum, P.I. fan enters t.c. as a search term. Without preg_quote(), this matches tic, tucker, and any other words whose first letter is t and third letter is c. Passing the pattern delimiter to preg_quote() as well makes sure that user input with forward slashes in it, such as CP/M, is also handled correctly.

See Also

Documentation on preg_quote() at *http://www.php.net/preg-quote* and quotemeta() at *http://www.php.net/quotemeta*.

13.9 Reading Records with a Pattern Separator

Problem

You want to read in records from a file, in which each record is separated by a pattern you can match with a regular expression.

Solution

Read the entire file into a string and then split on the regular expression:

```
$filename = '/path/to/your/file.txt';
$fh = fopen($filename, 'r') or die($php_errormsg);
$contents = fread($fh, filesize($filename));
fclose($fh);

$records = preg_split('/[0-9]+\) /', $contents);
```

Discussion

This breaks apart a numbered list and places the individual list items into array elements. So, if you have a list like this:

```
1) Gödel
2) Escher
3) Bach
```

You end up with a four-element array, with an empty opening element. That's because preg_split( ) assumes the delimiters are between items, but in this case, the numbers are before items:

```
Array
(
    [0] =>
    [1] => Gödel
    [2] => Escher
    [3] => Bach
)
```

From one point of view, this can be a feature, not a bug, since the *n*th element holds the *n*th item. But, to compact the array, you can eliminate the first element:

```
$records = preg_split('/[0-9]+\) /', $contents);
array_shift($records);
```

Another modification you might want is to strip new lines from the elements and substitute the empty string instead:

```
$records = preg_split('/[0-9]+\) /', str_replace("\n",'',$contents));
array_shift($records);
```

PHP doesn't allow you to change the input record separator to anything other than a newline, so this technique is also useful for breaking apart records divided by strings. However, if you find yourself splitting on a string instead of a regular expression, substitute explode( ) for preg_split( ) for a more efficient operation.

See Also

Recipe 18.5 for reading from a file; Recipe 1.11 for parsing CSV files.

CHAPTER 14

Encryption and Security

14.0 Introduction

In a perfect world, encryption wouldn't be necessary. Nosy people would keep their eyes on their own data, and a credit card number floating around the Internet would attract no special attention. In so many ways, however, our world isn't perfect, so we need encryption.

Encryption scrambles data. Some data scrambling can't be unscrambled without unreasonable amounts of processing. This is called *one-way encryption*. Other encryption methods work in two directions: data is encrypted; then it's decrypted.

PHP supplies tools to encrypt and secure your data. Some tools, such as the crypt( ) and md5( ) functions, are part of PHP's base set of functions, and some are extensions that need to be explicitly included when PHP is compiled (e.g., *mcrypt*, *mhash*, and cURL).

The crypt( ) function does one-way DES encryption using the first eight characters of plaintext to calculate the ciphertext. You pass it the plaintext to encrypt (and a salt, which strengthens the encryption), and it returns the encrypted ciphertext. PHP generates a random salt if you don't supply one:

```
print crypt('shrimp','34');
34b/4qaoXmcoY
```

If the constant CRYPT_MD5 is set to 1, crypt( ) can do MD5 encryption. To tell PHP to use MD5 encryption, start the salt with 1:

```
print crypt('shrimp','$1$seasalt!');
$1$seasalt!$C8bRD475BC3T4EvjjmR9I.
```

Recipe 14.4 discusses crypt( ). It is most widely used for encrypting passwords.

mcrypt is a more full-featured encryption library that offers different algorithms and encryption modes. Because it supports different kinds of encryption, *mcrypt* is especially helpful when you need to exchange encrypted data with other systems or with programs not written in PHP. *mcrypt* is discussed in detail in Recipe 14.7.

PHP gives you the tools to protect your data with robust encryption, but encryption is just part of the large and often complex security picture. Your encrypted data can be unlocked with a key, so protecting that key is very important. If your encryption keys are accessible to unauthorized users (because they're stored in a file accessible via your web server or because they're stored in a file accessible by other users in a shared hosting environment, for example), your data is at risk, no matter how airtight your chosen encryption algorithm is.

You need to determine how secure you want your data to be. Encrypting it is more secure but more complex. Simpler encoding hides your data from elementary prying eyes but offers less security. No encryption or security is absolute. Picking an appropriate security method means finding a place on the spectrum between convenience and protection. The more convenient (or computationally inexpensive) types of security generally provide less protection. Sometimes your goal isn't to protect data from prying eyes but to avoid the appearance of impropriety. Seeing a plaintext field in a form (or URL) named "Password" could be more disturbing to your users than the same data wrapped in Base64 encoding. Recipe 14.2 shows how to obscure data with Base64.

Sensitive data needs to be protected not just on the server but also when it's traveling on the network between your server and your users. Data sent over regular HTTP is visible to anybody with access to the network at any point between your server and a user. Recipe 14.10 discusses how to layer HTTP over SSL to prevent network snoopers from peeping at data as it passes by.

There are plenty of nontechnical prerequisites to tight security. Assigning passwords that are a random jumble of letters, numbers, and punctuation does no good if those passwords are so hard to remember that users write them on sticky notes attached to their monitors. As we have already said, security is not an absolute, but a tradeoff between convenience and protection. As you use the recipes in this chapter to protect your data, decide what is an acceptable risk for your data versus the corresponding appropriate level of inconvenience that security introduces.[*]

14.1   Keeping Passwords Out of Your Site Files

Problem

You need to use a password to connect to a database, for example. You don't want to put the password in the PHP files you use on your site in case those files are compromised.

---

[*] *Practical Unix and Internet Security*, by Simson Garfinkel and Gene Spafford (O'Reilly) offers some helpful and (not surprisingly) practical advice on how to think about the balancing act of risk management.

Solution

Store the password in an environment variable in a file that the web server loads when starting up; then, just reference the environment variable in your script:

```
mysql_connect('localhost',$_SERVER['MYSQL_USER'],$_SERVER['MYSQL_PASSWORD']);
```

Discussion

While this technique removes passwords from the source code of your pages, it does make them available in other places that need to be protected. Most importantly, make sure that there are no publicly viewable pages that call phpinfo( ). Because phpinfo( ) displays environment variables available to scripts, it displays the passwords put into environment variables.

Next, especially if you are in a shared hosting setup, make sure that the environment variables are set in such a way that they are available only to your virtual host, not to all shared hosting users. With Apache, you can do this by setting the variables in a separate file from the main configuration file:

```
SetEnv  MYSQL_USER      "susannah"
SetEnv  MYSQL_PASSWORD "y23a!t@ce8"
```

Inside the <VirtualHost> directive for the site in the main configuration file, include this separate file as follows:

```
Include "/usr/local/apache/database-passwords"
```

Make sure that the separate file that contains the passwords (e.g., */usr/local/apache/ database-passwords*) is not readable by any users other than the one that controls the appropriate virtual host. When Apache starts up and is reading in configuration files, it's usually running as root, so it is able to read the included file.

See Also

Documentation on Apache's Include directive at *http://httpd.apache.org/docs/mod/ core.html#include*.

14.2 Obscuring Data with Encoding

Problem

You want to prevent data being viewable as plaintext. For example, you don't want hidden form data to be revealed simply by someone viewing the source code of a web page.

Solution

Encode the data with base64_encode( ):

```
$personal_data = array('code' => 5123, 'blood_type' => 'O');
$info = base64_encode(serialize($personal_data));
print '<input type="hidden" name="info" value="'.$info.'">';
<input type="hidden" name="info"
value="YToyOntzOjQ6ImNvZGUiO2k6NTEyMztzOjEwOiJibG9vZF90eXBlIjtzOjE6Ik8iO30=">
```

Decode the data with base64_decode( ):

```
$personal_data = unserialize(base64_decode($_REQUEST['info']));
get_transfusion($personal_data['blood_type']);
```

Discussion

The Base64 algorithm encodes data as a string of letters, numbers, and punctuation marks. This makes it ideal for transforming binary data into a plaintext form and also for obfuscating data.

See Also

Documentation on base64_encode( ) at *http://www.php.net/base64-encode* and base64_decode( ) at *http://www.php.net/base64-decode*; the Base64 algorithm is defined in RFC 2045, available at *http://www.faqs.org/rfcs/rfc2045.html*.

14.3   Verifying Data with Hashes

Problem

You want to make sure users don't alter data you've sent them in a cookie or form element.

Solution

Along with the data, send an MD5 hash of the data with a secret word. When you receive the data back, compute the hash of the received value with the same secret word. If they don't match, the user has altered the data.

Here's how to print a hash in a hidden form field:

```
$secret_word = 'flyingturtle';
$id = 2836;
$hash = md5($secret_word . $id);

print<<<_HTML_
<input type="hidden" name="id" value="$id">
```

```
<input type="hidden" name="idhash" value="$hash">
_HTML_;
```

Here's how to verify the hidden form field data when it's submitted:

```
$secret_word = 'flyingturtle';

if (md5($secret_word . $_REQUEST['id']) == $_REQUEST['idhash']) {
    $id = $_REQUEST['id'];
} else {
    die("Invalid data in $_REQUEST[id]");
}
```

Discussion

When processing the submitted form data, compute the hash of the submitted value of $_REQUEST['id'] and the secret word. If it matches the submitted hash, the value of $_REQUEST['id'] has not been altered by the user. If the hashes don't match, you know that the value of $_REQUEST['id'] you received is not the same as the one you sent.

To use a verification hash with a cookie, add the hash to the cookie value with join():

```
$secret_word = 'flyingturtle';
$cookie_value = 'Ellen';
$hash = md5($secret_word . $cookie_value);

setcookie('name',join('|',array($cookie_value,$hash)));
```

Parse the hash from the cookie value with explode():

```
$secret_word = 'flyingturtle';
list($cookie_value,$cookie_hash) = explode('|',$_COOKIE['name'],2);
if (md5($secret_word . $cookie_value) == $cookie_hash) {
    $name = $cookie_value;
} else {
    die('Invalid data in $_COOKIE[name]');
}
```

Using a data-verification hash in a form or cookie obviously depends on the secret word used in hash computation. If a malicious user discovers your secret word, the hash offers no protection. Aside from guarding the secret word zealously, changing it frequently is a good idea. For an additional layer of protection, use different secret words, choosing the specific word to use in the hash based on some property of the $id value (10 different words selected by $id%10, for example). That way, damage is controlled if one of the words is compromised.

If you have the *mhash* module installed, you're not limited to MD5 hashes. *mhash* supports a number of different hash algorithms. For more information about *mhash*, see the *mhash* material in the online PHP manual or the *mhash* home page at *http://mhash.sourceforge.net/*.

See Also

Recipe 8.10 uses a verification hash for cookie-based authentication; Recipe 9.3 for an example of using hashes with hidden form variables; documentation on md5( ) at *http://www.php.net/md5* and the *mhash* extension at *http://www.php.net/mhash*.

14.4   Storing Passwords

Problem

You need to keep track of users' passwords so they can log in to your web site.

Solution

When a user signs up, encrypt her chosen password with crypt( ) and store the encrypted password in your database of users:

```
// encrypt the password
$encrypted_password = crypt($_REQUEST['password']);

// store $encrypted_password in the user database
$dbh->query('INSERT INTO users (username,password) VALUES (?,?)',
            array($_REQUEST['username'],$encrypted_password));
```

Then, when that user attempts to log in to your web site, encrypt the password she supplies with crypt( ) and compare it to the stored encrypted password. If the two encrypted values match, she has supplied the correct password:

```
$encrypted_password =
    $dbh->getOne('SELECT password FROM users WHERE username = ?',
                array($_REQUEST['username']));

if (crypt($_REQUEST['password'],$encrypted_password) == $encrypted_password) {
  // successful login
} else {
  // unsuccessful login
}
```

Discussion

Storing encrypted passwords prevents users' accounts from becoming compromised if an unauthorized person gets a peek at your username and password database. (Although such unauthorized peeks may foreshadow other security problems.)

When the password is initially encrypted, crypt( ) supplies two randomly generated characters of salt that get prepended to the encrypted password. Passing $encrypted_password to crypt( ) when testing a user-supplied password tells crypt( ) to use the same salt characters again. The salt reduces your vulnerability to dictionary attacks,

---

in which someone compares encrypted passwords with encrypted versions of common words. Still, it's a good idea to prevent users from choosing passwords that are simple words or other easier-to-crack combinations. Recipe 14.5 provides a function to filter out easily guessable passwords.

The crypt( ) function uses a one-way algorithm. This means it's currently impossible (or at least prohibitively computationally expensive) to turn a crypt( )-generated ciphertext back into plain text. This makes your stored passwords somewhat more secure, but it also means that you can't get at the plaintext of users' passwords even if you need to. So, for example, if a user forgets his password, you won't be able to tell him what it is. The best you can do is to reset the password to a new value and then tell the user the new password. A method for dealing with lost passwords is covered in Recipe 14.6.

See Also

Recipe 14.8 for information on storing encrypted data; documentation on crypt( ) at *http://www.php.net/crypt*.

14.5   Checking Password Strength

Problem

You want to make sure users pick passwords that are hard to guess.

Solution

Test a user's password choice with the pc_passwordcheck( ) function, shown later in Example 14-1. For example:

```
if ($err = pc_passwordcheck($_REQUEST['username'],$_REQUEST['password'])) {
    print "Bad password: $err";
    // Make the user pick another password
}
```

Discussion

The pc_passwordcheck( ) function, shown in Example 14-1, performs some tests on user-entered passwords to make sure they are harder to crack. It returns a string describing the problem if the password doesn't meet its criteria. The password must be at least six characters long and must have a mix of uppercase letters, lowercase letters, numerals, and special characters. The password can't contain the username either in regular order or reverse order. Additionally, the password can't contain a dictionary word. The filename for the word list used for dictionary checking is stored in $word_file.

The checks for the username or dictionary words in the password are also applied to a version of the password with letters substituted for lookalike numbers. For example, if the supplied password is w0rd$%, the function also checks the string word$% for the username and dictionary words. The "0" character is turned into an "o." Also, "5" is turned into "s," "3" into "e," and both "1" and "!" into "l" (el).

Example 14-1. pc_passwordcheck()

```
function pc_passwordcheck($user,$pass) {
    $word_file = '/usr/share/dict/words';

    $lc_pass = strtolower($pass);
    // also check password with numbers or punctuation subbed for letters
    $denum_pass = strtr($lc_pass,'5301!','seoll');
    $lc_user = strtolower($user);

    // the password must be at least six characters
    if (strlen($pass) < 6) {
        return 'The password is too short.';
    }

    // the password can't be the username (or reversed username)
    if (($lc_pass == $lc_user) || ($lc_pass == strrev($lc_user)) ||
        ($denum_pass == $lc_user) || ($denum_pass == strrev($lc_user))) {
        return 'The password is based on the username.';
    }

    // count how many lowercase, uppercase, and digits are in the password
    $uc = 0; $lc = 0; $num = 0; $other = 0;
    for ($i = 0, $j = strlen($pass); $i < $j; $i++) {
        $c = substr($pass,$i,1);
        if (preg_match('/^[[:upper:]]$/',$c)) {
            $uc++;
        } elseif (preg_match('/^[[:lower:]]$/',$c)) {
            $lc++;
        } elseif (preg_match('/^[[:digit:]]$/',$c)) {
            $num++;
        } else {
            $other++;
        }
    }

    // the password must have more than two characters of at least
    // two different kinds
    $max = $j - 2;
    if ($uc > $max) {
        return "The password has too many upper case characters.";
    }
    if ($lc > $max) {
        return "The password has too many lower case characters.";
```

Example 14-1. pc_passwordcheck( ) (continued)

```
    }
    if ($num > $max) {
        return "The password has too many numeral characters.";
    }
    if ($other > $max) {
        return "The password has too many special characters.";
    }

    // the password must not contain a dictionary word
    if (is_readable($word_file)) {
        if ($fh = fopen($word_file,'r')) {
            $found = false;
            while (! ($found || feof($fh))) {
                $word = preg_quote(trim(strtolower(fgets($fh,1024))),'/');
                if (preg_match("/$word/",$lc_pass) ||
                    preg_match("/$word/",$denum_pass)) {
                    $found = true;
                }
            }
            fclose($fh);
            if ($found) {
                return 'The password is based on a dictionary word.';
            }
        }
    }

    return false;
}
```

See Also

Helpful password choosing guidelines are available at *http://tns.sdsu.edu/security/passwd.html*.

14.6 Dealing with Lost Passwords

Problem

You want to issue a password to a user who claims he's lost his password.

Solution

Generate a new password and send it to the user's email address (which you should have on file):

```
// generate new password
$new_password = '';
$i = 8;
```

```
while ($i--) { $new_password .= chr(mt_rand(33,126)); }

// encrypt new password
$encrypted_password = crypt($new_password);

// save new encrypted password to the database
$dbh->query('UPDATE users SET password = ? WHERE username = ?',
            array($encrypted_password,$username));

// email new plaintext password to user
mail($email,"New Password","Your new password is $new_password");
```

Discussion

If a user forgets his password, and you store encrypted passwords as recommended in Recipe 14.4, you can't provide the forgotten password. The one-way nature of crypt( ) prevents you from retrieving the unencrypted password.

Instead, generate a new password and send that to his preexisting contact address. If you send the new password to an address you don't already have on file for that user, you don't have a way to verify that the new address really belongs to the user. It may be an attacker attempting to impersonate the real user.

Because the email containing the new password isn't encrypted, the code in the Solution doesn't include the username in the email message to reduce the chances that an attacker that eavesdrops on the email message can steal the password. To avoid disclosing a new password by email at all, let a user authenticate himself without a password by answering one or more personal questions (the answers to which you have on file). These questions can be "What was the name of your first pet?" or "What's your mother's maiden name?"—anything a malicious attacker is unlikely to know. If the user provides the correct answers to your questions, you can let him choose a new password.

One way to compromise between security and readability is to generate a password for a user out of actual words interrupted by some numbers.

```
$words =
array('dished','mother','basset','detain','sudden','fellow','logged','sonora',
      'earths','remove','dustin','snails','direct','serves','daring','cretan',
      'chirps','reward','snakes','mchugh','uphold','wiring','gaston','nurses',
      'regent','ornate','dogmas','singed','mended','hinges','latent','verbal',
      'grimes','ritual','drying','hobbes','chests','newark','sourer','rumple');

mt_srand((double) microtime() * 1000000);
$word_count = count($words);

$password = sprintf('%s%02d%s',
                    $words[mt_rand(0,$word_count - 1)],
                    mt_rand(0,99),
                    $words[mt_rand(0,$word_count - 1)]);

print $password;
```

This code produces passwords that are two six-letter words with two numbers between them, like `mother43hinges` or `verbal08chirps`. The passwords are long, but remembering them is made easier by the words in them.

See Also

Recipe 14.4 for information about storing encrypted passwords and Recipe 14.5 for details on checking password strength.

14.7 Encrypting and Decrypting Data

Problem

You want to encrypt and decrypt data using one of a variety of popular algorithms.

Solution

Use PHP's *mcrypt* extension:

```
$key  = 'That golden key that opes the palace of eternity.';
$data = 'The chicken escapes at dawn. Send help with Mr. Blue.';
$alg  = MCRYPT_BLOWFISH;
$mode = MCRYPT_MODE_CBC;

$iv = mcrypt_create_iv(mcrypt_get_iv_size($alg,$mode),MCRYPT_DEV_URANDOM);
$encrypted_data = mcrypt_encrypt($alg, $key, $data, $mode, $iv);
$plain_text = base64_encode($encrypted_data);

print $plain_text."\n";
$decoded = mcrypt_decrypt($alg,$key,base64_decode($plain_text),$mode,$iv);
print $decoded."\n";
NNB9WnuCYjyd3Y7vUh7XDfWFCWnQYOBsMehHNmBHbGOdJ3cM+yghABb/XyrJ+w3xz9tms74/a7O=
The chicken escapes at dawn. Send help with Mr. Blue.
```

Discussion

The *mcrypt* extension is an interface with *mcrypt*, a library that implements many different encryption algorithms. The data is encrypted and decrypted by mcrypt_encrypt( ) and mcrypt_decrypt( ), respectively. They each take five arguments. The first is the algorithm to use. To find which algorithms *mcrypt* supports on your system, call mcrypt_list_algorithms( ). The full list of *mcrypt* algorithms is shown in Table 14-1. The second argument is the encryption key; the third argument is the data to encrypt or decrypt. The fourth argument is the mode for the encryption or decryption (a list of supported modes is returned by mcrypt_list_modes( )). The fifth argument is an initialization vector (IV), used by some modes as part of the encryption or decryption process.

Table 14-1 lists all the possible *mcrypt* algorithms, including the constant value used to indicate the algorithm, the key and block sizes in bits, and whether the algorithm is supported by *libmcrypt* 2.2.x and 2.4.x.

Table 14-1. mcrypt algorithm constants

Algorithm constant	Description	Key size	Block size	2.2.x	2.4.x
MCRYPT_3DES	Triple DES	168 (112 effective)	64	Yes	Yes
MCRYPT_TRIPLEDES	Triple DES	168 (112 effective)	64	No	Yes
MCRYPT_3WAY	3way (Joan Daemen)	96	96	Yes	No
MCRYPT_THREEWAY	3way	96	96	Yes	Yes
MCRYPT_BLOWFISH	Blowfish (Bruce Schneier)	Up to 448	64	No	Yes
MCRYPT_BLOWFISH_COMPAT	Blowfish with compatibility to other implementations	Up to 448	64	No	Yes
MCRYPT_BLOWFISH_128	Blowfish	128	64	Yes	No
MCRYPT_BLOWFISH_192	Blowfish	192	64	Yes	
MCRYPT_BLOWFISH_256	Blowfish	256	64	Yes	No
MCRYPT_BLOWFISH_448	Blowfish	448	64	Yes	No
MCRYPT_CAST_128	CAST (Carlisle Adams and Stafford Tavares)	128	64	Yes	Yes
MCRYPT_CAST_256	CAST	256	128	Yes	Yes
MCRYPT_CRYPT	One-rotor Unix crypt	104	8		Yes
MCRYPT_ENIGNA	One-rotor Unix crypt	104	8	No	Yes
MCRYPT_DES	U.S. Data Encryption Standard	56	64	Yes	Yes
MCRYPT_GOST	Soviet Gosudarstvennyi Standard ("Government Standard")	256	64	Yes	Yes
MCRYPT_IDEA	International Data Encryption Algorithm	128	64	Yes	Yes
MCRYPT_LOKI97	LOKI97 (Lawrie Brown, Josef Pieprzyk)	128, 192, or 256	64	Yes	Yes
MCRYPT_MARS	MARS (IBM)	128–448	128	No	Yes
MCRYPT_PANAMA	PANAMA (Joan Daemen, Craig Clapp)	–	Stream	No	Yes
MCRYPT_RC2	Rivest Cipher 2	8–1024	64	No	Yes
MCRYPT_RC2_1024	Rivest Cipher 2	1024	64	Yes	No
MCRYPT_RC2_128	Rivest Cipher 2	128	64	Yes	No
MCRYPT_RC2_256	Rivest Cipher 2	256	64	Yes	No
MCRYPT_RC4	Rivest Cipher 4	Up to 2048	Stream	Yes	No
MCRYPT_ARCFOUR	Non-trademarked RC4 compatible	Up to 2048	Stream	No	Yes

Table 14-1. mcrypt algorithm constants (continued)

Algorithm constant	Description	Key size	Block size	2.2.x	2.4.x
MCRYPT_ARCFOUR_IV	Arcfour with Initialization Vector	Up to 2048	Stream	No	Yes
MCRYPT_RC6	Rivest Cipher 6	128, 192, or 256	128	No	Yes
MCRYPT_RC6_128	Rivest Cipher 6	128	128	Yes	No
MCRYPT_RC6_192	Rivest Cipher 6	192	128	Yes	No
MCRYPT_RC6_256	Rivest Cipher 6	256	128	Yes	No
MCRYPT_RIJNDAEL_128	Rijndael (Joan Daemen, Vincent Rijmen)	128	128	Yes	Yes
MCRYPT_RIJNDAEL_192	Rijndael	192	192	Yes	Yes
MCRYPT_RIJNDAEL_256	Rijndael	256	256	Yes	Yes
MCRYPT_SAFERPLUS	SAFER+ (based on SAFER)	128, 192, or 256	128	Yes	Yes
MCRYPT_SAFER_128	Secure And Fast Encryption Routine with strengthened key schedule	128	64	Yes	Yes
MCRYPT_SAFER_64	Secure And Fast Encryption Routine with strengthened key	64	64	Yes	Yes
MCRYPT_SERPENT	Serpent (Ross Anderson, Eli Biham, Lars Knudsen)	128, 192, or 256	128	No	Yes
MCRYPT_SERPENT_128	Serpent	128	128	Yes	No
MCRYPT_SERPENT_192	Serpent	192	128	Yes	No
MCRYPT_SERPENT_256	Serpent	256	128	Yes	No
MCRYPT_SKIPJACK	U.S. NSA Clipper Escrowed Encryption Standard	80	64	No	Yes
MCRYPT_TWOFISH	Twofish (Counterpane Systems)	128, 192, or 256	128	No	Yes
MCRYPT_TWOFISH_128	Twofish	128	128	Yes	No
MCRYPT_TWOFISH_192	Twofish	192	128	Yes	No
MCRYPT_TWOFISH_256	Twofish	256	128	Yes	No
MCRYPT_WAKE	Word Auto Key Encryption (David Wheeler)	256	32	No	Yes
MCRYPT_XTEA	Extended Tiny Encryption Algorithm (David Wheeler, Roger Needham)	128	64	Yes	Yes

Except for the data to encrypt or decrypt, all the other arguments must be the same when encrypting and decrypting. If you're using a mode that requires an initialization vector, it's okay to pass the initialization vector in the clear with the encrypted text.

The different modes are appropriate in different circumstances. Cipher Block Chaining (CBC) mode encrypts the data in blocks, and uses the encrypted value of each block (as well as the key) to compute the encrypted value of the next block. The initialization vector affects the encrypted value of the first block. Cipher Feedback (CFB) and Output Feedback (OFB) also use an initialization vector, but they encrypt data in units smaller than the block size. Note that OFB mode has security problems if you encrypt data in smaller units than its block size. Electronic Code Book (ECB) mode encrypts data in discreet blocks that don't depend on each other. ECB mode doesn't use an initialization vector. It is also less secure than other modes for repeated use, because the same plaintext with a given key always produces the same ciphertext. Constants to set each mode are listed in Table 14-2.

Table 14-2. mcrypt mode constants

Mode constant	Description
MCRYPT_MODE_ECB	Electronic Code Book mode
MCRYPT_MODE_CBC	Cipher Block Chaining mode
MCRYPT_MODE_CFB	Cipher Feedback mode
MCRYPT_MODE_OFB	Output Feedback mode with 8 bits of feedback
MCRYPT_MODE_NOFB	Output Feedback mode with *n* bits of feedback, where *n* is the block size of the algorithm used (*libmcrypt* 2.4 and higher only)
MCRYPT_MODE_STREAM	Stream Cipher mode, for algorithms such as RC4 and WAKE (*libmcrypt* 2.4 and higher only)

Different algorithms have different block sizes. You can retrieve the block size for a particular algorithm with mcrypt_get_block_size( ). Similarly, the initialization vector size is determined by the algorithm and the mode. mcrypt_create_iv( ) and mcrypt_get_iv_size( ) make it easy to create an appropriate random initialization vector:

```
$iv = mcrypt_create_iv(mcrypt_get_iv_size($alg,$mode),MCRYPT_DEV_URANDOM);
```

The first argument to mcrypt_create_iv( ) is the size of the vector, and the second is a source of randomness. You have three choices for the source of randomness. MCRYPT_DEV_RANDOM reads from the pseudodevice */dev/random*, MCRYPT_DEV_URANDOM reads from the pseudo-device */dev/urandom*, and MCRYPT_RAND uses an internal random number generator. Not all operating systems support random-generating pseudo-devices. Make sure to call srand( ) before using MCRYPT_RAND in order to get a nonrepeating random number stream.

The code and examples in this recipe are compatible with *mcrypt* 2.4. PHP's mcrypt interface supports both *mcrypt* 2.2 and *mcrypt* 2.4, but there are differences between the two. With *mcrypt* 2.2, PHP supports only the following *mcrypt* functions: mcrypt_ecb( ), mcrypt_cbc( ), mcrypt_cfb( ), mcrypt_ofb( ), mcrypt_get_key_size( ), mcrypt_get_block_size( ), mcrypt_get_cipher_name( ), and mcrypt_create_iv( ). To encrypt or decrypt data with *mcrypt* 2.2, call the appropriate mcrypt_*MODE*( ) function, based on what mode you want to use, and pass it an argument that instructs it to encrypt or decrypt. The following code is the *mcrypt* 2.2-compatible version of the code in the Solution:

```
$key  = 'That golden key that opes the palace of eternity.';
$data = 'The chicken escapes at dawn. Send help with Mr. Blue.';
$alg = MCRYPT_BLOWFISH;

$iv = mcrypt_create_iv(mcrypt_get_block_size($alg),MCRYPT_DEV_URANDOM);
$encrypted_data = mcrypt_cbc($alg,$key,$data,MCRYPT_ENCRYPT);
$plain_text = base64_encode($encrypted_data);

print $plain_text."\n";

$decoded = mcrypt_cbc($alg,$key,base64_decode($plain_text),MCRYPT_DECRYPT);

print $decoded."\n";
```

See Also

Documentation on the *mcrypt* extension at *http://www.php.net/mcrypt*; the *mcrypt* library is available at *http://mcrypt.hellug.gr/*; choosing an appropriate algorithm and using it securely requires care and planning: for more information about *mcrypt* and the cipher algorithms it uses, see the online PHP manual section on *mcrypt*, the *mcrypt* home page, and the manpages for */dev/random* and */dev/urandom*; good books about cryptography include *Applied Cryptography*, by Bruce Schneier (Wiley) and *Cryptography: Theory and Practice*, by Douglas R. Stinson (Chapman & Hall).

14.8 Storing Encrypted Data in a File or Database

Problem

You want to store encrypted data that needs to be retrieved and decrypted later by your web server.

Solution

Store the additional information required to decrypt the data (such as algorithm, cipher mode, and initialization vector) along with the encrypted information, but not the key:

```
// encrypt data
$alg  = MCRYPT_BLOWFISH;
$mode = MCRYPT_MODE_CBC;
$iv = mcrypt_create_iv(mcrypt_get_iv_size($alg,$mode),MCRYPT_DEV_URANDOM);
$ciphertext = mcrypt_encrypt($alg,$_REQUEST['key'],$_REQUEST['data'],$mode,$iv);

// save encrypted data
$dbh->query('INSERT INTO noc_list (algorithm,mode,iv,data) values (?,?,?,?)',
            array($alg,$mode,$iv,$ciphertext));
```

To decrypt, retrieve a key from the user and use it with the saved data:

```
$row = $dbh->getRow('SELECT * FROM noc_list WHERE id = 27');
$plaintext = mcrypt_decrypt($row->algorithm,$_REQUEST['key'],$row->data,
                            $row->mode,$row->iv);
```

Discussion

The *save-crypt.php* program shown in Example 14-2 stores encrypted data to a file.

Example 14-2. save-crypt.php

```
function show_form() {
    print<<<_FORM_
<form method="post" action="$_SERVER[PHP_SELF]">
<textarea name="data" rows="10" cols="40">
Enter data to be encrypted here.
</textarea>
<br>
Encryption Key: <input type="text" name="key">
<input name="submit" type="submit" value="save">
</form>
_FORM_;
}

function save_form() {
    $alg  = MCRYPT_BLOWFISH;
    $mode = MCRYPT_MODE_CBC;

    // encrypt data
    $iv = mcrypt_create_iv(mcrypt_get_iv_size($alg,$mode),MCRYPT_DEV_URANDOM);
    $ciphertext = mcrypt_encrypt($alg, $_REQUEST['key'],
                                 $_REQUEST['data'], $mode, $iv);

    // save encrypted data
    $filename = tempnam('/tmp','enc') or die($php_errormsg);
    $fh = fopen($filename,'w')        or die($php_errormsg);
    if (false === fwrite($fh,$iv.$ciphertext)) {
        fclose($fh);
        die($php_errormsg);
    }
    fclose($fh)                       or die($php_errormsg);

    return $filename;
}

if ($_REQUEST['submit']) {
    $file = save_form();
    print "Encrypted data saved to file: $file";
} else {
    show_form();
}
```

Example 14-3 shows the corresponding program, *get-crypt.php*, that accepts a file-name and key and produces the decrypted data.

Example 14-3. get-crypt.php

```
function show_form() {
    print<<<_FORM_
<form method="post" action="$_SERVER[PHP_SELF]">
Encrypted File: <input type="text" name="file">
<br>
Encryption Key: <input type="text" name="key">
<input name="submit" type="submit" value="display">
</form>
_FORM_;
}

function display() {
    $alg  = MCRYPT_BLOWFISH;
    $mode = MCRYPT_MODE_CBC;

    $fh = fopen($_REQUEST['file'],'r') or die($php_errormsg);
    $iv = fread($fh,mcrypt_get_iv_size($alg,$mode));
    $ciphertext = fread($fh,filesize($_REQUEST['file']));
    fclose($fh);

    $plaintext = mcrypt_decrypt($alg,$_REQUEST['key'],$ciphertext,$mode,$iv);
    print "<pre>$plaintext</pre>";
}

if ($_REQUEST['submit']) {
    display();
} else {
    show_form();
}
```

These two programs have their encryption algorithm and mode hardcoded in them, so there's no need to store this information in the file. The file consists of the initialization vector immediately followed by the encrypted data. There's no need for a delimiter after the initialization vector (IV), because mcrypt_get_iv_size( ) returns exactly how many bytes the decryption program needs to read to get the whole IV. Everything after that in the file is encrypted data.

Encrypting files using the method in this recipe offers protection if an attacker gains access to the server on which the files are stored. Without the appropriate key or tremendous amounts of computing power, the attacker won't be able to read the files. However, the security that these encrypted file provides is undercut if the data to be encrypted and the encryption keys travel between your server and your users' web browsers in the clear. Someone who can intercept or monitor network traffic can see data before it even gets encrypted. To prevent this kind of eavesdropping, use SSL.

An additional risk when your web server encrypts data as in this recipe comes from how the data is visible before it's encrypted and written to a file. Someone with root or administrator access to the server can look in the memory the web server process is using and snoop on the unencrypted data and the key. If the operating system swaps the memory image of the web server process to disk, the unencrypted data might also be accessible in this swap file. This kind of attack can be difficult to pull off but can be devastating. Once the encrypted data is in a file, it's unreadable even to an attacker with root access to the web server, but if the attacker can peek at the unencrypted data before it's in that file, the encryption offers little protection.

See Also

Recipe 14.10 discusses SSL and protecting data as it moves over the network; documentation on mcrypt_encrypt() at *http://www.php.net/mcrypt-encrypt*, mcrypt_decrypt() at *http://www.php.net/mcrypt-decrypt*, mcrypt_create_iv() at *http://www.php.net/mcrypt-create-iv*, and mcrypt_get_iv_size() at *http://www.php.net/mcrypt-get-iv-size*.

14.9 Sharing Encrypted Data with Another Web Site

Problem

You want to securely exchange data with another web site.

Solution

If the other web site is pulling the data from your site, put the data up on a password-protected page. You can also make the data available in encrypted form, with or without a password. If you need to push the data to another web site, submit the potentially encrypted data via POST to a password-protected URL.

Discussion

The following page requires a username and password and then encrypts and displays the contents of a file containing yesterday's account activity:

```
$user = 'bank';
$password = 'fas8uj3';

if (! (($_SERVER['PHP_AUTH_USER'] == $user) &&
       ($_SERVER['PHP_AUTH_PW'] == $password))) {
    header('WWW-Authenticate: Basic realm="Secure Transfer"');
    header('HTTP/1.0 401 Unauthorized');
```

```
        echo "You must supply a valid username and password for access.";
        exit;
    }

    header('Content-type: text/plain');
    $filename = strftime('/usr/local/account-activity.%Y-%m-%d',time() - 86400);
    $data = join('',file($filename));

    $alg  = MCRYPT_BLOWFISH;
    $mode = MCRYPT_MODE_CBC;
    $key  = "There are many ways to butter your toast.";

    // encrypt data
    $iv = $iv = mcrypt_create_iv(mcrypt_get_iv_size($alg,$mode),
                            MCRYPT_DEV_URANDOM);
    $ciphertext = mcrypt_encrypt($alg, $key, $data, $mode, $iv);

    print base64_encode($iv.$ciphertext);
```

Here's the corresponding code to retrieve the encrypted page and decrypt the information:

```
    $user = 'bank';
    $password = 'fas8uj3';
    $alg  = MCRYPT_BLOWFISH;
    $mode = MCRYPT_MODE_CBC;
    $key  = "There are many ways to butter your toast.";

    $fh = fopen("http://$user:$password@bank.example.com/accounts.php",'r')
        or die($php_errormsg);
    $data = '';
    while (! feof($fh)) { $data .= fgets($fh,1048576); }
    fclose($fh) or die($php_errormsg);
    $binary_data = base64_decode($data);
    $iv_size = mcrypt_get_iv_size($alg,$mode);
    $iv = substr($binary_data,0,$iv_size);
    $ciphertext = substr($binary_data,$iv_size,strlen($binary_data));

    print mcrypt_decrypt($alg,$key,$ciphertext,$mode,$iv);
```

The retrieval program does all the steps of the encryption program but in reverse. It retrieves the Base64 encoded encrypted data, supplying a username and password. Then, it decodes the data with Base64 and separates out the initialization vector. Last, it decrypts the data and prints it out.

In the previous examples, the username and password are still sent over the network in clear text, unless the connections happen over SSL. However, if you're using SSL, it's probably not necessary to encrypt the file's contents. We included both password-prompting and file encryption in these examples to show how it can be done.

There's one circumstance, however, in which both password protection and file encryption is helpful: if the file isn't automatically decrypted when it's retrieved. An automated program can retrieve the encrypted file and put it, still encrypted, in a place that can be accessed later. The decryption key thus doesn't need to be stored in the retrieval program.

See Also

Recipe 8.9 for information on using HTTP Basic authentication; Recipe 14.10 discusses SSL and protecting data as it moves over the network; documentation on mcrypt_encrypt( ) at *http://www.php.net/mcrypt-encrypt* and mcrypt_decrypt( ) at *http://www.php.net/mcrypt-decrypt.*

14.10 Detecting SSL

Problem

You want to know if a request arrived over SSL.

Solution

Test the value of $_SERVER['HTTPS']:

```
if ('on' == $_SERVER['HTTPS']) {
  print "The secret ingredient in Coca-Cola is Soylent Green.";
} else {
  print "Coca-Cola contains many delicious natural and artificial flavors.";
}
```

Discussion

SSL operates on a lower level than HTTP. The web server and a browser negotiate an appropriately secure connection, based on their capabilities, and the HTTP messages can pass over that secure connection. To an attacker intercepting the traffic, it's just a stream of nonsense bytes that can't be read.

Different web servers have different requirements to use SSL, so check your server's documentation for specific details. No changes have to be made to PHP to work over SSL.

In addition to altering code based on $_SERVER['HTTPS'], you can also set cookies to be exchanged only over SSL connections. If the last argument to setcookie( ) is 1, the browser sends the cookie back to the server only over a secure connection:

```
/* set an SSL-only cookie named "sslonly" with value "yes" that expires
 * at the end of the current browser session */
setcookie('sslonly','yes','','/','sklar.com',1);
```

Although the browser sends these cookies back to the server only over an SSL connection, the server sends them to the browser (when you call setcookie( ) in your page) whether or not the request for the page that sets the cookie is over SSL. If you're putting sensitive data in the cookie, make sure that you set the cookie only in an SSL request as well. Keep in mind as well that the cookie data is unencrypted on the user's computer.

See Also

Recipe 8.1 discusses setting cookies; documentation on setcookie( ) at *http://www.php.net/setcookie*.

14.11 Encrypting Email with GPG

Problem

You want to send encrypted email messages. For example, you take orders on your web site and need to send an email to your factory with order details for processing. By encrypting the email message, you prevent sensitive data such as credit card numbers from passing over the network in the clear.

Solution

Encrypt the body of the email message with GNU Privacy Guard (GPG) before sending it:

```
$message_body = escapeshellarg($message_body);
$gpg_path     = '/usr/local/bin/gpg';
$sender       = 'web@example.com';
$recipient    = 'ordertaker@example.com';
$home_dir     = '/home/web';
$user_env     = 'web';

$cmd = "echo $message_body | HOME=$home_dir USER=$user_env $gpg_path " .
       '--quiet --no-secmem-warning --encrypt --sign --armor ' .
       "--recipient $recipient --local-user $sender";

$message_body = `$cmd`;

mail($recipient,'Web Site Order',$message_body);
```

The email message can be decrypted by GPG, Pretty Good Privacy (PGP) or an email client plug-in that supports either program.

Discussion

PGP is a popular public key encryption program; GPG is an open-source program based on PGP. Because PGP in encumbered by a variety of patent and control issues, it's often easier to use GPG.

The code in the Solution invokes */usr/local/bin/gpg* to encrypt the message in $message_body. It uses the private key belonging to $sender and the public key belonging to $recipient. This means that only $recipient can decrypt the email message and when she does, she knows the message came from $sender.

Setting the HOME and USER environment variables tells GPG where to look for its keyring: *$HOME/.gnupg/secring.gpg*. The --quiet and --no-secmem-warning options suppress warnings GPG would otherwise generate. The --encrypt and --sign options tell GPG to both encrypt and sign the message. Encrypting the message obscures it to anyone other than the recipient. Signing it adds information so that the recipient knows who generated the message and when it was generated. The --armor option produces plaintext output instead of binary, so the encrypted message is suitable for emailing.

Normally, private keys are protected with a passphrase. If a private key protected by a passphrase is copied by an attacker, the attacker can't encrypt messages with the private key unless he also knows the passphrase. GPG prompts for the passphrase when encrypting a message. In this recipe, however, we don't want the private key of $sender to have a passphrase. If it did, the web site couldn't send new-order email messages without a human typing in the passphrase each time. Storing the passphrase in a file and providing it to GPG each time you encrypt offers no additional security over not having a passphrase in the first place.

The downside of using a key without a passphrase for encryption is that an attacker who obtains the secret key can send fake order emails to your order processor. This is a manageable risk. Since orders can be submitted via a web site in the first place, there is already a place where false information can be injected into the order process. Any procedures for catching bad orders can also be triggered by these potential fake emails. Also, once the key theft is discovered, and the problem that enabled the theft is fixed, the attacker is easily disabled by switching to a new private key.

See Also

The GNU Privacy Guard home page at *http://www.gnupg.org/* and the MIT PGP distribution site at *http://web.mit.edu/network/pgp.html*.

CHAPTER 15

Graphics

15.0 Introduction

With the assistance of the GD library, you can use PHP to create applications that use dynamic images to display stock quotes, reveal poll results, monitor system performance, and even create games. However it's not like using Photoshop or GIMP; you can't draw a line by moving your mouse. Instead, you need to precisely specify a shape's type, size, and position.

GD has an existing API, and PHP tries to follows its syntax and function-naming conventions. So, if you're familiar with GD from other languages, such as C or Perl, you can easily use GD with PHP. If GD is new to you, it may take a few minutes to figure it out, but soon you'll be drawing like Picasso.

The feature set of GD varies greatly depending on which version GD you're running and which features were enabled during configuration. Versions of GD up to 1.6 supported reading and writing GIFs, but this code was removed due to patent problems. Instead, newer versions of GD support JPEGs, PNGs, and WBMPs. Because PNGs are generally smaller than GIFs, allow you to use many more colors, have built-in gamma correction, and are supported by all major web browsers, the lack of GIF support is classified as a feature, not a bug. For more on PNG, go to *http:// www.libpng.org/pub/png/* or read Chapter 21, "PNG Format," of *Web Design in a Nutshell* written by Jennifer Niederst (O'Reilly).

Besides supporting multiple file formats, GD lets you draw pixels, lines, rectangles, polygons, arcs, ellipses, and circles in any color you want. Recipe 15.1 covers straight shapes, while Recipe 15.2 covers the curved ones. To fill shapes with a pattern instead of a solid color, see Recipe 15.3.

You can also draw text using a variety of font types, including built-in, TrueType, and PostScript Type 1 fonts. Recipe 15.4 shows the ins and outs of the three main text-drawing functions, and Recipe 15.5 shows how to center text within a canvas. These two recipes form the basis for Recipe 15.6, which combines an image template with real-time data to create dynamic images. GD also lets you make transparent GIFs and PNGs. Setting a color as transparent and using transparencies in patterns are discussed in Recipe 15.7.

Recipe 15.8 moves away from GD and shows how to securely serve images by restricting user access. Last, we provide an example application—taking poll results and producing a dynamic bar graph showing what percentage of users voted for each answer.

All these features work with GD 1.8.4, which is the latest stable version of the library. If you have an earlier version, you should not have a problem. However, if a particular recipe needs a specific version of GD, we note it in the recipe.

PHP also supports GD 2.x, which, as of this writing, is still in beta. Despite its beta status, the new version is relatively stable and has many new features. In particular, Version 2.x allows true-color images, which lets GD read in PNGs and JPEGs with almost no loss in quality. Also, GD 2.x supports PNG alpha channels, which allow you to specify a transparency level for each pixel.

Both versions of GD are available for download from the official GD site at *http://www.boutell.com/gd/*. The GD section of the online PHP Manual at *http://www.php.net/image* also lists the location of the additional libraries necessary to provide support for JPEGs and Type 1 fonts.

There are two easy ways to see which version, if any, of GD is installed on your server and how it's configured. One way is to call phpinfo( ). You should see --with-gd at the top under "Configure Command"; further down the page there is also a section titled "gd" that has more information about which version of GD is installed and what features are enabled. The other option is to check the return value of function_exists('imagecreate'). If it returns true, GD is installed. The imagetypes( ) function returns a bit field indicating which graphics formats are available. See *http://www.php.net/imagetypes* for more on how to use this function. If you want to use a feature that isn't enabled, you need to rebuild PHP yourself or get your ISP to do so.

The basic image generation process has three steps: creating the image, adding graphics and text to the canvas, and displaying or saving the image. For example:

```
$image = ImageCreate(200, 50);
$background_color = ImageColorAllocate($image, 255, 255, 255); // white
$gray            = ImageColorAllocate($image, 204, 204, 204); // gray

ImageFilledRectangle($image, 50, 10, 150, 40, $gray);

header('Content-type: image/png');
ImagePNG($image);
```

The output of this code, which prints a gray rectangle on a white background, is shown in Figure 15-1.

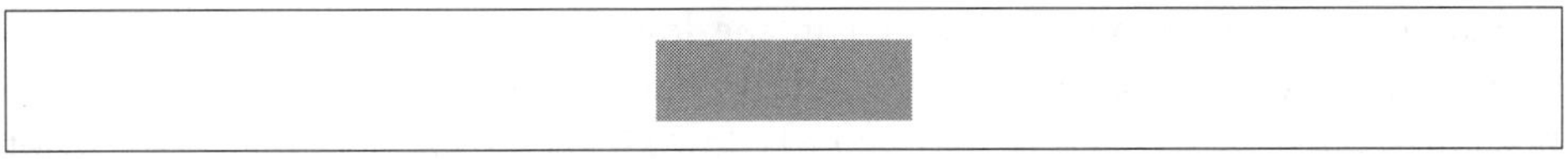

Figure 15-1. A gray rectangle on a white background

To begin, you create an image canvas. The ImageCreate( ) function doesn't return an actual image. Instead, it provides you with a handle to an image; it's not an actual graphic until you specifically tell PHP to write the image out. Using ImageCreate( ), you can juggle multiple images at the same time.

The parameters passed to ImageCreate( ) are the width and height of the graphic in pixels. In this case, it's 200 pixels across and 50 pixels high. Instead of creating a new image, you can also edit existing images. To open a graphic, call ImageCreateFromPNG( ) or a similarly named function to open a different file format. The filename is the only argument, and files can live locally or on remote servers:

```
// open a PNG from the local machine
$graph = ImageCreateFromPNG('/path/to/graph.png');

// open a JPEG from a remote server
$icon  = ImageCreateFromJPEG('http://www.example.com/images/icon.jpeg');
```

Once you have an editable canvas, you get access to drawing colors by calling ImageColorAllocate( ):

```
$background_color = ImageColorAllocate($image, 255, 255, 255); // white
$gray             = ImageColorAllocate($image, 204, 204, 204); // gray
```

The ImageColorAllocate( ) function takes an image handle to allocate the color to and three integers. The three integers each range from 0 to 255 and specify the red, green, and blue components of the color. This is the same RGB color combination that is used in HTML to set a font or background color. So, white is 255, 255, 255; black is 0, 0, 0, and everything else is somewhere in between.

The first call to ImageAllocateColor( ) sets the background color. Additional calls allocate colors for drawing lines, shapes, or text. Therefore, set the background color to 255, 255, 255 and then grab a gray pen with ImageAllocateColor($image, 204, 204, 204). It may seem odd that the background color is determined by the order ImageAllocateColor() is called and not by a separate function. But, that's how things work in GD, so PHP respects the convention.

Call ImageFilledRectangle( ) to place a box onto the canvas. ImageFilledRectangle( ) takes many parameters: the image to draw on, the x and y coordinates of the upper left corner of the rectangle, the x and y coordinates of the lower right corner of the rectangle, and finally, the color to use to draw the shape. Tell ImageFilledRectangle( ) to draw a rectangle on $image, starting at (50,10) and going to (150,40), in the color gray:

```
ImageFilledRectangle($image, 50, 10, 150, 40, $gray);
```

Unlike a Cartesian graph, (0,0) is not in the lower left corner; instead, it's in the upper left corner. So, the vertical coordinate of the spot 10 pixels from the top of a 50 pixel high canvas is 10 because it's 10 pixels down from the top of the canvas. It's not 40, because you measure from the top down, not the bottom up. And it's not –10, because down is considered the positive direction, not the negative one.

Now that the image is all ready to go, you can serve it up. First, send a Content-type header to let the browser know what type of image you're sending. In this case, we display a PNG. Next, have PHP write the PNG image out using ImagePNG( ). Once the image is sent, your task is over:

```
header('Content-Type: image/png');
ImagePNG($image);
```

To write the image to disk instead of sending it to the browser, provide a second argument to ImagePNG( ) with where to save the file:

```
ImagePng($image, '/path/to/your/new/image.png');
```

Since the file isn't going to the browser, there's no need to call header( ). Make sure to specify a path and an image name, and be sure PHP has permission to write to that location.

PHP cleans up the image when the script ends, but, if you wish to manually deallocate the memory used by the image, calling ImageDestroy($image) forces PHP to get rid of the image immediately.

15.1 Drawing Lines, Rectangles, and Polygons

Problem

You want to draw a line, rectangle, or polygon. You also want to be able to control if the rectangle or polygon is open or filled in. For example, you want to be able to draw bar charts or create graphs of stock quotes.

Solution

To draw a line, use ImageLine( ):

```
ImageLine($image, $x1, $y1, $x2, $y2, $color);
```

To draw an open rectangle, use ImageRectangle( ):

```
ImageRectangle($image, $x1, $y1, $x2, $y2, $color);
```

To draw a solid rectangle, use ImageFilledRectangle( ):

```
ImageFilledRectangle($image, $x1, $y1, $x2, $y2, $color);
```

To draw an open polygon, use ImagePolygon( ):

```
$points = array($x1, $y1, $x2, $y2, $x3, $y3);
ImagePolygon($image, $points, count($points)/2, $color);
```

To draw a filled polygon, use ImageFilledPolygon( ):

```
$points = array($x1, $y1, $x2, $y2, $x3, $y3);
ImageFilledPolygon($image, $points, count($points)/2, $color);
```

Discussion

The prototypes for all five functions in the Solution are similar. The first parameter is the canvas to draw on. The next set of parameters are the x and y coordinates to specify where GD should draw the shape. In ImageLine( ), the four coordinates are the end points of the line, and in ImageRectangle( ), they're the opposite corners of the rectangle. For example, ImageLine($image, 0, 0, 100, 100, $color) produces a diagonal line. Passing the same parameters to ImageRectangle( ) produces a rectangle with corners at (0,0), (100,0), (0,100), and (100,100). Both shapes are shown in Figure 15-2.

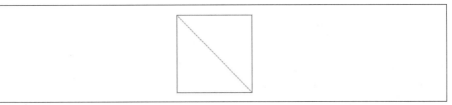

Figure 15-2. A diagonal line and a square

The ImagePolygon( ) function is slightly different because it can accept a variable number of vertices. Therefore, the second parameter is an array of x and y coordinates. The function starts at the first set of points and draws lines from vertex to vertex before finally completing the figure by connecting back to the original point. You must have a minimum of three vertices in your polygon (for a total of six elements in the array). The third parameter is the number of vertices in the shape; since that's always half of the number of elements in the array of points, a flexible value for this is count($points) / 2 because it allows you to update the array of vertices without breaking the call to ImageLine( ).

Last, all the functions take a final parameter that specifies the drawing color. This is usually a value returned from ImageColorAllocate( ) but can also be the constants IMG_COLOR_STYLED or IMG_COLOR_STYLEDBRUSHED, if you want to draw nonsolid lines, as discussed in Recipe 15.3.

These functions all draw open shapes. To get GD to fill the region with the drawing color, use ImageFilledRectangle( ) and ImageFilledPolygon( ) with the identical set of arguments as their unfilled cousins.

See Also

Recipe 15.2 for more on drawing other types of shapes; Recipe 15.3 for more on drawing with styles and brushes; documentation on ImageLine( ) at *http://www.php.net/imageline*, ImageRectangle( ) at *http://www.php.net/imagerectangle*, ImagePolygon( ) at *http://www.php.net/imagepolygon*, and ImageColorAllocate( ) at *http://www.php.net/imagecolorallocate*.

15.2   Drawing Arcs, Ellipses, and Circles

Problem

You want to draw open or filled curves. For example, you want to draw a pie chart showing the results of a user poll.

Solution

To draw an arc, use ImageArc( ):

```
ImageArc($image, $x, $y, $width, $height, $start, $end, $color);
```

To draw an ellipse, use ImageArc( ) and set $start to 0 and $end to 360:

```
ImageArc($image, $x, $y, $width, $height, 0, 360, $color);
```

To draw a circle, use ImageArc( ), set $start to 0, set $end to 360, and use the same value for both $width and $height:

```
ImageArc($image, $x, $y, $diameter, $diameter, 0, 360, $color);
```

Discussion

Because the ImageArc( ) function is highly flexible, you can easily create common curves such as ellipses and circles by passing it the right values. Like many GD functions, the first parameter is the canvas. The next two parameters are the x and y coordinates for the center position of the arc. After that comes the arc width and height. Since a circle is an arc with the same width and height, to draw a circle, set both numbers to your circle's diameter.

The sixth and seventh parameters are the starting and ending angles, in degrees. A value of 0 is at 3 o'clock. The arc then moves clockwise, so 90 is at 6 o'clock, 180 is at 9 o'clock, and 270 is at the top of the hour. (Be careful, this behavior is not consistent among all GD functions. For example, when you rotate text, you turn in a counter-clockwise direction.) Since the arc's center is located at ($x,$y), if you draw a semicircle from 0 to 180, it doesn't start at ($x,$y); instead, it begins at ($x+($diameter/2),$y).

As usual, the last parameter is the arc color.

For example, this draws an open black circle with a diameter of 100 pixels centered on the canvas, as shown in left half of Figure 15-3:

```
$image = ImageCreate(100,100);
$bg = ImageColorAllocate($image, 255, 255, 255);
$black = ImageColorAllocate($image, 0, 0, 0);
ImageArc($image, 50, 50, 100, 100, 0, 360, $black);
```

To produce a solid-colored ellipse or circle, call ImageFillToBorder():

```
ImageArc($image, $x, $y, $diameter, $diameter, 0, 360, $color);
ImageFillToBorder($image, $x, $y, $color, $color);
```

The ImageFillToBorder() function floods a region beginning at ($x,$y) with the color specified as the last parameter until it hits the edge of the canvas or runs into a line with the same color as the third parameter.

Incorporating this into the earlier example gives:

```
$image = ImageCreate(100,100);
$bg = ImageColorAllocate($image, 255, 255, 255);
$black = ImageColorAllocate($image, 0, 0, 0);
ImageArc($image, 50, 50, 100, 100, 0, 360, $black);
ImageFillToBorder($image, 50, 50, $black, $black);
```

The output is shown in the right half of Figure 15-3.

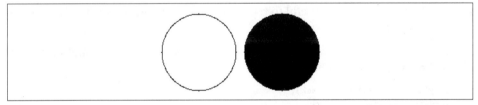

Figure 15-3. An open black circle and a filled black circle

If you're running GD 2.x, you can call ImageFilledArc() and pass in a final parameter that describes the fill style. GD 2.x also supports specific ImageEllipse() and ImageFilledEllipse() functions.

See Also

Recipe 15.1 for more on drawing other types of shapes; Recipe 15.3 for more on drawing with styles and brushes; documentation on ImageArc() at *http://www.php.net/imagearc*, ImageFilledArc() at *http://www.php.net/imagefilledarc*, and ImageFillToBorder() at *http://www.php.net/imagefilltoborder*.

15.3 Drawing with Patterned Lines

Problem

You want to draw shapes using line styles other than the default, a solid line.

Solution

To draw shapes with a patterned line, use ImageSetStyle( ) and pass in IMG_COLOR_
STYLED as the image color:

```
$black = ImageColorAllocate($image,   0,   0,   0);
$white = ImageColorAllocate($image, 255, 255, 255);

// make a two-pixel thick black and white dashed line
$style = array($black, $black, $white, $white);
ImageSetStyle($image, $style);

ImageLine($image, 0, 0, 50, 50, IMG_COLOR_STYLED);
ImageFilledRectangle($image, 50, 50, 100, 100, IMG_COLOR_STYLED);
```

Discussion

The line pattern is defined by an array of colors. Each element in the array is another pixel in the brush. It's often useful to repeat the same color in successive elements, as this increases the size of the stripes in the pattern.

For instance, here is code for a square drawn with alternating white and black pixels, as shown in left side of Figure 15-4:

```
$style = array($white, $black);
ImageSetStyle($image, $style);
ImageFilledRectangle($image, 0, 0, 49, 49, IMG_COLOR_STYLED);
```

This is the same square, but drawn with a style of five white pixels followed by five black ones, as shown in the middle of Figure 15-4:

```
$style = array($white, $white, $white, $white, $white,
               $black, $black, $black, $black, $black);
ImageSetStyle($image, $style);
ImageFilledRectangle($image, 0, 0, 49, 49, IMG_COLOR_STYLED);
```

Figure 15-4. Three squares with alternating white and black pixels

The patterns look completely different, even though both styles are just white and black pixels.

If the brush doesn't fit an integer number of times in the shape, it wraps around. In the previous examples, the square is 50 pixels wide. Since the first brush is 2 pixels long, it fits exactly 25 times; the second brush is 10 pixels, so it fits 5 times. But, if you make the square 45 by 45 and used the second brush, you don't get straight lines as you did previously, as shown in the right side of Figure 15-4:

```
ImageFilledRectangle($image, 0, 0, 44, 44, IMG_COLOR_STYLED);
```

See Also

Recipes 15.1 and 15.2 for more on drawing shapes; documentation on ImageSetStyle( ) at *http://www.php.net/imagesetstyle*.

15.4   Drawing Text

Problem

You want to draw text as a graphic. This allows you to make dynamic buttons or hit counters.

Solution

For built-in GD fonts, use ImageString( ):

```
ImageString($image, 1, $x, $y, 'I love PHP Cookbook', $text_color);
```

For TrueType fonts, use ImageTTFText( ):

```
ImageTTFText($image, $size, 0, $x, $y, $text_color, '/path/to/font.ttf',
             'I love PHP Cookbook');
```

For PostScript Type 1 fonts, use ImagePSLoadFont( ) and ImagePSText( ):

```
$font = ImagePSLoadFont('/path/to/font.pfb');
ImagePSText($image, 'I love PHP Cookbook', $font, $size,
            $text_color, $background_color, $x, $y);
```

Discussion

Call ImageString( ) to place text onto the canvas. Like other GD drawing functions, ImageString( ) needs many inputs: the image to draw on, the font number, the x and y coordinates of the upper right position of the first characters, the text string to display, and finally, the color to use to draw the string.

With ImageString( ), there are five possible font choices, from 1 to 5. Font number 1 is the smallest, while font 5 is the largest, as shown in Figure 15-5. Anything above or below that range generates a size equivalent to the closest legal number.

```
The quick brown fox jumps over the lazy dog.

The quick brown fox jumps over the lazy dog.

The quick brown fox jumps over the lazy dog.

The quick brown fox jumps over the lazy dog.

The quick brown fox jumps over the lazy dog.
```

Figure 15-5. Built-in GD font sizes

To draw text vertically instead of horizontally, use the function `ImageStringUp( )` instead. Figure 15-6 shows the output.

```
ImageStringUp($image, 1, $x, $y, 'I love PHP Cookbook', $text_color);
```

Figure 15-6. Vertical text

To use TrueType fonts, you must also install the FreeType library and configure PHP during installation to use FreeType. The FreeType main site is *http:// www.freetype.org*. To enable FreeType 1.x support, use `--with-ttf` and for FreeType 2.x, pass `--with-freetype-dir=DIR`.

Like `ImageString( )`, `ImageTTFText( )` prints a string to a canvas, but it takes slightly different options and needs them in a different order:

```
ImageTTFText($image, $size, $angle, $x, $y, $text_color, '/path/to/font.ttf',
             $text);
```

The `$size` argument is the font size in pixels; `$angle` is an angle of rotation, in degrees going counter-clockwise; and */path/to/font.ttf* is the pathname to TrueType font file. Unlike `ImageString( )`, (`$x,$y`) are the lower left coordinates of the baseline for the first character. (The baseline is where the bottom of most characters sit. Characters such as "g" and "j" extend below the baseline; "a" and "z" sit on the baseline.)

PostScript Type 1 fonts require *t1lib* to be installed. It can be downloaded from *ftp:// sunsite.unc.edu/pub/Linux/libs/graphics/* and built into PHP using `--with-t1lib`.

Again, the syntax for printing text is similar but not the same:

```
$font = ImagePSLoadFont('/path/to/font.pfb');
ImagePSText($image, $text, $font, $size, $text_color, $background_color, $x, $y);
ImagePSFreeFont($font);
```

First, PostScript font names can't be directly passed into `ImagePSText( )`. Instead, they must be loaded using `ImagePSLoadFont( )`. On success, the function returns a font resource usable with `ImagePSText( )`. In addition, besides specifying a text color, you also pass a background color to be used in antialiasing calculations. The ($x,$y) positioning is akin to the how the TrueType library does it. Last, when you're done with a font, you can release it from memory by calling ImagePSFreeFont().

Besides the mandatory arguments listed above, ImagePSText() also accepts four optional ones, in this order: space, tightness, angle, and antialias_steps. You must include all four or none of the four (i.e., you can't pass one, two, or three of these arguments). The first controls the size of a physical space (i.e., what's generated by hitting the space bar); the second is the tightness of the distance between letters; the third is a rotation angle, in degrees, counter-clockwise; and the last is an antialiasing value. This number must be either 4 or 16. For better looking, but more computationally expensive graphics, use 16 instead of 4.

By default, space, tightness, and angle are all 0. A positive number adds more space between words and letters or rotates the graphic counterclockwise. A negative number kerns words and letters or rotates in the opposite direction. The following example has the output shown in Figure 15-7:

```
// normal image
ImagePSText($image, $text, $font, $size, $black, $white, $x, $y,
            0, 0, 0, 4);

// extra space between words
ImagePSText($image, $text, $font, $size, $black, $white, $x, $y + 30,
            100, 0, 0, 4);

// extra space between letters
ImagePSText($image, $text, $font, $size, $black, $white, $x, $y + 60,
            0, 100, 0, 4);
```

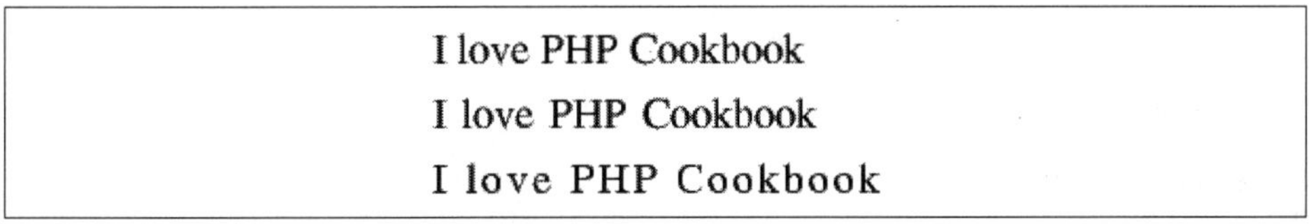

I love PHP Cookbook

I love PHP Cookbook

I love PHP Cookbook

Figure 15-7. Words with extra space and tightness

See Also

Recipe 15.5 for drawing centered text; documentation on ImageString() at *http://www.php.net/imagestring*, ImageStringUp() at *http://www.php.net/imagestringup*, ImageTTFText() at *http://www.php.net/imagettftext*, ImagePSText() at *http://www.php.net/imagepstext*, and ImagePSLoadFont() at *http://www.php.net/imagepsloadfont*.

15.5 Drawing Centered Text

Problem

You want to draw text in the center of an image.

Solution

Find the size of the image and the bounding box of the text. Using those coordinates, compute the correct spot to draw the text.

For built-in GD fonts, use the pc_ImageStringCenter( ) function shown in Example 15-1.

Example 15-1. pc_ImageStringCenter( )

```
function pc_ImageStringCenter($image, $text, $font) {

    // font sizes
    $width  = array(1 => 5, 6, 7, 8, 9);
    $height = array(1 => 6, 8, 13, 15, 15);

    // find the size of the image
    $xi = ImageSX($image);
    $yi = ImageSY($image);

    // find the size of the text
    $xr = $width[$font] * strlen($text);
    $yr = $height[$font];

    // compute centering
    $x = intval(($xi - $xr) / 2);
    $y = intval(($yi - $yr) / 2);

    return array($x, $y);
}
```

For example:

```
    list($x, $y) = pc_ImageStringCenter($image, $text, $font);
    ImageString($image, $font, $x, $y, $text, $fore);
```

For PostScript fonts, use the pc_ImagePSCenter( ) function shown in Example 15-2.

Example 15-2. pc_ImagePSCenter( )

```
function pc_ImagePSCenter($image, $text, $font, $size, $space = 0,
                          $tightness = 0, $angle = 0) {

    // find the size of the image
    $xi = ImageSX($image);
    $yi = ImageSY($image);
```

Example 15-2. pc_ImagePSCenter() (continued)

```
    // find the size of the text
    list($xl, $yl, $xr, $yr) = ImagePSBBox($text, $font, $size,
                                   $space, $tightness, $angle);

    // compute centering
    $x = intval(($xi - $xr) / 2);
    $y = intval(($yi + $yr) / 2);

    return array($x, $y);
}
```

For example:

```
    list($x, $y) = pc_ImagePSCenter($image, $text, $font, $size);
    ImagePSText($image, $text, $font, $size, $fore, $back, $x, $y);
```

For TrueType fonts, use the pc_ImageTTFCenter( ) function shown in Example 15-3.

Example 15-3. pc_ImageTTFCenter()

```
function pc_ImageTTFCenter($image, $text, $font, $size) {

    // find the size of the image
    $xi = ImageSX($image);
    $yi = ImageSY($image);

    // find the size of the text
    $box = ImageTTFBBox($size, $angle, $font, $text);

    $xr = abs(max($box[2], $box[4]));
    $yr = abs(max($box[5], $box[7]));

    // compute centering
    $x = intval(($xi - $xr) / 2);
    $y = intval(($yi + $yr) / 2);

    return array($x, $y);
}
```

For example:

```
    list($x, $y) = pc_ImageTTFCenter($image, $text, $font, $size);
    ImageTTFText($image, $size, $angle, $x, $y, $fore, $font, $text);
```

Discussion

All three solution functions return the x and y coordinates for drawing. Of course, depending on font type, size, and settings, the method used to compute these coordinates differs.

For PostScript Type 1 fonts, pass pc_ImagePSCenter( ) an image allocated from ImageCreate( ) (or one of its friends) and a number of parameters to specify how to draw the text. The first three parameters are required: the text to be drawn, the font, and the font size. The next three are optional: the space in a font, the tightness between letters, and an angle for rotation in degrees.

Inside the function, use ImageSX( ) and ImageSY( ) to find the size of the canvas; they return the width and height of the graphic. Then call ImagePSBBox( ). It returns four integers: the x and y coordinates of the lower-leftmost location the text and the x and y coordinates of the upper-rightmost location. Because the coordinates are relative to the baseline of the text, it's typical for these not to be 0. For instance, a lowercase "g" hangs below the bottom of the rest of the letters; so, in that case, the lower left y value is negative.

Armed with these six values, we can now calculate the correct centering values. Because coordinates of the canvas have (0,0) in the upper left corner, but ImagePSBText( ) wants the lower left corner, the formula for finding $x and $y isn't the same. For $x, we take the difference between the size of the canvas and the text. This gives the amount of whitespace that surrounds the text. Then we divide that number by two, to find the number of pixels we should leave to the left of the text. For $y, we do the same, but add $yi and $yr. By adding these numbers, we can find the coordinate of the far side of the box, which is what is needed here because of the inverted way the y coordinate is entered in GD.

We intentionally ignore the lower left coordinates in making these calculations. Because the bulk of the text sits above the baseline, adding the descending pixels into the centering algorithm actually worsens the code; it appears off-center to the eye.

To center text, put it together like this:

```
function pc_ImagePSCenter($image, $text, $font, $size, $space = 0,
                          $tightness = 0, $angle = 0) {

    // find the size of the image
    $xi = ImageSX($image);
    $yi = ImageSY($image);

    // find the size of the text
    list($xl, $yl, $xr, $yr) = ImagePSBBox($text, $font, $size,
                                    $space, $tightness, $angle);

    // compute centering
    $x = intval(($xi - $xr) / 2);
    $y = intval(($yi + $yr) / 2);

    return array($x, $y);
}

$image = ImageCreate(500,500);
$text = 'PHP Cookbook Rules!';
```

```
$font = ImagePSLoadFont('/path/to/font.pfb');
$size = 20;
$black = ImageColorAllocate($image, 0, 0, 0);
$white = ImageColorAllocate($image, 255, 255, 255);

list($x, $y) = pc_ImagePSCenter($image, $text, $font, $size);
ImagePSText($image, $text, $font, $size, $white, $black, $x, $y);
ImagePSFreeFont($font);

header('Content-type: image/png');
ImagePng($image);

ImageDestroy($image);
```

Unfortunately, this example doesn't work for GD's built-in fonts nor for TrueType fonts. There's no function to return the size of a string using the built-in fonts, and ImageTTFBBox( ) returns eight values instead of four. With a few modifications, however, we can accommodate these differences.

Because the built-in fonts are fixed-width, we can easily measure the size of a character to create a function that returns the size of the text based on its length. Table 15-1 isn't 100% accurate, but it should return results within one or two pixels, which should be good enough for most cases.

Table 15-1. GD Built-in font character sizes

Font number	Width	Height
1	5	6
2	6	8
3	7	13
4	8	15
5	9	15

Inside pc_ImageStringCenter( ), we calculate the length of the string as an integral multiple based on its length; the height is just one character high. Note that ImageString( ) takes its y coordinate as the uppermost part of the text, so we should switch the sign back to a minus when you compute $y.

Here is an example using all five fonts that centers text horizontally:

```
$text = 'The quick brown fox jumps over the lazy dog.';
for ($font = 1, $y = 5; $font <= 5; $font++, $y += 20) {
    list($x, $y) = pc_ImageStringCenter($image, $text, $font);
    ImageString($image, $font, $x, $y, $text, $color);
}
```

The output is shown in Figure 15-8.

For TrueType fonts, we need to use ImageTTFBBox( ) or the more modern ImageFtBBox( ). (The function with TTF in the name is for FreeType version 1.x; the

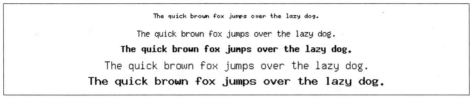

Figure 15-8. Centered GD built-in fonts

one with Ft is for FreeType 2.x.) It returns eight numbers: the (x,y) coordinates of the four corners of the text starting in the lower left and moving around counter clockwise. So, the second two coordinates are for the lower right spot, and so on.

To make pc_ImageTTFCenter( ), begin with pc_ImagePSCenter( ) and swap this line:

```
// find the size of the text
list($xl, $yl, $xr, $yr) = ImagePSBBox($text, $font, $size,
                                    $space, $tightness, $angle);
```

with these:

```
// find the size of the text
$box = ImageTTFBBox($size, $angle, $font, $text);

$xr = abs(max($box[2], $box[4]));
$yr = abs(max($box[5], $box[7]));
```

Here's an example of pc_ImageTTFCenter() in use:

```
list($x, $y) = pc_ImageTTFCenter($image, $text, $font, $size);
ImageTTFText($image, $size, $angle, $x, $y, $white, $black,
            '/path/to/font.ttf', $text);
```

See Also

Recipe 15.5 for more on drawing text; Recipe 15.6 for more on centering text; documentation on ImageSX( ) at *http://www.php.net/imagesx*, ImageSY( ) at *http://www.php.net/imagesy*, ImagePSBBox( ) at *http://www.php.net/imagepsbbox*, ImageTTFBBox( ) at *http://www.php.net/imagettfbbox*, ImageFtBBox( ) at *http://www.php.net/imageftbbox*.

15.6   Building Dynamic Images

Problem

You want to create an image based on a existing image template and dynamic data (typically text). For instance, you want to create a hit counter.

Solution

Load the template image, find the correct position to properly center your text, add the text to the canvas, and send the image to the browser:

```
// Configuration settings
$image    = ImageCreateFromPNG('button.png');
$text     = $_GET['text'];
$font     = ImagePSLoadFont('Times');
$size     = 24;
$color    = ImageColorAllocate($image,   0,   0,   0); // black
$bg_color = ImageColorAllocate($image, 255, 255, 255); // white

// Print centered text
list($x, $y) = pc_ImagePSCenter($image, $text, $font, $size);
ImagePSText($image, $text, $font, $size, $color, $bg_color, $x, $y);

// Send image
header('Content-type: image/png');
ImagePNG($image);

// Clean up
ImagePSFreeFont($font);
ImageDestroy($image);
```

Discussion

Building dynamic images with GD is easy; all you need to do is combine a few recipes together. At the top of the code in the Solution, we load in an image from a stock template button; it acts as the background on which we overlay the text. We define the text to come directly from the query string. Alternatively, we can pull the string from a database (in the case of access counters) or a remote server (stock quotes or weather report icons).

After that, we continue with the other settings: loading a font and specifying its size, color, and background color. Before printing the text, however, we need to compute its position; pc_ImagePSCenter( ) from Recipe 15.6 nicely solves this task. Last, we serve the image, and deallocate the font and image from memory.

For example, the following code generates a page of HTML and image tags using dynamic buttons, as shown in Figure 15-9:

```
<?php
if (isset($_GET['button'])) {

    // Configuration settings
    $image    = ImageCreateFromPNG('button.png');
    $text     = $_GET['button'];      // dynamically generated text
    $font     = ImagePSLoadFont('Times');
    $size     = 24;
    $color    = ImageColorAllocate($image,   0,   0,   0); // black
    $bg_color = ImageColorAllocate($image, 255, 255, 255); // white
```

```
    // Print centered text
    list($x, $y) = pc_ImagePSCenter($image, $text, $font, $size);
    ImagePSText($image, $text, $font, $size, $color, $bg_color, $x, $y);

    // Send image
    header('Content-type: image/png');
    ImagePNG($image);

    // Clean up
    ImagePSFreeFont($font);
    ImageDestroy($image);

} else {
?>
<html>
<head>
    <title>Sample Button Page</title>
</head>
<body>
    <img src="<?php echo $_SERVER['PHP_SELF']; ?>?button=Previous"
        alt="Previous" width="132" height="46">
    <img src="<?php echo $_SERVER['PHP_SELF']; ?>?button=Next"
        alt="Next"     width="132" height="46">
</body>
</html>
<?php
}
?>
```

Figure 15-9. Sample button page

In this script, if a value is passed in for $_GET['button'], we generate a button and send out the PNG. If $_GET['button'] isn't set, we print a basic HTML page with two embedded calls back to the script with requests for button images—one for a Previous button and one for a Next button. A more general solution is to create a separate *button.php* page that returns only graphics and set the image source to point at that page.

See Also

Recipe 15.5 for more on drawing text; Recipe 15.6 for more on centering text; an excellent discussion on dynamic image caching in Chapter 9, "Graphics," of *Programming PHP*, by Kevin Tatroe and Rasmus Lerdorf (O'Reilly).

15.7 Getting and Setting a Transparent Color

Problem

You want to set one of an image's colors as transparent. When the image is overlayed on a background, the background shows through the transparent section of the image.

Solution

Use `ImageColorTransparent( )`:

```
$color = ImageColorAllocate($image, $red, $green, $blue);
ImageColorTransparent($image, $color);
```

Discussion

Both GIFs and PNGs support transparencies; JPEGs, however, do not. To refer to the transparent color within GD, use the constant `IMG_COLOR_TRANSPARENT`. For example, here's how to make a dashed line that alternates between black and transparent:

```
// make a two-pixel thick black and white dashed line
$style = array($black, $black, IMG_COLOR_TRANSPARENT, IMG_COLOR_TRANSPARENT);
ImageSetStyle($image, $style);
```

To find the current transparency setting, take the return value of `ImageColorTransparent( )` and pass it to `ImageColorsForIndex( )`:

```
$transparent = ImageColorsForIndex($image, ImageColorTransparent($image));
print_r($transparent);
Array
(
    [red] => 255
    [green] => 255
    [blue] => 255
)
```

The `ImageColorsForIndex( )` function returns an array with the red, green, and blue values. In this case, the transparent color is white.

See Also

Documentation on `ImageColorTransparent( )` at *http://www.php.net/imagecolortransparent* and on `ImageColorsForIndex( )` at *http://www.php.net/imagecolorsforindex*.

15.8   Serving Images Securely

Problem

You want to control who can view a set of images.

Solution

Don't keep the images in your document root, but store them elsewhere. To deliver a file, manually open it and send it to the browser:

```
header('Content-Type: image/png');
readfile('/path/to/graphic.png');
```

Discussion

The first line in the Solution sends the `Content-type` header to the browser, so the browser knows what type of object is coming and displays it accordingly. The second opens a file off a disk (or from a remote URL) for reading, reads it in, dumps it directly to the browser, and closes the file.

The typical way to serve up an image is to use an `<img>` tag and set the `src` attribute to point to a file on your web site. If you want to protect those images, you probably should use some form of password authentication. One method is HTTP Basic Authentication, which is covered in Recipe 8.9.

The typical way, however, may not always be the best. First, what happens if you want to restrict the files people can view, but you don't want to make things complex by using usernames and passwords? One option is to link only to the files; if users can't click on the link, they can't view the file. They might, however, bookmark old files, or they may also try and guess other filenames based on your naming scheme and manually enter the URL into the browser.

If your content is embargoed, you don't want people to be able to guess your naming scheme and view images. When information is embargoed, a select group of people, usually reporters, are given a preview release, so they can write stories about the topic or be ready to distribute it the moment the embargo is lifted. You can fix this by making sure only legal content is under the document root, but this requires a lot of file shuffling back and forth from directory to directory. Instead, you can keep all the files in one constant place, and deliver only files that pass a check inside your code.

For example, let's say you have a contract with a publishing corporation to redistribute one of their comics on your web site. However, they don't want you to create a virtual archive, so you agree to let your users view only the last two weeks worth of strips. For everything else, they'll need to go to the official site. Also, you may get comics in advance of their publication date, but you don't want to let people get a free preview; you want them to keep coming back to your site on a daily basis.

Here's the solution. Files arrive named by date, so it's easy to identify which files belong to which day. Now, to lock out strips outside the rolling 14-day window, use code like this:

```
// display a comic if it's less than 14 days old and not in the future

// calculate the current date
list($now_m,$now_d,$now_y) = explode(',',date('m,d,Y'));
$now = mktime(0,0,0,$now_m,$now_d,$now_y);

// two hour boundary on either side to account for dst
$min_ok = $now - 14*86400 - 7200; // 14 days ago
$max_ok = $now + 7200;            // today

// find the time stamp of the requested comic
$asked_for = mktime(0,0,0,$_REQUEST['mo'],$_REQUEST['dy'],$_REQUEST['yr']);

// compare the dates
if (($min_ok > $asked_for) || ($max_ok < $asked_for)) {
    echo 'You are not allowed to view the comic for that day.';
} else {
    header('Content-type: image/png');
    readfile("/www/comics/$_REQUEST['mo']$_REQUEST['dy'] $_REQUEST['yr'].png");
}
```

See Also

Recipe 18.5 for more on reading files.

15.9 Program: Generating Bar Charts from Poll Results

When displaying the results of a poll, it can be more effective to generate a colorful bar chart instead of just printing the results as text. The function shown in Example 15-4 uses GD to create an image that displays the cumulative responses to a poll question.

Example 15-4. Graphical bar charts

```
function pc_bar_chart($question, $answers) {

    // define colors to draw the bars
    $colors = array(array(255,102,0), array(0,153,0),
                    array(51,51,204), array(255,0,51),
                    array(255,255,0), array(102,255,255),
                    array(153,0,204));

    $total = array_sum($answers['votes']);

    // define some spacing values and other magic numbers
    $padding = 5;
    $line_width = 20;
    $scale = $line_width * 7.5;
    $bar_height = 10;

    $x = $y = $padding;

    // allocate a large palette for drawing, since we don't know
    // the image length ahead of time
    $image = ImageCreate(150, 500);
    $bg_color = ImageColorAllocate($image, 224, 224, 224);
    $black = ImageColorAllocate($image, 0, 0, 0);

    // print the question
    $wrapped = explode("\n", wordwrap($question, $line_width));
    foreach ($wrapped as $line) {
        ImageString($image, 3, $x, $y , $line, $black);
        $y += 12;
    }

    $y += $padding;

    // print the answers
    for ($i = 0; $i < count($answers['answer']); $i++) {

        // format percentage
        $percent = sprintf('%1.1f', 100*$answers['votes'][$i]/$total);
        $bar = sprintf('%d', $scale*$answers['votes'][$i]/$total);

        // grab color
        $c = $i % count($colors); // handle cases with more bars than colors
        $text_color = ImageColorAllocate($image, $colors[$c][0],
                                $colors[$c][1], $colors[$c][2]);

        // draw bar and percentage numbers
        ImageFilledRectangle($image, $x, $y, $x + $bar,
                            $y + $bar_height, $text_color);
        ImageString($image, 3, $x + $bar + $padding, $y,
                    "$percent%", $black);

         $y += 12;
```

Example 15-4. Graphical bar charts (continued)

```
        // print answer
        $wrapped = explode("\n", wordwrap($answers['answer'][$i], $line_width));
        foreach ($wrapped as $line) {
            ImageString($image, 2, $x, $y, $line, $black);
            $y += 12;
        }

        $y += 7;
    }

    // crop image by copying it
    $chart = ImageCreate(150, $y);
    ImageCopy($chart, $image, 0, 0, 0, 0, 150, $y);

    // deliver image
    header ('Content-type: image/png');
    ImagePNG($chart);

    // clean up
    ImageDestroy($image);
    ImageDestroy($chart);
}
```

To call this program, create an array holding two parallel arrays: $answers['answer']
and $answer['votes']. Element $i of each array holds the answer text and the total
number of votes for answer $i. Figure 15-10 shows this sample output.

```
// Act II. Scene II.
$question = 'What a piece of work is man?';

$answers['answer'][ ] = 'Noble in reason';
$answers['votes'][ ]  = 29;

$answers['answer'][ ] = 'Infinite in faculty';
$answers['votes'][ ]  = 22;

$answers['answer'][ ] = 'In form, in moving, how express and admirable';
$answers['votes'][ ]  = 59;

$answers['answer'][ ] = 'In action how like an angel';
$answers['votes'][ ]  = 45;

pc_bar_chart($question, $answers);
```

Here the answers are manually assigned, but for a real poll, this data could be pulled
from a database instead.

This program is a good start, but because it uses the built-in GD fonts, there are a lot
of magic numbers embedded in the program corresponding to the font height and
width. Also, the amount of space between each answer is hardcoded. If you modify

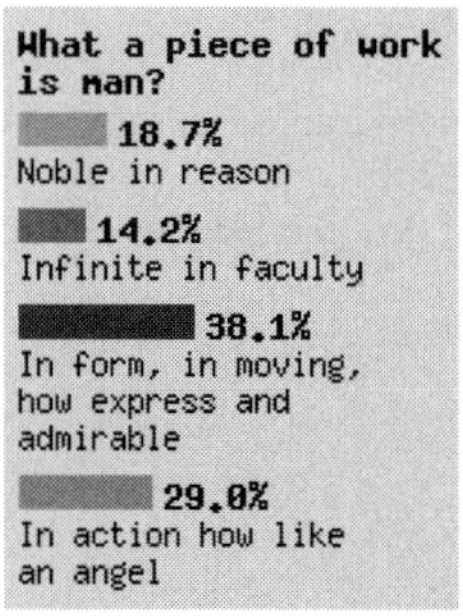

Figure 15-10. Graphical bar chart of poll results

this to handle more advanced fonts, such as PostScript or TrueType, you'll need to update the algorithms that control those numbers.

At the top of the function, a bunch of RGB combinations are defined; they are used as the colors to draw the bars. A variety of constants are broken out, such as $line_width, which is the maximum number of characters per line. The $bar_height variable determines how high the bars should be, and $scale scales the length of the bar as a function of the longest possible line. $padding is used to push the results five pixels away from the edge of the canvas.

We then make a very large canvas to draw the chart; later, we will crop the canvas down to size, but it can be difficult to know ahead of time how large our total size will be. The default background color of the bar chart is (224, 224, 224), or a light gray.

In order to restrict the width of the chart to a reasonable size, we use wordwrap( ) to break our $question down to size and explode( ) it on \n. This gives us an array of correctly-sized lines, which we loop on to print out one line at a time.

After printing the question, we move on to the answers. First, we format the results numbers with sprintf( ). To format the total percentage of votes for an answer as a floating-point number with one decimal point, we use %1.1f. To find the length of the bar corresponding to that number, you compute a similar number, but instead of multiplying it by 100, we multiply by a magic number, $scale, and return an integer.

The text color is pulled from the $colors array of RGB triplets. Then, we call ImageFilledRectangle( ) to draw the bar and ImageString( ) to draw the percentage text to the right of the bar. After adding some padding, we print the answer using the same algorithm used to print the question.

When all the answers have been printed, the total size of bar chart is stored in $y. Now we can correctly crop the graphic to size, but there's no ImageCrop( ) function. To work around this, we make a new canvas of the appropriate size and ImageCopy( ) over the part of the original canvas you want to keep. Then we serve the correctly sized image as a PNG using ImagePNG( ) and clean up with two calls to ImageDestroy( ).

As we mentioned at the beginning of this section, this is just a quick-and-dirty function to print bar charts. It works, and solves some problems, such a wrapped lines, but isn't 100% perfect. For instance, it's not very customizable. Many settings are baked directly into the code. Still, it shows how to put together a variety of GD's functions to create a useful graphical application.

CHAPTER 16

Internationalization and Localization

16.0 Introduction

While everyone who programs in PHP has to learn some English eventually to get a handle on its function names and language constructs, PHP can create applications that speak just about any language. Some applications need to be used by speakers of many different languages. Taking an application written for French speakers and making it useful for German speakers is made easier by PHP's support for internationalization and localization.

Internationalization (often abbreviated I18N[*]) is the process of taking an application designed for just one locale and restructuring it so that it can be used in many different locales. Localization (often abbreviated L10N[†]) is the process of adding support for a new locale to an internationalized application.

A locale is a group of settings that describe text formatting and language customs in a particular area of the world. The settings are divided into six categories:

LC_COLLATE
> These settings control text sorting: which letters go before and after others in alphabetical order.

LC_CTYPE
> These settings control mapping between uppercase and lowercase letters as well as which characters fall into the different character classes, such as alphanumeric characters.

LC_MONETARY
> These settings describe the preferred format of currency information, such as what character to use as a decimal point and how to indicate negative amounts.

---

[*] The word "internationalization" has 18 letters between the first "i" and the last "n."

[†] The word "localization" has 10 letters between the first "l" and the "n."

LC_NUMERIC

These settings describe the preferred format of numeric information, such as how to group numbers and what character is used as a thousands separator.

LC_TIME

These settings describe the preferred format of time and date information, such as names of months and days and whether to use 24- or 12-hour time.

LC_MESSAGES

This category contains text messages used by applications that need to display information in multiple languages.

There is also a metacategory, LC_ALL, that encompasses all the categories.

A locale name generally has three components. The first, an abbreviation that indicates a language, is mandatory. For example, "en" for English or "pt" for Portuguese. Next, after an underscore, comes an optional country specifier, to distinguish between different countries that speak different versions of the same language. For example, "en_US" for U.S. English and "en_GB" for British English, or "pt_BR" for Brazilian Portuguese and "pt_PT" for Portuguese Portuguese. Last, after a period, comes an optional character-set specifier. For example, "zh_TW.Big5" for Taiwanese Chinese using the Big5 character set. While most locale names follow these conventions, some don't. One difficulty in using locales is that they can be arbitrarily named. Finding and setting a locale is discussed in Recipes 16.1 through 16.3.

Different techniques are necessary for correct localization of plain text, dates and times, and currency. Localization can also be applied to external entities your program uses, such as images and included files. Localizing these kinds of content is covered in Recipes 16.4 through 16.8.

Systems for dealing with large amounts of localization data are discussed in Recipes 16.9 and 16.10. Recipe 16.9 shows some simple ways to manage the data, and Recipe 16.10 introduces GNU *gettext*, a full-featured set of tools that provide localization support.

PHP also has limited support for Unicode. Converting data to and from the Unicode UTF-8 encoding is addressed in Recipe 16.11.

16.1 Listing Available Locales

Problem

You want to know what locales your system supports.

Solution

Use the *locale* program to list available locales; *locale -a* prints the locales your system supports.

Discussion

On Linux and Solaris systems, you can find `locale` at */usr/bin/locale*. On Windows, locales are listed in the Regional Options section of the Control Panel.

Your mileage varies on other operating systems. BSD, for example, includes locale support but has no *locale* program to list locales. BSD locales are often stored in */usr/share/locale*, so looking in that directory may yield a list of usable locales.

While the locale system helps with many localization tasks, its lack of standardization can be frustrating. Systems aren't guaranteed to have the same locales or even use the same names for equivalent locales.

See Also

Your system's *locale(1)* manpage.

16.2 Using a Particular Locale

Problem

You want to tell PHP to use the settings of a particular locale.

Solution

Call `setlocale()` with the appropriate category and locale. Here's how to use the es_US (U.S. Spanish) locale for all categories:

```
setlocale(LC_ALL,'es_US');
```

Here's how to use the de_AT (Austrian German) locale for time and date formatting:

```
setlocale(LC_TIME,'de_AT');
```

Discussion

To find the current locale without changing it, call `setlocale()` with a NULL locale:

```
print setlocale(LC_ALL,NULL);
en_US
```

Many systems also support a set of aliases for common locales, listed in a file such as */usr/share/locale/locale.alias*. This file is a series of lines including:

```
russian          ru_RU.ISO-8859-5
slovak           sk_SK.ISO-8859-2
slovene          sl_SI.ISO-8859-2
slovenian        sl_SI.ISO-8859-2
spanish          es_ES.ISO-8859-1
swedish          sv_SE.ISO-8859-1
```

The first column of each line is an alias; the second column shows the locale and character set the alias points to. You can use the alias in calls to `setlocale()` instead of the corresponding string the alias points to. For example, you can do:

```
setlocale(LC_ALL,'swedish');
```

instead of:

```
setlocale(LC_ALL,'sv_SE.ISO-8859-1');
```

On Windows, to change the locale, visit the Control Panel. In the Regional Options section, you can pick a new locale and customize its settings.

See Also

Recipe 16.3 shows how to set a default locale; documentation on `setlocale()` at *http://www.php.net/setlocale*.

16.3 Setting the Default Locale

Problem

You want to set a locale that all your PHP programs can use.

Solution

At the beginning of a file loaded by the `auto_prepend_file` configuration directive, call `setlocale()` to set your desired locale:

```
setlocale(LC_ALL,'es_US');
```

Discussion

Even if you set up appropriate environment variables before you start your web server or PHP binary, PHP doesn't change its locale until you call `setlocale()`. After setting environment variable `LC_ALL` to es_US, for example, PHP still runs in the default C locale.

See Also

Recipe 16.2 shows how to use a particular locale; documentation on setlocale( ) at *http://www.php.net/setlocale* and auto_prepend_file at *http://www.php.net/manual/en/ configuration.directives.php#ini.auto-prepend-file.*

16.4 Localizing Text Messages

Problem

You want to display text messages in a locale-appropriate language.

Solution

Maintain a message catalog of words and phrases and retrieve the appropriate string from the message catalog before printing it. Here's a simple message catalog with some foods in American and British English and a function to retrieve words from the catalog:

```
$messages = array ('en_US' =>
           array(
             'My favorite foods are' => 'My favorite foods are',
             'french fries' => 'french fries',
             'biscuit'      => 'biscuit',
             'candy'        => 'candy',
             'potato chips' => 'potato chips',
             'cookie'       => 'cookie',
             'corn'         => 'corn',
             'eggplant'     => 'eggplant'
           ),
          'en_GB' =>
           array(
             'My favorite foods are' => 'My favourite foods are',
             'french fries' => 'chips',
             'biscuit'      => 'scone',
             'candy'        => 'sweets',
             'potato chips' => 'crisps',
             'cookie'       => 'biscuit',
             'corn'         => 'maize',
             'eggplant'     => 'aubergine'
           )
         );

function msg($s) {
  global $LANG;
  global $messages;
  if (isset($messages[$LANG][$s])) {
    return $messages[$LANG][$s];
  } else {
```

```
    error_log("l10n error: LANG: $lang, message: '$s'");
  }
}
```

Discussion

This short program uses the message catalog to print out a list of foods:

```
$LANG = 'en_GB';
print msg('My favorite foods are').":\n";
print msg('french fries')."\n";
print msg('potato chips')."\n";
print msg('corn')."\n";
print msg('candy')."\n";
My favourite foods are:
chips
crisps
maize
sweets
```

To have the program output in American English instead of British English, just set
$LANG to en_US.

You can combine the msg( ) message retrieval function with sprintf( ) to store
phrases that require values to be substituted into them. For example, consider the
English sentence "I am 12 years old." In Spanish, the corresponding phrase is
"Tengo 12 años." The Spanish phrase can't be built by stitching together transla-
tions of "I am," the numeral 12, and "years old." Instead, store them in the message
catalogs as sprintf( )-style format strings:

```
$messages = array ('en_US' => array('I am X years old.' => 'I am %d years old.'),
                   'es_US' => array('I am X years old.' => 'Tengo %d años.')
            );
```

You can then pass the results of msg( ) to sprintf( ) as a format string:

```
$LANG = 'es_US';
print sprintf(msg('I am X years old.'),12);
Tengo 12 años.
```

For phrases that require the substituted values to be in a different order in different
language, sprintf( ) supports changing the order of the arguments:

```
$messages = array ('en_US' =>
                   array('I am X years and Y months old.' =>
                       'I am %d years and %d months old.'),
                   'es_US' =>
                   array('I am X years and Y months old.' =>
                       'Tengo %2$d meses y %1$d años.')
            );
```

With either language, call sprintf( ) with the same order of arguments (i.e., first
years, then months):

```
$LANG = 'es_US';
print sprintf(msg('I am X years and Y months old.'),12,7);
Tengo 7 meses y 12 años.
```

In the format string, %2$ tells sprintf( ) to use the second argument, and %1$ tells it to use the first.

These phrases can also be stored as a function's return value instead of as a string in an array. Storing the phrases as functions removes the need to use sprintf( ). Functions that return a sentence look like this:

```
// English version
function i_am_X_years_old($age) {
  return "I am $age years old.";
}


// Spanish version
function i_am_X_years_old($age) {
  return "Tengo $age años.";
}
```

If some parts of the message catalog belong in an array, and some parts belong in functions, an object is a helpful container for a language's message catalog. A base object and two simple message catalogs look like this:

```
class pc_MC_Base {
  var $messages;
  var $lang;

  function msg($s) {
    if (isset($this->messages[$s])) {
      return $this->messages[$s];
    } else {
      error_log("l10n error: LANG: $this->lang, message: '$s'");
    }
  }

}

class pc_MC_es_US extends pc_MC_Base {

  function pc_MC_es_US() {
    $this->lang = 'es_US';
    $this->messages = array ('chicken' => 'pollo',
                'cow'     => 'vaca',
                'horse'   => 'caballo'
                );
  }

  function i_am_X_years_old($age) {
    return "Tengo $age años";
  }
}
```

```
class pc_MC_en_US extends pc_MC_Base {

  function pc_MC_en_US() {
    $this->lang = 'en_US';
    $this->messages = array ('chicken' => 'chicken',
                'cow'     => 'cow',
                'horse'   => 'horse'
                );
  }

  function i_am_X_years_old($age) {
    return "I am $age years old.";
  }
}
```

Each message catalog object extends the pc_MC_Base class to get the msg( ) method, and then defines its own messages (in its constructor) and its own functions that return phrases. Here's how to print text in Spanish:

```
$MC = new pc_MC_es_US;

print $MC->msg('cow');
print $MC->i_am_X_years_old(15);
```

To print the same text in English, $MC just needs to be instantiated as a pc_MC_en_US object instead of a pc_MC_es_US object. The rest of the code remains unchanged.

See Also

The introduction to Chapter 7 discusses object inheritance; documentation on sprintf( ) at *http://www.php.net/sprintf*.

16.5   Localizing Dates and Times

Problem

You want to display dates and times in a locale-specific manner.

Solution

Use strftime( )'s %c format string:

```
print strftime('%c');
```

You can also store strftime( ) format strings as messages in your message catalog:

```
$MC = new pc_MC_es_US;
print strftime($MC->msg('%Y-%m-%d'));
```

Discussion

The %c format string tells strftime( ) to return the preferred date and time representation for the current locale. Here's the quickest way to a locale-appropriate formatted time string:

```
print strftime('%c');
```

This code produces a variety of results:

```
Tue Aug 13 18:37:11 2002     // in the default C locale
mar 13 ago 2002 18:37:11 EDT // in the es_US locale
mar 13 aoû 2002 18:37:11 EDT // in the fr_FR locale
```

The formatted time string that %c produces, while locale-appropriate, isn't very flexible. If you just want the time, for example, you must pass a different format string to strftime( ). But these format strings themselves vary in different locales. In some locales, displaying an hour from 1 to 12 with an A.M./P.M. designation may be appropriate, while in others the hour should range from 0 to 23. To display appropriate time strings for a locale, add elements to the locale's $messages array for each time format you want. The key for a particular time format, such as %H:%M, is always the same in each locale. The value, however, can vary, such as %H:%M for 24-hour locales or %I:%M %P for 12-hour locales. Then, look up the appropriate format string and pass it to strftime( ):

```
$MC = new pc_MC_es_US;

print strftime($MC->msg('%H:%M'));
```

Changing the locale doesn't change the time zone, it changes only the formatting of the displayed result.

See Also

Recipe 3.4 discusses the format strings that strftime( ) accepts; Recipe 3.11 covers changing time zones in your program; documentation on strftime( ) at *http://www.php.net/strftime*.

16.6   Localizing Currency Values

Problem

You want to display currency amounts in a locale-specific format.

Solution

Use the pc_format_currency( ) function, shown in Example 16-1, to produce an appropriately formatted string. For example:

```
setlocale(LC_ALL,'fr_CA');
print pc_format_currency(-12345678.45);
(12 345 678,45 $)
```

Discussion

The pc_format_currency( ) function, shown in Example 16-1, gets the currency formatting information from localeconv( ) and then uses number_format( ) and some
logic to construct the correct string.

Example 16-1. pc_format_currency

```
function pc_format_currency($amt) {
    // get locale-specific currency formatting information
    $a = localeconv();

    // compute sign of $amt and then remove it
    if ($amt < 0) { $sign = -1; } else { $sign = 1; }
    $amt = abs($amt);
    // format $amt with appropriate grouping, decimal point, and fractional digits
    $amt = number_format($amt,$a['frac_digits'],$a['mon_decimal_point'],
                         $a['mon_thousands_sep']);

    // figure out where to put the currency symbol and positive or negative signs
    $currency_symbol = $a['currency_symbol'];
    // is $amt >= 0 ?
    if (1 == $sign) {
        $sign_symbol   = 'positive_sign';
        $cs_precedes   = 'p_cs_precedes';
        $sign_posn     = 'p_sign_posn';
        $sep_by_space  = 'p_sep_by_space';
    } else {
        $sign_symbol   = 'negative_sign';
        $cs_precedes   = 'n_cs_precedes';
        $sign_posn     = 'n_sign_posn';
        $sep_by_space  = 'n_sep_by_space';
    }
    if ($a[$cs_precedes]) {
        if (3 == $a[$sign_posn]) {
            $currency_symbol = $a[$sign_symbol].$currency_symbol;
        } elseif (4 == $a[$sign_posn]) {
            $currency_symbol .= $a[$sign_symbol];
        }
        // currency symbol in front
        if ($a[$sep_by_space]) {
            $amt = $currency_symbol.' '.$amt;
        } else {
            $amt = $currency_symbol.$amt;
        }
    } else {
        // currency symbol after amount
        if ($a[$sep_by_space]) {
            $amt .= ' '.$currency_symbol;
```

Example 16-1. pc_format_currency (continued)

```
    } else {
        $amt .= $currency_symbol;
    }
}
if (0 == $a[$sign_posn]) {
    $amt = "($amt)";
} elseif (1 == $a[$sign_posn]) {
    $amt = $a[$sign_symbol].$amt;
} elseif (2 == $a[$sign_posn]) {
    $amt .= $a[$sign_symbol];
}
    return $amt;
}
```

The code in pc_format_currency( ) that puts the currency symbol and sign in the correct place is almost identical for positive and negative amounts; it just uses different elements of the array returned by localeconv( ). The relevant elements of localeconv( )'s returned array are shown in Table 16-1.

Table 16-1. Currency-related information from localeconv( )

Array element	Description
currency_symbol	Local currency symbol
mon_decimal_point	Monetary decimal point character
mon_thousands_sep	Monetary thousands separator
positive_sign	Sign for positive values
negative_sign	Sign for negative values
frac_digits	Number of fractional digits
p_cs_precedes	1 if currency_symbol should precede a positive value, 0 if it should follow
p_sep_by_space	1 if a space should separate the currency symbol from a positive value, 0 if not
n_cs_precedes	1 if currency_symbol should precede a negative value, 0 if it should follow
n_sep_by_space	1 if a space should separate currency_symbol from a negative value, 0 if not
p_sign_posn	Positive sign position:
	• 0 if parenthesis should surround the quantity and currency_symbol
	• 1 if the sign string should precede the quantity and currency_symbol
	• 2 if the sign string should follow the quantity and currency_symbol
	• 3 if the sign string should immediately precede currency_symbol
	• 4 if the sign string should immediately follow currency_symbol
n_sign_posn	Negative sign position: same possible values as p_sign_posn

There is a function in the C library called strfmon( ) that does for currency what strftime( ) does for dates and times; however, it isn't implemented in PHP. The pc_format_currency( ) function provides most of the same capabilities.

See Also

Recipe 2.9 also discusses `number_format()`; documentation on `localeconv()` at *http://www.php.net/localeconv* and `number_format()` at *http://www.php.net/number-format*.

16.7 Localizing Images

Problem

You want to display images that have text in them and have that text in a locale-appropriate language.

Solution

Make an image directory for each locale you want to support, as well as a global image directory for images that have no locale-specific information in them. Create copies of each locale-specific image in the appropriate locale-specific directory. Make sure that the images have the same filename in the different directories. Instead of printing out image URLs directly, use a wrapper function similar to the `msg()` function in Recipe 16.4 that prints out locale-specific text.

Discussion

The `img()` wrapper function looks for a locale-specific version of an image first, then a global one. If neither are present, it prints a message to the error log:

```
$image_base_path = '/usr/local/www/images';
$image_base_url  = '/images';

function img($f) {
    global $LANG;
    global $image_base_path;
    global $image_base_url;

    if (is_readable("$image_base_path/$LANG/$f")) {
        print "$image_base_url/$LANG/$f";
    } elseif (is_readable("$image_base_path/global/$f")) {
        print "$image_base_url/global/$f";
    } else {
        error_log("l10n error: LANG: $lang, image: '$f'");
    }
}
```

This function needs to know both the path to the image file in the filesystem (`$image_base_path`) and the path to the image from the base URL of your site (*/images*). It uses the first to test if the file can be read and the second to construct an appropriate URL for the image.

A localized image must have the same filename in each localization directory. For example, an image that says "New!" on a yellow starburst should be called *new.gif* in both the *images/en_US* directory and the *images/es_US* directory, even though the file *images/es_US/new.gif* is a picture of a yellow starburst with "¡Nuevo!" on it.

Don't forget that the alt text you display in your image tags also needs to be localized. A complete localized <img> tag looks like:

```
printf('<img src="%s" alt="%s">',img('cancel.png'),msg('Cancel'));
```

If the localized versions of a particular image have varied dimensions, store image height and width in the message catalog as well:

```
printf('<img src="%s" alt="%s" height="%d" width="%d">',
       img('cancel.png'),msg('Cancel'),
       msg('img-cancel-height'),msg('img-cancel-width'));
```

The localized messages for img-cancel-height and img-cancel-width are not text strings, but integers that describe the dimensions of the *cancel.png* image in each locale.

See Also

Recipe 16.4 discusses locale-specific message catalogs.

16.8   Localizing Included Files

Problem

You want to include locale-specific files in your pages.

Solution

Dynamically modify the include_path once you've determined the appropriate locale:

```
$base = '/usr/local/php-include';
$LANG = 'en_US';

$include_path = ini_get('include_path');
ini_set('include_path',"$base/$LANG:$base/global:$include_path");
```

Discussion

The $base variable holds the name of the base directory for your included localized files. Files that are not locale-specific go in the *global* subdirectory of $base, and locale-specific files go in a subdirectory named after their locale (e.g., *en_US*). Prepending the locale-specific directory and then the global directory to the include path makes them the first two places PHP looks when you include a file. Putting the locale-specific directory first ensures that nonlocalized information is loaded only if localized information isn't available.

This technique is similar to what the img( ) function does in the Recipe 16.7. Here, however, you can take advantage of PHP's include_path feature to have the directory searching happen automatically. For maximum utility, reset include_path as early as possible in your code, preferably at the top of a file loaded via auto_prepend_file on every request.

See Also

Documentation on include_path at *http://www.php.net/manual/en/configuration.directives.php#ini.include-path* and auto_prepend_file at *http://www.php.net/manual/en/configuration.directives.php#ini.auto-prepend-file*.

16.9   Managing Localization Resources

Problem

You need to keep track of your various message catalogs and images.

Solution

Two techniques simplify the management of your localization resources. The first is making a new language's object, for example Canadian English, extend from a similar existing language, such as American English. You only have to change the words and phrases in the new object that differ from the original language.

The second technique: to track what phrases still need to be translated in new languages, put stubs in the new language object that have the same value as in your base language. By finding which values are the same in the base language and the new language, you can then generate a list of words and phrases to translate.

Discussion

The *catalog-compare.php* program shown in Example 16-2 prints out messages that are the same in two catalogs, as well as messages that are missing from one catalog but present in another.

Example 16-2. catalog-compare.php

```
$base = 'pc_MC_'.$_SERVER['argv'][1];
$other = 'pc_MC_'.$_SERVER['argv'][2];
```

Example 16-2. catalog-compare.php (continued)

```
require 'pc_MC_Base.php';
require "$base.php";
require "$other.php";

$base_obj = new $base;
$other_obj = new $other;

/* Check for messages in the other class that
 * are the same as the base class or are in
 * the base class but missing from the other class */
foreach ($base_obj->messages as $k => $v) {
    if (isset($other_obj->messages[$k])) {
        if ($v == $other_obj->messages[$k]) {
            print "SAME: $k\n";
        }
    } else {
        print "MISSING: $k\n";
    }
}

/* Check for messages in the other class but missing
 * from the base class */
foreach ($other_obj->messages as $k => $v) {
    if (! isset($base_obj->messages[$k])) {
        print "MISSING (BASE): $k\n";
    }
}
```

To use this program, put each message catalog object in a file with the same name as the object (e.g., the pc_MC_en_US class should be in a file named *pc_MC_en_US.php*, and the pc_MC_es_US class should be in a file named *pc_MC_es_US.php*). You then call the program with the two locale names as arguments on the command line:

```
% php catalog-compare.php en_US es_US
```

In a web context, it can be useful to use a different locale and message catalog on a per-request basis. The locale to use may come from the browser (in an Accept-Language header), or it may be explicitly set by the server (different virtual hosts may be set up to display the same content in different languages). If the same code needs to select a message catalog on a per-request basis, the message catalog class can be instantiated like this:

```
$classname = "pc_MC_$locale.php";

require 'pc_MC_Base.php';
require $classname.'.php';

$MC = new $classname;
```

See Also

Recipe 16.4 discusses message catalogs; Recipe 7.10 for information on finding the methods and properties of an object.

16.10 Using gettext

Problem

You want a comprehensive system to create, manage, and deploy message catalogs.

Solution

Use PHP's *gettext* extension, which allows you to use GNU's *gettext* utilities:

```
bindtextdomain('gnumeric','/usr/share/locale');
textdomain('gnumeric');

$languages = array('en_CA','da_DK','de_AT','fr_FR');
foreach ($languages as $language) {
  setlocale(LC_ALL, $language);
  print gettext(" Unknown formula")."\n";
}
```

Discussion

gettext is a set of tools that makes it easier for your application to produce multilingual messages. Compiling PHP with the --with-gettext option enables functions to retrieve the appropriate text from *gettext*-format message catalogs, and there are a number of external tools to edit the message catalogs.

With *gettext*, messages are divided into domains, and all messages for a particular domain are stored in the same file. bindtextdomain( ) tells *gettext* where to find the message catalog for a particular domain. A call to:

```
bindtextdomain('gnumeric','/usr/share/locale')
```

indicates that the message catalog for the gnumeric domain in the en_CA locale is in the file */usr/share/locale/en_CA/LC_MESSAGES/gnumeric.mo*.

The textdomain('gnumeric') function sets the default domain to gnumeric. Calling gettext( ) retrieves a message from the default domain. There are other functions, such as dgettext( ), that let you retrieve a message from a different domain. When gettext( ) (or dgettext( )) is called, it returns the appropriate message for the current locale. If there's no message in the catalog for the current locale that corresponds to the argument passed to it, gettext( ) (or dgettext( )) returns just its argument. As a result, if you haven't translated all your messages, your code prints out English (or whatever your base language is) for those untranslated messages.

Setting the default domain with `textdomain( )` makes each subsequent retrieval of a message from that domain more concise, because you just have to call `gettext('Good morning')` instead of `dgettext('domain','Good morning')`. However, if even `gettext('Good morning')` is too much typing, you can take advantage of an undocumented function alias: `_( )` for `gettext( )`. Instead of `gettext('Good morning')`, use `_('Good morning')`.

The *gettext* web site has helpful and detailed information for managing the information flow between programmers and translators and how to efficiently use *gettext*. It also includes information on other tools you can use to manage your message catalogs, such as a special GNU Emacs mode.

See Also

Documentation on *gettext* at *http://www.php.net/gettext*; the *gettext* library at *http://www.gnu.org/software/gettext/gettext.html*.

16.11 Reading or Writing Unicode Characters

Problem

You want to read Unicode-encoded characters from a file, database, or form; or, you want to write Unicode-encoded characters.

Solution

Use `utf8_encode( )` to convert single-byte ISO-8859-1 encoded characters to UTF-8:

```
print utf8_encode('Kurt Gödel is swell.');
```

Use `utf8_decode( )` to convert UTF-8 encoded characters to single-byte ISO-8859-1 encoded characters:

```
print utf8_decode("Kurt G\xc3\xb6del is swell.");
```

Discussion

There are 256 possible ASCII characters. The characters between codes 0 and 127 are standardized: control characters, letters and numbers, and punctuation. There are different rules, however, for the characters that codes 128–255 map to. One encoding is called ISO-8859-1, which includes characters necessary for writing most European languages, such as the ö in Gödel or the ñ in pestaña. Many languages, though, require more than 256 characters, and a character set that can express more than one language requires even more characters. This is where Unicode saves the day; its UTF-8 encoding can represent more than a million characters.

This increased functionality comes at the cost of space. ASCII characters are stored in just one byte; UTF-8 encoded characters need up to four bytes. Table 16-2 shows the byte representations of UTF-8 encoded characters.

Table 16-2. UTF-8 byte representation

Character code range	Bytes used	Byte 1	Byte 2	Byte 3	Byte 4
0x00000000 - 0x0000007F	1	0xxxxxxx			
0x00000080 - 0x000007FF	2	110xxxxx	10xxxxxx		
0x00000800 - 0x0000FFFF	3	1110xxxx	10xxxxxx	10xxxxxx	
0x00010000 - 0x001FFFFF	4	11110xxx	10xxxxxx	10xxxxxx	10xxxxxx

In Table 16-2, the x positions represent bits used for actual character data. The least significant bit is the rightmost bit in the rightmost byte. In multibyte characters, the number of leading 1 bits in the leftmost byte is the same as the number of bytes in the character.

See Also

Documentation on utf8_encode( ) at *http://www.php.net/utf8-encode* and utf8_decode( ) at *http://www.php.net/utf8-decode*; more information on Unicode is available at the Unicode Consortium's home page, *http://www.unicode.org*; the UTF-8 and Unicode FAQ at *http://www.cl.cam.ac.uk/~mgk25/unicode.html* is also helpful.

CHAPTER 17

Internet Services

17.0 Introduction

Before there was HTTP, there was FTP, NNTP, IMAP, POP3, and a whole alphabet soup of other protocols. Many people quickly embraced web browsers because the browser provided an integrated program that let them check their email, read newsgroups, transfer files, and view documents without worrying about the details surrounding the underlying means of communication. PHP provides functions, both natively and through PEAR, to use these other protocols. With them, you can use PHP to create web frontend applications that perform all sorts of network-enabled tasks, such as looking up domain names or sending web-based email. While PHP simplifies these jobs, it is important to understand the strengths and limitations of each protocol.

Recipes 17.1 to 17.3 cover the most popular feature of all: email. Recipe 17.1 shows how to send basic email messages. Recipe 17.2 describes MIME-encoded email, which enables you to send plain-text and HTML-formatted messages. The IMAP and POP3 protocols, which are used to read mailboxes, are discussed in Recipe 17.3.

The next two recipes discuss how to read newsgroups with NNTP. Newsgroups are similar to mailing lists, but instead of every person on the list receiving an email message, people can access a news server and view just the messages they're interested in. Newsgroups also allow threaded discussions, so its easy to trace a conversation through the archives. Recipe 17.4 discusses posting messages, while Recipe 17.5 covers retrieving messages.

Recipe 17.6 covers how to exchange files using FTP. FTP, or file transfer protocol, is a method for sending and receiving files across the Internet. FTP servers can require users to log in with a password or allow anonymous usage.

Searching LDAP servers is the topic of Recipe 17.7, while Recipe 17.8 discusses how to authenticate users against an LDAP server. LDAP servers are used as address books and as a centralized store for user information. They're optimized for information retrieval and can be configured to replicate their data to ensure high reliability and quick response times.

The chapter concludes with recipes on networking. Recipe 17.9 covers DNS lookups, both from domain name to IP and vice versa. The final recipe tells how to check if a host is up and accessible with PEAR's Ping module.

Other parts of the book deal with some network protocols as well. HTTP is covered in detail in Chapter 11. Those recipes discuss how to fetch URLs in a variety of different ways. Protocols that combine HTTP and XML are covered in Chapter 12. In that chapter, along with covering DOM and XSLT, we discuss the emerging area of web services, using the XML-RPC and SOAP protocols.

17.1   Sending Mail

Problem

You want to send an email message. This can be in direct response to a user's action, such as signing up for your site, or a recurring event at a set time, such as a weekly newsletter.

Solution

Use PEAR's Mail class:

```
require 'Mail.php';

$to = 'adam@example.com';

$headers['From'] = 'webmaster@example.com';
$headers['Subject'] = 'New Version of PHP Released!';

$body = 'Go to http://www.php.net and download it today!';

$message =& Mail::factory('mail');
$message->send($to, $headers, $body);
```

If you can't use PEAR's Mail class, use PHP's built-in mail( ) function:

```
$to = 'adam@example.com';
$subject = 'New Version of PHP Released!';
$body = 'Go to http://www.php.net and download it today!';

mail($to, $subject, $body);
```

Discussion

PEAR's Mail class allows you to send mail three ways. You indicate the method to use when instantiating a mail object with Mail::factory( ).

- To send mail using an external program such as *sendmail* or *qmail*, pass sendmail.
- To use an SMTP server, pass smtp.
- To use the built-in mail( ) function, pass mail. This tells Mail to apply the settings from your *php.ini*.

To use sendmail or smtp, you have to pass a second parameter indicating your settings. To use sendmail, specify a sendmail_path and sendmail_args:

```
$params['sendmail_path'] = '/usr/sbin/sendmail';
$params['sendmail_args'] = '-oi -t';

$message =& Mail::factory('sendmail', $params);
```

One good value for sendmail_path is */usr/lib/sendmail*. Unfortunately, *sendmail* tends to jump around from system to system, so it can be hard to track down. If you can't find it, try */usr/sbin/sendmail* or ask your system administrator.

Two useful flags to pass *sendmail* are -oi and -t. The -oi flag tells *sendmail* not to think a single dot (.) on a line is the end of the message. The -t flag makes *sendmail* parse the file for To: and other header lines.

If you prefer *qmail*, try using */var/qmail/bin/qmail-inject* or */var/qmail/bin/sendmail*.

If you're running Windows, you may want to use an SMTP server because most Windows machines don't have copies of *sendmail* installed. To do so, pass smtp:

```
$params['host'] = 'smtp.example.com';

$message =& Mail::factory('smtp', $params);
```

In smtp mode, you can pass five optional parameters. The host is the SMTP server hostname; it defaults to localhost. The port is the connection port; it defaults to 25. To enable SMTP authentication, set auth to true. To allow the server to validate you, set username and password. SMTP functionality isn't restricted to Windows; it also works on Unix servers.

If you don't have PEAR's Mail class, you can use the built-in mail( ) function. The program mail( ) uses to send mail is specified in the sendmail_path configuration variable in your *php.ini* file. If you're running Windows, set the SMTP variable to the hostname of your SMTP server. Your From address comes from the sendmail_from variable.

Here's an example that uses `mail( )`:

```
$to = 'adam@example.com';
$subject = 'New Version of PHP Released!';
$body = 'Go to http://www.php.net and download it today!';

mail($to, $subject, $body);
```

The first parameter is the recipient's email address, the second is the message subject, and the last is the message body. You can also add extra headers with an optional fourth parameter. For example, here's how to add `Reply-To` and `Organization` headers:

```
$to = 'adam@example.com';
$subject = 'New Version of PHP Released!';
$body = 'Go to http://www.php.net and download it today!';
$header = "Reply-To: webmaster@example.com\r\n"
          ."Organization: The PHP Group";

mail($to, $subject, $body, $header);
```

Separate each header with \r\n, but don't add \r\n following the last header.

Regardless of which method you choose, it's a good idea to write a wrapper function to assist you in sending mail. Forcing all your mail through this function makes it easy to add logging and other checks to every message sent:

```
function pc_mail($to, $headers, $body) {
    $message =& Mail::factory('mail');

    $message->send($to, $headers, $body);
    error_log("[MAIL][TO: $to]");
}
```

Here a message is written to the error log, recording the recipient of each message that's sent. This provides a time stamp that allows you to more easily track complaints that someone is trying to use the site to send spam. Another option is to create a list of "do not send" email addresses, which prevent those people from ever receiving another message from your site. You can also validate all recipient email addresses, which reduces the number of bounced messages.

See Also

Recipe 13.5 for a regular expression to validate email addresses; Recipe 17.2 for sending MIME email; Recipe 17.3 for more on retrieving mail; documentation on `mail( )` at *http://www.php.net/mail*; the PEAR `Mail` class at *http://pear.php.net/ package-info.php?package=Mail*; RFC 822 at *http://www.faqs.org/rfcs/rfc822.html*; O'Reilly publishes two books on sendmail, called *sendmail* by Bryan Costales with Eric Allman and *sendmail Desktop Reference* by Bryan Costales and Eric Allman.

17.2   Sending MIME Mail

Problem

You want to send MIME email. For example, you want to send multipart messages with both plain-text and HTML portions and have MIME-aware mail readers automatically display the correct portion.

Solution

Use the `Mail_mime` class in PEAR:

```
require 'Mail.php';
require 'Mail/mime.php';

$to = 'adam@example.com, sklar@example.com';

$headers['From'] = 'webmaster@example.com';
$headers['Subject'] = 'New Version of PHP Released!';

// create MIME object
$mime = new Mail_mime;

// add body parts
$text = 'Text version of email';
$mime->setTXTBody($text);

$html = '<html><body>HTML version of email</body></html>';
$mime->setHTMLBody($html);

$file = '/path/to/file.png';
$mime->addAttachment($file, 'image/png');

// get MIME formatted message headers and body
$body = $mime->get();
$headers = $mime->headers($headers);

$message =& Mail::factory('mail');
$message->send($to, $headers, $body);
```

Discussion

PEAR's `Mail_mime` class provides an object-oriented interface to all the behind-the-scenes details involved in creating an email message that contains both text and HTML parts. The class is similar to PEAR's `Mail` class, but instead of defining the body as a string of text, you create a `Mail_mime` object and call its methods to add parts to the body:

```
// create MIME object
$mime = new Mail_mime;

// add body parts
$text = 'Text version of email';
$mime->setTXTBody($text);

$html = '<html><body>HTML version of email</body></html>';
$mime->setHTMLBody($html);

$file = '/path/to/file.txt';
$mime->addAttachment($file, 'text/plain');

// get MIME formatted message headers and body
$body = $mime->get();
$headers = $mime->headers($headers);
```

The `Mail_mime::setTXTBody()` and `Mail_mime::setHTMLBody()` methods add the plain-text and HTML body parts, respectively. Here, we pass in variables, but you can also pass a filename for `Mail_mime` to read. To use this option, pass true as the second parameter:

```
$text = '/path/to/email.txt';
$mime->setTXTBody($text, true);
```

To add an attachment to the message, such as a graphic or an archive, call `Mail_mime::addAttachment()`:

```
$file = '/path/to/file.png';
$mime->addAttachment($file,'image/png');
```

Pass the function to the location to the file and its MIME type.

Once the message is complete, do the final preparation and send it out:

```
// get MIME formatted message headers and body
$body = $mime->get();
$headers = $mime->headers($headers);

$message =& Mail::factory('mail');
$message->send($to, $headers, $body);
```

First, you have the `Mail_mime` object provide properly formatted headers and body. You then use the parent `Mail` class to format the message and send it out with `Mail_mime::send()`.

See Also

Recipe 17.1 for sending regular email; Recipe 17.3 for more on retrieving mail; the PEAR `Mail_Mime` class at *http://pear.php.net/package-info.php?package=Mail_Mime*.

17.3 Reading Mail with IMAP or POP3

Problem

You want to read mail using IMAP or POP3, which allows you to create a web-based email client.

Solution

Use PHP's IMAP extension, which speaks both IMAP and POP3:

```
// open IMAP connection
$mail = imap_open('{mail.server.com:143}',        'username', 'password');
// or, open POP3 connection
$mail = imap_open('{mail.server.com:110/pop3}', 'username', 'password');

// grab a list of all the mail headers
$headers = imap_headers($mail);

// grab a header object for the last message in the mailbox
$last = imap_num_msg($mail);
$header = imap_header($mail, $last);

// grab the body for the same message
$body = imap_body($mail, $last);

// close the connection
imap_close($mail);
```

Discussion

The underlying library PHP uses to support IMAP and POP3 offers a seemingly unending number of features that allow you to essentially write an entire mail client. With all those features, however, comes complexity. In fact, there are currently 63 different functions in PHP beginning with the word imap, and that doesn't take into account that some also speak POP3 and NNTP.

However, the basics of talking with a mail server are straightforward. Like many features in PHP, you begin by opening the connection and grabbing a handle:

```
$mail = imap_open('{mail.server.com:143}', 'username', 'password');
```

This opens an IMAP connection to the server named *mail.server.com* on port 143. It also passes along a username and password as the second and third arguments.

To open a POP3 connection instead, append /pop3 to the end of the server and port. Since POP3 usually runs on port 110, add :110 after the server name:

```
$mail = imap_open('{mail.server.com:110/pop3}', 'username', 'password');
```

To encrypt your connection with SSL, add /ssl on to the end, just as you did with pop3. You also need to make sure your PHP installation is built with the --with-imap-ssl configuration option in addition to --with-imap. Also, you need to build the system IMAP library itself with SSL support. If you're using a self-signed certificate and wish to prevent an attempted validation, also add /novalidate-cert. Finally, most SSL connections talk on either port 993 or 995. All these options can come in any order, so the following is perfectly legal:

```
$mail = imap_open('{mail.server.com:993/novalidate-cert/pop3/ssl}',
                  'username', 'password');
```

Surrounding a variable with curly braces inside of a double-quoted string, such as {$var}, is a way to tell PHP exactly which variable to interpolate. Therefore, to use interpolated variables in this first parameter to imap_open( ), escape the opening {:

```
$server = 'mail.server.com';
$port = 993;

$mail = imap_open("\{$server:$port}", 'username', 'password');
```

Once you've opened a connection, you can ask the mail server a variety of questions. To get a listing of all the messages in your inbox, use imap_headers( ):

```
$headers = imap_headers($mail);
```

This returns an array in which each element is a formatted string corresponding to a message:

```
   A   189) 5-Aug-2002 Beth Hondl           an invitation (1992 chars)
```

Alternatively, to retrieve a specific message, use imap_header( ) and imap_body( ) to pull the header object and body string:

```
$header = imap_header($message_number);
$body   = imap_body($message_number);
```

The imap_header( ) function returns an object with many fields. Useful ones include subject, fromaddress, and udate. All the fields are listed in Table 17-2 in Recipe 17.5.

The body element is just a string, but, if the message is a multipart message, such as one that contains both a HTML and a plain-text version, $body holds both parts and the MIME lines describing them:

```
------=_Part_1046_3914492.1008372096119
Content-Type: text/plain; charset=us-ascii
Content-Transfer-Encoding: 7bit

Plain-Text Message

------=_Part_1046_3914492.1008372096119
Content-Type: text/html
Content-Transfer-Encoding: 7bit
```

```
<html>HTML Message</html>
------=_Part_1046_3914492.1008372096119--
```

To avoid this occurrence, use `imap_fetchstructure( )` in combination with `imap_fetchbody( )` to discover how the body is formatted and to extract just the parts you want:

```
// pull the plain text for message $n
$st = imap_fetchstructure($mail, $n);
if (!empty($st->parts)) {
    for ($i = 0, $j = count($st->parts); $i < $j; $i++) {
        $part = $st->parts[$i];
        if ($part->subtype == 'PLAIN') {
            $body = imap_fetchbody($mail, $n, $i+1);
        }
    }
} else {
    $body = imap_body($mail, $n));
}
```

If a message has multiple parts, `$st->parts` holds an array of objects describing them. The part property holds an integer describing the main body MIME type. Table 17-1 lists which numbers go with which MIME types. The subtype property holds the MIME subtype and tells if the part is plain, html, png, or another type, such as octet-stream.

Table 17-1. IMAP MIME type values

Number	MIME type	PHP constant	Description	Examples
0	text	TYPETEXT	Unformatted text	Plain text, HTML, XML
1	multipart	TYPEMULTIPART	Multipart message	Mixed, form data, signed
2	message	TYPEMESSAGE	Encapsulated message	News, HTTP
3	application	TYPEAPPLICATION	Application data	Octet stream, PDF, Zip
4	audio	TYPEAUDIO	Music file	MP3, RealAudio
5	image	TYPEIMAGE	Graphic image	GIF, JPEG, PNG
6	video	TYPEVIDEO	Video clip	MPEG, Quicktime
7	other	TYPEOTHER	Everything else	VRML models

See Also

Recipes 17.1 and 17.3 for more on sending mail; documentation on `imap_open( )` at *http://www.php.net/imap_open*, `imap_header( )` at *http://www.php.net/imap-header*, `imap-body( )` at *http://www.php.net/imap-body*, and IMAP in general at *http://www.php.net/imap*.

17.4 Posting Messages to Usenet Newsgroups

Problem

You want to post a message to a Usenet newsgroup, such as *comp.lang.php*.

Solution

Use `imap_mail_compose( )` to format the message, then write the message to the server using sockets:

```
$headers['from'] = 'adam@example.com';
$headers['subject'] = 'New Version of PHP Released!';
$headers['custom_headers'][] = 'Newsgroups: comp.lang.php';

$body[0]['type'] = TYPETEXT;
$body[0]['subtype'] = 'plain';
$body[0]['contents.data'] = 'Go to http://www.php.net and download it today!';

$post = imap_mail_compose($headers, $body);

$server = 'nntp.example.com';
$port = 119;

$sh = fsockopen($server, $port) or die ("Can't connect to $server.");
fputs($sh, "POST\r\n");
fputs($sh, $post);
fputs($sh, ".\r\n");
fclose($sh);
```

Discussion

No built-in PHP functions can post a message to a newsgroup. Therefore, you must open a direct socket connection to the news server and send the commands to post the message. However, you can use `imap_mail_compose( )` to format a post and create the headers and body for the message. Every message must have three headers: the From: address, the message Subject:, and the name of the newsgroup:

```
$headers['from'] = 'adam@example.com';
$headers['subject'] = 'New Version of PHP Released!';
$headers['custom_headers'][ ] = 'Newsgroups: comp.lang.php';
```

Create an array, $headers, to hold the message headers. You can directly assign the values for the From: and Subject: headers, but you can't do so for the Newsgroups: header. Because `imap_mail_compose( )` is most frequently used to create email messages, the Newsgroups: header is not a predefined header. To work around this, you must instead add it with the custom_headers array element.

There is a different syntax for the custom_headers. Instead of placing the lowercase header name as the element name and the header value as the array value, place the entire header as an array value. Between the header name and value, add a colon followed by a space. Be sure to correctly spell Newsgroups: with a capital N and final s.

The message body can contain multiple parts. As a result, the body parameter passed to imap_mail_compose( ) is an array of arrays. In the Solution, there was only one part, so we directly assign values to $body[0]:

```
$body[0]['type'] = TYPETEXT;
$body[0]['subtype'] = 'plain';
$body[0]['contents.data'] = 'Go to http://www.php.net and download it today!';
```

Each message part needs a MIME type and subtype. This message is ASCII, so the type is TYPETEXT, and the subtype is plain. Refer back to Table 17-1 in Recipe 17.3 for a listing of IMAP MIME type constants and what they represent. The contents.data field holds the message body.

To convert these arrays into a formatted string call imap_mail_compose($body, $headers). It returns a post that looks like this:

```
From: adam@example.com
Subject: New Version of PHP Released!
MIME-Version: 1.0
Content-Type: TEXT/plain; CHARSET=US-ASCII
Newsgroups: comp.lang.php

Go to http://www.php.net and download it today!
```

Armed with a post the news server will accept, call fsockopen( ) to open a connection:

```
$server = 'nntp.example.com';
$port = 119;

$sh = fsockopen($server, $port) or die ("Can't connect to $server.");
```

The first parameter to fsockopen( ) is the hostname of the server, and the second is the port to use. If you don't know the name of your news server, try the hostnames *news*, *nntp*, or *news-server* in your domain: for example, *news.example.com*, *nntp.example.com*, or *news-server.example.com*. If none of these work, ask your system administrator. Traditionally, all news servers use port 119.

Once connected, you send the message:

```
fputs($sh, "POST\r\n");
fputs($sh, imap_mail_compose($headers, $body));
fputs($sh, ".\r\n");
```

The first line tells the news server that you want to post a message. The second is the message itself. To signal the end of the message, place a period on a line by itself. Every line must have both a carriage return and a newline at the end. Close the connection by calling fclose($sh).

Every message on the server is given a unique name, known as a `Message-ID`. If you want to reply to a message, take the `Message-ID` of the original message and use it as the value for a `References` header:

```
// retrieved when reading original message
$message_id = '<20030410020818.33915.php@news.example.com>';

$headers['custom_headers'][] = "References: $message_id";
```

See Also

Recipe 17.5 for more on reading newsgroups; documentation on `imap_mail_compose()` at *http://www.php.net/imap-mail-compose*, `fsockopen()` at *http://www.php.net/ fsockopen*, `fputs()` at *http://www.php.net/fputs*, and `fclose()` at *http://www.php.net/ fclose*; RFC 977 at *http://www.faqs.org/rfcs/rfc977.html*.

17.5 Reading Usenet News Messages

Problem

You want to read Usenet news messages using NNTP to talk to a news server.

Solution

Use PHP's IMAP extension. It also speaks NNTP:

```
// open a connection to the nntp server
$server = '{news.php.net/nntp:119}';
$group = 'php.general'; // main PHP mailing list
$nntp = imap_open("$server$group", '', '', OP_ANONYMOUS);

// get header
$header = imap_header($nntp, $msg);

// pull out fields
$subj  = $header->subject;
$from  = $header->from;
$email = $from[0]->mailbox."@".$from[0]->host;
$name  = $from[0]->personal;
$date  = date('m/d/Y h:i A', $header->udate);

// get body
$body  = nl2br(htmlspecialchars(imap_fetchbody($nntp,$msg,1)));

// close connection
imap_close($nntp);
```

Discussion

Reading news from a news server requires you to connect to the server and specify a group you're interested in reading:

```
// open a connection to the nntp server
$server = "{news.php.net/nntp:119}";
$group = "php.general";
$nntp = imap_open("$server$group",'','',OP_ANONYMOUS);
```

The function imap_open( ) takes four parameters. The first specifies the news server to use and the newsgroup to read. The server here is *news.php.net*, the news server that mirrors all the PHP mailing lists. Add */nntp* to let the IMAP extension know you're reading news instead of mail, and specify 119 as a port; that's typically the port reserved for NNTP. NNTP stands for Network News Transport Protocol; it's used to communicate with news servers, just as HTTP communicates with web servers. The group is *php.general*, the main mailing list of the PHP community.

The middle two arguments to imap_open( ) are a username and password, in case you need to provide verification of your identity. Because *news.php.net* is open to all readers, leave them blank. Finally, pass the flag OP_ANONYMOUS, which tells IMAP you're an anonymous reader; it will not then keep a record of you in a special *.newsrc* file.

Once you're connected, you usually want to either get a general listing of recent messages or all the details about one specific message. Here's some code that displays recent messages:

```
// read and display posting index
$last = imap_num_msg($nntp);
$n = 10; // display last 10 messages

// table header
print <<<EOH
<table>
<tr>
    <th align="left">Subject</th>
    <th align="left">Sender</th>
    <th align="left">Date</th>
</tr>
EOH;

// the messages
for ($i = $last-$n+1; $i <= $last; $i++) {
    $header = imap_header($nntp, $i);

    if (! $header->Size) { continue; }

    $subj  = $header->subject;
    $from  = $header->from;
    $email = $from[0]->mailbox."@".$from[0]->host;
    $name  = $from[0]->personal ? $from[0]->personal : $email;
```

```
    $date   = date('m/d/Y h:i A', $header->udate);

print <<<EOM
<tr>
    <td><a href="$_SERVER[PHP_SELF]"?msg=$i\">$subj</a></td>
    <td><a href="mailto:$email">$name</a></td>
    <td>$date</td>
</tr>
EOM;
    }


// table footer
echo "</table>\n";
```

To browse a listing of posts, you need to specify what you want by number. The first post ever to a group gets number 1, and the most recent post is the number returned from imap_num_msg( ). So, to get the last $n messages, loop from $last-$n+1 to $last.

Inside the loop, call imap_header( ) to pull out the header information about a post. The header contains all the metainformation but not the actual text of the message; that's stored in the body. Because the header is usually much smaller than the body, this allows you to quickly retrieve data for many posts without taking too much time.

Now pass imap_header( ) two parameters: the server connection handle and the message number. It returns an object with many properties, which are listed in Table 17-2.

Table 17-2. imap_header() fields from a NNTP server

Name	Description	Type	Example
date or Date	RFC 822 formatted date: date('r')	String	Fri, 16 Aug 2002 01:52:24 -0400
subject or Subject	Message subject	String	Re: PHP Cookbook Revisions
message_id	A unique ID identifying the message	String	<20030410020818.33915.php@news.example.com>
newsgroups	The name of the group the message was posted to	String	php.general
toaddress	The address the message was sent to	String	php-general@lists.php.net
to	Parsed version of toaddress field	Object	mailbox: "php-general", host: "lists-php.net"
fromaddress	The address that sent the message	String	Ralph Josephs <ralph@example.net>
from	Parsed version of fromaddress field	Object	personal: "Ralph Josephs", mailbox: "ralph", host: "example.net"
reply_toaddress	The address you should reply to, if you're trying to contact the author	String	rjosephs@example.net
reply_to	Parsed version of reply_toaddress field	Object	Mailbox: "rjosephs", host: "example.net"

Table 17-2. imap_header() fields from a NNTP server (continued)

Name	Description	Type	Example
senderaddress	The person who sent the message; almost always identical to the `from` field, but if the `from` field doesn't uniquely identify who sent the message, this field does	String	Ralph Josephs <ralph@example.net>
sender	Parsed version of `senderaddress` field	Object	Personal: "Ralph Josephs", mailbox: "ralph", host: "example.net"
Recent	If the message is recent, or new since the last time the user checked for mail	String	Y or N
Unseen	If the message is unseen	String	Y or " "
Flagged	If the message is marked	String	Y or " "
Answered	If a reply has been sent to this message	String	Y or " "
Deleted	If the message is deleted	String	Y or " "
Draft	If the message is a draft	String	Y or " "
Size	Size of the message in bytes	String	1345
udate	Unix timestamp of message date	Int	1013480645
Mesgno	The number of the message in the group	String	34943

Some of the more useful fields are: size, subject, the from list, and udate. The size property is the size of the message in bytes; if it's 0, the message was either deleted or otherwise removed. The subject field is the subject of the post. The from list is more complicated. It's an array of objects; each element in the array holds an object with three properties: personal, mailbox and host. The personal field is the name of the poster: Homer Simpson. The mailbox field is the part of the email address before the @ sign: homer. The host is the part of the email address after the @ sign: thesimpsons.com. Usually, there's just one element in the from list array, because a message usually has just one sender.

Pull the $header->from object into $from because PHP can't directly access $header->from[0]->personal due to the array in the middle. Then combine $from[0]->mailbox and $from[0]->host to form the poster's email address. Use the ternary operator to assign the personal field as the poster's name, if one is supplied; otherwise, make it the email address.

The udate field is the posting time as an Unix timestamp. Use date( ) to convert it from seconds to a more human-friendly format.

You can also view a specific posting as follows:

```
// read and display a single message
$header = imap_header($nntp, $msg);
```

```
$subj   = $header->subject;
$from   = $header->from;
$email  = $from[0]->mailbox."@".$from[0]->host;
$name   = $from[0]->personal;
$date   = date('m/d/Y h:i A', $header->udate);
$body   = nl2br(htmlspecialchars(imap_fetchbody($nntp,$msg,1)));

print <<<EOM
<table>
<tr>
    <th align=left>From:</th>
    <td>$name &lt;<a href="mailto:$email">$email</a>&gt;</td>
</tr>
<tr>
    <th align=left>Subject:</th>
    <td>$subj</td>
</tr>
<tr>
    <th align=left>Date:</th>
    <td>$date</td>
</tr>
<tr>
    <td colspan="2">$body</td>
</tr>
</table>
EOM;
```

The code to grab a single message is similar to one that grabs a sequence of message headers. The main difference is that you define a $body variable that's the result of three chained functions. Innermost, you call imap_fetchbody( ) to return the message body; it takes the same parameters as imap_header( ). You pass that to htmlspecialchars( ) to escape any HTML that may interfere with yours. That result then is passed to nl2br( ), which converts all the carriage returns to XHTML <br /> tags; the message should now look correct on a web page.

To disconnect from the IMAP server and close the stream, pass the IMAP connection handle to imap_close( ):

```
// close connection when finished
imap_close($nntp);
```

See Also

Recipe 17.4 for more on posting to newsgroups; documentation on imap_open( ) at *http://www.php.net/imap-open*, imap_header( ) at *http://www.php.net/imap-header*, imap_body( ) at *http://www.php.net/imap-body*, and IMAP in general at *http://www.php.net/imap*; code to read newsgroups in PHP without using IMAP at *http://cvs.php.net/cvs.php/php-news-web*; RFC 977 at *http://www.faqs.org/rfcs/rfc977.html*.

Example 16-2. catalog-compare.php (continued)

```php
require 'pc_MC_Base.php';
require "$base.php";
require "$other.php";

$base_obj = new $base;
$other_obj = new $other;

/* Check for messages in the other class that
 * are the same as the base class or are in
 * the base class but missing from the other class */
foreach ($base_obj->messages as $k => $v) {
    if (isset($other_obj->messages[$k])) {
        if ($v == $other_obj->messages[$k]) {
            print "SAME: $k\n";
        }
    } else {
        print "MISSING: $k\n";
    }
}

/* Check for messages in the other class but missing
 * from the base class */
foreach ($other_obj->messages as $k => $v) {
    if (! isset($base_obj->messages[$k])) {
        print "MISSING (BASE): $k\n";
    }
}
```

To use this program, put each message catalog object in a file with the same name as the object (e.g., the pc_MC_en_US class should be in a file named *pc_MC_en_US.php*, and the pc_MC_es_US class should be in a file named *pc_MC_es_US.php*). You then call the program with the two locale names as arguments on the command line:

```
% php catalog-compare.php en_US es_US
```

In a web context, it can be useful to use a different locale and message catalog on a per-request basis. The locale to use may come from the browser (in an Accept-Language header), or it may be explicitly set by the server (different virtual hosts may be set up to display the same content in different languages). If the same code needs to select a message catalog on a per-request basis, the message catalog class can be instantiated like this:

```php
$classname = "pc_MC_$locale";

require 'pc_MC_Base.php';
require $classname.'.php';

$MC = new $classname;
```

The ftp_put( ) function takes a file on your computer and copies it to the remote server; ftp_get( ) copies a file on the remote server to your computer. In the previous code, $remote is the pathname to the remote file, and $local points at the file on your computer.

There are two final parameters passed to these functions. The FTP_ASCII parameter, used here, transfers the file as if it were ASCII text. Under this option, linefeed endings are automatically converted as you move from one operating system to another. The other option is FTP_BINARY, which is used for nonplaintext files, so no linefeed conversions take place.

Use ftp_fget( ) and ftp_fput( ) to download or upload a file to an existing open file pointer (opened using fopen( )) instead of to a location on the filesystem. For example, here's how to retrieve a file and write it to the existing file pointer, $fp:

```
$fp = fopen($file, 'w');
ftp_fget($c, $fp, $remote, FTP_ASCII)    or die("Can't transfer");
```

Finally, to disconnect from the remote host, call ftp_close( ) to log out:

```
ftp_close($c);                          or die("Can't close");
```

To adjust the amount of seconds the connection takes to time out, use ftp_set_option( ):

```
// Up the time out value to two minutes:
set_time_limit(120)
$c = ftp_connect('ftp.example.com');
ftp_set_option($c, FTP_TIMEOUT_SEC, 120);
```

The default value is 90 seconds; however, the default max_execution_time of a PHP script is 30 seconds. So, if your connection times out too early, be sure to check both values.

To use the cURL extension, you must download cURL from *http://curl.haxx.se/* and set the --with-curl configuration option when building PHP. To use cURL, start by creating a cURL handle with curl_init( ), and then specify what you want to do using curl_setopt( ). The curl_setopt( ) function takes three parameters: a cURL resource, the name of a cURL constant to modify, and value to assign to the second parameter. In the Solution, the CURLOPT_FILE constant is used:

```
$c = curl_init("ftp://$username:$password@ftp.example.com/$remote");
// $local is the location to store file on local client
$fh = fopen($local, 'w') or die($php_errormsg);
curl_setopt($c, CURLOPT_FILE, $fh);
curl_exec($c);
curl_close($c);
```

You pass the URL to use to curl_init( ). Because the URL begins with ftp://, cURL knows to use the FTP protocol. Instead of a separate call to log on to the remote server, you embed the username and password directly into the URL. Next, you set the location to store the file on your server. Now you open a file named $local for writing and pass the file handle to curl_setopt( ) as the value for CURLOPT_FILE. When cURL transfers the file, it automatically writes to the file handle. Once everything is configured, you call curl_exec( ) to initiate the transaction and then curl_close( ) to close the connection.

See Also

Documentation on the FTP extension at *http://www.php.net/ftp* and cURL at *http://www.php.net/curl*; RFC 959 at *http://www.faqs.org/rfcs/rfc969.html*.

17.7 Looking Up Addresses with LDAP

Problem

You want to query an LDAP server for address information.

Solution

Use PHP's LDAP extension:

```
$ds = ldap_connect('ldap.example.com')          or die($php_errormsg);
ldap_bind($ds)                                  or die($php_errormsg);
$sr = ldap_search($ds, 'o=Example Inc., c=US', 'sn=*') or die($php_errormsg);
$e  = ldap_get_entries($ds, $sr)                or die($php_errormsg);

for ($i=0; $i < $e['count']; $i++) {
    echo $info[$i]['cn'][0] . ' (' . $info[$i]['mail'][0] . ')<br>';
}

ldap_close($ds)                                 or die($php_errormsg);
```

Discussion

LDAP stands for Lightweight Directory Access Protocol. An LDAP server stores directory information, such as names and addresses, and allows you to query it for results. In many ways, it's like a database, except that it's optimized for storing information about people.

In addition, instead of the flat structure provided by a database, an LDAP server allows you to organize people in a hierarchical fashion. For example, employees may be divided into marketing, technical, and operations divisions, or they can be split regionally into North America, Europe, and Asia. This makes it easy to find all employees of a particular subset of a company.

When using LDAP, the address repository is called as a *data source*. Each entry in the repository has a globally unique identifier, known as a *distinguished name*. The distinguished name includes both a person's name, but also their company information. For instance, John Q. Smith, who works at Example Inc., a U.S. company has a distinguished name of `cn=John Q. Smith, o=Example Inc., c=US`. In LDAP, `cn` stands for common name, `o` for organization, and `c` for country.

You must enable PHP's LDAP support with `--with-ldap`. You can download an LDAP server from *http://www.openldap.org*. This recipe assumes basic knowledge about LDAP. For more information, read the articles on the O'Reilly Network at *http://www.onlamp.com/topics/apache/ldap*.

Communicating with an LDAP server requires four steps: connecting, authenticating, searching records, and logging off. Besides searching, you can also add, alter, and delete records.

The opening transactions require you to connect to a specific LDAP server and then authenticate yourself in a process known as *binding*:

```
$ds = ldap_connect('ldap.example.com')            or die($php_errormsg);
ldap_bind($ds)                                     or die($php_errormsg);
```

Passing only the connection handle, `$ds`, to `ldap_bind( )` does an anonymous bind. To bind with a specific username and password, pass them as the second and third parameters, like so:

```
ldap_bind($ds, $username, $password)              or die($php_errormsg);
```

Once logged in, you can request information. Because the information is arranged in a hierarchy, you need to indicate the base distinguished name as the second parameter. Finally, you pass in the search criteria. For example, here's how to find all people with a surname of `Jones` at company `Example Inc.` located in the country `US`:

```
$sr = ldap_search($ds, 'o=Example Inc., c=US', 'sn=Jones') or die($php_errormsg);
$e  = ldap_get_entries($ds, $sr)                           or die($php_errormsg);
```

Once `ldap_search( )` returns results, use `ldap_get_entries( )` to retrieve the specific data records. Then iterate through the array of entries, `$e`:

```
for ($i=0; $i < $e['count']; $i++) {
    echo $e[$i]['cn'][0] . ' (' . $e[$i]['mail'][0] . ')<br>';
}
```

Instead of doing `count($e)`, use the precomputed record size located in `$e['count']`. Inside the loop, print the first common name and email address for each record. For example:

```
David Sklar (sklar@example.com)
Adam Trachtenberg (adam@example.com)
```

The `ldap_search( )` function searches the entire tree equal to and below the distinguished name base. To restrict the results to a specific level, use `ldap_list( )`. Because the search takes place over a smaller set of records, `ldap_list( )` can be significantly faster than `ldap_search( )`.

See Also

Recipe 17.7 for authenticating users with LDAP; documentation on LDAP at *http://www.php.net/ldap*; RFC 2251 at *http://www.faqs.org/rfcs/rfc2251.html*.

17.8   Using LDAP for User Authentication

Problem

You want to restrict parts of your site to authenticated users. Instead of verifying people against a database or using HTTP Basic authorization, you want to use an LDAP server. Holding all user information in an LDAP server makes centralized user administration easier.

Solution

Use PEAR's Auth class, which supports LDAP authentication:

```
$options = array('host'     => 'ldap.example.com',
                 'port'     => '389',
                 'base'     => 'o=Example Inc., c=US',
                 'userattr' => 'uid');

$auth = new Auth('LDAP', $options);

// begin validation
// print login screen for anonymous users
$auth->start();

if ($auth->getAuth()) {
    // content for validated users
} else {
    // content for anonymous users
}

// log users out
$auth->logout();
```

Discussion

LDAP servers are designed for address storage, lookup, and retrieval, and so are better to use than standard databases like MySQL or Oracle. LDAP servers are very fast, you can easily implement access control by granting different permissions to different groups of users, and many different programs can query the server. For example, most email clients can use an LDAP server as an address book, so if you address a message to "John Smith," the server replies with John's email address, *jsmith@example.com*.

PEAR's `Auth` class allows you to validate users against files, databases, and LDAP servers. The first parameter is the type of authentication to use, and the second is an array of information on how to validate users. For example:

```
$options = array('host'     => 'ldap.example.com',
                 'port'     => '389',
                 'base'     => 'o=Example Inc., c=US',
                 'userattr' => 'uid');

$auth = new Auth('LDAP', $options);
```

This creates a new `Auth` object that validates against an LDAP server located at *ldap.example.com* and communicates over port 389. The base directory name is `o=Example Inc., c=US`, and usernames are checked against the `uid` attribute. The `uid` field stands for user identifier. This is normally a username for a web site or a login name for a general account. If your server doesn't store `uid` attributes for each user, you can substitute the `cn` attribute. The common name field holds a user's full name, such as "John Q. Smith."

The `Auth::auth()` method also takes an optional third parameter—the name of a function that displays the sign-in form. This form can be formatted however you wish; the only requirement is that the form input fields must be called `username` and `password`. Also, the form must submit the data using POST.

```
$options = array('host'     => 'ldap.example.com',
                 'port'     => '389',
                 'base'     => 'o=Example Inc., c=US',
                 'userattr' => 'uid');

function pc_auth_ldap_signin() {
    print<<<_HTML_
<form method="post" action="$_SERVER[PHP_SELF]">
Name: <input name="username" type="text"><br />
Password: <input name="password" type="password"><br />
<input type="submit" value="Sign In">
</form>
_HTML_;
}

$auth = new Auth('LDAP', $options, 'pc_auth_ldap_signin');
```

Once the `Auth` object is instantiated, authenticate a user by calling `Auth::start()`:

```
$auth->start();
```

If the user is already signed in, nothing happens. If the user is anonymous, the sign-in form is printed. To validate a user, `Auth::start()` connects to the LDAP server, does an anonymous bind, and searches for an address in which the user attribute specified in the constructor matches the username passed in by the form:

```
$options['userattr'] == $_POST['username']
```

If `Auth::start( )` finds exactly one person that fits this criteria, it retrieves the designated name for the user, and attempts to do an authenticated bind, using the designated name and password from the form as the login credentials. The LDAP server then compares the password to the `userPassword` attribute associated with the designated name. If it matches, the user is authenticated.

You can call `Auth::getAuth( )` to return a boolean value describing a user's status:

```
if ($auth->getAuth( )) {
    print 'Welcome member! Nice to see you again.';
} else {
    print 'Welcome guest. First time visiting?';
}
```

The `Auth` class uses the built-in session module to track users, so once validated, a person remains authenticated until the session expires, or you explicitly log them out with:

```
$auth->logout( );
```

See Also

Recipe 17.7 for searching LDAP servers; PEAR's `Auth` class at *http://pear.php.net/package-info.php?package=Auth*.

17.9   Performing DNS Lookups

Problem

You want to look up a domain name or an IP address.

Solution

Use gethostbyname( ) and gethostbyaddr( ):

```
$ip   = gethostbyname('www.example.com'); // 192.0.34.72
$host = gethostbyaddr('192.0.34.72'); // www.example.com
```

Discussion

You can't trust the name returned by gethostbyaddr( ). A DNS server with authority for a particular IP address can return any hostname at all. Usually, administrators set up DNS servers to reply with a correct hostname, but a malicious user may configure her DNS server to reply with incorrect hostnames. One way to combat this trickery is to call gethostbyname( ) on the hostname returned from gethostbyaddr( ) and make sure the name resolves to the original IP address.

If either function can't successfully look up the IP address or the domain name, it doesn't return false, but instead returns the argument passed to it. To check for failure, do this:

```
if ($host == ($ip = gethostbyname($host))) {
    // failure
}
```

This assigns the return value of gethostbyname( ) to $ip and also checks that $ip is not equal to the original $host.

Sometimes a single hostname can map to multiple IP addresses. To find all hosts, use gethostbynamel( ):

```
$hosts = gethostbynamel('www.yahoo.com');
print_r($hosts);
Array
(
    [0] => 64.58.76.176
    [1] => 64.58.76.224
    [2] => 64.58.76.177
    [3] => 64.58.76.227
    [4] => 64.58.76.179
    [5] => 64.58.76.225
    [6] => 64.58.76.178
    [7] => 64.58.76.229
    [8] => 64.58.76.223
)
```

In contrast to gethostbyname( ) and gethostbyaddr( ), gethostbynamel( ) returns an array, not a string.

You can also do more complicated DNS-related tasks. For instance, you can get the MX records using getmxrr( ):

```
getmxrr('yahoo.com', $hosts, $weight);
for ($i = 0; $i < count($hosts); $i++) {
    echo "$weight[$i] $hosts[$i]\n";
}
5 mx4.mail.yahoo.com
1 mx2.mail.yahoo.com
1 mx1.mail.yahoo.com
```

To perform zone transfers, dynamic DNS updates, and more, see PEAR's Net_DNS package.

See Also

Documentation on gethostbyname( ) at *http://www.php.net/gethostbyname*, gethostbyaddr( ) *http://www.php.net/gethostbyaddr*, gethostbynamel( ) at *http://www.php.net/gethostbynamel*, and getmxrr( ) at *http://www.php.net/getmxrr*; PEAR's Net_DNS package at *http://pear.php.net/package-info.php?package=Net_DNS*; *DNS and BIND* by Paul Albitz and Cricket Liu (O'Reilly) .

17.10 Checking if a Host Is Alive

Problem

You want to ping a host to see if it is still up and accessible from your location.

Solution

Use PEAR's Net_Ping package:

```
require 'Net/Ping.php';

$ping = new Net_Ping;
if ($ping->checkhost('www.oreilly.com')) {
    print 'Reachable';
} else {
    print 'Unreachable';
}

$data = $ping->ping('www.oreilly.com');
```

Discussion

The *ping* program tries to send a message from your machine to another. If everything goes well, you get a series of statistics chronicling the transaction. An error means that *ping* can't reach the host for some reason.

On error, Net_Ping::checkhost( ) returns false, and Net_Ping::ping( ) returns the constant PING_HOST_NOT_FOUND. If there's a problem running the *ping* program (because Net_Ping is really just a wrapper for the program), PING_FAILED is returned.

If everything is okay, you receive an array similar to this:

```
$results = $ping->ping('www.oreilly.com');

foreach($results as $result) { print "$result\n"; }
PING www.oreilly.com (209.204.146.22) from 192.168.123.101 :
    32(60) bytes of data.
40 bytes from www.oreilly.com (209.204.146.22): icmp_seq=0 ttl=239
    time=96.704 msec
40 bytes from www.oreilly.com (209.204.146.22): icmp_seq=1 ttl=239
    time=86.567 msec
40 bytes from www.oreilly.com (209.204.146.22): icmp_seq=2 ttl=239
    time=86.563 msec
40 bytes from www.oreilly.com (209.204.146.22): icmp_seq=3 ttl=239
    time=136.565 msec
40 bytes from www.oreilly.com (209.204.146.22): icmp_seq=4 ttl=239
    time=86.627 msec
```

```
--- www.oreilly.com ping statistics ---
5 packets transmitted, 5 packets received, 0% packet loss
round-trip min/avg/max/mdev = 86.563/98.605/136.565/19.381 ms
```

Net_Ping doesn't do any parsing of the data to pull apart the information, such as the packet loss percentage or the average round-trip time. However, you can parse it yourself:

```
$results = $ping->ping('www.oreilly.com');

// grab last line of array; equivalent to non-destructive array_pop()
// or $results[count($results) - 1]
$round_trip = end($results);
preg_match_all('#[ /]([.\d]+)#', $round_trip, $times);

// pull out the data
list($min,$avg,$max,$mdev) = $times[1];
// or print it out
foreach($times[1] as $time) { print "$time\n"; }
83.229
91.230
103.223
7.485
```

This regular expression searches for either a space or a slash. It then captures a sequence of one or more numbers and a decimal point. To avoid escaping /, we use the # nonstandard character as your delimiter.

See Also

PEAR's Net_Ping package at *http://pear.php.net/package-info.php?package=Net_Ping*.

17.11 Getting Information About a Domain Name

Problem

You want to look up contact information or other details about a domain name.

Solution

Use PEAR's Net_Whois class:

```
require 'Net/Whois.php';
$server = 'whois.networksolutions.com';
$query  = 'example.org';
$data = Net_Whois::query($server, $query);
```

Discussion

The Net_Whois::query( ) method returns a large text string whose contents reinforce how hard it can be to parse different Whois results:

```
Registrant:
Internet Assigned Numbers Authority (EXAMPLE2-DOM)
    4676 Admiralty Way, Suite 330
    Marina del Rey, CA 90292
    US

    Domain Name: EXAMPLE.ORG

    Administrative Contact, Technical Contact, Billing Contact:
        Internet Assigned Numbers Authority  (IANA)  iana@IANA.ORG
        4676 Admiralty Way, Suite 330
        Marina del Rey, CA 90292
        US
        310-823-9358
        Fax- 310-823-8649

    Record last updated on 07-Jan-2002.
    Record expires on 01-Sep-2009.
    Record created on 31-Aug-1995.
    Database last updated on 6-Apr-2002 02:56:00 EST.

    Domain servers in listed order:

    A.IANA-SERVERS.NET               192.0.34.43
    B.IANA-SERVERS.NET               193.0.0.236
```

For instance, if you want to parse out the names and IP addresses of the domain name servers, use this:

```
preg_match_all('/^\s*([\S]+)\s+([\d.]+)\s*$/m', $data, $dns,
               PREG_SET_ORDER);

foreach ($dns as $server) {
    print "$server[1] : $server[2]\n";
}
```

You must set $server to the correct Whois server for a domain to get information about that domain. If you don't know the server to use, query *whois.internic.net*:

```
require 'Net/Whois.php';

print Net_Whois::query('whois.internic.net','example.org');
[whois.internic.net]

Whois Server Version 1.3

Domain names in the .com, .net, and .org domains can now be registered
with many different competing registrars. Go to http://www.internic.net
for detailed information.
```

```
Domain Name: EXAMPLE.ORG
Registrar: NETWORK SOLUTIONS, INC.
Whois Server: whois.networksolutions.com
Referral URL: http://www.networksolutions.com
Name Server: A.IANA-SERVERS.NET
Name Server: B.IANA-SERVERS.NET
Updated Date: 19-aug-2002


>>> Last update of whois database: Wed, 21 Aug 2002 04:56:56 EDT <<<

The Registry database contains ONLY .COM, .NET, .ORG, .EDU domains and
Registrars.
```

The "Whois Server:" line says that the correct server to ask for information about *example.org* is *whois.networksolutions.com*.

See Also

PEAR's Net_Whois class at *http://pear.php.net/package-info.php?package=Net_Whois*.

CHAPTER 18

Files

18.0 Introduction

The input and output in a web application usually flow between browser, server, and database, but there are many circumstances in which files are involved too. Files are useful for retrieving remote web pages for local processing, storing data without a database, and saving information that other programs need access to. Plus, as PHP becomes a tool for more than just pumping out web pages, the file I/O functions are even more useful.

PHP's interface for file I/O is similar to C's, although less complicated. The fundamental unit of identifying a file to read from or write to is a *file handle*. This handle identifies your connection to a specific file, and you use it for operations on the file. This chapter focuses on opening and closing files and manipulating file handles in PHP, as well as what you can do with the file contents once you've opened a file. Chapter 19 deals with directories and file metadata such as permissions.

Opening */tmp/cookie-data* and writing the contents of a specific cookie to the file looks like this:

```
$fh = fopen('/tmp/cookie-data','w')      or die("can't open file");
if (-1 == fwrite($fh,$_COOKIE['flavor'])) { die("can't write data"); }
fclose($fh)                              or die("can't close file");
```

The function fopen() returns a file handle if its attempt to open the file is successful. If it can't open the file (because of incorrect permissions, for example), it returns false. Recipes 18.1 and 18.3 cover ways to open files.

The function fwrite() writes the value of the flavor cookie to the file handle. It returns the number of bytes written. If it can't write the string (not enough disk space, for example), it returns –1.

Last, fclose() closes the file handle. This is done automatically at the end of a request, but it's a good idea to explicitly close all files you open anyway. It prevents problems using the code in a command-line context and frees up system resources. It also allows you to check the return code from fclose(). Buffered data might not be actually written to disk until fclose() is called, so it's here that "disk full" errors are sometimes reported.

As with other processes, PHP must have the correct permissions to read from and write to a file. This is usually straightforward in a command-line context but can cause confusion when running scripts within a web server. Your web server (and consequently your PHP scripts) probably runs as a specific user dedicated to web serving (or perhaps as user nobody). For good security reasons, this user often has restricted permissions on what files it can access. If your script is having trouble with a file operation, make sure the web server's user or group—not yours—has permission to perform that file operation. Some web serving setups may run your script as you, though, in which case you need to make sure that your scripts can't accidentally read or write personal files that aren't part of your web site.

Because most file-handling functions just return false on error, you have to do some additional work to find more details about that error. When the track_errors configuration directive is on, each error message is put in the global variable $php_errormsg. Including this variable as part of your error output makes debugging easier:

```
$fh = fopen('/tmp/cookie-data','w')       or die("can't open: $php_errormsg");
if (-1 == fwrite($fh,$_COOKIE['flavor'])) { die("can't write: $php_errormsg") };
fclose($fh)                               or die("can't close: $php_errormsg");
```

If you don't have permission to write to the */tmp/cookie-data*, the example dies with this error output:

```
can't open: fopen("/tmp/cookie-data", "w") - Permission denied
```

There are differences in how files are treated by Windows and by Unix. To ensure your file access code works appropriately on Unix and Windows, take care to handle line-delimiter characters and pathnames correctly.

A line delimiter on Windows is two characters: ASCII 13 (carriage return) followed by ASCII 10 (linefeed or newline). On Unix, it's just ASCII 10. The typewriter-era names for these characters explain why you can get "stair-stepped" text when printing out a Unix-delimited file. Imagine these character names as commands to the platen in a typewriter or character-at-a-time printer. A carriage return sends the platen back to the beginning of the line it's on, and a line feed advances the paper by one line. A misconfigured printer encountering a Unix-delimited file dutifully follows instructions and does a linefeed at the end of each line. This advances to the next line but doesn't move the horizontal printing position back to the left margin. The next stair-stepped line of text begins (horizontally) where the previous line left off.

PHP functions that use a newline as a line-ending delimiter (for example, fgets()) work on both Windows and Unix because a newline is the character at the end of the line on either platform.

To remove any line-delimiter characters, use the PHP function `rtrim()`:

```
$fh = fopen('/tmp/lines-of-data.txt','r') or die($php_errormsg);
while($s = fgets($fh,1024)) {
    $s = rtrim($s);
    // do something with $s ...
}
fclose($fh)                            or die($php_errormsg);
```

This function removes any trailing whitespace in the line, including ASCII 13 and ASCII 10 (as well as tab and space). If there's whitespace at the end of a line that you want to preserve, but you still want to remove carriage returns and line feeds, use an appropriate regular expression:

```
$fh = fopen('/tmp/lines-of-data.txt','r') or die($php_errormsg);
while($s = fgets($fh,1024)) {
    $s = preg_replace('/\r?\n$/','',$s);
    // do something with $s ...
}
fclose($fh)                            or die($php_errormsg);
```

Unix and Windows also differ on the character used to separate directories in pathnames. Unix uses a slash (/), and Windows uses a backslash (\). PHP makes sorting this out easy, however, because the Windows version of PHP also understands / as a directory separator. For example, this code successfully prints the contents of *C:\Alligator\Crocodile Menu.txt*:

```
$fh = fopen('c:/alligator/crocodile menu.txt','r') or die($php_errormsg);
while($s = fgets($fh,1024)) {
    print $s;
}
fclose($fh)                                     or die($php_errormsg);
```

This piece of code also takes advantage of the fact that Windows filenames aren't case-sensitive. However, Unix filenames are.

Sorting out linebreak confusion isn't only a problem in your code that reads and writes files but in your source code as well. If you have multiple people working on a project, make sure all developers configure their editors to use the same kind of linebreaks.

Once you've opened a file, PHP gives you many tools to process its data. In keeping with PHP's C-like I/O interface, the two basic functions to read data from a file are `fread()`, which reads a specified number of bytes, and `fgets()`, which reads a line at a time (up to a specified number of bytes.) This code handles lines up to 256 bytes long:

```
$fh = fopen('orders.txt','r') or die($php_errormsg);
while (! feof($fh)) {
    $s = fgets($fh,256);
    process_order($s);
}
fclose($fh) or die($php_errormsg);
```

If *orders.txt* has a 300-byte line, fgets() returns only the first 256 bytes. The next fgets() returns the next 44 bytes and stops when it finds the newline. The next fgets() moves to the next line of the file. Examples in this chapter generally give fgets() a second argument of 1048576: 1 MB. This is longer than lines in most text files, but the presence of such an outlandish number should serve as a reminder to consider your maximum expected line length when using fgets().

Many operations on file contents, such as picking a line at random (see Recipe 18.10) are conceptually simpler (and require less code) if the entire file is read into a string or array. Recipe 18.5 provides a method for reading a file into a string, and the file() function puts each line of a file into an array. The tradeoff for simplicity, however, is memory consumption. This can be especially harmful when you are using PHP as a server module. Generally, when a process (such as a web server process with PHP embedded in it) allocates memory (as PHP does to read an entire file into a string or array), it can't return that memory to the operating system until it dies. This means that calling file() on a 1 MB file from PHP running as an Apache module increases the size of that Apache process by 1 MB until the process dies. Repeated a few times, this decreases server efficiency. There are certainly good reasons for processing an entire file at once, but be conscious of the memory-use implications when you do.

Recipes 18.20 through 18.23 deal with running other programs from within a PHP program. Some program-execution operators or functions offer ways to run a program and read its output all at once (backticks) or read its last line of output (system()). PHP can use pipes to run a program, pass it input, or read its output. Because a pipe is read with standard I/O functions (fgets() and fread()), you decide how you want the input and you can do other tasks between reading chunks of input. Similarly, writing to a pipe is done with fputs() and fwrite(), so you can pass input to a program in arbitrary increments.

Pipes have the same permission issues as regular files. The PHP process must have execute permission on the program being opened as a pipe. If you have trouble opening a pipe, especially if PHP is running as a special web server user, make sure the user is allowed to execute the program you are opening a pipe to.

18.1 Creating or Opening a Local File

Problem

You want to open a local file to read data from it or write data to it.

Solution

Use fopen( ):

```
$fh = fopen('file.txt','r') or die("can't open file.txt: $php_errormsg");
```

Discussion

The first argument to fopen( ) is the file to open; the second argument is the mode to open the file in. The mode specifies what operations can be performed on the file (reading and/or writing), where the file pointer is placed after the file is opened (at the beginning or end of the file), whether the file is truncated to zero length after opening, and whether the file is created if it doesn't exist, as shown in Table 18-1.

Table 18-1. fopen() file modes

Mode	Readable?	Writeable?	File pointer	Truncate?	Create?
r	Yes	No	Beginning	No	No
r+	Yes	Yes	Beginning	No	No
w	No	Yes	Beginning	Yes	Yes
w+	Yes	Yes	Beginning	Yes	Yes
a	No	Yes	End	No	Yes
a+	Yes	Yes	End	No	Yes

On non-POSIX systems, such as Windows, you need to add a b to the mode when opening a binary file, or reads and writes get tripped up on NUL (ASCII 0) characters:

```
$fh = fopen('c:/images/logo.gif','rb');
```

To operate on a file, pass the file handle returned from fopen( ) to other I/O functions such as fgets( ), fputs( ), and fclose( ).

If the file given to fopen( ) doesn't have a pathname, the file is opened in the directory of the running script (web context) or in the current directory (command-line context).

You can also tell fopen( ) to search for the file to open in the include_path specified in your *php.ini* file by passing 1 as a third argument. For example, this searches for *file.inc* in the include_path:

```
$fh = fopen('file.inc','r',1) or die("can't open file.inc: $php_errormsg");
```

See Also

Documentation on fopen( ) at *http://www.php.net/fopen*.

18.2 Creating a Temporary File

Problem

You need a file to temporarily hold some data.

Solution

Use tmpfile() if the file needs to last only the duration of the running script:

```
$temp_fh = tmpfile();
// write some data to the temp file
fputs($temp_fh,"The current time is ".strftime('%c'));
// the file goes away when the script ends
exit(1);
```

If the file needs to last longer, generate a filename with tempnam(), and then use fopen():

```
$tempfilename = tempnam('/tmp','data-');
$temp_fh = fopen($tempfilename,'w') or die($php_errormsg);
fputs($temp_fh,"The current time is ".strftime('%c'));
fclose($temp_fh) or die($php_errormsg);
```

Discussion

The function tmpfile() creates a file with a unique name and returns a file handle. The file is removed when fclose() is called on that file handle, or the script ends.

Alternatively, tempnam() generates a filename. It takes two arguments: the first is a directory, and the second is a prefix for the filename. If the directory doesn't exist or isn't writeable, tempnam() uses the system temporary directory—the TMPDIR environment variable in Unix or the TMP environment variable in Windows. For example:

```
$tempfilename = tempnam('/tmp','data-');
print "Temporary data will be stored in $tempfilename";
Temporary data will be stored in /tmp/data-GawVoL
```

Because of the way PHP generates temporary filenames, the filename tempnam() returns is actually created but left empty, even if your script never explicitly opens the file. This ensures another program won't create a file with the same name between the time that you call tempnam() and the time you call fopen() with the filename.

See Also

Documentation on tmpfile() at *http://www.php.net/tmpfile* and on tempnam() at *http://www.php.net/tempnam*.

18.3   Opening a Remote File

Problem

You want to open a file that's accessible to you via HTTP or FTP.

Solution

Pass the file's URL to fopen():

```
$fh = fopen('http://www.example.com/robots.txt','r') or die($php_errormsg);
```

Discussion

When fopen() is passed a filename that begins with *http://*, it retrieves the given page with an HTTP/1.0 GET request (although a Host: header is also passed along to deal with virtual hosts). Only the body of the reply can be accessed using the file handle, not the headers. Files can be read, not written, via HTTP.

When fopen() is passed a filename that begins with *ftp://*, it returns a pointer to the specified file, obtained via passive mode FTP. You can open files via FTP for either reading or writing, but not both.

To open URLs that require a username and a password with fopen(), embed the authentication information in the URL like this:

```
$fh = fopen('ftp://username:password@ftp.example.com/pub/Index','r');
$fh = fopen('http://username:password@www.example.com/robots.txt','r');
```

Opening remote files with fopen() is implemented via a PHP feature called the *URL fopen wrapper*. It's enabled by default but is disabled by setting allow_url_fopen to off in your *php.ini* or web server configuration file. If you can't open remote files with fopen(), check your server configuration.

See Also

Recipes 11.1 through 11.5, which discuss retrieving URLs; documentation on fopen() at *http://www.php.net/fopen* and on the URL fopen wrapper feature at *http://www.php.net/features.remote-files*.

18.4   Reading from Standard Input

Problem

You want to read from standard input.

Solution

Use fopen( ) to open *php://stdin*:

```
$fh = fopen('php://stdin','r') or die($php_errormsg);
while($s = fgets($fh,1024)) {
    print "You typed: $s";
}
```

Discussion

Recipe 20.3 discusses reading data from the keyboard in a command-line context. Reading data from standard input isn't very useful in a web context, because information doesn't arrive via standard input. The bodies of HTTP POST and file-upload requests are parsed by PHP and put into special variables. They can't be read on standard input, as they can in some web server and CGI implementations.

See Also

Recipe 20.3 for reading from the keyboard in a command-line context; documentation on fopen( ) at *http://www.php.net/fopen*.

18.5   Reading a File into a String

Problem

You want to load the entire contents of a file into a variable. For example, you want to determine if the text in a file matches a regular expression.

Solution

Use filesize( ) to get the size of the file, and then tell fread( ) to read that many bytes:

```
$fh = fopen('people.txt','r') or die($php_errormsg);
$people = fread($fh,filesize('people.txt'));
if (preg_match('/Names:.*(David|Susannah)/i',$people)) {
    print "people.txt matches.";
}
fclose($fh) or die($php_errormsg);
```

Discussion

To read a binary file (e.g., an image) on Windows, a b must be appended to the file mode:

```
$fh = fopen('people.jpg','rb') or die($php_errormsg);
$people = fread($fh,filesize('people.jpg'));
fclose($fh);
```

There are easier ways to print the entire contents of a file than by reading it into a string and then printing the string. PHP provides two functions for this. The first is fpassthru($fh), which prints everything left on the file handle $fh and then closes it. The second, readfile($filename), prints the entire contents of $filename.

You can use readfile() to implement a wrapper around images that shouldn't always be displayed. This program makes sure a requested image is less than a week old:

```
$image_directory = '/usr/local/images';

if (preg_match('/^[a-zA-Z0-9]+\.(gif|jpeg)$/',$image,$matches) &&
    is_readable($image_directory."/$image") &&
    (filemtime($image_directory."/$image") >= (time() - 86400 * 7))) {

  header('Content-Type: image/'.$matches[1]);
  header('Content-Length: '.filesize($image_directory."/$image"));

  readfile($image_directory."/$image");

} else {
  error_log("Can't serve image: $image");
}
```

The directory in which the images are stored, $image_directory, needs to be outside the web server's document root for the wrapper to be effective. Otherwise, users can just access the image files directly. You test the image for three things. First, that the filename passed in $image is just alphanumeric with an ending of either *.gif* or *.jpeg*. You need to ensure that characters such as .. or / are not in the filename; this prevents malicious users from retrieving files outside the specified directory. Second, use is_readable() to make sure you can read the file. Finally, get the file's modification time with filemtime() and make sure that time is after 86400 × 7 seconds ago. There are 86,400 seconds in a day, so 86400 × 7 is a week.* If all of these conditions are met, you're ready to send the image. First, send two headers to tell the browser the image's MIME type and file size. Then use readfile() to send the entire contents of the file to the user.

---

* When switching between standard time and daylight saving time, there are not 86,400 seconds in a day. See Recipe 3.10 for details.

See Also

Documentation on `filesize()` at *http://www.php.net/filesize*, `fread()` at *http://www.php.net/fread*, `fpassthru()` at *http://www.php.net/fpassthru*, and `readfile()` at *http://www.php.net/readfile*.

18.6 Counting Lines, Paragraphs, or Records in a File

Problem

You want to count the number of lines, paragraphs, or records in a file.

Solution

To count lines, use `fgets()`. Because it reads a line at a time, you can count the number of times it's called before reaching the end of a file:

```
$lines = 0;

if ($fh = fopen('orders.txt','r')) {
  while (! feof($fh)) {
    if (fgets($fh,1048576)) {
      $lines++;
    }
  }
}
print $lines;
```

To count paragraphs, increment the counter only when you read a blank line:

```
$paragraphs = 0;

if ($fh = fopen('great-american-novel.txt','r')) {
  while (! feof($fh)) {
    $s = fgets($fh,1048576);
    if (("\n" == $s) || ("\r\n" == $s)) {
      $paragraphs++;
    }
  }
}
print $paragraphs;
```

To count records, increment the counter only when the line read contains just the record separator and whitespace:

```
$records = 0;
$record_separator = '--end--';
```

```
if ($fh = fopen('great-american-novel.txt','r')) {
  while (! feof($fh)) {
    $s = rtrim(fgets($fh,1048576));
    if ($s == $record_separator) {
      $records++;
    }
  }
}
print $records;
```

Discussion

In the line counter, $lines is incremented only if fgets() returns a true value. As fgets() moves through the file, it returns each line it retrieves. When it reaches the last line, it returns false, so $lines doesn't get incorrectly incremented. Because EOF has been reached on the file, feof() returns true, and the while loop ends.

This paragraph counter works fine on simple text but may produce unexpected results when presented with a long string of blank lines or a file without two consecutive linebreaks. These problems can be remedied with functions based on preg_split(). If the file is small and can be read into memory, use the pc_split_paragraphs() function shown in Example 18-1. This function returns an array containing each paragraph in the file.

Example 18-1. pc_split_paragraphs()

```
function pc_split_paragraphs($file,$rs="\r?\n") {
    $text = join('',file($file));
    $matches = preg_split("/(.*?$rs)(?:$rs)+/s",$text,-1,
                        PREG_SPLIT_DELIM_CAPTURE|PREG_SPLIT_NO_EMPTY);
    return $matches;
}
```

The contents of the file are broken on two or more consecutive newlines and returned in the $matches array. The default record-separation regular expression, \r?\n, matches both Windows and Unix linebreaks. If the file is too big to read into memory at once, use the pc_split_paragraphs_largefile() function shown in Example 18-2, which reads the file in 4K chunks.

Example 18-2. pc_split_paragraphs_largefile()

```
function pc_split_paragraphs_largefile($file,$rs="\r?\n") {
    global $php_errormsg;

    $unmatched_text = '';
    $paragraphs = array();

    $fh = fopen($file,'r') or die($php_errormsg);
```

Example 18-2. pc_split_paragraphs_largefile() (continued)

```
while(! feof($fh)) {
    $s = fread($fh,4096) or die($php_errormsg);
    $text_to_split = $unmatched_text . $s;

    $matches = preg_split("/(.*?$rs)(?:$rs)+/s",$text_to_split,-1,
                        PREG_SPLIT_DELIM_CAPTURE|PREG_SPLIT_NO_EMPTY);

    // if the last chunk doesn't end with two record separators, save it
     * to prepend to the next section that gets read
    $last_match = $matches[count($matches)-1];
    if (! preg_match("/$rs$rs\$/",$last_match)) {
        $unmatched_text = $last_match;
        array_pop($matches);
    } else {
        $unmatched_text = '';
    }

    $paragraphs = array_merge($paragraphs,$matches);
}

// after reading all sections, if there is a final chunk that doesn't
 * end with the record separator, count it as a paragraph
if ($unmatched_text) {
    $paragraphs[] = $unmatched_text;
}
return $paragraphs;
}
```

This function uses the same regular expression as pc_split_paragraphs() to split the file into paragraphs. When it finds a paragraph end in a chunk read from the file, it saves the rest of the text in the chunk in $unmatched_text and prepends it to the next chunk read. This includes the unmatched text as the beginning of the next paragraph in the file.

See Also

Documentation on fgets() at *http://www.php.net/fgets*, on feof() at *http://www.php.net/feof*, and on preg_split() at *http://www.php.net/preg-split*.

18.7   Processing Every Word in a File

Problem

You want to do something with every word in a file.

Solution

Read in each line with fgets( ), separate the line into words, and process each word:

```
$fh = fopen('great-american-novel.txt','r') or die($php_errormsg);
while (! feof($fh)) {
    if ($s = fgets($fh,1048576)) {
        $words = preg_split('/\s+/',$s,-1,PREG_SPLIT_NO_EMPTY);
        // process words
    }
}
fclose($fh) or die($php_errormsg);
```

Discussion

Here's how to calculate average word length in a file:

```
$word_count = $word_length = 0;

if ($fh = fopen('great-american-novel.txt','r')) {
  while (! feof($fh)) {
    if ($s = fgets($fh,1048576)) {
      $words = preg_split('/\s+/',$s,-1,PREG_SPLIT_NO_EMPTY);
      foreach ($words as $word) {
        $word_count++;
        $word_length += strlen($word);
      }
    }
  }
}

print sprintf("The average word length over %d words is %.02f characters.",
              $word_count,
              $word_length/$word_count);
```

Processing every word proceeds differently depending on how "word" is defined. The code in this recipe uses the Perl-compatible regular-expression engine's \s whitespace metacharacter, which includes space, tab, newline, carriage return, and formfeed. Recipe 2.5 breaks apart a line into words by splitting on a space, which is useful in that recipe because the words have to be rejoined with spaces. The Perl-compatible engine also has a word-boundary assertion (\b) that matches between a word character (alphanumeric) and a nonword character (anything else). Using \b instead of \s to delimit words most noticeably treats differently words with embedded punctuation. The term 6 o'clock is two words when split by whitespace (6 and o'clock); it's four words when split by word boundaries (6, o, ', and clock).

See Also

Recipe 13.2 discusses regular expressions to match words; Recipe 1.4 for breaking apart a line by words; documentation on fgets( ) at *http://www.php.net/fgets*, on

---

preg_split() at *http://www.php.net/preg-split*, and on the Perl-compatible regular expression extension at *http://www.php.net/pcre*.

18.8 Reading a Particular Line in a File

Problem

You want to read a specific line in a file; for example, you want to read the most recent guestbook entry that's been added on to the end of a guestbook file.

Solution

If the file fits into memory, read the file into an array and then select the appropriate array element:

```
$lines = file('vacation-hotspots.txt');
print $lines[2];
```

Discussion

Because array indexes start at 0, $lines[2] refers to the third line of the file.

If the file is too big to read into an array, read it line by line and keep track of which line you're on:

```
$line_counter = 0;
$desired_line = 29;

$fh = fopen('vacation-hotspots.txt','r') or die($php_errormsg);
while ((! feof($fh)) && ($line_counter <= $desired_line)) {
    if ($s = fgets($fh,1048576)) {
        $line_counter++;
    }
}
fclose($fh) or die($php_errormsg);

print $s;
```

Setting $desired_line = 29 prints the 30th line of the file, to be consistent with the code in the Solution. To print the 29th line of the file, change the while loop line to:

```
while ((! feof($fh)) && ($line_counter < $desired_line)) {
```

See Also

Documentation on fgets() at *http://www.php.net/fgets* and feof() at *http://www.php.net/feof*.

18.9   Processing a File Backward by Line or Paragraph

Problem

You want to do something with each line of a file, starting at the end. For example, it's easy to add new guestbook entries to the end of a file by opening in append mode, but you want to display the entries with the most recent first, so you need to process the file starting at the end.

Solution

If the file fits in memory, use `file()` to read each line in the file into an array and then reverse the array:

```
$lines = file('guestbook.txt');
$lines = array_reverse($lines);
```

Discussion

You can also iterate through an unreversed array of lines starting at the end. Here's how to print out the last 10 lines in a file, last line first:

```
$lines = file('guestbook.txt');
for ($i = 0, $j = count($lines); $i <= 10; $i++) {
    print $lines[$j - $i];
}
```

See Also

Documentation on `file()` at *http://www.php.net/file* and `array_reverse()` at *http://www.php.net/array-reverse*.

18.10 Picking a Random Line from a File

Problem

You want to pick a line at random from a file; for example, you want to display a selection from a file of sayings.

Solution

Use the `pc_randomint()` function shown in Example 18-3, which spreads the selection odds evenly over all lines in a file.

Example 18-3. pc_randomint()

```
function pc_randomint($max = 1) {
  $m = 1000000;
  return ((mt_rand(1,$m * $max)-1)/$m);
}
```

Here's an example that uses the pc_randomint( ) function:

```
$line_number = 0;

$fh = fopen('sayings.txt','r') or die($php_errormsg);
while (! feof($fh)) {
    if ($s = fgets($fh,1048576)) {
        $line_number++;
        if (pc_randomint($line_number) < 1) {
            $line = $s;
        }
    }
}
fclose($fh) or die($php_errormsg);
```

Discussion

The pc_randomint( ) function computes a random decimal number between 0 and $max, including 0 but excluding $max. As each line is read, a line counter is incremented, and pc_randomint( ) generates a random number between 0 and $line_number. If the number is less than 1, the current line is selected as the randomly chosen line. After all lines have been read, the last line that was selected as the randomly chosen line is left in $line.

This algorithm neatly ensures that each line in an n line file has a $1/n$ chance of being chosen without having to store all n lines into memory.

See Also

Documentation on mt_rand( ) at *http://www.php.net/mt-rand.*

18.11 Randomizing All Lines in a File

Problem

You want to randomly reorder all lines in a file. You have a file of funny quotes, for example, and you want to pick out one at random.

Solution

Read all the lines in the file into an array with file(), and then shuffle the elements of the array:

```
$lines = file('quotes-of-the-day.txt');
$lines = pc_array_shuffle($lines);
```

Discussion

The pc_array_shuffle() function from Recipe 4.20 is more random than PHP's built-in shuffle() function, because it uses the Fisher-Yates shuffle, which equally distributes the elements throughout the array.

See Also

Recipe 4.19 for pc_array_shuffle(); documentation on shuffle() at *http://www.php.net/shuffle*.

18.12 Processing Variable Length Text Fields

Problem

You want to read delimited text fields from a file. You might, for example, have a database program that prints records one per line, with tabs between each field in the record, and you want to parse this data into an array.

Solution

Read in each line and then split the fields based on their delimiter:

```
$delim = '|';

$fh = fopen('books.txt','r') or die("can't open: $php_errormsg");
while (! feof($fh)) {
    $s = rtrim(fgets($fh,1024));
    $fields = explode($delim,$s);
    // ... do something with the data ...
}
fclose($fh) or die("can't close: $php_errormsg");
```

Discussion

To parse the following data in *books.txt*:

```
Elmer Gantry|Sinclair Lewis|1927
The Scarlatti Inheritance|Robert Ludlum|1971
```

```
The Parsifal Mosaic|Robert Ludlum|1982
Sophie's Choice|William Styron|1979
```

Process each record like this:

```
$fh = fopen('books.txt','r') or die("can't open: $php_errormsg");
while (! feof($fh)) {
    $s = rtrim(fgets($fh,1024));
    list($title,$author,$publication_year) = explode('|',$s);
    // ... do something with the data ...
}
fclose($fh) or die("can't close: $php_errormsg");
```

The line length argument to fgets() needs to be at least as long as the longest record, so that a record doesn't get truncated.

Calling rtrim() is necessary because fgets() includes the trailing whitespace in the line it reads. Without rtrim(), each $publication_year would have a newline at its end.

See Also

Recipe 1.11 discusses ways to break apart strings into pieces; Recipes 1.9 and 1.10 cover parsing comma-separated and fixed-width data; documentation on explode() at *http://www.php.net/explode* and rtrim() at *http://www.php.net/rtrim*.

18.13 Reading Configuration Files

Problem

You want to use configuration files to initialize settings in your programs.

Solution

Use parse_ini_file():

```
$config = parse_ini_file('/etc/myapp.ini');
```

Discussion

The function parse_ini_file() reads configuration files structured like PHP's main *php.ini* file. Instead of applying the settings in the configuration file to PHP's configuration, however, parse_ini_file() returns the values from the file in an array.

For example, when parse_ini_file() is given a file with these contents:

```
; physical features
eyes=brown
```

```
hair=brown
glasses=yes

; other features
name=Susannah
likes=monkeys,ice cream,reading
```

The array it returns is:

```
Array
(
    [eyes] => brown
    [hair] => brown
    [glasses] => 1
    [name] => Susannah
    [likes] => monkeys,ice cream,reading
)
```

Blank lines and lines that begin with ; in the configuration file are ignored. Other lines with name=value pairs are put into an array with the name as the key and the value, appropriately, as the value. Words such as on and yes as values are returned as 1, and words such as off and no are returned as the empty string.

To parse sections from the configuration file, pass 1 as a second argument to parse_ini_file( ). Sections are set off by words in square brackets in the file:

```
[physical]
eyes=brown
hair=brown
glasses=yes

[other]
name=Susannah
likes=monkeys,ice cream,reading
```

If this file is in */etc/myapp.ini*, then:

```
$conf = parse_ini_file('/etc/myapp.ini',1);
```

Puts this array in $conf:

```
Array
(
    [physical] => Array
        (
            [eyes] => brown
            [hair] => brown
            [glasses] => 1
        )

    [other] => Array
        (
            [name] => Susannah
            [likes] => monkeys,ice cream,reading
        )

)
```

Your configuration file can also be a valid PHP file that you load with require instead of parse_ini_file( ). If the file *config.php* contains:

```php
<?php

// physical features
$eyes = 'brown';
$hair = 'brown';
$glasses = 'yes';

// other features
$name = 'Susannah';
$likes = array('monkeys','ice cream','reading');
?>
```

You can set the variables $eyes, $hair, $glasses, $name, and $likes with:

```php
require 'config.php';
```

The configuration file loaded by require needs to be valid PHP—including the <?php start tag and the ?> end tag. The variables named in *config.php* are set explicitly, not inside an array, as in parse_ini_file( ). For simple configuration files, this technique may not be worth the extra attention to syntax, but it is useful for embedding logic in the configuration file:

```php
<?php

$time_of_day = (date('a') == 'am') ? 'early' : 'late';

?>
```

The ability to embed logic in configuration files is a good reason to make the files PHP code, but it is helpful also to have all the variables set in the configuration file inside an array. Upcoming versions of PHP will have a feature called *namespaces*, which is the ability to group variables hierarchically in different bunches; you can have a variable called $hair in two different namespaces with two different values. With namespaces, all the values in a configuration file can be loaded into the Config namespace so they don't interfere with other variables.

See Also

Documentation on parse_ini_file( ) at *http://www.php.net/parse-ini-file*; information about namespaces and other upcoming PHP language features is available at *http://www.php.net/ZEND_CHANGES.txt*.

18.14 Reading from or Writing to a Specific Location in a File

Problem

You want to read from (or write to) a specific place in a file. For example, you want to replace the third record in a file of 80-byte records, so you have to write starting at the 161st byte.

Solution

Use fseek() to move to a specific number of bytes after the beginning of the file, before the end of the file, or from the current position in the file:

```
fseek($fh,26);            // 26 bytes after the beginning of the file
fseek($fh,26,SEEK_SET);   // 26 bytes after the beginning of the file
fseek($fh,-39,SEEK_END);  // 39 bytes before the end of the file
fseek($fh,10,SEEK_CUR);   // 10 bytes ahead of the current position
fseek($fh,0);             // beginning of the file
```

The rewind() function moves to the beginning of a file:

```
rewind($fh);              // the same as fseek($fh,0)
```

Discussion

The function fseek() returns 0 if it can move to the specified position, otherwise it returns –1. Seeking beyond the end of the file isn't an error for fseek(). Contrastingly, rewind() returns 0 if it encounters an error.

You can use fseek() only with local files, not HTTP or FTP files opened with fopen(). If you pass a file handle of a remote file to fseek(), it throws an E_NOTICE error.

To get the current file position, use ftell():

```
if (0 === ftell($fh)) {
  print "At the beginning of the file.";
}
```

Because ftell() returns false on error, you need to use the === operator to make sure that its return value is really the integer 0.

See Also

Documentation on fseek() at *http://www.php.net/fseek*, ftell() at *http://www.php.net/ftell*, and rewind() at *http://www.php.net/rewind*.

18.15 Removing the Last Line of a File

Problem

You want to remove the last line of a file; for example, someone's added a comment to the end of your guestbook. You don't like it, so you want to get rid of it.

Solution

If the file is small, you can read it into an array with file() and then remove the last element of the array:

```
$lines = file('employees.txt');
array_pop($lines);
$file = join('',$lines);
```

Discussion

If the file is large, reading it into an array requires too much memory. Instead, use this code, which seeks to the end of the file and works backwards, stopping when it finds a newline:

```
$fh = fopen('employees.txt','r') or die("can't open: $php_errormsg");
$linebreak = $beginning_of_file = 0;

$gap = 80;
$filesize = filesize('employees.txt');
fseek($fh,0,SEEK_END);

while (! ($linebreak || $beginning_of_file)) {
    // save where we are in the file
    $pos = ftell($fh);

    /* move back $gap chars, use rewind() to go to the beginning if
     * we're less than $gap characters into the file */
    if ($pos < $gap) {
        rewind($fh);
    } else {
        fseek($fh,-$gap,SEEK_CUR);
    }

    // read the $gap chars we just seeked back over
    $s = fread($fh,$gap) or die($php_errormsg);

    /* if we read to the end of the file, remove the last character
     * since if it's a newline, we should ignore it */
    if ($pos + $gap >= $filesize) {
        $s = substr_replace($s,'',-1);
    }
```

```
        // move back to where we were before we read $gap chars into $s
        if ($pos < $gap) {
            rewind($fh);
        } else {
            fseek($fh,-$gap,SEEK_CUR);
        }

        // is there a linebreak in $s ?
        if (is_integer($lb = strrpos($s,"\n"))) {
            $linebreak = 1;
            // the last line of the file begins right after the linebreak
            $line_end = ftell($fh) + $lb + 1;
        }

        // break out of the loop if we're at the beginning of the file
        if (ftell($fh) == 0) { $beginning_of_file = 1; }

    }
    if ($linebreak) {
        rewind($fh);
        $file_without_last_line = fread($fh,$line_end) or die($php_errormsg);
    }
    fclose($fh) or die("can't close: $php_errormsg");
```

This code starts at the end of the file and moves backwards in $gap character chunks looking for a newline. If it finds one, it knows the last line of the file starts right after that newline. This position is saved in $line_end. After the while loop, if $linebreak is set, the contents of the file from the beginning to $line_end are read into $file_without_last_line.

The last character of the file is ignored because if it's a newline, it doesn't indicate the start of the last line of the file. Consider the 10-character file whose contents are asparagus\n. It has only one line, consisting of the word asparagus and a newline character. This file without its last line is empty, which the previous code correctly produces. If it starts scanning with the last character, it sees the newline and exits its scanning loop, incorrectly printing out asparagus without the newline.

See Also

Recipe 18.14 discusses fseek() and rewind() in more detail; documentation on array_pop() at *http://www.php.net/array-pop*, fseek() at *http://www.php.net/fseek*, and rewind() at *http://www.php.net/rewind*.

18.16 Modifying a File in Place Without a Temporary File

Problem

You want to change a file without using a temporary file to hold the changes.

Solution

Read the file into memory, make the changes, and rewrite the file. Open the file with mode r+ (rb+, if necessary, on Windows) and adjust its length with ftruncate() after writing out changes:

```
// open the file for reading and writing
$fh = fopen('pickles.txt','r+')          or die($php_errormsg);

// read the entire file into $s
$s = fread($fh,filesize('pickles.txt')) or die($php_errormsg);

// ... modify $s ...

// seek back to the beginning of the file and write the new $s
rewind($fh);
if (-1 == fwrite($fh,$s))                { die($php_errormsg); }

// adjust the file's length to just what's been written
ftruncate($fh,ftell($fh))                or die($php_errormsg);

// close the file
fclose($fh)                              or die($php_errormsg);
```

Discussion

The following code turns text emphasized with asterisks or slashes into text with HTML <b> or <i> tags:

```
$fh = fopen('message.txt','r+')          or die($php_errormsg);

// read the entire file into $s
$s = fread($fh,filesize('message.txt')) or die($php_errormsg);

// convert *word* to <b>word</b>
$s = preg_replace('@\*(.*?)\*@i','<b>$1</b>',$s);
// convert /word/ to <i>word</i>
$s = preg_replace('@/(.*?)/@i','<i>$1</i>',$s);

rewind($fh);
if (-1 == fwrite($fh,$s))                { die($php_errormsg); }
```

```
ftruncate($fh,ftell($fh))                    or die($php_errormsg);
fclose($fh)                                  or die($php_errormsg);
```

Because adding HTML tags makes the file grow, the entire file has to be read into memory and then processed. If the changes to a file make each line shrink (or stay the same size), the file can be processed line by line, saving memory. This example converts text marked with <b> and <i> to text marked with asterisks and slashes:

```
$fh = fopen('message.txt','r+')             or die($php_errormsg);

// figure out how many bytes to read
$bytes_to_read = filesize('message.txt');

// initialize variables that hold file positions
$next_read = $last_write = 0;

// keep going while there are still bytes to read
while ($next_read < $bytes_to_read) {

    /* move to the position of the next read, read a line, and save
     * the position of the next read */
    fseek($fh,$next_read);
    $s = fgets($fh,1048576)                  or die($php_errormsg);
    $next_read = ftell($fh);

    // convert <b>word</b> to *word*
    $s = preg_replace('@<b[^>]*>(.*?)</b>@i','*$1*',$s);
    // convert <i>word</i> to /word/
    $s = preg_replace('@<i[^>]*>(.*?)</i>@i','/$1/',$s);

    /* move to the position where the last write ended, write the
     * converted line, and save the position for the next write */
    fseek($fh,$last_write);
    if (-1 == fwrite($fh,$s))                { die($php_errormsg); }
    $last_write = ftell($fh);
}

// truncate the file length to what we've already written
ftruncate($fh,$last_write)                   or die($php_errormsg);

// close the file
fclose($fh)                                  or die($php_errormsg);
```

See Also

Recipes 11.9 and 11.10 for additional information on converting between ASCII and HTML; Recipe 18.14 discusses fseek( ) and rewind( ) in more detail; documentation on fseek( ) at *http://www.php.net/fseek*, rewind( ) at *http://www.php.net/rewind*, and ftruncate( ) at *http://www.php.net/ftruncate*.

18.17 Flushing Output to a File

Problem

You want to force all buffered data to be written to a filehandle.

Solution

Use `fflush()`:

```
fwrite($fh,'There are twelve pumpkins in my house.');
fflush($fh);
```

This ensures that "There are twelve pumpkins in my house." is written to $fh.

Discussion

To be more efficient, system I/O libraries generally don't write something to a file when you tell them to. Instead, they batch the writes together in a buffer and save all of them to disk at the same time. Using `fflush()` forces anything pending in the write buffer to be actually written to disk.

Flushing output can be particularly helpful when generating an access or activity log. Calling `fflush()` after each message to log file makes sure that any person or program monitoring the log file sees the message as soon as possible.

See Also

Documentation on `fflush()` at *http://www.php.net/fflush*.

18.18 Writing to Standard Output

Problem

You want to write to standard output.

Solution

Use echo or print:

```
print "Where did my pastrami sandwich go?";
echo  "It went into my stomach.";
```

Discussion

While print( ) is a function, echo is a language construct. This means that print( ) returns a value, while echo doesn't. You can include print( ) but not echo in larger expressions:

```
// this is OK
(12 == $status) ? print 'Status is good' : error_log('Problem with status!');

// this gives a parse error
(12 == $status) ? echo 'Status is good' : error_log('Problem with status!');
```

Use *php://stdout* as the filename if you're using the file functions:

```
$fh = fopen('php://stdout','w') or die($php_errormsg);
```

Writing to standard output via a file handle instead of simply with print( ) or echo is useful if you need to abstract where your output goes, or if you need to print to standard output at the same time as writing to a file. See Recipe 18.19 for details.

You can also write to standard error by opening *php://stderr*:

```
$fh = fopen('php://stderr','w');
```

See Also

Recipe 18.19 for writing to many filehandles simultaneously; documentation on echo at *http://www.php.net/echo* and on print( ) at *http://www.php.net/print*.

18.19 Writing to Many Filehandles Simultaneously

Problem

You want to send output to more than one file handle; for example, you want to log messages to the screen and to a file.

Solution

Wrap your output with a loop that iterates through your filehandles, as shown in Example 18-4.

Example 18-4. pc_multi_fwrite()

```
function pc_multi_fwrite($fhs,$s,$length=NULL) {
  if (is_array($fhs)) {
    if (is_null($length)) {
      foreach($fhs as $fh) {
        fwrite($fh,$s);
```

Example 18-4. pc_multi_fwrite() (continued)

```
      }
   } else {
     foreach($fhs as $fh) {
       fwrite($fh,$s,$length);
     }
   }
  }
}
```

Here's an example:

```
$fhs['file'] = fopen('log.txt','w') or die($php_errormsg);
$fhs['screen'] = fopen('php://stdout','w') or die($php_errormsg);

pc_multi_fwrite($fhs,'The space shuttle has landed.');
```

Discussion

If you don't want to pass a length argument to fwrite() (or you always want to), you can eliminate that check from your pc_multi_fwrite(). This version doesn't accept a $length argument:

```
function pc_multi_fwrite($fhs,$s) {
  if (is_array($fhs)) {
    foreach($fhs as $fh) {
      fwrite($fh,$s);
    }
  }
}
```

See Also

Documentation on fwrite() at *http://www.php.net/fwrite*.

18.20 Escaping Shell Metacharacters

Problem

You need to incorporate external data in a command line, but you want to escape out special characters so nothing unexpected happens; for example, you want to pass user input as an argument to a program.

Solution

Use escapeshellarg() to handle arguments:

```
system('ls -al '.escapeshellarg($directory));
```

Use escapeshellcmd( ) to handle program names:

```
system(escapeshellcmd($ls_program).' -al');
```

Discussion

The command line is a dangerous place for unescaped characters. Never pass unmodified user input to one of PHP's shell-execution functions. Always escape the appropriate characters in the command and the arguments. This is crucial. It is unusual to execute command lines that are coming from web forms and not something we recommend lightly. However, sometimes you need to run an external program, so escaping commands and arguments is useful.

escapeshellarg( ) surrounds arguments with single quotes (and escapes any existing single quotes). To print the process status for a particular process:

```
system('/bin/ps '.escapeshellarg($process_id));
```

Using escapeshellarg( ) ensures that the right process is displayed even if it has an unexpected character (e.g., a space) in it. It also prevents unintended commands from being run. If $process_id contains:

```
1; rm -rf /
```

then:

```
system("/bin/ps $process_id")
```

not only displays the status of process 1, but it also executes the command *rm -rf /*. However:

```
system('/bin/ps '.escapeshellarg($process_id))
```

runs the command */bin/ps 1; rm -rf*, which produces an error because "1-semicolon-space-rm-space-hyphen-rf" isn't a valid process ID.

Similarly, escapeshellcmd( ) prevents unintended command lines from execution. This code runs a different program depending on the value of $which_program:

```
system("/usr/local/bin/formatter-$which_program");
```

For example, if $which_program is pdf 12, the script runs */usr/local/bin/formatter-pdf* with an argument of 12. But, if $which_program is pdf 12; 56, the script runs */usr/local/bin/formatter-pdf* with an argument of 12, but then also runs the program 56, which is an error. To successfully pass the arguments to *formatter-pdf*, you need escapeshellcmd( ):

```
system(escapeshellcmd("/usr/local/bin/formatter-$which_program"));
```

This runs */usr/local/bin/formatter-pdf* and passes it two arguments: 12; and 56.

See Also

Documentation on system() at *http://www.php.net/system*, escapeshellarg() at *http://www.php.net/escapeshellarg*, and escapeshellcmd() at *http://www.php.net/escapeshellcmd*.

18.21 Passing Input to a Program

Problem

You want to pass input to an external program run from inside a PHP script. You might, for example, use a database that requires you to run an external program to index text and want to pass text to that program.

Solution

Open a pipe to the program with popen(), write to the pipe with fputs() or fwrite(), then close the pipe with pclose():

```
$ph = popen('program arg1 arg2','w')          or die($php_errormsg);
if (-1 == fputs($ph,"first line of input\n"))  { die($php_errormsg); }
if (-1 == fputs($ph,"second line of input\n")) { die($php_errormsg); }
pclose($ph)                                   or die($php_errormsg);
```

Discussion

This example uses popen() to call the *nsupdate* command, which submits Dynamic DNS Update requests to name servers:

```
$ph = popen('/usr/bin/nsupdate -k keyfile')                or die($php_errormsg);
if (-1 == fputs($ph,"update delete test.example.com A\n")) { die($php_errormsg); }
if (-1 == fputs($ph,"update add test.example.com 5 A 192.168.1.1\n"))
                                                          { die($php_errormsg); }
pclose($ph)                                               or die($php_errormsg);
```

Two commands are sent to *nsupdate* via popen(). The first deletes the *test.example.com* A record, and the second adds a new A record for *test.example.com* with the address 192.168.1.1.

See Also

Documentation on popen() at *http://www.php.net/popen* and pclose() at *http://www.php.net/pclose*; Dynamic DNS is described in RFC 2136 at *http://www.faqs.org/rfcs/rfc2136.html*.

18.22 Reading Standard Output from a Program

Problem

You want to read the output from a program; for example, you want the output of a system utility such as *route(8)* that provides network information.

Solution

To read the entire contents of a program's output, use the backtick (') operator:

```
$routing_table = `/sbin/route`;
```

To read the output incrementally, open a pipe with popen( ):

```
$ph = popen('/sbin/route','r') or die($php_errormsg);
while (! feof($ph)) {
    $s = fgets($ph,1048576)     or die($php_errormsg);
}
pclose($ph)                     or die($php_errormsg);
```

Discussion

The backtick operator (which is not available in safe mode), executes a program and returns all its output as a single string. On a Linux system with 448 MB of RAM, this command:

```
$s = `/usr/bin/free`;
```

puts this multiline string in $s:

```
                 total      used      free    shared    buffers     cached
Mem:            448620    446384      2236         0      68568     163040
-/+ buffers/cache:        214776    233844
Swap:           136512         0    136512
```

If a program generates a lot of output, it is more memory-efficient to read from a pipe one line at a time. If you're printing formatted data to the browser based on the output of the pipe, you can print it as you get it. This example prints information about recent Unix system logins formatted as an HTML table. It uses the */usr/bin/last* command:

```
// print table header
print<<<_HTML_
<table>
<tr>
 <td>user</td><td>login port</td><td>login from</td><td>login time</td>
 <td>time spent logged in</td>
</tr>
_HTML_;

// open the pipe to /usr/bin/last
```

```
$ph = popen('/usr/bin/last','r') or die($php_errormsg);
while (! feof($ph)) {
    $line = fgets($ph,80) or die($php_errormsg);

    // don't process blank lines or the info line at the end
    if (trim($line) && (! preg_match('/^wtmp begins/',$line))) {
        $user = trim(substr($line,0,8));
        $port = trim(substr($line,9,12));
        $host = trim(substr($line,22,16));
        $date = trim(substr($line,38,25));
        $elapsed = trim(substr($line,63,10),' ()');

        if ('logged in' == $elapsed) {
            $elapsed = 'still logged in';
            $date = substr_replace($date,'',-5);
        }

        print "<tr><td>$user</td><td>$port</td><td>$host</td>";
        print "<td>$date</td><td>$elapsed</td></tr>\n";
    }
}
pclose($ph) or die($php_errormsg);

print '</table>';
```

See Also

Documentation on popen() at *http://www.php.net/popen*, pclose() at *http://www.php.net/pclose*, and the backtick operator at *http://www.php.net/language.operators.execution*; safe mode is documented at *http://www.php.net/features.safe-mode*.

18.23 Reading Standard Error from a Program

Problem

You want to read the error output from a program; for example, you want to capture the system calls displayed by *strace(1)*.

Solution

Redirect standard error to standard output by adding 2>&1 to the command line passed to popen( ). Read standard output by opening the pipe in r mode:

```
$ph = popen('strace ls 2>&1','r') or die($php_errormsg);
while (!feof($ph)) {
    $s = fgets($ph,1048576)        or die($php_errormsg);
}
pclose($ph)                        or die($php_errormsg);
```

Discussion

In both the Unix *sh* and the Windows *cmd.exe* shells, standard error is file descriptor 2, and standard output is file descriptor 1. Appending 2>&1 to a command tells the shell to redirect what's normally sent to file descriptor 2 (standard error) over to file descriptor 1 (standard output). fgets( ) then reads both standard error and standard output.

This technique reads in standard error but doesn't provide a way to distinguish it from standard output. To read just standard error, you need to prevent standard output from being returned through the pipe. This is done by redirecting it to */dev/null* on Unix and NUL on Windows:

```
// Unix: just read standard error
$ph = popen('strace ls 2>&1 1>/dev/null','r') or die($php_errormsg);

// Windows: just read standard error
$ph = popen('ipxroute.exe 2>&1 1>NUL','r') or die($php_errormsg);
```

See Also

Documentation on popen( ) at *http://www.php.net/popen*; see your *popen(3)* manpage for details about the shell your system uses with popen( ); for information about shell redirection, see the Redirection section of the *sh(1)* manpage on Unix systems; on Windows, see the entry on redirection in the Command Reference section of your system help.

18.24 Locking a File

Problem

You want to have exclusive access to a file to prevent it from being changed while you read or update it. If, for example, you are saving guestbook information in a file, two users should be able to add guestbook entries at the same time without clobbering each other's entries.

Solution

Use flock( ) to provide advisory locking:

```
$fh = fopen('guestbook.txt','a')          or die($php_errormsg);
flock($fh,LOCK_EX)                         or die($php_errormsg);
fwrite($fh,$_REQUEST['guestbook_entry'])   or die($php_errormsg);
fflush($fh)                                or die($php_errormsg);
flock($fh,LOCK_UN)                         or die($php_errormsg);
fclose($fh)                                or die($php_errormsg);
```

Discussion

The file locking flock() provides is called *advisory* file locking because flock() doesn't actually prevent other processes from opening a locked file, it just provides a way for processes to voluntarily cooperate on file access. All programs that need to access files being locked with flock() need to set and release locks to make the file locking effective.

There are two kinds of locks you can set with flock(): exclusive locks and shared locks. An *exclusive lock*, specified by LOCK_EX as the second argument to flock(), can be held only by one process at one time for a particular file. A *shared lock*, specified by LOCK_SH, can be held by more than one process at one time for a particular file. Before writing to a file, you should get an exclusive lock. Before reading from a file, you should get a shared lock.

To unlock a file, call flock() with LOCK_UN as the second argument. It's important to flush any buffered data to be written to the file with fflush() before you unlock the file. Other processes shouldn't be able to get a lock until that data is written.

By default, flock() blocks until it can obtain a lock. To tell it not to block, add LOCK_NB to the second argument:

```
$fh = fopen('guestbook.txt','a')            or die($php_errormsg);
$tries = 3;
while ($tries > 0) {
    $locked = flock($fh,LOCK_EX | LOCK_NB);
    if (! $locked) {
        sleep(5);
        $tries--;
    } else {
        // don't go through the loop again
        $tries = 0;
    }
}
if ($locked) {
    fwrite($fh,$_REQUEST['guestbook_entry']) or die($php_errormsg);
    fflush($fh)                              or die($php_errormsg);
    flock($fh,LOCK_UN)                       or die($php_errormsg);
    fclose($fh)                              or die($php_errormsg);
} else {
    print "Can't get lock.";
}
```

When the lock is nonblocking, flock() returns right away even if it couldn't get a lock. The previous example tries three times to get a lock on *guestbook.txt*, sleeping five seconds between each try.

Locking with flock() doesn't work in all circumstances, such as on some NFS implementations. Also, flock() isn't supported on Windows 95, 98, or ME. To simulate file locking in these cases, use a directory as a exclusive lock indicator. This is a separate empty directory whose presence indicates that the data file is locked. Before opening a data file, create a lock directory and then delete the lock directory when you're finished working with the data file. Otherwise, the file access code is the same, as shown here:

```
$fh = fopen('guestbook.txt','a')          or die($php_errormsg);

// loop until we can successfully make the lock directory
$locked = 0;
while (! $locked) {
    if (@mkdir('guestbook.txt.lock',0777)) {
        $locked = 1;
    } else {
        sleep(1);
    }
}

if (-1 == fwrite($fh,$_REQUEST['guestbook_entry'])) {
    rmdir('guestbook.txt.lock');
    die($php_errormsg);
}
if (! fclose($fh)) {
    rmdir('guestbook.txt.lock');
    die($php_errormsg);
}
rmdir('guestbook.txt.lock')                or die($php_errormsg);
```

A directory is used instead of a file to indicate a lock because the mkdir() function fails to create a directory if it already exists. This gives you a way, in one operation, to check if the lock indicator exists and create it if it doesn't. Any error trapping after the directory is created, however, needs to clean up by removing the directory before exiting. If the directory is left in place, no future processes can get a lock by creating the directory.

If you use a file as a lock indicator, the code to create it looks like:

```
$locked = 0;
while (! $locked) {
    if (! file_exists('guestbook.txt.lock')) {
        touch('guestbook.txt.lock');
        $locked = 1;
    } else {
        sleep(1);
    }
}
```

This might fail under heavy load because you check for the lock's existence with file_exists() and then create the lock with touch(). After one process calls file_exists(), another might call touch() before the first calls touch(). Both processes would then think they've got exclusive access to the file when neither does. With mkdir() there's no gap between the checking for existence and creation, so the process that makes the directory is ensured exclusive access.

See Also

Documentation on flock( ) at *http://www.php.net/flock*.

18.25 Reading and Writing Compressed Files

Problem

You want to read or write compressed files.

Solution

Use PHP's *zlib* extension to read or write *gzip*'ed files. To read a compressed file:

```
$zh = gzopen('file.gz','r') or die("can't open: $php_errormsg");
while ($line = gzgets($zh,1024)) {
    // $line is the next line of uncompressed data, up to 1024 bytes
}
gzclose($zh) or die("can't close: $php_errormsg");
```

Here's how to write a compressed file:

```
$zh = gzopen('file.gz','w') or die("can't open: $php_errormsg");
if (-1 == gzwrite($zh,$s))   { die("can't write: $php_errormsg"); }
gzclose($zh)                 or die("can't close: $php_errormsg");
```

Discussion

The *zlib* extension contains versions of many file-access functions, such as fopen( ), fread( ), and fwrite( ) (called gzopen( ), gzread( ), gzwrite( ), etc.) that transparently compress data when writing and uncompress data when reading. The compression algorithm that *zlib* uses is compatible with the *gzip* and *gunzip* utilities.

For example, gzgets($zp,1024) works like fgets($fh,1024). It reads up to 1023 bytes, stopping earlier if it reaches EOF or a newline. For gzgets( ), this means 1023 uncompressed bytes.

However, gzseek( ) works differently than fseek( ). It only supports seeking a specified number of bytes from the beginning of the file stream (the SEEK_SET argument to fseek( )). Seeking forward (from the current position) is only supported in files opened for writing (the file is padded with a sequence of compressed zeroes). Seeking backwards is supported in files opened for reading, but it is very slow.

The *zlib* extension also has some functions to create compressed strings. The function gzencode( ) compresses a string and gives it the correct headers and formatting to be compatible with *gunzip*. Here's a simple *gzip* program:

```
$in_file = $_SERVER['argv'][1];
$out_file = $_SERVER['argv'][1].'.gz';
```

```
$ifh = fopen($in_file,'rb')  or die("can't open $in_file: $php_errormsg");
$ofh = fopen($out_file,'wb') or die("can't open $out_file: $php_errormsg");

$encoded = gzencode(fread($ifh,filesize($in_file)))
                        or die("can't encode data: $php_errormsg");

if (-1 == fwrite($ofh,$encoded)) { die("can't write: $php_errormsg"); }
fclose($ofh)                 or die("can't close $out_file: $php_errormsg");
fclose($ifh)                 or die("can't close $in_file: $php_errormsg");
```

The guts of this program are the lines:

```
$encoded = gzencode(fread($ifh,filesize($in_file)))
                        or die("can't encode data: $php_errormsg);
    if (-1 == fwrite($ofh,$encoded)) { die("can't write: $php_errormsg"); }
```

The compressed contents of $in_file are stored in $encoded and then written to
$out_file with fwrite( ).

You can pass a second argument to gzencode( ) that indicates compression level. Set
no compression with 0 and maximum compression with 9. The default level is 1. To
adjust the simple *gzip* program for maximum compression, the encoding line
becomes:

```
$encoded = gzencode(fread($ifh,filesize($in_file)),9)
                        or die("can't encode data: $php_errormsg);
```

You can also compress and uncompress strings without the *gzip*-compatibility headers by using gzcompress( ) and gzuncompress( ).

See Also

Recipe 18.26 for a program that extracts files from a ZIP archive; documentation on
the *zlib* extension at *http://www.php.net/zlib*; you can download *zlib* at *http://
www.gzip.org/zlib/*; the *zlib* algorithm is detailed in RFCs 1950 (*http://www.faqs.org/
rfcs/rfc1950.html*) and 1951 (*http://www.faqs.org/rfcs/rfc1951.html*).

18.26 Program: Unzip

The *unzip.php* program, shown in Example 18-5, extracts files from a ZIP archive. It
uses the pc_mkdir_parents( ) function which is defined in Recipe 19.10. The program also requires PHP's *zip* extension to be installed. You can find documentation
on the *zip* extension at *http://www.php.net/zip*.

This program takes a few arguments on the command line. The first is the name of
the ZIP archive it should unzip. By default, it unzips all files in the archive. If additional command-line arguments are supplied, it only unzips files whose name
matches any of those arguments. The full path of the file inside the ZIP archive must
be given. If *turtles.html* is in the ZIP archive inside the *animals* directory, *unzip.php*
must be passed *animals/turtles.html*, not just *turtles.html*, to unzip the file.

Directories are stored as 0-byte files inside ZIP archives, so *unzip.php* doesn't try to create them. Instead, before it creates any other file, it uses pc_mkdir_parents() to create all directories that are parents of that file, if necessary. For example, say *unzip.php* sees these entries in the ZIP archive:

```
animals (0 bytes)
animals/frogs/ribbit.html (2123 bytes)
animals/turtles.html   (1232 bytes)
```

It ignores *animals* because it is 0 bytes long. Then it calls pc_mkdir_parents() on *animals/frogs*, creating both *animals* and *animals/frogs*, and writes *ribbit.html* into *animals/frogs*. Since *animals* already exists when it reaches *animals/turtles.html*, it writes out *turtles.html* without creating any additional directories.

Example 18-5. unzip.php

```php
// the first argument is the zip file
$in_file = $_SERVER['argv'][1];

// any other arguments are specific files in the archive to unzip
if ($_SERVER['argc'] > 2) {
    $all_files = 0;
    for ($i = 2; $i < $_SERVER['argc']; $i++) {
        $out_files[$_SERVER['argv'][$i]] = true;
    }
} else {
    // if no other files are specified, unzip all files
    $all_files = true;
}

$z = zip_open($in_file) or die("can't open $in_file: $php_errormsg");
while ($entry = zip_read($z)) {

    $entry_name = zip_entry_name($entry);

    // check if all files should be unzipped, or the name of
    // this file is on the list of specific files to unzip
    if ($all_files || $out_files[$entry_name]) {

        // only proceed if the file is not 0 bytes long
        if (zip_entry_filesize($entry)) {
            $dir = dirname($entry_name);

            // make all necessary directories in the file's path
            if (! is_dir($dir)) { pc_mkdir_parents($dir); }

            $file = basename($entry_name);

            if (zip_entry_open($z,$entry)) {
                if ($fh = fopen($dir.'/'.$file,'w')) {
                    // write the entire file
                    fwrite($fh,
                        zip_entry_read($entry,zip_entry_filesize($entry)))
```

Example 18-5. unzip.php (continued)

```
                    or error_log("can't write: $php_errormsg");
                fclose($fh) or error_log("can't close: $php_errormsg");
            } else {
                error_log("can't open $dir/$file: $php_errormsg");
            }
            zip_entry_close($entry);
        } else {
            error_log("can't open entry $entry_name: $php_errormsg");
        }
    }
  }
}
```

See Also

Recipe 18.25 for reading and writing *zlib* compressed files; Recipe 19.10 for the pc_
mkdir_parents( ) function; documentation on the *zip* extension at *http://
www.php.net/zip*.

CHAPTER 19

Directories

19.0 Introduction

A filesystem stores a lot of additional information about files aside from their actual contents. This information includes such particulars as the file's size, what directory it's in, and access permissions for the file. If you're working with files, you may also need to manipulate this metadata. PHP gives you a variety of functions to read and manipulate directories, directory entries, and file attributes. Like other file-related parts of PHP, the functions are similar to the C functions that accomplish the same tasks, with some simplifications.

Files are organized with *inodes*. Each file (and other parts of the filesystem, such as directories, devices, and links) has its own inode. That inode contains a pointer to where the file's data blocks are as well as all the metadata about the file. The data blocks for a directory hold the names of the files in that directory and the inode of each file.

PHP provides two ways to look in a directory to see what files it holds. The first way is to use opendir() to get a directory handle, readdir() to iterate through the files, and closedir() to close the directory handle:

```
$d = opendir('/usr/local/images') or die($php_errormsg);
while (false !== ($f = readdir($d))) {
    // process file
}
closedir($d);
```

The second method is to use the directory class. Instantiate the class with dir(), read each filename with the read() method, and close the directory with close():

```
$d = dir('/usr/local/images') or die($php_errormsg);
while (false !== ($f = $d->read())) {
    // process file
}
$d->close();
```

Recipe 19.7 shows how to use opendir( ) or dir( ) to process each file in a directory. Making new directories is covered in Recipe 19.10 and removing directories in Recipe 19.11.

The filesystem holds more than just files and directories. On Unix, it can also hold symbolic links. These are special files whose contents are a pointer to another file. You can delete the link without affecting the file it points to. To create a symbolic link, use symlink( ):

```
symlink('/usr/local/images','/www/docroot/images') or die($php_errormsg);
```

This creates a symbolic link called *images* in */www/docroot* that points to */usr/local/ images*.

To find information about a file, directory, or link you must examine its inode. The function stat( ) retrieves the metadata in an inode for you. Recipe 19.2 discusses stat( ). PHP also has many functions that use stat( ) internally to give you a specific piece of information about a file. These are listed in Table 19-1.

Table 19-1. File information functions

Function name	What file information does the function provide?
file_exists( )	Does the file exist?
fileatime( )	Last access time
filectime( )	Last metadata change time
filegroup( )	Group (numeric)
fileinode( )	Inode number
filemtime( )	Last change time of contents
fileowner( )	Owner (numeric)
fileperms( )	Permissions (decimal, numeric)
filesize( )	Size
filetype( )	Type (fifo, char, dir, block, link, file, unknown)
is_dir( )	Is it a directory?
is_executable( )	Is it executable?
is_file( )	Is it a regular file?
is_link( )	Is it a symbolic link?
is_readable( )	Is it readable?
is_writable( )	Is it writeable?

On Unix, the file permissions indicate what operations the file's owner, users in the file's group, and all users can perform on the file. The operations are reading, writing, and executing. For programs, executing means the ability to run the program; for directories, it's the ability to search through the directory and see the files in it.

Unix permissions can also contain a setuid bit, a setgid bit, and a sticky bit. The setuid bit means that when a program is run, it runs with the user ID of its owner. The setgid bit means that a program runs with the group ID of its group. For a directory, the setgid bit means that new files in the directory are created by default in the same group as the directory. The sticky bit is useful for directories in which people share files because it prevents nonsuperusers with write permission in a directory from deleting files in that directory unless they own the file or the directory.

When setting permissions with chmod( ) (see Recipe 19.3), they must be expressed as an octal number. This number has four digits. The first digit is any special setting for the file (such as setuid or setgid). The second digit is the user permissions—what the file's owner can do. The third digit is the group permissions—what users in the file's group can do. The fourth digit is the world permissions—what all other users can do. To compute the appropriate value for each digit, add together the permissions you want for that digit using the values in Table 19-2. For example, a permission value of 0644 means that there are no special settings (the 0), the file's owner can read and write the file (the 6, which is 4 (read) + 2 (write)), users in the file's group can read the file (the first 4), and all other users can also read the file (the second 4). A permission value of 4644 is the same, except that the file is also setuid.

Table 19-2. File permission values

Value	Permission meaning	Special setting meaning
4	Read	setuid
2	Write	setgid
1	Execute	sticky

The permissions of newly created files and directories are affected by a setting called the *umask*, which is a permission value that is removed, or masked out, from the initial permissions of a file (0666 or directory (0777). For example, if the umask is 0022, the default permissions for a new file created with touch( ) or fopen( ) are 0644 and the default permissions for a new directory created with mkdir( ) are 0755. You can get and set the umask with the function umask( ). It returns the current umask and, if an argument is supplied to it, changes the umask to the value of that argument. For example, here's how to make the permissions on newly created files prevent anyone but the file's owner (and the superuser) from accessing the file:

```
$old_umask = umask(0077);
touch('secret-file.txt');
umask($old_umask);
```

The first call to umask( ) masks out all permissions for group and world. After the file is created, the second call to umask( ) restores the umask to the previous setting. When PHP is run as a server module, it restores the umask to its default value at the end of each request. Like other permissions-related functions, umask( ) doesn't work on Windows.

19.1 Getting and Setting File Timestamps

Problem

You want to know when a file was last accessed or changed, or you want to update a file's access or change time; for example, you want each page on your web site to display when it was last modified.

Solution

The `fileatime()`, `filemtime()`, and `filectime()` functions return the time of last access, modification, and metadata change of a file:

```
$last_access = fileatime('larry.php');
$last_modification = filemtime('moe.php');
$last_change = filectime('curly.php');
```

The `touch()` function changes a file's modification time:

```
touch('shemp.php');         // set modification time to now
touch('joe.php',$timestamp); // set modification time to $timestamp
```

Discussion

The `fileatime()` function returns the last time a file was opened for reading or writing. The `filemtime()` function returns the last time a file's contents were changed. The `filectime()` function returns the last time a file's contents or metadata (such as owner or permissions) were changed. Each function returns the time as an epoch timestamp.

A file's modification time can be updated with `touch()`. Without a second argument, `touch()` sets the modification time to the current date and time. To set a file's modification time to a specific value, pass that value as an epoch timestamp to `touch()` as a second argument.

This code prints the time a page on your web site was last updated:

```
print "Last Modified: ".strftime('%c',filemtime($_SERVER['SCRIPT_FILENAME']));
```

See Also

Documentation on `fileatime()` at *http://www.php.net/fileatime*, `filemtime()` at *http://www.php.net/filemtime*, and `filectime()` at *http://www.php.net/filectime*.

19.2   Getting File Information

Problem

You want to read a file's metadata; for example, permissions and ownership.

Solution

Use stat( ), which returns an array of information about a file:

```
$info = stat('harpo.php');
```

Discussion

The function stat( ) returns an array with both numeric and string indexes with information about a file. The elements of this array are in Table 19-3.

Table 19-3. Information returned by stat()

Numeric index	String index	Value
0	dev	Device
1	ino	Inode
2	mode	Permissions
3	nlink	Link count
4	uid	Owner's user ID
5	gid	Group's group ID
6	rdev	Device type for inode devices (-1 on Windows)
7	size	Size (in bytes)
8	atime	Last access time (epoch timestamp)
9	mtime	Last change time of contents (epoch timestamp)
10	ctime	Last change time of contents or metadata (epoch timestamp)
11	blksize	Block size for I/O (-1 on Windows)
12	blocks	Number of block allocated to this file

The mode element of the returned array contains the permissions expressed as a base 10 integer. This is confusing since permissions are usually either expressed symbolically (e.g., *ls*'s -rw-r--r-- output) or as an octal integer (e.g., 0644). To convert the permissions to a more understandable format, use base_convert( ) to change the permissions to octal:

```
$file_info = stat('/tmp/session.txt');
$permissions = base_convert($file_info['mode'],10,8);
```

This results in a six-digit octal number. For example, if *ls* displays the following about */tmp/session.txt*:

```
-rw-rw-r--    1 sklar    sklar         12 Oct 23 17:55 /tmp/session.txt
```

Then `$file_info['mode']` is 33204 and `$permissions` is 100664. The last three digits (664) are the user (read and write), group (read and write), and other (read) permissions for the file. The third digit, 0, means that the file is not setuid or setgid. The leftmost 10 means that the file is a regular file (and not a socket, symbolic link, or other special file).

Because `stat()` returns an array with both numeric and string indexes, using foreach to iterate through the returned array produces two copies of each value. Instead, use a for loop from element 0 to element 12 of the returned array.

Calling `stat()` on a symbolic link returns information about the file the symbolic link points to. To get information about the symbolic link itself, use `lstat()`.

Similar to `stat()` is `fstat()`, which takes a file handle (returned from `fopen()` or `popen()`) as an argument. You can use `fstat()` only on local files, however, not URLs passed to `fopen()`.

PHP's `stat()` function uses the underlying *stat(2)* system call, which is expensive. To minimize overhead, PHP caches the result of calling *stat(2)*. So, if you call `stat()` on a file, change its permissions, and call `stat()` on the same file again, you get the same results. To force PHP to reload the file's metadata, call `clearstatcache()`, which flushes PHP's cached information. PHP also uses this cache for the other functions that return file metadata: `file_exists()`, `fileatime()`, `filectime()`, `filegroup()`, `fileinode()`, `filemtime()`, `fileowner()`, `fileperms()`, `filesize()`, `filetype()`, `fstat()`, `is_dir()`, `is_executable()`, `is_file()`, `is_link()`, `is_readable()`, `is_writable()`, and `lstat()`.

See Also

Documentation on `stat()` at *http://www.php.net/stat*, `lstat()` at *http://www.php.net/lstat*, `fstat()` at *http://www.php.net/fstat*, and `clearstatcache()` at *http://www.php.net/clearstatcache*.

19.3 Changing File Permissions or Ownership

Problem

You want to change a file's permissions or ownership; for example, you want to prevent other users from being able to look at a file of sensitive data.

Solution

Use chmod( ) to change the permissions of a file:

```
chmod('/home/user/secrets.txt',0400);
```

Use chown( ) to change a file's owner and chgrp( ) to change a file's group:

```
chown('/tmp/myfile.txt','sklar');           // specify user by name
chgrp('/home/sklar/schedule.txt','soccer'); // specify group by name

chown('/tmp/myfile.txt',5001);              // specify user by uid
chgrp('/home/sklar/schedule.txt',102);      // specify group by gid
```

Discussion

The permissions passed to chmod( ) must be specified as an octal number.

The superuser can change the permissions, owner, and group of any file. Other users are restricted. They can change only the permissions and group of files that they own, and can't change the owner at all. Nonsuperusers can also change only the group of a file to a group they belong to.

The functions chmod( ), chgrp( ), and chown( ) don't work on Windows.

See Also

Documentation on chmod( ) at *http://www.php.net/chmod*, chown( ) at *http://www.php.net/chown*, and chgrp( ) at *http://www.php.net/chgrp*.

19.4 Splitting a Filename into Its Component Parts

Problem

You want to find a file's path and filename; for example, you want to create a file in the same directory as an existing file.

Solution

Use basename( ) to get the filename and dirname( ) to get the path:

```
$full_name = '/usr/local/php/php.ini';
$base = basename($full_name);  // $base is php.ini
$dir  = dirname($full_name);   // $dir is /usr/local/php
```

Use pathinfo() to get the directory name, base name, and extension in an associative array:

```
$info = pathinfo('/usr/local/php/php.ini');
```

Discussion

To create a temporary file in the same directory as an existing file, use dirname() to find the directory, and pass that directory to tempnam():

```
$dir = dirname($existing_file);
$temp = tempnam($dir,'temp');
$temp_fh = fopen($temp,'w');
```

The elements in the associative array returned by pathinfo() are dirname, basename, and extension:

```
$info = pathinfo('/usr/local/php/php.ini');
print_r($info);
Array
(
    [dirname] => /usr/local/php
    [basename] => php.ini
    [extension] => ini
)
```

You can also pass basename() an optional suffix to remove it from the filename. This sets $base to *php*:

```
$base = basename('/usr/local/php/php.ini','.ini');
```

Using functions such as basename(), dirname(), and pathinfo() is more portable than just separating a full filename on / because they use an operating-system appropriate separator. On Windows, these functions treat both / and \ as file and directory separators. On other platforms, only / is used.

There's no built-in PHP function to combine the parts produced by basename(), dirname(), and pathinfo() back into a full filename. To do this you have to combine the parts with . and /:

```
$dirname = '/usr/local/php';
$basename = 'php';
$extension = 'ini';

$full_name = $dirname . '/' . $basename . '.' . $extension;
```

You can pass a full filename produced like this to other PHP file functions on Windows, because PHP accepts / as a directory separator on Windows.

See Also

Documentation on basename() at *http://www.php.net/basename*, dirname() at *http://www.php.net/dirname*, and pathinfo() at *http://www.php.net/pathinfo*.

19.5   Deleting a File

Problem

You want to delete a file.

Solution

Use unlink():

```
unlink($file) or die ("can't delete $file: $php_errormsg");
```

Discussion

The function unlink() is only able to delete files that the user of the PHP process is able to delete. If you're having trouble getting unlink() to work, check the permissions on the file and how you're running PHP.

See Also

Documentation on unlink() at *http://www.php.net/unlink*.

19.6   Copying or Moving a File

Problem

You want to copy or move a file.

Solution

Use copy() to copy a file:

```
copy($old,$new) or die("couldn't copy $old to $new: $php_errormsg");
```

Use rename() to move a file:

```
rename($old,$new) or die("couldn't move $old to $new: $php_errormsg");
```

Discussion

On Unix, rename() can't move files across filesystems. To do so, copy the file to the new location and then delete the old file:

```
if (copy("/tmp/code.c","/usr/local/src/code.c")) {
  unlink("/tmp/code.c");
}
```

If you have multiple files to copy or move, call copy() or rename() in a loop. You can operate only on one file each time you call these functions.

See Also

Documentation on copy() at *http://www.php.net/copy* and rename() at *http://www.php.net/rename*.

19.7 Processing All Files in a Directory

Problem

You want to iterate over all files in a directory. For example, you want to create a select box in a form that lists all the files in a directory.

Solution

Get a directory handle with opendir() and then retrieve each filename with readdir():

```
$d = opendir('/tmp') or die($php_errormsg);
while (false !== ($f = readdir($d))) {
    print "$f\n";
}
closedir($d);
```

Discussion

The code in the solution tests the return value of readdir() with the nonidentity operator (!==) so that the code works properly with filenames that evaluate to false, such as a file named 0.

The function readdir() returns each entry in a directory, whether it is a file, directory, or something else (such as a link or a socket). This includes the metaentries "." (current directory) and ".." (parent directory). To just return files, use the is_file() function as well:

```
print '<select name="files">';
$d = opendir('/usr/local/upload') or die($php_errormsg);
while (false !== ($f = readdir($d))) {
    if (is_file("/usr/local/upload/$f")) {
        print '<option> ' . $f . '</option>';
    }
}
closedir($d);
print '</select>';
```

Because `readdir()` returns only the filename of each directory entry, not a full path-name, you have to prepend the directory name to $f before you pass it to is_file().

PHP also has an object-oriented interface to directory information. The `dir()` function returns an object on which you can call read(), rewind(), and close() methods, which act like the readdir(), rewinddir(), and closedir() functions. There's also a $path property that contains the full path of the opened directory.

Here's how to iterate through files with the object-oriented interface:

```
print '<select name="files">';
$d = dir('/usr/local/upload') or die($php_errormsg);
while (false !== ($f = $d->read())) {
    if (is_file($d->path.'/'.$f)) {
        print '<option> ' . $f . '</option>';
    }
}
$d->close();
```

In this example, $d->path is */usr/local/upload*.

See Also

Documentation on opendir() at *http://www.php.net/opendir*, readdir() at *http://www.php.net/readdir*, and the directory class at *http://www.php.net/class.dir*.

19.8 Getting a List of Filenames Matching a Pattern

Problem

You want to find all filenames that match a pattern.

Solution

If your pattern is a regular expression, read each file from the directory and test the name with preg_match():

```
$d = dir('/tmp') or die($php_errormsg);
while (false !== ($f = $d->read())) {
    // only match alphabetic names
    if (preg_match('/^[a-zA-Z]+$/',$f)) {
        print "$f\n";
    }
}
$d->close();
```

Discussion

If your pattern is a shell glob (e.g., *.*), use the backtick operator with *ls* (Unix) or *dir* (Windows) to get the matching filenames. For Unix:

```
$files = explode("\n",`ls -1 *.gif`);
foreach ($files as $file) {
  print "$b\n";
}
```

For Windows:

```
$files = explode("\n",`dir /b *.gif`);
foreach ($files as $file) {
  print "$b\n";
}
```

See Also

Recipe 19.7 details on iterating through each file in a directory; information about shell pattern matching is available at *http://www.gnu.org/manual/bash/html_node/bashref_35.html*.

19.9 Processing All Files in a Directory Recursively

Problem

You want to do something to all the files in a directory and in any subdirectories.

Solution

Use the pc_process_dir() function, shown in Example 19-1, which returns a list of all files in and beneath a given directory.

Example 19-1. pc_process_dir()

```
function pc_process_dir($dir_name,$max_depth = 10,$depth = 0) {
    if ($depth >= $max_depth) {
        error_log("Reached max depth $max_depth in $dir_name.");
        return false;
    }
    $subdirectories = array();
    $files = array();
    if (is_dir($dir_name) && is_readable($dir_name)) {
        $d = dir($dir_name);
        while (false !== ($f = $d->read())) {
            // skip . and ..
            if (('.' == $f) || ('..' == $f)) {
                continue;
            }
```

Example 19-1. pc_process_dir() (continued)

```
        if (is_dir("$dir_name/$f")) {
            array_push($subdirectories,"$dir_name/$f");
        } else {
            array_push($files,"$dir_name/$f");
        }
    }
    $d->close();
    foreach ($subdirectories as $subdirectory) {
        $files = array_merge($files,pc_process_dir($subdirectory,$max_depth,$depth+1));
    }
}
return $files;
}
```

Discussion

Here's an example: if */tmp* contains the files *a* and *b*, as well as the directory *c*, and */tmp/c* contains files *d* and *e*, pc_process_dir('/tmp') returns an array with elements */tmp/a*, */tmp/b*, */tmp/c/d*, and */tmp/c/e*. To perform an operation on each file, iterate through the array:

```
$files = pc_process_dir('/tmp');
foreach ($files as $file) {
    print "$file was last accessed at ".strftime('%c',fileatime($file))."\n";
}
```

Instead of returning an array of files, you can also write a function that processes them as it finds them. The pc_process_dir2() function, shown in Example 19-2, does this by taking an additional argument, the name of the function to call on each file found.

Example 19-2. pc_process_dir2()

```
function pc_process_dir2($dir_name,$func_name,$max_depth = 10,$depth = 0) {
    if ($depth >= $max_depth) {
        error_log("Reached max depth $max_depth in $dir_name.");
        return false;
    }
    $subdirectories = array();
    $files = array();
    if (is_dir($dir_name) && is_readable($dir_name)) {
        $d = dir($dir_name);
        while (false !== ($f = $d->read())) {
            // skip . and ..
            if (('.' == $f) || ('..' == $f)) {
                continue;
            }
            if (is_dir("$dir_name/$f")) {
                array_push($subdirectories,"$dir_name/$f");
            } else {
                $func_name("$dir_name/$f");
```

Example 19-2. pc_process_dir2() (continued)

```
        }
    }
    $d->close();
    foreach ($subdirectories as $subdirectory) {
        pc_process_dir2($subdirectory,$func_name,$max_depth,$depth+1);
    }
  }
}
```

The pc_process_dir2() function doesn't return a list of directories; instead, the function $func_name is called with the file as its argument. Here's how to print out the last access times:

```
function printatime($file) {
    print "$file was last accessed at ".strftime('%c',fileatime($file))."\n";
}

pc_process_dir2('/tmp','printatime');
```

Although the two functions produce the same results, the second version uses less memory because potentially large arrays of files aren't passed around.

The pc_process_dir() and pc_process_dir2() functions use a *breadth-first search*. In this type of search, the functions handle all the files in the current directory; then they recurse into each subdirectory. In a *depth-first search*, they recurse into a subdirectory as soon as the subdirectory is found, whether or not there are files remaining in the current directory. The breadth-first search is more memory efficient; each pointer to the current directory is closed (with $d->close()) before the function recurses into subdirectories, so there's only one directory pointer open at a time.

Because is_dir() returns true when passed a symbolic link that points to a directory, both versions of the function follow symbolic links as they traverse down the directory tree. If you don't want to follow links, change the line:

```
    if (is_dir("$dir_name/$f")) {
```

to:

```
    if (is_dir("$dir_name/$f") && (! is_link("$dir_name/$f"))) {
```

See Also

Recipe 6.9 for a discussion of variable functions; documentation on is_dir() at *http:// www.php.net/is-dir* and is_link() at *http://www.php.net/is-link*.

19.10 Making New Directories

Problem

You want to create a directory.

Solution

Use mkdir():

```
mkdir('/tmp/apples',0777) or die($php_errormsg);
```

Discussion

The second argument to mkdir() is the permission mode for the new directory, which must be an octal number. The current umask is taken away from this permission value to create the permissions for the new directory. So, if the current umask is 0002, calling mkdir('/tmp/apples',0777) sets the permissions on the resulting directory to 0775 (user and group can read, write, and execute; others can only read and execute).

PHP's built-in mkdir() can make a directory only if its parent exists. For example, if */tmp/a* doesn't exist, you can't create */tmp/a/b* until */tmp/a* is created. To create a directory and its parents, you have two choices: you can call your system's mkdir program, or you can use the pc_mkdir_parents() function, shown in Example 19-3. To use your system's *mkdir* program, on Unix, use this:

```
system('/bin/mkdir -p '.escapeshellarg($directory));
```

On Windows do:

```
system('mkdir '.escapeshellarg($directory));
```

You can also use the pc_mkdir_parents() function shown in Example 19-3.

Example 19-3. pc_mkdir_parents()

```
function pc_mkdir_parents($d,$umask = 0777) {
    $dirs = array($d);
    $d = dirname($d);
    $last_dirname = '';
    while($last_dirname != $d) {
        array_unshift($dirs,$d);
        $last_dirname = $d;
        $d = dirname($d);
    }

    foreach ($dirs as $dir) {
        if (! file_exists($dir)) {
            if (! mkdir($dir,$umask)) {
```

Example 19-3. pc_mkdir_parents() (continued)

```
              error_log("Can't make directory: $dir");
              return false;
         }
    } elseif (! is_dir($dir)) {
        error_log("$dir is not a directory");
        return false;
    }
  }
  return true;
}
```

For example:

```
  pc_mkdir_parents('/usr/local/upload/test',0777);
```

See Also

Documentation on mkdir() at *http://www.php.net/mkdir*; your system's *mkdir* documentation, such as the Unix *mkdir(1)* man page or the Windows *mkdir /?* help text.

19.11 Removing a Directory and Its Contents

Problem

You want to remove a directory and all of its contents, including subdirectories and their contents.

Solution

On Unix, use *rm*:

```
    $directory = escapeshellarg($directory);
    exec("rm -rf $directory");
```

On Windows, use *rmdir*:

```
    $directory = escapeshellarg($directory);
    exec("rmdir /s /q $directory");
```

Discussion

Removing files, obviously, can be dangerous. Be sure to escape $directory with escapeshellarg() so that you don't delete unintended files.

Because PHP's built-in directory removal function, rmdir(), works only on empty directories, and unlink() can't accept shell wildcards, calling a system program is much easier than recursively looping through all files in a directory, removing them, and then removing each directory. If an external utility isn't available, however, you can modify the pc_process_dir() function from Recipe 19.9 to remove each subdirectory.

See Also

Documentation on rmdir() at *http://www.php.net/rmdir*; your system's *rm* or *rmdir* documentation, such as the Unix *rm(1)* manpage or the Windows *rmdir /?* help text.

19.12 Program: Web Server Directory Listing

The *web-ls.php* program shown in Example 19-4 provides a view of the files inside your web server's document root, formatted like the output of the Unix command *ls*. Filenames are linked so that you can download each file, and directory names are linked so that you can browse in each directory, as shown in Figure 19-1.

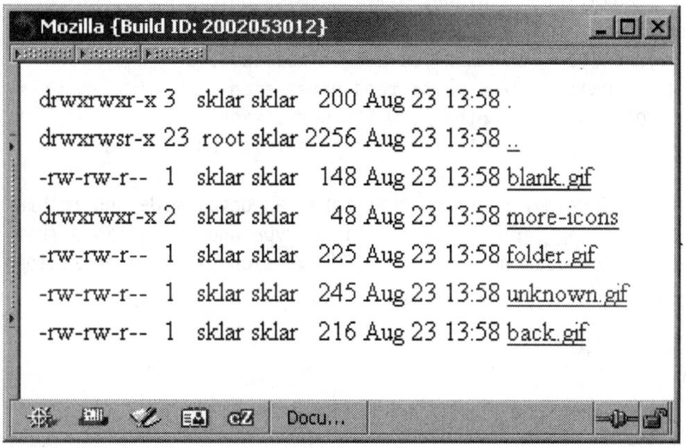

Figure 19-1. Web listing

Most lines in Example 19-4 are devoted to building an easy-to-read representation of the file's permissions, but the guts of the program are in the while loop at the end. The $d->read() method gets the name of each file in the directory. Then, lstat() retrieves information about that file, and printf() prints out the formatted information about that file.

The mode_string() functions and the constants it uses turn the octal representation of a file's mode (e.g., 35316) into an easier-to-read string (e.g., -rwsrw-r--).

Example 19-4. web-ls.php

```
/* Bit masks for determining file permissions and type. The names and values
 * listed below are POSIX-compliant, individual systems may have their own
 * extensions.
 */
```

Example 19-4. web-ls.php (continued)

```php
define('S_IFMT',0170000);    // mask for all types
define('S_IFSOCK',0140000);  // type: socket
define('S_IFLNK',0120000);   // type: symbolic link
define('S_IFREG',0100000);   // type: regular file
define('S_IFBLK',0060000);   // type: block device
define('S_IFDIR',0040000);   // type: directory
define('S_IFCHR',0020000);   // type: character device
define('S_IFIFO',0010000);   // type: fifo
define('S_ISUID',0004000);   // set-uid bit
define('S_ISGID',0002000);   // set-gid bit
define('S_ISVTX',0001000);   // sticky bit
define('S_IRWXU',00700);     // mask for owner permissions
define('S_IRUSR',00400);     // owner: read permission
define('S_IWUSR',00200);     // owner: write permission
define('S_IXUSR',00100);     // owner: execute permission
define('S_IRWXG',00070);     // mask for group permissions
define('S_IRGRP',00040);     // group: read permission
define('S_IWGRP',00020);     // group: write permission
define('S_IXGRP',00010);     // group: execute permission
define('S_IRWXO',00007);     // mask for others permissions
define('S_IROTH',00004);     // others: read permission
define('S_IWOTH',00002);     // others: write permission
define('S_IXOTH',00001);     // others: execute permission

/* mode_string() is a helper function that takes an octal mode and returns
 * a ten character string representing the file type and permissions that
 * correspond to the octal mode. This is a PHP version of the mode_string()
 * function in the GNU fileutils package.
 */
function mode_string($mode) {
  $s = array();

  // set type letter
  if (($mode & S_IFMT) == S_IFBLK) {
    $s[0] = 'b';
  } elseif (($mode & S_IFMT) == S_IFCHR) {
    $s[0] = 'c';
  } elseif (($mode & S_IFMT) == S_IFDIR) {
    $s[0] = 'd';
  } elseif (($mode & S_IFMT) ==  S_IFREG) {
    $s[0] = '-';
  } elseif (($mode & S_IFMT) ==  S_IFIFO) {
    $s[0] = 'p';
  } elseif (($mode & S_IFMT) == S_IFLNK) {
    $s[0] = 'l';
  } elseif (($mode & S_IFMT) == S_IFSOCK) {
    $s[0] = 's';
  }

  // set user permissions
  $s[1] = $mode & S_IRUSR ? 'r' : '-';
```

Example 19-4. web-ls.php (continued)

```php
  $s[2] = $mode & S_IWUSR ? 'w' : '-';
  $s[3] = $mode & S_IXUSR ? 'x' : '-';

  // set group permissions
  $s[4] = $mode & S_IRGRP ? 'r' : '-';
  $s[5] = $mode & S_IWGRP ? 'w' : '-';
  $s[6] = $mode & S_IXGRP ? 'x' : '-';

  // set other permissions
  $s[7] = $mode & S_IROTH ? 'r' : '-';
  $s[8] = $mode & S_IWOTH ? 'w' : '-';
  $s[9] = $mode & S_IXOTH ? 'x' : '-';

  // adjust execute letters for set-uid, set-gid, and sticky
  if ($mode & S_ISUID) {
    if ($s[3] != 'x') {
      // set-uid but not executable by owner
      $s[3] = 'S';
    } else {
      $s[3] = 's';
    }
  }

  if ($mode & S_ISGID) {
    if ($s[6] != 'x') {
      // set-gid but not executable by group
      $s[6] = 'S';
    } else {
      $s[6] = 's';
    }
  }

  if ($mode & S_ISVTX) {
    if ($s[9] != 'x') {
      // sticky but not executable by others
      $s[9] = 'T';
    } else {
      $s[9] = 't';
    }
  }

  // return formatted string
  return join('',$s);

}

// Start at the document root if not specified
if (isset($_REQUEST['dir'])) {
    $dir = $_REQUEST['dir'];
} else {
    $dir = '';
}
```

Example 19-4. web-ls.php (continued)

```php
// locate $dir in the filesystem
$real_dir = realpath($_SERVER['DOCUMENT_ROOT'].$dir);

// make sure $real_dir is inside document root
if (! preg_match('/^'.preg_quote($_SERVER['DOCUMENT_ROOT'],'/').'/',
                 $real_dir)) {
    die("$dir is not inside the document root");
}

// canonicalize $dir by removing the document root from its beginning
$dir = substr_replace($real_dir,'',0,strlen($_SERVER['DOCUMENT_ROOT']));

// are we opening a directory?
if (! is_dir($real_dir)) {
    die("$real_dir is not a directory");
}

// open the specified directory
$d = dir($real_dir) or die("can't open $real_dir: $php_errormsg");

print '<table>';

// read each entry in the directory
while (false !== ($f = $d->read())) {

    // get information about this file
    $s = lstat($d->path.'/'.$f);

    // translate uid into user name
    $user_info = posix_getpwuid($s['uid']);

    // translate gid into group name
    $group_info = posix_getgrgid($s['gid']);

    // format the date for readability
    $date = strftime('%b %e %H:%M',$s['mtime']);

    // translate the octal mode into a readable string
    $mode = mode_string($s['mode']);

    $mode_type = substr($mode,0,1);
    if (($mode_type == 'c') || ($mode_type == 'b')) {
        /* if it's a block or character device, print out the major and
         * minor device type instead of the file size */
        $major = ($s['rdev'] >> 8) & 0xff;
        $minor = $s['rdev'] & 0xff;
        $size = sprintf('%3u, %3u',$major,$minor);
    } else {
        $size = $s['size'];
    }
```

Example 19-4. web-ls.php (continued)

```
    // format the <a href=""> around the filename
    // no link for the current directory
    if ('.' == $f) {
        $href = $f;
    } else {
        // don't include the ".." in the parent directory link
        if ('..' == $f) {
            $href = urlencode(dirname($dir));
        } else {
            $href = urlencode($dir) . '/' . urlencode($f);
        }

        /* everything but "/" should be urlencoded */
        $href = str_replace('%2F','/',$href);

        // browse other directories with web-ls
        if (is_dir(realpath($d->path . '/' . $f))) {
            $href = sprintf('<a href="%s?dir=%s">%s</a>',
                            $_SERVER['PHP_SELF'],$href,$f);
        } else {
            // link to files to download them
            $href= sprintf('<a href="%s">%s</a>',$href,$f);
        }

        // if it's a link, show the link target, too
        if ('l' == $mode_type) {
            $href .= ' -&gt; ' . readlink($d->path.'/'.$f);
        }
    }

    // print out the appropriate info for this file
    printf('<tr><td>%s</td><td>%3u</td><td align="right">%s</td>
            <td align="right">%s</td><td align="right">%s</td>
            <td align="right">%s</td><td>%s</td></tr>',
        $mode,                  // formatted mode string
        $s['nlink'],            // number of links to this file
        $user_info['name'],     // owner's user name
        $group_info['name'],    // group name
        $size,                  // file size (or device numbers)
        $date,                  // last modified date and time
        $href);                 // link to browse or download
}

print '</table>';
```

19.13 Program: Site Search

You can use *site-search.php*, shown in Example 19-5, as a search engine for a small-to-medium size, file-based site.

The program looks for a search term (in $_REQUEST['term']) in all files within a specified set of directories under the document root. Those directories are set in $search_dirs. It also recurses into subdirectories and follows symbolic links but keeps track of which files and directories it has seen so that it doesn't get caught in an endless loop.

If any pages are found that contain the search term, it prints list of links to those pages, alphabetically ordered by each page's title. If a page doesn't have a title (between the <title> and </title> tags), the page's relative URI from the document root is used.

The program looks for the search term between the <body> and </body> tags in each file. If you have a lot of text in your pages inside <body> tags that you want to exclude from the search, surround the text that should be searched with specific HTML comments and then modify $body_regex to look for those tags instead. Say, for example, if your page looks like this:

```
<body>

// Some HTML for menus, headers, etc.

<!-- search-start -->

<h1>Aliens Invade Earth</h1>

<h3>by H.G. Wells</h3>

<p>Aliens invaded earth today. Uh Oh.</p>

// More of the story

<!-- search-end -->

// Some HTML for footers, etc.

</body>
```

To match the search term against just the title, author, and story inside the HTML comments, change $body_regex to:

```
$body_regex = '#<!-- search-start -->(.*' . preg_quote($_REQUEST['term'],'#').
              '.*)<!-- search-end -->#Sis';
```

If you don't want the search term to match text that's inside HTML or PHP tags in your pages, add a call to strip_tags() to the code that loads the contents of the file for searching:

```
// load the contents of the file into $file
$file = strip_tags(join('',file($path)));
```

Example 19-5. site-search.php

```
function pc_search_dir($dir) {
    global $body_regex,$title_regex,$seen;

    // array to hold pages that match
    $pages = array();

    // array to hold directories to recurse into
    $dirs = array();

    // mark this directory as seen so we don't look in it again
    $seen[realpath($dir)] = true;

    // if we can get a directory handle for this directory
    if (is_readable($dir) && ($d = dir($dir))) {
        // get each file name in the directory
        while (false !== ($f = $d->read())) {
            // build the full path of the file
            $path = $d->path.'/'.$f;
            // if it's a regular file and we can read it
            if (is_file($path) && is_readable($path)) {

                $realpath = realpath($path);
                // if we've seen this file already,
                if ($seen[$realpath]) {
                    // then skip it
                    continue;
                } else {
                    // otherwise, mark it as seen so we skip it
                    // if we come to it again
                    $seen[$realpath] = true;
                }

                // load the contents of the file into $file
                $file = join('',file($path));

                // if the search term is inside the body delimiters
                if (preg_match($body_regex,$file)) {

                    // construct the relative URI of the file by removing
                    // the document root from the full path
                    $uri = substr_replace($path,'',0,strlen($_SERVER['DOCUMENT_ROOT']));

                    // If the page has a title, find it
                    if (preg_match('#<title>(.*?)</title>#Sis',$file,$match)) {
```

Example 19-5. site-search.php (continued)

```
                        // and add the title and URI to $pages
                        array_push($pages,array($uri,$match[1]));
                    } else {
                        // otherwise use the URI as the title
                        array_push($pages,array($uri,$uri));
                    }
                }
            } else {
                // if the directory entry is a valid subdirectory
                if (is_dir($path) && ('.' != $f) && ('..' != $f)) {
                    // add it to the list of directories to recurse into
                    array_push($dirs,$path);
                }
            }
        }
        $d->close();
    }

    /* look through each file in each subdirectory of this one, and add
       the matching pages in those directories to $pages. only look in
       a subdirectory if we haven't seen it yet.
    */
    foreach ($dirs as $subdir) {
        $realdir = realpath($subdir);
        if (! $seen[$realdir]) {
            $seen[$realdir] = true;
            $pages = array_merge($pages,pc_search_dir($subdir));
        }
    }

    return $pages;
}

// helper function to sort matched pages alphabetically by title
function pc_page_sort($a,$b) {
    if ($a[1] == $b[1]) {
        return strcmp($a[0],$b[0]);
    } else {
        return ($a[1] > $b[1]);
    }
}

// array to hold the pages that match the search term
$matching_pages = array();
// array to hold pages seen while scanning for the search term
$seen = array();
// directories underneath the document root to search
$search_dirs = array('sports','movies','food');
// regular expression to use in searching files. The "S" pattern
// modifier tells the PCRE engine to "study" the regex for greater
// efficiency.
```

Example 19-5. site-search.php (continued)

```php
$body_regex = '#<body>(.*' . preg_quote($_REQUEST['term'],'#').
              '.*)</body>#Sis';

// add the files that match in each directory to $matching_pages
foreach ($search_dirs as $dir) {
    $matching_pages = array_merge($matching_pages,
                                  pc_search_dir($_SERVER['DOCUMENT_ROOT'].'/'.$dir));
}

if (count($matching_pages)) {
    // sort the matching pages by title
    usort($matching_pages,'pc_page_sort');
    print '<ul>';
    // print out each title with a link to the page
    foreach ($matching_pages as $k => $v) {
        print sprintf('<li> <a href="%s">%s</a>',$v[0],$v[1]);
    }
    print '</ul>';
} else {
    print 'No pages found.';
}
```

CHAPTER 20

Client-Side PHP

20.0 Introduction

PHP was created for web programming and is still used mostly for that purpose. However, newer versions of PHP are increasingly more capable as a general-purpose scripting language. Using PHP for scripts you run from the command line is especially helpful when they share code with your web applications. If you have a discussion board on your web site, you might want to run a program every few minutes or hours to scan new postings and alert you to any messages that contain certain keywords. Writing this scanning program in PHP lets you share relevant discussion-board code with the main discussion-board application. Not only does this save you time, but also helps avoid maintenance overhead down the road.

With the PHP-GTK extension, your command-line PHP programs can be full-featured GUI applications. These can also share code with PHP web applications and text-based command-line programs. Like PHP, PHP-GTK is cross-platform, so the same code runs on Unix and Windows.

The same PHP binary built to be executed as a CGI program can be run from the command line. To run a script, pass the script filename as an argument:

```
% php scan-discussions.php
```

On Unix, you can also use the "hash-bang" syntax at the top of your scripts to run the PHP interpreter automatically. If the PHP binary is in *usr/local/bin*, make the first line of your script:

```
#!/usr/local/bin/php
```

You can then run the script just by typing its name on the command line, as long as the file has execute permission.

Command-line PHP scripts almost always use the -q flag, which prevents PHP from printing HTTP response headers at the beginning of its output:

```
% php -q scan-discussions.php
```

You can also use this:

```
#!/usr/local/bin/php -q
```

Another helpful option on the command line is the -c flag, which lets you specify an alternate *php.ini* file to load settings from. If your default *php.ini* file is */usr/local/lib/php.ini*, it can be helpful to have a separate configuration file at */usr/local/lib/php-commandline.ini* with settings such as max_execution_time = 0; this ensures that your scripts don't quit after 30 seconds. Here's how to use this alternate file:

```
% php -q -c /usr/local/lib/php-commandline.ini scan-discussions.php
```

You can also use this :

```
#!/usr/local/bin/php -q -c /usr/local/lib/php-commandline.ini
```

If it's likely that you'll use some of your classes and functions both for the web and for the command line, abstract the code that needs to react differently in those different circumstances, such as HTML versus plain-text output or access to environment variables that a web server sets up. A useful tactic is to make your code aware of a global variable called $COMMAND_LINE. Set this to true at the top of your command-line scripts. You can then branch your scripts' behavior as follows:

```
if ($GLOBALS['COMMAND_LINE']) {
  print "Database error: ".mysql_error()."\n";
} else {
  print "Database error.<br>";
  error_log(mysql_error());
}
```

This code not only adjusts the output formatting based on the context it's executing in (\n versus <br>), but also where the information goes. On the command line, it's helpful to the person running the program to see the error message from MySQL, but on the Web, you don't want your users to see potentially sensitive data. Instead, the code outputs a generic error message and stores the details in the server's error log for private review.

Beginning with Version 4.3, PHP builds include a command-line interface (CLI) binary.* The CLI binary is similar to the CGI binary but has some important differences that make it more shell-friendly. Some configuration directives have hard-coded values with CLI; for example, the html_errors directive is set to false, and implicit_flush is set to true. The max_execution_time directive is set to 0, allowing unlimited program runtime. Finally, register_argc_argv is set to true. This means you can look for argument information in $argv and $argc instead of in $_SERVER['argv'] and $_SERVER['argc']. Argument processing is discussed in Recipes 20.1 and 20.2.

---

* The CLI binary can be built under 4.2.x versions by explicitly configuring PHP with --enable-cli.

The CLI binary accepts a slightly different set of arguments than the CGI binary. It doesn't accept the -q or -C flags because it does what these flags indicate by default. While -q tells the CGI binary not to print headers, the CLI binary never prints headers. Even the header( ) function produces no output under CLI. Similarly, the -C flag tells the CGI binary not to change to the directory of the script being run. The CLI binary never changes to the script directory.

The CLI binary also takes one new argument: -r. When followed by some PHP code without <?php and ?> script tags, the CLI binary runs the code. For example, here's how to print the current time:

```
% php -r 'print strftime("%c");'
```

Finally, the CLI binary defines handles to the standard I/O streams as the constants STDIN, STDOUT, and STDERR. You can use these instead of creating your own file handles with fopen( ):

```
// read from standard in
$input = fgets(STDIN,1024);

// write to standard out
fwrite(STDOUT,$jokebook);

// write to standard error
fwrite(STDERR,$error_code);
```

If you're using the CLI binary, you can use php_sapi_name( ) instead of $GLOBALS['COMMAND_LINE'] to test whether a script is running in a web or command-line context:

```
if ('cli' == php_sapi_name()) {
  print "Database error: ".mysql_error()."\n";
} else {
  print "Database error.<br>";
  error_log(mysql_error());
}
```

You can use the CLI binary or the CGI binary to run programs that use the PHP-GTK extension. This extension is an interface to the GTK+ toolkit, which is a library of widgets, screen drawing code, and other necessary functions for building a GUI application.

Widgets are GUI interface elements such as buttons, scrollbars, windows, menus, and select boxes. To build a PHP-GTK application, your code must create widgets and arrange them on the screen. Recipe 20.5 shows how to create and display a widget, Recipe 20.6 shows how to arrange multiple widgets for display together, and Recipe 20.8 explains how to display a menu bar.

Widgets communicate with each other and with the rest of your program using signals. When something happens to a widget, it emits a signal; for example, when a button is clicked, it emits a clicked signal. Recipe 20.7 discusses how to capture these signals and take action when one is emitted. The sample application in Recipe 20.10 combines PHP-GTK with some SOAP function calls to display weather conditions around the world.

To install PHP-GTK on Unix, download the latest version of PHP-GTK from *http://gtk.php.net/download.php* and the GTK+ libraries from *http://www.gtk.org/download*. You also need *libtool* 1.4.2, *automake* 1.4, and *autoconf* 2.13 (available at *http://www.gnu.org/directory/* if they're not already installed on your system).

Once you've downloaded all the necessary files and installed the support libraries and tools, unpack the PHP-GTK source distribution. In the PHP-GTK directory, run *./buildconf* to create configuration files, *./configure* to create makefiles, then *make* to build the PHP-GTK extension. Last, run *make install* to install the PHP-GTK extension in your PHP extensions directory. You can find detailed Unix installation instructions, including common build problems, at *http://gtk.php.net/manual/en/install.unix.php*.

To install PHP-GTK on Windows, no compiling is necessary. From *http://gtk.php.net/download.php*, you can download a compiled PHP-GTK extension and supporting libraries. Once you've downloaded and unzipped the Windows distribution, copy the files in the *php4* subdirectory to your PHP binary directory (or create one if it doesn't already exist). Copy the files in the *winnt\system32* subdirectory to your *system32* directory (*C:\WINNT\SYSTEM32* for Windows NT and Windows 2000; *C:\WINDOWS\SYSTEM32* for Windows 95 and Windows 98). If you don't already have a *php.ini* file in place, copy the *winnt\php.ini* file to your Windows directory (*C:\WINNT* or *C:\WINDOWS*). If you already have a *php.ini* file in place, add these lines to the end of it:

```
[PHP-GTK]
php-gtk.extensions = php_gtk_libglade.dll, php_gtk_sqpane.dll
```

Detailed Windows installation instructions are at *http://gtk.php.net/manual/en/install.win32.php*.

On either platform, once you've installed the PHP-GTK extension, you need to use the dl( ) function to load it in any script in which you want to use GTK functionality. On Windows:

```
if (! class_exists('gtk')) {
    dl('php_gtk.dll');
}
```

On Unix:

```
if (! class_exists('gtk')) {
    dl('php_gtk.so');
}
```

If you want the same script to run unaltered on Unix or Windows, you can load the PHP-GTK extension like this:

```
if (! class_exists('gtk')) {
    dl('php_gtk.'. (((strtoupper(substr(PHP_OS,0,3))) == 'WIN')?'dll':'so'));
}
```

The GTK+ toolkit is large and powerful. PHP-GTK makes it easy to create and manipulate GTK+ objects, but designing and planning a GUI application is still a significant task. In addition to the comprehensive PHP-GTK documentation at *http:// gtk.php.net/manual/*, also take advantage of the GTK+ documentation itself at *http:// developer.gnome.org/doc/API/gtk/index.html*. The C class and function names in the GTK+ documentation map almost directly to their PHP equivalents. Also, the tutorial at *http://www.gtk.org/tutorial/* is for GTK+ 2.0 (not 1.2), but it is still a good introduction to the concepts and practices of GTK+ application building.

20.1 Parsing Program Arguments

Problem

You want to process arguments passed on the command line.

Solution

Look in $_SERVER['argc'] for the number of arguments and $_SERVER['argv'] for their values. The first argument, $_SERVER['argv'][0], is the name of script that is being run:

```
if ($_SERVER['argc'] != 2) {
    die("Wrong number of arguments: I expect only 1.");
}

$size = filesize($_SERVER['argv'][1]);

print "I am $_SERVER[argv][0] and report that the size of ";
print "$_SERVER[argv][1] is $size bytes.";
```

Discussion

In order to set options based on flags passed from the command line, loop through $_SERVER['argv'] from 1 to $_SERVER['argc']:

```
for ($i = 1; $i < $_SERVER['argc']; $i++) {
    switch ($_SERVER['argv'][$i]) {
    case '-v':
        // set a flag
        $verbose = 1;
        break;
```

```
case '-c':
    // advance to the next argument
    $i++;
    // if it's set, save the value
    if (isset($_SERVER['argv'][$i])) {
        $config_file = $_SERVER['argv'][$i];
    } else {
        // quit if no filename specified
        die("Must specify a filename after -c");
    }
    break;
case '-q':
    $quiet = 1;
    break;
default:
    die('Unknown argument: '.$_SERVER['argv'][$i]);
    break;
}
}
```

In this example, the -v and -q arguments are flags that set $verbose and $quiet, but the -c argument is expected to be followed by a string. This string is assigned to $config_file.

See Also

Recipe 20.2 for more parsing arguments with *getopt*; documentation on $_SERVER['argc'] and $_SERVER['argv'] at http://www.php.net/reserved.variables.

20.2   Parsing Program Arguments with getopt

Problem

You want to parse program options that may be specified as short or long options, or they may be grouped.

Solution

Use PEAR's Console_Getopt class. Its getopt() method can parse both short-style options such as -a or -b and long-style options such as --alice or --bob:

```
$o = new Console_Getopt;

// accepts -a, -b, and -c
$opts = $o->getopt($_SERVER['argv'],'abc');

// accepts --alice and --bob
$opts = $o->getopt($_SERVER['argv'],'',array('alice','bob'));
```

Discussion

To parse short-style options, pass Console_Getopt::getopt( ) the array of command-line arguments and a string specifying valid options. This example allows -a, -b, or -c as arguments, alone or in groups:

```
$o = new Console_Getopt;
$opts = $o->getopt($_SERVER['argv'],'abc');
```

For the previous option string abc, these are valid sets of options to pass:

```
% program.php -a -b -c
% program.php -abc
% program.php -ab -c
```

The getopt( ) method returns an array. The first element in the array is a list of all of the parsed options that were specified on the command line, along with their values. The second element is any specified command-line option that wasn't in the argument specification passed to getopt( ). For example, if the previous program is run as:

```
% program.php -a -b sneeze
```

then $opts is:

```
Array
(
    [0] => Array
        (
            [0] => Array
                (
                    [0] => a
                    [1] =>
                )
            [1] => Array
                (
                    [0] => b
                    [1] =>
                )
        )
    [1] => Array
        (
            [0] => program.php
            [1] => sneeze
        )
)
```

Put a colon after an option in the specification string to indicate that it requires a value. Two colons means the value is optional. So, ab:c:: means that a can't have a value, b must, and c can take a value if specified. With this specification string, running the program as:

```
% program.php -a -b sneeze
```

makes $opts:

```
Array
(
    [0] => Array
        (
            [0] => Array
                (
                    [0] => a
                    [1] =>
                )
            [1] => Array
                (
                    [0] => b
                    [1] => sneeze
                )
        )
    [1] => Array
        (
            [0] => program.php
        )
)
```

Because sneeze is now set as the value of b, it is no longer in the array of unparsed options. Note that the array of unparsed options always contains the name of the program.

To parse long-style arguments, supply getopt( ) with an array that describes your desired arguments. Put each argument in an array element (leave off the leading --) and follow it with = to indicate a mandatory argument or = = to indicate an optional argument. This array is the third argument to getopt( ). The second argument (the string for short-style arguments) can be left blank or not, depending on whether you also want to parse short-style arguments. This example allows debug as an argument with no value, name with a mandatory value, and size with an optional value:

```
require 'Console/Getopt.php';
$o = new Console_Getopt;
$opts = $o->getopt($_SERVER['argv'],'',array('debug','name=','size=='));
```

These are valid ways to run this program:

```
% program.php --debug
% program.php --name=Susannah
% program.php --name Susannah
% program.php --debug --size
% program.php --size=56 --name=Susannah
% program.php --name --debug
```

The last example is valid (if counterproductive) because it treats --debug as the value of the name argument and doesn't consider the debug argument to be set. Values can be separated from their arguments on the command line by either a = or a space.

For long-style arguments, getopt( ) includes the leading -- in the array of parsed arguments; for example, when run as:

```
% program.php --debug --name=Susannah
```

$opts is set to:

```
Array
(
    [0] => Array
        (
            [0] => Array
                (
                    [0] => --debug
                    [1] =>
                )
            [1] => Array
                (
                    [0] => --name
                    [1] => Susannah
                )
        )
    [1] => Array
        (
            [0] => program.php
        )
)
```

We've been using $_SERVER['argv'] as the array of command-line arguments, which is fine by default. Console_Getopt provides a method, readPHPArgv( ), to look also in $argv and $HTTP_SERVER_VARS['argv'] for command-line arguments. Use it by passing its results to getopt( ):

```
require 'Console/Getopt.php';
$o = new Console_Getopt;
$opts = $o->getopt($o->readPHPArgv(),'',array('debug','name=','size=='));
```

Both getopt( ) and readPHPArgv( ) return a Getopt_Error object when these encounter an error; for example, having no option specified for an option that requires one. Getopt_Error extends the PEAR_Error base class, so you can use familiar methods to handle errors:

```
require 'Console/Getopt.php';
$o = new Console_Getopt;
$opts = $o->getopt($o->readPHPArgv(),'',array('debug','name=','size=='));

if (PEAR::isError($opts)) {
    print $opts->getMessage();
} else {
    // process options
}
```

See Also

Recipe 20.1 for parsing of program options without *getopt*; documentation on Console_Getopt at *http://pear.php.net/manual/en/core.console.getopt.php*.

20.3   Reading from the Keyboard

Problem

You need to read in some typed user input.

Solution

Use fopen( ) with the special filename *php://stdin*:

```
print "Type your message. Type '.' on a line by itself when you're done.\n";

$fh = fopen('php://stdin','r') or die($php_errormsg);
$last_line = false;  $message = '';
while (! $last_line) {
    $next_line = fgets($fp,1024);
    if (".\n" == $next_line) {
      $last_line = true;
    } else {
      $message .= $next_line;
    }
}

print "\nYour message is:\n$message\n";
```

If the Readline extension is installed, use readline( ):

```
$last_line = false; $message = '';
while (! $last_line) {
    $next_line = readline();
    if ('.' == $next_line) {
        $last_line = true;
    } else {
        $message .= $next_line."\n";
    }
}

print "\nYour message is:\n$message\n";
```

Discussion

Once you get a file handle pointing to *stdin* with fopen( ), you can use all the standard file-reading functions to process input (fread( ), fgets( ), etc.) The solution uses fgets( ), which returns input a line at a time. If you use fread( ), the input still needs to be newline-terminated to make fread( ) return. For example, if you run:

```
$fh = fopen('php://stdin','r') or die($php_errormsg);
$msg = fread($fh,4);
print "[$msg]";
```

And type in tomato and then a newline, the output is [toma]. The fread( ) grabs only four characters from *stdin*, as directed, but still needs the newline as a signal to return from waiting for keyboard input.

The Readline extension provides an interface to the GNU Readline library. The readline( ) function returns a line at a time, without the ending newline. Readline allows Emacs and *vi*-style line editing by users. You can also use it to keep a history of previously entered commands:

```
$command_count = 1;
while (true) {
    $line = readline("[$command_count]--> ");
    readline_add_history($line);
    if (is_readable($line)) {
        print "$line is a readable file.\n";
    }
    $command_count++;
}
```

This example displays a prompt with an incrementing count before each line. Since each line is added to the readline history with readline_add_history( ), pressing the up and down arrows at a prompt scrolls through the previously entered lines.

See Also

Documentation on fopen( ) at *http://www.php.net/fopen*, fgets( ) at *http://www.php.net/fgets*, fread( ) at *http://www.php.net/fread*, and the Readline extension at *http://www.php.net/readline*; the Readline library at *http://cnswww.cns.cwru.edu/php/chet/readline/rltop.html*.

20.4 Reading Passwords

Problem

You need to read a string from the command line without it being echoed as it's typed; for example, when entering passwords.

Solution

On Unix systems, use */bin/stty* to toggle echoing of typed characters:

```
// turn off echo
`/bin/stty -echo`;

// read password
$password = readline();

// turn echo back on
`/bin/stty echo`;
```

On Windows, use w32api_register_function( ) to import _getch( ) from *msvcrt.dll*:

```
// load the w32api extension and register _getch()
dl('php_w32api.dll');
w32api_register_function('msvcrt.dll','_getch','int');

while(true) {
    // get a character from the keyboard
    $c = chr(_getch());
    if ( "\r" == $c ||  "\n" == $c ) {
        // if it's a newline, break out of the loop, we've got our password
        break;
    } elseif ("\x08" == $c) {
        /* if it's a backspace, delete the previous char from $password */
        $password = substr_replace($password,'',-1,1);
    } elseif ("\x03" == $c) {
        // if it's Control-C, clear $password and break out of the loop
        $password = NULL;
        break;
    } else {
        // otherwise, add the character to the password
        $password .= $c;
    }
}
```

Discussion

On Unix, you use */bin/stty* to control the terminal characteristics so that typed characters aren't echoed to the screen while you read a password. Windows doesn't have */bin/stty*, so you use the W32api extension to get access _getch( ) in the Microsoft C runtime library, *msvcrt.dll*. The _getch( ) function reads a character without echoing it to the screen. It returns the ASCII code of the character read, so you convert it to a character using chr( ). You then take action based on the character typed. If it's a newline or carriage return, you break out of the loop because the password has been entered. If it's a backspace, you delete a character from the end of the password. If it's a Control-C interrupt, you set the password to NULL and break out of the loop. If none of these things are true, the character is concatenated to $password. When you exit the loop, $password holds the entered password.

The following code displays Login: and Password: prompts, and compares the entered password to the corresponding encrypted password stored in */etc/passwd*. This requires that the system not use shadow passwords.

```
print "Login: ";
$fh = fopen('php://stdin','r')   or die($php_errormsg);
$username = rtrim(fgets($fh,64)) or die($php_errormsg);

preg_match('/^[a-zA-Z0-9]+$/',$username)
    or die("Invalid username: only letters and numbers allowed");


print 'Password: ';
`/bin/stty -echo`;
$password = rtrim(fgets($fh,64)) or die($php_errormsg);
`/bin/stty echo`;
print "\n";

// nothing more to read from the keyboard
fclose($fh);

// find corresponding line in /etc/passwd
$fh = fopen('/etc/passwd','r')   or die($php_errormsg);
$found_user = 0;
while (! ($found_user || feof($fh))) {
    $passwd_line = fgets($fh,256);
    if (preg_match("/^$username:/",$passwd_line)) {
        $found_user = 1;
    }
}
fclose($fh);

$found_user or die ("Can't find user \"$username\"");

// parse the correct line from /etc/passwd
$passwd_parts = split(':',$passwd_line);

/* encrypt the entered password and compare it to the password in
   /etc/passwd */
$encrypted_password = crypt($password,
                            substr($passwd_parts[1],0,CRYPT_SALT_LENGTH));

if ($encrypted_password == $passwd_parts[1]) {
    print "login successful";
} else {
    print "login unsuccessful";
}
```

See Also

Documentation on readline( ) at *http://www.php.net/readline*, chr( ) at *http://www.php.net/chr*, on w32api_register_function( ) at *http://www.php.net/w32api-register-function*, and on _getch( ) at *http://msdn.microsoft.com/library/en-us/vccore98/HTML/_crt__getch.2c_._getche.asp*; on Unix, see your system's *stty(1)* manpage.

20.5   Displaying a GUI Widget in a Window

Problem

You want to display a window with a GUI widget, such as a button, in it.

Solution

Create the window, create the widget, and then add the widget to the window:

```
// create the window
$window = &new GtkWindow();

// create the button and add it to the window
$button = &new GTKButton('Click Me, Alice');
$window->add($button);

// display the window
$window->show_all();

// necessary so that the program exits properly
function shutdown() { gtk::main_quit(); }
$window->connect('destroy','shutdown');

// start GTK's signal handling loop
gtk::main();
```

Discussion

First, you create a window by instantiating a new GtkWindow object. GTK objects must be created as references: &new GtkWindow( ), not new GtkWindow( ). You then create a new GtkButton object with a label "Click Me, Alice". Passing $button to the window's add( ) method adds the button to the window. The show_all( ) method displays the window and any widgets inside of it. The only widget inside the window in this example is the button. The next two lines ensure that the program quits when the window is closed. The shutdown( ) function is a callback, as is explained later in Recipe 20.7.

The last line is necessary in all PHP-GTK programs. Calling gtk::main( ) starts the signal-handling loop. This means that the program waits for signals emitted by its GUI widgets and then responds to the signals as they occur. These signals are activities like clicking on buttons, resizing windows, and typing in text boxes. The only signal this program pays attention to is the destroy signal. When the user closes the program's main window, the destroy signal is emitted, and gtk::main_quit( ) is called. This function exits the program.

See Also

Documentation on the GtkWindow class at *http://gtk.php.net/manual/en/gtk.gtkwindow.php*, on GTKContainer::add() at *http://gtk.php.net/manual/en/gtk.gtkcontainer.method.add.php*, on GtkWidget::show_all() at *http://gtk.php.net/manual/en/gtk.gtkwidget.method.show_all.php*, on the GtkButton class at *http://gtk.php.net/manual/en/gtk.gtkbutton.php*, on gtk::main_quit() at *http://gtk.php.net/manual/en/gtk.method.main_quit.php*, on and gtk::main() at *http://gtk.php.net/manual/en/gtk.method.main.php*; the tutorial at *http://gtk.php.net/manual/en/tutorials.hellow.php* is a helpful introduction to basic GTK programming.

20.6   Displaying Multiple GUI Widgets in a Window

Problem

You want to display more than one widget in a window.

Solution

Add all of the widgets in a container, and then add the container in the window:

```
// create the window
$window = &new GtkWindow();

// create the container - GtkVBox aligns widgets vertically
$container = &new GtkVBox();

// create a text entry widget and add it to the container
$text_entry = &new GtkEntry();
$container->pack_start($text_entry);

// create a button and add it to the container
$a_button = &new GtkButton('Abort');
$container->pack_start($a_button);

// create another button and add it to the container
$r_button = &new GtkButton('Retry');
$container->pack_start($r_button);

// create yet another button and add it to the container
$f_button = &new GtkButton('Fail');
$container->pack_start($f_button);

// add the container to the window
$window->add($container);
```

```
// display the window
$window->show_all();

// necessary so that the program exits properly
function shutdown() { gtk::main_quit(); }
$window->connect('destroy','shutdown');

// start GTK's signal handling loop
gtk::main();
```

Discussion

A window is a container that can hold only one widget. To put multiple widgets in a window, you must place all widgets into a container that can hold more than one widget and then put that container in the window. This process can be nested: the widgets inside a container can themselves be containers.

In the Solution, widgets are added to a GtkVBox container, which aligns the child widgets vertically, as shown in Figure 20-1. The add( ) method adds widgets to the GtkVBox, but pack_start( ) is used instead so that the size of the container is automatically updated with each new widget.

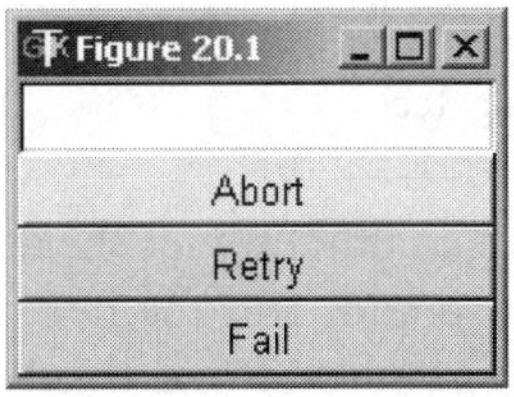

Figure 20-1. Widgets in a GtkVBox

GtkHBox is similar to GtkVBox. It aligns its child widgets horizontally instead of vertically. Figure 20-2 shows the four widgets from the Solution in a CtkHBox.

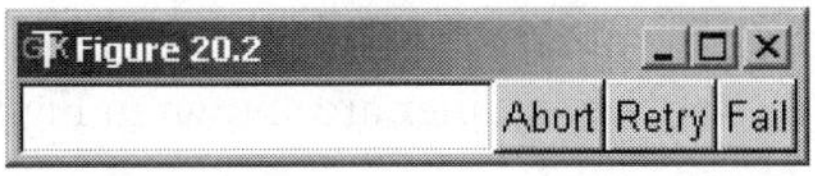

Figure 20-2. Widgets in a GtkHBox

GtkTable is a more flexible layout container; it aligns its child elements on a grid:

```
// create the window
$window = &new GtkWindow();

// create the container with 3 rows and 2 columns
$container = &new GtkTable(3,2);
```

```
// create a text entry widget and add it to the container
$text_entry = &new GtkEntry();
$container->attach($text_entry,0,2,0,1);

// create a button and add it to the container
$a_button = &new GtkButton('Abort');
$container->attach($a_button,0,1,1,2);

// create another button and add it to the container
$r_button = &new GtkButton('Retry');
$container->attach($r_button,1,2,1,2);

// create yet another button and add it to the container
$f_button = &new GtkButton('Fail');
$container->attach($f_button,0,2,2,3);

// add the container to the window
$window->add($container);

// display the window
$window->show_all();

// necessary so that the program exits properly
function shutdown() { gtk::main_quit(); }
$window->connect('destroy','shutdown');

// start GTK's signal handling loop
gtk::main();
```

Widgets are added to a GtkTable container with the attach( ) method. The first argument to attach( ) is the widget to add, and the next four arguments describe where in the grid to put the widget. The second and third arguments are the starting and ending columns for the widget. The fourth and fifth arguments are the starting and ending rows for the widget. For example:

```
$container->attach($text_entry,0,2,0,1)
```

means that the text-entry widget starts in column zero and ends in column two, spanning two columns. It starts at row zero and ends at row one, so it spans only one row. Rows and columns are numbered beginning with zero. The text entry and button widgets aligned in a GtkTable container are shown in Figure 20-3.

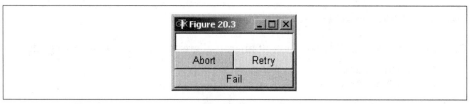

Figure 20-3. Widgets in a GtkTable

See Also

Documentation on containers at *http://gtk.php.net/manual/en/gtk.containers.wha-tare.php*, the GtkVBox class at *http://gtk.php.net/manual/en/gtk.gtkvbox.php*, the GtkHBox class at *http://gtk.php.net/manual/en/gtk.gtkhbox.php*, GtkBox::pack_start( ) at *http://gtk.php.net/manual/en/gtk.gtkbox.method.pack_start.php*, the GtkTable class at *http://gtk.php.net/manual/en/gtk.gtktable.php*, and GtkTable::attach( ) at *http:// gtk.php.net/manual/en/gtk.gtktable.method.attach.php*.

20.7 Responding to User Actions

Problem

You want to do something when a user clicks a button, chooses an item from a drop-down list, or otherwise interacts with a GUI widget.

Solution

Write a callback function and then associate the callback function with a signal using the connect( ) method:

```
// create the window
$window = &new GtkWindow();

// create a button with the current time as its label
$button = &new GtkButton(strftime('%c'));

// set the update_time() function as the callback for the "clicked" signal
$button->connect('clicked','update_time');

function update_time($b) {
    // the button's text is in a child of the button - a label widget
    $b_label = $b->child;
    // set the label text to the current time
    $b_label->set_text(strftime('%c'));
}

// add the button to the window
$window->add($button);

// display the window
$window->show_all();

// necessary so that the program exits properly
function shutdown() { gtk::main_quit(); }
$window->connect('destroy','shutdown');

// start GTK's signal handling loop
gtk::main();
```

Discussion

The code in the Solution displays a window with a button in it. On the button is the time, rendered by strftime('%c'). When the button is clicked, its label is updated with the current time.

The update_time( ) function is called each time the button is clicked because $button->connect('clicked','update_time') makes update_time( ) the callback function associated with the button's clicked signal. The first argument to the callback function is the widget whose signal triggered the call as its first argument. In this case, that means that $button is passed to update_time( ). You tell connect( ) to pass additional arguments to the callback by passing them to connect( ) after the callback function name. This example displays a window with a button and a separate label. The time is printed in the label and updated when the button is clicked:

```
// create the window
$window = &new GtkWindow();

// create a container for the label and the button
$container = &new GtkVBox();

// create a label showing the time
$label = &new GtkLabel(strftime('%c'));

// add the label to the container
$container->pack_start($label);

// create a button
$button = &new GtkButton('Update Time');

/* set the update_time() function as the callback for the "clicked" signal
   and pass $label to the callback */
$button->connect('clicked','update_time',$label);

function update_time($b,$lb) {
    $lb->set_text(strftime('%c'));
}

// add the button to the container
$container->pack_start($button);

// add the container to the window
$window->add($container);

// display the window
$window->show_all();

// necessary so that the program exits properly
function shutdown() { gtk::main_quit(); }
$window->connect('destroy','shutdown');
```

```
// start GTK's signal handling loop
gtk::main();
```

Because $label is on the list of arguments passed to $button->connect( ), $label is passed to update_time( ). Calling set_text( ) on $label updates the text displayed in the label.

See Also

Documentation on signals and callbacks at *http://gtk.php.net/manual/en/ gtk.signals.php*, on GtkObject::connect( ) at *http://gtk.php.net/manual/en/ gtk.gtkobject.method.connect.php*, and on GtkButton's clicked signal at *http:// gtk.php.net/manual/en/gtk.gtkbutton.signal.clicked.php*.

20.8   Displaying Menus

Problem

You want to display a menu bar at the top of a GTK window.

Solution

Create a GtkMenu. Create individual GtkMenuItem objects for each menu item you want to display and add each menu item to the GtkMenu with append( ). Then, create a root menu GtkMenuItem with the label that should appear in the menu bar (e.g., "File" or "Options"). Add the menu to the root menu with set_submenu( ). Create a GtkMenuBar and add the root menu to the menu bar with append( ). Finally, add the menu bar to the window:

```
// create the window
$window = &new GtkWindow();

// create a menu
$menu = &new GtkMenu();

// create a menu item and add it to the menu
$menu_item_1 = &new GtkMenuItem('Open');
$menu->append($menu_item_1);

// create another menu item and add it to the menu
$menu_item_2 = &new GtkMenuItem('Close');
$menu->append($menu_item_2);

// create yet another menu item and add it to the menu
$menu_item_2 = &new GtkMenuItem('Save');
$menu->append($menu_item_2);
```

```
// create a root menu and add the existing menu to it
$root_menu = &new GtkMenuItem('File');
$root_menu->set_submenu($menu);

// create a menu bar and add the root menu to it
$menu_bar = &new GtkMenuBar();
$menu_bar->append($root_menu);

// add the menu bar to the window
$window->add($menu_bar);

// display the window
$window->show_all();

// necessary so that the program exits properly
function shutdown() { gtk::main_quit(); }
$window->connect('destroy','shutdown');

// start GTK's signal handling loop
gtk::main();
```

Discussion

A menu involves a hierarchy of quite a few objects. The GtkWindow (or another container) holds the GtkMenuBar. The GtkMenuBar holds a GtkMenuItem for each top-level menu in the menu bar (e.g., "File," "Options," or "Help"). Each top-level GtkMenuItem has a GtkMenu as a submenu. That submenu contains each GtkMenuItem that should appear under the top-level menu.

As with any GTK widget, a GtkMenuItem object can have callbacks that handle signals. When a menu item is selected, it triggers the activate signal. To take action when a menu item is selected, connect its activate signal to a callback. Here's a version of the button-and-label time display from Recipe 20.7 with two menu items: "Update," which updates the time in the label, and "Quit," which quits the program:

```
// create the window
$window = &new GtkWindow();

// create a container for the label and the button
$container = &new GtkVBox();

// create a menu
$menu = &new GtkMenu();

// create a menu item and add it to the menu
$menu_item_1 = &new GtkMenuItem('Update');
$menu->append($menu_item_1);

// create another menu item and add it to the menu
$menu_item_2 = &new GtkMenuItem('Quit');
$menu->append($menu_item_2);
```

```
// create a root menu and add the existing menu to it
$root_menu = &new GtkMenuItem('File');
$root_menu->set_submenu($menu);

// create a menu bar and add the root menu to it
$menu_bar = &new GtkMenuBar();
$menu_bar->append($root_menu);

// add the menu to the container
$container->add($menu_bar);

// create a label showing the time
$label = &new GtkLabel(strftime('%c'));

// add the label to the container
$container->pack_start($label);

// create a button
$button = &new GtkButton('Update Time');

/* set the update_time() function as the callback for the "clicked" signal
   and pass $label to the callback */
$button->connect('clicked','update_time',$label);

function update_time($b,$lb) {
    $lb->set_text(strftime('%c'));
}

// add the button to the container
$container->pack_start($button);

// when the Update menu item is selected, call update_time()
$menu_item_1->connect('activate','update_time',$label);

// when the Quit menu item is selected, quit
$menu_item_2->connect('activate','shutdown');

// add the container to the window
$window->add($container);

// display the window
$window->show_all();

// necessary so that the program exits properly
function shutdown() { gtk::main_quit(); }
$window->connect('destroy','shutdown');

// start GTK's signal handling loop
gtk::main();
```

Callbacks are connected to the menu items with their connect( ) methods. The callbacks are connected to the activate signals towards the end of the code because the call to $menu_item_1->connect( ) passes $label to update_time( ). For $label to be successfully passed to update_time( ) while the program is running, connect( ) has to be called after $label is instantiated.

See Also

Documentation on the GtkMenu class at *http://gtk.php.net/manual/en/gtk.gtkmenu.php*, GtkMenuShell::append( ) at *http://gtk.php.net/manual/en/gtk.gtkmenushell.method. append.php*, the GtkMenuItem class at *http://gtk.php.net/manual/en/gtk.gtkmenuitem. php*, GtkMenuItem::set_submenu( ) at *http://gtk.php.net/manual/en/gtk.gtkmenuitem. method.set_submenu.php*, GtkMenuItem's activate signal at *http://gtk.php.net/manual/ en/gtk.gtkmenuitem.signal.activate.php*, and the GtkMenuBar class at *http://gtk.php.net/ manual/en/gtk.gtkmenubar.php*.

20.9 Program: Command Shell

The *command-shell.php* program shown in Example 20-1 provides a shell-like prompt to let you execute PHP code interactively. It reads in lines using readline( ) and then runs them with eval( ). By default, it runs each line after it's typed in. In multiline mode (specified with -m or --multiline), however, it keeps reading lines until you enter . on a line by itself; it then runs the accumulated code.

Additionally, *command-shell.php* uses the Readline word-completion features to more easily enter PHP functions. Enter a few characters and hit Tab to see a list of functions that match the characters you've typed.

This program is helpful for running snippets of code interactively or testing different commands. The variables, functions, and classes defined in each line of code stay defined until you quit the program, so you can test different database queries, for example:

```
% php -q command-shell.php
[1]> require 'DB.php';

[2]> $dbh = DB::connect('mysql://user:pwd@localhost/phpc');

[3]> print_r($dbh->getAssoc('SELECT sign,planet,start_day FROM zodiac WHERE element
LIKE "water"'));
Array
(
    [Cancer] => Array
        (
            [0] => Moon
            [1] => 22
        )
    [Scorpio] => Array
        (
            [0] => Mars
            [1] => 24
```

```
            )
        [Pisces] => Array
            (
                [0] => Neptune
                [1] => 19
            )
    )
```

The code for *command-shell.php* is in Example 20-1.

Example 20-1. command-shell.php

```php
// Load the readline library
if (! function_exists('readline')) {
    dl('readline.'. (((strtoupper(substr(PHP_OS,0,3))) == 'WIN')?'dll':'so'))
        or die("Readline library required\n");
}

// Load the Console_Getopt class
require 'Console/Getopt.php';

$o = new Console_Getopt;
$opts = $o->getopt($o->readPHPArgv(),'hm',array('help','multiline'));

// Quit with a usage message if the arguments are bad
if (PEAR::isError($opts)) {
    print $opts->getMessage();
    print "\n";
    usage();
}

// default is to evaluate each command as it's entered
$multiline = false;

foreach ($opts[0] as $opt) {
    // remove any leading -s
    $opt[0] = preg_replace('/^-+/','',$opt[0]);

    // check the first character of the argument
    switch($opt[0][0]) {
    case 'h':
        // display help
        usage();
        break;
    case 'm':
        $multiline = true;
        break;
    }
}

// set up error display
ini_set('display_errors',false);
ini_set('log_errors',true);
```

Example 20-1. command-shell.php (continued)

```php
// build readline completion table
$functions = get_defined_functions();
foreach ($functions['internal'] as $k => $v) {
    $functions['internal'][$k] = "$v(";
}
function function_list($line) {
    return $GLOBALS['functions']['internal'];
}
readline_completion_function('function_list');

$cmd = '';
$cmd_count = 1;

while (true) {
    // get a line of input from the user
    $s = readline("[$cmd_count]> ");
    // add it to the command history
    readline_add_history($s);
    // if we're in multiline mode:
    if ($multiline) {
        // if just a "." has been entered
        if ('.' == rtrim($s)) {
            // eval() the code
            eval($cmd);
            // clear out the accumulated code
            $cmd = '';
            // increment the command count
            $cmd_count++;
            // start the next prompt on a new line
            print "\n";
        } else {
            /* otherwise, add the new line to the accumulated code
               tacking on a newline prevents //-style comments from
               commenting out the rest of the lines entered
            */
            $cmd .= $s."\n";;
        }
    } else {
        // if we're not in multiline mode, eval() the line
        eval($s);
        // increment the command count
        $cmd_count++;
        // start the next prompt in a new line
        print "\n";
    }
}

// display helpful usage information
function usage() {
    $my_name = $_SERVER['argv'][0];
```

Example 20-1. command-shell.php (continued)

```
    print<<<_USAGE_
Usage: $my_name [-h|--help] [-m|--multiline]

  -h, --help: display this help
  -m, --multiline: execute accumulated code when "." is entered
                   by itself on a line. The default is to execute
                   each line after it is entered.

_USAGE_;
    exit(-1);
}
```

20.10 Program: Displaying Weather Conditions

The *gtk-weather.php* program shown in Example 20-2 uses SOAP and a weather web service to display weather conditions around the world. It incorporates a number of GTK widgets in its interface: menus, keyboard accelerators, buttons, a text entry box, labels, scrolled windows, and columned lists.

To use *gtk-weather.php*, first search for weather stations by typing a search term in the text-entry box and clicking the Search button. Searching for weather stations is shown in Figure 20-4.

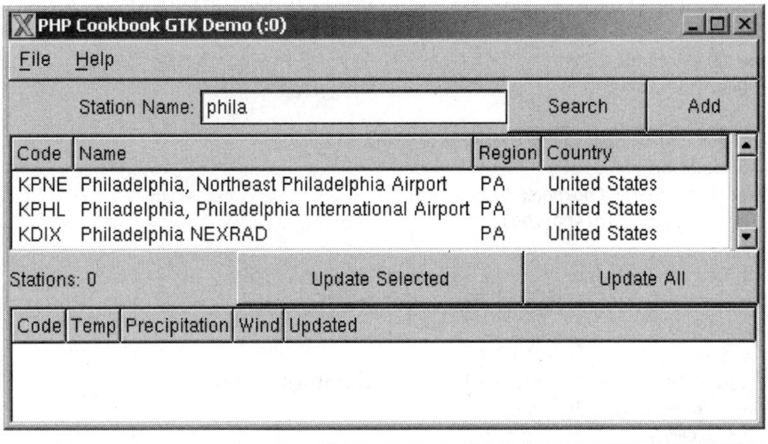

Figure 20-4. Searching for weather stations

Once you've retrieved a list of weather stations, you can get the conditions at a specific station by selecting the station and clicking the Add button. The station code and its current conditions are added to the list at the bottom of the window. You can search again and add more stations to the list. The *gtk-weather.php* window with a few added stations is shown in Figure 20-5.

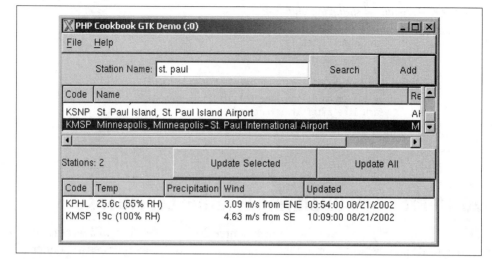

Figure 20-5. Added weather stations

The web service this program uses is called *GlobalWeather*; look for more information about it at *http://www.capescience.com/webservices/globalweather/index.shtml*.

Example 20-2. gtk-weather.php

```
// Load the GTK extension
dl('php_gtk.'. (((strtoupper(substr(PHP_OS,0,3))) == 'WIN')?'dll':'so'));

// Load the SOAP client class
require 'SOAP/Client.php';

// Create the main window and set its title and size
$window = &new GtkWindow();
$window->set_title('PHP Cookbook GTK Demo');
$window->set_default_size(500,200);

// The main layout container for the window is a VBox
$vbox = &new GtkVBox();
$window->add($vbox);

// Create a GtkAccelGroup to hold keyboard accelerators
$accelgroup = &new GtkAccelGroup();
$window->add_accel_group($accelgroup);

// Build the menu, starting with the GtkMenuBar. The arguments to
// pack_start() prevent the menu bar from expanding if the window does.
$menubar = &new GtkMenuBar();
$vbox->pack_start($menubar, false, false);

// Create the "File" menu and its keyboard accelerator
$menu_file_item = &new GtkMenuItem('_File');
$menu_file_item_label = $menu_file_item->child;
```

Example 20-2. gtk-weather.php (continued)

```
$menu_file_item->add_accelerator('activate',$accelgroup,
                                 $menu_file_item_label->parse_uline('_File'),
                                 GDK_MOD1_MASK,0);
// Add the "File" menu to the menu bar
$menubar->add($menu_file_item);

// Create the submenu for the options under "File"
$menu_file_submenu = &new GtkMenu();
$menu_file_item->set_submenu($menu_file_submenu);

// Create the "Quit" option under "File" and its accelerator
// GDK_MOD1_MASK means that the accelerator is Alt-Q, not Q
// GTK_ACCEL_VISIBLE means that the accelerator is displayed in the menu
$menu_file_choices_quit = &new GtkMenuItem('_Quit');
$menu_file_choices_quit_label = $menu_file_choices_quit->child;
$menu_file_choices_quit->add_accelerator('activate',$accelgroup,
    $menu_file_choices_quit_label->parse_uline('_Quit'),GDK_MOD1_MASK,
    GTK_ACCEL_VISIBLE);

// Add the "File | Quit" option to the "File" submenu
$menu_file_submenu->append($menu_file_choices_quit);

// Create the "Help" menu and its keyboard accelerator
$menu_help_item = &new GtkMenuItem('_Help');
$menu_help_item_label = $menu_help_item->child;
$menu_help_item->add_accelerator('activate',$accelgroup,
                                 $menu_help_item_label->parse_uline('_Help'),
                                 GDK_MOD1_MASK,0);
// Add the "Help" menu to the menu bar
$menubar->add($menu_help_item);

// Create the submenu for the options under "Help"
$menu_help_submenu = &new GtkMenu();
$menu_help_item->set_submenu($menu_help_submenu);

// Create the "About" option under "Help" and its accelerator
$menu_help_choices_about = &new GtkMenuItem('_About');
$menu_help_choices_about_label = $menu_help_choices_about->child;
$menu_help_choices_about->add_accelerator('activate',$accelgroup,
    $menu_help_choices_about_label->parse_uline('_About'),GDK_MOD1_MASK,
    GTK_ACCEL_VISIBLE);

// Add the "Help | About" option to the "Help" submenu
$menu_help_submenu->append($menu_help_choices_about);

// Layout the weather station searching widgets in a GtkTable
$table_1 = &new GtkTable(2,4);
$vbox->pack_start($table_1);

// Put a label on the left in the first row
$label_sn = &new GtkLabel('Station Name: ');
```

Example 20-2. gtk-weather.php (continued)

```
$label_sn->set_alignment(1,0.5);
$table_1->attach($label_sn,0,1,0,1, GTK_FILL);

// Put a text entry field in the middle of the first row
// The accelerator allows you to hit "Return" in the field to submit
$entry_sn = &new GtkEntry();
$entry_sn->add_accelerator('activate',$accelgroup,GDK_KEY_Return,0,0);
$table_1->attach($entry_sn,1,2,0,1, GTK_FILL);

// Put a scrolled window in the second row of the table
$scrolledwindow_1 = &new GtkScrolledWindow();
$scrolledwindow_1->set_policy(GTK_POLICY_AUTOMATIC, GTK_POLICY_AUTOMATIC);
$table_1->attach($scrolledwindow_1,0,4,1,2, GTK_EXPAND | GTK_SHRINK | GTK_FILL,
                 GTK_EXPAND | GTK_SHRINK | GTK_FILL);

// Put a columned list in the scrolled window. By putting the list inside
// the scrolled window instead of directly in the GtkTable, the window doesn't
// have to grow to a huge size to let you see everything in the list
$clist_sn = &new GtkCList(4,array('Code','Name','Region','Country'));
$scrolledwindow_1->add($clist_sn);

// Set the columns in the list to resize automatically
for ($i = 0; $i < 4; $i++) { $clist_sn->set_column_auto_resize($i,true); }

// Add a "Search" button to the first row
$button_search =&new GtkButton('Search');
$table_1->attach($button_search,2,3,0,1, GTK_FILL);

// Add an "Add" button to the first row
$button_add = &new GtkButton('Add');
$table_1->attach($button_add,3,4,0,1, GTK_FILL);

// Layout the weather conditions display widgets in another GtkTable
$table_2 = &new GtkTable(2,3);
$vbox->pack_start($table_2);

// Add a label displaying how many stations are shown
$label_st = &new GtkLabel('Stations: 0');
$label_st->set_alignment(0,0.5);
$table_2->attach($label_st,0,1,0,1, GTK_FILL);

// Add a button to update a single station
$button_update_sel = &new GtkButton('Update Selected');
$table_2->attach($button_update_sel,1,2,0,1, GTK_FILL);

// Add a button to update all stations
$button_update_all = &new GtkButton('Update All');
$table_2->attach($button_update_all,2,3,0,1, GTK_FILL);

// Add a columned list to hold the weather conditions at the stations
// This columned list also goes inside a scrolled window
$scrolledwindow_2 = &new GtkScrolledWindow();
```

Example 20-2. gtk-weather.php (continued)

```
$scrolledwindow_2->set_policy(GTK_POLICY_AUTOMATIC, GTK_POLICY_AUTOMATIC);
$table_2->attach($scrolledwindow_2,0,3,1,2, GTK_EXPAND | GTK_SHRINK | GTK_FILL,
                GTK_EXPAND | GTK_SHRINK | GTK_FILL);
$clist_st = &new GtkCList(5,array('Code','Temp','Precipitation','Wind','Updated'));
$scrolledwindow_2->add($clist_st);

// Set the columns in the list to resize automatically
for ($i = 0; $i < 5; $i++) { $clist_st->set_column_auto_resize($i,true); }

// Connect signals to callbacks

// Clicking on the "Search" button or hitting Return in the text entry field
// searches for weather stations whose name match the entered text
$button_search->connect('clicked','wx_searchByName',$entry_sn,$clist_sn,$window);
$entry_sn->connect('activate','wx_searchByName',$entry_sn,$clist_sn,$window);

// Clicking on the "Add" button adds the weather station to the bottom
// columned list
$button_add->connect('clicked','cb_add_station',$clist_sn,$clist_st,$label_st);

// Clicking on the "Update Selected" button updates the bottom columned list
// for a single station
$button_update_sel->connect('clicked','wx_update_report',$clist_st,$label_st,
                            'selected');
// Clicking on the "Update All" button updates all stations in the bottom
// columned list
$button_update_all->connect('clicked','wx_update_report',$clist_st,$label_st,
                            'all');

// Closing the window or selecting the "File | Quit" menu item exits the program
$window->connect('destroy','cb_shutdown');
$menu_file_choices_quit->connect('activate','cb_shutdown');

// Selecting the "Help | About" menu item shows an about box
$menu_help_choices_about->connect('activate','cb_about_box',$window);

// These callbacks keep track of the currently selected row (if any)
// in each columned list
$clist_sn->connect('select-row','cb_clist_select_row');
$clist_sn->connect('unselect-row','cb_clist_unselect_row');
$clist_st->connect('select-row','cb_clist_select_row');
$clist_st->connect('unselect-row','cb_clist_unselect_row');

// The interface has been set up and the signals we want to pay attention
// to have been connected to callbacks. Time to display the window and start
// the GTK signal handling loop.
$window->show_all();
gtk::main();

/*
 * CALLBACKS AND OTHER SUPPORT FUNCTIONS
 */
```

Example 20-2. gtk-weather.php (continued)

```php
// use the searchByName() function over SOAP to get a list of stations
// whose names match the given search term
function wx_searchByName($button,$entry,$clist,$window) {
    // instantiate a new SOAP client
    $sc = new SOAP_Client('http://live.capescience.com/ccx/GlobalWeather');

    $search_term = trim($entry->get_text());
    if ($search_term) {
        // call the remote function if a search term is provided
        $res = $sc->call('searchByName',
                        array(new SOAP_Value('name','string',$search_term)),
                        'capeconnect:GlobalWeather:StationInfo',
                        'capeconnect:GlobalWeather:StationInfo#searchByName');

        // pop up an error dialog if the SOAP function fails
        if (PEAR::isError($res)) {
            error_dialog($res->getMessage(),$window);
            return false;
        }
        // pop up an error dialog if there are no matches
        if (! is_array($res)) {
            error_dialog('No weather stations found.',$window);
            return false;
        }
        // add each station and its info to the columned list
        // wrapping the calls to append() with freeze() and thaw()
        // make all of the data appear at once
        $clist->freeze();
        $clist->clear();
        foreach ($res as $station) {
            $clist->append(array($station->icao,$station->name,
                                $station->region,$station->country));
        }
        $clist->thaw();
    }
}

// use the getWeatherReport function over SOAP to get the weather conditions
// at a particular station
function wx_getWeatherReport($code) {
    $sc = new SOAP_Client('http://live.capescience.com/ccx/GlobalWeather');
    $res = $sc->call('getWeatherReport',
                    array(new SOAP_Value('code','string',$code)),
                    'capeconnect:GlobalWeather:GlobalWeather',
                    'capeconnect:GlobalWeather:GlobalWeather#getWeatherReport');

    if (PEAR::isError($res)) {
        error_dialog($res->getMessage());
        return false;
    } else {
        return $res;
```

Example 20-2. gtk-weather.php (continued)

```
    }
}

// add the weather report in $res to the columned list $clist
// if $row is null, the report is appended to the list
// if $row is not null, the report replaces row $row in the list
function wx_add_report($clist,$label,$res,$row = null) {

    // format the timestamp
    $timestamp = str_replace('T',' ',$res->timestamp);
    $timestamp = str_replace('Z',' GMT',$timestamp);
    $timestamp = strftime('%H:%M:%S %m/%d/%Y',strtotime($timestamp));

    // format the wind information
    $wind = sprintf("%.2f m/s from %s",
                    $res->wind->prevailing_speed,
                    $res->wind->prevailing_direction->compass);

    $clist->freeze();
    if (! is_null($row)) {
        // replace the information in row number $row
        $clist->set_text($row,1,$res->temperature->string);
        $clist->set_text($row,2,$res->precipitation->string);
        $clist->set_text($row,3,$wind);
        $clist->set_text($row,4,$timestamp);
    } else {
        // add the information to the end of the columned list
        $clist->append(array($res->station->icao,
                            $res->temperature->string,
                            $res->precipitation->string,
                            $wind,
                            $timestamp));

        // update the columned list's internal row count
        $rows = 1 + $clist->get_data('rows');
        $clist->set_data('rows',$rows);
        // update the label that displays a station count
        $label->set_text("Stations: $rows");
    }
    $clist->thaw();
}

// update conditions for one station or all stations, depending on $mode
function wx_update_report($button,$clist,$label,$mode) {
    switch ($mode) {
    case 'selected':

        // if there is a row selected
        $selected_row = $clist->get_data('selected_row');
        if (($selected_row >= 0) && (! is_null($selected_row))) {
            $code = $clist->get_text($selected_row,0);
```

Example 20-2. gtk-weather.php (continued)

```php
            // get the report and update the columned list
            if ($res = wx_getWeatherReport($code)) {
                wx_add_report($clist,$label,$res,$selected_row);
            }
        }
        break;
    case 'all':
        // for each row in the columned list
        for ($i = 0, $j = $clist->get_data('rows'); $i < $j; $i++) {
            // get the report and update the list
            if ($res = wx_getWeatherReport($clist->get_text($i,0))) {
                wx_add_report($clist,$label,$res,$i);
            }
        }
        break;
    }
}

// add a station to the bottom list of weather reports
function cb_add_station($button,$clist,$clist_2,$label) {
    $selected_row = $clist->get_data('selected_row');
    // if there's a selected row in the top list of stations
    if ($selected_row >= 0) {
        $code = $clist->get_text($selected_row,0);
        // get the weather report for that station
        if ($res = wx_getWeatherReport($code)) {
            // find the row if this code is already in the list
            $row = null;
            for ($i = 0, $j = $clist_2->get_data('rows'); $i < $j; $i++) {
                if ($clist_2->get_text($i,0) == $code) {
                    $row = $i;
                }
            }
            // add the station and its report to the bottom list of
            // reports (or update the existing row)
            wx_add_report($clist_2,$label,$res,$row);
        }
    }
}

// update a columned list's internal selected row value when a row is selected
function cb_clist_select_row($clist,$row,$col,$e) {
    $clist->set_data('selected_row',$row);
}

// clear a columned list's internal selected row value when a row is unselected
function cb_clist_unselect_row($clist) {
    $clist->set_data('selected_row',-1);
}

// display the "About Box"
function cb_about_box($menu_item,$window) {
```

Example 20-2. gtk-weather.php (continued)

```
    $about_box = &new GtkDialog();
    $vbox = $about_box->vbox;
    $action_area = $about_box->action_area;
    $about_box->set_title('About');
    $label = &new GtkLabel("This is the PHP Cookbook PHP-GTK Demo.");
    $button = &new GtkButton('OK');
    $button->connect('clicked','cb_dialog_destroy',$about_box);
    $vbox->pack_start($label);
    $action_area->pack_start($button);
    $about_box->set_modal(true);
    $about_box->set_transient_for($window);
    $about_box->show_all();
}

// display an error dialog box
function error_dialog($msg,$window) {
    $dialog = &new GtkDialog();
    $vbox = $dialog->vbox;
    $action_area = $dialog->action_area;
    $dialog->set_title('Error');
    $label = &new GtkLabel("Error: $msg");
    $button = &new GtkButton('OK');
    $button->connect('clicked','cb_dialog_destroy',$dialog);
    $vbox->pack_start($label);
    $action_area->pack_start($button);
    $dialog->set_modal(true);
    $dialog->set_transient_for($window);
    $dialog->show_all();
}

// close a dialog box
function cb_dialog_destroy($button,$dialog) {
    $dialog->destroy();
}

// quit the main program
function cb_shutdown() { gtk::main_quit(); }
```

CHAPTER 21
PEAR

21.0 Introduction

PEAR is the PHP Extension and Application Repository, a collection of open source classes that work together. Developers can use PEAR classes to generate HTML, make SOAP requests, send MIME mail, and a variety of other common tasks. A pear is also a tasty fruit.

To find general information on PEAR, read the PEAR manual; to discover the latest PEAR packages, go to *http://pear.php.net*. A summary of each week's happenings can be found at *http://pear.php.net/weeklynews.php*.

Only a few core PEAR packages are bundled with the main PHP release. However, part of PEAR is a program called, appropriately enough, *pear*, that makes it easy for you to download and install additional PEAR packages. This program is also known as the PEAR package manager. Recipe 21.1 shows how to use the PEAR package manager.

PEAR packages divide into two major parts. One is the PHP Foundation Classes— object-oriented code written in PHP that's high quality and usable in production environments on any platform and web server. The other is PECL, or PHP Extension Code Library. PECL, pronounced pickle, is a series of extensions to PHP written in C. These extensions are just like ones distributed with the main PHP release, but they're of more specialized interest—such as an interface to the XMMS multimedia player or the ImageMagick graphics library.

Additionally, the PEAR package manager allows you to use the PEAR class management infrastructure with your personal projects. By creating your own packages that follow the PEAR format, your users can use *pear* to download and install the files from your project's web site.

This chapter explains how to find a PEAR package you may want to use and how to install it on your machine. Because PEAR has many classes, you need an easy way to browse them. Recipe 21.2 covers the different ways to find PEAR packages; once you've found a package's name, Recipe 21.3 shows how to view package details and information.

Once you locate a class you want to use, you need to run *pear* to transfer the class to your machine and install it in the correct location on your server. Installing PEAR packages and PECL extensions are the subjects of Recipe 21.4 and Recipe 21.5, respectively. Recipe 21.6 shows how discover if any upgrades are available to packages on your machine and how to install the latest versions. If you want to remove a package, see Recipe 21.7.

Finally, Recipe 21.8 describes how PEAR developers can write classes that abide by PEAR's coding standards and how to document your class with PHPDoc.

PHP 4.3 includes the first stable release of PEAR. Earlier copies of PHP bundled versions of PEAR prior to PEAR 1.0, but *pear* and the other packages weren't guaranteed to work, as they were still in beta. If you are having problems using PEAR, you should remove any old files that may be interfering with the release version. This includes the *pear* application itself; it can't always upgrade itself to the latest release.

If you can't upgrade to PHP 4.3 and need to bootstrap a copy of PEAR onto your system, run the following:

```
% lynx -source http://go-pear.org | php -q
Welcome to go-pear!

Go-pear will install the 'pear' command and all the files needed by
it.  This command is your tool for PEAR installation and maintenance.

Go-pear also lets you download and install the PEAR packages bundled
with PHP: DB, Net_Socket, Net_SMTP, Mail, XML_Parser.

If you wish to abort, press Control-C now, or press Enter to continue:
```

This downloads a PHP script from the PEAR web site and hands it to PHP for execution. The program downloads all files needed to run *pear* and gets you up and running.

On some Unix systems, you may need to run *links* instead of *lynx*. If you have the command-line version of PHP installed, remove the -q flag to PHP; the CLI version automatically suppresses HTTP headers. If *go-pear* seems to hang, set output_ buffering to off in your *php.ini* configuration file.

Installation on Windows is a two-step process:

```
C:\> php-cli -r 'readfile("http://go-pear.org");' > go-pear
c:\> php-cli go-pear
```

The *go-pear* script requires PHP 4.1 or greater. For the Windows installation, *php-cli* is the command-line version of PHP.

PHP installs PEAR by default, so if you're running PHP 4.3, you should be able to use PEAR without any additional setup.* Out of the box, PEAR installs *pear* in the same directory as *php* and places PEAR packages in *prefix/lib/php*.† To install PEAR in another directory, add `--with-pear=DIR` when configuring PHP.

Once a PEAR package is installed, use it in your PHP scripts by calling `require`. For example, here's how to include the Net_Dig package:

```
require 'Net/Dig.php';
```

If a package name contains an underscore, replace it with a slash, and add *.php* to the end.

Some packages may require you to include multiple classes, such as SOAP, so instead of requiring *SOAP.php*, you include *SOAP/Client.php* or *SOAP/Server.php*. Read the documentation to discover if a particular package requires nonstandard file includes.

Because PEAR packages are included as regular PHP files, make sure the directory containing the PEAR classes is in your `include_path`. If it isn't, `include` and `require` can't find PEAR classes.

To view instructions and examples showing how to use a particular PEAR class, check the PEAR Manual at *http://pear.php.net/manual/en/packages.php* or read the top section of the package's PHP files. For an example of a full-featured PEAR class in action, see the discussion of PEAR's database library in Recipe 10.3.

21.1 Using the PEAR Package Manager

Problem

You want to use the PEAR package manager, *pear*. This allows you to install new packages, and upgrade and get information about your existing PEAR packages.

Solution

To execute a command with the PEAR package manager, type the command name as the first argument on the command line:

```
% pear command
```

---

* If you disable building the command-line version of PHP with `--disable-cli`, PHP doesn't install PEAR.

† This is probably */usr/local/lib/php*.

Discussion

Here's how to list all installed PEAR packages with the `list` command:[*]

```
% pear list
Installed packages:
= == == == == == == == ==
+----------------+----------+--------+
| Package        | Version  | State  |
| Archive_Tar    | 0.9      | stable |
| Console_Getopt | 0.11     | beta   |
| DB             | 1.3      | stable |
| HTTP           | 1.2      | stable |
| Mail           | 1.0.1    | stable |
| Mail_Mime      | 1.2.1    | stable |
| Net_SMTP       | 1.0      | stable |
| Net_Socket     | 1.0.1    | stable |
| Net_URL        | 1.0.4    | stable |
| PEAR           | 0.91-dev | beta   |
| XML_Parser     | 1.0      | stable |
| XML_RPC        | 1.0.3    | stable |
+----------------+----------+--------+
```

For a list of all valid PEAR commands, use `list-commands`. Many commands also have abbreviated names; for example, `list` is also just `l`. These names are usually the first few letters of the command name. See Table 21-1 for a list of frequently used commands.

Table 21-1. PEAR package manager commands

Command name	Shortcut	Description
install	i	Download and install packages
upgrade	up	Upgrade installed packages
uninstall	un	Remove installed packages
list	l	List installed packages
list-upgrades	lu	List all available upgrades for installed packages
search	None	Search for packages

pear has commands both for using and for developing PEAR classes; as a result, you may not need all the commands. The package command, for example, creates a new PEAR package. If you only run other peoples' packages, you can safely ignore this command.

Like all programs, if you want to run *pear*, you must have permission to execute it. If you can run *pear* while running as root, but not as a regular user, make sure the group- or world-execute bit is set. Similarly, for some actions, *pear* creates a lock file

---

[*] In early versions of *pear*, this command was `list-installed`.

in the directory containing the PEAR files. You must have write permission to the file named *.lock* located in that directory.

To find where your PEAR packages are located, run the `config-get php_dir` command. You can check the value of the `include_path` by calling `ini_get('include_path')` from within PHP or by looking at your *php.ini* file. If you can't alter *php.ini* because you're in a shared hosting environment, add the directory to the `include_path` at the top of your script before including the file. See Recipe 8.23 for more on setting configuration variables from within PHP.

If you're behind a HTTP proxy server, configure PEAR to use it with the command:

```
% pear config-set http_proxy proxy.example.com:8080
```

You can configure PEAR package manager settings using:

```
% pear set-config setting value
```

Here *setting* is the name of the parameter to modify and *value* is the new value. To see all your current settings, use the `config-show` command:

```
% pear config-show
Configuration:
== == == == == == == =
+--------------------+----------------+------------------------------------+
| PEAR executables   | bin_dir        | /usr/local/bin                     |
| directory          |                |                                    |
| PEAR documentation | doc_dir        | /usr/local/lib/php/docs            |
| directory          |                |                                    |
| PHP extension      | ext_dir        | /usr/local/lib/php/extensions/no-de |
| directory          |                | bug-non-zts-20020429               |
| PEAR directory     | php_dir        | /usr/local/lib/php                  |
| PEAR data directory| data_dir       | /usr/local/lib/php/data             |
| PEAR test directory| test_dir       | /usr/local/lib/php/tests            |
| HTTP Proxy Server  | http_proxy     | <not set>                          |
| Address            |                |                                    |
| PEAR server        | master_server  | pear.php.net                       |
| PEAR password (for | password       | <not set>                          |
| maintainers)       |                |                                    |
| PEAR username (for | username       | <not set>                          |
| maintainers)       |                |                                    |
| Preferred Package  | preferred_state| stable                             |
| State              |                |                                    |
| Unix file mask     | umask          | 18                                 |
| Debug Log Level    | verbose        | 1                                  |
+--------------------+----------------+------------------------------------+
```

For a brief description of each configuration option, use the `config-help` command.

21.2 Finding PEAR Packages

Problem

You want a listing of PEAR packages. From this list you want to learn more about each package and decide if you want to install the package.

Solution

Browse packages at *http://pear.php.net/packages.php* or search for packages at *http://pear.php.net/package-search.php*. Use *pear*'s remote-list command to get listing of PEAR packages or the search command to search for packages.

Discussion

There are a few ways to review PEAR's packages. First, to browse the listings in a directory-style fashion, go to *http://pear.php.net/packages.php*. From there you can burrow into each individual PEAR category.

Alternatively, you can search through the listings at *http://pear.php.net/package-search.php*. The search page allows you to search by package name, author, category, and release date.

You can ask the PEAR package manager to provide you with a listing using the remote-list command:

```
% pear remote-list
Available packages:
==================
+----------------------+---------+
| Package              | Version |
| Archive_Tar          | 0.9     |
| Auth                 | 1.0.2   |

 ...

| XML_Transformer      | 0.3     |
| XML_Tree             | 1.1     |
+----------------------+---------+
```

The short form of remote-list is rl.

To search for package names from the command line, use the search command:

```
% pear search auth
Matched packages:
==================
```

```
+-----------+--------+-------+-----------------------------------+
| Package   | Latest | Local |                                   |
| Auth      | 1.0.2  | 1.0.2 | Creating an authentication system.|
| Auth_HTTP | 1.0.1  | 1.0.1 | HTTP authentication for PHP        |
+-----------+--------+-------+-----------------------------------+
```

This does a case-insensitive search of package names and returns the package name, the latest version number, the version you have installed (if any), and a short description about the package.

See Also

Recipe 21.3 to find out more information about a package.

21.3   Finding Information About a Package

Problem

You want to gather information about a package, such a description of what it does, who maintains it, what version you have installed, and which license it's released under.

Solution

If the package is installed on your machine, use the PEAR package manager's `info` command:

> % **pear info Net_URL**

Otherwise, use the `remote-info` command:

> % **pear remote-info SOAP**

You can also view the package's home page on *http://pear.php.net*.

Discussion

The `info` command provides summary information about a package:

```
% pear info Net_URL
About Net_URL-1.0.4
= == == == == == == == == ==
+-----------------+-------------------------------------------+
| Package         | Net_URL                                   |
| Summary         | Easy parsing of Urls                      |
| Description     | Provides easy parsing of URLs and their   |
|                 | constituent parts.                        |
| Maintainers     | Richard heyes <richard@php.net> (lead)    |
| Version         | 1.0.4                                     |
| Release Date    | 2002-07-27                                |
```

```
| Release License | BSD                 |
| Release State   | stable              |
| Release Notes   | License change      |
| Last Modified   | 2002-08-23          |
+-----------------+---------------------------------------------+
```

If you don't have the package installed, ask the remote server for a description:

```
% pear remote-info Net_URL
Package details:
== == == == == == == ==
+-------------+---------------------------------------+
| Latest      | 1.0.4                                 |
| Installed   | 1.0.4                                 |
| Package     | Net_URL                               |
| License     | BSD                                   |
| Category    | Networking                            |
| Summary     | Easy parsing of Urls                  |
| Description | Provides easy parsing of URLs and their |
|             | constituent parts.                    |
+-------------+---------------------------------------+
```

This request displays a slightly different set of information. It doesn't include the release data but does include the general PEAR category and the latest version number for the package.

The package home page provides a more complete view and also provides links to earlier releases, a change log, and browseable access to the CVS repository. You can also view package download statistics. Figure 21-1 shows a sample package information page.

See Also

Recipe 21.2 to search for packages.

21.4 Installing PEAR Packages

Problem

You want to install a PEAR package.

Solution

Download and install the package from your PEAR server using the PEAR package manager:

```
% pear install Package_Name
```

You can also install from any location on the Internet:

```
% pear install http://pear.example.com/Package_Name-1.0.tgz
```

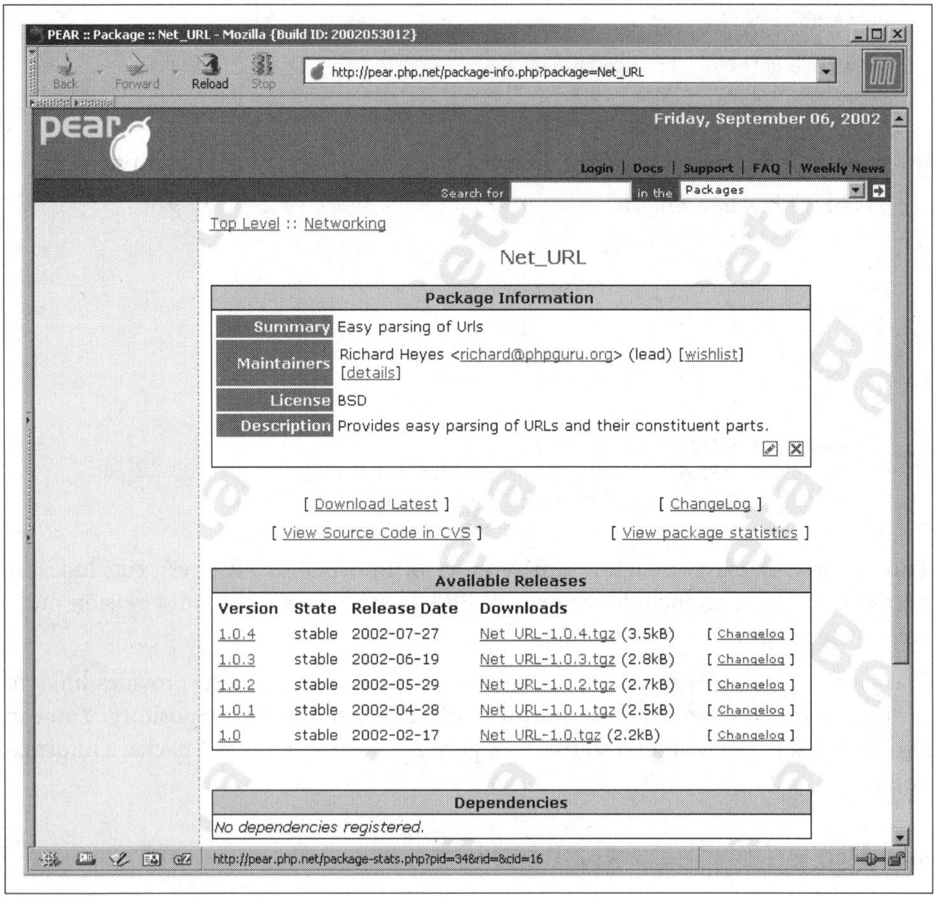

Figure 21-1. Net_URL Package Information page on PEAR web site

Here's how to install if you have a local copy of a package:

```
% pear install Package_Name-1.0.tgz
```

Discussion

To install PEAR packages, you need write permission where the packages are stored; this defaults to */usr/local/lib/php/*.

You can also request multiple packages at the same time:

```
% pear install HTML_Common HTML_Javascript
downloading HTML_Common-1.0.tgz ...
...done: 2,959 bytes
install ok: HTML_Common 1.0
downloading HTML_Javascript-1.0.0.tgz ...
...done: 4,141 bytes
install ok: HTML_Javascript 1.0.0
```

When installing a package, PEAR checks that you have all the necessary PHP functions and PEAR packages the new package depends on. If this check fails, PEAR reports on the dependencies:

```
% pear install HTML_Table
downloading HTML_Table-1.1.tgz ...
...done: 5,168 bytes

requires package `HTML_Common' >= 1.0
HTML_Table: dependencies failed
```

To fix this problem, download and install the missing packages first. If you want to ignore these dependencies, force installation with -n or --nodeps. You can then later install the required package.

See Also

Recipe 21.5 for information on installing PECL packages; Recipe 21.6 for more on upgrading an existing package; Recipe 21.7 to uninstall a package.

21.5 Installing PECL Packages

Problem

You want to install a PECL package; this builds a PHP extension written in C to use inside PHP.

Solution

Make sure you have all the necessary extension libraries and then use the PEAR package manager install command:

```
% pear install xmms
```

To use the extension from PHP, load it using dl( ):

```
dl('xmms.so');
```

Discussion

The frontend process for installing PECL packages is just like installing PEAR packages for code written in PHP. However, the behind-the-scenes tasks are very different. Because PECL extensions are written in C, the package manager needs to compile the extension and configure it to work with the installed version of PHP. As a result, at present, you can build PECL packages on Unix machines and on Windows machines if you use MSDev.

Unlike PHP-based PEAR packages, PECL extensions don't automatically inform you when you lack a library necessary to compile the extension. Instead, you are responsible for correctly preinstalling these files. If you are having trouble getting a PECL extension to build, check the *README* file and the other documentation that comes with the package. The package manager installs these files inside the *docs* directory under your PEAR hierarchy.

When you install a PECL extension, the PEAR package manager downloads the file, extracts it, runs *phpize* to configure the extension for the version of PHP installed on the machine, and then makes and installs the extension. It may also prompt you for the location of libraries:

```
% pear install xmms
downloading xmms-0.2.tgz ...
...done: 11,968 bytes
4 source files, building
running: phpize
PHP Api Version       : 20020307
Zend Module Api No    : 20020429
Zend Extension Api No : 20020731
Xmms library install dir? [autodetect] :
building in /var/tmp/pear-build-adam/xmms-0.2
running: /tmp/pearKIv63P/xmms-0.2/configure --with-xmms
running: make
xmms.so copied to /tmp/pearKIv63P/xmms-0.2/xmms.so
install ok: xmms 0.2
```

If these libraries are in a standard location, hitting Return selects the autodetect option. PHP then searches for the libraries and selects them; you don't need to enter an explicit pathname, as in the case of the xmms library shown earlier.

PECL extensions are stored in different places than non-PECL packages. If you want to run *pear*, you must be able to write inside the PHP *extensions* directory. Some PECL packages, such as xmms, install files in the same directory as the PHP binary. Because of this, you may want to install these packages while running as the same user you used to install PHP. Also, check the execute permissions of these files; because most PEAR files aren't executable, your umask may not provide those executable files with the correct set of permissions.

See Also

Recipe 21.4 for information on installing PEAR packages; Recipe 21.6 for more on upgrading an existing package; Recipe 21.7 to uninstall a package.

21.6 Upgrading PEAR Packages

Problem

You want to upgrade a package on your system to the latest version for additional functionality and bug fixes.

Solution

Find out if any upgrades are available and then tell *pear* to upgrade the packages you want:

```
% pear list-upgrades
% pear upgrade Package_Name
```

Discussion

Upgrading to a new version of a package is a simple task with the PEAR Package Manager. If you know a specific package is out of date, you can upgrade it directly. However, you may also want to just periodically check to see if any new releases are available.

To do this, user the `list-upgrades` command, which prints out a table showing package names, the new version number, and the size of the download:

```
% pear list-upgrades
Available Upgrades (stable):
============================
+-------------+---------+--------+
| Package     | Version | Size   |
| Archive_Tar | 0.9     | 8.9kB  |
| Auth        | 1.0.2   | 8.8kB  |
| Auth_HTTP   | 1.0.1   | 1.7kB  |
| DB          | 1.3     | 58kB   |
| HTTP        | 1.1     | 2.9kB  |
| Mail        | 1.0.1   | 11.6kB |
| Mail_Mime   | 1.2.1   | 15.0kB |
| Net_Ping    | 1.0.1   | 2.1kB  |
| Net_SMTP    | 1.0     | 2.8kB  |
| Net_Socket  | 1.0.1   | 3.5kB  |
| PEAR        | 0.9     | 40kB   |
| XML_Parser  | 1.0     | 4.8kB  |
| XML_RPC     | 1.0.3   | 11.9kB |
| XML_RSS     | 0.9.1   | 3.1kB  |
| XML_Tree    | 1.1     | 4.7kB  |
+-------------+---------+--------+
```

If you're up to date, *pear* prints:

```
No upgrades available
```

To upgrade a particular package, use the upgrade command. For example:

```
% pear upgrade DB
downloading DB-1.3.tgz ...
...done: 59,332 bytes
```

The short command for list-upgrades is lu; for upgrade it's up.

PEAR also has an RSS feed listing new packages available at *http://pear.php.net/rss.php*.

See Also

Recipes 21.4 and Recipe 21.5 for information on installing PEAR and PECL packages; Recipe 21.7 to uninstall a package; Recipe 12.11 for more on parsing RSS feeds.

21.7   Uninstalling PEAR Packages

Problem

You wish to remove a PEAR package from your system.

Solution

The uninstall command tells the PEAR package manager to delete packages:

```
% pear uninstall HTML_Common
uninstall HTML_Common ok
```

Discussion

Uninstalling a package removes it completely from your system. If you want to reinstall it, you must begin as if the package was never installed. PEAR doesn't warn you if you try to remove a package that's dependent on another package, so be careful when you uninstall.

There is no way to automatically roll back an upgrade to an earlier version of a package using uninstall. Also, PEAR complains if you try to install an earlier version over a later one. To force PEAR to overwrite a newer version, use install -f or install --force:

```
% pear install --force Net_URL
downloading Net_URL-1.0.4.tgz ...
...done: 3,540 bytes
install ok: Net_URL 1.0.4
```

The short command for uninstall is un.

See Also

Recipes 21.4 and Recipe 21.5 for information on installing PEAR and PECL packages.

21.8 Documenting Classes with PHPDoc

Problem

You want to be able to integrate documentation with your code.

Solution

Use PHPDoc. This allows PEAR to accurately list your class, and you can use the PHPDoc tools to automatically generate API documentation in HTML and XML.

PHPDoc syntax is based on Javadoc. The following tags are available for use: @access, @author, @package, @param, @return, @since, @var, and @version.

You can then use PEAR's PHPDoc utility to generate documentation.

Discussion

PHPDoc has a special inline documentation style. By formatting your comments in a particular way, the PHPDoc script can parse your code to not only generate which parameters a function take and what type of variable it returns, but also associate comments and other useful information with objects, functions, and variables.

PHPDoc comments are based on the same formatting and naming conventions as Javadoc. So, to flag a comment block to grab PHPDoc's attention, use a traditional C-style comment but use two asterisks after the opening slash:

```
/**
 * This is a PHPDoc comment block
 */
```

Inside of a block, certain keywords have special meaning. These keywords all begin with an at sign. Table 21-2 lists the keywords and what they stand for.

Table 21-2. PHPDoc keywords

Keyword	Meaning
@access	Method access: public or private
@author	Package author
@package	Package name
@param	Function parameter
@return	Function return value

Table 21-2. PHPDoc keywords (continued)

Keyword	Meaning
@see	See also reference
@since	Debut version of PHP
@var	Object variable
@version	Package release number

A more fully fleshed out example looks like this:

```
/**
 * Example_Class is a sample class for demonstrating PHPDoc
 *
 * Example_Class is a class that has no real actual code, but merely
 * exists to help provide people with an understanding as to how the
 * various PHPDoc tags are used.
 *
 * Example usage:
 * if (Example_Class::example()) {
 *     print "I am an example.";
 * }
 *
 * @package  Example
 * @author   David Sklar <david@example.com>
 * @author   Adam Trachtenberg <adam@example.com>
 * @version  $Revision: 1.30 $
 * @access   public
 * @see      http://www.example.com/pear
 */
class Example extends PEAR
{
    /**
     * returns the sample data
     *
     * @param  string  $sample the sample data
     * @return array    all of the exciting sample options
     * @access private
     */
    function _sampleMe($sample)
    {
```

Any text following a keyword is treated as the value assigned to it. So, in this example, the value of @package is "Example." It can be okay to have two instances of the same keyword, depending upon the situation. For instance, it's perfectly legal to have multiple @param keywords, but it's illegal to have multiple @return keywords.

PHPDoc and the PEAR web site use this information to generate hyperlinked references, so it's important to use a consistent naming scheme, or the cross-references won't work correctly.

To generate PHPDoc, first install the PHPDoc PEAR package. Inside that package is a program named *phpdoc*; run it from the command line, and use the -s flag to pass in the directory of the source files. By default, documentation is generated in */usr/ local/doc/pear/*, so be sure the *phpdoc* program has write permission to that location, or use -d to alter the destination directory.

To permanently modify the default values, edit the values at the top of the script. Pass -h for a listing of all possible command-line parameters.

PHPDoc isn't very efficient, so be patient. Generating documentation may take a while, depending upon the size of your files. A faster program is currently under development.

See Also

PEAR coding standards at *http://pear.php.net/manual/en/standards.php*; PHPDoc at *http://pear.php.net/package-info.php?package=PHPDoc*.

Index

Symbols

& (ampersand)
  & (logical AND) operator, 191
  argument separator for URLs, 181
  before function name, returning values by
    reference, 140
  before function parameter names, passing
    parameters by reference, 135
  converting to HTML entity, 181, 233,
    296
  placeholder in database queries, 256
< > (angle brackets)
  < and >, converting to HTML
    entities, 181, 233, 296
  <? and ?>, PHP start and end tags, 473
    programming conventions in this
      book, xix
  <<< in heredocs, 2, 12
  >& (redirection) operator, 486
* (asterisk)
  regular expression metacharacter, 344
  SQL and shell globbing wildcard, 259
@ (at sign) in PHPDoc commands, 565
\ (backslash)
  double-quoted string escape sequence, 2
  escaping for SQL, 242
  escaping regular expression pattern
    delimiters, 347
  escaping SQL and shell globbing
    wildcards, 259
  pathname separator on Windows, 456,
    500

` (backtick) operator, 484
  using with ls (Unix) or dir
    (Windows), 504
{ } (braces)
  array elements, resolving ambiguity
    about, 121
  dereferencing objects, 323
  in double-quoted strings, 2
  empty set, 110
  expressions between, evaluation in
    PHP, 121
  in variable interpolation, 433
[ ] (brackets)
  character classes in regular
    expressions, 345
  in double-quoted strings, 2
  variables, treating as arrays, 235
^ (caret)
  beginning of line anchor for patterns, 345
  inverting character class, 345
:: (colon) operator, accessing class methods
  or member variables, 150
, (comma)
  array elements, separating, 91
  data separated by, parsing, 14
$ (dollar sign)
  $_ in superglobal array names, 216
  in double-quoted strings, 2
  end of line anchor for patterns, 345
. (dot)
  . (current directory) and .. (parent
    directory), 502
  in HTML field name, converting to PHP
    variable, 234

We'd like to hear your suggestions for improving our indexes. Send email to *index@oreilly.com*.

. (dot) (*continued*)

recreating full filename from parts, 500

regular expression metacharacter, 344

string concatenation operator, 12

= (equal sign)

=& (assignment) operator, 140, 155

= (assignment) operator, == vs., 118

=> operator

instructing arrays to use different index, 78

specifying key/value pairs for arrays, 76

== (equality) operator, 93

=== (identity) operator, 118

!== (nonidentity) operator, 95, 502

#! (hash-bang) syntax, PHP scripts beginning with, 518

~ (logical NOT), 191

-> operator, accessing methods or member variables, 150

( ) (parentheses)

embedding comments in email addresses, 353

grouping characters and capturing in patterns, 344

% (percent sign)

SQL wildcard character, 258

strftime( ), formatting characters preceded by, 51

+ (plus sign)

+ operator, merging arrays, 89

regular expression metacharacter, 344

? (question mark)

?: (ternary) operator, 119

after quantifiers, for nongreedy matching, 350

placeholder in database queries, 255

regular expression metacharacter, 344

" (quotes, double)

converting to HTML entities, 181, 233, 296

in double-quoted strings, 2

escaping for SQL, 242

escaping in queried data, 258

in strings, 1

variable interpolation in a double-quoted string, 433

' (quotes, single)

escaping for SQL, 242

in command-line arguments, 482

in function return values, 143

marking strings in queried data, 258

in strings, 1

; (semicolon)

argument separator for URLs, 181

end of statement character, 3

/ (slash)

/** and */ in PHPDoc comments, 565

pathname separator on Unix, 456, 500

recreating full filename from parts, 500

regular expression pattern delimiters, 344, 347

_ (underscore)

_( ) alias for gettext( ), 424

_ _FILE_ _ and _ _LINE_ _ constants, 195

replacing . (dot) in variable names, 234

SQL wildcard character, 258

| (vertical bar), alternation in pattern matching, 345

Numbers

0 (zero)

as empty variable, 117

numbers beginning with, 61

return values from functions, 143

in string escape sequences, 2

A

abstraction layer for databases, 241

abusive users, program checking for, 210–214

Accept-Encoding header, 189

Accept-Language header, 422

access time for files, 496

access_log variables, 203

accounts, activating/deactivating for web site, 208–210

actions by user, responding to, 535

activate signal, 538

add( )

GtkVBox class, 533

GtkWindow class, 531

addAttachment( ) (Mail_mime), 431

addcslashes( ), 347

addHeader( ) (HTTP_Request), 287, 289

adding to a date, 61

addObjectMap( ) (SOAP_Server), 337

addresses

IP, looking up with DNS, 448

looking up with LDAP, 444

addslashes( ), 126

ADOdb (database abstraction layer), 249

advisory file locking, 487

M

magic quotes feature, 242, 250
    quoting of placeholder values and, 259
    unserializing data and, 126
mail
    MIME, 430
    reading with IMAP or POP3, 432
    sending, 427
    sending using external programs, 428
mail( ), 427
Mail class, 427
Mail::factory( ), 427
Mail_mime class, 430
Mail_mime::addAttachment( ), 431
Mail_mime::send( ), 431
Mail_mime::setHTMLBody( ), 431
Mail_mime::setTXTBody( ), 431
mailto: hyperlinks, converting text email
    addresses to, 343
main( ) (gtk), 531
man strftime, 51
mangle_email( ), 188
mantissa, 26
Manual (PEAR), web site, 554
marking up a web page, 293
markup languages
    HTML (see HTML)
    XML (see XML)
max( ), 96
maximal matching (see greedy matching)
mcrypt extension, 361, 371
    listing of encryption/decryption
        algorithms, 372
    Versions 2.2 and 2.4, 374
mcrypt_create_iv( ), 374
mcrypt_decrypt( ), 371
mcrypt_encrypt( ), 371
mcrypt_get_block_size( ), 374
mcrypt_get_iv_size( ), 374, 377
mcrypt_list_algorithms( ), 371
mcrypt_list_modes( ), 371
md5( ), 361
MD5 hash algorithm, 364
M_E built-in constant, 33
mean( ), 138
    passing array with variable arguments
        to, 137–139
memory, shared segments, 123
menus
    displaying in GTK window, 537–540
    dropdown, based on current date, 236

merging arrays, 88
    to find union, 107
message catalogs, 412
    catalog-compare.php program, 421
    creating, managing, and deploying with
        gettext, 423
    storing in objects, 414
    strftime( ) format strings as messages, 415
Message-ID, 437
message.php program, 275–280
messages
    formatting text messages for locales, 409
    localizing, 412
    posting to Usenet newsgroups, 435–437
    reading from Usenet
        newsgroups, 437–441
    threaded, storing and retrieving, 274–280
Metabase (database abstraction layer), 249
metacharacters, 344
    escaping in Perl-compatible regular
        expressions, 357
    shell, escaping in external files, 481
    URL, escaping, 126
metadata change of a file, 496
metasymbols, 345
method_exists( ), 264
methods, 148
    calling on object returned by another
        method, 156
    class
      inheritance by child classes, 151
      parent:: (prefacing parent
        methods), 151
    constructors
      class, 150
      defining for objects, 153
    namespaces and, 334
    object
      dynamic object instantiation and, 165
      finding, 163
      profiling execution of, 207
    overridden, accessing, 157
    polymorphism of, 160–162
    sorting arrays, 103
    XML-RPC
      associating with server and PHP
        functions, 331
      differences from PHP in naming, 327
    (see also functions)
mhash module, 365

nodes
  DOM XML
    adding attributes to, 315
    creating and appending, 314
    root node, getting, 316
    top-level or root, 314
  XML, 314
nonblocking file locks, 487
nongreedy matching, 350
nonidentity operator (!==), 95, 502
nonrelational databases supported by
    PHP, 238
non-true values, 143
notices, error messages flagged as, 191
notify-user.php program, 208
NOW( ) (SQL), 256
nsupdate command, 483
nth occurrence of a match, finding, 349
NUL characters
  opening binary files and, 458
  Windows, redirecting output to, 486
null characters
  escaping for SQL, 242
  trimming from strings, 13
number_format( ), 33, 417
numbers, 24–41
  bases other than decimal, 40
  beginning with zero, PHP treatment
    of, 61
  checking for specific data type, 26
  checking strings for valid number, 25
  converting between bases, 39
  converting to/from strings, 24
  exponents, 32
  floating-point
    comparing for equality, 26
    rounding, 27
  formatting, 33
  formatting for different locales, 409
    (see also locales; localization)
  integers (see integers)
  logarithms, 32
  printing correct plurals, 34
  random
    biased, generating, 31
    generated within a range, 29
    sources for initialization vectors, 374
  trigonometric functions, 36
    degrees, using, 37
  very large or very small, 37
numeric arrays, 75
  DB fetch mode, 251
  merging, 88

  merging, duplicate values and, 107
  mixing and matching with string keys, 79
  removing duplicate elements, 106
numeric sorting of arrays, 98
numeric strings, 25
numRows( ) (DB_Result), 257

O

ob_end_flush( ), 188
object-oriented interface to directory
    information, 503
object-oriented programming, PHP objects
    vs., 149
objects, 152–165
  arrays of, 76
  base, adding properties to, 164
  cloning, 154
  constructor method, defining, 153
  destroying, 154
  DOM nodes, 317
  GTK, 531
  instantiation of, 148, 149
    dynamic, 166
  languages stored in, 421
  for message catalogs, 414
  methods
    array sorting, use in, 103
    and properties, finding, 163
  PHP, traditional OO vs., 149
  properties of
    browser capabilities, 179
    interpolating into strings, 12
  references to, 155
  returned by another method, calling
    methods on, 156
  Simple Object Access Protocol (see SOAP)
  string representation of, 125
  Zend Engine 2 (ZE2) object model, 151
ob_start( ), 188
OCI8 interface (Oracle database), 239
OCIBindByName( ), 256
OCIExecute( ), 240, 256
OCIFetch( ), 240
OCILogin( ), 240
OCIParse( ), 240, 256
OCIPLogon( ), 241
OCIResult( ), 240
octal values, 40
  converting mode element of file
    information array to, 497
  \ddd, indicating with, 348
  in double-quoted strings, escaping, 2

About the Authors

David Sklar is an independent software development and strategic technology consultant. He was a cofounder and the Chief Technology Officer of Student.Com and TVGrid.Com. At both companies, David oversaw the architecture and development of varied systems to deliver personalized dynamic content to users around the world.

After discovering PHP as a solution to his web programming needs in 1996, he created the PX (*http://px.sklar.com/*), which enables PHP users to exchange programs. Since then, he has continued to rely on PHP for personal and professional projects.

When away from the computer, David eats mini-donuts, plays records, and likes to cook. He lives in New York City and has a degree in Computer Science from Yale University

Adam Trachtenberg is working on getting an MBA from Columbia Business School. At business school, he is focusing on General Management and Operations, with an emphasis on the field of technology. Adam also has a BA from Columbia University. As an undergraduate, he majored in Mathematics and his other studies included Computer Science and Chinese.

Before returning to school, he cofounded and served as Vice President for Development at two companies, Student.Com and TVGrid.Com. At both firms, he led the front- and middle-end web site design and development, worked on corporate planning and strategy, and served as liaison between the product and marketing teams.

During study breaks, Adam enjoys playing squash, reading fiction, and eating in New York City's many wonderful restaurants. He wishes he was better at playing pool, knew the constellations, and was handy around the house.

Colophon

Our look is the result of reader comments, our own experimentation, and feedback from distribution channels. Distinctive covers complement our distinctive approach to technical topics, breathing personality and life into potentially dry subjects.

The animal on the cover of *PHP Cookbook* is a Galapagos land iguana (*Conolophus subcristatus*). Once abundant in the Galapagos Islands, this iguana proved tasty to the settlers of the early 1800s, and domestic animals later introduced on the islands played further havoc with the reptile's home and food supply. Today there are no iguanas left on Santiago Island and very few left on the other islands.

Distantly related to the green iguana of the South American continent, Galapagos land iguanas can be over three feet long, with males weighing up to 30 pounds. Their tough, scaly skin is yellow with scattered patches of white, black, brown, and rust.

These lizards resemble mythical creatures of the past—dragons with long tails, clawed feet, and spiny crests. In reality, however, they are harmless.

Land iguanas live in the drier areas of the islands and in the morning are found basking in the sun. During midday, however, they seek the shade of cactus, rocks, and trees. To conserve body heat at night, they sleep in burrows dug in the ground.

These reptiles are omnivores, but they generally depend on low-growing plants and shrubs, as well as the fallen fruits and pads of cactus trees. These plants provide most of the moisture they need; however, they will drink fresh water whenever it's available.

Depending on their size, land iguanas reach maturity between 8 and 15 years of age. They congregate and mate during specific periods, which vary from island to island. The females then migrate to suitable areas to nest. After digging a burrow, the female lays 2 to 20 eggs in the nest. She then defends the covered nest site to prevent other females from nesting in the same spot.

Young iguanas hatch 85 to 110 days later and take about a week to dig their way out of the nest. Normally, if hatchlings survive the first year when food is often scarce and native predators such as hawks, egrets, herons, and snakes are a danger, they can live for more than 60 years. In reality, predation by feral cats is far worse because the young must survive and grow for at least three to four years before becoming large enough that cats can't kill them.

Mary Anne Weeks Mayo was the production editor and copyeditor for *PHP Cookbook*. Sarah Jane Shangraw proofread the book. Darren Kelly and Jane Ellin provided quality control. Julie Flanagan, Brian Sawyer, Genevieve d'Entremont, and Judy Hoer provided production assistance. Ellen Troutman-Zaig wrote the index.

Emma Colby designed the cover of this book, based on a series design by Edie Freedman. The cover image is a 19th-century engraving from the Dover Pictorial Archive. Emma produced the cover layout with QuarkXPress 4.1 using Adobe's ITC Garamond font.

David Futato designed the interior layout. This book was converted to FrameMaker 5.5.6 with a format conversion tool created by Erik Ray, Jason McIntosh, Neil Walls, and Mike Sierra that uses Perl and XML technologies. The text font is Linotype Birka; the heading font is Adobe Myriad Condensed; and the code font is Lucas-Font's TheSans Mono Condensed. The illustrations that appear in the book were produced by Robert Romano and Jessamyn Read using Macromedia FreeHand 9 and Adobe Photoshop 6. This colophon was compiled by Mary Anne Weeks Mayo.

Related Titles Available from O'Reilly

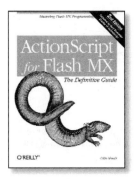

Web Programming

ActionScript Cookbook

ActionScript for Flash MX Pocket Reference

ActionScript for Flash MX: The Definitive Guide, *2nd Edition*

Creating Applications with Mozilla

Dynamic HTML: The Definitive Reference, *2nd Edition*

Flash Remoting: The Definitive Guide

Google Hacks

Google Pocket Guide

HTTP: The Definitive Guide

JavaScript & DHTML Cookbook

JavaScript Pocket Reference, *2nd Edition*

JavaScript: The Definitive Guide, *4th Edition*

PHP Pocket Reference, *2nd Edition*

Programming ColdFusion MX, *2nd Edition*

Programming PHP

Web Database Applications with PHP and MySQL

Webmaster in a Nutshell, *3rd Edition*

Web Authoring and Design

Building Database-Driven Web Sites with Dreamweaver MX

Cascading Style Sheets: The Definitive Guide

CSS Pocket Reference

Dreamweaver MX 2004: The Missing Manual

Dreamweaver MX: The Missing Manual

HTML & XHTML: The Definitive Guide, *5th Edition*

HTML Pocket Reference, *2nd Edition*

Information Architecture for the World Wide Web, *2nd Edition*

Learning Web Design, *2nd Edition*

Web Design in a Nutshell, *2nd Edition*

Web Administration

Apache Cookbook

Apache Pocket Reference

Apache: The Definitive Guide, *3rd Edition*

Essential Blogging

Perl for Web Site Management

Web Performance Tuning, *2nd Edition*

O'REILLY®

Our books are available at most retail and online bookstores.

To order direct: 1-800-998-9938 • *order@oreilly.com* • *www.oreilly.com*

Online editions of most O'Reilly titles are available by subscription at *safari.oreilly.com*

Keep in touch with O'Reilly

1. Download examples from our books

To find example files for a book, go to:

www.oreilly.com/catalog

select the book, and follow the "Examples" link.

2. Register your O'Reilly books

Register your book at *register.oreilly.com*

Why register your books?
Once you've registered your O'Reilly books you can:

- Win O'Reilly books, T-shirts or discount coupons in our monthly drawing.
- Get special offers available only to registered O'Reilly customers.
- Get catalogs announcing new books (US and UK only).
- Get email notification of new editions of the O'Reilly books you own.

3. Join our email lists

Sign up to get topic-specific email announcements of new books and conferences, special offers, and O'Reilly Network technology newsletters at:

elists.oreilly.com

It's easy to customize your free elists subscription so you'll get exactly the O'Reilly news you want.

4. Get the latest news, tips, and tools

www.oreilly.com

- "Top 100 Sites on the Web"—PC Magazine
- CIO Magazine's Web Business 50 Awards

Our web site contains a library of comprehensive product information (including book excerpts and tables of contents), downloadable software, background articles, interviews with technology leaders, links to relevant sites, book cover art, and more.

5. Work for O'Reilly

Check out our web site for current employment opportunities:

jobs.oreilly.com

6. Contact us

O'Reilly & Associates, Inc.
1005 Gravenstein Hwy North
Sebastopol, CA 95472 USA

TEL: 707-827-7000 or 800-998-9938
          (6am to 5pm PST)

FAX: 707-829-0104

order@oreilly.com
For answers to problems regarding your order or our products. To place a book order online, visit:

www.oreilly.com/order_new

catalog@oreilly.com
To request a copy of our latest catalog.

booktech@oreilly.com
For book content technical questions or corrections.

corporate@oreilly.com
For educational, library, government, and corporate sales.

proposals@oreilly.com
To submit new book proposals to our editors and product managers.

international@oreilly.com
For information about our international distributors or translation queries. For a list of our distributors outside of North America check out:

international.oreilly.com/distributors.html

adoption@oreilly.com
For information about academic use of O'Reilly books, visit:

academic.oreilly.com

O'REILLY®

Our books are available at most retail and online bookstores.
To order direct: 1-800-998-9938 • *order@oreilly.com* • *www.oreilly.com*
Online editions of most O'Reilly titles are available by subscription at *safari.oreilly.com*

How to stay in touch with O'Reilly

1.   Visit our award-winning web site

http://www.oreilly.com/

★ "Top 100 Sites on the Web"—PC Magazine
★ CIO Magazine's Web Business 50 Awards

Our web site contains a library of comprehensive product information (including book excerpts and tables of contents), downloadable software, background articles, interviews with technology leaders, links to relevant sites, book cover art, and more. File us in your bookmarks or favorites!

2.   Join our email mailing lists

Sign up to get email announcements of new books and conferences, special offers, and O'Reilly Network technology newsletters at:

http://elists.oreilly.com

It's easy to customize your free elists subscription so you'll get exactly the O'Reilly news you want.

3.   Get examples from our books

To find example files for a book, go to:

http://www.oreilly.com/catalog

select the book, and follow the "Examples" link.

4.   Work with us

Check out our web site for current employment opportunities:

http://jobs.oreilly.com/

5.   Register your book

Register your book at:

http://register.oreilly.com

6.   Contact us

O'Reilly & Associates, Inc.
1005 Gravenstein Hwy North
Sebastopol, CA 95472 USA
TEL: 707-827-7000 or 800-998-9938
            (6am to 5pm PST)
FAX: 707-829-0104

order@oreilly.com
For answers to problems regarding your order or our products. To place a book order online visit:

http://www.oreilly.com/order_new/

catalog@oreilly.com
To request a copy of our latest catalog.

booktech@oreilly.com
For book content technical questions or corrections.

corporate@oreilly.com
For educational, library, government, and corporate sales.

proposals@oreilly.com
To submit new book proposals to our editors and product managers.

international@oreilly.com
For information about our international distributors or translation queries. For a list of our distributors outside of North America check out:

http://international.oreilly.com/distributors.html

adoption@oreilly.com
For information about academic use of O'Reilly books, visit:

http://academic.oreilly.com

O'REILLY®

To order: *800-998-9938* • *order@oreilly.com* • *www.oreilly.com*
Online editions of most O'Reilly titles are available by subscription at *safari.oreilly.com*
Also available at most retail and online bookstores.